Oxford Dictionary of Idioms

John Ayto is an experienced lexicographer and author of many language titles, including *The Oxford Essential Guide to the English Language*, *The Longman Register of New Words*, the *Bloomsbury Dictionary of Word Origins*, *Twentieth Century Words*, and *Wobbly Bits and Other Euphemisms*. He was also editor of the nineteenth edition of *Brewer's Dictionary of Phrase and Fable*.

Oxford Dictionary of

Idioms

THIRD AND FOURTH EDITIONS

Edited by John Ayto

SECOND EDITION

Edited by Judith Siefring

FIRST EDITION

Edited by Jennifer Speake

Great Clarendon Street, Oxford, OX2 6DP,
United Kingdom

Oxford University Press is a department of the University of Oxford. It furthers the University's objective of excellence in research, scholarship, and education by publishing worldwide. Oxford is a registered trade mark of Oxford University Press in the UK and in certain other countries

First edition 1999
Second edition 2004
Third edition 2009, issued as an Oxford University Press paperback 2010
Fourth edition 2020

Published in the United States of America by Oxford University Press
198 Madison Avenue, New York, NY 10016, United States of America

British Library Cataloguing in Publication Data
Data available

Library of Congress Control Number: 2020935404

ISBN 978-0-19-884562-1

Printed and bound in Great Britain by
Clays Ltd, Elcograf S.p.A.

Contents

Preface

to the Third Edition

To begin at the beginning: what is an idiom? Perhaps the shortest meaningful answer to that question would be 'a phrase that behaves like a word'. We are used to thinking of words as the lowest common denominators of meaning. But then consider, for example, the phrase *a pig in a poke*. What can we make of that if we try to interpret it word by word? Even if we know what a poke is (or was), which most people probably do not, it would make very little sense. Or take the phrase *haul someone over the coals*. Its literal meaning would, in virtually any context, be totally inappropriate. Understanding each individual word does not get us very close to the meaning of the phrase; we have to interpret the phrase as a whole, almost as if it was a single word in its own right. It is phrases like these that are known as 'idioms', and they form the subject matter of this dictionary.

Understandability is not an all-or-nothing matter. There is no way you could guess that *kick the bucket* means 'to die'. At the other end of the spectrum, the meaning of the fixed phrase *go wrong* is fairly transparent. Between these two extremes there is a whole range of gradations. For instance, it is much easier to interpret *ahead of its time* than *kick the bucket*, but most people would probably reckon it to be less literal than *go wrong*. And some phrases contain elements that are more metaphorical than the rest of the phrase: in *get down to brass tacks*, for example, we can recognize *get down to* from other similar expressions (such as *get down to business*), but the meaning of *brass tacks* (if you do not know it) is entirely unguessable.

So, semantic opaqueness is one key feature of an idiom. The other is that the elements (words) of which they are made up are more or less firmly fixed, and in most cases there is little or no leeway for changing them. This operates on two levels: idioms tend not to have the full range of grammatical possibilities that a similar non-idiomatic phrase would have. For example, many verbal idioms cannot be turned into the passive (so you can say 'Fred kicked the bucket' but not 'the bucket was kicked by Fred'). And the key words in an idiom usually resist being substituted (*rare as hen's teeth*, for instance, can become *scarce as hen's teeth*, or even *like hen's teeth*, but not *rare as chicken's teeth*).

The *Oxford Dictionary of Idioms* collects together over 6,000 such expressions from contemporary and historical English and from around the English-speaking world. It explains their meaning, but in many cases it also gives an illustrative quotation (obtained not only from printed texts—from novels to guidebooks, broadsheet newspapers to teenage magazines—but also from a range of online sources) or a note on the origin or evolution of the idiom or on the scope of its current usage, with the overall aim of providing a well-rounded portrait of the phrase.

An index section at the end of the book groups together idioms that share a common theme or subject, so giving readers a vivid snapshot of those areas and aspects of life that have generated a particularly rich variety of figurative expressions.

John Ayto
London 2009

Preface

to the Fourth Edition

Lexicography is an ongoing game of catch-up. The English language has moved on since the previous edition of this dictionary was published, not least in the proliferation of idiomatic expressions, and a host of new entrants have made their way into this fourth edition (for example, *hard yards*, *heavy lifting*, *kick the can down the road*, *my way or the highway*, *talk to the hand*, *wind your neck in*). For the most part this new material comes from the ongoing third edition of the *Oxford English Dictionary* or is based on evidence gathered for the *OED*. That is also the origin of most of the quotations included here.

As in the previous edition, a generous provision of cross references means that users are quickly guided to the information they need. However, in order to avoid very long entries consisting of little or nothing besides cross references, at entries for high-frequency words, such as *go* and *take*, readers are advised to look up a more salient component word in the idiom they are searching for. So, for example, someone trying to find *take the biscuit* at *take* will be prompted to look up the main word in the idiom—in this case, *biscuit*.

John Ayto
London 2019

A

A1 excellent; first-rate.

ⓘ The full form of this expression is *A1 at Lloyd's*. In Lloyd's Register of Shipping, the phrase was used of ships in first-class condition as to the hull (A) and stores (1). The US equivalent is *A No. 1*; both have been in figurative use since the mid 19th century.

from A to B from your starting point to your destination; from one place to another.

2013 *Daily Telegraph* Tourists aren't interested in getting from A to B at maximum speed. They are interested in cost.

from A to Z over the entire range; in every particular.

ⓘ Dorothy Parker (allegedly) subverted the phrase with her comment on a performance of Katherine Hepburn's: She ran the whole gamut of the emotions from A to B.

2008 *Guardian* Mohammed admitted last year to plotting 'from A to Z' the hijacking of four passenger planes that crashed into the World Trade Centre, the Pentagon and a Pennsylvania field.

aback

take someone aback shock, surprise, or disconcert someone.

ⓘ The phrase is frequently used in the passive form (*be taken aback*): this was adopted in the mid 19th century from earlier (mid 18th-century) nautical terminology, to describe the situation of a ship with its sails pressed back against the mast by a headwind, preventing forward movement.

1991 Kathleen Jones *Learning Not To Be First* They were taken aback by the shabbiness of the hotel and lack of cleanliness in the city generally.

ABC

as easy (*or* simple) as ABC extremely easy or straightforward.

ⓘ From the 15th to the 17th century, a child's first spelling and reading book was commonly called an *ABC*, and this led to the development of its metaphorical use, 'the basic elements or rudiments of something'.

abdabs

give someone the screaming abdabs induce an attack of extreme anxiety or irritation in someone.

ⓘ *Abdabs* (or *habdabs*) is mid-20th-century slang whose origin is unknown. The word is sometimes also used to mean an attack of delirium tremens.

abet

aid and abet: *see* AID.

abode

your humble abode: *see* HUMBLE.

about

be not about to do something be unwilling to do something.

have your wits about you: *see* WIT.

know what you are about be aware of the implications of your actions or of a situation, and of how best to deal with them. Informal

1993 *Ski Survey* He ran a 3-star guest house before this, so knows what he is about.

up and about: *see* UP.

above

above board: *see* BOARD.

above yourself conceited; arrogant.

1999 Frank McCourt *'Tis* Many a man made his way in America by the sweat of his brow and his strong back and it's a good thing to learn your station in life and not be getting above yourself.

not be above — be capable of stooping to (an unworthy act).

2011 *Daily Telegraph* Even William's successor, Queen Victoria, was not above going what many people felt was improperly far to further the cause of her beloved Melbourne and Disraeli.

Abraham

in Abraham's bosom in heaven, the place of rest for the souls of the blessed. dated

ⓘ The phrase is taken from Luke 16:22: 'And it came to pass, that the beggar died, and was carried by the angels into Abraham's bosom'. In the Bible, *Abraham* was the Hebrew patriarch from whom all Jews traced their descent.

a

absence

conspicuous by your absence: *see* CONSPICUOUS.

acceptable

the acceptable face of the tolerable or attractive manifestation or aspect of (something generally regarded as unattractive or reprehensible).

ⓘ The seed of this idiom was 'the unacceptable face of capitalism', a phrase used in 1973 by the British prime minister Edward Heath with reference to a large payment made by a commercial company to a former cabinet minister.

2004 Norman Lebrecht *La Scena Musicale* Christopher Hogwood was the acceptable face of early music, a conductor who never allowed dogmas of authenticity to overwhelm musicality.

accident

an accident waiting to happen ❶ a potentially disastrous situation, usually caused by negligent or faulty procedures. ❷ a person certain to cause trouble.

❶ **2004** *IndieLondon film reviews* The K-19 was an accident waiting to happen (its nuclear reactor sacrificed safety margins in favour of power and compactness).

accidents will happen however careful you try to be, it is inevitable that some unfortunate or unforeseen events will occur.

ⓘ This phrase is a shortened form of the early 19th-century proverb 'accidents will happen in the best regulated families'.

a chapter of accidents: *see* CHAPTER.

accidentally

accidentally on purpose: *see* PURPOSE.

accord

of your own accord voluntarily or without outside intervention.

with one accord in a united way.

account

a blow-by-blow account: *see* BLOW-BY-BLOW.

give a good (*or* bad) account of yourself make a favourable (*or* unfavourable) impression through your performance or actions.

on no account under no circumstances.

settle (*or* square) accounts with someone ❶ pay money owed to someone. ❷ have revenge on someone.

take something into account (*or* take account of something) consider something along with other factors before reaching a decision.

there's no accounting for tastes it's impossible to explain why different people like different things, especially those things which the speaker considers unappealing. proverb

ⓘ Since the late 18th century, this has been the usual English form of the Latin expression *de gustibus non est disputandum* 'there is no disputing about tastes'.

turn to (good) account turn (something) to your advantage.

ace

have an ace up your sleeve have an effective resource or piece of information kept hidden until it is necessary to use it; have a secret advantage.

ⓘ The ace is the highest playing card in its suit in many card games, so a cheating player might well hide one to use against an unwary opponent. A North American variant is *an ace in the hole*. The next two idioms are also based on this meaning of *ace*.

hold all the aces have all the advantages.

play your ace use your best resource.

within an ace of very close to.

ⓘ *Ace* here has the figurative meaning of 'a tiny amount' and is used with reference to the single spot on the playing card. The phrase was first recorded in the early 18th century.

Achilles

an Achilles heel a person's only vulnerable spot; a serious or fatal weakness.

ⓘ In Greek mythology, the nymph Thetis dipped her infant son Achilles in the water of the River Styx to make him immortal, but the heel by which she held him was not touched by the water; he was ultimately killed in battle by an arrow wound in this one vulnerable spot.

2013 *New Zealand Herald* Our economy's Achilles heel is our inability to turn enough of our resources into high-value goods that sell for a premium overseas.

acid

the acid test a situation or event which finally proves whether something is good or bad, true or false, etc.

ⓘ The original use of the phrase was to denote a method of testing for gold with nitric acid (gold being resistant to the effects of nitric acid).

1990 *Which?* These deals are designed to encourage impulse buying, so the acid test is whether you would have bought anyway.

come the acid be unpleasant or offensive; speak in a caustic or sarcastic manner. informal

put the acid on someone try to extract a loan or favour from someone. Australian & New Zealand informal

acquaintance

have a nodding acquaintance with someone or something: *see* NODDING.

scrape acquaintance with: *see* SCRAPE.

acquired

an acquired taste a thing that you come to like over time.

acre

God's acre: *see* GOD.

hell's half acre: *see* HELL.

across

across the board applying to all.

ⓘ In the USA, this expression refers literally to a horse-racing bet in which equal amounts are staked on the same horse to win or finish in the first three in a race.

2014 *Daily Telegraph* Mrs May initially said it was right to 'look across the board at all other options that are available'.

be across something fully understand the details or complexity of an issue or situation. Australian

act

act (*or* be) your age behave in a manner appropriate to your age and not to someone much younger.

2000 Will Self *How the Dead Live* Don't be a fool, girl ... Act yer age—think!

act the goat: *see* GOAT.

act of God an instance of uncontrollable natural forces in operation.

ⓘ This phrase is often used in insurance contracts to refer to incidents such as lightning strikes or floods.

catch someone in the act surprise someone in the process of doing something wrong.

a class act: *see* CLASS.

clean up your act: *see* CLEAN.

do a disappearing act: *see* DISAPPEARING.

get your act together organize yourself in the manner required in order to achieve something. informal

2002 *New York Times* There are still many who think all that the dirty, homeless man on the corner talking to himself needs is just to get his act together.

a hard (*or* tough) act to follow an achievement or performance which sets a standard difficult for others to measure up to.

2012 *Diamond Geezer* Having said that, there's not the same buzz, is there? Maybe that's because the Olympics are a tough act to follow.

in on the act involved in a particular activity in order to gain profit or advantage. informal

2013 *Daily Telegraph* Even the royals seem to have got in on the act, with the gift shop at Kensington Palace selling Grenadier Guards sleepsuits (£22.99) and Buckingham Palace flogging a Guardsman babygro for £12.95.

the old pals act: *see* OLD.

read someone the riot act: *see* READ.

action

action stations an order or warning to prepare for action.

ⓘ Originally, this was an order to naval personnel to go to their allocated positions ready to engage the enemy.

man of action a man whose life is characterized by physical activity or deeds rather than by words or intellectual matters.

a piece of the action: *see* PIECE.

where the action is where important or interesting things are happening. informal

1971 *Gourmet* You can dine outside, weather permitting, or in the bar where the action is.

a

actress

as the actress said to the bishop used humorously to call attention to a sexual *double entendre*, especially an unintended one.

ℹ The cast of characters can be reversed without changing the meaning of the expression: *as the bishop said to the actress*. The allusion is presumably to the punchline of some now long-forgotten joke.

2005 *New Zealand Listener* Some of Charles's antipodean witticisms— . . . 'it all became too big for me, as the actress said to the bishop'—sounded several centuries old.

actual

your actual — the real, genuine, or important thing specified. informal

1968 Kenneth Williams *Diary* There's no doubt about it, on a good day, I look quite lovely in your actual gamin fashion.

Adam

not know someone from Adam not know or be completely unable to recognize the person in question. informal

the old Adam unregenerate human nature.

ℹ In Christian symbolism, *the old Adam* represents sinful humanity as contrasted with *the second Adam*, Jesus Christ.

1993 *Outdoor Canada* It is the Old Adam in us. We are descendants of a long line of dirt farmers, sheepherders . . . and so forth.

add

add fuel to the fire: *see* FUEL.

add insult to injury: *see* INSULT.

adder

deaf as an adder: *see* DEAF.

admirable

an admirable Crichton a person who excels in all kinds of studies and pursuits, or who is noted for supreme competence.

ℹ This expression originally referred to James Crichton of Clunie (1560–85?), a Scottish nobleman renowned for his intellectual and physical prowess. In J. M. Barrie's play *The Admirable Crichton* (1902), the eponymous hero is a butler who takes charge when his master's family is shipwrecked on a desert island.

adrift

cast (*or* **cut**) **someone adrift** ❶ leave someone in a boat or other craft which has nothing to secure or guide it. ❷ abandon or isolate someone.

❷ **2013** *The Age* (Melbourne) Certain solidly performing ministers have been cut adrift, sent to the backbench in shame for campaigning internally against her.

advance

any advance on —? any higher bid than —?

ℹ This phrase is said by an auctioneer to elicit a higher bid, and so is used figuratively as a query about general progress in a particular matter.

advantage

have the advantage of be in a stronger position than. dated

take advantage of ❶ make good use of the opportunities offered by (something). ❷ exploit or make unfair use of for your own benefit. ❸ (of a man) seduce (especially a sexually inexperienced person). dated

turn something to advantage (*or* **to your advantage**) handle or respond to something in such a way as to benefit from it.

advisement

take something under advisement reserve judgement while considering something. North American

advocate

play devil's advocate: *see* DEVIL.

afraid

afraid of your own shadow: *see* SHADOW.

Africa

for Africa in abundance; in large numbers. South African informal

1980 Christopher Hope *A Separate Development* An entire museum of vintage stuff including . . . Bentleys for Africa.

after

be after doing something be on the point of doing something or have just done it. Irish

1988 Roddy Doyle *The Commitments* I'm after rememberin'. I forgot to bring mine back. It's under me bed.

again

come again?: *see* COME.

— rides again: *see* RIDE.

against

up against it: *see* UP.

age

act your age: *see* ACT.

the awkward age: *see* AWKWARD.

of a certain age used euphemistically to avoid specifying the age of someone (typically a woman) of middle age or beyond.

ℹ The phrase, first recorded in 1754, may have been inspired by French *d'un certain âge*.

2003 *Architectural Review* Text . . . is in readable white sans-serif type . . . and, happily for potential clients of a certain age, it's adjustable with the browser's View/Text Size command.

come of age ❶ (of a person) reach adult status. ❷ (of a movement or activity) become fully established.

for a coon's age: *see* COON.

in a dog's age: *see* DOG.

in this day and age: *see* DAY.

feel your age become aware that you are growing older and less energetic.

a golden age: *see* GOLDEN.

under age not yet adult according to the law.

agenda

a hidden agenda: *see* HIDDEN.

agony

pile on the agony: *see* PILE.

prolong the agony: *see* PROLONG.

agree

agree to differ cease to argue about something because neither party will compromise or be persuaded.

agreement

a gentleman's agreement: *see* GENTLEMAN.

ahead

ahead of the game ahead of your competitors or peers in the same sphere of activity.

1996 *Daily Telegraph* The smart money headed for Chinatown, where you can pick up all those Eastern looks the designers are promoting for next spring ahead of the game.

ahead of your (*or* its) time innovative and radical by the standards of the time.

streets ahead: *see* STREET.

aid

aid and abet help and encourage (someone) to do something wrong, especially to commit a crime.

2013 Shaun Attwood *Jon's Jail Journal* We could get fined and who knows, we could cop our own charges of aiding and abetting an escape.

in aid of in support of; for the purpose of raising money for. chiefly British

2013 *Farmers Weekly* They're hoping to raise £10,000 in aid of the charities, to be split between Cancer Research UK and Worcester Samaritans.

what's this in aid of? what is the purpose of this? British informal

air

airs and graces an affected manner of behaving, designed to attract or impress. British

build castles in the air: *see* CASTLE.

clear the air: *see* CLEAR.

give yourself airs act pretentiously or snobbishly.

ℹ *Air* in the sense of 'an affected manner' has been current since the mid 17th century; from the early 18th century the plural form has been more usual in this derogatory sense.

1948 Christopher Bush *The Case of the Second Chance* It was said she gave herself airs, and it was also hinted that she was no better—as they say—than she might be.

a

hot air: *see* HOT.

in the air felt widely or generally to be happening or about to happen.

into (*or* out of) thin air: *see* THIN.

on (*or* off) the air being (*or* not being) broadcast on radio or television.

take the air walk or stroll out of doors.

up in the air (of a plan or issue) still to be settled; unresolved.

2013 *The Register* It's clear that HTML5 is the future, but whether or not that future needs to include DRM is up in the air.

walk on air feel elated.

1977 Bernard MacLaverty *Secrets* 'I'm sure you're walking on air,' my mother said to Paul at his wedding.

aisle

have people rolling in the aisles ❶ make an audience laugh uncontrollably. ❷ be very amusing. informal

❶ **1940 P. G. Wodehouse** *Quick Service* I made the speech of a lifetime. I had them tearing up the seats and rolling in the aisles.

knock them in the aisles: *see* KNOCK

lead someone up the aisle get married to someone.

aitch

drop your aitches: *see* DROP.

Aladdin

an Aladdin's cave a place full of valuable objects.

an Aladdin's lamp a talisman that enables its owner to fulfil every desire.

ⓘ In the *Arabian Nights* tale of Aladdin, the hero finds a magic lamp in a cave. He discovers that rubbing it summons a powerful genie who is able to carry out all his wishes.

alarm

alarms and excursions confused activity and uproar. humorous

ⓘ *Alarm* was formerly spelled *alarum*, representing a pronunciation with a rolling of the 'r'; the phrase was originally a call summoning soldiers to arms. The whole phrase is used in stage directions in Shakespeare to indicate a battle scene.

albatross

albatross round someone's neck something that is burdensome to someone and hinders their progress, especially arising from some misdeed of their own in the past.

ⓘ From the *albatross* shot dead by the sailor in Coleridge's poem *The Rime of the Ancient Mariner* (1798), which brought his ship bad luck. The bird was hung round his neck as a sign of his guilt.

2000 *Sunday Herald* Being the offspring of a famous guy has become an albatross round the neck of many a budding young lion.

ale

cakes and ale: *see* CAKE.

alec

smart alec: *see* SMART.

alight

set the world alight: *see* SET.

alive

alive and kicking prevalent and very active. informal

2013 *New Zealand Herald* According to Statistics NZ, 78 per cent of rural households had access to the internet in 2012. Dial-up is alive and kicking in the hinterland.

alive and well still existing or active (often used to deny rumours or beliefs that something has disappeared or declined).

ⓘ A frequent extension of the phrase, with reference to a person, is *alive and well and living in* (a particular country, city, etc.).

2013 *CNN Newsroom* This is very significant because this tells you that racism is still alive and well.

eat someone alive: *see* EAT.

all

all along all the time; from the beginning.

all and sundry everyone.

2013 *New Statesman* Steal enough from people and you are considered a rotter by all and sundry, at least until you've murdered a few outlaws to balance it out.

all comers anyone who chooses to take part in an activity, typically a competition.

2012 *New York Times* They often take all comers—clever teenagers, 25-year-old ex-drifters, middle-aged downsizees in need of retraining—and let them study as needed.

be all ears: *see* EAR.

all ends up: *see* END.

be all eyes: *see* EYE.

all found: *see* FOUND.

all gas and gaiters: *see* GAS.

all-in ❶ with everything included. ❷ exhausted. British informal

all in all all things considered; on the whole.

all in a day's work: *see* DAY.

be all mouth (and no trousers): *see* MOUTH.

all my eye and Betty Martin: *see* **my eye** *at* EYE.

all of as much as (often used ironically of an amount considered very small by the speaker or writer).

> **2014** *Daily Telegraph* The agenda-setting breakfast news on France Inter radio ... led on Monday morning with Paris taxi drivers going on strike, followed by an item on cigarette prices rising, before devoting all of two minutes to the latest twist in the presidential soap opera.

all of a sudden: *see* SUDDEN.

be all one to make no difference to someone.

all out using all your strength or resources.

all over the place in a state of confusion or disorganization. informal

> ℹ Other variants of this phrase include *all over the map* and *all over the lot* which are North American, and *all over the shop* which is mainly British.

> **2013 Derek Lowe** *Corante—In the Pipeline* The sticky-compound problem is always out there, where various substances decide that they like the plastic walls of the apparatus a lot more than they like being in solution. That'll throw your numbers all over the place.

all the rage: *see* RAGE.

all roads lead to Rome: *see* ROME.

all round ❶ in all respects. ❷ for or by each person.

all-singing, all-dancing with every possible attribute; able to perform any necessary function. British informal

> ℹ This phrase is used particularly in the area of computer technology, but it was originally used to describe show-business acts. Ultimately, it may come from a series of 1929 posters which advertised the addition of sound to motion pictures. The first Hollywood musical, MGM's *Broadway Melody*, was promoted with the slogan *All Talking All Singing All Dancing*.

> **2013** *Bit-Tech Hardware* You can go all out with an all-singing, all-dancing automatic bit of kit such as the Lamptron CW611, but for far less than half the price you can own a manual one too.

all Sir Garnet: *see* GARNET.

all systems go: *see* SYSTEM.

all that glitters is not gold: *see* GLITTER.

be all that be very attractive or good. US informal

> **2002** *Guardian* I can't believe how she throws herself at guys, she thinks she's all that.

not all there not in full possession of your mental faculties. informal

be all things to all men: *see* THING.

be all very well used to criticize or reject a favourable or consoling remark. informal

all wet: *see* WET.

— and all used to emphasize something additional that is being referred to. informal

> **1992 Kenichi Ohmae** *The Borderless World* You can whip up nationalist passions and stage-manage protectionist rallies, bonfires and all.

be all go: *see* GO.

be all hat and no cattle: *see* HAT.

be all up with: *see* UP.

a bit of all right: *see* BIT.

for all — in spite of —.

> **1989** *Independent* For all their cruel, corrupt and reckless vices, the Maharajahs were worshipped as gods by tens of thousands of their subjects.

go all the way: *see* WAY.

I'm all right, Jack: *see* JACK.

it takes all sorts: *see* SORT.

not for all the tea in China: *see* TEA.

on all fours with: *see* FOUR.

be struck all of a heap: *see* HEAP.

when all is said and done: *see* SAID.

you can't win them all: *see* WIN.

all-clear

give (*or* **get) the all-clear** indicate (*or* get a sign) that a dangerous situation is now safe.

> ℹ In wartime an 'all-clear' signal or siren is often sounded to indicate that a bombing raid is over.

a

alley

a blind alley: *see* BLIND.

up your alley: *see* **up your street** *at* STREET.

allowance

make allowance(s) for ❶ take into consideration when planning something. ❷ treat leniently on account of mitigating circumstances.

ally

pass in your ally die. Australian informal

ⓘ In this phrase, an *ally* is a toy marble made of marble, alabaster, or glass.

alone

go it alone act by yourself without assistance. informal

along

along about round about a specified time or date. North American informal or dialect

1989 *Motor Trend* Along about this time, it had started raining, so they red-flagged the race for a change to rain tires.

alpha

alpha and omega ❶ the beginning and the end. ❷ the essence or most important features.

ⓘ *Alpha* and *omega* are respectively the first and last letters of the Greek alphabet. Christians use the phrase as a title for Jesus Christ, taking it from Revelation 1:8: 'I am Alpha and Omega, the beginning and the ending, saith the Lord'.

❷ **1994** *BBC Holidays* At Cambridge . . . you'll find the alpha and omega of American academic life: historic Harvard and space-age MIT (Massachusetts Institute of Technology).

alphabet

alphabet soup incomprehensible or confusing language, typically containing many abbreviations or symbols. informal

ⓘ The expression alludes to a kind of clear soup containing pasta in the form of letters.

2000 *Montreal Mirror* Like the IMF, WB, WTO and the rest of the alphabet soup, the FTAA is yet another engine of global capital.

altar

sacrifice someone or something on the altar of make someone or something suffer in the interests of (someone or something else).

2012 *Daily Telegraph* We had . . . a flourishing community of craftsmen making quality accessories and ready to wear, but inverted snobbery sacrificed them on the altar of mass production.

altogether

in the altogether without any clothes on; naked. informal

2003 *Scotland on Sunday* I spend a good deal of my professional life naked. Not naked as in baring my soul, but as in the altogether, baring my bits to total strangers.

amber

a fly in amber: *see* FLY.

American

as American as apple pie typically American in character.

2012 *DVD Verdict* There are more movies about baseball than any other sport . . . Perhaps it's the allure that comes from being the nation's pastime, a sport as American as apple pie.

the American dream the ideal by which equality of opportunity is available to any American, allowing the highest aspirations and goals to be achieved.

amiss

take something amiss to be offended by something that is said, especially by misunderstanding the intention behind it. British

something would not come (*or* go) amiss the specified thing would be welcome and useful. British

amok

run amok behave uncontrollably and disruptively.

ⓘ *Amok*, formerly also spelt *amuck*, comes from the Malay word *amuk*, meaning 'in a homicidal frenzy', in which sense it was first introduced into English in the early 16th century.

2013 *Mac Observer* Steve Jobs was always adamant that no powerful vice president ran amok and destroyed a clear customer-directed vision.

analysis

in the final analysis when everything has been considered (used to suggest that the following statement expresses the basic truth about a complex situation).

ancient

ancient as the hills: *see* HILL.

the ancient of Days a biblical title for God, taken from Daniel 7:9.

angel

the angel in the house a woman who is completely devoted to her husband and family.

ⓘ This was the title of a collection of poems on married love by Coventry Patmore (1823–96), and it is now mainly used ironically.

on the side of the angels on the side of what is right.

ⓘ In a speech in Oxford in November 1864 the British statesman Benjamin Disraeli alluded to the controversy over the origins of humankind then raging in the wake of the publication of Charles Darwin's *On the Origin of Species* (1859): 'Is man an ape or an angel? Now I am on the side of the angels' (*The Times* 26 Nov. 1864).

anger

more in sorrow than in anger: *see* SORROW.

angry

angry young man a young man who feels and expresses anger at the conventional values of the society around him.

ⓘ Originally, this term referred to a member of a group of socially conscious writers in Britain in the 1950s, in particular the playwright John Osborne. The phrase, the title of a book (1951) by Leslie Paul, was used of Osborne in the publicity material for his play *Look Back in Anger* (1956), in which the characteristic views of the angry young men were articulated by the anti-hero Jimmy Porter.

animal

no such animal used to express the idea that nothing of the type mentioned exists. informal

ⓘ The phrase appears to have originated in the caption to a cartoon in *Life* magazine in 1907, in which someone is looking at a camel.

party animal: *see* PARTY.

Anne

Queen Anne's dead: *see* QUEEN.

another

another place the other house of the UK parliament (used in the Commons to refer to the Lords, and vice versa). British

have (got) another think coming: *see* THINK.

just another day at the office: *see* OFFICE.

tell me another: *see* TELL.

tomorrow is another day: *see* TOMORROW.

answer

the answer's a lemon: *see* LEMON.

answers on a postcard used to suggest that there is no plausible or reasonable answer to a question.

ⓘ The phrase originated as a call for responses to a radio competition or quiz; the fact that the answer could be fitted on to a postcard suggests little in-depth analysis is expected.

a dusty answer: *see* DUSTY.

know (*or* have) all the answers be confident in your knowledge of something, typically without justification. informal

not take no for an answer: *see* NO.

ant

have ants in your pants be fidgety or restless. informal

ante

up (*or* raise) the ante increase what is at stake or under discussion, especially in a conflict or dispute.

ⓘ *Ante* comes from Latin, in which it means 'before'. As an English noun it was originally (in the early 19th century) a term in poker and similar gambling games, meaning 'a stake put up by a player before drawing cards'.

2012 *DVD Verdict* It's not hard to take a movie like *The French Connection* for granted. There have been plenty of crime thrillers in the four decades since which have upped the ante significantly.

any

not be having any of it be absolutely unwilling to cooperate. informal

a

anyone

anyone's game an evenly balanced contest.

anyone's guess: *see* GUESS.

be anyone's (of a person) be open to sexual advances from anyone. informal

anything

anything but not at all (used for emphasis).

anything goes: *see* GOES.

not make anything of: *see* **make nothing of** *at* MAKE.

apart

come apart at the seams: *see* SEAM.

poles apart: *see* POLE.

take someone or something apart: *see* TAKE.

worlds apart: *see* WORLD.

ape

go ape go wild; become violently excited. informal

ℹ Originally mid-20th-century North American slang, this expression possibly refers to the 1933 movie *King Kong*, which stars a giant ape-like monster.

apology

an apology for a very poor example of.

1998 Imogen de la Bere *The Last Deception of Palliser Wentwood* It's an apology for a bridge, built of left-over stones.

with apologies to used before the name of an author or artist to indicate that something is a parody or adaptation of their work.

2001 *This Old House* With apologies to Robert Frost, boundary expert Walter Robillard says, 'Good fences on the proper line make good neighbours'.

appeal

appeal from Philip drunk to Philip sober ask someone to reconsider, with the suggestion that an earlier opinion or decision represented only a passing mood.

ℹ This phrase comes from an anecdote told by the Roman historian and moralist Valerius Maximus concerning an unjust judgement given by King Philip of Macedon: the woman condemned by Philip declared that she would appeal to him once again, but this time when he was sober.

appeal to Caesar appeal to the highest possible authority.

ℹ The allusion is to the claim made by the apostle Paul to have his case heard in Rome, which was his right as a Roman citizen: 'I appeal unto Caesar' (Acts 25:11).

appearance

keep up appearances maintain an impression of wealth, well-being, or respectability.

to (*or* **by**) **all appearances** as far as can be seen.

2009 *Bright Lights Film Journal* McQueen sat in his hot tub overlooking the beach, taking dope, his hair frizzy, unkempt, a can of beer in his hand, to all appearances an old hippie passing the time.

appetite

whet someone's appetite: *see* WHET.

apple

apple of discord a subject of dissension.

ℹ This expression refers to the Greek myth in which a golden apple inscribed 'for the fairest' was contended for by the goddesses Hera, Athene, and Aphrodite.

the apple of your eye a person or thing of whom you are extremely fond and proud.

ℹ In Old English, the phrase referred to the pupil of the eye, considered to be a globular solid body; it came to be used as a symbol of something cherished and watched over.

apples and oranges (of two people or things) irreconcilably or fundamentally different. North American

a rotten (*or* **bad**) **apple** a bad person in a group, typically one whose behaviour is likely to have a corrupting influence on the rest. informal

she's apples used to indicate that everything is in good order and there is nothing to worry about. Australian informal

ℹ *Apples and spice* or *apples and rice* is Australian rhyming slang for *nice*.

apple cart

upset the apple cart wreck an advantageous project or disturb the status quo.

ℹ The use of a cart piled high with apples as a metaphor for a satisfactory but possibly precarious state of affairs is recorded in various expressions from the late 18th century onwards.

2008 *Guardian* Regulators ... may be selected so as to give government a quiet life and not upset the apple cart too much.

apple pie

as American as apple pie: *see* AMERICAN.

in apple-pie order in perfect order or neatness.

🛈 The origin of the phrase, which is first recorded in 1780, is unclear. It may be traceable back to Old French *cap a pie* 'head to foot'; it may be an alteration of French *nappe pliée* 'folded cloth' (which is where 'apple-pie bed' comes from); or it may simply be a reference to a literal apple pie.

approval

on approval (of goods) supplied on condition that they may be returned if not satisfactory.

seal (*or* stamp) of approval an indication or statement that something is accepted or regarded favourably.

🛈 This expression stems from the practice of putting a stamp (or formerly a seal) on official documents.

apron

tied to someone's apron strings too much under the influence and control of someone (especially used to suggest that a man is too much influenced by his mother).

apropos

apropos of nothing having no relevance to any previous discussion or situation.

area

a grey area: *see* GREY.

a no-go area: *see* NO-GO.

argue

argue the toss dispute a decision or choice already made. informal, chiefly British

🛈 The *toss* in this phrase is the tossing of a coin to decide an issue in a simple and unambiguous way according to the side of the coin visible when it lands.

ark

out of the ark extremely old-fashioned.

🛈 The ark referred to is the biblical Noah's ark (Genesis 6–7), in which Noah endeavoured to save his family and two of every kind of animal from the Flood.

arm

babe in arms: *see* BABE.

a call to arms a call to make ready for confrontation.

chance your arm: *see* CHANCE.

cost an arm and a leg be extremely expensive. informal

give an arm and a leg for pay a high price for.

keep someone or something at arm's length avoid intimacy or close contact with someone or something.

the long arm of coincidence the far-reaching power of coincidence.

the long (*or* strong) arm of the law the police seen as a far-reaching or intimidating power.

as long as your arm very long. informal

put the arm on attempt to force or coerce someone to do something. North American informal

a shot in the arm: *see* SHOT.

twist someone's arm: *see* TWIST.

up in arms about protesting angrily about something.

2013 Ben *Silent Words Speak Loudest* They're not the only ones up in arms about the proposed new regulations, which could potentially result in restrictions on charities campaigning during election periods.

with open arms with great affection or enthusiasm.

would give your right arm for be willing to pay a high price for; greatly desire to have or do. informal

armchair

an armchair critic a person who knows about a subject only by reading or hearing about it and criticizes without active experience or first-hand knowledge.

🛈 The phrase *armchair critic* is first recorded in 1896, but the concept was around at least a decade earlier: in 1886 Joseph Chamberlain sneered at opponents as 'arm-chair politicians'. Another common variation on the theme is

a

armchair traveller, meaning 'someone who travels in their imagination only'.

armed

armed at all points prepared in every particular.

armed to the teeth ❶ carrying a lot of weapons. ❷ heavily equipped.

armour

a chink in someone's armour: *see* CHINK.

hog in armour: *see* HOG.

a knight in shining armour: *see* KNIGHT.

armpit

up to your armpits deeply involved in a particular unpleasant situation or enterprise. chiefly US

army

an army marches on its stomach: *see* STOMACH.

you and whose army? used to express disbelief in someone's ability to carry out a threat. informal

around

have been around have a lot of varied experience of the world, especially a lot of sexual experience. informal

what goes around comes around: *see* GOES.

arrow

arrow of time (*or* **time's arrow**) the direction of travel from past to future in time considered as a physical dimension.

slings and arrows: *see* SLING.

a straight arrow an honest or genuine person. North American

arse

vulgar slang

arse about face contrary to what is usual, expected, or logical.

> **2005** *Dangermaus* Leading judges in Ireland have denied that the justice system in Ireland is 'arse about face' as controversy grew over sentencing of a convicted sex-offender in Dublin.

a face like a slapped (*or* **smacked**) **arse** a miserable or discontented facial expression.

> **2018 Mark Billingham** *The Killing Habit* There's really no point walking out of here with a face like a smacked arse, because it's the best you're going to get.

get off your arse stop being lazy.

get your arse into gear begin to move or take action, especially belatedly; hurry.

go arse over tit fall over in a sudden or dramatic way.

kiss my arse: *see* KISS.

kiss someone's arse: *see* KISS.

lick someone's arse: *see* LICK.

my arse! used to express strong contradiction or disbelief.

> **2005** *Barbelith Underground Forums* Opera my arse, it's a musical with a Napoleon complex. Though I still liked it.

not know your arse from your elbow be totally ignorant or incompetent.

a pain in the arse: *see* PAIN.

art

art for art's sake the idea that a work of art has no purpose beyond itself.

> ⓘ This phrase is the slogan of artists who hold that the chief or only aim of a work of art is the self-expression of the individual artist who creates it.

be art and part of be an accessory or participant in; be deeply involved in.

> ⓘ *Be art and part of* was originally a Scottish legal expression: *art* referred to the bringing about of an action and *part* to participation in it.

have something down to a fine art: *see* FINE ART.

the noble art: *see* NOBLE.

state of the art: *see* STATE.

artful

as artful as a wagonload of monkeys: *see* MONKEY.

article

an article of faith a firmly held belief.

> ⓘ *Article* is here used in the sense of 'a statement or item in a summary of religious belief'.

> **2013** *New Statesman* The people who run MI5 are bureaucrats. It is a *Mail* article of faith that such people are lazy, good-for-nothing time-servers.

the finished article: *see* FINISHED.

the genuine article: *see* GENUINE.

as

as and when used to refer to an uncertain future event.

> **2013** *Bit-Tech Gaming* Murfy moves automatically as and when he's needed, but for him to perform an action requires the player to press a button.

as if! used to express the speaker's belief that something is very doubtful or unlikely. informal

as it were in a way (used to be less precise).

> **1991** *Atlantic* Jazz audiences permit older musicians to go on suiting up, as it were, until they drop.

as you do used to suggest that something is done habitually or in the normal course of events (or, ironically, to suggest that it is abnormal).

> **2014** *Independent* Greer longed someday to own a small part of arid desert land so she could set it free, turn feral again. That never happened. Then, in 2001, the middle-aged feminist went through an epiphany. As you do. It wasn't a toy boy or sudden urge to take off to the Andes. Her life was taken over by a forest, sixty hectares of rock, trees and scrub.

ascendant

in the ascendant rising in power or influence.

> ℹ This expression has been in figurative use since the late 16th century. Literally, in technical astrological use, an *ascendant* is the sign of the zodiac that is just rising above the eastern horizon at a particular moment.

ash

dust and ashes: *see* DUST.

in sackcloth and ashes: *see* SACKCLOTH.

rake over the ashes: *see* RAKE.

rise from the ashes: *see* RISE.

turn to ashes in your mouth become bitterly disappointing or worthless.

> ℹ This phrase alludes to the Dead Sea fruit, a legendary fruit which looked appetizing but turned to smoke and ashes when someone tried to eat it. The fruit is described in the *Travels* attributed to the 14th-century writer John de Mandeville.

> **2004** *New Zealand Listener* Sir Roger somehow morphs into a sort of bad teddy bear, and Prince David's freedom and joy turn to ashes in his mouth.

aside

take (*or* draw) someone aside move someone away from a group of people in order to talk to them privately.

ask

ask for the moon: *see* MOON.

ask me another! used to say emphatically that you do not know the answer to a question. informal

> ℹ The underlying idea is that you might know the answer to another question, even though you do not know this one.

ask no odds: *see* ODDS.

a big ask a difficult demand to fulfil. informal

don't ask me! used to indicate that you do not know the answer to a question and that you are surprised or irritated to be questioned. informal

I ask you! an exclamation of shock or disapproval intended to elicit agreement from your listener. informal

if you ask me used to emphasize that a statement is your personal opinion. informal

asking

be asking for trouble (*or* be asking for it) behave in a way that is likely to result in difficulty for yourself. informal

for the asking used to indicate that someone can easily have something if they want it.

> **2012** *New York Times* A testament to her standing is the opening she has to become president of the World Bank... It would be Mrs Clinton's for the asking.

asleep

asleep at the wheel not attentive or alert; inactive. informal

> ℹ The image here is of falling asleep while driving a car. A North American variant is *asleep at the switch*, which refers to the points lever or switch on a railway.

> **2003** *Guardian* Rowling has not been asleep at the wheel in the three years since the last Potter novel, and I am pleased to report that she has not confused sheer length with inspiration.

fall asleep die. euphemistic

a

ass

North American vulgar slang

bust your ass try very hard to do something.

chew someone's ass reprimand someone severely.

cover your ass take steps to protect yourself.

drag (*or* haul) ass hurry or move fast.

kick (some) ass (*or* kick someone's ass): *see* KICK.

kiss ass: *see* KISS.

kiss someone's ass: *see* KISS.

no skin off your ass: *see* SKIN.

not give a rat's ass not care at all about something.

a pain in the ass: *see* PAIN.

a piece of ass: *see* PIECE.

put someone's ass in a sling: *see* SLING.

tits and ass: *see* **tits and bums** *at* TIT.

whip (*or* bust) someone's ass use physical force to beat someone in a fight.

work your ass (*or* butt) off work extremely hard.

at

at it engaged in some activity, typically a reprehensible one.

> **1993 G. F. Newman** *Law & Order* Oh, don't take me for a complete idiot, Jack. I know you're at it.

at that in addition; furthermore (used for emphasis at the end of a statement).

> **2014** *CNN—The Situation Room* We know there's a settlement out there for the players, a large one at that.

where it's at the most fashionable place, possession, or activity. informal

> **1990 Ellen Feldman** *Looking for Love* New York is where it's at, stylewise.

atmosphere

an atmosphere that you could cut with a knife a general feeling of great tension or malevolence.

attached

no strings attached: *see* STRING.

attendance

dance attendance on: *see* DANCE.

auld

for auld lang syne for old times' sake.

> ℹ The phrase literally means 'for old long since' and is the title and refrain of a song by Robert Burns (1788).

aunt

my giddy aunt: *see* GIDDY.

auspice

under the auspices of with the help, support, or protection of.

> ℹ *Auspice* (since the late 18th century almost always used in the plural) comes from the Latin word *auspicium*, which means the act of divination carried out by an *auspex* in ancient Rome. The *auspex* observed the flight of birds in order to foretell future events. If the omens were favourable he was seen as the protector of the particular enterprise foretold.

authority

have something on good authority have ascertained something from a reliable source.

awakening

a rude awakening: *see* RUDE.

away

away with something used as an exhortation to overcome or be rid of something.

get away with you! used to express scepticism.

far and away: *see* FAR.

out and away: *see* OUT.

when the cat's away, the mice will play: *see* CAT.

awe

shock and awe: *see* SHOCK.

awkward

the awkward age adolescence.

the awkward squad a squad composed of recruits and soldiers who need further training.

> ℹ Shortly before his death the Scottish poet Robert Burns is reported to have said, 'Don't let the awkward squad fire over me'. Nowadays,

the expression is often used to refer to a group of people who are regarded as tiresome or difficult to deal with.

axe

have an axe to grind have a private, sometimes malign, motive for doing or being involved in something.

ℹ The expression originated in a story told by the American statesman and scientist Benjamin Franklin and was used first in the USA, especially with reference to politics, but it is now in general use.

2011 *Financial Times* It is not impossible to imagine a scenario . . . where losses might stir up a row; particularly if political groups had an axe to grind, as in Switzerland.

aye

the ayes have it the affirmative votes are in the majority.

ℹ *Aye* is an archaic or dialect word meaning 'yes', now used in standard speech only when voting. Compare with **the noes have it** (*at* NO).

2000 *Guardian* The arguments will continue. But we think the 'ayes' have it.

Bb

B

plan B an alternative strategy.

> **2012** *CNN transcripts* But if the economy doesn't get better, you have to ask yourself the question, Ali, what do we do next? What's plan B?

babe

babe in arms ❶ an innocent, inexperienced, or gullible person. ❷ something very young or new.

> ❷ **2005 Lee Marshall** *Travel Intelligence* Compared to the French Riviera—which is the Olduvai Gorge of Sunbathing Man—the Costa Smeralda is a babe in arms.

babes in the wood inexperienced people in a situation calling for experience.

> ⓘ The *babes in the wood* are characters in an old ballad *The Children in the Wood*, which dates from the 16th century. The two children are abandoned in the wood by their wicked uncle who wishes to steal their inheritance. The children die of starvation and robins cover their bodies with leaves; the uncle and his accomplice are subsequently brought to justice.

baby

be someone's baby (of a project) be instigated and developed by one particular person; be someone's creation or special concern. informal

be left holding the baby: *see* HOLDING.

tar baby: *see* TAR.

throw the baby out with the bathwater discard something valuable along with other things that are inessential or undesirable.

> ⓘ This phrase is based on a German saying recorded from the early 16th century but not introduced into English until the mid 19th century, by the Scottish historian and philosopher Thomas Carlyle. He identified it as German and gave it in the form, 'You must empty out the bathing-tub, but not the baby along with it.'

> **2009 Erica Bartle** *Girl with Satchel* We last redesigned when we went bimonthly in 2004 and while we haven't stood still since then, we just felt a bit of a refresh was due. We have endeavoured not to throw the baby out with the bathwater, and there are lots of things we have left the same.

wet the baby's head: *see* WET.

bachelor

confirmed bachelor: *see* CONFIRMED.

back

at the back of your mind not consciously or specifically thought of or remembered but still part of your general awareness.

back and fill ❶ go in contrary directions ❷ be indecisive, temporize, vacillate. chiefly North American

> ⓘ The expression was originally nautical: to *back* is to sail backwards, to *fill*, to sail forwards (from the notion of the wind filling the sails).

> ❷ **2003** *Commonweal* Even as she wants to advance boldly, therefore, she is required by the evidence to back and fill, leaving the reader with a bewildering combination of affirmation and qualification.

back in the day: *see* DAY.

a back number ❶ an issue of a periodical before the current one. ❷ a person whose ideas or methods are out of date and who is no longer relevant or useful.

back o' Bourke the outback. Australian informal

> ⓘ *Bourke* is the name of a town in north-west New South Wales.

the back of beyond a very remote or inaccessible place.

> **2008** *Strange Horizons* Naomi lives in Quebec's back of beyond with her two furry companions—one human, one canid.

back of the net: *see* NET.

back to basics: *see* BASIC.

back to the drawing board used to indicate that an idea or scheme has been unsuccessful and a new one must be devised.

> ⓘ An architectural or engineering project is at its earliest phase when it exists only as a plan on a *drawing board*.

> **2012** *Daily Telegraph* Lawyers representing opponents of the scheme ... are urging the

High Court to force the government to go back to the drawing board and declare the scheme illegal.

back to square one back to the starting point, with no progress made.

ⓘ *Square one* may be a reference to a board game such as Snakes and Ladders, or may come from the notional division of a football pitch into eight numbered sections for the purpose of early radio commentaries.

back the wrong horse make a wrong or inappropriate choice.

be on (*or* get off) someone's back nag (*or* stop nagging) someone. informal

behind someone's back without a person's knowledge and in an unfair or dishonourable way.

break the back of ❶ accomplish the main or hardest part of a task. ❷ overwhelm or defeat.

by the back door using indirect or dishonest means to achieve an objective.

cover your back: *see* COVER.

get someone's back up make someone annoyed or angry.

ⓘ This phrase developed as an allusion to the way a cat arches its back when it is angry or threatened.

get your own back: *see* GET.

have eyes in the back of your head: *see* EYE.

have someone's back support and protect someone.

2018 Mel Sherrat *Hush Hush* 'The Steeles won't protect you when all this goes pear-shaped'. 'Eddie has my back .... He'll look out for me because I look out for him'.

like the back of a bus: *see* BUS.

know something like the back of your hand be entirely familiar with something.

make a rod for your own back: *see* ROD.

mind your back: *see* MIND.

not in my back yard: *see* NOT.

on the back burner: *see* BURNER.

on the back of following on from (and perhaps as a consequence of).

2002 *Irish Examiner* After the Vatican called in the Israeli and American ambassadors for talks yesterday, and with world oil prices rising on the back of the soaring Middle East crisis, US President George Bush finally relented to mounting international pressure.

on the back of an envelope: *see* ENVELOPE.

on your back in bed recovering from an injury or illness.

pat someone on the back: *see* PAT.

put your back into approach (a task) with vigour.

see the back of be rid of (an unwanted person or thing). British informal

the shirt off your back: *see* SHIRT.

slap someone on the back: *see* SLAP.

someone's back is turned someone's attention is elsewhere.

1989 Orson Scott Card *Prentice Alvin* That prentice of yours look strong enough to dig it hisself, if he doesn't lazy off and sleep when your back is turned.

a stab in the back: *see* STAB.

take a back seat take or be given a less important position or role. Compare with **in the driver's seat** (*at* DRIVER).

turn your back on ❶ ignore (someone) by turning away from them. ❷ reject or abandon (a person or thing that you were previously involved with).

watch your back: *see* WATCH.

with your back to (*or* up against) the wall in a desperate situation.

you scratch my back and I'll scratch yours: *see* SCRATCH.

backbone

put backbone into someone encourage someone to behave resolutely.

ⓘ As a metaphor for 'firmness of character', *backbone* dates from the mid 19th century.

2004 *First Things Magazine* We can look for no figure such as Niebuhr to put backbone into liberal Protestantism. It is dead and cannot be revived.

to the backbone in every respect; through and through.

back-seat

a back-seat driver ❶ a passenger in a vehicle who constantly gives the driver unwanted advice on how to drive. ❷ someone who lectures and criticizes the person actually in control of something.

backwards

bend over backwards to do something make every effort, especially to be fair or helpful. informal

know something backwards be entirely familiar with something.

2005 *This is Wiltshire* There are 98 pages in this report, and I know it backwards.

bacon

save someone's bacon: *see* **save someone's skin** *at* SAVE.

bring home the bacon ❶ supply material provision or support. ❷ achieve success. informal

ⓘ This phrase probably derives from the much earlier *save your bacon*, recorded from the mid 17th century. In early use *bacon* also referred to fresh pork, the meat most readily available to rural people.

❷ **2009** *Guardian 'Cloudy with a Chance of Meatballs'* has been bringing home the bacon at the UK box office for almost a fortnight.

bad

a bad apple: *see* **a rotten apple** *at* APPLE.

bad blood: *see* BLOOD.

bad cess: *see* CESS.

a bad day at the office an instance or brief period of comparative lack of success, regarded as being uncharacteristic and temporary.

2010 *Irish Times* The great sportsmen and women occasionally endure a bad day at the office without a scintilla of blame being attached.

bad hair day a day on which everything seems to go wrong, characterized as a day on which your hair is particularly unmanageable.

2010 *The Register* I found the Street View ... took a while to load, and sometimes didn't load at all. Maybe my net connection's having a bad hair day.

a bad lot: *see* LOT.

a bad quarter of an hour a short but very unpleasant period of time; an unnerving experience.

ⓘ *A bad quarter of an hour* is a translation of the French phrase *un mauvais quart d'heure*, which has also been current in English since the mid 19th century.

a bad workman blames his tools: *see* WORKMAN.

be bad news: *see* NEWS.

give a dog a bad name: *see* DOG.

give something up as a bad job: *see* JOB.

have got it bad (*or* **badly**) be very powerfully affected emotionally, especially by love. informal

in bad with out of favour with. North American informal

2003 *The Nation* His undiplomatic pugnacity put him in bad with his boss, Henry Kissinger, but won him a ticket to the Senate.

my bad used to acknowledge responsibility for a mistake. North American informal

too bad used to indicate that something is regrettable but now beyond retrieval. informal

turn up like a bad penny: *see* PENNY.

bag

bag and baggage with all your belongings.

ⓘ The most celebrated use of this now rather dated phrase was by the British statesman William Gladstone, who in 1876 wrote that the Turks should get out of the Balkans 'bag and baggage' (i.e. completely).

a bag of bones an emaciated person or animal. Compare with **be skin and bone** *at* SKIN.

a bag (*or* **bundle**) **of nerves** a person who is extremely timid or tense. informal

a bag of spanners used to characterize someone's face or appearance as ugly, morose, hostile, etc. informal

2011 *Daily Telegraph* I thought of my grandmother pointing to a run-down terrace, face like a bag of spanners: 'Bug-ridden,' she'd say.

a bag (*or* **whole bag**) **of tricks** a set of ingenious plans, techniques, or resources. informal

bag some Zs: *see* **catch some Zs** *at* Zs

be left holding the bag: *see* **be left holding the baby** *at* HOLDING.

in the bag ❶ (of something desirable) as good as secured. ❷ drunk. US informal

let the cat out of the bag: *see* CAT.

mixed bag: *see* MIXED.

pack your bag: *see* PACK.

rough as bags: *see* ROUGH.

bait

fish or cut bait: *see* FISH.

rise to the bait: *see* RISE.

baker

a baker's dozen thirteen.

ⓘ This expression arose from the former bakers' practice of adding an extra loaf to a dozen sold to a retailer, this representing the latter's profit.

the butcher, the baker, the candlestick-maker: *see* BUTCHER.

balance

in the balance uncertain; at a critical stage.

on balance when all factors have been taken into consideration.

tip (*or* turn) the balance: *see* **tip the scales** *at* TIP.

weigh something in the balance carefully ponder or assess the merits and demerits of something. dated

ⓘ The image is of a pair of old-fashioned scales with two pans in which the positive and negative aspects of something can be set against each other. The expanded phrase *weighed in the balance and found wanting* meaning 'having failed to meet the test of a particular situation' is also found, and is an allusion to the biblical book of Daniel, where such a process formed part of the judgement made on King Belshazzar.

bald

as bald as a coot completely bald.

ⓘ The coot (*Fulica atra*) has a broad white patch extending up from the base of its bill.

ball

a ball and chain a severe hindrance.

ⓘ Originally, *a ball and chain* referred to a heavy metal ball attached by a chain to the leg of a prisoner or convict to prevent their escape. The term has latterly been used with wry misogynistic humour to refer to a wife.

the ball is in someone's court it is that particular person's turn to act next.

ⓘ This expression is a metaphor from tennis or a similar ball game where different players use particular areas of a marked court.

a ball of fire a person who is full of energy and enthusiasm.

ⓘ In the early 19th century this phrase was also used to mean 'a glass of brandy'.

ball the jack go fast; hurry. North American informal

ⓘ The expression has its origins in US railway terminology, where *highball* is a signal to proceed and *jack* is a locomotive.

behind the eight ball: *see* EIGHT.

belle of the ball: *see* BELLE.

drop the ball: *see* DROP.

have a ball enjoy yourself greatly; have fun. informal

ⓘ A 'ball' in this context is a party or celebration (originally an African American usage).

have the ball at your feet have your best opportunity of succeeding.

have a lot on the ball have a lot of ability. US

keep the ball rolling maintain the momentum of an activity.

keep your eye on (*or* take your eye off) the ball keep (*or* fail to keep) your attention focused on the matter in hand.

on the ball alert to new ideas, methods, and trends. informal

1998 Romesh Gunesekera *Sandglass* It's big business now, you know. You have to be on the ball: go, go, go all the time.

play ball work willingly with others; cooperate. informal

ⓘ The literal sense of *play ball* is 'play a team ball game such as baseball'.

start the ball rolling set an activity in motion; make a start.

the whole ball of wax everything. North American informal

ⓘ The origins of the phrase (first recorded in the mid 20th century) remain unclear.

a whole new ball game a completely new set of circumstances. informal

ⓘ The phrase originated in North America, where a *ball game* is a baseball match.

2014 Cecilia Bedella *Adventures of Cecilia Bedella* Granted I had a broken ankle as an excuse in November and December, but the New Year is a whole new ball game. I'll step it up in 2014!

ballistic

go ballistic fly into a rage. informal

2012 *The Age* (Melbourne) Personally, Holocaust denial does it for me. I go ballistic in the face of such outrage.

b

balloon

go down like a lead balloon: *see* LEAD.

when (*or* before) the balloon goes up when (*or* before) the action or trouble starts. informal

ℹ The balloon alluded to is probably one released to mark the start of an event.

1959 *Punch* The international rules of war are apt to be waived when the balloon goes up.

ballpark

in the ballpark in a particular area or range. informal

ℹ The phrase originated in the USA, where a *ballpark* is a baseball ground.

balls

have someone or something by the balls have complete control over someone or something. vulgar slang

bamboo

the bamboo curtain an impenetrable political, economic, and cultural barrier between China and non-Communist countries.

ℹ Formed on the pattern of **the iron curtain** (*see at* IRON), this phrase dates back to the 1940s.

banana

banana oil nonsensical talk; bullshit. US and Australian informal

banana republic a small tropical state, especially one in central America, whose economy is regarded as wholly dependent on its fruit-exporting trade. derogatory

go bananas ❶ become extremely angry or excited. ❷ go mad. informal

❶ **2013** *Business Insider* Twitter's revenue growth, meanwhile, should still be accelerating ... when the company goes public. And Wall Street goes bananas about growth like that.

second banana the second most important person in an organization or activity. informal, chiefly North American

top banana the most important person in an organization or activity. informal, chiefly North American

ℹ The two expressions above originated in US theatrical slang. The *top banana* was originally the comedian who topped the bill in a show, while the *second banana* was the supporting comedian.

banana skin

slip on a banana skin: *see* SLIP.

band

to beat the band: *see* BEAT.

when the band begins to play when matters become serious.

bandwagon

jump on the bandwagon join others in doing something or supporting a cause that is fashionable or likely to be successful.

ℹ *Bandwagon* was originally the US term for a large wagon able to carry a band of musicians in a procession.

bandy

bandy words argue pointlessly or rudely.

bang

bang for your (*or* the) buck value for money; performance for cost. US informal

2011 *DVD Verdict* It's a very well appointed disc that has plenty for fans to explore, and should make you feel like you get a ton of bang for your buck.

bang goes — used to express the sudden or complete destruction of something, especially a plan or ambition.

1895 George Bernard Shaw *Letter* Somebody will give a surreptitious performance of it: and then bang goes my copyright.

bang on exactly right. British informal

bang (*or* knock) people's heads together: *see* HEAD.

bang to rights: *see* RIGHT.

bang your head against a brick wall: *see* HEAD.

get a bang out of derive excitement or pleasure from. North American informal

1931 Damon Runyon *Guys and Dolls* He seems to be getting a great bang out of the doings.

go with a bang happen with obvious success.

bank

break the bank ❶ (in gambling) win more money than is held by the bank. ❷ cost more than you can afford. informal

laugh all the way to the bank: *see* LAUGH.

banner

under the banner of ❶ claiming to support (a particular cause or set of ideas). ❷ as part of (a particular group or organization).

baptism

a baptism of fire a difficult introduction to a new job or activity.

ⓘ A *baptism of fire* was originally a soldier's initiation into battle.

2011 *New Zealand Herald* Hiring and firing dogged Maori TV in its early days. Notably it had a baptism of fire in 2002 over hiring its foundation chief executive, Canadian John Davy.

bar

bar none with no exceptions.

1866 M. E. Braddon *Lady's Mile* Your 'Aspasia' is the greatest picture that ever was painted—'bar none'.

behind bars in prison.

lower (*or* raise) the bar lower (or raise) the standards which need to be met in order to qualify for something.

prop up the bar: *see* PROP.

bare

the bare bones the basic facts about something, without any detail.

bargain

into the bargain in addition to what has already been mentioned or was expected.

ⓘ The usual American English version of the phrase is *in the bargain*.

bargepole

would not touch someone or something with a bargepole used to express an emphatic refusal to have anything to do with someone or something. informal

ⓘ A *bargepole* is used to propel a barge and to fend off obstacles. The equivalent US expression substitutes a *ten-foot pole*.

bark

bark up the wrong tree pursue a mistaken or misguided line of thought or course of action. informal

ⓘ The metaphor is of a dog that has mistaken the tree in which its quarry has taken refuge and is barking at the foot of the wrong one.

1969 Alan Bennett *Forty Years On* For sovereign states to conclude agreements on the basis of a mutual fondness for dogs seems to me to be barking up the wrong tree.

keep a dog and bark yourself: *see* DOG.

my dogs are barking: *see* DOG.

someone's bark is worse than their bite someone is not as ferocious as they appear or sound.

barred

no holds barred: *see* HOLD.

barrel

a barrel of laughs a source of fun or amusement. informal

2012 *Bookslut* The poems aren't Pound at his luminous best, nor even mid-quality Pound. In fact, they're Pound at his monomaniacal worst: not exactly a barrel of laughs (especially dismal because that's how Pound intended these poems).

get someone over a barrel get someone in a helpless position; have someone at your mercy. informal

ⓘ This phrase perhaps refers to the condition of a person who has been rescued from drowning and is placed over a barrel to clear their lungs of water.

lock, stock, and barrel: *see* LOCK.

scrape the barrel: *see* SCRAPE.

with both barrels with unrestrained force or emotion. informal

ⓘ The barrels in question are the two barrels of a firearm.

barrelhead

on the barrelhead: *see* **on the nail** *at* NAIL.

barricade

man (*or* go to) the barricades strongly protest against a government or other institution or its policy.

base

cover all the bases: *see* COVER.

get to first base achieve the first step towards your objective. informal, chiefly North American

1962 P. G. Wodehouse *Service with a Smile* She gives you the feeling that you'll never get to first base with her.

off base mistaken. North American informal

1947 *Time* Your Latin American department was off base in its comparison of the Portillo Hotel in Chile with our famous Sun Valley.

touch base briefly make or renew contact with someone or something. informal

1984 Armistead Maupin *Babycakes* In search of a routine, he touched base with his launderette, his post office, his nearest market.

🛈 *Base* in these three phrases refers to each of the four points in the angles of the 'diamond' in baseball, which a player has to reach in order to score a run.

bash

have a bash make an attempt; try. informal

basic

back to basics abandoning complication and sophistication to concentrate on the most essential aspects of something.

🛈 *Back to basics* is often used to suggest the moral superiority of the plain and simple, as in a speech made in 1993 by the British Conservative prime minister John Major, who spearheaded the government's campaign for the regeneration of basic family and educational values in the 1990s.

basinful

have had a basinful have had more than enough of something; wish to have no more. informal

2005 *Sunday Times* Blunkett has had to endure what he would call a basinful of intrusion into his private life.

basket

basket case a person or thing regarded as useless or unable to cope. informal

🛈 The expression evolved from a US slang term for a soldier who had lost all four limbs in action and was thus unable to move independently.

2004 *Royal Academy Magazine* The transformation of Liverpool from urban basket case to textbook case for design-led regeneration has been one of the most remarkable turnarounds in recent city history.

bat

bat a thousand be enjoying great success. US informal

🛈 The metaphor comes from baseball, where someone who was literally 'batting a thousand' would have a perfect batting average.

2002 *DVD Verdict* Their first film, *Suture*, garnered them serious critical acclaim and with *The Deep End*, they are now batting a thousand.

blind as a bat: *see* BLIND.

carry your bat: *see* CARRY.

have bats in the (*or* your) belfry be eccentric or crazy. informal

🛈 This expression refers to the way in which bats in an enclosed space fly about wildly if they are disturbed.

***c*.1901 G. W. Peck** *Peck's Red-Headed Boy* They all thought a crazy man with bats in his belfry had got loose.

like a bat out of hell very fast and wildly. informal

1995 Patrick McCabe *The Dead School* Like a bat out of hell that Joe Buck gets on out of the apartment and doesn't stop running till he reaches Times Square.

not bat an eyelid (*or* eye) show no emotional or other reaction. informal

🛈 *Bat* in this sense is perhaps a dialect and US variant of the verb *bate* meaning 'lower or let down'. The variant *not blink an eye* is also found.

2012 Ben *Silent Words Speak Loudest* When a man wearing nothing but socks and a hat walks on stage ... Kay does not bat an eyelid, simply dropping his trousers and carrying on with the song.

off your own bat at your own instigation; spontaneously. British

🛈 The *bat* referred to in this phrase is a cricket bat.

2002 *Sydney Morning Herald* They seem oblivious of the fact ... that it was Democrats' policy at the time, not something that Lees did off her own bat but something that ... the party went into the election supporting.

right off the bat at the very beginning; straight away. North American

bated

with bated breath in great suspense; very anxiously or excitedly.

ⓘ *Baited*, which is sometimes seen, is a misspelling, since *bated* in this sense is a shortened form of *abated*, the idea being that your breathing is lessened under the influence of extreme suspense.

bath

take a bath suffer a heavy financial loss. informal

2012 *New Zealand Herald* While MediaWorks' bankers decide whether they would be prepared to take a bath on their debts, Ironbridge says its restructuring plans are continuing.

take an early bath: *see* EARLY.

baton

pass (*or* hand) on the baton hand over a particular duty or responsibility.

ⓘ In athletics, the *baton* is the short stick or rod passed from one runner to the next in a relay race. The related phrases *pick up* or *take up the baton* mean 'accept a duty or responsibility'. Compare with **hand on the torch** (*at* TORCH).

under the baton of (of an orchestra or choir) conducted by.

ⓘ The *baton* here is the rod used by the conductor.

batten

batten down the hatches prepare for a difficulty or crisis.

ⓘ *Batten down the hatches* was originally a nautical term meaning 'make a ship's hatches secure with gratings and tarpaulins' in expectation of stormy weather.

1998 *Oldie* They endured the hard pounding of the Seventies, when Labour battened down the hatches, and soldiered through the follies of the early Eighties.

battery

recharge your batteries: *see* RECHARGE.

battle

battle of the giants a contest between two pre-eminent parties.

ⓘ This expression may be a reference to the battle between the giants and gods in Greek mythology.

battle royal a fiercely contested fight or dispute.

In the 18th and 19th centuries the term was often applied to a cockfight between several birds.

2012 *Mac Observer* That's the same Judge Lucy Koh who is currently presiding over the patent battle royal between Apple and Samsung.

battle stations used as a command or signal to military personnel to take up their positions in preparation for battle. chiefly US

half the battle an important step towards achieving something.

a losing battle: *see* LOSING.

a pitched battle: *see* PITCHED.

a running battle: *see* RUNNING.

bay

bay at the moon: *see* MOON.

bay for blood demand punishment or retribution.

bring someone or something to bay trap or corner a person or animal being hunted or chased.

ⓘ This phrase was originally a medieval hunting term, referring to the position of the quarry when it is cornered by the baying hounds. An animal cornered in this way is said to *stand at bay*.

hold (*or* keep) someone or something at bay prevent someone or something from approaching or having an effect.

be

-to-be of the future.

2005 John Telfer Brown *Scotwise* Mum-to-be Nicola Leary went through two days of torture after a blundering doctor told her that her baby had died in her womb.

be there for someone: *see* THERE.

the be-all and end-all a feature of an activity or a way of life that is of greater importance than any other. informal

beach

not the only pebble on the beach: *see* PEBBLE.

bead

draw (*or* get) a bead on take aim at with a gun. chiefly North American

2010 *Flash Fiction Online* I drew a bead on the center of Mendez's chest. Then I thought: Sure, one of us has a blank in his rifle. But the odds are that mine is live.

b

beam

a beam in your eye a fault that is greater in yourself than in the person you are finding fault with.

ℹ This phrase comes from Matthew 7:3: 'Why beholdest thou the mote that is in thy brother's eye, but considerest not the beam that is in thy own eye?' *Beam* here means 'large piece of timber'. For **a mote in someone's eye**, *see* MOTE.

broad in the beam: *see* BROAD.

off (*or* **way off) beam** on the wrong track; mistaken. informal

ℹ Originally, this phrase referred to the radio beam or signal used to guide aircraft.

2004 Dave Weedon *Backword* George Orwell wasn't wrong about much but he was way off beam with his famously jaundiced view of sport.

on your beam ends near the end of your resources; desperate.

ℹ The *beam* referred to here is one of the main horizontal transverse timbers of a wooden ship; compare with **broad in the beam** (*at* BROAD). The phrase originated as the nautical term *on her beam ends*, and was used of a ship that had heeled over on its side and was almost capsizing.

bean

full of beans lively; in high spirits. informal

ℹ This phrase was originally used by people who work with horses, and referred to the good condition of a horse fed on beans.

give someone beans scold or deal severely with a person. informal

a hill (*or* **row) of beans** something of little importance or value. informal

2013 Tim Harford *Undercover Economist* This is the point: none of these losses will amount to a hill of beans. I expect to waste a few hours and a few quid. I don't expect to regret any of it.

know how many beans make five be intelligent; have your wits about you. British informal

not have a bean be penniless. informal

ℹ *Bean* was an early-19th-century slang term for a golden guinea or sovereign. In the sense of 'a coin', it now survives only in this phrase.

not know beans about know nothing about. North American informal

2001 *Hudson Review* One tires of reading collections of prose by poets who may know their craft from holes in the ground but don't appear to know beans about anything else.

spill the beans: *see* SPILL.

bear

bear the brunt of: *see* BRUNT.

bear fruit: *see* FRUIT.

bear in mind: *see* MIND.

bring something to bear (on something) ❶ aim (a weapon) (at something). ❷ muster and use something to effect (on something).

Do bears shit in the woods? used to indicate that something is blatantly obvious. informal

2005 Mark Barton *Losing Today: Mark's Tales* Do we review demos, he asked on the accompanying note—hey, do bears shit in woods—course we do, especially when they are as fine as this.

grin and bear it: *see* GRIN.

have your cross to bear: *see* CROSS.

like a bear with a sore head (of a person) very irritable. British informal

loaded for bear fully prepared for any eventuality, typically a confrontation or challenge. North American informal

ℹ The image here may be of a hunting gun loaded and ready to shoot a bear.

not bear thinking about be too terrible to contemplate.

beard

beard the lion in his den (*or* **lair)** confront or challenge someone on their own ground.

ℹ This phrase developed partly from the idea of being daring enough to take a lion by the hair on its chin and partly from the use of *beard* as a verb to mean 'face', i.e. to face a lion in his den.

beast

big beast: *see* BIG.

the nature of the beast: *see* NATURE.

beat

beat a hasty retreat withdraw, typically in order to avoid something unpleasant.

In former times, a drumbeat could be used to keep soldiers in step while they were retreating.

beat about the bush discuss a matter without coming to the point; be ineffectual and waste time.

This phrase is a metaphor which originated in the shooting or netting of birds; compare with **beat the bushes** below.

2013 *Scary Duck* Pete was—and let's not beat about the bush—the school git, who lived permanently under the wing of his over-protective mother.

beat someone at their own game use someone's own methods to outdo them in their chosen activity.

beat the bejesus out of someone: *see* BEJESUS.

beat your breast: *see* BREAST.

beat the bushes search thoroughly. North American informal

This expression originates from the way in which hunters walk through undergrowth wielding long sticks which are used to force birds or animals out into the open where they can be shot or netted.

beat the clock perform a task quickly or within a fixed time limit.

beat the daylights out of: *see* DAYLIGHT.

beat the drum for: *see* DRUM.

beat the Dutch: *see* DUTCH.

beat someone hollow: *see* HOLLOW.

beat your (*or* the) meat (of a man) masturbate. vulgar slang

beat the pants off prove to be vastly superior to. informal

1990 Paul Auster *The Music of Chance* 'Not bad, kid,' Nashe said. 'You beat the pants off me.'

beat a path to someone's door (of a large number of people) hasten to make contact with someone regarded as interesting or inspiring.

This phrase developed from the idea of a large number of people trampling down vegetation to make a path: compare with **off the beaten track** (*at* BEATEN).

beat the rap: *see* RAP.

beat the system succeed in finding a means of getting round rules, regulations, or other means of control.

beat someone to it succeed in doing something or getting somewhere before someone else, to their annoyance.

beat someone to the punch: *see* PUNCH.

if you can't beat them, join them if you are unable to outdo rivals in some endeavour, you might as well cooperate with them and gain whatever advantage possible by doing so. humorous.

miss a beat: *see* MISS.

a stick to beat someone or something with: *see* STICK.

to beat the band in such a way as to surpass all competition. North American informal

1995 Patrick McCabe *The Dead School* He was polishing away to beat the band.

beaten

beaten (*or* pipped) at the post defeated at the last moment.

The *post* alluded to here is the marker at the end of a race.

off the beaten track (*or* path) ❶ in or into an isolated place. ❷ unusual.

❷ **1992 Iain Banks** *The Crow Road* 'Your Uncle Hamish . . .' She looked troubled. 'He's a bit off the beaten track, that boy.'

beautiful

the beautiful game football.

The phrase has been attributed to the Brazilian footballer Pelé, who called his autobiography *My Life and the Beautiful Game* (1977), although in fact there is earlier evidence of it being applied to cricket.

the beautiful people ❶ fashionable, glamorous, and privileged people. ❷ (in the 1960s) hippies.

❶ **2005 Ron Mwangaguhunga** *The Corsair* It's our job to manufacture Eurogods for the masses to worship. We discover, and if we cannot discover, we manufacture the beautiful people. C'est tout!

the body beautiful an ideal of physical beauty.

2009 Erica Bartle *Girl with Satchel* The issue (body image campaigning, that is) is overwhelmingly complicated, what with all of popular culture geared towards the worship of the (slim, blemish-free) body beautiful.

small is beautiful: *see* SMALL.

beaver

an eager beaver: *see* EAGER.

work like a beaver work steadily and industriously. informal

ⓘ The beaver is referred to here because of the industriousness with which it constructs the dams necessary for its aquatic dwellings. The image is similarly conjured up by the phrase *beaver away* meaning 'work hard'.

beck

at someone's beck and call always having to be ready to obey someone's orders immediately.

ⓘ *Beck* in the sense of 'a significant gesture of command' comes from the verb *beck*, a shortened form of *beckon*. It is now found mainly in this phrase.

bed

bed and breakfast ❶ overnight accommodation and breakfast next morning as offered by hotels etc. ❷ designating financial transactions in which shares are sold and then bought back the next morning.

a bed of nails a problematic or uncomfortable situation.

ⓘ A *bed of nails* was originally a board with nails pointing out of it, lain on by Eastern fakirs and ascetics.

a bed of roses a situation or activity that is comfortable or easy.

die in your bed: *see* DIE.

fall out of bed suffer financial or commercial collapse. North American informal euphemistic

get out of bed on the wrong side be bad-tempered all day long.

in bed with ❶ having sexual intercourse with. ❷ in undesirably close association with. informal

❷ **2000** *Snowboard UK* Jackson lies like an oasis of culture and good coffee in a state that is otherwise firmly in bed with gun culture.

put something to bed ❶ complete the editing of a newspaper, magazine, etc. and send it for printing. ❷ deal with something conclusively. informal

❷ **2013** *Daily Telegraph* It is earnestly to be hoped that it will be us—the Scottish people—who will decide next Sept 18 that they wish their country to remain a part of Britain. In so doing, they will thus put to bed for ever the divisive and distracting issue of Scotland's constitutional future.

reds under the bed: *see* RED.

you have made your bed and must lie in it you must accept the consequences of your own actions.

bedpost

between you and me and the bedpost (*or* the gatepost *or* the wall) in strict confidence. informal

ⓘ The *bedpost*, *gatepost*, or *wall* is seen as marking the boundary beyond which the confidence must not go.

bedroom

bedroom eyes a look suggestive of sexual invitation. informal

bedside

bedside manner a doctor's approach or attitude to a patient.

2012 *Daily Telegraph* A caring, competent doc with a good bedside manner and a plan to save your life is far more comforting than sweet-sounding words.

bee

the bee's knees something or someone outstandingly good. informal

ⓘ *The bee's knees* was first used to refer to something small and insignificant, but it quickly developed its current, completely opposite meaning.

have a bee in your bonnet have an obsessive preoccupation with something. informal

ⓘ This expression, along with *have bees in the head* or *bees in the brain*, was first used to refer to someone who was regarded as crazy or eccentric.

the birds and the bees: *see* BIRD.

busy bee: *see* BUSY.

beef

where's the beef? used to complain that something is too insubstantial. informal

beeline

make a beeline for go rapidly and directly towards.

ⓘ The phrase refers to the straight line supposedly taken instinctively by a bee returning to its hive.

2013 *The Age* (Melbourne) Salam made a beeline for the Australian High Commission in Nicosia but, for once, he didn't land on his feet: his request to see an Australian diplomat was refused.

been

been (*or* been and gone) and — used to express surprise or annoyance at someone's actions. British informal

been there, done that: *see* THERE.

beer

beer and skittles amusement. British

ℹ This phrase comes from the proverb *life isn't all beer and skittles*. The game of skittles is used as a prime example of a form of light-hearted entertainment.

small beer: *see* SMALL.

beetroot

red as a beetroot: *see* RED.

before

before you can say Jack Robinson: *see* JACK.

before you can say knife: *see* KNIFE.

beg

beg the question ❶ raise a point that has not been dealt with; invite an obvious question. ❷ avoid the question ❸ assume the truth of an argument or of a proposition to be proved, without arguing it.

ℹ The original meaning of the phrase *beg the question* belongs to the field of logic and is a translation of Latin *petitio principii*, literally meaning 'laying claim to a principle', i.e. assume the truth of something that ought to be proved first. For many traditionalists this remains the only correct meaning, but far commoner in English today is the first sense here, 'invite an obvious question'.

beg yours I beg your pardon. Australian & New Zealand

beggar

beggar belief (*or* description) be too extraordinary to be believed (*or* described).

beggars can't be choosers people with no other options must be content with what is offered. proverb

begging

go begging ❶ (of an article) be available. ❷ (of an opportunity) not be taken.

beginner

beginner's luck good luck supposedly experienced by a beginner at a particular game or activity.

beginning

the beginning of the end the event or development to which the conclusion or failure of something can be traced.

ℹ In 1942 Winston Churchill, reporting on the Allied victory at the battle of Alamein, said 'This is not the end. It is not even the beginning of the end. But it is, perhaps, the end of the beginning.'

1992 H. Norman Schwartzkopf *It Doesn't Take a Hero* I heard about D-Day on the radio. The announcer quoted Ohio governor John Bricker's now-famous line that this was 'the beginning of the end of the forces of evil'.

behold

lo and behold: *see* LO.

bejesus

informal

beat the bejesus out of someone hit someone very hard or for a long time.

scare the bejesus out of someone frighten someone very much.

2001 *GQ* This place is going to scare the bejesus out of the fuddy-duddy Sloaney-Pony set.

ℹ *Bejesus* is an alteration of the exclamation *by Jesus!* It is often found in its Anglo-Irish form *bejasus* or *bejabers*.

belfry

have bats in the belfry: *see* BAT.

believe

believe you me used to emphasize the truth of a statement.

believing

seeing is believing: *see* SEEING.

b

bell

bell, book, and candle a formula for laying a curse on someone.

ℹ This expression alludes to the closing words of the rite of excommunication, 'Do to the book, quench the candle, ring the bell', meaning that the service book is closed, the candle put out, and the passing bell rung, as a sign of spiritual death.

bell the cat take the danger of a shared enterprise upon yourself.

ℹ *Bell the cat* alludes to the fable in which mice or rats have the idea of hanging a bell around the cat's neck so as to have warning of its approach, the only difficulty being to find one of their number willing to undertake the task.

bells and smells used depreciatively to denote the Anglo-Catholic or High Church wing of the Church of England.

ℹ The allusion is to the altar bells and incense used in Roman Catholic services.

bells and whistles attractive additional features or trimmings. informal

ℹ The *bells and whistles* originally referred to were those found on old fairground organs. Nowadays, the phrase is often used in computing jargon to mean 'attractive but superfluous facilities'.

as clear (*or* sound) as a bell perfectly clear (*or* sound).

1993 *Independent* We spent a few thousand on redecoration, but basically the place was sound as a bell.

give someone a bell telephone someone. British informal

hell's bells: *see* HELL.

ring a bell revive a distant recollection; sound familiar. informal

saved by the bell: *see* SAVED.

with bells on enthusiastically. North American informal

1989 Mary Gordon *The Other Side* So, everybody's waiting for you with bells on.

belle

belle of the ball the most admired and successful woman on a particular occasion.

ℹ The *belle of the ball* was originally the girl or woman regarded as the most beautiful and popular at a dance.

belly

fire in the belly: *see* FIRE.

go belly up fail or go out of business, especially by going bankrupt. informal

ℹ The implied comparison is with a dead fish or other animal floating upside down in the water. *See also* **go tits up** *at* TIT.

2014 *New Zealand Herald* The collapse of US investment bank Bear Stearns six months before Lehman's went belly up . . . might serve just as well as the GFC-starter.

bellyful

have a bellyful of become impatient after prolonged experience of someone or something. informal

below

below stairs in the basement of a house, in particular as the part occupied by servants. British dated

down below: *see* DOWN.

sit below the salt: *see* SALT.

belt

below the belt unfair or unfairly; not in keeping with the rules.

ℹ In boxing, a blow *below the belt* is a low, and therefore unlawful, blow.

belt and braces (of a policy or action) providing double security by using two means to achieve the same end. British

ℹ This meaning developed from the idea of a literal *belt* and *braces* holding up a pair of loose-fitting trousers.

2002 *Digital Photography Made Easy* Oddly, the manual is also on CD, which seems a bit belt and braces (though useful if you lose the original).

tighten your belt cut your expenditure; live more frugally.

under your belt ❶ (of food or drink) consumed. ❷ safely or satisfactorily achieved, experienced, or acquired.

bend

bend someone's ear talk to someone, especially with great eagerness or in order to ask a favour. informal

bend your elbow drink alcohol. North American *See also* **lift your elbow** *at* ELBOW.

bend the knee: *see* **bow the knee** *at* BOW.

bend over backwards: *see* BACKWARDS.

round the bend (*or* twist) crazy; mad. informal

2010 *Eye Weekly* (Toronto) The director of *The Wages of Fear* and *Diabolique* set out to portray the madness of a hotelier driven round the bend by suspicions of his wife's infidelity.

bended

on bended knee kneeling, especially when pleading or showing great respect.

ⓘ *Bended* was the original past participle of *bend*, but in Middle English it was superseded in general use by *bent*. It is now archaic and survives only in this phrase.

benefit

give someone the benefit of — explain or recount to someone at length (often used ironically when someone pompously or impertinently assumes that their knowledge or experience is superior to that of the person to whom they are talking).

2011 *Daily Telegraph* He said it was 'those who are not bursting into the media to give us the benefit of their latest opinion', who were getting on with the job of making efficient savings.

the benefit of the doubt a concession that someone or something must be regarded as correct or justified, if the contrary has not been proved.

bent

bent out of shape angry or agitated. North American informal

1994 David Spencer *Alien Nation 6: Passing Fancy* Max Corigliano was there . . . and bent out of shape about having been made to wait so long.

berry

as brown as a berry: *see* BROWN.

berth

give someone or something a wide berth stay away from someone or something.

ⓘ *Berth* is a nautical term which originally referred to the distance that ships should keep away from each other or from the shore, rocks, etc., in order to avoid a collision. Therefore, the literal meaning of the expression is 'steer a ship well clear of something while passing it'.

besetting

besetting sin a fault to which a person or institution is especially prone; a characteristic weakness.

ⓘ The verb *beset* literally means 'surround with hostile intent', so the image is of a sin besieging or pressing in upon a person.

1974 Donal Scannell *Mother Knew Best* Mother said vanity was a besetting sin which Amy resented, to say the least of it.

beside

beside yourself overcome with worry, grief, or anger; distraught.

best

at the best of times even in the most favourable circumstances.

best bib and tucker: *see* BIB.

the best thing since sliced bread: *see* BREAD.

do your level best: *see* LEVEL.

give it your best shot: *see* SHOT.

man's best friend: *see* MAN.

put your best foot forward: *see* FOOT.

with the best will in the world: *see* WILL.

the best of both worlds: *see* WORLD.

the best of British used to wish someone well in an enterprise, especially when you are almost sure it will be unsuccessful. informal

ⓘ This phrase is an abbreviation of *the best of British luck to you*.

give someone or something best admit the superiority of; give way to. British

2004 *Sunday Business Post* That was always one thing that the Irish race was always noted for, the one place where the world had to give us best.

make the best of it ❶ derive what limited advantage you can from something unsatisfactory or unwelcome. ❷ use resources as well as possible.

ⓘ The first sense is often found in the form *make the best of a bad job*, meaning 'do something as well as you can under difficult circumstances'.

your best bet the most favourable option available in particular circumstances.

six of the best a caning as a punishment, traditionally with six strokes of the cane.

ⓘ *Six of the best* was formerly a common punishment in boys' schools, but it is now chiefly historical in its literal sense and tends to be used figuratively or humorously.

with the best of them as well or as much as anyone.

2000 *DVD Verdict* Lewis is cold, arrogant, even violent, but can turn on the charm and tinkle the ivories with the best of them.

bet

all bets are off the outcome of a particular situation is unpredictable. informal

don't bet on it used to express doubt about an assertion or situation. informal

you bet you may be absolutely certain. informal

2010 *Manchester Music* Would people still come? You bet: sold out in advance, but then it is one hell of a line-up.

you can bet your boots (*or* bottom dollar *or* life) you may be absolutely certain. informal

bet the farm risk everything that you own on a bet, investment, or enterprise. North American informal

hedge your bets: *see* HEDGE.

a safe bet a certainty.

ⓘ *A safe bet* originally referred to a horse that was confidently expected to win a race.

2002 *Observer* It is a safe bet that as the Western world gets fatter, the people on its television screens will continue to get thinner.

betide

woe betide: *see* WOE.

better

against your better judgement: *see* JUDGEMENT.

the — the better used to emphasize the importance or desirability of the quality or thing specified.

1986 Patrick Leigh Fermor *Between the Woods & the Water* He had a passion for limericks, the racier the better.

better the devil you know it's wiser to deal with an undesirable but familiar person or situation than to risk a change that might lead to a situation with worse difficulties or a person whose faults you have yet to discover.

ⓘ This phrase is a shortened form of the proverb *better the devil you know than the devil you don't know.*

better late than never it's preferable for something to happen or be done belatedly than not at all.

be better than a poke in the eye with a sharp stick: *see* POKE.

better safe than sorry it's wiser to be cautious and careful than to be hasty or rash and so do something that you may later regret.

ⓘ Apparently the expression is quite recent in this form (mid 20th century); *better be sure than sorry* is recorded from the mid 19th century.

2012 *New Zealand Herald* We were told to get the heck out. I was going to stay, but it's better to be safe than sorry.

the better to — so as to — better.

1986 Peter Mathiessen *Men's Lives* Francis ran both motors with their housings off, the better to tinker with them.

get the better of win an advantage over someone; defeat or outwit someone.

go one better ❶ narrowly surpass a previous effort or achievement. ❷ narrowly outdo another person.

no better than you should (*or* ought to) be regarded as sexually promiscuous or of doubtful moral character.

ⓘ This phrase dates back to the early 17th century. Used typically of a woman, it is now rather dated.

1998 *Spectator* 'She's no better than she ought to be.' (British mothers of my generation... often used that enigmatic phrase. They would use it about female neighbours of whom they disapproved, or women in low-cut dresses on television.)

seen better days: *see* DAY.

so much the better: *see* MUCH.

think better of: *see* THINK.

your better half your husband or wife. humorous

your better nature: *see* NATURE.

betting

the betting is that it is likely that. informal

Betty Martin

all my eye and Betty Martin: *see* **my eye** *at* EYE.

between

between the devil and the deep blue sea: *see* DEVIL.

between a rock and a hard place: *see* ROCK.

between you and me in confidence; confidentially.

ⓘ The alternative version *between you and I* is often used, but it is frowned on by sticklers for correct usage (*me* is the form of the pronoun that follows a preposition). A further alternative that avoids the problem is *between ourselves*. An informal extended version is *between you, me, and the gatepost*.

few and far between: *see* FEW.

betwixt

betwixt and between neither one thing nor the other. informal

ⓘ *Betwixt* is now poetic or archaic and is seldom found outside this phrase.

beyond

the back of beyond: *see* BACK.

beyond the black stump: *see* STUMP.

beyond the pale: *see* PALE.

get beyond a joke: *see* JOKE.

it's beyond me it's too astonishing, puzzling, etc. for me to understand or explain. informal

bib

your best bib and tucker your best clothes. informal

ⓘ *Bib and tucker* originally referred to certain items of women's clothing. A *bib* is a garment worn over the upper front part of the body (e.g. the bib of an apron), and a *tucker* was a decorative piece of lace formerly worn on a woman's bodice.

stick (*or* poke) your bib in interfere. Australian & New Zealand informal

biblical

know someone in the biblical sense: *see* KNOW.

bicky

big bickies a large sum of money Australian informal

ⓘ *Bickies* is an abbreviation of *biscuits*.

1981 *Canberra Times* Appearance money is another claim which we think will succeed... Just showing up is worth big bickies.

bid

bid fair to seem likely to. archaic or literary

bide

bide your time wait quietly for a good opportunity.

ⓘ *Bide* in the sense of *await* is now only found in this expression. It has been superseded by *abide* in most of its other senses.

2009 *Matairea* We've been playing a waiting game, working on the boat, biding our time, until the strong southeasterlies lessen for just a few days.

big

a big ask: *see* ASK.

big beast a person of high status and wide influence. informal

2013 *Daily Telegraph* Mr Clegg, who beat Mr Huhne to the Liberal Democrat leadership in 2007, said the former minister was a 'big beast' who should be in the Cabinet.

big bickies: *see* BICKY.

the big boys: *see* BOY.

Big Brother: *see* BROTHER.

big bucks: *see* BUCK.

the big C: *see* C.

a big cheese an important and influential person. informal

ⓘ Other versions of this phrase substitute *fish*, *gun*, *noise*, *shot*, or *wheel* for *cheese*. These are mainly self-explanatory, with the exception of *cheese* itself, which is of doubtful origin but may be from Persian and Urdu *chīz* meaning 'thing'. As a phrase, *big cheese* seems to have originated in early 20th-century US slang, as did *big noise*. *Big wheel* in this metaphorical sense (as opposed to the fairground ride known as a Ferris wheel) and *big shot* are similarly US in origin (mid 20th century). *Big fish* may have connotations either of something it is desirable for you to catch or of the metaphorical expression a *big fish in a small pond*.

big deal: *see* DEAL.

the big enchilada: *see* ENCHILADA.

the big five a name given by hunters to the five largest and most dangerous African mammals: rhinoceros, elephant, buffalo, lion, and leopard.

big girl's blouse: *see* BLOUSE.

big (*or* heavy) hitter a person with considerable power and influence (as contrasted with those who have less).

2004 *Film Inside Out* Ollie Trinke . . . is a big hitter in the music PR world of Manhattan.

big jobs: *see* JOB.

the big lie a gross distortion or misrepresentation of the facts, especially when used as a propaganda device by a politician or official body.

the big — -o used to denote an age ending in a zero, especially as marked by a landmark birthday. informal

the big smoke ❶ London. British informal ❷ any large town. chiefly Australian

the big stick the use or threat of force or power. informal

ⓘ In a speech in 1903, President Theodore Roosevelt, discoursing on US foreign policy, referred to the 'old adage': 'Speak softly and carry a big stick.'

the big Three, Four, etc. the dominant group of three, four, etc. informal

2013 *Daily Telegraph* Before BR the tendency was always towards simplification, resulting in the amalgamation of 120 companies into the 'Big Four' in 1923.

big time on a large scale; to a great extent. informal

2006 *Metro* (Toronto) Wow, some of these people look like they just got beat down big time.

the big time the highest or most successful level in a career, especially in entertainment.

big white chief: *see* CHIEF.

bite the big one: *see* BITE.

give someone the big e reject someone, typically in an insensitive or dismissive way. British informal

ⓘ The e in the phrase is from *elbow*: *give someone the big elbow* has the same meaning.

make it big become very successful or famous. informal

talk big: *see* TALK.

that's big of you used as an ironic comment on the meagreness of someone's generosity.

think big be ambitious. informal

too big for your boots conceited. informal

what's the big idea? used to remonstrate with someone who has rudely inconvenienced you. informal

bigger

have eyes bigger than your stomach: *see* EYE.

bike

get off your bike become annoyed. Australian & New Zealand informal

1939 Xavier Herbert *Capricornia* 'I tell you I saw no-one.' 'Don't get off your bike, son.—I know you're tellin' lies.'

on your bike! ❶ go away! ❷ take action! British informal

ⓘ Sense 2 became a catchphrase in 1980s Britain, when it was used as an exhortation to the unemployed to show initiative in their attempt to find work. It was taken from a speech by the Conservative politician Norman Tebbit in which he said of his unemployed father: 'He did not riot, he got on his bike and looked for work.'

bill

bill and coo exchange caresses or affectionate words; behave or talk in a very loving or sentimental way. informal, dated

ⓘ The image is of two doves, a long-established symbol of mutual love (*bill* denotes touching beaks).

a clean bill of health a declaration or confirmation that someone is healthy or something is in good condition.

ⓘ In the mid 18th century, a *bill of health* was an official certificate given to the master of a ship on leaving port; if *clean*, it certified that there was no infection either in the port or on board the vessel.

fit (*or* fill) the bill be suitable for a particular purpose.

ⓘ *Bill* in this context is a printed list of items on a theatrical programme or advertisement.

foot the bill be responsible for paying for something.

sell someone a bill of goods deceive or swindle someone, usually by persuading them to accept something untrue or undesirable.

ⓘ A *bill of goods* is a consignment of merchandise.

1968 *Globe & Mail (Toronto)* There was no production bonus . . . We were sold a bill of goods.

top (*or* head) the bill be the main performer or act in a show, play, etc.

billy-o

like billy-o very much, hard, or strongly. British informal

2007 *Diamond Geezer* A dodgy knee joint was to blame, half of which has now been replaced by a pseudo-bionic implant (and which hurts like billy-o when you bend it, so I'm told).

bird

the bird has flown the person you are looking for has escaped or gone away.

a bird in (the) hand something that you have securely or are sure of.

ℹ This phrase refers to the proverb *a bird in hand is worth two in the bush*, current in English since the mid 15th century.

a bird of passage someone who is always moving on.

ℹ Literally, a *bird of passage* is a migrant bird.

a bird's-eye view a general view from above.

the birds and the bees basic facts about sex and reproduction as told to a child. informal

birds of a feather people with similar tastes, interests, etc.

ℹ This phrase comes from the proverb *birds of a feather flock together*, which has been current in this form since the late 16th century. Its origins may ultimately lie in the Apocrypha: 'the birds will resort unto their like' (Ecclesiasticus 27:9).

be a box of birds: *see* BOX.

do bird serve a prison sentence. British informal

ℹ In this phrase *bird* comes from rhyming slang *birdlime* 'time'.

early bird: *see* EARLY.

flip someone the bird stick your middle finger up at someone as a sign of contempt or anger. informal, chiefly US

2019 Sarah Baxter *Sunday Times* In shock, he manages to walk stiffly from the wreckage. 'I'm such a fool,' he mutters, fearing the royal life of confinement has got him in the end. But not yet, dammit. As the credits roll, he flips the bird at his critics, clambers back into the driving seat of his replacement Land Rover and speeds off without a seatbelt.

give someone (*or* get) the bird boo or jeer at someone (*or* be booed or jeered at). British informal

ℹ This phrase first appeared in early 19th-century theatrical slang as *the big bird*, meaning 'a goose'. This was because the hissing of geese could be compared to the audience's hissing at an act or actor of which it disapproved.

have a bird be very shocked or agitated. North American informal

1992 *Globe & Mail (Toronto)* The Washington press corps would have a bird if the president-to-be appointed his wife to a real job.

kill two birds with one stone: *see* KILL.

a little bird told me used as a teasing way of saying that you do not intend to divulge how you came to know something.

rare bird: *see* RARE.

strictly for the birds not worth consideration; unimportant. informal

ℹ This expression was originally US army slang. It may be an allusion to the way in which birds eat the droppings of horses and cattle.

birthday

in your birthday suit naked. humorous

biscuit

have had the biscuit be no longer good for anything; be done for. Canadian informal

1994 *Equinox* I thought I'd had the biscuit. I was more than 12 kilometres from camp, I didn't have a coat . . . and it was about 40 below.

take the biscuit (*or* cake) be the most remarkable. informal

1925 P. G. Wodehouse Letter Of all the poisonous, foul, ghastly places, Cannes takes the biscuit with absurd ease.

bishop

as the actress said to the bishop: *see* ACTRESS.

bit

a bit much somewhat excessive or unreasonable.

a bit of all right a pleasing person or thing, especially a woman regarded sexually. British informal

a bit of crackling: *see* CRACKLING.

bit of fluff (*or* skirt *or* stuff) a woman regarded in sexual terms. British informal

2000 *Sunday Herald* There is so much stuff you get put up for where you are obviously just the bit of fluff, even if you have brains and wear trousers all the time. It's hard as well for women to keep their career going.

bit of rough: *see* ROUGH.

b

bit on the side ❶ a person with whom you are unfaithful to your partner. ❷ a relationship involving being unfaithful to your partner. ❸ money earned outside your normal job. informal

bits and pieces (*or* bobs) an assortment of small or unspecified items.

champ at the bit: *see* CHAMP.

do your bit make a useful contribution to an effort or cause. informal

ⓘ The exhortation to *do your bit* was much used during World War 1, but the expression was current in the late 19th century.

get the bit between your teeth begin to tackle a problem or task in a determined or independent way.

ⓘ The metal bit in a horse's mouth should lie on the fleshy part of its gums; if a headstrong horse grasps the bit between its teeth it can evade the control of the reins and its rider.

in bits very upset or emotionally affected. British informal

2019 *Evening Standard* Jayden's uncle Josh Grant ... told the Evening Standard 'I'm in bits. It's a sad time. He was a good kid.'

a nasty bit of work: *see* **a nasty piece of work** *at* NASTY.

naughty bits: *see* NAUGHTY.

not a bit of it not at all; on the contrary.British

2008 Christopher Stocks *Forgotten Fruits* Were strawberry breeders so careless, and so little concerned with history? Not a bit of it.

to bits very much. informal

1998 *Times* A succession of elderly ladies explained how, as young women, they had fancied him to bits.

bite

bite someone's head off: *see* HEAD.

a bite at the cherry: *see* CHERRY.

bite the big one die. North American informal

1996 Tom Clancy *Executive Orders* The Premier of Turkmenistan bit the big one, supposedly an automobile accident.

bite the bullet face up to doing something difficult or unpleasant; stoically avoid showing fear or distress.

ⓘ This phrase dates from the days before anaesthetics, when wounded soldiers were given a bullet or similar solid object to clench between their teeth when undergoing surgery.

2019 *Radio Times* Patients include an anxious young man who, having avoided a vasectomy for a long time, has finally bitten the bullet and come in for the procedure.

bite the dust ❶ be killed. ❷ fail. informal

bite the hand that feeds you deliberately hurt or offend a benefactor; act ungratefully.

2011 *The Age* (Melbourne) Easy to point the blame at politicians, but they are funded by business interests. They will never bite the hand that feeds them.

bite off more than you can chew take on a commitment you cannot fulfil.

bite your lip: *see* LIP.

bite your tongue make a desperate effort to avoid saying something.

2018 Mel Sherratt *Hush Hush* She would bite her tongue and say nothing when Eddie thought he was the head of the family, telling Jade what to do.

put the bite on blackmail; extort money from. North American & Australian informal

1955 Ray Lawler *Summer of the Seventeenth Doll* Your money's runnin' out you know you can't put the bite on me any more.

someone's bark is worse than their bite: *see* BARK.

take a bite out of reduce by a significant amount. informal

biter

the biter bit (*or* bitten) a person who has done harm has been harmed in a similar way.

ⓘ *Biter* was a late 17th-century term for a fraudster or trickster. In this sense it now survives only in this phrase.

2000 *Locus* The most common plot device in Lee's stories is the classic 'biter bitten' resolution.

bitten

be bitten by the bug: *see* BUG.

I could have bitten my tongue off used to convey that you profoundly and immediately regret having said something.

once bitten, twice shy: *see* ONCE.

bitter

a bitter pill: *see* PILL.

to the bitter end persevering to the end, whatever the outcome.

ⓘ The phrase may be associated with a nautical word *bitter*, denoting the last part of a cable inboard of the *bitts* (a pair of posts on the deck of a ship for fastening cables), perhaps influenced by the biblical phrase 'her end is bitter as wormwood' (Proverbs 5:4).

black

be in someone's black books be in disfavour with someone.

ⓘ Although a *black book* was generally an official book in which misdemeanours and their perpetrators were noted down, this phrase perhaps originated in the black-bound book in which evidence of monastic scandals and abuses was recorded by Henry VIII's commissioners in the 1530s, before the suppression of the monasteries.

beyond the black stump: *see* STUMP.

black and blue covered in bruises, (as if) from a severe beating.

black box an automatic apparatus, the internal operations of which are mysterious to non-experts.

ⓘ *Black* does not refer to the colour of the device but to the arcane nature of its functions. Originally Royal Air Force slang for a navigational instrument in an aircraft, the phrase is now used in aviation specifically to refer to the flight recorder.

the black dog a metaphorical representation of melancholy or depression. informal

ⓘ The expression is particularly associated with the British politician and war leader Winston Churchill, who used it to characterize the fits of depression from which he periodically suffered.

2019 Russell Lewis *Endeavour* 'Was he much given to leaving you alone of an evening without saying where he was going?' 'When the black dog was on him.'

black hat: *see* HAT.

a black mark against someone something that someone has done that is disliked or disapproved of by other people.

ⓘ The literal meaning of the phrase is a black cross or spot marked against the name of a person who has done something wrong.

the black sheep a person considered to have brought discredit upon a family or other group; a bad character.

a black spot a place that is notorious for something, especially a high crime or accident rate.

2012 *Daily Telegraph* Despite Hackney's reputation as an unemployment black spot, there are more artists per square foot there than in any other London borough.

in the black not owing any money; solvent.

in black and white ❶ in writing or in print, and regarded as more reliable than by word of mouth. ❷ in terms of clearly defined opposing principles or issues.

the man in black a football referee. informal

ⓘ The officials in football traditionally wear all black.

men in black anonymous dark-clothed men who supposedly visit people who have reported an encounter with a UFO or an alien in order to prevent them publicizing it. informal

the new black ❶ a colour that is currently so popular that it rivals the traditional status of black as the most reliably fashionable colour. ❷ something which is suddenly extremely popular or fashionable.

❶ **2003** *Guardian* We've been down this road before, brown is the new black.

❷ **2011** *The Age* (Melbourne) Because, now that frivolous public liability claims have slowed, corpo bullying has become the new black.

not as black as you are painted not as bad as you are said to be. informal

ⓘ The proverb *the devil is not as black as he is painted*, first recorded in English in the mid 16th century, was used as a warning not to base your fears of something on exaggerated reports.

the pot calling the kettle black: *see* POT.

swear black is white: *see* SWEAR.

blackboard

blackboard jungle a school, or schools in general, with violent and uncontrollable pupils.

blame

a bad workman blames his tools: *see* WORKMAN.

b

blank

a blank cheque unlimited scope, especially to spend money.

ℹ A *blank cheque* is literally one in which the amount of money to be paid has not been filled in by the payer.

draw a blank elicit no response; be unsuccessful.

ℹ A *blank* was originally a lottery ticket that did not win a prize.

fire blanks: *see* FIRE.

blanket

born on the wrong side of the blanket illegitimate. dated

a wet blanket: *see* WET.

blarney

have kissed the blarney stone be eloquent and persuasive.

ℹ A stone at Blarney Castle near Cork in Ireland is said to give the gift of persuasive speech to anyone who kisses it; from this comes the verb *blarney*, meaning 'talk in a flattering way'.

blast

a blast from the past something powerfully nostalgic, especially an old pop song. informal

2016 *Central Coast Express Advocate* (Australia) Bursting with character and old-world charm, this circa 1928 California bungalow is a real blast from the past.

blaze

blaze a trail be the first to do something and so set an example for others to follow.

ℹ *Blaze* in this sense comes ultimately from an Old Norse noun meaning 'a white mark on a horse's face'. In its literal sense, *blazing a trail* refers to the practice of making white marks on trees by chipping off bits of their bark, thereby indicating your route to those who are following you.

like blazes very fast or forcefully. informal

ℹ *Blazes* in this context refers to the flames of hell; *go to blazes!* is a dated equivalent of *go to hell!*

blazing

with guns blazing: *see* GUN.

bleed

bleed someone dry (*or* **white**) drain someone of all their money or resources.

ℹ Since the late 17th century *bleeding* has been a metaphor for extorting money from someone. *White* refers to the physiological effect of losing blood.

1982 William Haggard *The Mischief-Makers* Her husband had been a wealthy man, the lady's solicitors sharp and ruthless, and her husband had been bled white to get rid of her.

bleeding

bleeding heart a person considered to be dangerously soft-hearted, typically someone too liberal or left-wing in their political beliefs. informal

2005 *DVD Verdict* Ed Bannon is the lone voice of antagonistic reason in an army filled with lily-livered bleeding hearts.

bleeds

my heart bleeds for you I sympathize very deeply with you.

ℹ This image was used by Chaucer and Shakespeare to express sincere anguish. Nowadays, the phrase most often indicates the speaker's belief that the person referred to does not deserve the sympathy they are seeking.

bless

bless you! said to a person who has just sneezed.

bless your little cotton socks: *see* SOCK.

not have a penny to bless yourself with: *see* PENNY.

blessing

a blessing in disguise an apparent misfortune that eventually has good results.

count your blessings: *see* COUNT.

a mixed blessing: *see* MIXED.

blind

a blind alley a course of action that does not deliver any positive results.

2013 *New Statesman* They are well aware of the gilded complacency that dulls Cameron's appeal, especially to squeezed households. But they want that flaw to discredit the rest of his project to reform the party. According to this view, the Camerоons led the Tories down a blind alley of cosmopolitan elitism.

as blind as a bat having very bad eyesight. informal

ⓘ This expression probably arose from the bat's nocturnal habits and its disorientated flutterings if disturbed by day. The poor eyesight of bats (and less frequently, moles) has been proverbial since the late 16th century.

a blind bit of — the smallest bit of—; no — at all. informal

2007 *Daily Telegraph* His two great fears were that the technology might not be robust enough to use in casework, and that, even if it were, no one would take a blind bit of notice.

a blind date a social meeting, usually with the object of starting a romance, between two people who have not met each other before.

the blind leading the blind a situation in which the ignorant or inexperienced are instructed or guided by someone equally ignorant or inexperienced.

ⓘ This phrase alludes to the proverb *when the blind lead the blind, both shall fall into the ditch*, quoting Matthew 15:14.

a blind spot ❶ an area into which you cannot see. ❷ an aspect of something that someone knows or cares little about.

ⓘ These general senses appear to have developed from a mid-19th-century cricketing term for the spot of ground in front of a batsman where a ball pitched by the bowler leaves the batsman undecided whether to play forward to it or back.

blind someone with science use special or technical knowledge and vocabulary to confuse someone.

rob someone blind: *see* ROB.

swear blind: *see* SWEAR.

turn a blind eye pretend not to notice.

ⓘ This phrase is said to be a reference to Admiral Horatio Nelson (1758–1805), who lifted a telescope to his blind eye at the Battle of Copenhagen (1801), thereby ensuring that he failed to *see* his superior's signal to discontinue the action. A less usual version, referring directly to this story, is *turn a Nelson eye*.

blinder

play a blinder perform very well. informal

ⓘ Dating from the 1950s, *blinder* is a colloquial term for 'a dazzlingly good match performance', especially in football, rugby, or cricket.

2001 *Sun* Gilles will start and I would just love him to play a blinder and score a couple of goals to knock Southampton out of the cup.

blinding

effing and blinding: *see* EFFING.

blink

in the blink of an eye very quickly. informal

2013 *Believer Magazine* Look how many bugs there are. They're taking over the world. We have only one species and we could go extinct in the blink of an eye.

on the blink (of a machine) not working properly; out of order. informal

block

a chip off the old block: *see* CHIP.

a new kid on the block a newcomer to a particular place or sphere of activity. informal

ⓘ This phrase was originally American: the *block* referred to is a block of buildings between streets.

2013 *PC World* Chrome OS, developed by Google, is the new kid on the block. It's a Web-centric platform that basically makes the browser itself the operating system.

have been around the block a few times (of a person) have a lot of experience. North American informal

knock someone's block off: *see* KNOCK.

on the block for sale at auction. chiefly North American

ⓘ The *block* in this phrase was the platform on which, in former times, a slave stood to be auctioned.

put the blocks on prevent from proceeding.

ⓘ A *block* of wood or other material placed in front of a wheel prevents forward movement.

put your head (*or* neck) on the block put your position or reputation at risk by proceeding with a particular course of action. informal

ⓘ This phrase alludes to the *block* of wood on which a condemned person was formerly beheaded.

blood

bay for blood: *see* BAY.

blood and guts violence and bloodshed, especially in fiction. informal

b

blood and iron military force rather than diplomacy.

ⓘ *Blood and iron* is a translation of German *Blut und Eisen*, a phrase particularly associated with a speech made by the German statesman Bismarck (1815–98) in the Prussian House of Deputies in 1886.

blood and thunder unrestrained and violent action or behaviour, especially in sport or fiction. informal

ⓘ *Blood and thunder* is often used to describe sensational literature, and in the late 19th century gave rise to *penny bloods* as a term for cheap sensational novels.

blood is thicker than water family loyalties are stronger than other relationships.

blood on the carpet used to refer in an exaggerated way to a serious disagreement or its aftermath.

1984 *Times* The last thing I want now is blood on the boardroom carpet.

blood, sweat, and tears extremely hard work; unstinting effort.

ⓘ In May 1940 Winston Churchill made a speech in the House of Commons in which he declared: 'I have nothing to offer but blood, toil, tears, and sweat.'

blood will tell family characteristics cannot be concealed. proverb

first blood the first point or advantage gained in a contest.

ⓘ *First blood* is literally 'the first shedding of blood', especially in a boxing match or formerly in duelling with swords.

flesh and blood: *see* FLESH.

freeze your blood: *see* FREEZE.

have blood on your hands be responsible for the death of someone.

in cold blood: *see* COLD.

in your blood ingrained in or fundamental to your character.

like getting blood out of (*or* **from**) **a stone** extremely difficult and frustrating.

ⓘ A North American variant of this expression is *like getting blood out of a turnip*.

make your blood boil infuriate you.

make your blood curdle fill you with horror.

make your blood run cold horrify you.

ⓘ The previous three phrases all come from the medieval physiological scheme of the four humours in the human body (melancholy, phlegm, blood, and choler). Under this scheme blood was the hot, moist element, so the effect of horror or fear in making the blood run cold or curdling (solidifying) it was to make it unable to fulfil its proper function of supplying the body with vital heat or energy. The blood boiling was a supposedly dangerous overreaction to strong emotion.

new (*or* **young**) **blood** new (*or* younger) members of a group, especially those admitted as an invigorating force.

a rush of blood: *see* RUSH.

smell blood: *see* SMELL.

someone's blood is up someone is in a fighting mood.

spit blood: *see* SPIT.

stir the blood: *see* STIR.

sweat blood: *see* SWEAT.

taste blood achieve an early success that stimulates further efforts.

there is bad blood between — there is long-standing hostility between the parties mentioned.

2001 Hugh Collins *No Smoke* There are occasional square-gos sometimes, but there's no bad blood between rival gangs.

your (own) flesh and blood: *see* FLESH.

bloody

bloody (*or* **bloodied**) **but unbowed** proud of what you have achieved despite having suffered great difficulties or losses.

give someone a bloody nose: *see* NOSE.

bloom

the bloom is off the rose something is no longer new, fresh, or exciting. North American

blot

blot your copybook tarnish your good reputation. British

ⓘ A *copybook* was an exercise book with examples of handwriting for children to copy as they practised their own writing.

a blot on the escutcheon something that tarnishes your reputation.

ⓘ An *escutcheon* was a family's heraldic shield, and so also a record and symbol of its honour.

a blot on the landscape something ugly that spoils the appearance of a place; an eyesore.

1962 *Listener* Charabancs and monstrous hordes of hikers are blots upon the landscape.

blouse

big girl's blouse a weak, cowardly, or oversensitive man. British informal

blow

ℹ For idioms containing *blow*, see the entry for the main word in the idiom (for example, **blow your own trumpet** at TRUMPET).

blow-by-blow

a blow-by-blow account a detailed narrative of events as they happened.

blowed

I'll be blowed used to express surprise, annoyance, etc. informal, dated

blown

be blown off course have your plans disrupted by some circumstance.

ℹ This phrase is a nautical metaphor: contrary winds turn a sailing ship away from its intended course.

be blown out of the water (of a person, idea, or project) be shown to lack credibility or viability.

1997 *Daily Mail* Things finally seem to be looking up for Kelly—which is more than can be said for Biff, whose romantic plans are blown out of the water by Linda.

blue

between the devil and the deep blue sea: *see* DEVIL.

blue on blue used to denote an (inadvertent) attack by a military force on members of its own side. British

ℹ The expression derives from the use of blue on maps to designate one's own forces.

2004 *BBC Press Release* If I had been told on the day that Christopher died that it had been blue on blue, I could have coped with that, things do happen in war, mistakes are made, casualties, it happens.

blues and twos the siren and blue flashing lights of an emergency-service vehicle. British informal

ℹ The *twos* refers to the vehicles' two-tone siren.

2003 *Bolton Evening News* They will go out with local officers and really learn the craft of being a beat bobby rather than just going out in blues and twos.

a bolt from the blue: *see* BOLT.

boys in blue: *see* BOY.

clear blue water: *see* CLEAR

do something until you are blue in the face persist in trying your hardest at an activity but without success. informal

once in a blue moon very rarely; practically never. informal

ℹ The colour *blue* was an arbitrary choice in this phrase. To say that the moon is blue is recorded in the 16th century as a way of indicating that something could not be true.

out of the blue without warning; very unexpectedly. informal

ℹ This phrase refers to a blue (i.e. clear) sky, from which nothing unusual is expected.

scream blue murder: *see* MURDER.

talk a blue streak speak continuously and at great length. North American informal

ℹ A *blue streak* refers to something like a flash of lightning in its speed and vividness.

the thin blue line: *see* THIN.

true blue genuine.

ℹ The sense of someone being *true blue* may derive from the idea of someone being genuinely aristocratic, or having 'blue blood'. In recent times, the term *true blue* has become particularly associated with loyal supporters of the British Conservative party.

the wide (*or* wild) blue yonder the sky or sea; the far or unknown distance.

ℹ The phrase comes from 'Army Air Corps' (1939), a song by Robert Crawford: 'Off we go into the wild blue yonder, Climbing high into the sun'.

blue-arsed

like a blue-arsed fly: *see* FLY.

blue-eyed

a blue-eyed boy the favourite of someone in authority.

ℹ The significance of *blue eyes* may be their association with the innocence and charm of a very young child. The term is first recorded in a novel by P. G. Wodehouse in 1924.

2009 *Times of India* What is the secret to making a comeback? The examples are many: cricketer Sourav Ganguly, who fought politics and became the blue-eyed boy of cricket.

blue-sky

blue-sky research research that is not directed towards any immediate or definite commercial goal.

2005 *Wired* The Science and Technology Directorate ... places wagers on almost-there technology that it hopes the public sector will embrace—and it leaves blue-sky research to others.

bluff

call someone's bluff challenge someone to carry out a stated intention, in the expectation of being able to expose it as a false pretence.

ℹ In the game of poker (which was formerly also known by the name of *bluff*), *calling someone's bluff* meant making an opponent show their hand in order to reveal that its value was weaker than their heavy betting suggested.

blush

at first blush at the first glimpse or impression.

spare (*or* save) someone's blushes refrain from causing someone embarrassment.

board

above board honest; not secret.

ℹ *Above board* was originally a gambling term, indicating fair play by players who kept their hands above the *board* (i.e. the table).

across the board: *see* ACROSS.

go by the board (of something planned or previously upheld) be abandoned, rejected, or ignored.

ℹ In former times, *go by the board* was a nautical term meaning 'fall overboard' and was used of a mast falling past the *board* (i.e. the side of the ship).

on board as a member of a team or group. informal

ℹ *On board* literally means on or in a ship, aircraft, or other vehicle, or (of a jockey) riding a horse.

stiff as a board: *see* STIFF.

sweep the board: *see* SWEEP.

take something on board fully consider or assimilate a new idea or situation. informal

tread (*or* walk) the boards appear on stage as an actor. informal

boat

be in the same boat be in the same unfortunate or difficult circumstances as others. informal

burn your boats: *see* BURN.

float someone's boat: *see* FLOAT.

miss the boat: *see* MISS.

off the boat recently arrived from a foreign country, and by implication naive or an outsider. informal, often offensive

push the boat out be lavish in your spending or celebrations. British informal

ℹ *Push the boat out* apparently originated as mid 20th-century naval slang meaning 'pay for a round of drinks'.

rock the boat say or do something to disturb an existing situation and upset other people. informal

2001 Reginald Hill *Dialogues of the Dead* Having got back to something like an even keel with the super, it would be foolish to risk rocking the boat by letting personal dislike cloud his judgment.

bob

bob and weave make rapid bodily movements up and down and from side to side.

Bob's your uncle everything is fine; problem solved. British informal

ℹ *Bob* is a familiar form of the name *Robert*. The origin of the phrase is often said to be in the controversial appointment in 1887 of the young Arthur Balfour to the important post of Chief Secretary for Ireland by his uncle Lord Salisbury, whose first name was Robert. The problem with this explanation is that the phrase is not recorded until the 1930s.

2011 *Guardian* All you need to do is chuck together some random images, edit them and, Bob's your uncle, you've made yourself something 'postmodern'.

bobtail

rag, tag, and bobtail: *see* RAG.

body

body and soul involving every aspect of a person; completely.

the body beautiful: *see* BEAUTIFUL.

body blow a severe disappointment or crushing setback.

2004 *BBC News: Business* Energywatch said next month's increases were 'a body blow to consumers'. 'This price rise is going to add millions to bills.'

keep body and soul together manage to stay alive, especially in difficult circumstances.

know where the bodies are buried have the security deriving from personal knowledge of an organization's confidential affairs and secrets. informal

over my dead body: *see* DEAD.

boil

go off the boil pass the stage at which interest, excitement, activity, etc. is at its greatest.

it all boils down to it amounts to or is in essence.

ⓘ *Boiling down* a liquid means reducing its volume and concentrating it by evaporation.

1998 *Times* And why are deals getting more complex? Unsurprisingly it all boils down to profit.

lance the boil: *see* LANCE.

make your blood boil: *see* BLOOD.

boiling

keep the pot boiling maintain the momentum or interest value of something.

bold

as bold as brass confident to the point of impudence.

ⓘ *Brass* is used in this phrase as a metaphorical representation of a lack of shame, as it was in the old expression *a brass face*, meaning 'an impudent person'. *See also* **brass neck** *at* BRASS.

bollocks

the dog's bollocks: *see* DOG.

bolt

a bolt from the blue a sudden and unexpected event or piece of news.

ⓘ The phrase refers to the unlikelihood of a thunderbolt coming out of a clear blue sky.

have shot your bolt have done all that is in your power. informal

ⓘ In this idiom, the *bolt* referred to is a thick, heavy arrow for a crossbow.

2003 *Scotland on Sunday* McGeechan, for all his magnificent record with Scotland and the British Lions, shot his bolt a long time ago and should never have returned for a second spell as head coach three years ago.

make a bolt for try to escape by moving suddenly towards something.

ⓘ A *bolt* here is a sudden spring or start into rapid motion, typically that made by a horse breaking into an uncontrollable gallop.

nuts and bolts: *see* NUT.

bomb

go down a bomb be very well received. British informal

ⓘ This phrase is especially used of entertainment and in this context is the opposite of **go down like a lead balloon** (*see* LEAD).

go like a bomb ❶ be very successful. ❷ (of a vehicle or person) move very fast. British informal

put a bomb under ❶ take drastic steps to rouse (an inactive or dilatory person) to action. ❷ have a profound or radical effect on (something, especially something that has been accepted or unchanged for a long time). informal

❷ **2003 John Ray** *Dissecting Leftism* In my academic posting of May 16th about psychopathy, I report findings that should put a bomb under a major field of psychological research.

bond

someone's word is their bond: *see* WORD.

Bondi

give someone Bondi attack someone savagely. Australian informal

ⓘ A *bondi* (also spelled *boondie, bundi, or bundy*) is a heavy Aboriginal club. The preferred spelling in the idiom, and its capitalization, are due to association with the Sydney suburb of *Bondi*.

bone

a bag of bones: *see* BAG.

the bare bones: *see* BARE.

be skin and bones: *see* SKIN.

a bone of contention a subject or issue over which there is continuing disagreement.

ℹ The idea is of a bone thrown into the midst of a number of dogs and causing a fight between them.

a bone in your leg (*or* **head**) a (feigned) reason for idleness. informal

close to (*or* **near**) **the bone** ❶ (of a remark) penetrating and accurate to the point of causing hurt or discomfort. ❷ (of a joke or story) likely to cause offence because near the limit of decency.

cut (*or* **pare**) **something to the bone** reduce something to the bare minimum.

dry as a bone: *see* DRY.

have a bone on have an erection of the penis. slang

2010 Stephen Hunter *Dead Zero* Maybe the great Bob Lee Swagger has a bone on, and he's come down here to Chinatown to get it off.

have a bone to pick with someone have reason to disagree or be annoyed with someone. informal

ℹ A *bone to pick* (or *gnaw*) has been a metaphor for a problem or difficulty to be thought over since the mid 16th century.

in your bones felt, understood, or believed very deeply or instinctively.

jump someone's bones: *see* JUMP.

make no bones about something have no hesitation in stating or dealing with something, however unpleasant, awkward, or distasteful it is.

ℹ This expression, which dates back to the 16th century, may originally have referred to eating a bowl of soup in which no bones were found and which was therefore easily eaten.

make old bones; *see* OLD.

not a — bone in your body not the slightest trace of the specified quality.

2014 Stephen May *Wake up Happy Every Day* I haven't got a Sapphic bone in my body, worse luck.

point the bone at betray someone; cause someone's downfall. Australian

ℹ The phrase comes from an Australian Aboriginal ritual, in which a bone is pointed at a victim so as to curse them and cause their sickness or death.

to the bone ❶ (of a wound) so deep as to expose the victim's bone. ❷ affecting a person in a very penetrating way.

to your bones (*or* **to the bone**) in a very fundamental way (used to emphasize that a person possesses a specified quality as an essential or innate aspect of their personality).

2003 *Eve* Gloria is known today to be a conservative to her bones—a true monarchist.

work your fingers to the bone work very hard.

boner

pull a boner make a stupid mistake. North American informal

bonnet

have a bee in your bonnet: *see* BEE.

boo

wouldn't say boo to a goose (of a person) very shy or reticent.

1948 P. G. Wodehouse *Uncle Dynamite* She looks on you as a . . . poor, spineless sheep who can't say boo to a goose.

booay

up the booay completely wrong or astray. Australian & New Zealand

ℹ Literally, *booay* denotes a remote rural district. The term comes from *Puhoi*, the name of a district to the north of Auckland, New Zealand.

book

be in someone's black books: *see* BLACK.

bell, book, and candle: *see* BELL.

bring someone to book bring someone to justice; punish someone.

by the book strictly according to the rules.

close the books make no further entries at the end of an accounting period; cease trading.

a closed book: *see* CLOSED.

cook the books: *see* COOK.

crack a book: *see* CRACK.

in my book in my opinion; to me.

in someone's bad (*or* **good**) **books** in disfavour (*or* favour) with someone.

make (*or* **open**) **a book** take bets and pay out winnings on the outcome of a race or other contest or event.

on the books contained in a list of members, employees, or clients.

one for the book something particularly noteworthy. informal

ⓘ The expression is based on the notion of a sporting or other achievement that merits a permanent record.

read someone like a book: *see* READ.

suit someone's book be convenient or acceptable to someone. British

take a leaf out of someone's book: *see* LEAF.

throw the book at charge or punish someone as severely as possible or permitted. informal

ⓘ The 'book' is an imaginary codification of misdemeanours and their punishments.

a turn-up for the book: *see* TURN-UP.

wrote the book on: *see* WROTE.

boom

boom boom! an exclamation made after delivering the punchline of a joke. British informal

ⓘ The phrase was popularized by the fox puppet Basil Brush, a character in a British television comedy show.

lower the boom on: *see* LOWER.

boot

boots and all completely. Australian & New Zealand informal

1947 Dan Davin *The Rest of Our Lives* The next thing he'll do is counter-attack, boots and all.

the boot is on the other foot the situation has reversed.

ⓘ A North American variant is *the shoe is on the other foot.*

die with your boots on: *see* DIE.

fill someone's boots: *see* **fill someone's shoes** *at* FILL.

fill your boots: *see* FILL.

get the boot be dismissed from your job or position. informal

ⓘ *Get the boot* comes from the idea of being literally kicked out, as does *give someone the boot*. A facetious expansion of this idiom is *get the Order of the Boot*.

hang up your boots: *see* HANG.

lick someone's boots: *see* LICK.

put the boot in treat someone brutally, especially when they are vulnerable. British informal

ⓘ The literal sense is 'kick someone hard when they are already on the ground'.

seven-league boots the ability to travel very fast on foot.

ⓘ This phrase comes from the fairy story of Hop o' my Thumb, in which magic boots enable the wearer to travel seven leagues at each stride (a 'league' is an old measure of length, equal to about three miles).

shake in your boots: *see* **shake in your shoes** *at* SHAKE.

to boot as well; in addition. informal

ⓘ *Boot* here has nothing to do with footwear but comes from an Old English word meaning 'good, profit, or advantage'. It survives for the most part only in this phrase and in *bootless* meaning 'unavailing or profitless'.

2014 Jayne *Our Great Southern Land* I have really got to applaud the builders next door; . . . they've restumped the house while extending it and have done a bloody ripper of a job to boot.

too big for your boots: *see* BIG.

tough as old boots: *see* TOUGH.

you can bet your boots: *see* BET.

your heart sinks into your boots used to express a feeling of sudden sadness or dismay.

booted

suited and booted: *see* SUITED.

bootstrap

pull (*or* drag) yourself up by your own bootstraps improve your position by your own efforts.

ⓘ A *bootstrap* is sometimes sewn into the back of boots to help with pulling them on. This idiom has given rise to the computing term *bootstrapping*, meaning the process of loading a program into a computer by means of a few initial instructions which enable the introduction of the rest of the program from an input device. We now refer to the process of starting a computer as *booting* or *booting up*.

booty

shake your booty dance energetically. informal

ⓘ *Booty* in this context means 'buttocks' (it originated in African American slang in the 1920s, probably as an alteration of *botty*, itself a shortened form of *bottom*).

b

borak

poke borak at make fun of someone. Australian & New Zealand, dated

ⓘ *Borak* was used in 19th-century Australian English to mean 'nonsense or rubbish'. It was originally a pidgin term and was based on the Aboriginal word *burag* meaning 'no, not'.

1960 Eric North *Nobody Stops Me* I... subscribed to his ravings about women, while everybody else about the place poked borak at him.

bore

bore the pants off: *see* **scare the pants off** *at* PANTS.

born

be born with a silver spoon in your mouth: *see* SILVER.

born and bred by birth and upbringing.

1991 Sharon Kay Penman *The Reckoning* I was being tended by a most unlikely nurse, an Irish sprite who spoke French as if she was Paris born and bred.

born in the purple: *see* PURPLE.

born on the wrong side of the blanket: *see* BLANKET.

in all my born days ever, in my whole life (often used to express surprise or shock at something you have not encountered before).

2000 Voyle A. Glover *Western Fiction* Bruther, that was the best feed I ever had in all my born days.

not know you are born be unaware how easy your life is. informal

there's one (*or* a sucker) born every minute there are many stupid or gullible people about (used as a comment on a particular situation in which someone has been or is about to be deceived). informal

to the manner born: *see* MANNER.

I wasn't born yesterday used to indicate that you are not foolish or gullible.

borne

be borne in on (*or* upon) come to be realized by.

borrow

borrow trouble take needless action that may have bad effects. North American

borrowed

living on borrowed time continuing to survive against expectations (used with the implication that this will not be for much longer).

borrowed plumes a pretentious display not rightly your own.

ⓘ This phrase refers to the fable of the jay which dressed itself in the peacock's feathers.

bosom

in Abraham's bosom: *see* ABRAHAM.

a viper in your bosom: *see* VIPER.

boss

show someone who's boss make it clear that it is yourself who is in charge.

both

the best of both worlds: *see* WORLD.

cut both ways: *see* CUT.

have it both ways benefit from two incompatible ways of thinking or behaving.

2005 *New Yorker* Consistency means we cannot have it both ways.

bothered

hot and bothered in a state of anxiety or physical discomfort, especially as a result of being pressured.

bottle

chief cook and bottle-washer: *see* CHIEF.

crack a bottle: *see* CRACK.

have (*or* show) a lot of bottle have (*or* show) boldness or initiative. British informal

ⓘ *Bottle* in the sense 'courage, nerve' comes from *bottle and glass*. That is rhyming slang for *arse*, which itself came in 20th-century British slang to mean 'courage'. So if you have *lost your bottle* (in effect, 'lost your arse'), or *your bottle has fallen out*, your courage has failed you. The derived verb *bottle out* (or *bottle it*) means 'fail to do something as a result of losing your nerve'.

hit (*or* be on) the bottle start to drink alcohol heavily, especially in an attempt to escape from one's problems. informal

let the genie out of the bottle: *see* GENIE.

b

bottom

be bumping along the bottom (of an economy or industry) be at the lowest point in its performance without improving or deteriorating further.

bottom drawer: *see* DRAWER.

the bottom falls (*or* drops) out of something something fails or collapses totally.

the bottom line: *see* LINE.

bottoms up! used to express friendly feelings towards your companions before drinking. informal

ⓘ The expression refers to the raising of a glass towards the horizontal.

from the bottom of your heart: *see* HEART.

from top to bottom: *see* TOP.

get to the bottom of find an explanation for (a mystery).

rock bottom: *see* ROCK.

scrape the bottom of the barrel: *see* SCRAPE.

touch bottom: *see* TOUCH.

you can bet your bottom dollar: *see* **you can bet your boots** *at* BET.

bought

have bought it be killed. informal

bounce

bounce an idea off someone share an idea with another person in order to get feedback on it and refine it. informal

bounce off the walls be full of nervous excitement or agitation. North American informal

a dead cat bounce: *see* DEAD.

on the bounce ❶ as something rebounds. ❷ in quick succession. informal

❷ **2001** *Greyhound Star* He has now won twelve races on the bounce, including three big competitions.

bound

by leaps and bounds: *see* LEAP.

duty-bound: *see* DUTY.

honour-bound: *see* HONOUR.

I'll be bound used to emphasize that one is sure of something. British

know no bounds be so great as to seem limitless; be unconfined.

2002 *Film Inside Out* His imagination knows no bounds. He can fib his way out of every situation.

bounden

a bounden duty a responsibility regarded by yourself or others as obligatory.

ⓘ *Bounden* as the past participle of *bind* is now archaic in all contexts and is seldom found except in this phrase.

bountiful

Lady Bountiful: *see* LADY.

Bourke

back o' Bourke: *see* BACK.

bow

bow and scrape behave in an obsequious way to someone in authority.

bow down in the house of Rimmon pay lip service to a principle; sacrifice your principles for the sake of conformity.

ⓘ *Rimmon* was a god worshipped in ancient Damascus; the source of this phrase is Naaman's request in 2 Kings 5:18, 'when I bow down myself in the house of Rimmon, the Lord pardon thy servant in this thing'.

bow (*or* bend) the knee (to) kneel in submission; submit.

have a second string to your bow: *see* STRING.

make your bow make your first formal appearance in a particular role.

take a bow ❶ (of an actor or entertainer) acknowledge applause after a performance. ❷ used to tell someone that they should feel themselves worthy of applause.

a warning shot across the bows a statement or gesture intended to frighten someone into changing their course of action.

ⓘ Literally, a shot fired in front of the bows of a ship is one which is not intended to hit it but to make it stop or alter course.

bowl

a bowl of cherries: *see* CHERRY.

goldfish bowl: *see* GOLDFISH.

b

box

back in your box no longer conspicuous or calling attention to yourself; returned to a low profile. informal

> **2002** *Sunday Herald* Since the invasion of Kuwait, Saddam Hussein has been put back in his box and has hardly stirred against the West.

black box: *see* BLACK.

Box and Cox used to refer to an arrangement whereby people make use of the same accommodation or facilities at different times. British

> ⓘ The phrase comes from the title of a play (1847) by J. M. Morton, in which two characters, John *Box* and James *Cox*, unknowingly become tenants of the same room.

box clever act so as to outwit someone. British informal

> **1950 Alexander Baron** *There's No Home* If you box clever and keep your mouth shut . . . you ought to be able to count on a suspended sentence.

box the compass ❶ recite the compass points in correct order. ❷ make a complete change of direction.

> ⓘ The word *box* in this nautical expression may have come from Spanish *bojar* 'sail round'.

be a box of birds be fine or happy. Australian & New Zealand

a box of tricks an ingenious gadget. informal

in the wrong box placed unsuitably or awkwardly; in difficulty or at a disadvantage.

> ⓘ This phrase perhaps arose with reference to an apothecary's boxes, from which a mistaken choice might have provided poison instead of medicine.

out of the box unusually good. Australian & New Zealand informal

out of your box intoxicated with alcohol or drugs. British informal

Pandora's box: *see* PANDORA.

think outside the box have ideas that are original, creative, or innovative. informal

tick all the (right) boxes: *see* TICK.

box seat

in the box seat in an advantageous position.

boy

the big boys men or organizations considered to be the most powerful and successful. informal

> **2004 Richard Valot** *Earth vs Mars* I don't have time to argue about every trivial little concern you may have, Hank. Leave the decision-making to the big boys.

a blue-eyed boy: *see* BLUE-EYED.

the boy next door: *see* NEXT.

boys in blue policemen; the police. informal

boys will be boys childish, irresponsible, or mischievous behaviour is typical of boys or young men. proverb

golden boy: *see* GOLDEN.

jobs for the boys: *see* JOB.

man and boy: *see* MAN.

the old boy network: *see* OLD.

one of the boys accepted by a group of men.

sort out the men from the boys: *see* MAN.

braces

belt and braces: *see* BELT.

brain

cudgel your brain: *see* CUDGEL.

have something on the brain be obsessed with something. informal

nappy brain: *see* NAPPY.

pick someone's brains: *see* PICK.

rack your brains: *see* RACK.

shit for brains: *see* SHIT.

branch

hold out an olive branch: *see* OLIVE.

root and branch: *see* ROOT.

brass

as bold as brass: *see* BOLD.

brass monkey used in various phrases to refer to extremely cold weather.

> ⓘ *Brass monkey* comes from the mid-20th-century vulgar slang expression 'cold enough to freeze the balls off a brass monkey', the origin of which has been debated. One suggestion relates it to brass trays known as *monkeys* on which cannon balls were once stowed aboard warships.

1994 *Camping Magazine* David will be doing his best to show you how to keep warm under canvas even if the temperature outside has dipped to brass monkey level.

the brass ring success, especially as a reward for ambition or hard work. North American informal

ⓘ This phrase refers to the reward of a free ride on a merry-go-round given to the person who succeeds in hooking a brass ring suspended over the horses.

brass neck cheek or effrontery. informal

get (*or* **come**) **down to brass tacks** start to consider the essential facts or practical details; reach the real matter in hand. informal

1932 T. S. Eliot *Sweeney Agonistes* That's all the facts when you come to brass tacks: Birth, and copulation, and death.

not a brass farthing no money or assets at all. informal

part brass rags with: *see* RAG.

where there's muck there's brass: *see* MUCK.

brave

brave new world a new and hopeful period in history resulting from major changes in society.

ⓘ This phrase comes ultimately from Shakespeare's *The Tempest*, but is more often used with allusion to Aldous Huxley's ironical use of the phrase as the title of his 1932 novel *Brave New World*.

fortune favours the brave: *see* FORTUNE.

put a brave face on something: *see* FACE.

breach

step into the breach take the place of someone who is suddenly unable to do a job or task.

ⓘ In military terms a *breach* is a gap in fortifications made by enemy guns or explosives. In this context, to *stand in the breach* is to bear the brunt of an attack when other defences or expedients have failed.

bread

the best (*or* **greatest**) **thing since sliced bread** a notable new idea, person, or thing (used to express real or ironic appreciation). informal

ⓘ This phrase alludes to the mid 20th-century advertising promotions for packed, pre-sliced loaves.

bread and circuses material benefits and entertainment employed by rulers or political parties to keep the masses happy and docile.

ⓘ *Bread and circuses* is a translation of the Latin phrase *panem et circenses*, which appeared in Juvenal's *Satires*, and which alludes to the Roman emperors' organization of grain handouts and gladiatorial games for the populace.

break bread with share a meal with someone. dated

cast your bread upon the waters do good without expecting gratitude or immediate reward.

ⓘ This expression comes from Ecclesiastes 11:1: 'Cast thy bread upon the waters: for thou shalt find it after many days'.

have your bread buttered on both sides be in a state of easy prosperity.

know on which side your bread is buttered know where your advantage lies.

2018 Robert Goddard *Panic Room* He had noticed the same spatial discrepancy ... as Don had, but had not made the slightest fuss when told to disregard it. He clearly knew which side his bread was buttered.

man cannot live by bread alone people have spiritual as well as physical needs.

ⓘ This phrase comes from Matthew 4:4 (quoting Deuteronomy 8:3), where the passage continues 'but by every word that proceedeth out of the mouth of God'.

someone's bread and butter someone's livelihood; routine work to provide an income.

2013 *New York Metro: Pop Music* On Perry's new album, *Prism*, there are a few bustling dance songs and one goofy party tune .... But her bread and butter is the inspirational anthem, songs like Firework and the walloping jock jam Roar.

someone's daily bread the money or food that someone needs in order to live.

take the bread out of people's mouths deprive people of their livings, especially by competition or unfair working practices.

want your bread buttered on both sides want more than is practicable or than is reasonable to expect. informal

bread-and-butter

a bread-and-butter letter a guest's written thanks for hospitality.

b

breadth

a hair's breadth: *see* HAIR.

the length and breadth of: *see* LENGTH.

break

break it down! stop it! desist! Australian informal

break a leg! good luck! theatrical slang

give me a break! used to express contemptuous disagreement or disbelief about something that has been said.

give someone a break stop putting pressure on someone about something. informal

make a break for make a sudden dash in the direction of, usually in a bid to escape.

that's (*or* them's) the breaks that's the way things turn out (used to express resigned acceptance of a situation). North American informal

ℹ For other idioms containing *break*, see the entry for the main word in the idiom (for example, **break wind** at WIND).

breakfast

bed and breakfast: *see* BED.

a dog's breakfast: *see* DOG.

have someone for breakfast deal with or defeat someone with contemptuous ease. informal

breast

beat your breast make a great show of sorrow or regret.

make a clean breast of something: *see* CLEAN.

breath

a breath of fresh air ❶ a small amount of or a brief time in the fresh air. ❷ a refreshing change, especially a new person on the scene.

the breath of life a thing that someone needs or depends on.

ℹ *Breath of life* is a biblical phrase: 'And the Lord God formed man of the dust of the ground, and breathed into his nostrils the breath of life' (Genesis 2:7).

don't hold your breath used to indicate that something is very unlikely to happen.

in the same (*or* the next) breath as the next in a series of statements, contradicting a previous one.

save your breath not bother to say something because it is pointless.

take someone's breath away fill someone with awed respect or delight or with shocked or scandalized disbelief; astonish someone.

> **1988 Janet Frame** *The Carpathians* The speed of the process took everyone's breath away.

take a deep breath pause in order to gather your thoughts or calm yourself before taking important action.

> **2005** *USA Today* What does the small business do when the engine that drives its business backfires? There are several steps to take. First, take a deep breath and don't do anything sudden.

under your breath in a very quiet voice; almost inaudibly.

waste your breath talk or give advice without effect.

with bated breath: *see* BATED.

breathe

breathe down someone's neck ❶ constantly check up on someone. ❷ follow closely behind someone.

breathe fire: *see* FIRE.

breathe (freely) again relax after being frightened or tense about something.

breathe your last die. dated

live and breathe something: *see* LIVE.

bred

born and bred: *see* BORN.

breed

a breed apart a kind of person or thing that is very different from the norm.

a dying breed: *see* DYING.

breeze

shoot the breeze: *see* SHOOT.

brick

bang your head against a brick wall: *see* HEAD.

a brick short of a load (of a person) stupid. informal

ⓘ This is one of a number of humorous variations on the theme of someone not possessing their proper share of brains or intelligence; compare, for example, with **a sandwich short of a picnic** (*at* SANDWICH).

be bricking it be extremely apprehensive. informal

ⓘ The expression is a euphemistic condensation of *be shitting bricks* (*see* SHIT).

2005 *The Press* (York) If I was going to be on my own, I'd be bricking it but there are six of us, we're all part of a team, so we'll be sharing the experience, and I'm happy with that.

be built like a brick shithouse: *see* SHITHOUSE.

bricks and mortar ❶ buildings, typically houses. ❷ a house considered in terms of its value as an investment. ❸ used as a modifier to denote a business that operates conventionally rather than (or as well as) over the Internet.

❶ **2012** *The Age* Much of the cost of child-care fees includes the cost of land and bricks and mortar, that is land and buildings that have to be acquired to provide a dedicated child-care facility.

❸ **2013** *New Zealand Herald* While in bricks and mortar stores most of the year's Christmas sales happen in the few weeks before December 25, in digital the holiday rush tends to happen earlier.

come down like a ton of bricks exert crushing weight, force, or authority against someone. informal

come up against (*or* hit) a brick wall encounter an insuperable problem or obstacle while trying to do something.

drop a brick: *see* DROP.

hit the bricks go on strike. US informal

make bricks without straw try to accomplish something without proper or adequate material, equipment, or information.

ⓘ The allusion here is to Exodus 5:6–19 where 'without straw' meant 'without having straw provided', as the Israelites were required to gather straw for themselves in order to make the bricks required by their Egyptian taskmasters. A misinterpretation has led to the current sense.

be shitting bricks: *see* SHIT.

bridesmaid

always the bridesmaid used to refer pityingly to someone who seems always to be allocated to a subsidiary function, and is never invited to take the lead.

ⓘ The expression probably originated in the words of a 1917 song by Charles Collins, Fred W Leigh, and Lily Morris: 'Why am I always the bridesmaid, never the blushing bride?'.

bridge

a bridge too far ❶ a step or act that is regarded as being too drastic or impracticable to take or contemplate. ❷ something that is very difficult to achieve.

ⓘ The phrase comes from the title of Cornelius Ryan's book *A Bridge Too Far* (1974), popularized by Richard Attenborough's film (1977) of the same name, concerning the Allied airborne landings in Holland in 1944. Officially named 'Operation Market Garden', they were intended to capture eleven bridges over the Rhine to facilitate the invasion of Germany, but the bridge at Arnhem proved impossible to take.

❶ **2018 Linwood Barclay** *A Noise Downstairs* Sleepwalking was one thing. But inventing messages from the dead and having no memory of it? That was a bridge too far.

build bridges promote friendly relations between groups.

burn your bridges: *see* **burn your boats** *at* BURN.

cross that bridge when you come to it deal with a problem when and if it arises.

2012 *Globe and Mail* (Toronto) Would the Palestinian Authority consider closing the Canadian representative's office in Ramallah, if Ottawa closes the Palestinian office, Ms Ashrawi was asked. 'We'll cross that bridge when we come to it,' she replied.

water under the bridge: *see* WATER.

brief

hold no brief for not support or argue in favour of.

ⓘ The *brief* referred to is the summary of the facts and legal points in a case given to a barrister to argue in court.

bright

bright and early very early in the morning.

as bright as a button intelligently alert and lively. informal

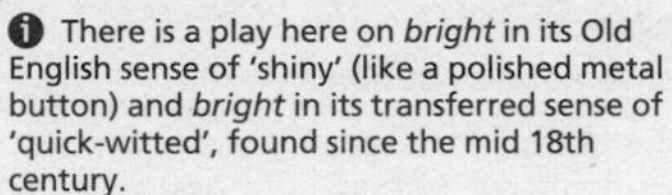

ⓘ There is a play here on *bright* in its Old English sense of 'shiny' (like a polished metal button) and *bright* in its transferred sense of 'quick-witted', found since the mid 18th century.

the bright lights the glamour and excitement of a big city.

bright spark a clever person (often used ironically to or of a person who has done something you consider stupid). British informal

bright young thing a wealthy, pleasure-loving, and fashionable young person.

ⓘ The term was originally applied in the 1920s to a member of a young fashionable group of people noted for their exuberant and outrageous behaviour.

look on the bright side be optimistic or cheerful in spite of difficulties.

bright-eyed

bright-eyed and bushy-tailed alert and lively; eager. informal

brimstone

fire and brimstone: *see* FIRE.

bring

bring it on! used as a defiant challenge to carry out a threat. informal

2013 *New Zealand Herald* If any political party wants to have that political debate with me on the campaign trail, bring it on.

ⓘ For other idioms containing *bring*, see the entry for the main word in the idiom (for example, **bring the house down** at HOUSE).

Bristol

shipshape and Bristol fashion: *see* SHIPSHAPE.

British

the best of British: *see* BEST.

the British disease a problem or failing supposed to be characteristically British, especially (formerly) a proneness to industrial unrest. informal

broad

broad in the beam wide in the hips. informal

ⓘ A *beam* was one of the horizontal transverse timbers in a wooden ship, and so the word came to refer to a ship's breadth at its widest point. It is from this sense that the current meaning of *broad in the beam* developed.

in broad daylight used generally to express surprise or outrage at someone's daring to carry out a particular act, especially a crime, during the day, when anyone could *see* it.

it's as broad as it's long there's no significant difference between two possible alternatives. informal

broke

go for broke risk everything in an all-out effort. informal

if it ain't broke don't fix it if something is reasonably successful or effective, there is no need to change or replace it. informal

broken

a broken reed: *see* REED.

broker

an honest broker: *see* HONEST.

broo

on the broo claiming unemployment benefit. Scottish informal

ⓘ *Broo*, also spelt *buroo*, is a colloquial alteration of *bureau*, meaning a labour exchange or social security office.

broom

a new broom a newly appointed person who is likely to make far-reaching changes.

ⓘ This phrase comes from the proverb *a new broom sweeps clean*.

broth

a broth of a boy a lively boy. Irish

too many cooks spoil the broth: *see* COOK.

brother

be your brother's keeper be responsible for the behaviour of a relative, friend, or associate.

ⓘ The phrase originated in the Bible (Genesis 4:9): 'And the Lord said unto Cain, Where is Abel thy brother? And he said, I know not: Am I my brother's keeper?'

Big Brother the state perceived as a sinister force supervising citizens' lives.

ⓘ *The expression* comes from the slogan *Big Brother is watching you* in George Orwell's novel *1984*.

brought

like something the cat brought in: *see* CAT.

brow

by the sweat of your brow: *see* SWEAT.

brown

as brown as a berry (of a person) very suntanned.

in a brown study in a reverie; absorbed in your thoughts.

ⓘ The earliest meaning of *brown* in English was simply 'dark'. From this, an extended sense of 'gloomy or serious' developed and it is apparently from this sense that we get the phrase *in a brown study*.

2001 *New York Review of Books* When he isn't stirring up mischief, or conniving for gold, or composing beautiful poetry, he's apt to be sunk in a brown study.

brownie

brownie point an imaginary award given to someone who does good deeds or tries to please. informal

ⓘ The *Brownies* are the junior wing of the Guides, for girls aged 7 to 10; the organization awards points and badges for proficiency in various activities.

bruising

cruising for a bruising: *see* CRUISING.

brunt

bear the brunt of be the person to suffer the most as the result of (an attack, misfortune, etc.).

ⓘ The origin of *brunt* is unknown, and may be onomatopoeic. The sense has evolved from the specific ('a sharp or heavy blow') to the more general ('the shock or violence of an attack').

brush

tar people with the same brush: *see* TAR.

bubble

burst someone's bubble: *see* BURST.

on the bubble (of a sports player or team) occupying the last qualifying position in a team or for a tournament, and liable to be replaced by another. North American informal

ⓘ This expression comes from *sit on the bubble*, with the implication that the bubble may burst.

buck

bang for your buck: *see* BANG.

big bucks a lot of money. informal

the buck stops here (*or* **with someone**) the responsibility for something cannot or should not be passed to someone else. informal

ⓘ Famously, *the buck stops here* was the wording of a sign on the desk of US President Harry S. Truman. Compare with **pass the buck** below.

buck your ideas up make more effort; become more energetic and hardworking. informal

ⓘ *Buck* here refers to the lively action of a horse jumping with all its feet together and its back arched. *Buck up* in its modern senses of 'cheer up' and 'hurry up' is first found in late 19th-century school slang.

buck the trend run counter to the general direction of affairs.

2013 *Business Insider* Markets in Asia and the Pacific closed mostly lower. Japan's Nikkei was off 0.41%. Korea's Kospi was down 0.04%. Hong Kong's Hang Seng bucked the trend, finishing 0.39% higher.

make a fast buck earn money easily and quickly. informal

pass the buck shift the responsibility for something to someone else. informal

ⓘ In the 19th century a *buck* was an object placed as a reminder in front of the person whose turn it was to deal in the game of poker. The object used was often a buckhorn knife: hence *buck*.

2013 *New Statesman* The time has come to lay these problems at fashion's door, because they must take their fair share of responsibility. Whoever inevitably passes the buck about what goes on outside the Stockholm Centre for Eating Disorders will demonstrate the industry's unwillingness to ever involve themselves in anything beyond how a gypsy skirt hangs.

b

bucket

a drop in a bucket: *see* DROP.

kick the bucket: *see* KICK.

sweat buckets: *see* SWEAT.

Buckley

Buckley's chance a forlorn hope; no chance at all. Australian & New Zealand informal

ⓘ The phrase is often shortened simply to *Buckley's*. Who or what *Buckley* was remains uncertain: the name is sometimes said to refer to William Buckley, a convict transported to Australia in 1802 who escaped and lived with the Aborigines for many years, despite dire predictions as to his chances of survival.

1948 Vance Palmer *Golconda* Buckley's chance we have of getting our price if we're left to face the companies alone.

bud

nip something in the bud: *see* NIP.

buff

in the buff naked. informal

ⓘ The original meaning of *buff* in English was 'buffalo', and it later came to mean 'ox hide' or 'the colour of ox hide'. *In the buff* itself comes from *buff* leather, a type of yellowish-beige ox hide formerly used in military uniform, the colour of which was regarded as comparable to that of human skin.

steady the Buffs!: *see* STEADY.

buffers

hit the buffers come to a sudden unsuccessful end. British informal

bug

have (*or* be bitten by) the bug develop a sudden strong enthusiasm for something.

snug as a bug: *see* SNUG.

bugger

vulgar slang

bugger all nothing.

bugger me used to express surprise or amazement.

play silly buggers act in a foolish way.

buggery

like buggery to the maximum degree or extent. British vulgar slang

2002 'Sputnik' *That Day in September* 'You can't die of cracked ribs, y'know.' 'They just hurt like buggery, that's all.'

Buggins

Buggins's turn appointment in rotation rather than by merit.

ⓘ *Buggins* is used here to represent a typical or generic surname.

build

build bridges: *see* BRIDGE.

build castles in the air: *see* CASTLE.

built

be built like a brick shithouse: *see* SHITHOUSE.

built on sand without secure foundations; liable to collapse.

ⓘ This phrase comes from the biblical parable contrasting the wise man who built his house on rock with the fool who built his on sand (Matthew 7:24–7).

Rome was not built in a day: *see* ROME.

bulge

have (*or* get) the bulge on have or get an advantage over. British informal

bulging

bulging at the seams: *see* SEAM.

bull

like a bull at a gate hastily and without thought.

like a bull in a china shop behaving recklessly and clumsily in a place or situation where you are likely to cause damage or injury.

a red rag to a bull: *see* RED.

shoot the bull: *see* **shoot the breeze** *at* SHOOT.

take (*or* grab) the bull by the horns deal bravely and decisively with a difficult, dangerous, or unpleasant situation.

2000 Andrew Calcutt *Brit Cult* The government has failed to take the bull by the horns, thereby granting 'hunt sabs' a new lease of life.

bullet

bite the bullet: *see* BITE.

dodge the bullet: *see* DODGE.

sweat bullets: *see* SWEAT.

bully

bully for —! well done!; good for (you, them, etc.)!

ⓘ This expression takes its origin from the US colloquial sense of *bully* meaning 'first-rate', recorded since the mid 19th century.

bum

bums on seats the audience at a theatre, cinema, or other entertainment, viewed as a source of income. informal

bum steer a piece of false information or guidance. informal, chiefly North American

ⓘ In this context, *bum* means 'bad, worthless', and *steer* 'advice' or 'guidance' (it has no connection with young bulls).

give someone (*or* get) the bum's rush ❶ forcibly eject someone (*or* be forcibly ejected) from a place or gathering. ❷ abruptly dismiss someone (*or* be abruptly dismissed) for a poor idea or performance. chiefly North American

❶ **1998** *Spectator* When ... James Cameron wrote an uproariously funny piece about the hotel's iniquities ... he was promptly given the bum's rush.

on the bum travelling rough and with no fixed home; vagrant. North American

tits and bums: *see* TIT.

bump

a bump in the road a problem or setback. informal

be bumping along the bottom: *see* BOTTOM.

things that go bump in the night: *see* THING.

bumper

bumper-to-bumper ❶ very close together, as cars in a traffic jam. ❷ (chiefly of an insurance policy) comprehensive; all-inclusive.

bun

have a bun in the oven be pregnant. informal

bunch

bunch of fives ❶ a fist. ❷ a punch. British informal

bundle

bundle of joy a baby, especially one who is newly born or whose birth is keenly anticipated.

a bundle of nerves: *see* **a bag of nerves** *at* BAG.

a bundle of fun (*or* laughs) something extremely amusing or pleasant. informal

drop your bundle panic or lose one's self-control. Australian & New Zealand informal

ⓘ This expression comes from an obsolete sense of *bundle* meaning 'swag' or 'a traveller's or miner's bundle of personal belongings'.

go a bundle on be very keen on or fond of. British informal

ⓘ In this idiom, *bundle* is being used in the late 19th-century US slang sense of a bundle of money, i.e. a large sum. To *go a bundle on* was originally early 20th-century slang for betting a large sum of money on a horse.

1968 Adam Diment *Bang Bang Birds* I don't go a bundle on being told I'm a pro.

bung

go bung ❶ die. ❷ fail or go bankrupt. Australian & New Zealand informal

ⓘ In this sense *bung* comes from Yagara, an extinct Aboriginal language.

❷ **1951 Jean Devanny** *Travel in North Queensland* 'The stations would go bung without the Abos', one of the missionaries told me.

bunk

do a bunk make a hurried and furtive departure. British informal

2004 *Scotland on Sunday* There were rumours after Nessy left. She'd done a bunk with the provy money. She'd gone away with another man.

bunny

not a happy bunny: *see* HAPPY.

burden

the white man's burden the task, believed by white colonizers to be incumbent upon them, of imposing Western civilization on the black inhabitants of European colonies. dated

ⓘ *The white man's burden* comes from Rudyard Kipling's poem of that title (1899), originally referring specifically to the United States' role in the Philippines.

b

burgers

flip burgers: *see* FLIP.

burl

give it a burl attempt to do something. Australian & New Zealand informal

1953 T. A. G. Hungerford *Riverslake* Well you want to give it a burl—you want to come?

burn

burn your boats (*or* **bridges**) commit yourself irrevocably.

ⓘ In a military campaign, burning your boats or bridges would make escape or retreat impossible.

burn the candle at both ends ❶ lavish energy or resources in more than one direction at the same time. ❷ go to bed late and get up early.

burn your fingers: *see* FINGER.

burn the midnight oil read or work late into the night.

burn rubber: *see* RUBBER.

crash and burn: *see* CRASH.

go for the burn push your body to the extremes when practising a form of physical exercise. informal

ⓘ The *burn* referred to is the burning sensation caused in muscles by strenuous exertion.

have money to burn: *see* MONEY.

money burns a hole in your pocket: *see* MONEY.

someone's ears are burning: *see* EAR.

slow burn a state of slowly mounting anger or annoyance. informal

burner

on the back (*or* **front**) **burner** having low (*or* high) priority. informal

ⓘ The metaphor here is from cooking on a stove with several burners of varying heat: food cooking at a lower temperature on a back burner receives or requires less frequent attention than that cooking at a high temperature on a front burner. Compare with the mainly North American expression *cook on the front burner* meaning 'be on the way to rapid success'.

burnt

burnt to a cinder (*or* **crisp**) completely burnt through, leaving only the charred remnant.

burr

a burr under (*or* **in**) **your saddle** a persistent source of irritation. North American informal

burst

burst someone's bubble shatter someone's illusions about something or destroy their sense of well-being.

bursting

bursting at the seams: *see* SEAMS.

Burton

go for a Burton meet with disaster; be ruined, destroyed, or killed. British informal

ⓘ This phrase first appeared in mid-20th-century air force slang, meaning 'be killed in a crash'. It has been suggested that it refers to Burton's, the British men's outfitters, or to Burton, a kind of ale, but these are folk etymologies with no definite evidence to support them, and the origin of the phrase remains uncertain.

bury

bury the hatchet end a quarrel or conflict and become friendly.

ⓘ This expression makes reference to a Native American custom of burying a hatchet or tomahawk to mark the conclusion of a peace treaty.

bury your head in the sand ignore unpleasant realities; refuse to face facts.

ⓘ This expression alludes to the belief that ostriches bury their heads in the sand when pursued, thinking that as they cannot *see* their pursuers the pursuers cannot *see* them.

bus

like the back of a bus (of a face) very ugly. informal

2004 *Waterford News and Star* What's so great about a guy that has rotting teeth, lungs of tar and bless the poor bloke but the back of a bus does him fair enough justice.

miss the bus: *see* **miss the boat** *at* MISS.

b

bush

beat about the bush: *see* BEAT.

beat the bushes: *see* BEAT.

bush telegraph: *see* TELEGRAPH.

go bush leave your usual surroundings; run wild.

ⓘ *Bush* in the sense of 'wild, wooded, or uncleared country' became current among English speakers during 19th-century British colonial expansion. In South Africa it may have been adopted directly from Dutch *bosch*.

Sydney or the bush: *see* SYDNEY.

bushel

hide your light under a bushel: *see* HIDE.

business

the business end the part of a tool, weapon, etc. that carries out the object's particular function. informal

1936 Richmal Crompton *Sweet William* The business end of a geometrical compass was jabbed into Douglas's arm.

do the business ❶ do what is required or expected; achieve the desired result. British informal ❷ have sexual intercourse. vulgar slang

do your business defecate. informal euphemistic

in business able to begin operations. informal

in the business of engaged in or prepared to engage in

2013 *Telegraph* I'm not in the business of making excuses, and I think it's always important to acknowledge in any project where things may have gone wrong.

like nobody's business in no ordinary way; to an extremely intense degree. informal

1991 Elspeth Barker *O Caledonia* They spread like nobody's business. They're a really pernicious weed.

mean business: *see* MEAN.

busman

a busman's holiday a holiday or form of recreation that involves doing the same thing that you do at work.

ⓘ From the late 19th century, a popular form of working-class recreation was to take an excursion by bus.

bust

a busted flush someone or something that has not fulfilled expectations; a failure. US informal

ⓘ In the game of poker, *a busted flush* is a sequence of cards of one suit that you fail to complete.

bust your (*or* someone's) ass: *see* ASS.

bust your (*or* someone's) chops: *see* CHOP.

bust a gut make a strenuous effort. informal.

2001 David Moody *Autumn* I don't want to bust a gut building something up if we're just going to end up prisoners here.

fit to bust with great energy.

2008 *Salmagundi* She ushered me into the dentist's lair, where I found him laughing fit to bust, and the nurse had a fit of uncontrollable giggling of her own.

busy

as busy as a bee very busy or industrious.

busy bee an industrious person

butcher

the butcher, the baker, the candlestick-maker people of all kinds.

ⓘ This phrase comes from the traditional nursery rhyme *Rub-dub-dub, Three men in a tub*.

have a butcher's have a look. British informal

ⓘ *Butcher's* comes here from *butcher's hook*, rhyming slang for 'look'.

butt

butt heads engage in conflict or be in strong disagreement. North American

kick (someone's) butt: *see* **kick (someone's) ass** *at* KICK.

butter

have (*or* want) your bread buttered on both sides: *see* BREAD.

like a knife through butter: *see* KNIFE.

look as if butter wouldn't melt in your mouth appear deceptively gentle or innocent. informal

someone's bread and butter: *see* BREAD.

b

butterfly

break a butterfly on a wheel use unnecessary force in destroying something fragile or insignificant.

ⓘ In former times, *breaking someone upon the wheel* was a form of punishment or torture which involved fastening criminals to a wheel so that their bones would be broken or dislocated.

2002 *Times* There were plenty of implausibilities in *Ella and the Mothers*, if you stopped and thought about it too much, but that would be to break a butterfly upon a wheel.

the butterfly effect the phenomenon whereby a minute localized change in a complex system can have large effects elsewhere.

ⓘ The expression comes from chaos theory. In 1979, Edward N. Lorenz gave a paper to the American Association for the Advancement of Science entitled 'Does the flap of a butterfly's wings in Brazil set off a tornado in Texas?'

have butterflies in your stomach have a queasy feeling because you are nervous. informal

button

as bright as a button: *see* BRIGHT.

button your lip remain silent. informal

on the button ❶ punctually. ❷ exactly right. informal, chiefly US

press the button initiate an action or train of events. informal

ⓘ During the Cold War period, this expression was often used with reference to the possible action of the US or Soviet presidents in starting a nuclear war.

press the panic button: *see* PANIC.

push (*or* **press**) **someone's buttons** be successful in arousing or provoking a reaction in someone. informal

buy

buy the farm die. North American informal

ⓘ This expression originated as US military slang, probably with the meaning that the pilot (or owner) of a crashed plane owes money to the farmer whose property or land is damaged in the crash.

buy time adopt tactics which delay an event temporarily so as to have longer to improve your own position.

by

by and large on the whole; everything considered.

ⓘ Originally this phrase was used in a nautical context, describing the handling of a ship both to the wind and off it.

by the by (*or* **bye**) incidentally; parenthetically.

bygones

let bygones be bygones forgive and forget past offences or causes of conflict.

C

the big C cancer. informal

caboodle

the whole caboodle (*or* **the whole kit and caboodle**) the whole lot. informal

ⓘ *Caboodle* may come from the Dutch word *boedel* meaning 'possessions'.

cackle

cut the cackle stop talking aimlessly and come to the point. informal

cadenza

have a cadenza be extremely agitated. South African informal

ⓘ *Cadenza* is an Italian term for a virtuoso solo passage near the end of a piece of music. This informal sense probably comes from Danny Kaye's humorous 1940s recording 'The Little Fiddle', in which the various instruments of the orchestra are explained in anthropomorphic terms: 'Along came a handsome young trumpet. When he clasps his eyes on the little fiddle his heart went zing. And he gets so excited he has a big cadenza.'

1991 David Capel *Personality* The Conservative party is having a cadenza about 'subliminal messages' on the SABC's news logo.

Caesar

appeal to Caesar: *see* APPEAL.

Caesar's wife a person who is required to be above suspicion.

ⓘ This expression comes ultimately from Plutarch's account of Julius Caesar's decision to divorce his wife Pompeia. The libertine Publius Clodius, who was in love with Pompeia, smuggled himself into the house in which the women of Caesar's household were celebrating a festival, thereby causing a scandal. Caesar refused to bring charges against Clodius, but divorced Pompeia; when questioned he replied 'I thought my wife ought not even to be under suspicion'.

cage

rattle someone's cage: *see* RATTLE.

cahoots

in cahoots working or conspiring together, often dishonestly; in collusion. informal

ⓘ *In cahoots* is recorded in the early 19th century, in the south and west of the USA, in the sense of 'partnership'. The origin of *cahoot* is uncertain; it may come either from the French word *cahute* meaning 'a hut' or from *cohort*.

2018 Linwood Barclay *A Noise Downstairs* If Bill and Charlotte had been in cahoots—boy, there was a word she hadn't thought of in years—then some of the responsibility would have been lifted from her shoulders.

Cain

mark of Cain: *see* MARK.

raise Cain create trouble or a commotion. informal

ⓘ The sense of *raise* in this expression is that of summoning a spirit, especially an evil one; similar sayings include *raise the Devil* and *raise hell*. A mid-19th-century expression originating in the USA, the particular form *raise Cain* is possibly a euphemism to avoid using the words *Devil* or *hell*. Cain, according to the biblical book of Genesis, was the first murderer.

cake

cakes and ale merrymaking.

1601 William Shakespeare *Twelfth Night* Dost thou think because thou art virtuous there shall be no more cakes and ale?

you can't have your cake and eat it you can't enjoy both of two desirable but mutually exclusive alternatives. proverb

ⓘ The puzzlement sometimes caused by this formulation can be dispersed by reversing it: if you have eaten your cake, you no longer have it.

the cherry on the cake: *see* CHERRY.

the icing on the cake: *see* ICING.

a piece of cake something easily achieved. informal

sell (*or* **go**) **like hot cakes** be sold quickly and in large quantities.

a slice of the cake: *see* SLICE.

take the cake: *see* TAKE.

ⓘ In most of these idioms *cake* is used as a metaphor for something pleasant or desirable.

calf

a golden calf: *see* GOLDEN.

kill the fatted calf: *see* FATTED.

call

don't call us, we'll call you used as a dismissive way of saying that someone has not been successful in an audition or job application. informal

good call (*or* **bad call**) used to express approval (*or* criticism) of a person's decision or suggestion. informal

ⓘ Originally *good call* or *bad call* referred to decisions made by referees or umpires in a sports match.

ⓘ For other idioms containing *call*, see the entry for the main word in the idiom (for example, **call it quits** at QUITS).

calm

the calm before the storm: *see* **the lull before the storm** *at* STORM.

camp

have a foot in both camps: *see* FOOT.

camper

not a happy camper: *see* HAPPY.

can

can it! ❶ stop talking; be quiet. ❷ stop doing something. North American informal

carry the can: *see* CARRY.

in the can completed and available for use.

ⓘ In recording or film-making, something that is *in the can* has been captured on tape or film.

kick the can down the road: *see* KICK.

no can do: *see* NO.

(open up) a can of worms (discover or bring to light) a complicated matter likely to prove awkward or embarrassing. informal

2013 *DVD Verdict* Even if you buy the official story—'that Lee Harvey Oswald acted alone as the only shooter before being killed by the patriotic but misguided Jack Ruby'—the death of John F. Kennedy opened up so many cans of worms, exposing our involvement in Cuba, drug running, and sexual scandals at all levels of government.

candle

bell, book, and candle: *see* BELL.

burn the candle at both ends: *see* BURN.

cannot hold a candle to be nowhere near as good as. informal

ⓘ In the 16th century, an assistant would literally *hold a candle to* his superior by standing beside him with a candle to provide enough light for him to work by. The modern version suggests that the subordinate is so far inferior that he is unfit to perform even this humble task.

not worth the candle not justifiable because of the trouble or cost involved.

ⓘ The idea behind this idiom is that expenditure on a candle to provide light for an activity would not be recouped by the profits from that activity. The expression comes from the French phrase *le jeu ne vaut pas la chandelle*, 'the game is not worth the candle'.

2010 *Guardian* The argument that being able to deploy missiles off another country's coast without anyone being any the wiser is valid, but consider the costs against the benefits. Is the game worth the candle?

candlestick

the butcher, the baker, the candlestick-maker: *see* BUTCHER.

cannon

a loose cannon: *see* LOOSE.

canoe

paddle your own canoe: *see* PADDLE.

canter

at a canter without much effort; easily. British

ⓘ *At a canter* is a horse-racing metaphor: a horse has to make so little effort that it can win at the easy pace of a canter rather than having to gallop.

canvas

under canvas ❶ in a tent or tents. ❷ with sails spread.

by a canvas by a small margin.

ⓘ The tapered front end of a racing boat was formerly covered with canvas to prevent water being taken on board. In this context, to win *by a canvas* meant to win by the length between the tip of the bow and the first rower.

cap

cap in hand humbly asking for a favour.

ⓘ To have your cap in your hand, and therefore to have your head uncovered, is a mark of respect and also of subordination. The idea of a cap as a begging bowl into which coins can be dropped may also be present. A North American version of this expression is *hat in hand*.

a feather in your cap: *see* FEATHER.

fling your cap over the windmill(s): *see* WINDMILL.

if the cap fits, wear it used as a way of suggesting that someone should accept a generalized remark or criticism as applying to themselves.

ⓘ Early examples of this saying show that the *cap* in question was originally a fool's cap. The variant *if the shoe fits, wear it* is also found, mainly in North America.

put on your thinking cap: *see* THINKING.

set your cap at try to attract as a suitor. dated

to cap it all: *see* **to top it all** *at* TOP.

capital

with a capital — used to give emphasis to the word or concept in question.

2008 *Independent* We just went shopping. It was mad with a capital 'M'.

carbon

carbon copy a person or thing identical or very similar to another.

ⓘ The expression comes from the idea of an exact copy of written or typed material made by using *carbon* paper.

card

get your cards be dismissed from your employment. British informal

ⓘ *Cards* are the national insurance card and other documents relating to an employee that were in the past retained by the employer during the period that the employee worked for them. *Give someone their cards* means 'make someone redundant'.

have a card up your sleeve have a plan or asset that is kept secret until it is needed. British

hold all the cards be in the strongest or most advantageous position.

a house of cards: *see* HOUSE.

keep (*or* play) your cards close to your chest (*or* vest) be extremely secretive and cautious about something. informal

ⓘ The previous two idioms both refer to a hand of cards in a card game. If you hold all the cards you have a winning hand, while card players who hold their cards close to their bodies ensure that no opponent can look at them.

mark someone's card: *see* MARK.

on the cards possible or likely.

ⓘ This phrase, a North American variant of which is *in the cards*, probably refers to the practice of using playing cards or tarot cards to foretell the future.

play the — card exploit the specified issue or idea mentioned, especially for political advantage.

ⓘ In modern usage the phrase is most commonly deployed as *play the race card*, with reference to race relations, but it is first recorded in the remark of Lord Randolph Churchill (1886) that, concerning Irish Home Rule, 'the Orange card would be the one to play'.

2018 Mel Sherratt *Hush Hush* Her shoulders drooped again, thinking of her daughter, and her granddaughter. It wasn't entirely Jade's fault, but she did play the victim card far too often.

play your cards right make the best use of your assets and opportunities.

put (*or* lay) your cards on the table be completely open and honest in declaring your resources, intentions, or attitude.

show your cards: *see* **show your hand** *at* SHOW.

care

not care a hoot: *see* HOOT.

not care two straws care little or not at all.

take care said to someone on leaving them.

ⓘ The usage arose out of the original, more literal sense, 'be cautious'.

take care of ❶ deal with (something). ❷ put (a person) out of action by killing them, abducting them, etc.; dispose of.

carpet

blood on the carpet: *see* BLOOD.

chew the carpet: *see* CHEW.

a magic carpet a means of sudden and effortless travel.

❶ In fairy tales, a *magic carpet* is able to transport a person sitting on it to any place they desire.

on the carpet ❶ (of a topic or problem) under discussion. ❷ (of a person) being severely reprimanded by someone in authority. informal

❶ *Carpet* in both these senses originally meant 'table covering', and referred to 'the carpet of the council table', a table around which a problem was debated (as in sense 1) or before which a person would be summoned for reprimand (as in sense 2). The informal use of *carpet* as a verb meaning 'reprove' dates from mid 19th century.

the red carpet: *see* RED.

sweep something under the carpet hide or ignore a problem or difficulty in the hope that it will be forgotten.

2013 *National Business Review* (New Zealand) No one in this government has the balls to address this issue—they just sweep it under the carpet.

carrot

carrot and stick the promise of reward combined with the threat of force or punishment.

❶ The image in this expression is of offering a carrot to a donkey to encourage it to move and using a stick to beat it if it refuses to budge.

2013 *New Zealand Herald* It is a case of the carrot and stick approach to welfare, with a bit of encouragement offered before benefits are cut off.

carry

carry all before you overcome all opposition.

carry your bat (of an opening batsman or top-order batsman) remain not out at the end of your team's completed innings.

carry the can take responsibility for a mistake or misdeed. British informal

❶ The origin of this expression and the nature of the *can* involved are both uncertain, though the idiom appears to have started life as early 20th-century naval or military slang. It has been speculated that it may originally have alluded to one man carrying a container of beer for all his companions, or having to return the empty container at the end of the drinking session.

1999 Shyama Perera *Haven't Stopped Dancing Yet* When something goes wrong in our family, why's it always me who carries the can?

carry the day: *see* DAY.

carry a torch for: *see* TORCH.

carry weight be influential or important.

fetch and carry: *see* FETCH.

cart

in the cart in trouble or difficulty. British informal

❶ A cart was formerly used to take convicted criminals to the public gallows and to expose prostitutes and other offenders to public humiliation in the streets.

put the cart before the horse reverse the proper order or procedure of something.

❶ A medieval version of this expression was *set the oxen before the yoke*. The version with *horse* and *cart* dates from the early 16th century.

2013 *Age* (Melbourne) 'It's putting the cart before the horse,' she said. 'You can't really assess parenting competencies before there is a child. There may not even be a child.'

carved

be carved in stone: *see* STONE.

case

be on (*or* get off) someone's case start (*or* stop) criticizing or hounding someone. informal

a case in point an instance or example that illustrates what is being discussed.

case the joint reconnoitre a place before carrying out a robbery. informal

make a federal case out of something: *see* FEDERAL.

a hard case: *see* HARD.

rest your case: *see* REST.

cash

cash in your chips die. informal

❶ The counters used in various gambling games are called *chips*. They are converted into cash at the conclusion of the game.

cash in hand payment for goods and services by money in the form of notes and coins.

❶ *Cash in hand* is mainly used to distinguish between cash payment and payment by cheque or card, especially with reference to being paid in this way in order to avoid having to declare the amount earned to the tax authorities.

cast

cast something in someone's teeth reject defiantly or refer reproachfully to a person's previous action or statement.

> ℹ For other idioms containing *cast*, see the entry for the main word in the idiom (for example, **cast your bread upon the waters** at BREAD).

castle

build castles in the air (*or* **in Spain**) have a visionary and unattainable scheme; daydream.

> ℹ The concept was known to St Augustine (354–430), who uses the phrase *subtracto fundamento in aere aedificare* meaning 'build on air without foundation'. *Castles in the air* has been the version predominant in English since the late 16th century, but *castles in Spain*, from Old French *châteaux en Espagne*, was used in the late medieval period and occasionally in more recent times. The form of the saying in Old French, known from the 13th century, may refer to the fact that much of Spain in the Middle Ages was under Moorish control, so any scheme to build castles there was clearly unlikely to succeed.

king of the castle: *see* KING.

cat

all cats are grey in the dark the qualities that distinguish people from one another are obscured in some circumstances, and if they can't be perceived they don't matter. proverb

> ℹ The US version of this proverb is *at night all cats are gray*.

bell the cat: *see* BELL.

the cat has got someone's tongue someone is remaining silent.

a cat may look at a king even a person of low status or importance has rights. proverb

> **1998** *Times* A cat may look at a king. The cat may be wrong in its conclusions, but others, following its gaze, can draw their own.

curiosity killed the cat: *see* CURIOSITY.

a dead cat bounce: *see* DEAD.

enough to make a cat laugh extremely ridiculous or ironic. informal

> ℹ This expression dates from the mid 19th century and is associated with the story of Puss in Boots.

fat cat: *see* FAT.

fight like cat and dog (*or* **cats and dogs**) (of two people) be continually arguing with one another.

> **2013 Andrew** *The 4th Avenue Blues* Mom and I used to consistently fight like cats and dogs. It is hard to believe now, but I grew up at odds with my mother all the time.

let the cat out of the bag reveal a secret, especially carelessly or by mistake.

> ℹ A similar metaphorical use of *bag* may be found in the French phrase *vider le sac*, literally 'empty the bag', meaning 'tell the whole story'.

> **1996 Bernard Connolly** *The Rotten Heart of Europe*Tim Renton . . . at odds with his leader on Europe, let the cat out of the bag when he told a television audience, 'we need a strong Europe to maintain our independence from the United States and the Pacific Rim'.

like a cat on a hot tin roof (*or* **on hot bricks**) very agitated, restless, or anxious.

like the cat that's got (*or* **who's stolen**) **the cream** self-satisfied; having achieved your objective. informal, chiefly British

like herding cats used to refer to a difficult or impossible task, typically an attempt to organize a group of people. informal

like a scalded cat: *see* SCALDED.

like something the cat brought in (of a person) very dirty, bedraggled, or exhausted. informal

> **1996 Frank McCourt** *Angela's Ashes* One of them says we look like something the cat brought in and Malachy has to be held back from fighting them.

no room to swing a cat: *see* ROOM.

not a cat in hell's chance no chance at all. informal

> ℹ This expression is often shortened to *not a cat's chance*.

> **2001 James Hamilton-Paterson** *Loving Monsters* There isn't, of course, a cat in hell's chance that I shall ever *see* 1999 as you, I and Dr Faruli know perfectly well.

play cat and mouse with manoeuvre in a way designed alternately to provoke and thwart an opponent.

> ℹ The image here is of the way that a cat toys with a mouse, pretending to release it and then pouncing on it again.

put (*or* **set**) **the cat among the pigeons** say or do something that is likely to cause trouble or controversy. British

> ℹ This expression was first recorded in John Stevens's *New Spanish and English Dictionary* (1706), where it is explained as referring to a

man coming into the company of a group of women. The idiom **flutter the dovecotes** (*see* FLUTTER) is based on the same idea of a group of pigeons as a tranquil or harmless community.

2000 Adrian Hastings *Oxford Companion to Christian Thought* John put the cat among the pigeons by establishing in 1960 a new Roman Secretariat of Christian Unity.

C

rain cats and dogs: *see* RAIN.

see which way the cat jumps *see* what direction events are taking before committing yourself.

1990 Dennis Kavanagh *Thatcherism* She borrowed Kipling's words: 'I don't spend a lifetime watching which way the cat jumps. I know really which way I want the cat to go.'

that cat won't jump that suggestion is implausible or impracticable. informal

1965 Simon Troy *No More a-Roving* If you're telling me she fell in, just like that—oh no! That cat won't jump.

there's more than one way to skin a cat: *see* SKIN.

when the cat's away, the mice will play people will naturally take advantage of the absence of someone in authority to do as they like. proverb

whip the cat: *see* WHIP.

catbird

in the catbird seat in a superior or more advantageous position. North American informal

ℹ This expression is first recorded in James Thurber's short story 'The Catbird Seat' (1942), where it is attributed to the sports broadcaster Red Barber. A literal catbird is a type of North American bird that has a song somewhat reminiscent of a cat's mewing. The allusion in the idiom may be to a cat sitting in a high position from which it can ambush birds.

catch

ℹ For idioms containing *catch*, see the entry for the main word in the idiom (for example, **catch your death** at DEATH).

catch-22

a catch-22 situation a dilemma or difficulty from which there is no escape because of mutually conflicting or dependent conditions.

ℹ The classic statement of this paradoxical situation is in Joseph Heller's novel *Catch-22* (1961), from which the expression is taken: 'Orr would be crazy to fly more missions and sane if he didn't, but if he was sane he had to fly them. If he flew them he was crazy and didn't have to; but if he didn't want to he was sane and had to.' Heller's choice of the number 22 was purely arbitrary: there were no Catches-1 to 21.

2013 *Telegraph* It's the ultimate catch 22, because if they do what Marine A was convicted of, then under British law you're a murderer. If you stay and try to treat him then potentially you and your team are going to get surrounded and killed.

catch-up

play catch-up try to equal a competitor in a sporting event.

cat's whiskers

the cat's whiskers an excellent person or thing. informal

ℹ Other similar phrases include *the cat's pyjamas* and the chiefly North American *the cat's miaou*.

caught

be caught in the crossfire: *see* CROSSFIRE.

be caught short: *see* SHORT.

cause

make common cause with unite with in order to achieve a shared aim.

2013 *Washington Post* I look to liberals to make common cause with the underprivileged, the unfortunate and the weak. If that doesn't describe the people of Syria, then what does?

a rebel without a cause: *see* REBEL.

caution

throw caution to the wind (*or* **winds**) act in a completely reckless manner.

cave

keep cave act as lookout. school slang

ℹ *Cave* is a Latin word meaning 'beware!' Pronounced as one or two syllables, *cave* was the traditional warning uttered by a schoolchild to let others know that a teacher was approaching.

caviar

caviar to the general a good thing that is not appreciated by the ignorant.

ℹ This phrase comes from Shakespeare's *Hamlet*, where Hamlet commends a play with the words: 'the play, I remember, pleased not the million; 'twas caviar to the general'.

ceiling

hit the ceiling fly into a sudden rage.

2004 Scarlett Elizabeth Cooper *Nuts & Bolts* When Dr John Pulaski arrived home that night, he hit the ceiling. 'Why are you bringing other people into our home?' he demanded of his wife.

cell

little grey cells: *see* GREY.

cent

two cents an unsolicited opinion. North American informal

ℹ A lengthier version of the expression is two cents' worth.

2012 *CNN transcripts* It's an election year, so it's no surprise politicians are giving their two cents about what Americans want and what they need.

centre

left, right, and centre: *see* LEFT.

Cerberus

a sop to Cerberus: *see* SOP.

ceremony

stand on ceremony insist on the observance of formalities; behave formally.

without ceremony without preamble or politeness.

certain

of a certain age: *see* AGE.

cess

bad cess to a curse on. chiefly Irish

ℹ The origin of *cess* in this expression is probably linked to the historical requirement for Irish households to provide the soldiers of their English overlords with provisions at the low prices 'assessed' by the government. Alternatively, the word could be a shortened form of *success*.

chafe

chafe at the bit: *see* **champ at the bit** *at* CHAMP.

chaff

separate the wheat from the chaff: *see* WHEAT.

chain

a ball and chain: *see* BALL.

pull (*or* **yank**) **someone's chain** tease someone, especially by leading them to believe something that isn't true. US informal

chalice

a poisoned chalice: *see* POISONED.

chalk

as different as chalk and cheese (*or* **like chalk and cheese**) fundamentally different or incompatible. British

ℹ The opposition of *chalk* and *cheese* hinges on their being totally different in all qualities other than their rather similar appearance.

by a long chalk by far. British

ℹ This expression is based on the old custom of marking up points scored in a game with chalk on a blackboard, as is its opposite *not by a long chalk* meaning 'by no means; not at all'.

chalk and talk teaching by traditional methods focusing on the blackboard and presentation by the teacher as opposed to more informal or interactive methods. British

walk the chalk: *see* WALK.

champ

champ (*or* **chafe**) **at the bit** be restlessly impatient, especially to start doing something.

ℹ *Champ at the bit* is used literally of a spirited horse that tugs at the bit in its mouth in its eagerness to move. *Champ* means 'bite' or 'chew'; in present-day usage it is often replaced in the idiom by its variant *chomp*.

chance

chance your arm (*or* **luck**) undertake something although it may be dangerous or unsuccessful; take a risk. British informal

chance would be a fine thing used to express a belief that something desirable that has just been mentioned is unlikely to happen. informal

fancy your chances: *see* FANCY.

half a chance: *see* HALF.

in the last chance saloon: *see* LAST.

not a cat in hell's chance: *see* CAT.

not a chance in hell: *see* HELL.

not a Chinaman's chance: *see* CHINAMAN.

not a dog's chance: *see* DOG.

not have the ghost of a chance: *see* GHOST.

on the off chance just in case.

> **1992 Neal Stephenson** *Snow Crash* They upload staggering quantities of useless information to the database, on the off chance that some of it will eventually be useful.

a sporting chance: *see* SPORTING.

change

change gear: *see* GEAR.

change hands ❶ (of a business or building) pass to a different owner. ❷ (of money or a marketable commodity) pass to another person in the course of a business transaction.

change horses in midstream: *see* HORSE.

a change is as good as a rest a change of work or occupation can be as restorative or refreshing as a period of relaxation. proverb

a change of heart a move to a different opinion or attitude.

the change of life the menopause. informal euphemistic

change of scene: *see* SCENE.

change your tune express a very different opinion or behave in a very different way, usually in response to a change in circumstances.

chop and change: *see* CHOP.

get no change out of fail to get information or a desired reaction from. British informal

ring the changes vary the ways of expressing, arranging, or doing something.

> ⓘ In bell-ringing, the *changes* are the different sequences in which a peal of bells may be rung.

chapter

chapter and verse an exact reference or authority.

> ⓘ *Chapter and verse* was originally used to refer to the numbering of passages in the Bible. It is now also used more generally to refer to any (usually written) authority for something.

a chapter of accidents a series of unfortunate events.

> ⓘ This expression was apparently coined by Lord Chesterfield in a letter to Solomon Dayrolles in 1753: 'The chapter of knowledge is a very short, but the chapter of accidents is a very long one'.

charge

lay a charge make an accusation.

> **1989 Tony Parker** *A Place Called Bird* We have domestic assaults. The complainant lays a charge.

return to the charge make a further attempt at something, especially in arguing a point. dated

> ⓘ *Charge* here is used in the sense of a headlong rush forward, usually associated with attacking soldiers in a battle.

charity

charity begins at home a person's first responsibility is for the needs of their own family and friends. proverb

cold as charity: *see* COLD.

charm

work like a charm be completely successful or effective.

> ⓘ *Charm* here means a magic spell or lucky talisman.

Charybdis

Scylla and Charybdis: *see* SCYLLA.

chase

chase the dragon take heroin (sometimes mixed with another smokable drug) by heating it in tinfoil and inhaling the fumes through a tube or roll of paper.

> ⓘ *Chase the dragon* is reputedly a translation from Chinese. The expression apparently refers to the undulating movements of the fumes up and down the tinfoil, resembling those of the tail of a dragon, a creature found in many Chinese myths.

chase the game (in football and other sports) adopt attacking tactics, especially when losing, at the risk of being vulnerable to counter-attack.

chase rainbows: *see* RAINBOW.

chase your (own) tail keep on doing something futile. informal

cut to the chase come to the point. North American informal.

ⓘ In this idiom, *cut* is being used in the cinematographic sense 'move to another shot in a film'. Chase scenes are a particularly exciting feature of some films, and the idiom expresses the idea of ignoring any preliminaries and coming immediately to the most important part.

2018 Ruth Ware *The Death of Mrs Westaway* Clearly there's something he's circling around, and I for one would like to cut to the chase and find out what it is.

go and chase yourself! go away! informal

a wild goose chase: *see* WILD.

chattering

the chattering classes articulate and educated people considered as a social group given to the expression of liberal opinions about society and culture. derogatory

cheap

cheap and cheerful simple and inexpensive. British

cheap and nasty of low cost and bad quality. British

cheap as chips extremely inexpensive. British informal

2003 *Croydon Guardian* Sutton Arena is 'cheap as chips', with athletics sessions costing as little as 80p, according to the borough's leisure boss.

cheap at the price well worth having, regardless of the cost.

ⓘ A frequently heard variant of this expression, *cheap at half the price*, while used to mean exactly the same, is, logically speaking, nonsense, since *cheap at twice the price* is the actual meaning intended.

check

check someone or something skeef give someone or something a dirty look; look askance at someone or something. South African

ⓘ Afrikaans *skeef* means 'crooked, askew'.

check you goodbye. South African informal

cheddar

hard cheddar: *see* **hard cheese** *at* CHEESE.

cheek

cheek by jowl close together; side by side.

ⓘ *Jowl* here is used in the sense 'cheek'; the phrase was originally *cheek by cheek*.

tongue in cheek: *see* TONGUE.

turn the other cheek refrain from retaliating when you have been attacked or insulted.

ⓘ This expression comes from Matthew 5:39: 'But I say unto you, That ye resist not evil: but whosoever shall smite thee on thy right cheek, turn to him the other also'.

cheer

of good cheer cheerful or optimistic. archaic

ⓘ The exhortation to *be of good cheer* occurs in several passages of the New Testament in the Authorized Version of the Bible (for example in Matthew 9:2, John 16:33, and Acts 27:22). In Middle English, *cheer* had the meaning 'face'. This sense of *cheer* is now obsolete, but the related senses of 'countenance' and 'demeanour as reflected in the countenance' survive in a number of phrases, including *in good cheer* and the archaic *what cheer*? 'how are you?'.

three cheers for — three successive hurrahs expressing (sometimes ironic) appreciation or congratulation of someone or something.

ⓘ Qualified approval or mild enthusiasm is sometimes expressed by *two cheers for —*, as in the title of E. M. Forster's book *Two Cheers for Democracy* (1951).

2010 *Guardian* So we got Theresa May! She . . . wasn't good enough to be involved with the manifesto; she wasn't good enough to be part of the negotiating team. But apparently she's good enough to be home secretary. Three cheers for that!

cheese

a big cheese: *see* BIG.

as different as chalk and cheese: *see* CHALK.

hard cheese used to express sympathy over a petty matter. British informal

ⓘ *Cheese* is sometimes facetiously replaced by the more specific *cheddar*.

2012 Tony Drury. *Megan's Game* Hard cheddar. So your Dad's in prison.

say cheese said by a photographer to encourage the subject to smile.

cheque

a blank cheque: *see* BLANK.

rubber cheque: *see* RUBBER.

chequered flag

take the chequered flag finish first in a race.

ℹ In motor racing a *chequered flag* is used to signify that the winner has passed the finishing post.

cherry

a bite at the cherry an attempt or chance to do something.

ℹ This phrase is often used in the negative, to express the idea that you will not get a second chance (*a second bite at the cherry*). If you take two attempts to do something, especially some quite small task, this is taking *two bites at the* (*same*) *cherry* or *another bite at the cherry*.

a bowl of cherries a very pleasant or enjoyable situation or experience.

the cherry on the cake a desirable feature perceived as the finishing touch to something that is already inviting or worth having.

lose your cherry lose your virginity. informal

pop someone's cherry have sexual intercourse with a girl or woman who is a virgin. informal

Cheshire

grin like a Cheshire cat have a broad fixed smile on your face.

ℹ The Cheshire cat with its broad grin is best known for its appearance (and disappearance) in Lewis Carroll's *Alice's Adventures in Wonderland* (1865), but the expression is recorded from the first half of the 19th century. Its origins remain enigmatic, although it has been claimed that Cheshire cheeses were at one time marked with the face of a smiling cat. (There is no such breed as an actual 'Cheshire cat'.)

chest

hope chest: *see* HOPE.

get something off your chest say something that you have wanted to say for a long time, resulting in a feeling of relief. informal

put hair on your chest: *see* HAIR.

chestnut

an old chestnut a joke, story, or subject that has become tedious and boring as a result of its age and constant repetition.

ℹ The most likely source for this sense of *chestnut* is in the following exchange between two characters, Zavior and Pablo, in William Dimond's play *Broken Sword* (1816): ZAVIOR ... When suddenly from the thick boughs of a cork tree—PABLO. (Jumping up) A chesnut, Captain, a chesnut ... Captain, this is the twenty-seventh time I have heard you relate this story, and you invariably said, a chesnut, until now.

pull someone's chestnuts out of the fire succeed in a hazardous undertaking for someone else's benefit.

ℹ This expression refers to the fable of a monkey using a cat's paw (or in some versions a dog's paw) to rake out roasting chestnuts from a fire. *Cat's paw* is sometimes used as a term for someone who is used by another person as a tool or stooge.

chew

ℹ For idioms containing *chew*, see the entry for the main word in the idiom (for example, **bite off more than you can chew** at BITE).

chick

neither chick nor child no children at all. North American or dialect

chicken

a chicken-and-egg problem an unresolved question as to which of two things caused the other.

ℹ This expression comes from the traditional riddle: 'which came first, the chicken or the egg?'

chickens come home to roost your past mistakes or wrongdoings will eventually be the cause of present troubles.

ℹ This phrase comes from the proverb *curses, like chickens, come home to roost*.

1997 Arundhati Roy *The God of Small Things* He knew, had known, that one day History's twisted chickens would come home to roost.

chicken feed a paltry sum of money. informal

count your chickens: *see* COUNT.

no (spring) chicken not a young person. euphemistic

2005 Molly Hart *Road to Ruination* She must've been in at least her mid-forties, she was no spring chicken, but she looked good for her age.

running (*or* rushing) about like a headless chicken acting in a panic-stricken manner and not thinking clearly about what should be done.

ⓘ A decapitated chicken may continue to flap about for a few moments before finally expiring.

chief

big white chief a person in authority. humorous

ⓘ This expression supposedly represents Native American speech, and also occurs as *great white chief*.

1971 Roger Busby *Deadlock* You'd think he was the bloody big white chief instead of an OB technician.

chief cook and bottle-washer a person who performs a variety of important but routine tasks. informal

too many chiefs and not enough Indians used to describe a situation where there are too many people giving orders and not enough people to carry them out.

child

child's play a task which is very easily accomplished.

neither chick nor child: *see* CHICK.

with child pregnant. archaic

chimney

smoke like a chimney: *see* SMOKE.

chin

keep your chin up remain cheerful in difficult circumstances. informal

lead with your chin: *see* LEAD.

stick your chin out show firmness or fortitude.

take it on the chin endure or accept misfortune courageously.

ⓘ The image here is of a boxing blow taken squarely on the chin.

2013 *Telegraph* Hervey Saumade, of the leftist FO union, took the report's unflattering conclusions on the chin, saying: 'We have to accept criticism.'

china

like a bull in a china shop: *see* BULL.

not for all the tea in China: *see* TEA.

Chinaman

not a Chinaman's chance not even a very slight chance.

ⓘ *Chinaman* is now widely regarded as an offensive way of referring to a Chinese person, so the expression is best avoided.

1952 Frank Yerby *A Woman Called Fancy* You haven't a Chinaman's chance of raising that money in Boston.

chink

a chink in someone's armour a weak point in someone's character, arguments, or ideas which makes them vulnerable to attack or criticism.

chip

cash in your chips: *see* CASH.

cheap as chips: *see* CHEAP.

a chip off the old block someone who resembles their parent, especially in character. informal

ⓘ A *chip* in this expression means something which forms a portion of, or is derived from, a larger or more important thing, and which retains the characteristic qualities of that superior thing. In 1781 Edmund Burke commented on Pitt the Younger's maiden speech in Parliament by saying he was: 'Not merely a chip of the old "block", but the old block itself'.

a chip on your shoulder a strong and usually long-standing inclination to feel resentful or aggrieved, often about a particular thing; a sense of inferiority characterized by a quickness to take offence. informal

ⓘ In 1830 the *Long Island Telegraph* described the practice which gave rise to this expression: 'When two churlish boys were *determined* to fight, a *chip* would be placed on the shoulder of one, and the other demanded to knock it off at his peril'.

have had your chips be dead, dying, or out of contention. British informal

spit chips: *see* SPIT.

when the chips are down when you find yourself in a very serious and difficult situation. informal

ⓘ *Chips* in this phrase, and in **have had your chips** above, are gambling chips.

choice

Hobson's choice no choice at all.

ⓘ Thomas Hobson, to whom this expression refers, was a carrier at Cambridge in the early 17th century, who would not allow his clients their own choice of horse from his stables as he insisted on hiring them out in strict rotation. They were offered the 'choice' of the horse nearest the door or none at all. *Hobson's choice* is also mid-20th-century British rhyming slang for *voice*.

be spoilt for choice: *see* SPOILT.

you pays your money and you takes your choice: *see* PAY.

choose

pick and choose: *see* PICK.

choosers

beggars can't be choosers: *see* BEGGAR.

chop

bust someone's chops nag or criticize someone. North American informal

bust your chops exert yourself. North American informal

chop and change change your opinions or behaviour repeatedly and abruptly, often for no good reason. British informal

ⓘ Both *chop* and *change* originally had the sense of 'barter', 'exchange', or 'buy and sell', but as this sense of *chop* became dated the meaning of the whole expression shifted to its present one.

chop logic argue in a tiresomely pedantic way; quibble.

ⓘ *Chop* is here used in the 16th-century sense meaning 'bandy words'. This sense is now obsolete, and the sense of *chop* used in this phrase was later wrongly understood as 'cut something into small pieces'.

lick (*or* smack) your chops: *see* **lick (*or* smack) your lips** *at* LICK.

not much chop no good; not up to much. Australian & New Zealand informal

ⓘ The sense of *chop* in this expression originated in the Hindi word *chāp* meaning 'official stamp'. Europeans in the Far East extended the use of the word to cover documents such as passports to which an official stamp or impression was attached and in China it came to mean 'branded goods'. From this, in the late 19th century, *chop* was used to refer to something that had 'class' or had been validated as genuine or good.

1947 Dan Davin *The Gorse Blooms Pale* I know it's not been much chop so far but we're only getting started.

chord

strike (*or* touch) a chord say or do something which affects or stirs the emotions of others.

strike (*or* touch) the right chord skilfully appeal to or arouse a particular emotion in others.

Christmas

like turkeys voting for Christmas: *see* TURKEY.

chuck

chuck it down rain heavily. informal

chump

off your chump crazy. British informal

ⓘ The literal sense of *chump* meaning 'a broad, thick block of wood' led in the mid 19th century to its humorous use to mean 'head', with the implication of 'blockhead'.

chunks

blow chunks vomit. North American informal

church

poor as a church mouse: *see* POOR.

cigar

close but no cigar (of an attempt) almost but not quite successful. North American informal

ⓘ This phrase possibly originated as a consoling comment to or about a man who put up a good, but not winning, performance in a competition or especially a fairground test of strength in which the prize was a cigar.

2010 *Guardian* He's too old to be in porn, and it's the wrong month for nude calendars. So who is he: the newest Chippendale? Close, but no cigar. He's the former ballet dancer who is now White House chief of staff.

cinder

burnt to a cinder: *see* BURNT.

circle

circle the wagons (of a group) unite in defence of a common interest. North American informal

ⓘ The expression reflects a common method of defence against marauders adopted by wagon trains in the American Old West.

In South Africa the Afrikaans word *laager*, meaning 'a defensive circle of ox wagons', is used in similar metaphorical contexts.

come (*or* **turn**) **full circle** return to a past position or situation, often in a way considered to be inevitable.

go round in circles do something for a long time without achieving anything but purposeless repetition. informal

run round in circles be fussily busy with little result. informal

square the circle: *see* SQUARE.

the wheel has turned (*or* **come**) **full circle** the situation has returned to what it was in the past, as if completing a cycle.

ℹ This phrase comes from Shakespeare's *King Lear*: 'The wheel is come full circle'. The wheel referred to is that which the goddess Fortune was said to turn as a symbol of random luck or change.

circumstance

pomp and circumstance: *see* POMP.

circus

bread and circuses: *see* BREAD.

a three-ring circus ❶ a circus with three rings for simultaneous performances. ❷ a public spectacle, especially one with little substance.

❷ 2003 *TroppoArmadillo* You can understand why the Justices … didn't want Eastman turning the High Court into a three ring circus.

citizen

citizen of the world a person who is at home in any country.

civil

keep a civil tongue in your head speak politely and calmly, without rudeness.

civilization

the end of civilization as we know it: *see* END.

claim

claim to fame a reason for being regarded as unusual or noteworthy (often used when the reason cited is comical, bizarre, or trivial).

clam

happy as a clam: *see* **happy as a sandboy** *at* HAPPY.

clanger

drop a clanger: *see* DROP.

clap

clap eyes on: *see* EYE.

clap someone in jail (*or* **irons**) put someone in prison (*or* in chains).

Clapham

the man on the Clapham omnibus: *see* MAN.

clapper

like the clappers very fast or very hard. British informal

ℹ *Clappers* may refer to the striking part of a bell, or it may refer to a device in a mill for striking or shaking the hopper in order to make the grain move down to the millstones. The phrase *like the clappers* developed as mid-20th-century RAF slang, and is sometimes found in the form *like the clappers of hell*.

1992 Jeff Torrington *Swing Hammer Swing!* Why should a hearse be going like the clappers through the streets of Glasgow at this time of night?

claret

tap someone's claret make someone's nose bleed by a blow with the fist. informal, dated

class

the chattering classes: *see* CHATTERING.

a class act a person or thing displaying impressive and stylish excellence. informal

claw

get (*or* **sink**) **your claws into** ❶ enter into a possessive relationship with (someone). informal ❷ criticize vituperatively. informal

red in tooth and claw: *see* RED.

clay

have feet of clay: *see* FOOT.

clean

clean (*or* **neat**) **as a new pin:** *see* PIN.

C

clean as a whistle ❶ extremely clean or clear. ❷ free of incriminating evidence. informal

a clean bill of health: *see* BILL.

a clean sheet (*or* **slate**) an absence of existing restraints or commitments.

> **2003** *Guardian* Given a clean slate and an impressive budget, I would love to programme a festival . . . that exposed audiences to completely new forms of music-making at their best and most diverse.

clean someone's clock ❶ give someone a beating. ❷ defeat or surpass someone decisively. North American informal

> ℹ *Clock* is used here in the slang sense of 'face'.

clean house eliminate corruption or inefficiency. North American

clean up your act behave in a more acceptable manner. informal

come clean be completely honest and frank. informal

have clean hands (*or* **keep your hands clean**) be uninvolved and blameless with regard to an immoral act.

keep a clean sheet (in a football match) prevent the opposing side from scoring.

keep your nose clean: *see* NOSE.

make a clean break remove yourself completely and finally from a situation or relationship.

make a clean breast of something (*or* **of it**) confess your mistakes or wrongdoings.

> ℹ In former times, many people believed that the breast or chest was where a person's conscience was located. The breast is still used metaphorically to represent the seat of the emotions.

make a clean sweep ❶ remove all unwanted people or things ready to start afresh. ❷ win all of a group of similar or related sporting competitions, events, or matches.

Mr Clean an honourable or incorruptible politician.

show someone a clean pair of heels: *see* HEEL.

squeaky clean: *see* SQUEAKY.

cleaner

take someone to the cleaners ❶ take all of someone's money or possessions in a dishonest or unfair way. ❷ inflict a crushing defeat on someone.

clear

clear the air defuse or clarify an angry, tense, or confused situation by frank discussion.

> ℹ This expression comes from the idea that a thunderstorm makes the air less humid.

clear as a bell: *see* BELL.

clear blue water an obvious and decisive gap between you and your rivals. British

> ℹ The expression originated in the 1990s as a political slogan characterizing the ideological gap between the British Conservative party (whose traditional colour is blue) and its political opponents, which right-of-centre Conservatives wished to be as wide as possible.

as clear as day very easy to see or understand.

clear your desk leave your job, especially having been dismissed.

clear as mud not at all easy to understand. informal

clear away the cobwebs: *see* **blow away the cobwebs** *at* COBWEB.

clear the decks prepare for a particular event or goal by dealing beforehand with anything that might hinder progress.

> ℹ In the literal sense, *clear the decks* meant to remove obstacles or unwanted items from the decks of a ship before a battle at sea.

the coast is clear: *see* COAST.

crystal clear: *see* CRYSTAL.

in clear not in code.

> **1966 Robert Sheckley** *Mindswap* Thus, he crosscircuited his fear of embarrassment, and spoke to his oldest friend in clear.

in the clear ❶ no longer in danger or suspected of something. ❷ with nothing to hinder someone in achieving something.

out of a clear (blue) sky as a complete surprise.

> **1992** *New Yorker* The latest revelations . . . about the marriage of the Prince and Princess of Wales may have induced disbelief, but they did not come out of a clear blue sky.

see your way clear to do (*or* **doing**) **something** find that it is possible or convenient to do something.

steer clear of: *see* STEER.

cleft

be (*or* **be caught) in a cleft stick** be in a difficult situation, when any action you take will have adverse consequences. chiefly British

ⓘ *Cleft* is one of the forms of the past participle of *cleave*, in its basic meaning of 'divide with a cutting blow' or 'split'.

clever

as clever as a wagonload of monkeys: *see* **as artful as a wagonload of monkeys** *at* MONKEY.

box clever: *see* BOX.

too clever by half annoyingly proud of your intelligence or skill. informal

click

clicks and mortar used to refer to a traditional business that has expanded its activities to operate also on the Internet.

click into place become suddenly clear and understandable.

ⓘ *Click into place* is used literally of an object, especially part of a mechanism, to mean 'fall smoothly into its allotted position'.

click your fingers at: *see* **snap your fingers at** *at* FINGER.

cliff

fall off the (*or* **a) cliff** decline or diminish precipitously.

2014 Doug Kass *Doug Kass on the Market* Despite a widespread belief that housing activity will fall off the cliff, the rise in home prices ... continues apace.

climb

climb the walls feel frustrated, helpless, and trapped. informal

have a mountain to climb: *see* MOUNTAIN.

clip

at a clip at a time; all at once. US informal

2000 Anthony Bourdain *Kitchen Confidential* I peeled 75 pounds of shrimp at a clip.

clip someone's wings prevent someone from acting freely.

ⓘ *Clip someone's wings* comes from the phrase *clip a bird's wings*, which means 'trim the feathers of a bird so that it cannot fly'.

clock

beat the clock: *see* BEAT.

clean someone's clock: *see* CLEAN.

round (*or* **around) the clock** all day and all night; ceaselessly.

1992 Susan Sontag *The Volcano Lover* The mountain was ... guarded round the clock by a ring of armed soldiers mounted on nervous horses.

turn back the clock return to the past or to a previous way of doing things.

watch the clock wait eagerly for the end of working hours.

ⓘ It is from this expression that the word *clock-watcher* has developed, referring to someone who is determined not to work more than their allotted hours.

clockwork

like clockwork ❶ very smoothly and easily, with no disruptions or problems. ❷ with mechanical regularity.

clog

clogs to clogs in three generations the return of a family to poverty after one generation of prosperity.

pop your clogs: *see* POP.

close

run someone close ❶ almost defeat a person or team in a contest. ❷ almost match the same standards or level of achievement as someone else.

too close to call (of a contest, race, etc.) so evenly balanced that it is impossible to predict the outcome with confidence. informal

ⓘ For other idioms containing *close*, see the entry for the main word in the idiom (for example, **close ranks** at RANK).

closed

behind closed doors (of an action) done in a secretive or furtive way; hidden from public view.

a closed book a thing of which you have no knowledge or understanding.

1944 Frank Clune *The Red Heart* The desert is an open book to the man of the Vast Open Spaces, but to the schoolmaster it was a closed book.

closet

out of the closet out into the open. informal

ℹ *Closet*, the normal North American term for 'cupboard' or 'wardrobe', is used in the Bible to typify privacy and seclusion (for example in Luke 12:3: 'that which ye have spoken in the ear in closets shall be proclaimed upon the housetops'). *Come out of the closet* means 'cease hiding a secret about yourself' or 'make public your intentions'. It is now most commonly, though not always, used in connection with someone making their homosexuality public.

1998 *Spectator* The Prime Minister's entourage could not conceal its glee at the results of their boss coming out of the closet.

cloth

cloth ears an inability to hear or understand clearly. British informal derogatory

cut from the same cloth of the same nature.

2011 *DVD Verdict* Nestled right in the middle is King George VI, a man who seems cut from the same cloth as Chamberlain in his apparent shyness.

cut your coat according to your cloth undertake only what you have the money or ability to do and no more. proverb

man of the cloth: *see* MAN.

out of (the) whole cloth wholly fabricated; with no basis in fact or reality. North American informal

1991 Ron Rosenbaum *Travels with Dr. Death* The fact that her murder is officially 'unsolved' is irritating, yes, but not justification for creating conspiracy theories out of the whole cloth.

clothes

steal someone's clothes: *see* STEAL.

clothing

a wolf in sheep's clothing: *see* WOLF.

cloud

on cloud nine extremely happy.

ℹ *On cloud nine* refers to a ten-part classification of clouds in which *nine* was second highest. A dated variant of the expression is *on cloud seven*.

under a cloud under suspicion or discredited.

1992 Alasdair Gray *Poor Things* The career of this once famous soldier began as well as ended under a cloud.

with your head in the clouds (of a person) out of touch with reality; daydreaming.

cloven

a cloven hoof a symbol or indication of evil.

ℹ Traditional pictures of the Devil show him with the head and torso of a man but the legs and cloven hoofs of a goat. Therefore, a *cloven hoof* is a giveaway sign of the Devil.

1959 François Mauriac *A Woman of Pharisees* She had been a trial to him from the beginning, and now the cloven hoof was beginning to show.

clover

in clover in ease and luxury.

ℹ This sense of the phrase is a reference to clover's being particularly attractive to livestock, as in the expression *happy as a pig in clover*.

club

in the club (*or* **the pudding club**) pregnant. British informal

1993 Carl MacDougall *The Lights Below* Must be serious if you're drinking with the old man. Did you stick her in the club?

join (*or* **welcome to**) **the club** used as a humorous exclamation to express solidarity with someone else who is experiencing problems or difficulties that the speaker has already experienced.

the mile-high club: *see* MILE.

clue

not have a clue know nothing about something or about how to do something. informal

clutch

clutch at straws: *see* STRAW.

coach

drive a coach and horses through make something entirely useless or ineffective. British

ℹ An early example of this idiom is found in this statement by the Irish lawyer Stephen Rice (1637–1715): 'I will drive a coach and six horses through the Act of Settlement'. Early versions of the phrase also refer to a space big enough to *turn a coach and six* (or *four*) (i.e. horses) in, but the context, following Rice's declaration, is very often that of rendering a law or regulation ineffective.

2013 *Telegraph* This is yet another example of the spurious deployment of human rights arguments to drive a coach and horses through our immigration controls.

coal

coals to Newcastle something brought or sent to a place where it is already plentiful.

ℹ Coal from Newcastle-upon-Tyne in northern England was famously abundant in previous centuries, and *carry coals to Newcastle* has been an expression for an unnecessary activity since the mid 17th century.

haul someone over the coals reprimand someone severely.

ℹ This expression originated in a form of torture that involved dragging the victim over the coals of a slow fire.

heap coals of fire on someone's head go out of your way to cause someone to feel remorse. British

ℹ This phrase is of biblical origin: 'if thine enemy hunger, feed him; if he thirst, give him drink: for in so doing thou shalt heap coals of fire on his head' (Romans 12:20).

pour on coal: *see* POUR.

rake over (old) coals: *see* RAKE.

coalface

at the coalface engaged in work at an active rather than a theoretical level in a particular field. British

2012 *Nottingham Post* My vigorous ... manner and bright-eyed optimism belie my 40 years at the coalface of newspaper journalism.

coast

the coast is clear there is no danger of being observed or caught.

ℹ *The coast is clear* originally meant that there were no enemies guarding a sea coast who would prevent an attempt to land or embark.

coat

cut your coat according to your cloth: *see* CUT.

trail your coat: *see* TRAIL.

coat-tail

on someone's coat-tails undeservedly benefiting from another's success.

1964 *Economist* Mr Robert Kennedy cannot be sure of riding the coat-tails of Mr Johnson in New York.

cob

have (*or* get) a cob on be annoyed or in a bad mood. British informal

ℹ The origin of *cob* in this sense is not known.

Cobley

Uncle Tom Cobley and all: *see* UNCLE.

cobweb

blow (*or* clear) away the cobwebs banish a state of lethargy; enliven or refresh yourself.

cock

a cock-and-bull story a ridiculous and implausible story.

ℹ The expression 'talk of a cock and a bull' is recorded from the early 17th century, and apparently refers to an original story or fable which is now lost.

at full cock (of a firearm) with the cock lifted to the position at which the trigger will act.

at half cock: *see* HALF.

cock a leg (especially of a male dog) urinate. informal euphemistic

cock a snook: *see* SNOOK.

cock of the walk someone who dominates others within a group.

ℹ The places in which cocks bred for fighting were kept were known as *walks*: one cock would be kept in each walk and would tolerate no other birds in its space.

cock your ear listen attentively to or for something.

ℹ The image here is of a dog raising its ears to an erect position.

cocked hat

knock something into a cocked hat ❶ put a definitive end to something. ❷ be very much better than someone or something.

ℹ A *cocked hat* is a hat with the brim permanently turned up, especially a style of three-cornered hat worn from the late 18th century to the early 19th century.

C

cockle

warm the cockles of someone's heart give someone a comforting feeling of pleasure or contentment.

ℹ This phrase perhaps arose as a result of the resemblance in shape between a heart and a cockleshell.

cocoa

I should cocoa (*or* coco) used to express scornful rejection of a ridiculous suggestion. British slang

ℹ *Cocoa* is short for (the fairly rare) rhyming slang *coffee and cocoa* 'say so'. The phrase was popularized in the 1950s by the BBC radio programme *The Billy Cotton Bandshow*.

2008 Andrew Sanger *J-Word* Do they show you that you are appreciated? Do they make things as easy for you as they possibly can? Do they heck. I should cocoa.

code

bring something up to code renovate an old building or update its features in line with the latest building regulations. North American

coffee

wake up and smell the coffee: *see* WAKE.

coffin

a nail in the coffin: *see* NAIL.

cog

cog in the wheel (*or* machine) a person who plays a small mundane (perhaps vital but generally unacknowledged or unappreciated) role in a large enterprise.

coign

coign of vantage a favourable position for observation or action. literary

ℹ The literal sense of a *coign of vantage* is 'a projecting corner of a wall or building'; the phrase appears in Shakespeare's *Macbeth* in Duncan's description of the nesting places of the swifts at Macbeth's castle. The word *quoin* meaning 'an external angle of a building' still exists in English, but the archaic spelling *coign* survives mainly in this phrase.

coil

shuffle off this mortal coil die. literary

ℹ *Shuffle off this mortal coil* is a quotation from Shakespeare's *Hamlet*. *This mortal coil* is sometimes used independently to mean 'the fact or state of being alive', with the suggestion that this is a troublesome state, since *coil* retains here its archaic sense of 'turmoil'.

1986 Dudley Moore *Off-Beat* He was just one of a number of distinguished composers who have shuffled off their mortal coil in a variety of unusual ways.

coin

the other side of the coin the opposite or contrasting aspect of a matter. Compare with **the reverse of the medal** (*at* MEDAL).

pay someone back in their own coin retaliate by similar behaviour.

to coin a phrase ❶ said ironically when introducing a banal remark or cliché. ❷ said when introducing a new expression or a variation on a familiar one.

coincidence

the long arm of coincidence: *see* ARM.

cold

catch a cold (*or* catch cold) ❶ become infected with a cold. ❷ encounter trouble or difficulties, especially financial ones. informal

❷ **2001** *Financial Times* Most observers expect house prices to rise . . . depending on whether the UK economy continues to grow smoothly or whether it catches a cold from the US.

as cold as charity very cold.

cold comfort poor or inadequate consolation.

ℹ This expression, together with the previous idiom, reflects a traditional view that charity is often given in a perfunctory or uncaring way. The words *cold* (as the opposite of 'encouraging') and *comfort* have been associated since the early 14th century, but perhaps the phrase is most memorably linked for modern readers with the title of Stella Gibbons's 1933 parody of sentimental novels of rural life, *Cold Comfort Farm*.

cold feet loss of nerve or confidence.

come (*or* bring) in from the cold gain (*or* grant) acceptance. informal

2013 *Telegraph* The French, who were not fully integrated into the Nato military, were always outside the central group, until

President Sarkozy brought them in from the cold a few years ago.

in the cold light of day when you have had time to consider a situation objectively.

the cold shoulder a show of intentional unfriendliness; rejection.

ⓘ The underlying allusion is probably to the notion of 'coldly' (i.e. unfeelingly) partially turning your back on someone. The link with the idea of (inhospitably) offering someone a cold roast shoulder of meat to eat remains, despite occasional 19th-century references to a *cold shoulder of mutton* in this sense, unsubstantiated. The verb *cold-shoulder*, meaning 'reject or be deliberately unfriendly', comes from the phrase.

cold steel weapons such as swords and knives collectively.

in a cold sweat: *see* SWEAT.

go cold turkey suddenly and completely stop taking drugs.

ⓘ The image is of one of the possible unpleasant side effects of this, involving bouts of shivering and sweating that cause goose flesh or goose pimples, a bumpy condition of the skin which resembles the flesh of a dead plucked turkey.

go hot and cold: *see* HOT.

have someone cold have someone at your mercy. US informal

1988 Rodney Hall *Kisses of the Enemy* He waited in his office for news of violence, knowing that then he would have the troublemakers cold.

in cold blood without feeling or mercy; ruthlessly.

ⓘ According to medieval physiology blood was naturally hot, and so this phrase refers to an unnatural state in which someone can carry out a (hot-blooded) deed of passion or violence without the normal heating of the blood. Compare with **make your blood curdle** and **make your blood run cold** (*at* BLOOD).

leave someone cold fail to interest or excite someone.

1993 James Merril *A Different Person* I might have waxed sentimental over the ruins of Catullus's garçonnière but places that 'breathe History' have always left me cold.

left out in the cold ignored; neglected.

make your blood run cold: *see* BLOOD.

out cold completely unconscious.

pour (*or* throw) cold water on be discouraging or negative about a plan or suggestion.

2013 *New Zealand Herald* A former security consultant pours cold water on New Zealand being under threat. 'Anyone who is willing to talk to media about such targeted attacks would not have been involved in dealing with them,' he says.

collar

feel someone's collar arrest or legally apprehend someone.

ⓘ The image here is of using a person's collar as a means of getting a secure grip on them.

hot under the collar: *see* HOT.

collect

collect dust: *see* **gather dust** *at* DUST.

collision

on a collision course adopting an approach that is certain to lead to conflict with another person or group.

ⓘ This phrase is also used literally to mean 'going in a direction that will lead to a violent crash with another moving object or person'.

colour

lend (*or* give) colour to make something seem true or probable.

2002 *Taipei Times* The timing of Chen's remarks appears to lend color to the interpretation that his move was reactive rather than proactive.

see the colour of someone's money receive some evidence of forthcoming payment from a person.

colours

nail (*or* pin) your colours to the mast declare openly and firmly what you believe or favour.

sail under false colours disguise your true nature or intentions.

show your (true) colours reveal your real character or intentions, especially when these are disreputable or dishonourable.

with flying colours: *see* FLYING.

ⓘ The distinguishing ensign or flag of a ship or regiment was known as its *colours*, and the word is used in this sense in these four idioms. A ship on illegal business or in time of war may fly a bogus flag in order to deceive and would therefore be *sailing under false colours*.

column

dodge the column: *see* DODGE.

fifth column: *see* FIFTH.

come

as — as they come used to describe someone or something that is a supreme example of the quality specified.

> **2014** *New York Times* Our reviewer . . . called 'Wave' an 'unforgettable book that isn't only as unsparing as they come, but also defiantly flooded with light.'

come the — play the part of; behave like. informal

> **1992 Jeff Torrington** *Swing Hammer Swing!* Don't come the innocent with me.

come again? used to ask someone to repeat or explain something they have said. informal

come it over seek to impose on or to impress deceptively. informal

come off it! said when vigorously expressing disbelief. informal

come to that (*or* **if it comes to that**) said to introduce an additional significant point. informal

> **1998 Martin Booth** *The Industry of Souls* I am sure you would not wish your son to hear of his father's waywardness. Or your wife, come to that.

have it coming to you be due for retribution on account of something bad that you have done. informal

how come? said when asking how or why something happened or is the case. informal

> **2013 Scary Duck** All of Jesus' mates were fishermen, so how come they only had two fishes between them?

not know if you are coming or going be confused, especially as a result of being very busy. informal

where someone is coming from someone's meaning, motivation, or personality. informal

> ℹ For other idioms containing *come*, see the entry for the main word in the idiom (for example, **come a cropper** at CROPPER).

comer

all comers: *see* ALL.

comfort

cold comfort: *see* COLD.

too — for comfort causing physical or mental unease by an excess of the specified quality.

> **2013** *Farmers Weekly* Potatoes dominate the rotation . . . with sugar beet, oilseed rape, winter wheat and poppies also grown—the latter having replaced vining peas when crop prices became too volatile for comfort.

too close for comfort dangerously or uncomfortably near.

commando

go commando wear no underpants. informal

common

as common as muck: *see* MUCK.

common or garden of the usual or ordinary type. British informal

> ℹ *Common or garden* was originally used to describe a plant in its most familiar domesticated form, e.g. 'the common or garden nightshade'.

> **1964 Leonard Woolf** *Letter* I certainly do not agree that the unconscious mind reveals deeper truths about someone else than plain common or garden common sense does.

the common touch the ability to get on with or appeal to ordinary people.

> ℹ An obsolete sense of *common* (which comes from Latin *communis* meaning 'affable') may have influenced this phrase, as may a Shakespearean phrase used in his play about the great exponent of the common touch, King Henry V, on the eve of the battle of Agincourt: 'a little touch of Harry in the night'.

> **1910 Rudyard Kipling** *If* If you can talk with crowds and keep your virtue, Or walk with Kings—nor lose the common touch . . .

make common cause with: *see* CAUSE.

company

be (*or* **err**) **in good company** be in the same situation as someone important or respected.

part company: *see* PART.

present company excepted: *see* PRESENT.

two's company used to indicate that two people, especially lovers, should be left alone together.

> ℹ The expression is a curtailed version of the proverb 'Two's company, three's a crowd' (or, in an alternative formulation, 'Two's company, three's none').

compare

compare notes exchange ideas, opinions, or information about a particular subject.

compass

box the compass: *see* BOX.

compliment

left-handed compliment: *see* LEFT-HANDED.

return the compliment ❶ give a compliment in return for another. ❷ retaliate or respond in kind.

con

pros and cons: *see* PRO.

conclusion

a foregone conclusion: *see* FOREGONE.

jump (*or* **leap**) **to conclusions** (*or* **the conclusion that**)**:** *see* JUMP.

try conclusions with engage in a trial of skill or argument with. formal

1902 G. S. Whitmore *The Last Maori War in New Zealand* Te Kooti's prestige enormously increased by an apparent unwillingness to try conclusions with him, even with an immensely superior force and in the open plains.

concert

in concert ❶ acting jointly. ❷ (of music or a performer) giving a public performance live.

❶ **2013** *Independent* The more SMEs take this hardline approach, the more effective it is likely to be—especially if they act in concert.

concrete

be set in concrete (of a policy or idea) be fixed and unalterable.

confirmed

confirmed bachelor a male homosexual. euphemistic, dated

conjure

a name to conjure with a person who is important within a particular sphere of activity.

ℹ The image here is of magically summoning a spirit to do your bidding by invoking a powerful name or using a spell.

1954 Iris Murdoch *Under the Net* His name, little known to the public, is one to conjure with in Hollywood.

conspicuous

conspicuous by your absence obviously not present in a place where you should be.

ℹ This phrase was coined by Lord John Russell in a speech made in 1859. He acknowledged as his source for the idea a passage in Tacitus describing a procession of images at a funeral: the fact that those of Cassius and Brutus were absent attracted a great deal of attention.

conspiracy

a conspiracy of silence an agreement to say nothing about an issue that should be generally known.

ℹ This expression appears to have originated with the French philosopher Auguste Comte (1798–1857).

contemplate

contemplate your navel: *see* NAVEL.

content

to your heart's content to the full extent of your desires.

ℹ *Heart's content* was used by Shakespeare in *Henry VI, Part 2* (1593) and in *The Merchant of Venice* (1596) in the sense of 'complete inward satisfaction'.

contention

bone of contention: *see* BONE.

contest

no contest ❶ a decision by the referee to declare a boxing match invalid on the grounds that one or both of the boxers are not making serious efforts. ❷ a competition, comparison, or choice of which the outcome is a foregone conclusion.

ℹ This expression is mainly found in the USA, and is perhaps influenced by the plea of *nolo contendere* (I do not wish to contend) in US law, meaning that the defendant in a criminal prosecution accepts conviction but does not admit guilt.

contradiction

contradiction in terms a statement or group of words associating objects or ideas which are incompatible.

2013 *DVD Verdict* Her character is a contradiction in terms. One minute, she's dead set against playing up her looks to make a dollar, the next she is eagerly doing so.

converted

preach to the converted: *see* PREACH.

conviction

have the courage of your convictions: *see* COURAGE.

coo

bill and coo: *see* BILL.

cooee

within cooee of within reach of; near to. Australian

ℹ *Cooee* originated as an Aboriginal word used as a shout to attract attention, and was adopted by European settlers in Australia. The literal meaning of the phrase *within cooee of* is 'within hailing distance of'.

cook

chief cook and bottle-washer: *see* CHIEF.

cook the books alter records, especially accounts, with fraudulent intent or in order to mislead. informal

ℹ *Cook* has been used since the mid 17th century in this figurative sense of 'tamper with' or 'manipulate'.

cook on the front burner be on the right lines; be on the way to rapid success. North American informal

ℹ Another version of this phrase is *cook with gas*.

cook someone's goose spoil someone's plans; cause someone's downfall. informal

ℹ The underlying idea of this phrase seems to be that a goose was cherished and fattened up for a special occasion, and therefore to cook it prematurely meant to spoil the plans for a feast.

too many cooks spoil the broth if too many people are involved in a task or activity, it will not be done well. proverb

1997 *Times* Too many cooks spoil the broth and at Apple there is now the equivalent of Marco Pierre White, Anton Mosimann and Nico Ladenis.

cookie

toss your cookies: *see* TOSS.

the way (*or* how) the cookie crumbles how things turn out (often used of an undesirable but unalterable situation). informal, chiefly North American

with your hand in the cookie jar engaged in surreptitious theft from your employer. North American informal

cool

blow your cool lose your composure; become angry or agitated. informal

cool as a cucumber perfectly cool or self-possessed.

2013 *DVD Verdict* Crenna looks like he does in most of his movies: cool as a cucumber because he's got his shit together, a guy who ain't afraid to take charge when Ashland begins to show signs he's gone bonkers.

cool it behave in a less excitable way. informal

cool your heels: *see* HEEL.

lose your cool lose control of your temper or emotions. informal

play it cool make an effort to be or appear to be calm and unemotional. informal

too cool for school very cool or fashionable. informal

coon

for (*or* in) a coon's age a very long time. North American informal

1951 William Styron *Lie Down in Darkness* I haven't seen him in a coon's age.

a gone coon a person or thing in desperate straits or as good as dead. US informal

ℹ *Coon* in these idioms is an informal abbreviation of *raccoon*. Raccoons were hunted for their fur, and *a gone coon* was one that had been cornered so that it could not escape.

coop

fly the coop: *see* FLY.

coot

bald as a coot: *see* BALD.

cop

cop a feel succeed in fondling someone's genitals or other intimate body parts. slang

2006 *DVD Verdict* Long before Salem slaughtered its witches, Count DeMarco was gathering up gals in and around the greater New York area and performing perverted Satanic rites on them. This usually consisted of copping a feel and then biting their boobies.

cop hold of take hold of. British

ℹ A slang word meaning 'catch', *cop* probably originated in northern English dialect.

cop a packet ❶ be killed, especially in battle. ❷ contract a venereal disease. informal euphemistic

cop a plea engage in plea bargaining. North American

good cop, bad cop used to refer to a police interrogation in which one officer feigns a sympathetic or protective attitude while another adopts an aggressive approach.

it's a fair cop an admission that the speaker has been caught doing wrong and deserves punishment.

not much cop not very good. British informal

ℹ *Cop* is used here in the sense of 'an acquisition'.

2012 *Diamond Geezer* The predominant colours at Kew, at present, are green and brown. That's grass and branches, mostly, which is great if you like trees and shrubs but not much cop if you prefer flowers.

copybook

blot your copybook: *see* BLOT.

cord

cut the cord cease to rely on someone or something influential or supportive and begin to act independently.

ℹ The image here is of the cutting of a baby's umbilical cord at birth.

corn

corn in Egypt a plentiful supply.

ℹ This expression comes from the aged Jacob's instructions to his sons in Genesis 42:2: 'Behold, I have heard that there is corn in Egypt: get you down thither, and buy for us from thence'.

earn your corn: *see* EARN.

corner

cut corners undertake something in what appears to be the easiest, quickest, or cheapest way, often by omitting to do something important or ignoring rules.

ℹ This phrase comes from *cutting (off) the corner*, which means 'taking the shortest course by going across and not round a corner'.

the elephant in the corner: *see* ELEPHANT.

fight your corner defend your position or interests.

the four (*or* **far**) **corners of the world** (*or* **earth**) remote regions of the earth, far away from each other.

2012 *Telegraph* As always, there are the usual 'nominees' and some newcomers, some famous and some unknowns, hailing from the four corners of the earth.

in someone's corner on someone's side; giving someone support.

ℹ This idiom and *fight your corner* are boxing metaphors and refer to the diagonally opposite corners taken by opponents in a boxing match. Trainers and assistants are in a boxer's corner to offer support and encouragement between rounds.

(just) around (*or* **round**) **the corner** very near.

paint yourself into a corner: *see* PAINT.

a tight corner: *see* TIGHT.

turn the corner pass the critical point and start to improve.

correct

all present and correct: *see* PRESENT.

corridor

the corridors of power the senior levels of government or administration, where covert influence is regarded as being exerted and significant decisions are made.

ℹ This expression comes from the title of C. P. Snow's novel *The Corridors of Power* (1964).

the corridor of uncertainty (in cricket) a line of bowling just outside the off stump, which makes the batsman uncertain whether to play at the ball or not.

ℹ The expression is particularly associated with the cricket commentaries of the former Yorkshire and England batsman Sir Geoffrey Boycott (b.1940).

cosh

under the cosh under pressure; in a difficult situation.

C

cost

at all costs (*or* **at any cost**) regardless of the price to be paid or the effort needed.

cost an arm and a leg: *see* ARM.

count the cost: *see* COUNT.

cotton

bless your little cotton socks: *see* SOCK.

cotton wool

wrap someone in cotton wool be over-protective towards someone.

couch

couch potato someone who watches a lot of television, eats junk food, and takes little or no physical exercise. informal

> ❶ *Couch potato* was a humorous American coinage using the image of a person with the physical shape of a potato slouching on a sofa or couch. Originally, the phrase relied on a pun with *tuber* in the slang term *boob tuber*, which referred to someone devoted to watching the *boob tube* or television.

on the couch undergoing psychoanalysis or psychiatric treatment.

counsel

a counsel of despair an action to be taken when all else fails.

> **2003** *Guardian* This is not a counsel of despair. The argument in favour of the euro can be won, as Winning From Behind, a pamphlet published today by Britain in Europe, argues.

a counsel of perfection advice that is ideal but not feasible.

> **1986 E. Hall** in *Home Owner Manual* Twice yearly desludging has been recommended but this is probably a counsel of perfection.

keep your own counsel say nothing about what you think or plan.

count

— and counting used to indicate that a number or amount is going up and is set to rise further.

> ❶ The expression originated in the terminology of countdowns (e.g. for the launch of a rocket), to indicate that a count was still in progress (as in 'T minus 15 minutes *and counting*')—although in a literal countdown, of course, the number goes down rather than up.

> **2000** *Art Business News* In recent years, the number of millionaires in this country has doubled to 8 million and counting.

count your blessings be grateful for what you have.

> **2003** *The Hindu: Literary Review* At forty you ruminate. Mostly about life and what it has done to you. At forty you count your blessings. And accept the bitter dollops that have been flung your way.

count your chickens treat something that has not yet happened as a certainty. informal

> ❶ This phrase refers to the proverb *don't count your chickens before they're hatched.*

count the cost calculate the consequences of something, typically a careless or foolish action.

> **2004** *The Mercury* (Hobart) Aaron Mauger is on standby as the All Blacks count the cost of Saturday's loss.

count noses: *see* NOSE.

count the pennies: *see* PENNY.

count sheep: *see* SHEEP.

count something on the fingers of one hand used to emphasize the small number of a particular thing.

> **2012** *The Stage* The number of UK resorts that feature professional summer shows, set in theatre venues with six-nights-a-week programmes, can be counted on the fingers of one hand.

count to ten count to ten under your breath in order to prevent yourself from reacting angrily to something.

out for the count unconscious or soundly asleep.

> ❶ A North American variant of the phrase is *down for the count*. In boxing, the *count* is the ten-second period, counted out loud by the referee, during which a boxer who has been knocked to the ground may regain his feet: if he fails to do so he must concede victory to his opponent. A boxer who manages to rise within the count of ten is said to 'beat the count'.

stand up and be counted state publicly your support for someone or something.

take the count (of a boxer) be knocked out.

countenance

out of countenance disconcerted or unpleasantly surprised.

> ❶ *Countenance* here has the sense of 'confidence of demeanour or calmness of expression'.

counter

over the counter by ordinary retail purchase, with no need for a prescription or licence.

run counter to be or develop in conflict with.

under the counter (*or* table) (with reference to goods bought or sold) surreptitiously and usually illegally.

2014 *Independent* Pete Russell's Gallery Bookshop at 20 D'Arblay Street in Soho sometimes had copies of *Naked Lunch*, but very much under the counter, and they were expensive.

country

a country mile a very long way; a very large margin. informal

2001 *Sunday Business Post* He's definitely the best barrister there—by a country mile.

go (*or* appeal) to the country test public opinion by dissolving Parliament and holding a general election. British

it's a free country: *see* FREE.

line of country a subject about which a person is skilled or knowledgeable. British

unknown country an unfamiliar place or topic.

🛈 The Latin equivalent, *terra incognita*, is also used in English.

courage

Dutch courage: *see* DUTCH.

have (*or* lack) the courage of your convictions act (*or* fail to act) on your beliefs despite danger or disapproval.

2012 *Washington Post* He ... told us a couple of war and political stories, the moral of which was to have the courage of your convictions, to have a stiff spine and a good argument, to be respectful and to laugh off... some of the sillier objections we received.

screw up your courage: *see* SCREW.

take your courage in both hands nerve yourself to do something that frightens you.

course

be blown off course: *see* BLOWN.

horses for courses: *see* HORSE.

a matter of course: *see* MATTER.

on a collision course: *see* COLLISION.

par for the course: *see* PAR.

run (*or* take) its course complete its natural development without interference.

stay the course: *see* STAY.

court

the ball is in someone's court: *see* BALL.

have your day in court have a chance to make your case in a court of law.

a friend at court: *see* FRIEND.

hold court be the centre of attention amidst a crowd of your admirers.

laugh someone or something out of court: *see* LAUGH.

pay court to pay flattering attention to (someone) in order to win favour.

Coventry

send someone to Coventry refuse to associate with or speak to someone. chiefly British

🛈 This expression, which dates from the mid 18th century, is thought by some to stem from the extreme unpopularity of soldiers stationed in Coventry, who were cut off socially by the citizens. Another suggestion is that the phrase arose because Royalist prisoners were sent to Coventry during the English Civil War, the city being staunchly Parliamentarian.

cover

blow someone's cover discover or expose someone's real identity.

break cover emerge into the open; suddenly leave a place of shelter.

🛈 *Break cover* originally referred to a hunted animal emerging from the undergrowth in which it had been hiding.

cover all the bases deal with something thoroughly. informal

cover the waterfront cover every aspect of something. North American informal

2013 *New Statesman* Public service broadcasting had a responsibility to 'cover the waterfront', he argued, especially because of the way the press now failed in this task. Very different viewpoints have to be got across.

cover your ass: *see* ASS.

cover your back foresee and avoid the possibility of attack or criticism. informal

cover your tracks conceal evidence of what you have done.

C

cow

have a cow become angry, excited, or agitated. North American informal

ⓘ The reference is probably to the eye-watering pain that would be caused by giving birth to a cow.

1990 Susin Nielsen *Wheels* 'Don't have a cow,' she said huffily. 'It's no big deal.'

a sacred cow an idea, custom, or institution held, especially unreasonably, to be above questioning or criticism.

ⓘ *Sacred cow* originally referred to the veneration of the cow as a sacred animal in the Hindu religion.

2013 *New Zealand Herald* Everyone knows it's time New Zealand started thinking smarter. That extends especially to the sacred cows like our targeted benefits system.

until the cows come home for an indefinitely long time. informal

Cox

Box and Cox: *see* BOX.

crab

catch a crab (in rowing) make a faulty stroke in which the oar is jammed under water or misses the water altogether.

crack

crack heads together: *see* **bang heads together** *at* BANG.

crack a book open a book and read it; study. North American informal

crack a bottle open a bottle, especially of wine, and drink it.

crack a crib break into a house. British informal, dated

the crack of dawn very early in the morning.

ⓘ *Crack* here means the instant of time occupied by the crack of a whip.

crack of doom a peal of thunder announcing the Day of Judgement.

ⓘ The idea of thunder announcing the Last Judgement comes from several passages in the book of Revelation (e.g., 6:1, 8:5).

a fair crack of the whip fair treatment; a chance to participate or compete on equal terms. British informal

1989 T. M. Albert *Tales of the Ulster Detective* You might think that the police concocted the circumstances to deny these men a fair crack of the whip.

crack wise make jokes. North American informal

have a crack at make an attempt at doing, achieving, or winning (something).

paper over the cracks: *see* PAPER.

slip (*or* **fall**) **through the cracks** escape from or be missed by something organized to catch or deal with you.

cracked

cracked up to be asserted to be (used to indicate that someone or something has been described too favourably). informal

ⓘ This expression stems from the use of *crack* as an adjective to mean 'pre-eminent', a sense dating from the late 18th century.

1986 Willy Russell *Shirley Valentine* Our Brian suddenly realised that the part of Joseph wasn't as big as it had been cracked up to be.

cracking

get cracking act quickly and energetically. informal

crackling

a bit of crackling an attractive woman regarded as a sexual object. British informal

1968 Peter Dickinson *Skin Deep* 'You know her?' 'I do, sir. Nice bit of crackling, she is.'

cradle

from the cradle to the grave all through a person's life, from beginning to end.

cramp

cramp someone's style prevent a person from acting freely or naturally. informal

cranny

every nook and cranny: *see* NOOK.

crap

cut the crap get to the point; state the real situation. vulgar slang

crash

crash and burn fail spectacularly. informal

2013 *New Zealand Herald* People who are high-flyers in their early corporate career can crash and burn if they are narcissists.

craw

stick in your craw make you angry or irritated.

ⓘ Literally, this phrase means 'stick in your throat'. A *craw* is the crop of a bird or insect; the transferred sense of the word to refer to a person's gullet, originally humorous, is now almost entirely confined to this expression. Compare with **stick in your gizzard** (*at* GIZZARD).

crawl

make your skin crawl cause you to feel an unpleasant sensation like something moving over your skin, as a symptom of fear or disgust.

crazy

crazy like a fox very cunning or shrewd.

cream

the cream of the crop the very best of a particular type; the *crème de la crème*.

cream your jeans experience strong emotions of delight and excitement. informal

ⓘ The expression is based on the idea of sexual excitement so overwhelmingly strong as to cause inadvertent emissions.

like the cat that's got the cream: *see* CAT.

peaches and cream: *see* PEACH.

creature

creature of habit a person who follows an unvarying routine.

credit

credit where credit is due praise should be given when it is deserved, even when you are reluctant to give it.

ⓘ This sentiment was earlier expressed in the form *honour where honour is due*, following the Authorized Version of the Bible: 'Render therefore to all their dues: tribute to whom tribute is due; custom to whom custom; fear to whom fear; honour to whom honour' (Romans 13:7).

creek

be up the creek without a paddle be in severe difficulty, usually with no means of extricating yourself from it. informal

ⓘ Often shortened to *be up the creek*, this expression is recorded in the mid 20th century as military slang for 'lost' (for example, while on a patrol).

up shit creek: *see* SHIT.

creep

give someone the creeps induce a feeling of fear or revulsion in someone.

2012 Mike Heuring *Mr Dilettante* Mike Huckabee is an excellent speaker, but he's always given me the creeps in a Robert Mitchum/*Night of the Hunter* sort of way.

make your flesh creep (*or* crawl): *see* FLESH.

crest

on the crest of a wave at a very successful point.

Crichton

an admirable Crichton: *see* ADMIRABLE.

cricket

a cricket score (in sports other than cricket) an unusually high score. British informal

not cricket contrary to traditional standards of fairness or rectitude. British informal

ⓘ The game of cricket, with its traditional regard for courtesy and fair play, has been a metaphor for these qualities since at least the mid 19th century.

crimp

put a crimp in have an adverse effect on. informal

1990 Walter Stewart *Right Church, Wrong Pew* Well, that maybe puts a crimp in my theory.

crisp

burnt to a crisp: *see* **burnt to a cinder** *at* BURNT.

critic

an armchair critic: *see* ARMCHAIR.

crock

a crock of shit nonsense. US vulgar slang

ⓘ A crock is an earthenware pot.

2018 Linwood Barclay *A Noise Downstairs* Anna wanted to look her in the eye when she asked her some of the same things she'd asked Bill Myers. And for sure, she'd ask about his call to her about the printer. What a crock of shit that was.

crocodile

crocodile tears a display of insincere grief.

ℹ This expression draws on the ancient belief that crocodiles wept while luring or devouring their prey.

C

crook

be crook on be annoyed by. Australian & New Zealand informal

by hook or by crook: *see* HOOK.

go crook ❶ lose your temper; become angry. ❷ become ill. Australian & New Zealand informal

ℹ *Crook* in late 19th-century Australian slang meant 'bad' or 'unpleasant'.

❶ **1950** *Coast to Coast 1949–50* What'd you do if you were expelled? Y'r old man'd go crook, I bet.

crop

the cream of the crop: *see* CREAM.

neck and crop: *see* NECK.

cropper

come a cropper ❶ fall heavily. ❷ suffer a defeat or disaster. informal

ℹ Sense 1 appears to have originated in mid-19th-century hunting jargon, and possibly came from the phrase *neck and crop* meaning 'bodily' or 'completely'.

❷ 1980 **Shirley Hazzard** *The Transit of Venus* He had seen how people came a cropper by giving way to impulse.

cross

at cross purposes misunderstanding or having different aims from one another.

cross as two sticks very annoyed or grumpy. British informal

ℹ This expression is a play on the two senses of *cross*, firstly 'bad-tempered' and secondly 'intersecting'.

cross your fingers (*or* keep your fingers crossed) hope that your plans will be successful; trust in good luck.

ℹ The gesture of putting your index and middle fingers across each other as a sign of hoping for good luck is a scaled-down version of the Christian one of making the sign of the Cross with your whole hand and arm as a request for divine protection. It is also superstitiously employed when telling a deliberate lie, with the idea of warding off the evil that might be expected to befall a liar. The abbreviated *fingers crossed* is often used as if as a charm, to keep ill luck at bay.

2014 Stuart Ian Burns *Feeling Listless* Hopefully 2014 won't include another hernia or anything else which requires an operation, fingers crossed.

cross the floor join the opposing side in Parliament. British

ℹ The floor of the UK House of Commons is the open space separating members of the Government and Opposition parties, who sit on benches facing each other across it.

cross my heart used to emphasize the truthfulness and sincerity of what you are saying or promising. informal

ℹ The full version of this expression is *cross my heart and hope to die*, and is sometimes reinforced by making a sign of the Cross over your chest.

cross your mind: *see* MIND.

cross someone's palm with silver pay someone for a favour or service. often humorous

ℹ *Crossing someone's palm with silver* was originally connected with the telling of fortunes, when the client would literally trace out the sign of a cross on the hand of the fortune-teller with a silver coin.

cross the Rubicon: *see* RUBICON.

cross swords have an argument or dispute.

ℹ Originally, this expression had the literal sense of 'fight a duel'.

cross that bridge when you come to it: *see* BRIDGE.

dot the i's and cross the t's: *see* DOT.

have your cross to bear suffer the troubles that life brings.

ℹ The reference here is to Jesus (or Simon of Cyrene) carrying the Cross to Calvary before the Crucifixion. The image is also used metaphorically in the New Testament (for example, in Matthew 10:38: 'And he that taketh not his cross and followeth after me is not worthy of me').

crossed

get your wires (*or* lines) crossed have a misunderstanding.

ℹ Wires being crossed originally referred to a faulty telephone connection ('a crossed line'), which resulted in another call or calls being heard.

crossfire

(be caught) in the crossfire suffer damage or harm inadvertently as the result of the conflict between two other people or groups.

ℹ The literal sense of the phrase, in a military context, is 'be trapped (and possibly killed) by being between two opposing sides who are shooting at each other'.

2012 *Telegraph* City authorities halted all Christmas displays after finding themselves in the crossfire between supporters of traditional Christmas celebrations and their secular opponents.

crossroads

at a (*or* the) crossroads at a critical point, when decisions with far-reaching consequences must be made.

dirty work at the crossroads: *see* DIRTY.

crow

as the crow flies used to refer to a shorter distance in a straight line across country rather than the distance as measured along a more circuitous road.

eat crow: *see* EAT.

stone the crows!: *see* **stone me!** *at* STONE.

crowd

crowd the mourners exert undue pressure on someone. US informal

far from the madding crowd: *see* MADDING.

pass in a crowd be not conspicuously below the average, especially in terms of appearance.

crown

to crown it all as the final event in a series of particularly fortunate or unfortunate events. British

the jewel in the crown: *see* JEWEL.

crowning

crowning glory ❶ the best and most notable aspect of something. ❷ a person's hair. informal

cruel

be cruel to be kind act towards someone in a way which seems harsh but will ultimately be of benefit.

ℹ In Shakespeare's *Hamlet*, 'I must be cruel only to be kind' was Hamlet's explanation of his reasons for bullying his mother about her second marriage.

cruising

cruising for a bruising heading or looking for trouble. informal, chiefly North American

2010 *Motley Fool* The price appreciation in China's real estate market has been steep and reversion to the mean tells us the sector may be cruising for a bruising, or at least a correction.

crumb

crumbs from someone's (*or* a rich man's) table an unfair and inadequate or unsatisfactory share of something.

ℹ Luke 16:21 describes the beggar Lazarus as 'desiring to be fed with the crumbs which fell from the rich man's table'.

crumble

the way (*or* how) the cookie crumbles: *see* COOKIE.

crunch

when (*or* if) it comes to the crunch when (*or* if) a point is reached or an event occurs such that immediate and decisive action is required. informal

cruse

a widow's cruse: *see* WIDOW.

crust

the upper crust: *see* UPPER.

cry

cry for the moon: *see* MOON.

cry foul protest strongly about a real or imagined wrong or injustice.

ℹ *Foul* in this context means *foul play*, a violation of the rules of a game to which attention is drawn by shouting 'foul!'

2013 *Telegraph* Multi-ethnic Malaysia is known for its relatively moderate version of

Islam, but conservatives frequently cry foul when a line is deemed to have been crossed.

cry from the heart a passionate and honest appeal or protest.

❶ The French equivalent *cri de coeur* has also been in use in English since the early 20th century.

cry over spilt milk: *see* MILK.

cry stinking fish disparage your own efforts or products.

❶ This expression stems from the practice of street vendors crying their wares (i.e. shouting and praising their goods) to attract customers. If a vendor were to cry 'stinking fish', he could not expect to attract many.

1991 *Independent on Sunday* I want to use the Home Affairs Committee Report for those in racing to go forward together and at last to stop crying 'stinking fish'.

cry wolf: *see* WOLF.

be a far cry from: *see* FAR.

in full cry expressing an opinion loudly and forcefully.

❶ *Full cry* originated and is still used as a hunting expression referring to a pack of hounds all baying in pursuit of their quarry.

a shoulder to cry on: *see* SHOULDER.

crying

for crying out loud used to express your irritation or impatience. informal

1941 Rebecca West *Black Lamb and Grey Falcon* For crying out loud, why did you do it?

crystal

crystal clear ❶ completely transparent and unclouded. ❷ unambiguous; easily understood.

cuckoo

cuckoo in the nest an unwelcome intruder in a place or situation.

❶ The female cuckoo often lays its eggs in other birds' nests. Once hatched, the cuckoo fledgling pushes the other birds' fledglings out of the nest.

cucumber

cool as a cucumber: *see* COOL.

cud

chew the cud ❶ (of a ruminant animal) further chew partly digested food. ❷ think or talk reflectively.

❷ 1992 *DJ* We chewed the cud, drank a few beers and at the end of the meal, Malu asked if I wanted to hit a club.

cudgel

cudgel your brain (*or* brains) think hard about a problem.

❶ This expression was used by Shakespeare in *Hamlet*: 'Cudgel thy brains no more about it'.

take up the cudgels start to support someone or something strongly.

cue

on cue at the correct moment.

take your cue from follow the example or advice of.

❶ *Cue* in both of these idioms is used in the theatrical sense of 'the word or words that signal when another actor should speak or perform a particular action'.

cuff

off the cuff without preparation. informal

❶ This expression refers to impromptu notes made on a speaker's shirt cuffs as an aid to memory.

on the cuff ❶ on credit. US informal ❷ beyond what is appropriate or conventional. New Zealand

❶ 1992 **Sandra Birdsell** *The Chrome Suite* Their surveillance system keeps a beady eye open and they don't let you buy groceries on the cuff.

culture

culture vulture a person who is very interested in the arts, especially to an obsessive degree.

❶ The image of a *vulture* here is of a greedy and often undiscriminating eater.

cup

in your cups while drunk. informal

❶ *In your cups* is now used mainly to mean 'drunk', but in former times the phrase could also mean 'during a drinking bout'. Either could be intended in the passage in the Apocrypha regarding the strength of wine: 'And when they are in their cups, they forget their love both to friends and brethren, and a little after draw out swords' (1 Esdras 3:22).

1948 Vladimir Nabokov *Letter* I have received your letter . . . and can only excuse its contents by assuming that you were in your cups when you wrote it.

not your cup of tea not what you like or are interested in. informal

cupboard

the cupboard is bare all available resources have been exhausted.

2009 *Guardian* You'd have to be a fool not to know that tomorrow is poorer than today. Why wait until the cupboard is bare and the only option is the big bang approach?

a skeleton in the cupboard: *see* SKELETON.

curate

a curate's egg something that is partly good and partly bad.

ⓘ This expression stems from a *Punch* cartoon produced in 1895, showing a meek curate breakfasting with his bishop. BISHOP: I'm afraid you've got a bad egg, Mr Jones. CURATE: Oh no, my Lord, I assure you! Parts of it are excellent!

curdle

make your blood curdle: *see* BLOOD.

cure

kill or cure: *see* KILL.

curiosity

curiosity killed the cat being inquisitive about other people's affairs may get you into trouble. proverb

curl

curl the mo succeed brilliantly; win. Australian informal

ⓘ The image is of a man triumphantly curling the ends of his moustache (*mo* is short for *moustache*).

make someone's hair curl shock or horrify someone. informal

ⓘ This expression may have developed in the mid 20th century as a dramatic or humorous variation of **make someone's hair stand on end** (*see* HAIR).

make someone's toes curl: *see* TOE.

curlies

get someone by the short and curlies: *see* SHORT.

current

pass current be generally accepted as true or genuine. British, dated

ⓘ *Pass current* originally referred to the currency of a genuine coin, as opposed to a counterfeit one.

curry

curry favour ingratiate yourself with someone through obsequious behaviour.

ⓘ *Curry* here means 'groom a horse or other animal' with a coarse brush or comb. The phrase is an early 16th-century alteration of the Middle English *curry favel*, *Favel* (or *Fauvel*) being the name of a chestnut horse in an early 14th-century French romance who epitomized cunning and duplicity. From this 'to groom Favel' came to mean to use on him the cunning which he personified. It is unclear whether the bad reputation of chestnut horses existed before the French romance, but the idea is also found in 15th-century German in the phrase *den fahlen hengst reiten* (ride the chestnut horse) meaning 'behave deceitfully'.

curtain

the bamboo curtain: *see* BAMBOO.

bring down the curtain on bring to an end.

ⓘ The curtain referred to is the one lowered at the front of the stage in a theatre at the end of a performance.

an iron curtain: *see* IRON.

ring down the curtain: *see* RING.

curve

behind (*or* **ahead of**) **the curve** behind (*or* in advance of) the current trend.

ⓘ The expression is probably based on the notion of the *curve* of a graph.

2005 *Stylus Magazine* Everyone knows the cultural stereotype—the Japanese are hopelessly, adorably behind the curve when it comes to Western music styles.

throw a curve cause confusion or consternation by acting unexpectedly. US informal

ⓘ *Curve* is short for *curve ball*, a term in baseball for a delivery in which the pitcher causes the ball to deviate from a straight path by imparting spin.

cushion

cushion the blow: *see* **soften the blow** *at* SOFTEN.

custom

C

old Spanish customs: *see* SPANISH.

cut

a cut above superior to. informal

1998 *Spectator* Samuel was a scholar . . . and his contributions are a cut above the rest.

be cut out for (*or* to be) have exactly the right qualities for (a particular role, task, or job). informal

ℹ The sense of *cut out* here is 'formed or fashioned by cutting', as the pieces of a garment are cut out from the fabric.

2013 *New Statesman* Not cut out for heavy work, Nighy was sent down the middle of the concrete pillars to clean their wire interiors, a job that struck him as particularly absurd, given that no one could ever see the result of his labour.

cut and run make a speedy or sudden departure from an awkward or hazardous situation rather than confront or deal with it. informal

ℹ *Cut and run* was originally an early 18th-century nautical phrase, meaning 'sever the anchor cable because of an emergency and make sail immediately'.

cut both ways ❶ (of a point or statement) serve both sides of an argument. ❷ (of an action or process) have both good and bad effects.

ℹ The image behind this expression is that of a double-edged weapon (*see* **double-edged sword** *at* DOUBLE-EDGED).

❶ 1998 **Sanjida O'Connell** *Angel Bird* Words have the power to cut both ways and I was not strong enough to wield them

cut it meet the required standard. informal

2014 Eric S. Raymond *Armed and Dangerous* It's a problem that requires a much higher-level analysis than simply looking at the strict definitions. There's no single Obvious Right Thing, so a simple algorithm won't cut it.

cut it out used to ask someone to stop doing or saying something that is annoying or offensive. informal

make (*or* miss) the cut come up to (*or* fail to come up to) a required standard.

ℹ In golf, a player has to equal or better a particular score in order to avoid elimination from the last two rounds of a four-round tournament. If the player succeeds, they *make the cut*.

ℹ For other idioms containing *cut*, see the entry for the main word in the idiom (for example, **cut the mustard** at MUSTARD).

cylinder

firing on all cylinders: *see* FIRING.

dab

be a dab hand at be expert at.

ⓘ *Dab* in this sense is recorded since the late 17th century, but its origin is unknown.

2013 *Daily Telegraph* Pope Francis starts his day at 4.15 am, is a dab hand at making paella and once gave a baby a dummy dipped in whisky to stop it crying.

dag

rattle your dags hurry up. Australian & New Zealand informal

ⓘ *Dags* are the excreta-clotted lumps of wool at the rear end of a sheep, which, in heavily fouled animals, rattle as they run.

dagger

at daggers drawn in a state of bitter enmity.

ⓘ The image here is of the drawing of daggers as the final stage in a confrontation before actual fighting breaks out. Although recorded in 1668, the expression only became common from the early 19th century onwards.

look daggers at glare angrily or venomously at.

ⓘ The expression *speak daggers* is also found, and is used by Shakespeare's Hamlet in the scene in which he reproaches his mother.

daily

someone's daily bread: *see* BREAD.

daisy

fresh as a daisy very bright and cheerful. informal

ⓘ This expression alludes to a daisy reopening its petals in the early morning or to its welcome appearance in springtime. The freshness of daisies has been a literary commonplace since at least the late 14th century, when it was used by Chaucer.

pushing up the daisies dead and buried. informal

ⓘ This phrase, a humorous early 20th-century euphemism, is now the most frequently used of several daisy-related expressions for being in the grave. Other idioms include *under the daisies* and *turn your toes up to the daisies*, both dating from the mid 19th century.

dale

up hill and down dale: *see* HILL.

damage

damaged goods a person who is regarded as inadequate or impaired in some way. informal

2012 *Washington Post* He … issued an apology that I believe was heartfelt and he should have. But life will go on. He's not damaged goods, in my estimation, to the extent that he'll never work again in the business.

what's the damage? used to ask the cost of something. informal

dammit

as near as dammit (*or* damn it) as close to being accurate as makes no difference. informal

damn

damn all nothing at all. British informal

damn someone or something with faint praise praise someone or something so unenthusiastically as to imply condemnation.

ⓘ This expression comes from the poet Alexander Pope's 'Epistle to Dr Arbuthnot' (1735): 'Damn with faint praise, assent with civil leer, And without sneering, teach the rest to sneer'.

2013 *The Age* (Melbourne) Some commentators have damned the government with faint praise, saying there is 'not a lot that is wildly illogical' or admiring the changes' 'virtue in clarity' in terms of the 'plain English' titles.

not give a damn not care at all. informal

1998 Penelope Lively *Spiderweb* The boys knew that the teachers didn't like them and they didn't give a damn.

not worth a damn having no value or validity at all. informal

damned

damned if you do and damned if you don't in some situations whatever you do is likely to attract criticism.

2012 *The Age* (Melbourne) As a single Dad, you're damned if you do and damned if you don't. I can't win either way, which is why I've stopped trying to please her.

d

well I'm (*or* I'll be) damned used to express surprise. informal

damnedest

do (*or* try) your damnedest do or try your utmost to do something.

ℹ The superlative form of the adjective *damned* is used here as a noun and can mean either 'your worst' or (more usually now) 'your best', depending on the context.

Damocles

sword of Damocles: *see* SWORD.

Damon

Damon and Pythias two faithful friends.

ℹ Phintias (the more correct form of the name) was condemned to death for plotting against Dionysius I of Syracuse. To enable Phintias to go to arrange his affairs, Damon offered to take his friend's place in Dionysius' prison and to be executed in his stead if he failed to return. Phintias returned just in time to redeem Damon, and Dionysius was so impressed by their friendship that he pardoned and released Phintias as well.

damp

a damp squib an unsuccessful attempt to impress; an anticlimax.

ℹ This expression stems from the idea that a squib, a type of small firework, will not have the desired explosive effect if it is damp.

damper

put a (*or* the) damper (*or* dampener) on have a depressing, subduing, or inhibiting effect on someone or something.

damsel

damsel in distress a young woman in trouble. humorous

ℹ *Damsel in distress* makes humorous reference to the ladies in chivalric romances whose sole purpose was to be rescued from peril by a **knight in shining armour** (*see* KNIGHT).

dance

dance attendance on do your utmost to please someone by attending to all their needs or requests.

ℹ The expression originally referred to someone waiting 'kicking their heels' until an important person summoned them or would see them.

1999 Shyama Perera *I Haven't Stopped Dancing Yet* Tammy and I sat on a vinyl bench seat and watched the visiting flow while Jan disappeared to dance attendance on her mother.

dance to someone's tune comply completely with someone's demands and wishes.

lead someone a (merry) dance cause someone a great deal of trouble or worry. British

2013 *Independent* Almost 70 years after that night ... Henry James wrote one of his most famous novels, *The Aspern Papers*. It was the result of a conversation with a friend about an American collector, Captain Silsbee, who had been led a merry dance by an aged Claire Clairmont, who had held out the promise of some letters of Shelley's and Byron's only to pressure the hapless Silsbee into marrying her spinster niece.

song and dance: *see* SONG.

dander

get your dander up lose your temper; become angry.

ℹ The origin of *dander* in this originally US expression is uncertain; neither *dandruff* nor *dunder* (meaning 'the ferment of molasses') seems entirely plausible.

dandy

fine and dandy: *see* FINE.

dangling

keep someone dangling keep someone, especially a would-be suitor, in an uncertain position.

dark

a dark horse a person, especially a competitor, about whom little is known.

ℹ The expression was originally horse-racing slang. The earliest recorded use was by Benjamin Disraeli in 1831: 'A dark horse, which had never been thought of... rushed past the grand stand in sweeping triumph'.

keep someone in the dark ensure that someone remains in a state of ignorance about something.

2003 *Village Voice* It's payback time for an administration that . . . has ignored lawmakers and . . . deliberately kept them in the dark.

keep something dark keep something secret from other people.

1993 *New York Review of Books* Ottoline was determined to keep her affair with Russell safe from Bloomsbury's prying eyes and she and Russell went to Feydeauesque lengths to keep their secret dark.

a leap in the dark: *see* LEAP.

a shot (*or* stab) in the dark an act whose outcome cannot be foreseen; a mere guess.

ⓘ The metaphorical use of *in the dark* to mean 'in a state of ignorance' dates from the late 17th century.

whistle in the dark: *see* WHISTLE.

darken

never darken someone's door (*or* doorstep) keep away from someone's home permanently.

1988 Salman Rushdie *The Satanic Verses* They couldn't lock her away in any old folks' home, sent her whole family packing when they dared to suggest it, never darken her doorstep, she told them, cut the whole lot off without a penny or a by your leave.

dash

cut a dash be stylish or impressive in your dress or behaviour.

ⓘ As a noun, *dash* in the sense of 'showy appearance' is now found only in this expression, but this sense does also survive in the adjective *dashing*.

do your dash exhaust your energies or chances. Australian informal

1973 Chester Eagle *Who Could Love the Nightingale?* 'Keep going,' she said. 'Keep going.' 'I've done my dash, Marg, in every sense of the words.'

date

a blind date: *see* BLIND.

pass your sell-by date: *see* PASS.

daunted

nothing daunted: *see* NOTHING.

Davy Jones's locker

go to Davy Jones's locker be drowned at sea.

ⓘ Davy Jones is identified in Tobias Smollett's *Peregrine Pickle* (1751) as 'the fiend that presides over all the evil spirits of the deep', but the origin of the name is uncertain.

dawn

the crack of dawn: *see* CRACK.

a false dawn: *see* FALSE.

day

all in a day's work (of something unusual or problematic) accepted as part of someone's normal routine or as a matter of course.

the ancient of Days: *see* ANCIENT.

any day ❶ at any time. ❷ used to express your strong preference for something under any circumstances.

❷ **2003** *Royal Academy Magazine* Give me Bruegel rather than Michelangelo any day.

as clear as day: *see* CLEAR.

at the end of the day: *see* END.

back in the day in former times.

2018 Isabelle Grey *Wrong Way Home* If there was some kind of corrupt relationship between Owen and DI Jupp back in the day, maybe he still imagines the police are open to negotiation.

bad hair day: *see* BAD.

call it a day decide or agree to stop doing something, either temporarily or permanently.

ⓘ This expression comes from the idea of having done a day's work; in the mid 19th century, the form was *call it half a day*.

carry (*or* win) the day be victorious or successful.

ⓘ The sense of *day* used here is 'the day's work on the field of battle'.

day in, day out continuously or repeatedly over a long period of time.

day of reckoning the time when past mistakes or misdeeds must be punished or paid for; a testing time when the degree of your success or failure will be revealed.

ⓘ This expression refers to the Day of Judgement, on which, according to Christian tradition, human beings will have to answer to God for their transgressions.

don't give up the day job used as a humorous way of recommending someone not to pursue an alternative career at which they are unlikely to be successful. informal

1996 **Charlie Higson** *Getting Rid of Mr Kitchen* 'You are the worst beggar I have ever encountered,' I said. 'Don't give up the day job.'

d

every dog has his day: *see* DOG.

from day one from the very beginning.

2013 *New Zealand Herald* For sudden deaths like this ... they ought to go in with quite a suspicious mind from day one and treat it like a crime scene from the first moment.

give someone the time of day: *see* TIME.

have had your (*or* its) day be no longer popular, successful, or influential.

have seen (*or* known) better days be in a worse state than in the past; have become old, worn-out, or shabby.

if he (*or* she) is a day at least (added to a statement about the age of a person or thing).

1992 Shashi Tharoor *Show Business* Lawrence must be fifty if he's a day.

in all my born days: *see* BORN.

in the cold light of day: *see* COLD.

in this day and age at the present time.

2003 *Film Inside Out* The idea of girls becoming a commodity, to be traded as slaves, seems totally alien in this day and age.

just another day at the office: *see* OFFICE.

know the time of day: *see* TIME.

late in the day: *see* LATE.

make a day (*or* night) of it devote a whole day (*or* night) to an activity, typically an enjoyable one.

make someone's day make an otherwise ordinary or dull day pleasingly memorable for someone.

ⓘ The expression is particularly associated with the character 'Dirty Harry' (police detective Harry Callahan) played by Clint Eastwood in the film *Sudden Impact* (1983) who, when threatened by a criminal, points his gun at him and says 'Go ahead, make my day' (i.e. by giving Harry an excuse to shoot).

night and day: *see* NIGHT.

not someone's day used to convey that someone has suffered a day of successive misfortunes. informal

1997 A. Sivanandan *When Memory Dies* He sighed inwardly, this was not his day.

the old days: *see* OLD.

one of these days at some unspecified time in the future.

1924 P.G. Wodehouse *Ukridge* 'Don't you worry, you'll get your money back ... ' 'When?' 'One of these days,' said Ukridge, buoyantly. 'One of these days.'

one of those days a day when several things go wrong.

the order of the day: *see* ORDER.

pass the time of day: *see* TIME.

plain as day: *see* PLAIN.

a red letter day: *see* RED.

Rome was not built in a day: *see* ROME.

save the day: *see* SAVE.

seize the day: *see* SEIZE.

someone's (*or* something's) days are numbered someone or something will not survive or remain in a position of power for much longer.

2001 *Business Asia* Daewoo's former chairman Kim Woo Choong's days are numbered after Korean authorities issued a warrant for his arrest.

that will be the day something is very unlikely to happen. informal

1991 Alistair Campbell *Sidewinder* 'Now for my proposal, which you'll find irresistible.' 'That'll be the day.'

those were the days used to assert that a particular past time was better in comparison with the present.

1997 Brenda Clough *How Like a God* 'Those were the days,' Rob said. 'B.C.—before children! Remember?'

your salad days: *see* SALAD.

daylight

beat the (living) daylights out of give (someone) a very severe beating. informal

ⓘ *Daylight* or *daylights* has been used from the mid 18th century as a metaphor for 'eyes', and here has the extended sense of any vital organ of the body.

daylight robbery blatant and unfair overcharging. British informal

2005 *MotleyFool.co.uk: Comment* Have you seen the price of potted plants and fruit trees in garden centres recently? It's daylight robbery.

frighten (*or* scare) the (living) daylights out of give someone a very severe fright.

ℹ This expression was a mid-20th-century development from *beat the living daylights out of*, on the premise that the effect of extreme fear is as drastic as physical violence.

1955 Frank Yerby *The Treasure of Pleasant Valley* Didn't mean to hit him . . . Meant to throw close to him and scare the living daylights out of him.

in broad daylight: *see* BROAD.

see daylight begin to understand what was previously puzzling or unclear.

dead

better dead than red: *see* RED.

cut someone dead completely ignore someone.

dead and buried used to emphasize that something is finally and irrevocably in the past.

dead as a (*or* the) dodo ❶ no longer alive. ❷ no longer effective, valid, or interesting. informal

ℹ The name *dodo* comes from Portuguese *duodo* meaning 'simpleton'. It was applied to the large flightless bird of Mauritius because the bird had no fear of man and so was easily killed, being quickly wiped out by visiting European sailors. The dodo's fate has made it proverbial for something that is long dead and the name has been used metaphorically for an old-fashioned, stupid, or unenlightened person since the 19th century.

2000 John Caughie *Television Drama* The once pleasant family hour is now as dead as a dodo.

dead as a doornail (*or* as mutton) completely dead.

ℹ A *doornail* was one of the large iron studs formerly often used on doors for ornamentation or for added strength; the word occurred in various alliterative phrases (e.g. *deaf as a doornail* and *dour as a doornail*) but *dead as a doornail* is now the only one in common use.

a dead cat bounce a misleading sign of vitality in something that is really moribund. informal

ℹ A dead cat might bounce if it is dropped from a great height: the fact of it bouncing does not reliably indicate that the cat is alive after all. The expression was coined in the late 20th century by Wall Street traders to refer to a situation in which a stock or company on a long-term, irrevocable downward trend suddenly shows a small temporary improvement.

dead from the neck (*or* chin) up stupid. informal

1990 *Film Comment* Steward subscribes to the notion that all women are 'nitwits and lunkheads, dead from the neck up'.

dead in the water unable to function effectively.

ℹ *Dead in the water* was originally used of a ship and in this context means 'unable to move'.

2013 *Daily Telegraph* The relationship had been dead in the water for some time.

a dead letter a law or practice no longer observed.

ℹ This phrase was originally used with reference to passages in the biblical epistles in which St Paul compares the life-giving spirit of the New Testament with what he sees as the dead 'letter' of the Mosaic law. Later (until the late 19th century) *Dead-letter Office* was the name given to the organization that dealt with unclaimed mail or mail that could not be delivered for any reason. The expression has been used metaphorically for an obsolete or unobserved law since the mid 17th century.

2013 *CNN transcripts* Immigration reform is a dead letter because those 80 people in the House are simply not going to pass it.

dead meat in serious trouble. informal

1989 Tracy Kidder *Among Schoolchildren* You're dead meat, I'm gonna get you after school.

dead men's shoes: *see* SHOE.

the dead of night the quietest, darkest part of the night.

the dead of winter the coldest part of winter.

ℹ The sense of *dead* here and in the previous idiom developed in the 16th century from *dead time of —*, meaning the period most characterized by lack of signs of life or activity.

dead on your feet extremely tired. informal

ℹ This expression was a development from the phrase *dead tired*, as an exaggerated way of expressing a feeling of exhaustion. *Dead* is sometimes also used on its own to mean 'exhausted'.

dead to the world fast asleep; unconscious. informal

2000 Michael Ondaatje *Anil's Ghost* The nurse tried to wake him, but he was dead to the world.

dead wood people or things that are no longer useful or productive.

2003 *Architectural Review* Academics cement themselves like limpets to whomever will give them tenure. Australian universities are full of dead wood.

drop dead: *see* DROP.

flog a dead horse: *see* FLOG.

from the dead ❶ from a state of death. ❷ from a period of obscurity or inactivity.

get the dead needle: *see* NEEDLE.

knock someone dead: *see* KNOCK.

make a dead set at make a determined attempt to win the affections of. British

ℹ Dating from the early 19th century, this was originally a sporting idiom, referring to the manner in which a dog such as a setter or pointer stands stock still with its muzzle pointing in the direction of game.

over my dead body used to emphasize that you completely oppose something and would do anything to prevent it from happening. informal

wouldn't be seen (*or* caught) dead in (*or* with *or* at) — used to express strong dislike or disinclination for a particular thing or situation. informal

2011 *The Age* (Melbourne) And if you're drinking coffee, feel free to make it the sort of ridiculously fluffy and chocolate-crusted cappuccino you wouldn't normally be seen dead with.

deaf

deaf as an adder (*or* a post) completely or extremely deaf.

ℹ The traditional deafness of an adder is based on an image in Psalm 58:4: 'the deaf adder that stoppeth her ear'.

dialogue of the deaf: *see* DIALOGUE.

fall on deaf ears (of a statement or request) be ignored by others.

1990 Ellen Kuzwayo *Sit Down and Listen* All efforts by her husband to dissuade her from wishing to leave fell on deaf ears.

turn a deaf ear refuse to listen or respond to a statement or request.

deal

a big deal a thing considered important. informal

big deal! used to express contempt for something regarded as impressive or important by another person. informal

cut a deal come to an arrangement, especially in business; make a deal. North American informal

ℹ *Cut* here relates to the informal sense of the noun *cut* as 'a share of profits'.

a done deal: *see* DONE.

a fair deal: *see* FAIR.

a raw (*or* rough) deal a situation in which someone receives unfair or harsh treatment. informal

the real deal: *see* REAL.

a square deal a fair bargain or treatment.

ℹ *Square* here has the sense of 'honest', which as an adjective was associated originally with honourable play at cards. *See also* **on the square** *at* SQUARE.

wheel and deal: *see* WHEEL.

dear

for dear life: *see* LIFE.

dearest

your nearest and dearest: *see* NEAREST.

death

at death's door so ill that you may die.

2005 Andre66 *A Beautiful Revolution* Cough, cough, splutter, splutter; I don't feel very well. I feel shit. I'm at death's door. The end of the world is nigh.

be the death of cause someone's death.

ℹ *Be the death of* is generally used as an exaggerated or humorous way of describing the effects of laughter, embarrassment, boredom, or similar emotions.

2002 R. J. Bailey *Far in the Hills* Those stairs will be the death of me. I gotta give up them ready rolls!

be frightened to death be made very alarmed and fearful. informal

be in at the death ❶ be present when a hunted animal is caught and killed. ❷ be present when something fails or comes to an end.

catch your death (of cold) catch a severe cold or chill. informal

a death's head at the feast: *see* FEAST.

dice with death: *see* DICE.

die a (*or* the) death come to an end; cease or fail to be popular or successful.

1999 *Linedancer* Our industry must expand . . . otherwise it will die a death with just a few clubs remaining.

do something to death perform or repeat something so frequently that it becomes tediously familiar.

a fate worse than death: *see* FATE.

kiss of death: *see* KISS.

like death warmed up extremely tired or ill. informal

ℹ *Like death warmed up* was originally military slang, recorded from the 1930s. The North American version is *like death warmed over*.

like grim death: *see* GRIM.

a matter of life and death: *see* LIFE.

sick to death: *see* SICK.

sign your own death warrant: *see* SIGN.

deceive

flatter to deceive: *see* FLATTER.

decent

do the decent thing take the most honourable or appropriate course of action even if it is not necessarily in your own interests.

deck

clear the decks: *see* CLEAR.

hit the deck fall to or throw yourself on the ground. informal

not playing with a full deck mentally deficient. North American informal

ℹ A *deck* in this phrase is a pack of playing cards.

on deck ready for action or work. North American

ℹ This expression refers to a ship's main deck as the place where the crew musters to receive orders for action.

declare

declare an interest: *see* INTEREST.

deep

dig deep ❶ give money or other resources generously. ❷ make a great effort to do something. informal

ℹ The idea here is of thrusting your hands deep into your pockets to find money with which to pay for something.

❷ **1991** *Sports Illustrated* You really have to dig deep night after night to get up for every game.

go off (*or* go in off) the deep end give way immediately to anger or emotion. informal

ℹ This expression refers to the deep end of a swimming pool, where the diving board is located. In the USA the phrase has also developed the meaning 'go mad', but in either sense the underlying idea is of a sudden explosive loss of self-control.

have deep pockets: *see* POCKET.

in deep water (*or* waters) in trouble or difficulty. informal

ℹ *In deep water* is a biblical metaphor; see, for example, Psalm 69:14: 'let me be delivered from them that hate me, and out of the deep waters'.

jump (*or* be thrown) in at the deep end face a difficult problem or undertaking with little experience of it. informal

still waters run deep: *see* STILL.

take a deep breath: *see* BREATH.

degree

one degree under slightly unwell. informal

to the nth degree: *see* NTH.

delicate

in a delicate condition pregnant. archaic

deliver

deliver the goods: *see* **come up with the goods** *at* GOOD.

signed, sealed, and delivered: *see* SIGN.

stand and deliver! a highwayman's order to hand over money and valuables. historical

delusion

delusions of grandeur a false impression of your own importance.

ℹ This expression is the equivalent of the French phrase *folie de grandeur*, which came into English in the late 19th century and is still used today.

demon

like a demon: *see* **like the devil** *at* DEVIL.

den

beard the lion in his den: *see* BEARD.

the lion's den: *see* LION.

depth

hidden depths admirable but previously unnoticed qualities.

out of your depth unable to cope due to lack of ability or knowledge.

ℹ Literally, if you are *out of your depth* you are in water too deep to stand in.

plumb the depths: *see* PLUMB.

derry

have a derry on someone be prejudiced against someone. Australian & New Zealand

ℹ This expression refers to the traditional song refrain *derry down*, and was a late 19th-century adaptation of **have a down on** (*see* DOWN).

1948 David Ballantyne *The Cunninghams* She didn't like the Baptists though, had a derry on that crowd ever since Hilda took her to an evening service.

desert

rats deserting a sinking ship: *see* RAT.

deserts

get (*or* receive) your just deserts receive what you deserve, especially appropriate punishment.

design

have designs on aim to obtain something desired, especially in an underhand way.

2003 *Economist* Hardliners . . . think America has designs on its oil, and will act against Iran once it has disposed of Saddam Hussein.

desire

leave much (*or* a lot) to be desired be highly unsatisfactory.

your heart's desire: *see* HEART.

desk

clear your desk: *see* CLEAR.

despite

despite yourself used to indicate that you did not intend to do the thing mentioned.

2010 *Believer Magazine* Woolf didn't hate Dutton. He was just baffled by him. And, despite himself, fascinated by him.

details

the gory details: *see* GORY.

deuce

informal, dated

a (*or* the) deuce of a — something very bad or difficult of its kind.

1933 John Galsworthy *The End of the Chapter* It seems there's a deuce of a fuss in the Bolivian papers.

the deuce to pay trouble to be expected.

like the deuce very fast.

ℹ *Deuce* was first used in 17th-century English in various exclamatory expressions in which it was equated with 'bad luck' or 'mischief', because in dice-playing two (= deuce) is the lowest and most unlucky throw. From this there soon developed the sense of *deuce* as 'the devil' (i.e. bad luck or mischief personified). *Deuce* as a euphemism for the devil occurs in a number of expressions, including those above.

device

leave someone to their own devices leave someone to do as they wish without supervision.

ℹ *Device* in the sense of 'inclination' or 'fancy' now only occurs in the plural, and is found only in this expression or in the phrase *devices and desires*, as quoted from the General Confession in the Book of Common Prayer.

devil

be a devil! said when encouraging someone to do something that they are hesitating to do. informal

better the devil you know: *see* BETTER.

between the devil and the deep blue sea caught in a dilemma; trapped between two equally dangerous alternatives.

devil-may-care cheerfully or defiantly reckless.

a (*or* the) devil of a — something very large or bad of its kind. informal

1919 Katherine Mansfield *Letter* We had the devil of a great storm last night, lasting for hours, thunder, lightning, rain & I had appalling nightmares!

the devil's in the detail the details of a matter are its most tricky or problematic aspect.

the devil's own — a very difficult or great —. informal

2003 *This Is Essex* Once the sheds and fences go up it's the devil's own job to get them down.

the devil to pay serious trouble to be expected.

ⓘ This expression refers to the bargain formerly supposed to be made between magicians and the devil, the former receiving extraordinary powers or wealth in return for their souls.

the devil you know something or someone bad that you are familiar with and have accommodated yourself to or can cope with.

ⓘ The expression is a shortened version of the proverb 'Better *the devil you know* than the one you don't'.

give the devil his due if someone or something generally considered bad or undeserving has any redeeming features these should be acknowledged. proverb

like the devil (*or* a demon) with great speed or energy.

the luck of the devil: *see* LUCK.

play devil's advocate take a side in an argument that is the opposite of what you really want or think.

ⓘ A translation of the Latin phrase *advocatus diaboli, devil's advocate* is the popular name for the official in the Roman Catholic Church who puts the case against a candidate for canonization or beatification; he is more properly known as *promotor fidei* 'promoter of the faith'.

2011 *The Charade Goes On* Since my earliest days to today, I'm cynical but a dreamer with an idealistic streak. I love a good argument, to play devil's advocate, to see both sides of the coin almost endlessly.

play the devil (*or* Old Harry) with damage or affect greatly.

ⓘ *Old Harry* has been a nickname for the devil in northern England since the 18th century.

raise the devil make a noisy disturbance. informal

sell your soul (to the devil): *see* SELL.

speak (*or* talk) of the devil said when a person appears just after being mentioned.

ⓘ This phrase stems from the superstition that the devil will manifest himself if his name is spoken.

sup (*or* dine) with the devil have dealings with a cunning or malevolent person.

ⓘ The proverb *he who sups with the devil should have a long spoon* is used especially to urge someone dealing with a person of this type to take care.

the world, the flesh, and the devil: *see* WORLD.

dialogue

dialogue of the deaf a discussion in which each party is unresponsive to what the others say.

ⓘ The French equivalent *dialogue des sourds* is also sometimes used in English.

diamond

diamond cut diamond a situation in which a sharp-witted or cunning person meets their match. British

1863 Charles Reade *Hard Cash* He felt . . . sure his employer would outwit him if he could; and resolved it should be diamond cut diamond.

rough diamond: *see* ROUGH.

dice

dice with death take serious risks.

ⓘ *Dice with* is used here in the general sense of 'play a game of chance with'. In the mid 20th century *dice with death* was a journalistic cliché used to convey the risks taken by racing drivers; the expression seems for some time to have been especially connected with motoring, although it is now used of other risky activities. It gave rise to the use of *dicing* as a slang word among drivers for 'driving in a race', and it can be compared with *dicey* meaning 'dangerous', a word which originated in 1950s air-force slang.

load the dice against: *see* LOAD.

no dice used to refuse a request or indicate that there is no chance of success. North American informal

1990 Paul Auster *The Music of Chance* Sorry kid. No dice. You can talk yourself blue in the face, but I'm not going.

roll the dice: *see* ROLL.

slice and dice: *see* SLICE.

throw of the dice a risky attempt to do or achieve something

2009 *Guardian* A report . . . warning that a third Heathrow runway could become a white elephant looks like a last throw of the dice before the government approves the project.

Dick

Tom, Dick, and Harry: *see* TOM.

dicky bird

not a dicky bird not a word; nothing at all. informal

ⓘ *Dicky bird* is rhyming slang for 'word'.

1988 Glenn Patterson *Burning Your Own* Sammy put his ear to where he thought its heart ought to be: not a dickybird.

d

dictionary

have swallowed a dictionary use long and obscure words when speaking. informal

dido

cut didoes perform mischievous tricks or deeds. North American informal

ⓘ The origin of *didoes* remains unknown.

die

die a death: *see* DEATH.

die hard disappear or change very slowly.

ⓘ This expression seems to have been used first of criminals who died resisting to the last on the Tyburn gallows in London. At the battle of Albuera in 1811, during the Peninsular War, William Inglis, commander of the British 57th Regiment of Foot, exhorted his men to 'die hard'; they acted with such heroism that the regiment earned the nickname Die-hards. The name was attached later in the century to various groupings in British politics who were determinedly opposed to change. The word *diehard* is still often used of someone who is stubbornly conservative or reactionary.

die in your bed suffer a peaceful death from natural causes.

die in harness die before retirement.

ⓘ This expression is drawing a comparison between a person at work and a horse in harness drawing a plough or cart.

2013 *Daily Telegraph* Helen McElhone ... was a Glasgow housewife who took over from her Labour MP husband when he died in harness, and in less than nine months in the Commons proved a doughty fighter for better housing and social conditions.

die in the last ditch die desperately defending something; die fighting to the last extremity.

ⓘ This expression comes from a remark attributed to King William III (1650–1702). Asked whether he did not *see* that his country was lost, he is said to have responded: 'There is one way never to *see* it lost, and that is to die in the last ditch'. *Last-ditch* is often used as an adjective meaning 'desperately resisting to the end'.

the die is cast an event has happened or a decision has been taken that cannot be changed.

ⓘ This expression has its origins in Julius Caesar's remark as he was about to cross the river Rubicon, making him technically an invader of Italy (*see* RUBICON), as reported by the Roman historian Suetonius: *jacta alea esto* 'let the die be cast' (i.e. 'roll the dice').

die like a dog die in degrading circumstances.

die like flies: *see* FLY.

die on the vine be unsuccessful at an early stage. Compare with **wither on the vine** (*at* WITHER).

die on your feet come to a sudden or premature end. informal

die with your boots on die while actively occupied.

ⓘ *Die with your boots on* was apparently first used in the late 19th century of the deaths of cowboys and others in the American West who were killed in gun battles or hanged.

do or die: *see* DO.

never say die used to encourage someone not to give up hope in a difficult situation.

straight as a die ❶ absolutely straight. ❷ entirely open and honest.

ⓘ A *die* here is an engineer's tool for cutting grooves.

❶ **1920** *Blackwood's Magazine* The ... Ganges Canal ... runs straight as a die between its wooded banks.

to die for extremely good or desirable. informal

1990 *Los Angeles* Farther down the street is Tutti's, an Italian deli-restaurant that serves up ... hazelnut torte to die for.

differ

agree to differ: *see* AGREE.

difference

same difference: *see* SAME.

split the difference: *see* SPLIT.

different

as different as chalk and cheese: *see* CHALK.

a different kettle of fish: *see* KETTLE.

different strokes for different folks different things please or are effective with different people. proverb

ⓘ This chiefly US expression was used as a slogan in the early 1970s in a Texan drug abuse project.

march to a different tune (*or* drum): *see* MARCH.

sing a different tune: *see* SING.

dig

dig deep: *see* DEEP.

dig the dirt (*or* dig up dirt) discover and reveal damaging information about someone. informal

ⓘ *Dirt* is commonly used as a metaphor for unsavoury gossip or scandal, as in, for example, **dish the dirt** (*see* DISH).

dig in your heels resist stubbornly; refuse to give in.

ⓘ The image here is of a horse or other animal obstinately refusing to be led or ridden forwards. *Dig in your heels* is the commonest form, but *dig in your toes* and *dig in your feet* are also found.

dig yourself into a hole (*or* dig a hole for yourself) get yourself into an awkward or restrictive situation.

dig your own grave do something foolish which causes you to fail or leads to your downfall.

1995 Colin Bateman *Divorcing Jack* Then I thought about Patricia again and how much I was missing her and how I'd dug my own grave over the phone.

dig a pit for try to trap.

ⓘ This is a common biblical metaphor: for example, in Jeremiah 18:20 we find 'they have digged a pit for my soul'.

dignity

beneath your dignity of too little importance or value for you to do it.

ⓘ The Latin equivalent is *infra dignitatem*, and the humorous abbreviation of this, *infra dig*, is sometimes used in informal contexts.

stand on your dignity insist on being treated with due respect.

dim

take a dim view of: *see* VIEW.

dime

a dime a dozen very common and of no particular value. US informal

ⓘ A dime is a small US coin worth ten cents which occurs in various US expressions as a metaphor for cheapness or smallness.

1998 *New Scientist* Of course, medical breakthroughs are not a dime a dozen.

drop the dime on: *see* DROP.

get off the dime be decisive and show initiative. US informal

2001 *U.S. News & World Report* Congress must get off the dime and redeem the commitments that President Bush made to New York City.

on a dime ❶ (of a manoeuvre that can be performed by a moving vehicle or person) within a small area or short distance. ❷ quickly or instantly. US informal

ⓘ The British equivalent to sense 1 is **on a sixpence** (*see* SIXPENCE).

diminishing

the law of diminishing returns used to refer to the point at which the level of profits or benefits to be gained is reduced to less than the amount of money or energy invested.

ⓘ This expression originated in the early 19th century with reference to the profits from agriculture.

dine

wine and dine someone: *see* WINE.

dinkum

fair dinkum ❶ genuine or true. ❷ (of behaviour) acceptable. Australian & New Zealand informal

ⓘ As a noun *dinkum*, recorded from the late 19th century, was an English dialect word meaning 'hard work, honest toil'; it now mainly features as an adjective in various Australian and New Zealand expressions.

dinner

a dog's dinner: *see* DOG.

done like (a) dinner utterly defeated or outwitted. Australian & Canadian informal

1978 C. Green *The Sun Is Up* I had old Splinters Maloney the fishing inspector knocking on me door wanting to see me licence. Of course I was done like a dinner.

dressed up like a dog's dinner: *see* DOG.

more — than someone has had hot dinners someone's experience of a specified activity or phenomenon is vastly greater than someone else's. British informal

2011 *Guardian* Seems like a nice guy who makes movies to pay for his international golf touring lifestyle.... He's done more films than I've had hot dinners, so of course he's made a wedge.

dinner pail

hand in your dinner pail die. informal

ℹ A *dinner pail* was the bucket in which a workman formerly carried his dinner; compare with **kick the bucket** (*at* KICK).

dint

by dint of by means of.

ℹ *Dint* in the sense of 'blow' or 'stroke' is now archaic, and in the sense of 'application of force' survives only in this phrase.

dip

dip your pen in gall write unpleasantly or spitefully.

ℹ *Gall* is another word for bile, the bitter secretion of the liver; it is used in many places in the Bible as a metaphor for bitterness or affliction. *See also* **wormwood and gall** *at* WORMWOOD.

dip your toe into something begin to do or test something cautiously.

ℹ The image here is of putting your toe briefly into water in order to check the temperature.

dip your wick: *see* WICK.

dirt

dig (up) the dirt: *see* DIG.

do someone dirt harm someone maliciously. informal

1939 Nathaniel West *The Day of the Locust* I remember those who do me dirt and those who do me favors.

drag someone through the dirt: *see* DRAG.

eat dirt: *see* EAT.

treat someone like dirt treat someone contemptuously or unfairly.

2013 Margaret Pomeranz and **David Stratton** *At the Movies* What is the point of being a god if all it means is that you are treated like dirt and as an alien by everyone?

dirty

the dirty end of the stick the difficult or unpleasant part of a task or situation. informal

ℹ A less house-trained version of the idiom is *the shitty end of the stick*.

2000 *Sunday Times* (Johannesburg) I still feel a bit sorry for Hugh, he always seems to get the dirty end of the stick.

dirty weekend a weekend devoted to clandestine sexual activity. informal

2011 *Guardian* So Chinese tourists would flock over to Hong Kong for a dirty weekend and a showing of *Sex and Zen* in 3D.

dirty work at the crossroads illicit or underhand dealing. humorous

ℹ This expression is recorded from the early 20th century and may reflect the fact that crossroads, the traditional burial site for people who had committed suicide, were once viewed as sinister places.

1914 P. G. Wodehouse *The Man Upstairs* A conviction began to steal over him that some game was afoot which he did not understand, that—in a word—there was dirty work at the crossroads.

do the dirty on someone cheat or betray someone. British informal

down and dirty: *see* DOWN.

get your hands dirty (*or* dirty your hands) ❶ do manual, menial, or other hard work. ❷ become directly involved in dishonest or dishonourable activity. informal

❶ **2013** *Adventures of Cecilia Bedella* The thing that resonated most with me this re-read was the juxtaposition of Sunshine's primal urge to make food and feed it to people (a metaphor for creation and nurture), and her mission/calling to do what she can to destroy evil (killing, getting her hands dirty).

play dirty act in a dishonest or unfair way. informal

quick and dirty: *see* QUICK.

talk dirty speak about sex in a way considered to be coarse or obscene. informal

wash your dirty linen in public: *see* LINEN.

disappearing

do a disappearing act go away without being seen to go, especially when someone is looking for you.

ℹ The suggestion here is that the person has vanished as completely and inexplicably as things vanish in a magician's act.

disaster

a recipe for disaster: *see* RECIPE.

discord

apple of discord: *see* APPLE.

discount

five-finger discount: *see* FIVE.

discretion

discretion is the better part of valour it's better to avoid a dangerous situation than to confront it. proverb

disease

the British disease: *see* BRITISH.

disguise

a blessing in disguise: *see* BLESSING.

dish

dish the dirt reveal or spread scandalous information or gossip. informal

2013 *Daily Telegraph* Dr Lipscomb leaned heavily on the insight gained from the *Secret Life Of* series, which delves deep into the lives of historical figures and dishes the dirt on their hitherto unexplored secret lives.

dishwater

dull as dishwater: *see* DULL.

dismal

the dismal science a derogatory epithet applied, usually facetiously, to economics.

distance

go the distance complete a difficult task or endure an ordeal.

ⓘ *Go the distance* is a metaphor from boxing that means, when used of a boxer, 'complete a fight without being knocked out' or, when used of a boxing match, 'last the scheduled length'. In the USA there is an additional baseball-related sense: 'pitch for the entire length of a game'.

2013 *Pop Matters* So many people have tried and so many have failed and very few have, as you say, gone the distance.

within spitting distance within a very short distance.

1991 *Time* His reputation as a hard-boiled novelist is within spitting distance of Hammett's and Chandler's.

within striking distance near enough to hit or achieve.

distress

damsel in distress: *see* DAMSEL.

ditchwater

dull as ditchwater: *see* **dull as dishwater** *at* DULL.

dive

duck and dive: *see* DUCK.

take a dive ❶ (of a boxer or footballer) pretend to fall so as to deceive an opponent or referee. ❷ (of prices, hopes, fortunes, etc.) fall suddenly and significantly. informal

❷ **2013** *Mac Observer* Their stock took a dive because investors have mistaken Apple's public dormancy over the past several months for having lost their spark.

divide

divide and rule (*or* conquer) the policy of maintaining supremacy over your opponents by encouraging dissent between them, thereby preventing them from uniting against you.

ⓘ This is a maxim associated with a number of rulers, and is found in Latin as *divide et impera* and in German as *entzwei' und gebiete*. Since the early 17th century, English writers have often wrongly attributed it to the Italian political philosopher Niccolò Machiavelli (1469–1527).

divided

divided against itself (of a group which should be a unified whole) split by factional interests.

ⓘ This expression originates in Jesus's words in Matthew 12:25: 'every city or house divided against itself shall not stand'.

a house divided: *see* HOUSE.

Dixie

whistle Dixie engage in unrealistic fantasies; waste your time. US ℹ *Dixie* as an informal name for the Southern states of the USA probably comes from the *Mason-Dixon line,* the boundary between Maryland and Pennsylvania established in the 1760s by Charles Mason and Jeremiah Dixon and taken as the northern limit of the slave-owning states. The marching song 'Dixie' (in full 'Dixie's Land') (1859) was popular with Confederate soldiers in the American Civil War.

2001 *New York Times* These guys are just whistling Dixie . . . They're ignoring the basic issues that everyone's been pointing out to them for a decade.

dizzy

dizzy heights a position of great and impressive eminence or importance. informal

2013 Steve Coogan *Independent* I'm delighted to be writing my memoir. It promises to be a sojourn through the faltering first steps of a lower middle-class boy who watched television to the dizzy heights of a man who achieved not only a multi-Bafta-winning status on television but also became fully middle-class and managed to annoy the *Daily Mail* at the same time.

do

do a — behave in a manner characteristic of a specified person or thing. informal

2001 *Times* One reporter even got the brigadier in charge to 'do a Blair' and come over all emotional while discussing the cull.

do one escape by running away; make off. British informal

ℹ The expression seems to have originated in the Liverpool area, perhaps as a condensed form of *do a runner* (*see* RUNNER).

do or die persist in the face of great danger, even if death is the result.

2012 *CNN transcipts* If Ron Paul does well, it potentially could hurt Jon Huntsman. This is do or die for Jon Huntsman in New Hampshire. As you know, he's invested all of his effort in New Hampshire. He's got to do well.

dos and don'ts rules of behaviour.

2002 Gaurav Sabnis *Vantage Point* He told us a long list of dos and don'ts (the former outnumbering the latter by a wide margin) and warned us to be on our best behaviour.

ℹ For other idioms containing *do,* see the entry for the main word in the idiom (for example, **do the trick** at TRICK).

dock

in dock ❶ (of a ship) moored in a dock. ❷ (of a person) not fully fit and out of action. British informal ❸ (of a vehicle) in a garage for repairs.

in the dock under investigation or scrutiny for suspected wrongdoing or harm caused. British

ℹ In a court of law, the dock is the enclosure where the defendant stands during a trial.

2013 *New Statesman* Public schools are firmly in the dock, accused of the contradictory positions of utilising clinical efficiency in killing and of amateur incompetence and other-worldliness.

doctor

be just what the doctor ordered be very beneficial or desirable under the circumstances. informal

1948 Gore Vidal *The City and the Pillar* The waiter brought her a drink. 'Just what the doctor ordered,' she said, smiling at him.

go for the doctor make an all-out effort. Australian informal

dodge

dodge the bullet avoid a possibly deserved fate. informal

2012 Eric S. Raymond *Armed & Dangerous* So you are giving an example of how people don't get sued for singing in their backyard, or are you claiming that they do but here just dodged the bullet?

dodge the column shirk your duty; avoid work. British informal

ℹ *Column* is a military term which refers to the usual formation of troops for marching.

dodo

dead as a dodo: *see* DEAD.

dog

the black dog: *see* BLACK.

call off the (*or* your) dogs stop attacking or persecuting someone or causing others to do so on your behalf.

die like a dog: *see* DIE.

dog-and-pony show an elaborate display or performance designed to attract people's attention. North American informal

2002 *St. Louis* (Missouri) *Post-Dispatch* The FAA delayed several American Airlines flights . . . for several hours. The fact of the matter is, it's nothing more than a dog-and-pony show to give us this sense of security.

dog eat dog a situation of fierce competition in which people are willing to harm each other in order to succeed.

🛈 This expression makes reference to the proverb *dog does not eat dog*, which dates back to the mid 16th century in English and before that to Latin *canis caninam non est* 'a dog does not eat dog's flesh'.

1998 Rebecca Ray *A Certain Age* It's dog eat dog, it's every man for himself... Right from the start, fighting amongst ourselves for the few decent wages left.

dog in the manger a person inclined to prevent others from having or using things that they do not want or need themselves.

🛈 This expression comes from the fable of the dog that lay in a manger to prevent the ox and horse from eating the hay.

the dog's bollocks the best person or thing of its kind. British vulgar slang

a dog's dinner (*or* breakfast) a poor piece of work; a mess. British informal

🛈 The image is of a dog's meal of jumbled-up scraps.

2000 *Independent* He was rightly sacked because he had made such a dog's dinner of an important job.

a dog's life an unhappy existence full of problems or unfair treatment.

1987 Fannie Flagg *Fried Green Tomatoes at the Whistle Stop Cafe* The judge's daughter had just died a couple of weeks ago, old before her time and living a dog's life on the outskirts of town.

dog tired extremely tired; utterly worn out. informal

🛈 The image here, and in the variant *dog weary*, is of a dog exhausted after a long chase or hunt.

dogs of war ❶ the havoc accompanying military conflict. literary ❷ mercenary soldiers.

🛈 This phrase is from Shakespeare's *Julius Caesar*: 'let slip the dogs of war'. The image is of hunting dogs being loosed from their leashes to pursue their prey.

❷ **1998** *Times* The good guys... may have broken the rules by employing dogs of war.

dressed (up) like a dog's dinner wearing ridiculously smart or ostentatious clothes. British informal

every dog has his (*or* its) day everyone will have good luck or success at some point in their lives. proverb

fight like cat and dog: *see* CAT.

give a dog a bad name it is very difficult to lose a bad reputation, even if it is unjustified.

🛈 This is a shortened version of the proverb *give a dog a bad name and hang him*, which was known from the early 18th century.

go to the dogs deteriorate shockingly, especially in behaviour or morals. informal

🛈 The underlying reference may be to the fate of worn-out horses, sent to the knacker's yard on the way to becoming dog food

2002 Norman Lebrecht *The Song of Names* Country's going to the dogs. Used to be the finest railway in the world, now look at it.

the hair of the dog: *see* HAIR.

have a dog in the fight be an interested party; have a stake in the outcome of a process. informal

help a lame dog over a stile come to the aid of a person in need.

in a dog's age in a very long time. North American informal

keep a dog and bark yourself pay someone to work for you and then do the work yourself.

2001 *United Press International Newswire* Investors can monitor their portfolios ... but mainly let the chosen professionals do their job. After all, why keep a dog and bark yourself?

let the dog see the rabbit let someone get on with work they are ready and waiting to do. informal

🛈 This phrase comes from greyhound racing, where the dogs chase a mechanical rabbit around a track.

let sleeping dogs lie: *see* SLEEPING.

like a dog with two tails showing great pleasure; delighted.

🛈 The image here is of a dog wagging its tail as an expression of happiness.

love me, love my dog: *see* LOVE.

my dogs are barking my feet are aching. British informal, dated

not a dog's chance no chance at all.

put on the dog behave in a pretentious or ostentatious way. North American informal

🛈 *Dog* was late 19th-century US slang for 'style' or a 'flashy display'.

d

1962 Anthony Gilbert *No Dust in the Attic* Matron put on a lot of dog about the hospital's responsibility.

rain cats and dogs: *see* RAIN.

see a man about a dog used euphemistically when leaving to go to the lavatory or if you do not wish to disclose the nature of the errand you are about to undertake. humorous

sick as a dog: *see* SICK.

the tail wags the dog: *see* TAIL.

there's life in the old dog yet: *see* LIFE.

throw someone to the dogs discard someone as worthless.

you can't teach an old dog new tricks you cannot make people change their ways. proverb

doggo

lie doggo remain motionless or quiet. British

ℹ *Lie doggo* is of uncertain origin, but probably arose from a dog's habit of lying motionless or apparently asleep but nonetheless alert.

doghouse

in the doghouse (*or* dogbox) in disgrace or disfavour. informal

1963 Pamela Hansford Johnson *Night & Silence* He'd been getting bad grades, he was in the dog-house as it was.

doing

nothing doing: *see* NOTHING.

dollar

be dollars to doughnuts that be a certainty that. North American informal

1936 James Curtis *The Gilt Kid* If he were seen it was dollars to doughnuts that he would be arrested.

look like a million dollars: *see* MILLION.

top dollar: *see* TOP.

you can bet your bottom dollar: *see* **you can bet your boots** *at* BET.

dolly

trolley dolly: *see* TROLLEY.

done

a done deal a plan or project that has been finalized or accomplished.

2009 *Independent* A project to have members of the public occupying the vacant fourth plinth in Trafalgar Square as living sculptures ... is currently 'an aspiration, not a done deal'.

be done and dusted: *see* DUSTED.

done for in a situation so bad that it is impossible to get out of it. informal

1993 *Catholic Herald* Don't you realise that without that contract we're done for?

done in extremely tired. informal

2010 Jon McGregor *Even the Dogs* You need some help rolling that fag, you look done in.

done like (a) dinner: *see* DINNER.

over and done with: *see* OVER.

donkey

donkey work the boring or laborious part of a job; drudgery.

2005 *The Register* I get the Systems guys to do all the donkey work once I'm sure it's up and running properly.

for donkey's years for a very long time. informal

ℹ *For donkey's years* is a pun referring to the length of a donkey's ears and playing on a former pronunciation of *years* as *ears*.

2013 *Daily Telegraph* Mrs Lynch said the stealing had gone on 'for donkey's years', and the family had to go to court as a last resort because 'we just couldn't go on'.

talk the hind leg off a donkey: *see* TALK.

doodah

all of a doodah very agitated or excited. informal

ℹ The nonsense word *doodah* is the refrain of the song 'Camptown Races', originally sung by slaves on American plantations.

doom

crack of doom: *see* CRACK.

doom and gloom a general feeling of pessimism or despondency.

ℹ This expression, sometimes found as *gloom and doom*, was particularly pertinent to fears about a nuclear holocaust during the cold war period of the 1950s and 1960s. It became a catchphrase in the 1968 film *Finian's Rainbow*.

doomsday

till doomsday for ever.

ℹ *Doomsday* means literally 'judgement day', the Last Judgement of Christian tradition.

door

as one door closes, another opens you shouldn't be discouraged by failure, as other opportunities will soon present themselves. proverb

at death's door: *see* DEATH.

beat a path to someone's door: *see* BEAT.

behind closed doors: *see* CLOSED.

blow the doors off be considerably better or more successful than. North American informal

by the back door: *see* BACK.

close its doors (of a business) close down or fail. euphemistic

close (*or* shut) the door on (*or* to) exclude the opportunity for; refuse to consider.

2014 *Daily Telegraph* Harman is developing a software barrier which might not be able to prevent a cyber attacker from making mischief with your route guidance, but would firmly close the door on any attempt to attack the operational side of the car.

door to door ❶ (of a journey) from start to finish. ❷ visiting all the houses in an area to sell or publicize something.

have a foot in the door: *see* FOOT.

keep the wolf from the door: *see* WOLF.

knock on the door: *see* KNOCK.

lay something at someone's door regard or name someone as responsible for something.

ℹ This phrase may have arisen from the practice of leaving an illegitimate baby on the doorstep of the man who was identified as its father.

leave the door open for ensure that there is still an opportunity for something.

never darken someone's door: *see* DARKEN.

open the door to create an opportunity for.

2014 *New Zealand Herald* Opponents will also claim that this is the thin end of the republican wedge and will open the door to the introduction of a republic.

show someone the door: *see* SHOW.

a toe in the door: *see* TOE.

doornail

dead as a doornail: *see* DEAD.

doorstep

on your (*or* the) doorstep very near; close at hand.

2011 *Better Farming—Ontario Community of Professional Farmers* It doesn't make sense to send taxpayers' money out of the province when we have fresh, affordable food on our doorstep.

Dorothy

a friend of Dorothy: *see* FRIEND.

dose

a dose of your own medicine: *see* MEDICINE.

in small doses experienced or engaged in a little at a time.

2013 *DVD Verdict* Jeong is an actor of considerable comedic talents, but his Chow is a character who works only in small doses.

like a dose of salts very fast and efficiently. British informal

ℹ The *salts* referred to in this expression are laxatives (e.g. Epsom salts).

1991 Peter Carey *The Tax Inspector* She's going to go through your old man like a dose of salts.

dot

dot the i's and cross the t's ensure that all details are correct. informal

join up the dots: *see* JOIN.

on the dot exactly on time. informal

ℹ The 'dot' referred to is that appearing on a clock face to mark the hour.

1998 *Oldie* The Conditions of Sale state that the buyer has to pay the auctioneer on the dot.

the year dot a very long time ago. British informal

ℹ The 'dot' probably represents a hypothetical number preceding 'one'.

2010 *Guardian* Work out how much the City has earned for the UK since the year dot. Subtract the cost of the financial crisis. If you think the result is a negative number please book yourself on an evening class in remedial mathematics.

dotted

sign on the dotted line: *see* SIGN.

double

at (*or* on) the double at running speed; very fast.

ℹ This modern generalized sense has developed from the mid-19th-century military use of *double pace* to mean twice the number of steps per minute of *slow pace*.

d

double bubble a doubly satisfying outcome; two for the price of one. British informal

2005 *Dooyoo.co.uk discussions: Terrorism* Some will give their cause a religious stamp of approval, combining a fear of their God with the fear of their behaviour, which is double bubble as far as the terrorist is concerned.

double or nothing a gamble to decide whether a loss or debt should be doubled or cancelled.

ℹ A British variant of *double or nothing* is *double or quits*.

double-edged

a double-edged sword (*or* weapon) a course of action or situation having both positive and negative effects.

2000 *Investor* A rising pound is a double-edged sword when investing overseas.

doubt

the benefit of the doubt: *see* BENEFIT.

doubting

a doubting Thomas a person who refuses to believe something without having incontrovertible proof; a sceptic.

ℹ In the Bible, the apostle Thomas said that he would not believe that Christ had risen from the dead until he had seen and touched his wounds (John 20:24–9).

doughnuts

be dollars to doughnuts that: *see* DOLLAR.

dovecote

flutter the dovecotes: *see* FLUTTER.

down

down and dirty ❶ unprincipled; unpleasant. ❷ energetically earthy, direct, or sexually explicit. North American informal

down and out beaten in the struggle of life; completely without resources or means of livelihood.

ℹ The phrase *down and out* comes from boxing, and refers to a boxer who is knocked out by a blow. Since the early 20th century the noun *down-and-out* has been used to describe a person without money, a job, or a place to live.

down below used euphemistically to refer to the genitalia, the urinary system, or any other embarrassing parts or functions of the lower abdomen.

ℹ An alternative formula is *down there*.

2004 *Observer Music Monthly Magazine* I also noticed that one of his nails was far shorter than the rest. 'What's up with that one?' I asked. 'That's so I don't hurt the ladies down below when I'm using my finger on them,' he said.

down in the dumps: *see* DUMPS.

down in the mouth (of a person or their expression) unhappy or dejected. informal

down on your luck experiencing a period of bad luck. informal

down the hatch: *see* HATCH.

down the road in the future; later on. informal, chiefly North American

ℹ An Australian variant of this phrase is *down the track*.

down the tube (*or* tubes) lost or wasted. informal

2001 *High Country News* I've already lost my alfalfa crop; that's about $20,000 down the tubes.

down tools stop work, typically as a form of industrial action. British informal

go down the pan: *see* PAN.

have (*or* put) someone or something down as judge someone or something to be a particular type or class of person or thing.

1914 M. A. Von Arnim *The Pastor's Wife* The other excursionists were all in pairs; they thought Ingeborg was too, and put her down at first as the German gentleman's wife because he did not speak to her.

have a (*or* be) down on disapprove of; feel hostile or antagonistic towards. informal

kick someone when they are down: *see* KICK.

suit someone or something down to the ground: *see* SUIT.

d

downgrade

on the downgrade in decline. North American

ⓘ *Downgrade* was originally used literally of a downward slope.

1953 William Burroughs *Letter* As a matter of fact the whole region is on the downgrade. The rubber business is shot, the cocoa is eat up with broom rot.

downhill

be downhill all the way ❶ be easy in comparison with what came before. ❷ become worse or less successful.

go downhill become worse; deteriorate.

downwardly

downwardly mobile: *see* MOBILE.

dozen

a baker's dozen: *see* BAKER.

a dime a dozen: *see* DIME.

six of one and half a dozen of the other: *see* SIX.

talk nineteen to the dozen: *see* TALK.

drag

drag ass: *see* ASS.

drag and drop (in computing) move (an image or highlighted text) to another part of the screen using a mouse or similar device.

drag your feet (*or* heels) (of a person or organization) be deliberately slow or reluctant to act.

1994 *Nature Conservancy* We can't afford to drag our feet until a species is at the brink of extinction.

drag someone or something through the dirt (*or* mud) make damaging allegations about someone or something.

2011 *The Age* (Melbourne) Capitalism has been dragged through the dirt in recent times and some key thinkers are tending to its wounds.

dragon

chase the dragon: *see* CHASE.

sow (*or* plant) dragon's teeth take action that is intended to prevent trouble, but which actually brings it about.

ⓘ In Greek legend, Cadmus killed a dragon and sowed its teeth, which sprang up as armed men; these men then killed one another, leaving just five survivors who became the ancestors of the Thebans.

drain

down the drain totally wasted or spoilt. informal

1930 W. Somerset Maugham *The Breadwinner* All his savings are gone down the drain.

laugh like a drain: *see* LAUGH.

drainpipe

like a rat up a drainpipe: *see* RAT.

drama

make a drama out of exaggerate the importance of a minor problem or incident. informal

draught

feel the draught experience an adverse change in your financial circumstances. informal

1992 *Daily Express* Redland . . . felt the draught of George Wimpey's interim profits slide.

draw

ⓘ For idioms containing *draw*, see the entry for the main word in the idiom (for example, **draw a blank** at BLANK).

drawer

bottom drawer the collection of linen, clothes, and household items assembled by a woman in preparation for her marriage.

ⓘ The *bottom drawer* was the traditional place for storing such articles. The US equivalent is *hope chest*.

hewers of wood and drawers of water: *see* HEWER.

top drawer: *see* TOP.

drawing

back to the drawing board: *see* BACK.

on the drawing board (of an idea, scheme, or proposal) under consideration; not yet put into practice.

ⓘ To get something *off the drawing board* is to put something into action or to realize the first stages of a project.

drawn

at daggers drawn: *see* DAGGER.

dream

the American dream: *see* AMERICAN.

beyond your wildest dreams bigger, better, or to a greater extent than it would be reasonable to expect or hope for.

in your dreams used to assert that something much desired is not likely ever to happen.

> **2002** *New Yorker* Before falling asleep, I try to imagine myself as . . . a savvy entrepreneur with her own catering business. In your dreams, as they say.

like a dream very well or successfully. informal

> **2004** *Canadian Yachting* It steers like a dream.

love's young dream: *see* LOVE.

never in your wildest dreams used to emphasize that something is beyond the scope of your imagination.

> **2013 Rashmi Bansal** *Youth Curry* Over 400,000 copies sold, 9 language editions, hundreds of emails from grateful readers. Never in my wildest dreams did I imagine such an outcome when I took up this project.

dressed

all dressed up and (*or* with) nowhere (*or* no place) to go prepared for action but having nothing to do or unable to be proceeded with. informal

> ⓘ The expression is an adaptation of the title of a song (1913) by Silvio Hein and Benjamin Burt, 'When You're All Dressed Up and No Place to Go'.

> **2004** *Time* Because Jeffords' departure put control of Senate committees in Democratic hands, President Bush's proposed National Missile Defense (NMD) is now all dressed up with nowhere to go.

dressed to kill wearing attractive and flamboyant clothes in order to make a striking impression.

dressed up like a dog's dinner: *see* DOG.

dressed (up) to the nines: *see* NINE.

mutton dressed as lamb: *see* MUTTON.

dried

cut and dried (of a situation, issue, or ideas) completely settled or decided.

> ⓘ A distinction was originally made between the *cut and dried* herbs sold in herbalists' shops and growing herbs.

drink

be meat and drink to: *see* MEAT.

drink like a fish drink excessive amounts of alcohol, especially habitually.

drink someone under the table consume more alcohol than your drinking companion without becoming as drunk. informal

drink with the flies: *see* FLY.

I'll drink to that said in order to express your agreement with or approval of a statement.

drive

drive a coach and horses through: *see* COACH.

drive something home: *see* HOME.

let drive attack with blows, missiles, or criticism.

> **1926** *Travel* I let drive for the point of his chin, and he went down and out for a full count.

driven

pure as the driven snow: *see* PURE.

driver

in the driver's (*or* driving) seat in charge of a situation.

> **2014** *FreakyTrigger* Congratulations to Cameroon who are in the Group A driving seat with a tight win. 3 points to them.

driving

what someone is driving at the point that someone is attempting to make.

> **1986 Robert Sproat** *Stunning the Punters* Martin is always saying things where I can't *see* what he's driving at.

drop

at the drop of a hat without delay or good reason. informal

> **1991** *Independent* These days Soviet visas are issued at the drop of a hat.

drag and drop: *see* DRAG.

drop your aitches fail to pronounce the 'h' sound, especially at the beginning of words.

ℹ In Britain, *dropping your aitches* is considered by some to be a sign of a lack of education or of inferior social class.

1903 George Bernard Shaw *Man & Superman* This man takes more trouble to drop his aitches than ever his father did to pick them up.

drop the ball make a mistake; mishandle things. North American informal

drop a brick make an indiscreet or embarrassing remark. British informal

drop your bundle: *see* BUNDLE.

drop a clanger make an embarrassing or foolish mistake. British informal

ℹ Dropping something that makes a loud clang attracts attention; this mid-20th-century expression is used especially in the context of a very embarrrassing or tactless act or remark made in a social situation.

2003 Jozef Imrich *A Media Dragon* I don't live my life in a simplistic way. Sometimes I drop a clanger, sometimes I make a mistake, other times I get it right

drop dead ❶ die suddenly and unexpectedly. ❷ used as an expression of intense scorn or dislike. informal

ℹ This idiom is the source of the adjective *drop-dead*, which is used to emphasize how attractive someone or something is, as in *drop-dead gorgeous*.

drop the (*or* a) dime on inform on someone to the police. US informal

1990 Scott Turow *The Burden of Proof* Dixon says he's thought it over, the best course for him is just to drop the dime on John.

drop your guard: *see* GUARD.

drop a hint (*or* drop hints) let fall a hint or hints, as if casually or unconsciously.

drop someone or something like a hot potato: *see* HOT.

drop someone in it place someone in an embarrassing or awkward situation. informal

drop someone a line send someone a note or letter in a casual manner.

a drop in the ocean (*or* in a bucket) a very small amount compared with what is needed or expected.

1995 Ian Rankin *Let It Bleed* A few million was a drop in the ocean, hardly a ripple.

drop like flies: *see* **die like flies** *at* FLY.

drop names: *see* NAME.

drop the pilot: *see* PILOT.

drop your trousers deliberately let your trousers fall down, especially in a public place.

fit (*or* ready) to drop worn out; exhausted.

have the drop on have the advantage over. informal

ℹ *Have the drop on* was originally a mid-19th-century US expression used literally to mean that you have the opportunity to shoot before your opponent can use their weapon.

2000 *Clay Shooting* He always seems to have the drop on me by one bird no matter how hard I try.

your jaw drops: *see* JAW.

let it drop (*or* rest) say or do no more about a matter or problem.

let something drop (*or* fall) casually reveal a piece of information.

the penny drops: *see* PENNY.

shop till you drop: *see* SHOP.

you could hear a pin drop: *see* PIN.

drown

drown your sorrows forget your problems by getting drunk.

drowned

like a drowned rat extremely wet and bedraggled.

drug

a drug on the market an unsaleable or valueless commodity.

ℹ *Drug* in the sense of 'a commodity for which there is no demand' is recorded from the mid 17th century, but it is not clear from the word's history whether it is the same word as the medicinal substance.

2007 *The Age* (Melbourne) Both artists are a bit of a drug on the market in American and European collections but in the context of this exhibition they recover their voices and reassert their significance.

drum

beat (*or* bang) the drum for (*or* of) be ostentatiously in support of.

march to a different drum: *see* MARCH.

d

drunk

drunk as a lord (*or* skunk) extremely drunk.

dry

bleed someone dry: *see* BLEED.

come up dry be unsuccessful. North American

1988 James Trefil *The Dark Side of the Universe* Attempts to *see* this decay with extremely sensitive experiments have so far come up dry.

dry as a bone: ❶ extremely dry. ❷ extremely thirsty.

dry as dust ❶ extremely dry. ❷ extremely dull.

ℹ Sense 2 is represented in the fictitious character of the antiquarian Dr Jonas Dryasdust, to whom Sir Walter Scott addressed the prefatory epistle of *Ivanhoe* and some other novels.

hang someone out to dry: *see* HANG.

high and dry: *see* HIGH.

home and dry: *see* HOME.

keep your powder dry: *see* POWDER.

run dry (especially of a source of money or information) be completely used up.

suck someone dry: *see* SUCK.

there wasn't a dry eye in the house everyone in the audience of a film, play, speech, etc. was moved to tears.

duck

break your duck ❶ score the first run of your innings. cricket ❷ make your first score or achieve a particular feat for the first time. British

duck and dive use your ingenuity to deal with or evade a situation.

2012 *New Statesman* Undoubtedly there are issues with some wealthy people ducking and diving, but on the face of it these figures show a progressive tax system at work.

fine weather for ducks: *see* WEATHER.

duck soup an easy task, or someone easy to overcome. North American informal

ℹ The precise origins of the metaphor remain obscure. It was popularized as the title of a Marx Brothers' film (1933).

get (*or* have) your ducks in a row get (*or* have) your facts straight; get (*or* have) everything organized. North American informal

ℹ The underlying image may be of a mother duck getting all her ducklings to follow behind in a line.

1996 *Brew Your Own* You really want to have all your ducks in a row before the meeting.

like a dying duck in a thunderstorm having a dejected or hopeless expression. informal

ℹ The miserable demeanour of ducks during thunder has been proverbial since the late 18th century.

1933 Agatha Christie *Lord Edgware Dies* You did look for all the world like a dying duck in a thunderstorm.

lame duck a person or thing that is powerless or in need of help. informal

ℹ In the mid 18th century, *lame duck* was used in a stock-market context, with reference to a person or company that could not fulfil their financial obligations. Later, from the mid 19th century, it was used specifically with reference to US politicians in the final period of office, after the election of their successor.

2014 *Daily Telegraph* Chataway spent much time brokering the survival of lame ducks: the collapsed Upper Clyde Shipyards under new ownership, Cammell Laird, Rootes Motors . . . , BSA and International Computers.

take to something like a duck to water take to something very readily.

1960 C. Day Lewis *Buried Day* I had taken to vice like a duck to water, but it ran off me like water from a duck's back.

like water off a duck's back a remark or incident which has no apparent effect on a person.

play ducks and drakes with trifle with; treat frivolously.

ℹ This expression comes from the game of *ducks and drakes*, played by throwing a flat stone across the surface of water in such a way as to make it skim and skip before it finally sinks. The game was known by this name by the late 16th century, and it was already a metaphor for an idle or frivolous activity in the early 17th century.

sitting duck: *see* SITTING.

duckling

an ugly duckling: *see* UGLY.

dudgeon

in high dudgeon in a state of deep resentment.

ℹ The origin of *dudgeon* in the sense of 'ill humour' is unknown, and it is almost always found in this phrase. However, other adjectives are sometimes used instead of *high*, for example *deep* or *great*.

1938 Zane Grey *Raiders of the Spanish Peaks* Neale left in high dudgeon to take his case to his court of appeal—his mother.

due

give the devil his due: *see* DEVIL.

duff

up the duff pregnant. British informal

1994 *Daily Telegraph* At 19, he was married ('only because she was up the duff' he explains gallantly).

duke

duke it out fight it out. North American informal

ⓘ *Dukes* or *dooks* are 'fists', especially when raised in a fighting position. The word comes from rhyming slang *Duke of Yorks*, 'forks' (i.e. fingers).

dull

dull as dishwater (*or* ditchwater) extremely dull.

dull the edge of make less sensitive, interesting, or effective.

ⓘ The image here is of making a knife's edge blunt.

never a dull moment used to express the idea of constant (and sometimes perhaps excessive) variety and excitement. informal

dummy

sell someone a dummy (chiefly in rugby or soccer) deceive an opponent by feigning a pass or kick.

spit (out) the dummy: *see* SPIT.

dumper

into the dumper into a bad or worse state or condition. North American informal

1991 *Tucson Weekly* J. Fife III peaked well before his run for governor ... and has been sliding into the dumper ever since.

dumps

down in the dumps (of a person) depressed or unhappy. informal

ⓘ In early 16th-century English *dump* had the meaning 'a fit of depression', a sense now surviving only in this expression.

dust

bite the dust: *see* BITE.

dry as dust: *see* DRY.

dust and ashes used to convey a feeling of great disappointment or disillusion about something.

ⓘ Often found in the fuller form *turn to dust and ashes in your mouth*, the phrase is used in the Bible as a metaphor for worthlessness, for example in Genesis 18:27 and the Book of Job 30:19. It derives from the legend of the Sodom apple, or Dead Sea fruit, whose attractive appearance tempted people, but which tasted only of dust and ashes when eaten.

the dust settles things quieten down.

2013 Idiot Savant *No Right Turn* While it may still take some years for the constitutional dust to settle, marriage equality is now going to be the law of the land in the US.

eat someone's dust: *see* EAT.

gather (*or* collect) dust remain unused.

kick up (a) dust create a disturbance. informal

kiss the dust: *see* KISS.

not see someone for dust find that a person has made a hasty departure.

1978 Patricia Grace *Mutuwhenua* You didn't *see* this Maori for dust ... Out the door, on the bike, and away.

raise a dust ❶ cause turmoil. ❷ obscure the truth. British

shake the dust off your feet: *see* SHAKE.

throw dust in someone's eyes mislead someone by misrepresentation or diverting attention from a point.

dusted

be done and dusted (of a project) be completely finished or ready. informal

dusty

a dusty answer a curt and unhelpful reply. British

ⓘ The source of this expression is probably a passage in George Meredith's *Modern Love* (1862): 'Ah, what a dusty answer gets the soul when hot for certainties in this our life!'

not so dusty (of a person's health or situation) fairly good. British informal, dated

d

Dutch

do the Dutch commit suicide. North American informal

ℹ *Dutch* is short for 'the Dutch act': apparently in the 19th century, when the expression originated, the Dutch had a reputation in America for attempting suicide.

Dutch courage bravery induced by drinking alcohol.

ℹ The phrase *Dutch courage* stems from a long-standing British belief that the Dutch are extraordinarily heavy drinkers.

a Dutch uncle a kindly but authoritative figure.

ℹ *Dutch* here probably means no more than that the person described is not a genuine blood relation. In the mid 19th century *I will talk to him like a Dutch uncle* (meaning 'I will give him a lecture') was noted as being an American expression.

2006 Digby *Hullabaloo* In the past when these situations would flare up, Israel would take an aggressive action to demonstrate that it wasn't a pushover and the US would step in like a Dutch uncle and reluctantly pull the pissed-off Israelis back.

go Dutch share the cost of something equally.

ℹ An outing or entertainment paid for in this way is a *Dutch treat* and sharing the cost of a meal in a restaurant is *eating Dutch*.

1993 *Vanity Fair* He insists on buying his own tickets, 'going Dutch', as he puts it.

in Dutch in trouble. US informal, dated

1939 Raymond Chandler *The Big Sleep* And for that amount of money you're willing to get yourself in Dutch with half the law enforcement of this country?

that beats the Dutch that is extraordinary or startling. US

Dutchman

I'm a Dutchman used to express your disbelief or as a way of underlining an emphatic assertion. British

1994 Ian Botham *My Autobiography* I read somewhere that Warne said he had been possessed by demons. Well, in that case I'm a Dutchman.

duty

a bounden duty: *see* BOUNDEN.

duty bound morally or legally obliged to do something.

dwaal

in a dwaal in a dreamy, dazed, or absent-minded state. South African

ℹ The word *dwaal* is Afrikaans.

1985 Paul Slabolepszy *Saturday Night at the Palace* Yassas—Carstens!! Wake up, man. You in a real dwaal tonight.

dyed

dyed in the wool (of a person) completely and permanently fixed in a particular belief or opinion; inveterate.

ℹ If yarn is dyed in the raw state, it produces a more even and permanent colour.

dying

like a dying duck in a thunderstorm: *see* DUCK.

to your dying day for the rest of your life.

1967 George Mackay Brown *A Calendar of Love* This one always was and ever will be to his dying day a garrulous long-winded old man.

dyke

put your finger in the dyke attempt to stem the advance of something undesirable which threatens to overwhelm you. informal

ℹ This expression stems from the story of a small Dutch boy who saved his community from flooding by placing his finger in a hole in a dyke.

e

give someone the big e: *see* BIG.

eager

an eager beaver a person who is very enthusiastic about work. informal

eagle

an eagle eye a keen or close watch

> **2010** *Guardian* Howells ... told Radio 4's *Today* programme that his committee ... kept 'an eagle eye' on MI5 and MI6 to ensure they operate within the law.

ear

be all ears be listening eagerly and attentively. informal

be in someone's ear talk insistently to someone in an annoying way. informal

> **2011** *Seeking Alpha* When I would be doing CNBC spots and got on the subject of Europe, the producers would be in my ear, asking me specifically not to use that phrase because it had become so tired.

bend someone's ear: *see* BEND.

bring something (down) about your ears bring something, especially misfortune, on yourself.

cloth ears: *see* CLOTH.

cock your ear: *see* COCK.

fall on deaf ears: *see* DEAF.

a flea in your ear: *see* FLEA.

give someone (*or* get) a thick ear: *see* THICK.

have (*or* gain) someone's ear have (*or* gain) access to and influence with someone.

> **2006** *Economist* A group of free-market economists gained his ear, preaching privatisation.

have something by the ears keep or obtain a secure hold on.

> **1949 Dylan Thomas** *Letter* I am tangled in hack-work. Depression has me by the ears.

have something coming out of your ears have a substantial or excessive amount of something. informal

> **1997** *Daily Express* In terms of advice ... Jill's had suggestions coming out of her ears.

have (*or* keep) an ear to the ground be well informed about events and trends.

> ❶ The idea behind this phrase is that by putting your ear against the ground you would be able to hear approaching footsteps.

have a tin ear: *see* TIN.

have a word in someone's ear: *see* WORD.

in one ear and out the other heard but disregarded or quickly forgotten.

lend an ear: *see* LEND.

listen with half an ear not give your full attention to someone or something.

make a pig's ear of: *see* PIG.

make a silk purse out of a sow's ear: *see* SILK.

music to your ears: *see* MUSIC.

out on your ear dismissed or ejected ignominiously. informal

> **2005 Chris Cleave** *Incendiary* Whenever I could squeeze a fiver out of the shopping money I used to stash it under the carpet just in case my husband blew everything one day and they chucked us out on our ear.

pin your ears back: *see* PIN.

play something by ear ❶ perform music without having to read from a score. ❷ proceed instinctively according to results and circumstances rather than according to rules or a plan. informal

> ❷ **1992 Paul Auster** *Leviathan* The only condition was that Sachs arrive at Maria's house promptly at ten o'clock, and from then on they would play it by ear.

prick up your ears: *see* PRICK.

set by the ears cause to quarrel.

someone's ears are burning someone is subconsciously aware of being talked about, especially in their absence.

> ❶ The superstition that your ears tingle when you are being talked about is recorded from the mid 16th century. Originally it was the left ear only that was supposed to do so.

someone's ears are flapping someone is listening intently in order to overhear something not intended for them. informal

stop your ears: *see* STOP.

turn a deaf ear: *see* DEAF.

up to your ears in very busy with or deeply involved in. informal

walls have ears: *see* WALL.

wet behind the ears: *see* WET.

early

bright and early: *see* BRIGHT.

early bird a person who gets up, arrives, or acts before the usual or expected time.

ⓘ This expression comes from the saying *the early bird catches the worm*, meaning that the person who takes the earliest opportunity to do something will gain an advantage over others.

early doors early on, especially in a game or contest. British informal

ⓘ Apparently this expression arose with reference to a period of admission to a music hall ending some time before the start of the performance and giving a better choice of seating.

2003 *Guardian* Jeremy Vine, hosting Radio 2's music industry debate last night, got a dig in early doors about his hallowed predecessor on the station.

it's early days it is too soon to be sure how a particular situation will develop. British informal

take an early bath ❶ be sent off in a game of football or other sport. ❷ fail early on in a race or contest. informal

ⓘ The allusion is to the bath or shower taken by players at the end of a match.

❷ **1992** *Bowlers' World* Defending champion Dave Phillips took an early bath losing all his three opening qualifying games.

earn

earn your corn put in a lot of effort for your wages. British informal

earn your keep be worth the time, money, or effort spent on you.

earner

a nice little earner a profitable activity or business. British informal

ⓘ The phrase was popularized by its use in the ITV comedy drama *Minder* (1979–94).

2010 *Guardian* I had no idea that so many profit driven companies were involved handling cases such as yours. It must be a nice little earner for the Tories' friends.

earth

come back (down) to earth (*or* bring someone back (down) to earth) return or make someone return suddenly to reality after a period of daydreaming or euphoria.

2003 *Guardian* When you start to believe you're in with a shout, the big boys have a nasty habit of bringing you down to earth with a bump.

cost (*or* charge *or* pay) the earth cost (*or* charge *or* pay) a large amount of money. British informal

the earth moved (*or* did the earth move for you?) you had (*or* did you have?) an orgasm. humorous

the ends of the earth: *see* END.

go to earth go into hiding.

ⓘ *Go to earth* is used literally of a hunted animal hiding in a burrow or earth. Compare with **go to ground** (*at* GROUND).

like nothing on earth very strange. informal

2005 *AC on Bike* All would have been well except Emma decided that she had to have something to eat. What turned up was quite a surprise. It looked like black pudding but tasted like nothing on earth.

promise someone the earth: *see* **promise someone the moon** *at* MOON.

run someone or something to earth (*or* ground) find someone or something, usually after a long search.

ⓘ This is an idiom from hunting, especially foxhunting, its literal meaning being 'chase a hunted animal to its lair and corner it there'.

the salt of the earth: *see* SALT.

earthly

not stand (*or* have) an earthly have no chance at all. British informal

easy

an easy touch: *see* **a soft touch** *at* TOUCH.

as easy as winking: *see* WINKING.

come easy to present little difficulty to.

1989 Tony Parker *A Place Called Bird* College was a lot harder than High School, book work didn't come easy to me there.

easier said than done more easily talked about than put into practice.

easy as ABC: *see* ABC.

easy as falling off a log very easy. informal

ⓘ This expression was originally a mid-19th-century American one, but it is now in general use. It was used around the year 1880 by Mark Twain in the alternative form *rolling off a log*.

easy as pie very easy. informal

ⓘ *Pie* as a metaphor for something pleasant was originally late 19th-century US slang. Compare with **nice as pie** and **pie in the sky** (*at* PIE).

easy come, easy go used to indicate that something acquired without effort or difficulty may be lost or spent casually and without regret.

ⓘ Although recorded in this exact form only from the mid 19th century, *easy come, easy go* had parallels in medieval French and in the English sayings *light come, light go* (mid 16th century) and *quickly come, quickly go* (mid 19th century).

easy does it approach a task carefully and slowly. informal

easy meat a person or animal overcome, outwitted, or persuaded without difficulty. informal

easy on the eye (*or* ear) pleasant to look at (*or* listen to). informal

ⓘ *Easy on the eye* originated in the late 19th century as a US expression describing a pretty woman, a context in which it is still often used.

easy street a state of financial comfort or security. informal

free and easy: *see* FREE.

go (*or* be) easy on someone be less harsh on or critical of someone. informal

go easy on (*or* with) something be sparing or cautious in your use or consumption of something. informal

have it easy be free from difficulties, especially those normally associated with a particular situation or activity. informal

I'm easy said by someone when offered a choice to indicate that they have no particular preference. informal

of easy virtue (of a woman) promiscuous.

ⓘ *Easy* in the sense of 'sexually compliant' is found in Shakespeare's *Cymbeline*: 'Not a whit, Your lady being so easy'.

take the easy way out ❶ extricate yourself from a difficult situation by choosing a course of action offering the least effort, worry, or inconvenience, even though a more honourable alternative exists. ❷ commit suicide. euphemistic

take it easy ❶ approach a task or activity gradually or carefully. ❷ relax.

eat

could eat a horse: *see* HORSE.

dog eat dog: *see* DOG.

eat someone alive ❶ (of insects) bite someone many times. ❷ exploit someone's weakness ruthlessly. informal

eat crow be humiliated by your defeats or mistakes. North American informal

ⓘ In the USA 'boiled crow' has been a metaphor for something extremely disagreeable since the late 19th century.

eat dirt suffer insults or humiliation. informal

ⓘ In the USA *eat dirt* also has the sense of 'make a humiliating retraction' or 'eat your words'.

eat someone's dust fall far behind someone in a competitive situation. North American informal

1993 *Fiddlehead* She let everybody know she was moving on to True Love and they could eat her dust.

eat your heart out ❶ suffer from excessive longing, especially for someone or something unattainable. ❷ used to indicate that you think someone will feel great jealousy or regret about something.

❷ **1997 Christina Reid** *Clowns* Wait'll you see my new frock. Joan Collins eat your heart out.

eat someone out of house and home eat a lot of someone else's food. informal

eat humble pie: *see* HUMBLE.

eat like a horse: *see* HORSE.

eat salt with: *see* SALT.

eat your words retract what you have said, especially when forced to do so.

I'll eat my hat used to indicate that you think a particular thing is extremely unlikely to happen.

you can't have your cake and eat it: *see* CAKE.

eating

have someone eating out of your hand have someone completely under your control.

1987 Bernard MacLaverty *The Great Profundo* One of my main difficulties is that I'm not good with an audience. There's guys can come out and have a crowd eating out of their hand right away with a few jokes.

the proof of the pudding is in the eating: *see* PROOF.

what's eating you (*or* him *or* her)? what is worrying or annoying you (*or* him *or* her)? informal

ebb

at a low ebb in an especially poor state.

ebb and flow a recurrent or rhythmical pattern of coming and going or decline and regrowth.

ℹ This expression makes reference to the regular movement of the tides, where *ebb* means move away from the land and *flow* move back towards it.

echo

applaud (*or* cheer) someone to the echo applaud (*or* cheer) someone very enthusiastically.

eclipse

in eclipse ❶ (of a celestial object) obscured by another or the shadow of another. ❷ losing or having lost significance, power, or prominence.

❷ **2011** *Real Clear Markets* The American labor market has been in eclipse for decades, but public-sector unions were one of its few remaining bastions. Now, their power too is waning

economical

economical with the truth used euphemistically to describe a person or statement that lies or deliberately withholds information.

ℹ The phrase *economy of truth* was used in the 18th century by the orator Edmund Burke (1729–97), while in the 19th century Mark Twain observed 'Truth is the most valuable thing we have. Let us economize it' (*Following the Equator*, 1897). The present phrase became current after its use in the 'Spycatcher' trial in the New South Wales Supreme Court: Robert Armstrong, head of the British Civil Service, was reported as saying of a letter: 'It contains a misleading impression, not a lie. It was being economical with the truth.'

2003 *Observer* He is ruthless in pursuit of commercial goals, otherwise he would not have been so economical with the truth two months ago when he ruled out any notion of signing Beckham.

edge

dull the edge of: *see* DULL.

on edge tense, nervous, or irritable.

on the edge of your seat (*or* chair) very excited or tense and giving your full attention to something. informal

on a knife-edge: *see* KNIFE-EDGE.

set someone's teeth on edge cause someone to feel intense discomfort or irritation.

ℹ This is an expression used in the Bible to describe the unpleasant sensation caused by eating something bitter or sour: 'every man that eateth the sour grape, his teeth shall be set on edge' (Jeremiah 31:30).

1997 Kate O'Riordan *The Boy in the Moon* Julia's voice sustained a quavery note that set Brian's teeth on edge.

take the edge off something reduce the intensity or effect of something, especially something unpleasant or severe.

edgeways

get a word in edgeways contribute to a conversation with difficulty because the other speaker talks almost incessantly.

effing

effing and blinding using vulgar expletives; swearing.

ℹ *Effing* and *blinding* here are euphemisms for taboo or vulgar slang words: *effing* represents the initial letter of *fuck*, and *blinding* reflects the now obsolete use of *blind* in mild curses (e.g. *blind me*, which became *blimey*).

2018 Peter Robinson *Careless Love* They were certainly a foul-mouthed pair, the Hadfield siblings.... Still, if Ronald Hadfield wanted to go around effing and blinding, who was she to complain?

egg

a curate's egg: *see* CURATE.

don't put all your eggs in one basket don't risk everything on the success of one venture. proverb

2013 *Better Farming—Ontario Community of Professional Farmers* Any business knows it's not a safe play to have all your eggs in one basket, so that is why a company like Harmony likely decided to go after the small and mid range customers so their business model was diverse and not reliant on one big customer.

go suck an egg go away (used as an expression of anger or scorn). North American informal *See also* **teach your grandmother to suck eggs** *at* GRANDMOTHER.

> **1993** *Virginian Pilot & Ledger-Star (Norfolk, Va.)* A place [in the country] where you can drop a line in the water from your back yard and tell the rest of the world to go suck an egg.

kill the goose that lays the golden egg: *see* GOOSE.

lay an egg be completely unsuccessful; fail badly. North American informal

sure as eggs is eggs: *see* SURE.

walk on eggs: *see* WALK.

with egg on your face appearing foolish or ridiculous. informal

Egypt

corn in Egypt: *see* CORN.

eight

behind the eight ball at a disadvantage; baffled. North American

> ❶ The black ball is numbered eight in a variety of the game of pool known as *eight-ball pool*.

one over the eight slightly drunk. British informal

> ❶ The idea behind this idiom is that a drinker can reasonably be expected to consume eight glasses of beer without becoming drunk. The expression was originally armed forces' slang from the early 20th century.

elbow

at your elbow close at hand; nearby.

bend the elbow: *see* BEND.

give someone the elbow reject or dismiss someone. informal

> ❶ The image is of nudging someone aside in a rough or contemptuous manner.

lift your (*or* the) elbow consume alcohol to excess.

more power to your elbow!: *see* POWER.

not know your arse from your elbow: *see* ARSE.

out at elbows wearing shabby or ragged clothing. dated

up to your elbows in ❶ with your hands plunged into. ❷ deeply involved in. informal

element

in (*or* out of) your element in (*or* out of) your accustomed or preferred environment, where you feel confident and at ease, often in performing a particular activity.

elephant

the elephant in the corner (*or* room) an embarrassing or awkward topic that everyone is aware of but no one wishes to discuss.

> **2003** *CNN* Of course, the elephant in the corner for all these developments is Yasser Arafat, the chairman of the Palestinian Authority.
>
> **2004** *New York Times* When it comes to the rising price of oil, the elephant in the room is the ever-weakening United States dollar..

see the elephant see the world; get experience of life. US

> ❶ An *elephant* is used here to symbolize or typify something which is extremely remarkable or exotic.
>
> **2003** *Boston Review* His experience [during World War I] as a pilot was limited to a few practice flights in Canada, and the war was over before his squadron had a chance to go see the elephant in the sky above Verdun.

a white elephant: *see* WHITE.

eleventh

at the eleventh hour at the latest possible moment.

> ❶ This expression originally referred to Jesus's parable of the labourers hired right at the end of the day to work in the vineyard (Matthew 20:1–16).

Elysian

the Elysian Fields heaven. literary

> ❶ Homer describes the Elysian Fields (called *Elysium* by Latin writers) as the happy land in which the blessed spirits live in the afterlife.

emotional

tired and emotional: *see* TIRED.

empty

be running on empty have exhausted all your resources or sustenance.

> ❶ The image is of a vehicle's fuel tank that has run dry. The same idea is expressed by *be running on fumes*.

2019 *Guardian* All that remains are tired minds and tired bodies. None more so than Theresa May's: the prime minister is running on fumes.

empty nester a person whose children have grown up and left home. informal

empty vessels make most noise (*or* sound) those with least wisdom or knowledge are always the most talkative. proverb

ℹ *Vessel* here refers to a hollow container, such as a bowl or cask, rather than a ship.

e

enchilada

the big enchilada a person or thing of great importance. North American informal

the whole enchilada the whole situation; everything. North American informal

2013 *PC World* We're naming what we think are the 10 best new features in Word 13. (We reviewed the whole enchilada last December, when it became available to Microsoft TechNet subscribers. You can read our opinion here.)

ℹ *Enchilada* is an American Spanish word for a tortilla served with chilli sauce and a filling of meat or cheese.

end

all ends up completely. informal

2018 Simon Wilde *England: The Biography* 'If I am beaten all ends up and get away with it, I have forgotten about it as soon as the bowler starts his run for the next delivery,' he [Herbert Sutcliffe] once said.

at the end of the day when everything is taken into consideration. British informal

2013 *New Zealand Herald* At the end of the day, for an event of this magnitude, we believe the pricing is in line with what we've seen and also in line with what's happened previously.

at the end of your tether having no patience, resources, or energy left to cope with something.

ℹ A North American variant of this expression is *at the end of your rope*, and in both cases the image is that of a grazing animal tethered on a rope that allows it a certain range in which to move but which at full stretch prohibits further movement.

at a loose end: *see* LOOSE END.

at your wit's end: *see* WIT.

the beginning of the end: *see* BEGINNING.

be on the receiving end: *see* RECEIVING.

be thrown in at the deep end: *see* DEEP.

burn the candle at both ends: *see* BURN.

the business end: *see* BUSINESS.

come to a sticky end: *see* STICKY.

the dirty end of the stick: *see* DIRTY.

end in tears have an unhappy or unpleasant outcome (often used as a warning). British

1992 Iain Banks *The Crow Road* Well, let them get married. The earlier the better; it would end in tears. Let them rush into it, let them repent at leisure.

end it all commit suicide.

2012 *Guardian* When he subsequently loses the girl of his fancy, Jimmy can be seen speeding towards the edge of a cliff in a bid to end it all—only for an empty scooter to crash on to the rocks below.

the end justifies the means wrong or unfair methods may be used if the overall goal is good.

ℹ The Roman poet Ovid expresses this concept in *Heroides* as *exitus acta probat* meaning 'the outcome justifies the actions'.

the end of civilization as we know it ❶ the complete collapse of ordered society. ❷ used to indicate that someone is being alarmist or is overreacting to a trivial inconvenience or blunder as if it were enormously significant and catastrophic.

ℹ This expression is supposedly a cinematic cliché, and was actually used in the film *Citizen Kane* (1941): 'a project which would mean the end of civilization as we know it'.

2010 *Guardian* For Labour to stagger on for another term would be good neither for the country nor for the party ... Some Labour politicians privately acknowledge this ... But publicly, they continue to insist that a victory for anyone else will be the end of civilisation as we know it.

the ends of the earth the most distant parts of the world.

the end of the road (*or* line) the point beyond which progress or survival cannot continue.

end of story used to emphasize that there is nothing more to add on the subject just mentioned. informal

ℹ The phrase is sometimes abbreviated to simply *end of*.

2012 *The Age* (Melbourne) The West Australian Commissioner for Corporate Affairs had asked whether it was a trade union, and had been told it wasn't a trade union. Which it wasn't. End of story.

2016 **Chris Lang** *Dark Heart* It was Kashell, on his own. Personal revenge. End of.

the end of the world a complete disaster. informal

ⓘ This expression comes from the idea of the termination of life on earth as the ultimate catastrophe, but is often used with the negative as a reassurance that a mistake or setback is not that important.

2014 Stuart Ian Burns *Feeling Listless* I woke up from my hernia operation ... realising that having a hernia wasn't the end of the world.

get (*or* have) your end away have sex. British vulgar slang

get the wrong end of the stick: *see* WRONG.

go off the deep end: *see* DEEP.

keep (*or* hold) your end up perform well in a difficult or competitive situation. informal

light at the end of the tunnel: *see* LIGHT.

make (both) ends meet earn or have enough money to live on without getting into debt.

2014 *Daily Telegraph* We wanted to use the banner to say that we are finding it hard to make ends meet after the demolition. We are like beggars, begging for food.

make someone's hair stand on end: *see* HAIR.

a means to an end: *see* MEAN.

never (*or* not) hear the end of something be continually reminded of an unpleasant topic or cause of annoyance.

2002 *Observer* If it was Ireland or Wales we'd support them, but not England. It's a minority nations thing. If England was to win, we'd never hear the end of it.

no end to a great extent; very much. informal

1984 James Kelman *The Busconductor Hines* McCulloch gives him a go at the wheel at certain remote terminuses at specific times of the late night and early morning and his confidence grows no end.

no end of something a vast number or amount of something. informal

2014 *Independent* Parkes and his co-writer, musician JS Rafaeli, have no end of yarns to tell.

odds and ends: *see* ODDS.

play both ends against the middle keep your options open by supporting or favouring opposing sides.

the sharp end: *see* SHARP.

the thick end of something: *see* THICK.

the thin end of the wedge: *see* THIN.

to the bitter end: *see* BITTER.

a — to end all —s something so impressive of its kind that nothing that follows will have the same impact. informal

ⓘ The First World War was often referred to as *the war to end all wars*, from the mistaken belief that it would make all subsequent wars unnecessary.

1971 Bessie Head *Maru* It was a wedding to end all weddings.

e

enemy

be your own worst enemy act contrary to your own interests; be self-destructive.

1993 Richard Lowe & William Shaw *Travellers* We convinced ourselves that everything was against us but the truth was we were probably our own worst enemies.

public enemy number one: *see* PUBLIC.

England

lie back and think of England: *see* LIE.

Englishman

an Englishman's home is his castle an English person's home is a place where they may do as they please and from which they may exclude anyone they choose. British proverb

enough

enough is as good as a feast moderation is more satisfying than excess. proverb

enough is enough no more will be tolerated.

2013 *Daily Telegraph* Mr Duncan Smith will say, 'But for those who aren't doing all they could, or who we think are cheating the system, it is time to make very clear that enough is enough. No attendance, no benefit.'

enough said there is no need to say more; all is understood. *See also* **nuff said** *at* NUFF.

enough to make a cat laugh: *see* CAT.

enter

enter into the spirit: *see* SPIRIT.

enter the lists: *see* LISTS.

envelope

on the back of an envelope used in reference to calculations or plans of the most sketchy kind.

2013 *Daily Telegraph* This two-boat, dual use idea has been dreamt up at the last minute on the back of an envelope, with no financial analysis.

push the envelope (*or* the edge of the envelope) approach or extend the limits of what is possible. informal

ⓘ This expression was originally aviation slang and related to graphs of aerodynamic performance on which the *envelope* is the boundary line representing an aircraft's capabilities.

2013 *New York Times* Like so many [Robert] Stone characters, Brookman and Maud like to push the envelope; they enjoy the frisson of danger and are prone to equate heedlessness with freedom.

e

épater

épater les bourgeois shock people who have attitudes or views regarded as conventional or complacent.

ⓘ The French phrase is generally used in English, there being no exact English equivalent. 'Il faut épater les bourgeois' ('one must astonish the bourgeois') was a comment attributed to the French poet and critic Charles Baudelaire.

2008 *Believer Magazine* On and off the water, he was omnipotent and inscrutable, wearing trench coats or top hats down to the beach, shooting rockets off the pier, painting swastikas on his board (less fascist impulse than a last ditch effort to epater les bourgeois).

equal

first among equals the person or thing having the highest status in a group.

ⓘ This expression is a translation of the Latin phrase *primus inter pares*, which is also used in English.

other (*or* all) things being equal provided that other factors or circumstances remain the same.

2014 *New Zealand Herald* All other things being equal, a carrier with a higher number of seats available will need to protect a lower percentage of seats and hence release a relatively greater number of lower priced fares.

some — are more equal than others although members of a society or group appear to be equal, in reality some receive better treatment than others.

ⓘ The phrase originated in George Orwell's *Animal Farm* (1945), where it characterizes the true state of affairs in a supposedly egalitarian community of farm animals: 'All animals are equal but some animals are more equal than others.'

err

err on the right side act so that the most likely mistake to be made is the least harmful one.

err on the side of act with a specified bias towards something.

1936 William Gerhardie *Of Mortal Love* When after lunch Dinah went up to her room she found that her things had been moved to another room, erring on the side of modesty.

to err is human, to forgive divine it is human nature to make mistakes yourself while finding it hard to forgive others. proverb

errand

errand of mercy a journey or mission carried out to help someone in difficulty or danger.

error

trial and error: *see* TRIAL.

escutcheon

a blot on your escutcheon: *see* BLOT.

essence

of the essence critically important.

1990 Louis de Bernières *The War of Don Emmanuel's Nether Parts* Gentlemen, we have before us an important mission for which speed and efficiency are of the essence, and where surprise is the key element.

eternal

the Eternal City a name for the city of Rome.

eternal triangle a relationship between three people, typically a couple and the lover of one of them, involving sexual rivalry.

hope springs eternal: *see* HOPE.

even

break even reach a point in a business venture where the profits are equal to the costs.

don't get mad, get even: *see* GET.

an even break a fair chance. informal

ⓘ This phrase is perhaps best known from W. C. Fields's catchphrase 'Never give a sucker an even break'. It is said to have originated in the 1923 musical *Poppy*, and was also the title of one of Fields's films (1941).

even Stephens (*or* Stevens) an even chance.

1990 Alan Duff *Once Were Warriors* And I give her half. Clean down the middle. Even stevens. I don't try and cheat her out of her share.

get (*or* be) even with inflict similar trouble or harm on someone as they have inflicted on you. informal

on an even keel ❶ (of a ship or aircraft) not tilting to one side. ❷ (of a person or situation) functioning normally after a period of difficulty.

❷ **2013** *Alf Grumble* When you bet your future on the loser it takes gall to expect Govt help to get you back on an even keel.

event

be wise after the event: *see* WISE.

happy event: *see* HAPPY.

ever

it was ever thus (*or* so) used as a humorous way of suggesting that despite claims of things having been better in the past nothing much alters. informal

2013 *Daily Telegraph* So all is not divine harmony within the Vatican, but a cursory reading of the 2,000-year history of the papacy suggests it was ever thus—schisms, factions and even, some stories go, a woman in disguise on Saint Peter's throne.

every

every last (*or* single) used to emphasize every member of a group.

1991 Colin Dexter *The Jewel That Was Ours* One clue unfinished in a Listener puzzle, and he would strain the capacity of every last brain-cell to bursting point until he had solved it.

every man for himself everyone must take care of themselves and their own interests and safety.

ⓘ This expression has been used since medieval times, but from the mid 16th century onwards it has often been expanded to *every man for himself and the devil take the hindmost* or, less commonly, *every man for himself and God for us all*.

2012 Bruce Schneier *Schneier on Security* Taken together, our findings show that human behaviour in life-and-death situations is best captured by the expression 'every man for himself'.

every man Jack: *see* JACK.

every which way in all directions; in a disorderly fashion. North American informal

everything

everything in the garden is lovely: *see* GARDEN.

evil

the evil eye a gaze or stare superstitiously believed to cause harm.

the lesser evil: *see* LESSER.

a necessary evil: *see* NECESSARY.

put off the evil day (*or* hour) postpone something unpleasant for as long as possible.

example

make an example of punish as a warning or deterrent to others.

excepted

present company excepted: *see* PRESENT.

exception

the exception that proves the rule a particular case that is so unusual that it is evidence of the validity of the rule that generally applies.

ⓘ This phrase comes from the Latin legal maxim *exceptio probat regulum in casibus non exceptis* 'exception proves the rule in the cases not excepted'. This in fact meant that the recognition of something as an exception proved the existence of a rule, but the idiom is popularly used or understood to mean 'a person or thing that does not conform to the general rule affecting others of that class'

2013 *DVD Verdict* The life of Malcolm X is the exception that proves the rule that people don't lead narratively interesting lives.

take exception to object strongly to.

excursion

alarms and excursions: *see* ALARM.

excuse

excuse my French: *see* FRENCH.

exercise

the object of the exercise: *see* OBJECT.

e

exeunt

exeunt omnes everyone leaves or goes away.

ℹ The Latin phrase *exeunt omnes* means 'all go out', and was used originally as a stage direction in a printed play to indicate that all the actors leave the stage.

exhibition

make an exhibition of yourself behave in a very foolish or ill-judged way in public.

expect

what can (*or* do) you expect? used to emphasize that there was nothing unexpected about a person or event.

ℹ A more elaborate statement of the same sentiment is the proverb *what can you expect from a pig but a grunt?*

expedition

a fishing expedition: *see* FISHING.

extra

go the extra mile: *see* MILE.

extreme

terminate with extreme prejudice: *see* TERMINATE.

eye

an eagle eye: *see* EAGLE.

the evil eye: *see* EVIL.

an eye for an eye and a tooth for a tooth used to refer to the belief that retaliation in kind is the appropriate way to deal with an offence or crime.

ℹ This expression refers to the law of retribution as set out in the Old Testament (Exodus 21:24), known as *lex talionis*.

the eye of a needle a very small opening or space (used to emphasize the impossibility of a projected endeavour).

ℹ This phrase comes from Matthew 19:24: 'It is easier for a camel to go through the eye of a needle, than for a rich man to enter the kingdom of God'.

2001 *FourFourTwo* Able to thread a pass through the eye of a needle, he can play in the centre or on either flank.

the eye of the storm ❶ the calm region at the centre of a storm or hurricane. ❷ the most intense part of a tumultous situation.

❷ **2012** *Guardian* There is a performance of eerie potency and poignancy from Annika Wedderkopp, playing Klara, the little girl in the eye of the storm.

the apple of your eye: *see* APPLE.

be all eyes be watching eagerly and attentively.

2002 John McGahern *That they may face the Rising Sun* When Patrick Ryan drew up in an expensive car that dropped him at the church he was all eyes.

a beam in your eye: *see* BEAM.

bedroom eyes: *see* BEDROOM.

catch someone's eye ❶ be noticed by someone. ❷ attract someone's attention by making eye contact with them.

clap (*or* lay *or* set) eyes on see. informal

1992 Barry Unsworth *Sacred Hunger* If we go by the indications of the play, these two charmers have never clapped eyes on a man before, never flirted, never known the sweets of love.

close (*or* shut) your eyes to refuse to notice or acknowledge something unwelcome or unpleasant.

do someone in the eye defraud, thwart, or humiliate someone.

1930 J. B. Priestley *Angel Pavement* He'd invented the job five minutes before, just to do mother in the eye.

eyes down! be ready to concentrate fully on the matter before you.

ℹ The expression originated as an injunction (in full 'Eyes down for a full house!') to give your full attention to your card when a game of bingo was about to start.

eyes out on stalks full of eager curiosity or amazement. informal

2012 *Manchester Music* You can tell the people who have never seen them before by the fact that their eyes are out on stalks as the lights go up.

feast your eyes on: *see* FEAST.

get (*or* keep) your eye in become (*or* remain) able to make good judgements about a task or occupation in which you are engaged. British

give someone the (glad) eye look at someone in a way that clearly indicates your sexual interest in them. informal

1992 James Meek *Last Orders* If it was an attractive woman, men would give her the eye.

a gleam in someone's eye: *see* GLEAM.

go eyes out make every effort. Australian informal

half an eye a slight degree of perception or attention.

1962 Cyprian Ekwensi *Burning Grass* His sandals were new because it was market day; or perhaps he had half an eye to some maiden.

have an eye for be able to recognize, appreciate, and make good judgements about a particular thing.

2003 *Observer* Europe's oldest continually inhabited city is Cádiz, founded by the Phoenicians in 1100 BC, but those wily Phoenicians, with an eye for a good setting, founded 'Malaka' further along the Andalucian coast a few hundred years later in 800 BC.

have (*or* with) an eye for (*or* on *or* to) the main chance look or be looking for an opportunity to take advantage of a situation for personal gain, especially when this is financial.

ⓘ This expression is taken from the use of *main chance* in the gambling game of hazard, where it refers to a number (5, 6, 7, or 8) called by a player before throwing the dice.

have eyes bigger than your stomach have asked for or taken more food than you can actually eat.

have eyes in the back of your head observe everything that is happening even when this is apparently impossible.

1991 Barbara Anderson *Girls High* They were all in Miss Royston's class who said that she had eyes in the back of her head and they half believed it, because how else did she know.

have eyes like a hawk miss nothing of what is going on around you.

have eyes like saucers: *see* SAUCER.

have square eyes: *see* SQUARE.

have stars in your eyes: *see* STAR.

have your eye on ❶ keep under careful observation. ❷ hope or plan to acquire.

❶ **2009** *Diamond Geezer* The BBC must be unblemishable. I've got my eye on a few programmes which I suspect might be breaking the BBC Trust's new Extra-Rigid Code of Prim and Proper Conduct.

❷ **2012 Snotty Grrl** I went ahead and bought a skirt and cardigan I've had my eye on since January that both just went on sale.

here's mud in your eye!: *see* MUD.

hit someone in the eye (*or* between the eyes) be very obvious or impressive. informal

2001 *Independent* When I saw the technology in operation, it hit me between the eyes. I was happy to give him £20,000, and became a non-executive director.

in the blink of an eye: *see* BLINK.

in the eyes of in the opinion of.

in your mind's eye: *see* MIND.

in a pig's eye: *see* PIG.

in the public eye: *see* PUBLIC.

in the twinkling of an eye: *see* **in a twinkling** *at* TWINKLING.

in the wink of an eye: *see* WINK.

keep an eye out (*or* open) for look out for something with particular attention.

2004 *Wanderlust* Along the way I kept an eye open for some of Hong Kong's rarest wildlife.

2005 Zadie Smith *On Beauty* OK—we got to keep an eye out for Jerome, though—he's about.

keep a weather eye on: *see* WEATHER.

keep your eye on the ball: *see* BALL.

keep your eyes open (*or* peeled *or* skinned) be on the alert; watch carefully or vigilantly for something.

leap to the eye: *see* LEAP.

look someone in the eye: *see* LOOK.

make eyes at someone look at someone in a way that makes it clear you find them sexually attractive.

make sheep's eyes at someone: *see* SHEEP.

meet your eye: *see* MEET.

meet someone's eye: *see* MEET.

more to someone or something than meets the eye: *see* MEET.

a mote in someone's eye: *see* MOTE.

my eye (*or* all my eye and Betty Martin) nonsense. informal, dated

ⓘ Who or what *Betty Martin* was has never been satisfactorily explained. Another version of the saying also in use in the late 18th century was *all my eye and my elbow.*

1991 Robertson Davies *Murther & Walking Spirits* Of course many of the grievances are all my eye and Betty Martin (Anna has picked up this soldier's phrase from her husband and likes to use it to show how thoroughly British she has become).

one in the eye for a disappointment or setback for someone or something, especially one that is perceived as being well deserved.

only have eyes for be exclusively interested in or attracted to.

open someone's eyes enlighten someone about certain realities; cause someone to realize or discover something.

1998 Scoular Anderson *1314 & All That* These events opened his eyes to what had happened to his country. Now his one wish was that Scotland should be independent.

pipe your eye: *see* PIPE.

pull the wool over someone's eyes: *see* WOOL.

a roving eye: *see* ROVING.

the scales fall from someone's eyes: *see* SCALE.

see eye to eye have similar views or attitudes to something; be in full agreement.

2010 Peter Murray *Skippy Dies* For a while now, your father and I haven't been seeing eye to eye. It's not ... anybody's fault, it's just the way relationships sometimes go.

—'s-eye view a view from the position or standpoint of the person or thing specified.

ℹ The most common versions of this phrase are **bird's-eye view** (*see* BIRD) and **worm's-eye view** (*see* WORM).

1982 Ian Hamilton *Robert Lowell* There is a kind of double vision: the child's eye view judged and interpreted by the ironical narrator.

shut your eyes to be wilfully ignorant of.

2009 Oona Eisenstadt *Hopeless but not Serious* Insofar as you have achieved some level of happiness, it has been hard-won, and arises not from shutting your eyes to the problems that exist in the world but from acting well.

spit in the eye of: *see* SPIT.

there's more to someone or something than meets the eye: *see* MEET.

there wasn't a dry eye in the house: *see* DRY.

turn a blind eye: *see* BLIND.

a twinkle in someone's eye: *see* TWINKLE.

up to your eyes in very busy with or deeply involved in. informal

what the eye doesn't see, the heart doesn't grieve over if you're unaware of an unpleasant fact or situation you can't be troubled by it. proverb

wipe someone's eye: *see* WIPE.

with one eye on giving some but not all your attention to.

1977 Craig Thomas *Firefox* With one eye on the JPT (jet-pipe temperature) gauge he opened the throttles until the rpm gauges were at fifty-five percent and the whine had increased comfortably.

with your eyes open (*or* with open eyes) fully aware of the risks and other implications of an action or situation.

1999 Salman Rushdie *The Ground Beneath Her Feet* I've always liked to stick my face right up against the hot sweaty broken surface of what was being done, with my eyes open.

with your eyes shut (*or* closed) ❶ without having to make much effort; easily. ❷ without considering the possible difficulties or consequences.

❶ **1994** *New Scientist* I can knock off pages of eco-babble for the UN with my eyes shut.

eyeball

eyeball to eyeball face to face with someone, especially in an aggressive way.

eyeballs out with maximum physical effort. informal

give someone the hairy eyeball stare at someone in a disapproving or angry way, especially with your eyelids partially lowered. North American informal

1992 Guy Vanderhaeghe *Things As They Are* The commissioner giving him the hairy eyeball all through the service didn't do anything for Reg's increasing bad humour either.

up to the (*or* your) eyeballs used to emphasize the extreme degree of an undesirable situation or condition. informal

2000 *Time* Consumers are up to their eyeballs in debt, and the strain shows.

eyebrow

raise your eyebrows (*or* an eyebrow) show surprise, disbelief, or mild disapproval.

eyelash

by an eyelash by a very small margin.

flutter your eyelashes: *see* FLUTTER.

eyelid

not bat an eyelid: *see* BAT.

eye teeth

cut your eye teeth: *see* **cut your teeth** *at* CUT.

give your eye teeth for go to any lengths in order to obtain something.

ℹ The *eye teeth* are the two canine teeth in the upper jaw.

1930 W. Somerset Maugham *Cakes & Ale* He'd give his eye-teeth to have written a book half as good.

face

the acceptable face of: *see* ACCEPTABLE.

arse about face: *see* ARSE.

be written all over your face: *see* WRITTEN.

blow up in your face (of an action, plan, or situation) go drastically wrong with damaging effects to yourself.

do something until you are blue in the face: *see* BLUE.

a face as long as a fiddle a dismal face.

a face like a slapped (*or* smacked) arse: *see* ARSE.

face the music be confronted with the unpleasant consequences of your actions.

face to face ❶ in direct personal contact. ❷ in a position in which you must confront a difficulty.

fly in the face of: *see* FLY.

get out of someone's face stop harassing or annoying someone. North American informal

have the (brass) face to have the effrontery to do something. dated

in your face aggressively obvious; assertive. informal

> **1996** *Sunday Telegraph* The . . . campaign reflects a growing trend of aggressive and 'in your face' advertisement that is alarming many within the industry.

laugh in someone's face: *see* LAUGH.

laugh on the other side of your face: *see* LAUGH.

let's face it let's be honest, admitting unpalatable facts.

> **2002** *DVD Verdict* There's never much need or reason to slow down and ponder characterization or plot—I mean, let's face it, this isn't Shakespeare.

lose face suffer a loss of respect; be humiliated.

> ℹ This expression was originally associated with China and was a translation of the Chinese idiom *tiu lien*.

make (*or* pull) a face (*or* faces) produce an expression on your face that shows dislike, disgust, or some other negative emotion, or that is intended to be amusing.

not just a pretty face: *see* PRETTY.

off your face very drunk or under the influence of illegal drugs. informal

> **2019** *Observer* I should clarify that there is no suggestion that the whole steepest street issue got screwed up because everyone involved was off their face on Guinness.

on the face of it without necessarily knowing all of the relevant facts; at first glance.

put a brave (*or* bold *or* good) face on something act as if something unpleasant or upsetting is not as bad as it really is.

put your face on apply make-up to your face. informal

rearrange someone's face: *see* REARRANGE.

save face retain respect; avoid humiliation.

> **1994 Thomas Boswell** *Cracking Show* And Rose got to save face, at least in his own eyes, with one last brassy news conference.

save someone's face enable someone to avoid humiliation.

set your face against oppose or resist with determination.

show your face: *see* SHOW.

shut your face (*or* trap) be silent; stop talking. informal

someone's face fits someone has the necessary qualities for something, especially beyond formal qualifications (with the implication of personal or social compatibility).

> **2010** *Daily Telegraph* The Equalities Minister and Labour's Deputy Leader said many people still only get on because 'their face fits' or because of 'connections'.

throw something back in someone's face reject something in a brusque or ungracious manner.

wash its face: *see* WASH.

fact

a fact of life something that must be accepted and cannot be changed, however unpalatable.

the facts of life information about sexual functions and practices, especially as given to children or teenagers.

fade

do a fade run away. informal

> **1990 Stephen King** *The Stand* Two days ago, he would probably have done a fade himself if he had seen someone.

fail

without fail absolutely predictably; with no exception or cause for doubt.

> ℹ *Fail* as a noun in the sense of 'failure or deficiency' is now only found in this phrase.

faint

damn someone or something with faint praise: *see* DAMN.

a faint heart timidity or lack of willpower preventing you from achieving your objective.

> ℹ *Faint heart never won fair lady* is a proverb which dates in this wording from the early 17th century; the idea, however, was around at least two centuries earlier.

faintest

not have the faintest (idea) have no idea. informal

fair

bid fair to: *see* BID.

fair and square ❶ with absolute accuracy. ❷ honestly and straightforwardly.

a fair crack of the whip: *see* CRACK.

a fair deal equitable treatment.

fair dinkum: *see* DINKUM.

fair dos used to request just treatment or to accept that it has been given. British informal

fair game: *see* GAME.

fair play to someone used as an expression of approval when someone has done something praiseworthy or the right thing under the circumstances.

fair's fair used to request just treatment or assert that an arrangement is just. informal

> **2013 Margaret Pomeranz** and **David Stratton** *At the Movies* I also figured out why movies like this are reviewed—you have to try and appeal to everybody, to maintain the ratings. Fair's fair! But please put the quality Venice film reviews up on the site from your trip.

a fair-weather friend: *see* FRIEND.

for fair completely and finally. US informal

> **1960 John Barth** *The Sot-Weed Factor* And when the matter of hostages arose, the mother had said 'Pray God they will take Harry, for then we'd be quit of him for fair, and not a penny poorer.'

get a fair shake: *see* SHAKE.

in a fair way to do something likely to achieve something.

it's a fair cop: *see* COP.

no fair unfair (often used in or as a petulant protestation). North American informal

play fair observe principles of justice; avoid cheating.

be set fair (of the weather) be fine and likely to stay fine for a time. British

fairy

(away) with the fairies giving the impression of being mad, distracted, or in a dreamworld.

faith

an article of faith: *see* ARTICLE.

fall

fall over yourself be excessively eager (to do something).

take the fall receive blame or punishment, typically in the place of another person. North American informal

> ℹ In late 19th-century criminals' slang *fall* could mean an 'an arrest', and this was later extended to mean 'a term of imprisonment'. From this the US term *fall guy* meaning 'a scapegoat' developed in the early 20th century.
> ℹ For other idioms containing *fall*, see the entry for the main word in the idiom (for example, **fall foul of** at FOUL).

false

a false dawn a misleadingly hopeful sign.

ℹ A false dawn is literally a transient light in the sky which precedes the rising of the sun by about an hour, commonly seen in Eastern countries.

2013 *Daily Telegraph* And the economy, after several false dawns, is edging towards recovery.

play someone false prove treacherous or deceitful towards someone; let someone down.

sail under false colours: *see* COLOUR.

f

fame

claim to fame: *see* CLAIM.

family

the (*or* your) family jewels a man's genitals. informal

in the family way pregnant. informal

sell the family silver part with a valuable resource in order to gain an immediate advantage.

ℹ In 1985, the former British prime minister Harold Macmillan made a speech to the Tory Reform Group on the subject of privatization (the selling off of nationalized industries to private companies). He likened it to the selling of heirlooms by impoverished aristocratic families: 'First of all the Georgian silver goes...'.

famous

famous for being famous having no recognizable reason for your fame other than high media exposure.

famous for fifteen minutes (especially of an ordinary person) enjoying a brief period of fame before fading back into obscurity.

ℹ In 1968, the pop artist Andy Warhol (1927–87) predicted that 'in the future everybody will be world famous for fifteen minutes'. Short-lived celebrity or notoriety is now often referred to as *fifteen minutes of fame*.

famous last words said as an ironic comment on or reply to an overconfident assertion that may well soon be proved wrong by events.

ℹ This expression apparently originated as a catchphrase in mid-20th-century armed forces' slang.

2011 Andrew *The 4th Avenue Blues* So far, so good! No disappearing acts going on around here. Those may be my famous last words so I better knock on wood.

fan

fan the flames (of something) cause an emotion, such as anger or hatred, to become stronger.

when the shit hits the fan: *see* SHIT.

fancy

fancy your (*or* someone's) chances believe that you (*or* someone else) are likely to be successful.

Fanny Adams

sweet Fanny dams: *see* SWEET.

fantastic

trip the light fantastic: *see* TRIP.

far

be a far cry from be very different from.

1987 *National Geographic* 'I walk out and hire a helicopter... an expensive way to mine.' And a far cry from the ancient Maori canoe expeditions... to hunt for jade.

far and away by a very large amount.

2014 *CNN transcripts* Hillary Clinton, of course, is far and away the favourite. She has a whopping 73 percent—who can beat her?

far be it from (*or* for) me to used to express reluctance, especially to do something which you think may be resented.

far from the madding crowd: *see* MADDING.

far gone ❶ advanced in time. ❷ in a bad or worsening state. ❸ very intoxicated or ill. informal

few and far between: *see* FEW.

so far, so good progress has been satisfactory up to now.

2013 *Independent* Community development finance institutions might have a role to play. So far, so good. The problem is the data throws up some mixed messages.

a — too far one regarded as a step or stage beyond what is safe, sensible, or desirable.

2013 *Daily Telegraph* 'What exactly is the downside,' he asked, 'apart from fewer fags sold?' This proved a provocation too far for Mr Davies. He could contain his disgust no longer.

fare-thee-well

to a fare-thee-well to perfection; thoroughly. US

ℹ This expression is of late 18th-century American origin, and is also found in the form *to a fare-you-well*.

1911 R. D. Saunders *Colonel Todhunter* The fight's begun, and we've got to rally around old Bill Strickland to a fare-you-well.

farm

bet the farm: *see* BET.

buy the farm: *see* BUY.

farthing

not a brass farthing: *see* BRASS.

fashion

after a fashion to a certain extent but not perfectly or satisfactorily.

like (*or* as if) it is going out of fashion (*or* style) in great quantities and without restraint.

2004 *Daily Dispatch (South Africa) Online* On the romantic front, it is action all the way; and you might be spending money like it's going out of fashion in order to keep yourself in style.

fast

fast and furious lively and exciting.

2000 *Independent* We understand that the bidding was fast and furious right up to the last minute.

hard and fast: *see* HARD.

make a fast buck: *see* BUCK.

play fast and loose ignore your obligations; be unreliable.

ℹ *Fast and loose* was the name of an old fairground game, in which a punter was challenged to pin an intricately folded belt, garter, or other piece of material to a surface. The person running the game would inevitably show that the item had not been securely fastened or made 'fast', and so the punter would lose their money. The phrase came to be used to indicate inconstancy.

2013 *Daily Telegraph* It seems the First Minister has been playing fast and loose with the facts on EU entry and has been spectacularly caught out.

in the fast lane where life is exciting or highly pressured.

pull a fast one try to gain an unfair advantage by rapid action of some sort. informal

ℹ This phrase was originally early-20th-century US slang and is also found as *put over a fast one*.

2012 Bryan Caplan, Arnold Kling & David Henderson *Library of Economics & Liberty* The Chinese negotiator that got the British to take Hong Kong thought he'd pulled a fast one precisely because it was pretty much a barren island at the time.

thick and fast: *see* THICK.

fat

chew the fat (*or* rag) chat in a leisurely way, usually at length. informal

1986 Tom Clancy *Red Storm Rising* Four-star admirals didn't chew the fat with newly frocked commanders unless they had nothing better to do.

fat cat a wealthy and powerful person, especially a businessman or politician. informal, derogatory

2013 *CNN transcripts* Her parties ... would be Nobel Prize winners and the top people in, who contributed to our society. It wasn't as it is today, a lot of fat cats and fund raisers.

the fat is in the fire something has been said or done that is about to cause trouble or anger.

ℹ This expression refers to the sizzling and spitting caused by a spillage of cooking fat into an open flame. It was first used, in the mid 16th century, to indicate the complete failure of a plan or enterprise.

it isn't over till the fat lady sings: *see* LADY.

live off (*or* on) the fat of the land have the best of everything.

ℹ In Genesis 45:18, Pharaoh tells Joseph's brothers: 'ye shall eat the fat of the land'. *Fat* meaning 'the best part' or 'choicest produce' is now found only in this expression.

fate

a fate worse than death a terrible experience, especially that of seduction or rape.

2013 *New Statesman* After she escapes with Booker, going back to this life of nothing, of confinement, is a fate worse than death.

seal someone's fate make it inevitable that something unpleasant will happen to someone.

tempt fate: *see* TEMPT.

father

at your father's knee: *see* **at your mother's knee** *at* KNEE.

founding father: *see* FOUNDING.

how's your father sexual intercourse. British informal euphemistic, dated

ⓘ A pre-World War I music-hall catchphrase, *how's your father* was earlier used to mean 'nonsense' before acquiring its later sexual sense. It is used also to refer to a man's penis.

like father, like son a son's character or behaviour can be expected to resemble that of his father.

ⓘ The Latin version of this expression is *qualis pater, talis filius*. The female equivalent, *like mother, like daughter*, is based on Ezekiel 16:44: 'Behold, every one that useth proverbs shall use this proverb against thee, saying, As is the mother, so is the daughter'.

fatted

kill the fatted calf produce a lavish celebratory feast.

ⓘ The allusion is to the New Testament story of the prodigal son (Luke 15:11–32), in which the forgiving father orders his best calf to be killed in order to provide a feast to celebrate the return of his wayward son. *Fatted* is an archaic form of the verb *fat* meaning 'make or become fat'. Nowadays we use the forms *fatten* and *fattened*.

fault

— to a fault (of someone or something displaying a particular commendable quality) to an extent verging on excess.

1995 Bill Bryson *Notes from a Small Island* Anyway, that's the kind of place Bournemouth is—genteel to a fault and proud of it.

favour

curry favour: *see* CURRY.

do me a favour used as a way of expressing brusque dismissal or rejection of a remark or suggestion.

1993 Merv Grist *Life at the Tip* Do me a favour, Webley couldn't even pass a mug of tea across the counter last season, let alone pass a ball.

do someone a favour do something for someone as an act of kindness. British informal

fortune favours the brave: *see* FORTUNE.

favourite

favourite son a famous man who is particularly popular and praised for his achievements in his native area.

ⓘ In the USA, the term is used specifically of a person supported as a presidential candidate by delegates from the candidate's home state.

play favourites show favouritism towards someone or something. chiefly North American

fear

no fear used as an emphatic expression of denial or refusal. British informal

put the fear of God in (*or* into) someone cause someone to be very frightened.

without fear or favour not influenced by any consideration of the people involved in a situation; impartially.

2013 *Daily Telegraph* Around the world there are hundreds of millions of people who enjoy freedom, who are able to say what they want to say without fear or favour because of her.

feast

feast your eyes on gaze at with pleasure.

feast of reason intellectual talk.

ⓘ This expression comes from the poet Alexander Pope's description of congenial conversation in *Imitations of Horace*: 'The feast of reason and the flow of soul'.

feast or famine either too much of something or too little.

a ghost (*or* spectre) at the feast someone or something that brings gloom or sadness to an otherwise pleasant or celebratory occasion.

ⓘ The *ghost* or *spectre* of Banquo at the feast in Shakespeare's *Macbeth* is the most famous literary instance of this. There are other versions of the expression. *A skeleton at the feast* dates from the mid 19th century and probably refers to the ancient Egyptian practice of having the coffin of a dead person, adorned with a painted portrait of the deceased, present at a funeral banquet. *A death's head at the feast* alludes to the use of a *death's head* or skull as a *memento mori* (an object which serves as a reminder of death).

a movable feast an event which takes place at no regular time.

ⓘ In a religious context a movable feast is a feast day (especially Easter Day and the other Christian holy days whose dates are related to it) which does not occur on the same calendar date each year.

feather

birds of a feather: *see* BIRD.

a feather in your cap an achievement to be proud of.

ⓘ Originally (in the late 17th century), a feather in your cap was taken as a sign of foolishness. However, by the mid 18th century the phrase was acquiring its modern positive sense.

2009 *DVD Verdict* With Koch Lorber's new DVD release of the film, viewers may now determine whether the filmmaker's swan song represents another feather in his cap or an unfortunate footnote.

feather your (own) nest make money, usually illicitly and at someone else's expense.

ⓘ This phrase refers to the way in which some birds use feathers (their own or another bird's) to line the interior of their nest.

2012 *Daily Telegraph* The Duke ... has stirred latent antimonarchist sentiments in Spain with the suggestion that he used his royal influence to feather his own nest.

fine feathers: *see* FINE.

in fine (*or* high) feather in good spirits.

ⓘ The image here is of a bird in its breeding plumage, when it is in peak condition.

ruffle someone's feathers: *see* RUFFLE.

show the white feather: *see* WHITE.

spit feathers: *see* SPIT.

tar and feather: *see* TAR.

you could have knocked me down with a feather: *see* KNOCK.

federal

make a federal case out of something elevate something relatively trivial into a matter of great concern. US informal

fed up

fed up to the teeth (*or* back teeth) extremely annoyed.

feed

chicken feed: *see* CHICKEN.

feed the fishes ❶ be dead from drowning. ❷ vomit over the side of a boat. informal

feeding frenzy an episode of frantic competition or rivalry for something.

ⓘ The term originally denoted literally an aggressive and competitive group attack on prey by a number of sharks or piranhas.

2000 *Larry King Live* (CNN) Haven't we learned today the way this story has unfolded ... to guess that this was yet another successful Republican attempt to manipulate the political process and generate a media feeding frenzy which the media has again fallen for?

feel

ⓘ For idioms containing *feel*, see the entry for the main word in the idiom (for example, **feel no pain** at PAIN).

feelings

hard feelings: *see* HARD.

fell

in (*or* at) one fell swoop all in one go.

ⓘ This expression comes from Macduff's appalled reaction to the murder of his wife and children in Shakespeare's *Macbeth*: 'Oh hell-kite! ... All my pretty chickens, and their dam At one fell swoop?'

felt

make your presence felt: *see* PRESENCE.

fence

mend fences: *see* MEND.

over the fence unreasonable or unacceptable. Australian & New Zealand informal

1964 *Sydney Morning Herald* Some publications which unduly emphasize sex were 'entirely over the fence'.

rush your fences: *see* RUSH.

sit on the fence avoid making a decision or choice.

ⓘ The two sides of a fence are seen here as representing the two opposing or conflicting positions or interests involved in a particular debate or situation.

2012 Eric S. Raymond *Armed & Dangerous* Nobody is left in much doubt which way you stand on issues and this makes you an easier target for the haters/losers than somebody who sits on the fence most of the time.

fetch

fetch and carry go backwards and forwards bringing things to someone in a servile fashion.

ⓘ This phrase was originally used to refer to a dog retrieving game that had been shot.

fettle

in fine fettle in very good condition.

ⓘ *Fettle* was recorded in a mid-18th-century glossary of Lancashire dialect as meaning 'dress, case, condition'. It is now seldom found outside this phrase and its variants, which include *in good fettle* and *in high fettle*.

fever

fever pitch a state of extreme excitement.

2007 *Independent* Britain's lust for canine crossbreeds has reached fever pitch this year, as dog lovers have discovered the novel joys of the labradoodle.

f

few

few and far between scarce or infrequent.

have a few drink enough alcohol to be slightly drunk. informal

1991 James Kelman *Events in Yer Life* In fact it's hard to talk politics at all down there. I tend to keep my mouth shut. Unless I've had a few.

a man of few words: *see* WORD.

fiddle

a face as long as a fiddle: *see* FACE.

fiddle while Rome burns be concerned with relatively trivial matters while ignoring the serious or disastrous events going on around you.

ⓘ This phrase comes from the Roman biographer and historian Suetonius' description of the behaviour of the Roman emperor Nero during the great fire that destroyed much of Rome in AD 64.

fit as a fiddle in very good health.

hang up your fiddle retire from business; give up an undertaking. chiefly US

hang up your fiddle when you come home cease to be cheerful or entertaining when you are in the company of your family. chiefly US

on the fiddle engaged in cheating or swindling. informal

ⓘ *Fiddle* was late 19th-century US slang for a 'swindle'.

play second fiddle to take a subordinate role to someone or something.

ⓘ The expression derives from the respective roles of the fiddles or violins in an orchestra. Both *play first fiddle* and *play third fiddle* are much less common. The implication of *playing second fiddle* is often that it is somewhat demeaning.

1998 *Times* In *A Yank at Oxford* she played second fiddle to Vivien Leigh, which never got anyone very far.

there's many a good tune played on an old fiddle: *see* TUNE.

field

the Elysian fields: *see* ELYSIAN.

fresh fields and pastures new: *see* PASTURE.

from left field: *see* LEFT.

have a field day have full scope for action, success, or excitement, especially at the expense of others.

ⓘ Originally, a *field day* was literally a day on which military manoeuvres were held as an exercise.

2005 *DVD Verdict* Hitchcock would have had a field day with this story—he would have injected a far more sinister sensibility.

hold the field remain the most important.

1991 *Twentieth Century British History* What analyses of AIDS policies hold the field?

play the field indulge in a series of sexual relationships without committing yourself to anyone. informal

1936 Louis Lefko *Public Relations* He hasn't any steady. He plays the field—blonde, brunette, or what have you.

fierce

something fierce to a great and almost overwhelming extent; intensely or furiously. North American informal

1986 Monica Hughes *Blaine's Way* Maud had trapped my right arm against the chair and it was getting pins and needles something fierce.

fifteen

famous for fifteen minutes: *see* FAMOUS.

fifth

fifth column an organized group of people sympathizing with and working for the enemy within a country at war or otherwise under attack.

ⓘ *Fifth column* is a translation of the Spanish phrase *quinta columna*: during the Spanish Civil War, an extra body of supporters was claimed by General Mola as being within Madrid when he besieged the city with four columns of Nationalist forces in 1936.

take (*or* plead) the fifth (in the USA) exercise the right of refusing to answer questions in order to avoid incriminating yourself.

ℹ The reference in this phrase is to Article V of the ten original amendments (1791) to the Constitution of the United States, which states that 'no person . . . shall be compelled in any criminal case to be a witness against himself'.

2013 *CNN transcripts* We're still awaiting Lois Lerner's testimony before a House Oversight Committee. She's the IRS official in charge of the unit that oversaw tax exempt status. She is expected to plead the fifth.

fig

in full fig wearing the smart clothes appropriate for an event or occasion. informal

ℹ *Fig* in the sense of 'dress or equipment' is now used only in this phrase, which was first recorded in the mid 19th century.

not give (*or* care) a fig not have the slightest concern about.

ℹ *Fig* was formerly used in a variety of expressions to signify something regarded as valueless or contemptible.

fight

fight fire with fire use the weapons or tactics of your enemy or opponent, even if you find them distasteful.

2011 *BusinessPundit* Maybe it's the idea of 'fighting fire with fire', but using malaria to fight syphilis sounds like burning down your house just to kill the roaches.

fight the good fight do your best always to live up to the tenets of your religion, especially Christianity.

ℹ The expression originated in the Bible: '*Fight the good fight* of faith, lay hold on eternal life' (1 Timothy 6:12).

fight like cat and dog: *see* CAT.

fight or flight the instinctive physiological response to a threatening situation, which readies you either to resist violently or to run away.

fight shy of be unwilling to undertake or become involved with.

2013 *Daily Telegraph* If you are going to have a review of the police, is a Royal Commission the best vehicle? Governments over the years have fought shy of them.

a fight to the finish: *see* FINISH.

fight tooth and nail: *see* TOOTH.

fight your corner: *see* CORNER.

have a dog in the fight: *see* DOG.

live to fight another day: *see* LIVE.

pick a fight: *see* PICK.

figure

cut a — figure present yourself or appear in a particular way.

1994 *Vanity Fair* David has cut a dashing figure on the international social scene.

figure of fun a person who is considered ridiculous.

1990 Richard Critchfield *Among the British* [Reagan] was the first American leader in my lifetime who was widely regarded over here as a figure of fun.

go figure! work it out for yourself (used to suggest that the conclusion to be drawn about something is obvious). North American informal

2014 Shaun Attwood *Jon's Jail Journal* The legislative record from that time frame clearly shows legislators wanted a paved highway to facilitate the movement of illegal alcohol through Arizona. Go figure. All I can say about this is, only in Arizona.

file

rank and file: *see* RANK.

fill

fill the bill: *see* BILL.

fill your boots take full advantage of an opportunity to benefit yourself. British informal

2011 *New Statesman* The banking crisis, MPs' expenses. Journalists hacking phones. From them all a something for nothing culture. Take what you can. Fill your boots. Who cares as long as you can get away with it.

fill someone's shoes (*or* boots) take over someone's function or duties and fulfil them satisfactorily. informal

have had your fill of have had as much or many of something as you want or can bear.

final

the final straw: *see* **the last straw** *at* STRAW.

find

find your feet ❶ stand up and become able to walk. ❷ establish yourself in a particular situation or enterprise.

❷ **1990 V. S. Naipaul** *India* In Calcutta he stayed with some friend or distant relation until he found his feet.

find God experience a religious conversion or awakening.

find it in your heart to do something allow or force yourself to do something.

1988 Richard Rayner *Los Angeles Without a Map* Could you find it in your heart to lend me, say, $2,500?

scratch a — and find a —: *see* SCRATCH.

speak as you find: *see* SPEAK.

finder

finders keepers (losers weepers) used, often humorously, to assert that whoever finds something by chance is entitled to keep it (and the person who lost it will just have to lament its loss). informal

ⓘ This expression has been widely used since the early 19th century, although the idea goes back much further and is found in the work of the Roman dramatist Plautus. A variant sometimes heard is *findings keepings*.

fine

chance would be a fine thing: *see* CHANCE.

cut it (*or* things) fine allow a very small margin of something, usually time.

fine and dandy excellent. informal

2013 *New Zealand Herald* On the surface everything looks fine and dandy, but if you look more closely you find that certain sectors—steel and cement for example—are not doing well at all.

fine feathers beautiful clothes.

ⓘ The proverb *fine feathers make fine birds*, meaning that an eye-catching appearance makes a person seem beautiful or impressive, has been known in England since the late 19th century. It is recorded in the early 16th century in French as *les belles plumes font les beaux oiseaux*.

in fine feather: *see* FEATHER.

in fine fettle: *see* FETTLE.

not to put too fine a point on it to speak bluntly.

one fine day at some unspecified or unknown time.

1990 Wilfred Sheed *Essays in Disguise* If Sydney blew away one fine day, Melbourne could easily take its place as a center of mateship and conspicuous democracy.

fine art

have (*or* get) something down to a fine art achieve a high level of skill, facility, or accomplishment in some activity through experience.

finer

the finer points of the more complex or detailed aspects of.

finest

your finest hour the time of your greatest success.

1940 W. S. Churchill *Speech to House of Commons* Let us therefore brace ourselves to that duty, and so bear ourselves that, if the British Commonwealth and its Empire lasts for a thousand years, men will still say, 'This was their finest hour'.

—'s finest the police of a specified city. North American informal

2000 Nelson DeMille *The Lion's Game* As I indicated, I was a homicide detective, one of New York's Finest.

fine-tooth comb

with a fine-tooth comb (of examination or analysis) extremely thorough and detailed.

ⓘ A literal fine-tooth comb is one with narrow teeth that are close together.

2011 *Daily Telegraph* Despite the fine-tooth comb applied to the evidence four years ago by the press ..., fascinating new details emerge from her account.

finger

be all fingers and thumbs be clumsy or awkward in your actions. British informal

ⓘ In the mid 16th century this idea was expressed in the form *each finger is a thumb*. *All thumbs* developed in the 19th century as an expression indicating a complete lack of dexterity.

burn your fingers (*or* get your fingers burned/burnt) suffer unpleasant consequences as a result of your actions.

2014 *Derby Telegraph* Don't play games in love unless you want to get your fingers burned.

count something on the fingers of one hand: *see* COUNT.

cross your fingers: *see* CROSS.

get (*or* pull) your finger out cease prevaricating and start to act. British informal

give someone the finger make a gesture with the middle finger raised as an obscene sign of contempt. North American informal

ℹ Since 1976, this gesture has sometimes been called the *Rockefeller Gesture* after Nelson Rockefeller was seen making it on a news film.

have a finger in every pie be involved in a large and varied number of activities or enterprises.

have a finger in the pie be involved in a matter, especially in an annoyingly interfering way.

have your fingers in the till: *see* TILL.

have (*or* keep) your finger on the pulse be aware of all the latest news or developments.

have green fingers: *see* GREEN.

have more something in your little finger than someone else has in their whole body have immeasurably more of a particular quality than the other named person has. informal

2005 *The Register* You, sir, are no Steve Jobs who, I suggest, has more business acumen in his little finger than you have in your whole body.

lay a finger on touch someone, usually with the intention of harming them.

1993 Tony Parker *May the Lord in His Mercy be Kind to Belfast* The one thing I'll say about my husband is he never laid a finger on the children and he never hit me in front of them.

let something slip through your fingers: *see* SLIP.

lift a finger: *see* LIFT.

point the finger openly accuse someone or apportion blame.

2004 *Guardian* This, of course, leads many to point the finger at schools.

put something on the long finger postpone consideration of something; put something off. Irish

put the finger on inform against someone to the authorities. informal

put your finger in the dyke: *see* DYKE.

put your finger on identify something exactly.

1988 Glenn Patterson *Burning Your Own* There was something about the dinette that struck him as peculiar, but he couldn't quite put his finger on it.

snap (*or* click) your fingers make a sharp clicking sound by bending the last joint of the middle finger against the thumb and suddenly releasing it, typically in order to attract attention in a peremptory way or to accompany the beat of music.

stick to someone's fingers (of money) be embezzled by a person. informal

sticky fingers: *see* STICKY.

twist (*or* wind *or* wrap) someone around your little finger have the ability to make someone do whatever you want.

work your fingers to the bone: *see* BONE.

your fingers itch you are longing or impatient to do something.

2013 *Express* If you are saddled with chalky soil and your fingers itch to take on rhododendrons, camellias, pieris or other lime-haters, the solution is simple.

fingertip

at your fingertips (especially of information) readily available.

by your fingertips only with difficulty; barely.

2009 Iain Pears *Stone's Fall* A few houses were owned by shopkeepers or clerks desperately clinging to respectability by their fingertips.

to your fingertips totally; completely.

1991 *Sun* McMahon, a professional to his fingertips, gave it his best shot even though an injury at this delicate stage could have sabotaged the last big move of his career.

finish

a fight to the finish a fight, contest, or match which only ends with the complete defeat of one of the parties involved.

finished

the finished article something that is complete and ready for use.

fire

a ball of fire: *see* BALL.

a baptism of fire: *see* BAPTISM.

breathe fire be fiercely angry.

ⓘ The implied comparison in this expression is with a fire-breathing dragon.

catch fire ❶ begin to burn. ❷ become interesting or exciting; flourish.

❷ **2015** *Wall Street Journal* Dozens of gender-neutral pronouns have been put forth over the years, including 'thon', 'xe' and 'ze', but all have failed to catch fire.

draw someone's fire attract hostility or criticism away from a more important target.

the fat is in the fire: *see* FAT.

fight fire with fire: *see* FIGHT.

fire and brimstone the supposed torments of hell.

ⓘ In the Bible, fire and brimstone are the means of divine punishment for the wicked (see, for example, Genesis 19:24 or Revelation 21:8). *Brimstone* (from the Old English word *brynstān* meaning 'burning stone') is an archaic word for 'sulphur' and is now rarely found outside this phrase.

fire blanks (of a man) be infertile. informal

ⓘ The expression is based on the idea of a gun firing blank cartridges.

fire in the (*or* your) belly a powerful sense of ambition or determination.

2010 *Crisis* She's walking proof that with a little fire in the belly and support, dreams for success come true.

go through fire (and water) face any peril.

ⓘ This phrase originally referred to the medieval practice of trial by ordeal, which could take the form of making an accused person hold or walk on red-hot iron or of throwing them into water.

hang fire: *see* HANG.

have many irons in the fire: *see* IRON.

hire and fire: *see* HIRE.

light a fire under someone stimulate someone to work or act more quickly or enthusiastically. North American

no smoke without fire: *see* SMOKE.

out of the frying pan into the fire: *see* FRYING.

play with fire take foolish risks.

pull someone's chestnuts out of the fire: *see* CHESTNUT.

set the world on fire: *see* **set the world alight** *at* WORLD.

under fire ❶ being shot at. ❷ being rigorously criticized.

❷ **2014** *Daily Telegraph* The newspaper of Italy's anti-immigrant Northern League party has come under fire for a new feature listing the daily whereabouts of the country's first black cabinet minister.

where's the fire? used to ask someone why they are in such a hurry or in a state of agitation. informal

1963 J. F. Straker *Final Witness* 'Where's the fire, dear boy?' he drawled. 'Do we really have to run for it?'

fireman

visiting fireman: *see* VISITING.

firing

firing on all (four) cylinders working or functioning at a peak level.

ⓘ This expression is a metaphor from an internal-combustion engine: a cylinder is said to be firing when the fuel inside it is ignited.

2004 *Natural Health* Winter bugs usually strike when it's least convenient, so ensuring your immune system is firing on all cylinders is essential.

in the firing line in a situation where you are subject to criticism or blame because of your responsibilities or position.

2001 *Sunday Business Post* Once again the International Monetary Fund is in the firing line after the financial collapse in Argentina.

firm

be on firm ground be sure of your facts or secure in your position, especially in a discussion.

a firm hand strict discipline or control.

ⓘ Often used in the the fuller form, *a firm hand on the reins* (or *the tiller*), this phrase is employing the image of controlling a horse by using the reins (or a boat using the tiller).

the Old Firm: *see* OLD.

first

at first blush: *see* BLUSH.

at first hand directly or from personal experience.

cast the first stone: *see* STONE.

first among equals: *see* EQUAL.

first blood: *see* BLOOD.

first come, first served used to indicate that people will be dealt with strictly in the order in which they arrive or apply.

first off as a first point; first of all. informal

2010 Jon McGregor *Even the Dogs* There's a patch in the underpass we'll try first off, ... should get enough for the first bag of the day.

first past the post ❶ (of a contestant, especially a horse, in a race) winning a race by being the first to reach the finishing line. ❷ denoting an electoral system whereby a candidate or party is selected by achievement of a simple majority. British

first thing early in the morning; before anything else.

first things first important matters should be attended to before anything else.

ⓘ *First Things First* was the title of a book by George Jackson, subtitled 'Addresses to young men' (1894).

first up ❶ first of all. ❷ at the first attempt. Australian

get to first base: *see* BASE.

in the first flush: *see* FLUSH.

of the first order (*or* magnitude) used to denote something that is excellent or considerable of its kind.

ⓘ In astronomy, magnitude is a measure of the degree of brightness of a star. Stars *of the first magnitude* are the most brilliant.

of the first water extreme or unsurpassed of its kind.

ⓘ If a diamond or other gem is *of the first water* it possesses the greatest possible degree of brilliance and transparency. In this metaphorical use, however, the phrase often refers to someone or something regarded as undesirable, e.g. *a bore of the first water*.

fish

big fish: *see* **big cheese** *at* BIG.

a big fish in a small (*or* little) pond a person seen as important and influential only within the limited scope of a small organization or group.

cry stinking fish: *see* CRY.

a different kettle of fish: *see* KETTLE.

drink like a fish: *see* DRINK.

feed the fishes: *see* FEED.

fish in troubled waters make a profit out of trouble or upheaval.

fish or cut bait stop vacillating and decide to act on or disengage from something. North American informal

a fish out of water a person who is in a completely unsuitable environment or situation.

1991 Margaret Weiss *King's Test* He realized that he was a fish out of water—a pilot in the midst of marines.

have other (*or* bigger) fish to fry have other or more important matters to attend to.

1985 Gregory Benford *Artifact* Kontos can throw a fit back there, chew the rug, anything—it won't matter. His government has bigger fish to fry.

like shooting fish in a barrel done very easily.

1992 Laurie Colwin *Home Cooking* I fear that's the urgency of greed. Picking cultivated berries is like shooting fish in a barrel.

neither fish nor fowl (nor good red herring) of indefinite character and difficult to identify or classify.

ⓘ This expression arose with reference to dietary laws formerly laid down by the Church during periods of fasting or abstinence.

a pretty kettle of fish: *see* KETTLE.

a queer fish: *see* QUEER.

soup and fish: *see* SOUP.

there are plenty more fish in the sea used to console someone whose romantic relationship has ended by pointing out that there are many other people with whom they may have a successful relationship in the future.

ⓘ This expression alludes to the proverb *there are as good fish in the sea as ever came out of it*.

fishing

a fishing expedition a search or investigation undertaken with the hope, though not the stated purpose, of discovering information.

2013 Idiot Savant *No Right Turn* The police broke the law here, using a search warrant essentially to mount a fishing expedition rather than seize specified items of evidence.

fist

an iron fist in a velvet glove: *see* **an iron hand in a velvet glove** *at* IRON.

the mailed fist: *see* MAILED.

make a — fist of do something to a specified degree of success. informal

2013 *Daily Telegraph* Building a business is tough, but he was making a good fist of it and there were always plenty of customers in there.

make money hand over fist: *see* HAND.

fit

give someone a fit greatly shock, frighten, or anger someone. informal

in fits in a state of hysterical amusement. informal

in (*or* by) fits and starts with irregular bursts of activity.

ⓘ For other idioms containing *fit*, see the entry for the main word in the idiom (for example, **fit to bust** at BUST).

five

the big five: *see* BIG.

bunch of fives: *see* BUNCH.

five-finger discount an act of shoplifting. North American informal

give someone five slap someone's palm as a gesture of celebration or greeting. informal, chiefly North American

ⓘ *Five* refers to the five fingers of the hand.

know how many beans make five: *see* BEAN.

nine to five: *see* NINE.

take five take a short break; relax.

ⓘ *Five* here is short for 'a five-minute break'.

fix

fix someone's wagon bring about someone's downfall; spoil someone's chances of success. US

1951 Truman Capote *The Grass Harp* She said her brother would fix my wagon, which he did . . . I've still got a scar where he hit me.

get a fix on ❶ determine the position of (an aircraft, ship, etc.) by visual or radio bearings or astronomical observation. ❷ assess or determine the nature or facts of; obtain a clear understanding of. informal

❷ **2013** *Knowledge at Wharton* It is difficult to get a fix on the number of taxis in India. Estimates vary anywhere from 500,000 to around one million.

if it ain't broke don't fix it: *see* BROKE.

flag

fly the flag ❶ (of a ship) be registered to a particular country and sail under its flag. ❷ represent or demonstrate support for your country, political party, or organization, especially when you are abroad.

ⓘ In sense 2, the forms *show the flag*, *carry the flag*, and *wave the flag* are also found.

❷ **1996** *Hello!* She flew the flag for British tennis in the Eighties.

keep the flag flying ❶ represent your country or organization, especially when abroad. ❷ show continued commitment to something, especially in the face of adversity.

ⓘ This expression comes from the practice in naval warfare of lowering the flag on a defeated ship to signify a wish to surrender.

put the flags (*or* flag) out celebrate publicly.

show the flag (of a naval vessel) make an official visit to a foreign port, especially as a show of strength.

wrap (*or* drape) yourself in the flag make an excessive show of your patriotism, especially for political ends. chiefly North American

2011 *Daily Telegraph* From Gordon Brown wrapping himself gratuitously in the flag in 2006, to David Cameron promising to put the 'Great' back into Great Britain—when politicos start talking about patriotism the public's response runs from groan to cringe.

flagpole

run something up the flagpole test the popularity of a new idea or proposal.

ⓘ The idea behind this expression is of hoisting a particular flag to see if it provokes the positive response of a salute.

flame

fan the flames: *see* FAN.

like a moth to the flame: *see* MOTH.

an old flame a former lover. informal

shoot someone or something down in flames: *see* SHOOT.

flapping

someone's ears are flapping: *see* EAR.

flash

flash in the pan a thing or person whose sudden but brief success is not repeated or repeatable.

🛈 This phrase developed from the operation of a flintlock or matchlock firearm, when the flash from the priming gunpowder in the 'pan' failed to ignite the charge in the barrel, so that the gun did not fire.

2014 *New Statesman* Some have been celebrities for a long time, drawing the devoted to kiss their knees (more of that later). Others are mere flashes in the pan, so to speak.

quick as a flash (especially of a person's response or reaction) happening or made very quickly.

flat

fall flat fail completely to produce the intended or expected effect.

fall flat on your face ❶ fall over forwards. ❷ fail in an embarrassingly obvious way.

flat as a pancake: *see* PANCAKE.

flat as a tack in very low spirits or lacking in energy. informal

🛈 The idea underlying the expression is of a tack that has been hammered in so that none of it protrudes.

flat out ❶ as fast or as hard as possible. informal ❷ without hesitation or reservation; unequivocally. chiefly North American

❶ **2013** *Daily Telegraph* In April this year another commissioner, Stephen Betts, who oversees the Norfolk force, was forced to apologise after saying skilled drivers should be allowed to drive 'flat out' on the motorway.

❷ **2013 Bryan Caplan, Arnold Kling & David Henderson** *Library of Economics & Liberty—Econlog* That's just a flat false and ugly accusation, based on a fundamental misunderstanding of the concept of the government's responsibility. It is actually quite appalling Yglesias would insinuate or flat out state otherwise.

in (*or* into) a flat spin in (*or* into) a state of agitation or panic. British informal

🛈 A flat spin is literally an aerobatic manoeuvre in which an aircraft descends in tight circles while remaining almost horizontal.

2004 *BBC Popular Music Reviews* Not only is this album rich in highly slanderous spurts, there is also enough copyright violation here to send any record company lawyer in to a flat spin.

on the flat ❶ on level ground as opposed to uphill. ❷ (of a horse race) on an open course as opposed to one with jumps.

that's flat used to indicate that you have reached a decision and will not be persuaded to change your mind. informal

flat-footed

catch someone flat-footed take someone by surprise or at a disadvantage. informal

🛈 The opposite of *flat-footed* in this metaphorical sense is **on your toes** (*see* TOE).

2013 *CNN Transcripts* We live in a world that is changing rapidly. And in both the United States and in Mexico, we can't be caught flat-footed as the world advances.

flatter

flatter to deceive encourage on insufficient grounds and cause disappointment.

1913 *Field* Two furlongs from home Maiden Erlegh looked most dangerous, but he flattered only to deceive.

flatting

go flatting leave the family home to live in a flat. Australian & New Zealand

flavour

flavour of the month someone or something that enjoys a short period of great popularity; the current fashion.

🛈 This phrase originated in a marketing campaign in American ice-cream parlours in the 1940s, when a particular flavour of ice cream would be singled out each month for special promotion.

flea

fit as a flea in very good health.

🛈 The phrase makes reference to a flea's agility.

a flea in your ear a sharp reproof.

🛈 Formerly *a flea in your ear* also meant something that agitates or alarms you, as does the French phrase *avoir la puce à l'oreille*. Nowadays, it is often found in the phrases *give someone a flea in the ear* or *send someone away with a flea in their ear*.

flesh

flesh and blood used to refer to a person's physical body and their needs and frailties, often as opposed to their mind or soul.

f

2010 *The Hindu Literary Review* A touch of meanness would go a long way in redeeming him from being a victim to a flesh and blood character we can empathise with.

your (own) flesh and blood near relatives; close family.

go the way of all flesh die or come to an end.

ℹ In the Authorized Version of the Bible *all flesh* is used to refer to all human and animal life.

in the flesh in person rather than via a telephone, film, article, etc.

make someone's flesh creep (*or* crawl) cause someone to feel fear, horror, or disgust.

press (the) flesh: *see* PRESS.

put flesh on (the bones of) something add more details to something which exists only in a draft or outline form.

a thorn in someone's flesh: *see* **a thorn in someone's side** *at* THORN.

the world, the flesh, and the devil: *see* WORLD.

your pound of flesh: *see* POUND.

flex

flex your muscles give a show of strength or power.

2012 *New Zealand Herald* A pioneer of IT outsourcing, the Bangalore-based firm has clients in 32 countries across the globe and is now looking to flex its muscles in the South Pacific.

flick

give someone the flick (*or* get the flick) reject someone (*or* be rejected) in a casual or offhand way. informal, chiefly Australian

flight

fight or flight: *see* FIGHT.

in full flight escaping as rapidly as possible.

1938 *Life* A week later General Cedillo was reported in full flight through the bush, with Federal troops hot on his heels.

fling

fling your cap over the windmill(s): *see* WINDMILL.

flip

flip someone the bird: *see* BIRD.

flip burgers work as a cook in a fast-food restaurant. North American informal

flip your lid suddenly go mad or lose your self-control. informal

ℹ A chiefly US variant of this phrase is *flip your wig*.

flit

do a moonlight flit: *see* MOONLIGHT.

float

float someone's boat appeal to or excite someone, especially sexually. informal

flog

flog a dead horse waste energy on a lost cause or unalterable situation.

1971 *Cabinet Maker & Retail Furnisher* If this is the case, we are flogging a dead horse in still trying to promote the scheme.

flood

be in full flood ❶ (of a river) be swollen and overflowing its banks. ❷ have gained momentum; be at the height of activity.

❷ **1991** *Journal of Theological Studies* There is too much detail for comfort... which is somewhat confusing when exposition is in full flood.

floodgates

open the floodgates remove the last restraint holding back an outpouring of something powerful or substantial.

2014 *Daily Telegraph* Many MPs fear that the charter, which sets out the right to marry and found a family and the right to fair treatment at work, will open the floodgates to a wave of human rights-based legal actions.

floor

cross the floor: *see* CROSS.

from the floor (of a speech or question) delivered by an individual member at a meeting or assembly, rather than by a representative on the platform.

take the floor ❶ begin to dance on a dance floor. ❷ speak in a debate or assembly.

wipe the floor with: *see* WIPE.

flotsam

flotsam and jetsam useless or discarded objects.

ℹ *Flotsam* refers to the wreckage of a ship or its cargo found floating on or washed up by the sea, while *jetsam* is unwanted material thrown overboard from a ship and washed ashore. The two nouns are seldom used independently, almost always appearing together in this phrase.

flow

ebb and flow: *see* EBB.

go with the flow be relaxed; accept a situation. informal

ℹ The image here is of going with the current of a stream rather than trying to swim against it.

2006 *Place in Sun* Basically, running a business out here is very complicated. It's important, though, that you go with the flow, don't argue and don't question things too much.

in full flow ❶ talking fluently and easily and showing no sign of stopping. ❷ performing vigorously and enthusiastically.

flower

the flower of — the finest individuals out of a number of people or things.

ℹ Middle and early modern English did not recognize the modern distinction in spelling and sense between *flower* and *flour*, and the earliest instances of this expression relate to the sense that in modern English would be spelt *flour*, referring to the finest part of the wheat.

2011 *New York Times* In this hecatomb along the minor rivers of Flanders and Picardy, the British people lost the cream of their working class and the flower of their aristocracy.

hearts and flowers: *see* HEART.

flown

the bird has flown: *see* BIRD.

fluff

bit of fluff: *see* BIT.

flush

a busted flush: *see* BUST.

in the first flush in a state of freshness and vigour.

ℹ The exact origins of *flush* as a noun are unknown; early senses share the idea of a sudden rush or abundance of something (e.g. water, growth of grass, or emotion).

1997 Tom Petsinis *The French Mathematician* A month ago, in the first flush of enthusiasm... I tackled the classic problem of trisecting an angle using only a compass and straightedge.

flutter

flutter the dovecotes alarm, startle, or upset a sedate or conventionally minded community.

ℹ This expression may come from Shakespeare's *Coriolanus*: 'like an eagle in a dove-cote, I Fluttered your Volscians in Corioli'. Compare with **put the cat among the pigeons** (*at* CAT).

1992 *Daily Telegraph* It is however the arrival of Michael Heseltine at the DTI that will flutter the dovecotes most of all.

flutter your eyelashes open and close your eyes rapidly in a coyly flirtatiousmanner.

fly

as the crow flies: *see* CROW.

die (*or* drop) like flies die or collapse in large numbers.

drink with the flies drink alone. Australian & New Zealand informal

1963 D. Whitington *Mile Pegs* 'Have a drink?' the larrikin invited. 'Or do you prefer drinking with the flies?'

fly the coop make your escape. informal

2013 *New York Times* Leonard is the product of a wild imagination and a troubled home. His burned-out rocker father flew the coop some years ago; his mother, a fashion designer, is so checked out she doesn't remember his birthday.

fly the flag: *see* FLAG.

fly high be very successful; prosper.

ℹ The noun *high-flyer* (or *high-flier*) meaning 'a successful and ambitious person' developed from this phrase in the mid 17th century.

a fly in amber a curious relic of the past, preserved into the present.

ℹ The image is of the fossilized bodies of insects which are often found preserved in amber.

fly in the face of be openly at variance with (what is usual or expected).

a fly in the ointment a minor irritation or other factor that spoils the success or enjoyment of something.

ⓘ This expression alludes to Ecclesiastes 10:1: 'Dead flies cause the ointment of the apothecary to send forth a stinking savour'.

2013 *New Zealand Herald* The X2 wins on a design basis, and its battery life led the pack hands down thanks to the additional battery in its keyboard dock. About the only fly in the ointment is the lack of any real processing muscle.

fly a kite try something out to test opinion. informal

ⓘ A historical sense of this phrase was 'raise money by an accommodation bill', meaning to raise money on credit, and this sense of testing public opinion of your creditworthiness gave rise to the current figurative sense. The US phrase *go fly a kite!* means 'go away!'.

fly the nest (of a young person) leave their parent's home to set up home elsewhere. informal

ⓘ The image here is of a young bird's departure from its nest on becoming able to fly. Compare with **empty nester** (*at* EMPTY).

fly off the handle lose your temper suddenly and unexpectedly. informal

ⓘ This expression uses the image of a loose head of an axe flying off its handle while the axe is being swung.

a fly on the wall an unnoticed observer of a particular situation.

ⓘ This expression is often used as an adjective, as in a *fly-on-the-wall documentary*, where it refers to a film-making technique in which events are merely observed and presented realistically with minimum interference, rather than acted out under direction.

the fur will fly: *see* FUR.

let fly attack physically or verbally.

2013 Mark Heuring *Mr Dilettante* Some things have changed—with increased maturity, she's less likely to let fly with a cutting remark than she was then.

like a blue-arsed fly in an extremely hectic or frantic way. British vulgar slang

ⓘ The 'blue-arsed fly' referred to is a bluebottle, well known for its frenetic buzzing about.

1998 Rebecca Ray *A Certain Age* I'm not going to run around like a blue-arsed fly pandering to you and your bloody room, alright?

on the fly ❶ while in motion. ❷ while busy or active. ❸ (of an addition or modification in computing) carried out during the running of a program without interrupting the run.

pigs might fly: *see* PIG.

there are no flies on — the person mentioned is very quick and astute.

ⓘ Early instances of this expression suggest that it originated with reference to cattle who were so active that no flies settled on them. The phrase was noted in the mid 19th century as being very common in Australia as a general expression of approbation. In the USA it could also be used to convey that the person in question was of superior breeding or behaved honestly.

wouldn't hurt (*or* harm) a fly used to emphasize how inoffensive and harmless a person or animal is.

flyer

take a flyer take a chance. chiefly North American

1998 *Times* Or we [i.e. journalists] can take a flyer: share a hunch and risk coming a cropper.

flying

keep the flag flying: *see* FLAG.

with flying colours with distinction.

ⓘ Formerly, in military contexts, *flying colours* meant having the regimental flag flying as a sign of success or victory; a conquered army usually had to *lower* (or *strike*) *its colours*.

Flynn

be in like Flynn seize an opportunity; be successful. Australian

ⓘ The *Flynn* referred to in this expression is Errol Flynn (1909–59), the Australian-born actor, who had a reputation as a notable playboy.

1987 Kathy Lette *Girls' Night Out* Russell brightened. 'Really?' I'm in, he thought to himself. I'm in like Flynn. 'You really *see* it that way?' He slid his arms around her.

foam

foam at the mouth: *see* **froth at the mouth** *at* FROTH.

fog

in a fog in a state of perplexity; unable to think clearly or understand something.

foggiest

not have the foggiest (idea *or* notion) have no idea at all. informal, chiefly British

fold

return to the fold come back to the community of beliefs or principles you originally belonged to, having previously repudiated it.

ⓘ The image is of a lost sheep returning to its fold. It can be expressed in various other wordings (e.g. 'They welcomed him *back to the fold*').

2004 *The Cherwell Magazine Online* Blair's sudden rush to get it onto the statute books in time for the 2005 election is a shrewd political manoeuvre designed to encourage the party faithful, many of whom were alienated over Iraq, to return to the fold.

follow

follow in someone's footsteps: *see* FOOTSTEP.

follow your nose ❶ trust to your instincts. ❷ move along guided by your sense of smell. ❸ go straight ahead.

follow suit ❶ (in bridge, whist, and other card games) play a card of the suit led. ❷ conform to another's actions.

❷ **2002** *History of Scotland* The first Earl of Huntly was a Gordon by adoption. Many other lesser men followed suit, assuming the surname of so successful a family.

food

food for thought something that warrants serious consideration or reflection.

food for worms: *see* WORM.

fool

a fool and his money are soon parted a foolish person spends money carelessly and will soon be penniless. proverb

fools rush in where angels fear to tread people without good sense or judgement will have no hesitation in tackling a situation that even the wisest would avoid. proverb

be no (*or* nobody's) fool be a shrewd or prudent person.

fool's gold something deceptively attractive and promising in appearance.

ⓘ *Fool's gold* is the name popularly given to any yellow metal, such as pyrite or chalcopyrite, that may be mistaken for gold.

2003 *Nation* Many good people have been euchred into falling for the current fool's gold—politicians and lobbyists calling for 'universal healthcare'.

more fool — used as an exclamation indicating that a specified person is unwise to behave in such a way.

2002 *Pride* Any self-respecting female should be wise enough to steer clear of Romeo rats and, if you don't, then more fool you.

not suffer fools gladly: *see* SUFFER.

there's no fool like an old fool the foolish behaviour of an older person seems especially foolish as they are expected to think and act more sensibly than a younger one. proverb

you could have fooled me! used to express cynicism or doubt about an assertion. informal

foot

cold feet: *see* COLD.

dead on your feet: *see* DEAD.

die on your feet: *see* DIE.

dig in your feet: *see* **dig in your heels** *at* DIG.

drag your feet: *see* DRAG.

fall (*or* land) on your feet achieve a fortunate outcome to a difficult situation.

ⓘ This expression comes from cats' supposed ability always to land on their feet, even if they fall or jump from a very high point.

2011 *The Age* (Melbourne) The only downside is that you will be alright, won't you, you will fall on your feet while rest of us deal with the economic holocaust you unleashed.

feet first ❶ with the feet in front. ❷ dead, as in a coffin.

find your feet: *see* FIND.

foot the bill: *see* BILL.

from head to foot: *see* **from head to toe** *at* HEAD.

get itchy feet: *see* ITCHY.

get (*or* start) off on the right (*or* wrong) foot make a good (*or* bad) start at something, especially a task or relationship.

2003 George Best *Scoring at Half-time* Ron got off on the wrong foot, I fear, when he immediately began to refer to Denis Law as 'the old man'.

get your feet under the table establish yourself securely in a new situation. chiefly British

get your feet wet begin to participate in an activity.

have the ball at your feet: *see* BALL.

have feet of clay have a fatal flaw in a character that is otherwise powerful or admirable.

ℹ This expression alludes to the biblical account of a magnificent statue seen in a dream by Nebuchadnezzar, king of Babylon. It was constructed from fine metals, all except for its feet which were made of clay; when these were smashed, the whole statue was brought down and destroyed. Daniel interprets this to signify a future kingdom that will be 'partly strong, and partly broken', and will eventually fall (Daniel 2:31–5).

have a foot in both camps have an interest or stake in two parties or sides without commitment to either.

1992 *Community Care* As EWOs [Education Welfare Officers] we have a foot in both camps. We work with the children and their families and the school and bring the two together.

have (*or* get) a foot (*or* toe) in the door have (*or* gain) a first introduction to a profession or organization or, more broadly, a (first) chance of ultimately achieving what you want.

have one foot in the grave be near death through old age or illness. informal, often humorous

have (*or* keep) your feet on the ground be (*or* remain) practical and sensible.

have something at your feet have something in your power or command.

have two left feet: *see* LEFT.

keep your feet manage not to fall.

my foot! used to express strong contradiction or disbelief. informal

the patter of tiny feet: *see* PATTER.

put your best foot forward embark on an undertaking with as much speed, effort, and determination as possible.

put your feet up take a rest, especially when reclining with your feet raised and supported.

put foot hurry up; get a move on. South African informal

put your foot down ❶ adopt a firm policy when faced with opposition or disobedience. ❷ make a motor vehicle go faster by pressing the accelerator pedal with your foot. British informal

put your foot in it (*or* put your foot in your mouth) say or do something tactless or embarrassing; commit a blunder or indiscretion. informal

2014 *North Devon Journal* He … has been a master of faux pas (the act of putting your foot in it, in layman's terms) throughout his life.

put a foot wrong make any mistake in performing an action.

2012 *Canberra Times* The royal couple never put a foot wrong in the style stakes.

be rushed (*or* run) off your feet be kept extremely busy. informal

set foot on (*or* **in**) enter; go into.

ℹ The phrase is usually used in negatives or questions.

shake the dust off your feet: *see* SHAKE.

shoot yourself in the foot: *see* SHOOT.

sit at someone's feet: *see* SIT.

six feet under: *see* SIX.

someone's feet won't touch the ground someone will be summarily and vigorously punished or ejected. informal

2010 *Daily Telegraph* What about the 'doomsday' scenario, which must have been made much more likely after the PM's horrendous gaffe yesterday, where Labour don't just lose but lose badly? In that case, Mr Brown's feet won't touch the ground and open warfare will break out in the People's Party.

stand on your own (two) feet be or become self-reliant or independent.

sweep someone off their feet quickly and overpoweringly charm someone.

take the weight off your feet: *see* WEIGHT.

think on your feet: *see* THINK.

under your feet in your way.

vote with your feet: *see* VOTE.

wait on someone hand and foot: *see* HAND.

walk someone off their feet: *see* WALK.

footloose

footloose and fancy-free without any commitments or responsibilities; free to act or travel as you please.

ℹ *Footloose* was used literally in the late 17th century to mean 'free to move the feet'. The sense 'without commitments' originated in late 19th-century US usage. *Fancy* in *fancy-free* is used in the sense of 'love' or 'the object of someone's affections'.

footsie

play footsie with someone ❶ touch someone's feet lightly with your own feet, usually under a table, as a playful expression of romantic interest. ❷ work with someone in a cosy and covert way.

footstep

follow (*or* tread) in someone's footsteps do as another person did before, especially in making a journey or following an occupation.

for

be for it be in imminent danger of punishment or other trouble. British informal

> **2010 Jayne** *Our Great Southern Land* I come in peace. But if any of that lot in there catch you watching that in here you'll be for it.

there's (*or* that's) — for you used ironically to indicate a particularly good example of a quality or thing mentioned.

> **1982 William Least Heat-Moon** *Blue Highways* Satchel Paige—there's a name for you—old Satch could fire the pill a hundred and five miles an hour.

— for (the usually specified country) used to indicate that someone does or can do the specified activity with great enthusiasm or tirelessness. British informal

> **2012** *Daily Telegraph* My rose-tinted recollection of those days had me sailing through university in an indolent vinous haze, partying for England, playing lots of cricket, achieving a good degree without writing an essay or visiting a library.

forbid

God (*or* Heaven) forbid used to express a fervent wish that something should not happen.

> **2013** *New Statesman* Hopefully this will be to somewhere civilised like the Inn at Whitewell or Sharrow Bay. But if, God forbid, it's Carlisle or Leeds, be sure to let any minor discomfiture be reflected in your review.

forbidden

forbidden fruit a thing that is desired all the more because it is not allowed.

> ℹ The original *forbidden fruit* was that forbidden to Adam in the Garden of Eden: 'But of the tree of the knowledge of good and evil, thou shalt not eat of it' (Genesis 2:17).

force

by main force: *see* MAIN.

force someone's hand make someone act prematurely or do something they dislike.

force the issue compel the making of an immediate decision.

force the pace adopt a fast pace in a race in order to tire out your opponents quickly.

in force in great strength or numbers.

> **1989 Amy Wilentz** *The Rainy Season* They turned out in force, armed with machetes and cocomacaques.

foregone

a foregone conclusion a result that can be predicted with certainty.

forelock

take time by the forelock seize an opportunity. literary

> ℹ The Latin writer Phaedrus described Opportunity or Occasion as being bald except for a long forelock, a personification that was illustrated in Renaissance emblem books and was applied also to Time.

touch (*or* tug) your forelock raise a hand to your forehead in deference when meeting a person of higher social rank.

fork

Morton's fork: *see* MORTON.

forked

with forked tongue untruthfully or deceitfully. humorous

> ℹ The image is of the forked tongue of a snake, snakes being traditional symbols of treachery and deceit.

> **2010** *Mail & Guardian* (South Africa) Let the reader then beware; this is double-jeopardy territory, confessions of a books editor who might speak with forked tongue.

forlorn

a forlorn hope a faint remaining hope or chance; a desperate attempt.

> ℹ This expression developed in the mid 16th century from the Dutch expression *verloren hoop* 'lost troop'. The phrase originally denoted a band of soldiers picked to begin an attack, many of whom would not survive; the equivalent French phrase is *enfants perdus* 'lost children'. The current sense, which dates from the mid 17th century, arose from a misunderstanding of the etymology.

form

a matter of form: *see* MATTER.

true to form: *see* TRUE.

fort

hold the fort take responsibility for a situation while someone is absent.

Forth Bridge

paint the Forth Bridge: *see* PAINT.

fortitude

intestinal fortitude: *see* INTESTINAL.

fortune

fortune favours the brave a successful person is often one who is willing to take risks. proverb

the fortunes of war the unpredictable events of war.

a hostage to fortune: *see* HOSTAGE.

a small fortune a large amount of money. informal

soldier of fortune: *see* SOLDIER.

the wheel of Fortune: *see* WHEEL.

forty

forty winks a short sleep or nap, especially during the day. informal

ⓘ This expression dates from the early 19th century, but *wink* in the sense of 'a closing of the eyes for sleep' is found from the late 14th century.

foul

cry foul: *see* CRY.

fall foul of come into conflict with and be undermined by.

2004 *Sunday Business Post* Australia's biggest wine-maker, Foster's Group, is the latest company to fall foul of the wine surplus, which is set to continue for at least two years.

foul your own nest do something damaging or harmful to yourself or your own interests.

ⓘ The proverb *it's an ill bird that fouls its own nest*, used of a person who criticizes or abuses their own country or family, has been found in English since the early 15th century.

run foul of come into conflict with; go against.

ⓘ This expression is nautical in origin: when used of a ship it means 'collide or become entangled with an obstacle or another vessel'. Both literal and figurative uses were current by the late 17th century.

found

all found (of an employee's wages) with board and lodging provided free. British dated

founding

founding father someone who establishes an institution.

ⓘ *Founding Father* is used in particular of an American statesman at the time of the Revolution, especially a member of the Federal Constitutional Convention of 1787.

four

the four corners of the world: *see* CORNER.

on all fours with equal with; presenting an exact analogy with.

2004 *TroppoArmadillo* [He] set forward his own conclusions, which ... may not be precisely on all fours with what was said by the learned Chief Justice.

to the four winds: *see* **to the wind** *at* WIND.

fourth

the fourth estate the press; the profession of journalism.

ⓘ The three traditional Estates of the Realm (the Crown, the House of Lords, and the House of Commons) are now viewed as having been joined by the press, which is regarded as having equal power. As early as 1843 Lord Macaulay stated: 'The gallery in which the reporters sit has become a fourth estate of the realm'.

the fourth wall ❶ the space which separates a performer or performance from an audience. ❷ the conceptual barrier between any fictional work and its viewers or readers.

fowl

neither fish nor fowl (nor good red herring): *see* FISH.

fox

crazy like a fox: *see* CRAZY.

shoot someone's fox: *see* SHOOT.

frame

be in (*or* out of) the frame ❶ be (*or* not be) eligible or the centre of attention. ❷ under suspicion or wanted (*or* not) by the police.

frame of mind a particular mood that influences your attitude or behaviour.

Frankenstein

Frankenstein's monster a thing that becomes terrifying or destructive to its maker.

ⓘ *Frankenstein* was the title of a novel written in 1818 by Mary Shelley. The scientist Frankenstein creates and brings to life a manlike monster which eventually turns on him and destroys him; Frankenstein is not the name of the monster itself, as is often assumed.

1991 John Kingdom *Local Government & Politics in Britain* The factories of the bourgeoisie had created another dangerous by-product, a Frankenstein's monster posing a constant sense of threat—the working class.

free

for free without cost or payment; free of charge. informal

1957 Godfrey Smith *The Friends* Back home we pay if we're ill... You don't expect to be ill for free.

free and easy informal and relaxed.

free, gratis, and for nothing without charge. humorous

a free hand freedom to act at your own discretion.

free rein: *see* REIN.

a free ride used to refer to a situation in which someone benefits without having to make a fair contribution.

home free: *see* HOME.

it's a free country said when asserting that a course of action is not illegal or forbidden, often in justification of it.

make free with treat without ceremony or proper respect; take liberties with.

there's no such thing as a free lunch: *see* LUNCH.

walk free be released from custody having been exonerated.

ⓘ The expression is often used with the underlying implication that the person concerned did not deserve release.

2013 *The Age* (Melbourne) It's a decision that sees him still in jail after his co-accused walked free on parole in 2004.

freeze

freeze the balls off a brass monkey: *see* **brass monkey** *at* BRASS.

freeze your blood fill you with feelings of fear or horror.

ⓘ According to the medieval physiological scheme of the four humours in the human body (melancholy, phlegm, blood, and choler), blood was the hot, moist element, so the effect of horror or fear in making the blood cold was to make it unable to fulfil its proper function of supplying the body with vital heat or energy. Compare with **make your blood run cold** (*at* BLOOD).

until hell freezes over: *see* HELL.

French

excuse (*or* pardon) my French used to apologize for swearing. informal

ⓘ *French* has been used since the late 19th century as a euphemism for bad language.

2018 Isabelle Grey *Wrong Way Home* 'Fuck.' Colin threw himself back in his leather executive chair. 'Excuse my French.'

take French leave make an unannounced or unauthorized departure.

ⓘ This expression stems from the custom prevalent in 18th-century France of leaving a reception or entertainment without saying goodbye to your host or hostess.

frenzy

feeding frenzy: *see* FEED.

fresh

be fresh out of something have just sold or run out of a supply of something. informal

break fresh ground: *see* **break new ground** *at* GROUND.

a breath of fresh air: *see* BREATH.

fresh as a daisy: *see* DAISY.

fresh blood: *see* **new blood** *at* BLOOD.

fresh fields and pastures new: *see* PASTURE.

friend

a fair-weather friend someone who cannot be relied on in a crisis.

2013 *Daily Telegraph* It destroys any pretence that the EU has at its heart a belief in democracy, or in those warm words so often repeated about it being the guardian of essential 'European' qualities. In truth it was only a fair-weather friend and its behaviour in this storm, as in others, is to drop these benevolent ideas like hot stones.

a friend at court a person in a position to use influence on your behalf.

a friend of Dorothy a homosexual person. informal euphemistic

ℹ The expression alludes to Dorothy Gale, the young heroine of Frank L. Baum's *The Wizard of Oz* (1900), played in the 1939 film version by Judy Garland, who later became a gay icon.

friends in high places people in senior positions who are able and willing to use their influence on your behalf.

man's best friend: *see* MAN.

fright

look a fright have a dishevelled or grotesque appearance. informal

frighten

frighten the horses: *see* HORSE.

frighten the life out of: *see* LIFE.

frighten the (living) daylights out of: *see* DAYLIGHT.

frightened

frightened of your own shadow: *see* **afraid of your own shadow** *at* SHADOW.

be frightened out of your wits: *see* WIT.

be frightened to death: *see* DEATH.

frightener

put the frighteners on threaten or intimidate. British informal

ℹ Literally, a *frightener* is a thug who intimidates victims on behalf of a gang.

2011 *New Statesman* My guess is that something very serious happened at the end of August and early September that put the frighteners on UK policymakers.

fritz

go (*or* be) on the fritz (of a machine) stop working properly. North American informal

ℹ The nature of any connection with *Fritz*, the derogatory nickname for a German, is uncertain. The related phrase *put the fritz on* means 'put a stop to something'.

frog

have a frog in your throat lose your voice or find it hard to speak because of hoarseness or an apparent impediment in your throat. informal

mad as a box of frogs: *see* MAD.

front

front of house ❶ the parts of a theatre in front of the proscenium arch. ❷ the business of a theatre that concerns the audience, such as ticket sales.

lead from the front: *see* LEAD.

on the front burner: *see* **on the back burner** *at* BURNER.

frosty

it'll be a frosty Friday (in July) used to indicate that something is very unlikely to happen. Canadian informal

1990 Walter Stewart *Right Church, Wrong Pew* It would be a frosty Friday in the middle of July before he would discuss personal affairs with the press.

froth

froth (*or* foam) at the mouth be very angry.

ℹ This phrase stems from the involuntary production of large amounts of saliva from the mouth during a seizure or fit.

fruit

bear fruit have good results.

ℹ This expression is a biblical metaphor, found, for example, in Matthew 13:23: 'But he that received seed into the good ground is he that heareth the word, and understandeth it; which also beareth fruit, and bringeth forth, some an hundredfold, some sixty, some thirty'.

forbidden fruit: *see* FORBIDDEN.

low-hanging fruit: *see* LOW.

fruitcake

nutty as a fruitcake: *see* NUTTY.

fry

have other fish to fry: *see* FISH.

frying

out of the frying pan into the fire from a bad situation to one that is worse.

fuck

vulgar slang

fuck all absolutely nothing. British

ⓘ An embellished version of the phrase, *sweet fuck all*, has been euphemized as **sweet Fanny Adams** (see SWEET).

not give a fuck not care at all.

ⓘ The expression is sometimes elaborated to *not give a flying fuck*.

2018 Linwood Barclay *A Noise Downstairs* I know this is a pigsty. I am aware that I'm living in a hellhole. The thing is, I don't give a flying fuck.

fudge

fudge factor a figure which is included in a calculation in order to account for some unquantified but significant phenomenon or to ensure a desired result.

ⓘ *Fudge*, apparently originating in the mid 18th century as an exclamation of disgust or irritation, later acquired a specific verbal sense in printers' jargon, meaning to 'do work imperfectly or as best you can with the materials available'.

fuel

add fuel to the fire (*or* flames) (of a person or circumstance) cause a situation or conflict to become more intense, especially by provocative comments.

full

full of yourself very self-satisfied and with an exaggerated sense of self-worth; bumptious.

to the full to the greatest possible extent.

ⓘ For other idioms containing *full*, see the entry for the main word in the idiom (for example, **full of beans** at BEAN).

fullness

the fullness of your (*or* the) heart great or overwhelming emotion. literary

in the fullness of time after a due length of time has elapsed; eventually.

fumes

be running on fumes: *see* **be running on empty** *at* EMPTY.

fun

a bundle of fun: *see* BUNDLE.

figure of fun: *see* FIGURE.

fun and games amusing and enjoyable activities.

ⓘ The phrase is often used ironically, to refer to activities that are far from amusing (e.g. things that are frustratingly difficult, or nefarious goings-on).

2007 Mohsin Hamid *The Reluctant Fundamentalist* Aside from light-hearted banter of this kind, there would be little in the way of fun and games at the workplace.

like fun ❶ vigorously or quickly. dated British ❷ an ironic exclamation of contradiction or disbelief in response to a statement. dated, chiefly North American

poke fun at: *see* POKE.

fund

in funds having money to spend. British

funeral

it's (*or* that's) someone's funeral used to warn someone that an unwise act or decision is their own responsibility. informal

2009 digby *Hullabaloo* The right is planning to bring up the Schiavo mess in the confirmation hearings. If they want to remind the country of that circus, it's their funeral.

funny

see the funny side of something appreciate the humorous aspect of a situation or experience.

fur

be all fur coat and no knickers have an impressive or sophisticated appearance which belies the fact that there is nothing to substantiate it. British informal

fur and feather game animals and birds.

the fur will fly there will be serious, perhaps violent, trouble. informal

ⓘ This phrase originated in the early 19th century, in the USA. The image is of a furious fight between dogs or cats.

furious

fast and furious: *see* FAST.

furiously

give someone furiously to think: *see* THINK.

furniture

part of the furniture a person or thing that has been somewhere so long as to seem a permanent, unquestioned, or invisible feature of the scene. informal

furrow

plough a lonely furrow: *see* PLOUGH.

fury

like fury with great energy or effort. informal

> **1994–5** *Game Gazette* I was to fish it [the Zambesi] for the legendary Tiger fish . . . that . . . has a mouth of teeth like a canteen of cutlery and fights like fury.

fuse

blow a fuse lose your temper. informal

> ℹ The metaphor is of the failure of an electrical circuit or engine as a result of overheating.

have (*or* be on) a short fuse have a tendency to lose your temper quickly.

light the fuse: *see* LIGHT.

fussy

not be fussy not be very concerned about something, especially a decision that is to be made. informal

future

future shock a state of distress or disorientation due to rapid social or technological change.

> ℹ This phrase was coined by the American writer Alvin Toffler (1928–2016) in *Horizon* (1965), where he defines it as 'the dizzying disorientation brought on by the premature arrival of the future'.

once and future: *see* ONCE.

Gg

gab

the gift of the gab: *see* GIFT.

gaff

blow the gaff reveal or let out a plot or secret. British informal, dated

ℹ The word *gaff* is recorded from the early 19th century, but its origins are uncertain.

gaiety

the gaiety of nations general cheerfulness or amusement. British

ℹ In *The Lives of the English Poets*, Samuel Johnson wrote about the death of the great actor David Garrick (1717–79), remarking that it 'has eclipsed the gaiety of nations and impoverished the public stock of harmless pleasure'.

gain

no pain, no gain: *see* PAIN.

gaiters

all gas and gaiters: *see* GAS.

gall

dip your pen in gall: *see* DIP.

wormwood and gall: *see* WORMWOOD.

gallery

play to the gallery act in an exaggerated or histrionic manner, especially in order to appeal to popular taste.

ℹ From the mid 17th century the highest seating in a theatre was called the gallery, and it was here that the cheapest seats—and the least refined members of the audience—were to be found. This figurative expression dates from the late 19th century.

game

ahead of the game: *see* AHEAD.

anyone's game: *see* ANYONE.

beat someone at their own game: *see* BEAT.

the beautiful game: *see* BEAUTIFUL.

chase the game: *see* CHASE.

fair game someone or something considered a reasonable target for criticism, exploitation, or attack.

fun and games: *see* FUN.

as game as Ned Kelly very brave. Australian

ℹ Ned Kelly (1855–80) was a famous Australian outlaw, the leader of a band of horse and cattle thieves and bank raiders operating in Victoria; he was eventually hanged at Melbourne. An alternative Australian formulation is *as game as a meatant* (meatants are truculent Australian insects with a fierce bite).

have (*or* put) your game face on have (or adopt) a look or manner characterized by single-minded dedication, determination, or seriousness. chiefly North American

2012 *New York Times* Whether he is shooting pool, preparing for a meeting on world affairs or trying to pick up a tough spare at the bowling alley, President Obama seemingly always has his game face on.

the game is up the plan, deception, or crime is revealed or foiled.

game on ❶ a signal for play to begin in a game or match. ❷ said when a contest seems about to begin in earnest. ❸ said when you feel that a situation is about to develop in your favour. informal

ℹ The expression seems to have originated in the game of darts.

❷ **2006** *Sunday Mail* (Brisbane) It's game on as Australia's largest car makers, Holden and Toyota, clash with their locally made sedans.

game over said when a situation is regarded as hopeless or irreversible.

ℹ This expression probably comes from the use of the phrase at the conclusion of a computer game.**2009 Shaun Ellis** & **Penny Junor** *The Man Who Lives with Wolves* If you inadvertently surprised a bear . . . it could be game over very quickly.

game, set, and match used to indicate a decisive victory.

ℹ The expression comes from the formula for announcing the result at the end of a tennis match.

give the game away inadvertently reveal something secret or concealed.

the Great Game ❶ spying. ❷ the rivalry between Britain and Russia in central Asia during the 19th century.

ℹ The phrase was first used by Rudyard Kipling in *Kim* (1901).

have skin in the game: *see* SKIN.

a mug's game: *see* MUG.

the name of the game: *see* NAME.

off (*or* on) your game playing badly (*or* well).

on the game involved in prostitution. British informal

ℹ The phrase itself apparently dates from the late 19th century, but *game* in the sense of 'sexual activity' is much older. Shakespeare talks of 'daughters of the game' in *Troilus and Cressida* (1606) and from the early 17th century *gamester* was a term used to describe a lewd person.

the only game (*or* show) in town the best or most important of its kind; the only thing worth concerning yourself with. informal

2012 *The Australian* Australia needs to move quickly ... and not remain fixated on China as the only game in town.

play games deal with someone or something in a way that lacks due seriousness or respect or deviates from the truth.

2000 Mike Gayle *Turning Thirty* I couldn't stand him at first. I'd have a conversation with him and would come away feeling like he was playing games with me.

play someone's game advance another's plans, whether intentionally or not.

play the game behave in a fair or honourable way; abide by the rules or conventions.

1993 Andy McNab *Bravo Two Zero* Shorncliffe was a nightmare, but I learned to play the game. I had to—there was nothing else for me.

play a waiting game: *see* WAITING.

talk a good game: *see* TALK.

two can play at that game: *see* TWO.

up your game: *see* UP.

what's your (*or* the) game? what's going on?; what are you up to? informal

gamekeeper

poacher turned gamekeeper: *see* POACHER.

gamut

run the gamut experience, display, or perform the complete range of something.

ℹ *Gamut* is a contraction of medieval Latin *gamma ut, gamma* being the lowest note in the medieval musical scale and *ut* the first of the six notes forming a hexachord. Together, therefore, they represent the full range of notes of which a voice or an instrument is capable. The American writer Dorothy Parker (1893–1967) is famous for (allegedly) remarking sarcastically of a performance by Katherine Hepburn 'She ran the whole gamut of the emotions from A to B.'

1996 *Europe: Rough Guide* Russia's hotels run the gamut from opulent citadels run as joint-ventures with foreign firms to seedy pits inhabited by mobsters.

gangbusters

go gangbusters proceed very vigorously or successfully. North American informal

ℹ Literally, a *gangbuster* is 'a person who assists in the vigorous or violent break-up of criminal gangs', from which the more general sense of 'a successful person' has developed. The phrase *like gangbusters* means 'vigorously and successfully'.

2012 Andrew *The 4th Avenue Blues* The railroads have been going gangbusters lately with lots of tonnage to haul as the economy revives.

gap

stop a gap: *see* STOP.

garbage

garbage in, garbage out incorrect or poor quality input inevitably produces faulty output.

ℹ This expression is often abbreviated as *GIGO*. The phrase originated in the mid 20th century in the field of computing, but it can now have a more general application.

2013 *CNN Transcripts* My main message was that this is one of the most poorly conducted investigations I had ever seen outside of a third world country. It was frightenly bad. And of course, you know, garbage in, garbage out.

garden

common or garden: *see* COMMON.

everything in the garden is lovely (*or* rosy) all is well. informal ℹ *Everything in the garden is lovely* was an early 20th-century catchphrase, originating in a song popularized by the English music-hall artiste Marie Lloyd (1870–1922), and is used as an expression of general satisfaction and contentment.

lead someone up the garden path give someone misleading clues or signals. informal

ℹ The earliest (early 20th-century) examples of this phrase use just *garden* rather than *garden path*, which suggests that the original context was of someone enticing a person they wanted to seduce or flirt with out into a garden. A North American variant of the phrase is *lead someone down the garden path*.

Garnet

all Sir Garnet highly satisfactory. informal, dated

ℹ Sir Garnet Wolseley (1833–1913), leader of several successful military expeditions, was associated with major reforms in the army. He was the model for the 'modern Major-General' in Gilbert and Sullivan's *The Pirates of Penzance*.

garters

have someone's guts for garters: *see* GUTS.

gas

all gas and gaiters a satisfactory state of affairs. informal, dated

ℹ This expression was first recorded in Charles Dickens' *Nicholas Nickleby* (1839): 'All is gas and gaiters'.

1961 P. G. Wodehouse *Ice in the Bedroom* She cries 'Oh, Freddie darling!' and flings herself into his arms, and all is gas and gaiters again.

cook with gas: *see* **cook on the front burner** *at* COOK.

run out of gas run out of energy; lose momentum. North American informal

step on the gas press on the accelerator to make a car go faster. North American informal

gasket

blow a gasket ❶ suffer a leak in a gasket of an engine. ❷ lose your temper. informal

gasp

your (*or* the) last gasp the point of death, exhaustion, or completion.

1996 Will Hutton *The State We're In* The failure of the 1994 rail strike was the last gasp of an old order.

gate

get (*or* be given) the gate be dismissed from a job. North American informal

like a bull at a gate: *see* BULL.

gatepost

between you and me and the gatepost: *see* **between you and me and the bedpost** at BEDPOST.

g

gather

gather dust: *see* DUST.

gauntlet

run the gauntlet go through an intimidating or dangerous crowd, place, or experience in order to reach a goal.

ℹ This phrase alludes to the former military practice of punishing a wrongdoer by forcing him to run between two lines of men armed with sticks, who beat him as he passed. *Gauntlet* here has nothing to do with a glove, but is a version of an earlier word *gantlope*, itself taken from Swedish *gatloppe*, which meant 'lane course'.

throw down (*or* take up) the gauntlet issue (*or* accept) a challenge.

ℹ In medieval times, a person issued a challenge by throwing their gauntlet (i.e. glove) to the ground; whoever picked it up was deemed to have accepted the challenge.

gear

change gear begin to move or act differently, usually more rapidly.

ℹ This expression derives from literally engaging a different gear of a motor vehicle in order to alter its speed. Compare with *in gear* (with a gear engaged, and so ready for action) and its opposite *out of gear*. To *move up a gear* means literally 'change to a higher gear'; the phrase is often used figuratively to mean 'put more effort into an activity'. To *go* (or *move*) *through the gears* is metaphorically to 'operate with increasing force or intensity through successive stages of an activity'.

get your arse into gear: *see* ARSE.

give someone the gears harass or pester someone. Canadian

1989 Guy Vanderhaeghe *Homesick* Whenever Daniel gave him the gears about overdressing, the old man grew sulky and grouchy.

general

caviar to the general: *see* CAVIAR.

Genghis Khan

somewhere to the right of Genghis Khan: *see* RIGHT.

g

genie

let the genie out of (*or* put the genie back in) the bottle let loose (*or* bring back under control) an unpredictable force, course of events, etc.

ℹ A *genie* or *jinnee* in Arabian stories is a spirit that can adopt various forms and take a mischievous or benign hand in human affairs. The genie generally inhabits a lamp (compare with **Aladdin's lamp** *at* ALADDIN) or bottle from which someone can release it by the appropriate words or actions. The Arabic word appears in English in various transliterations; *genie* derives from French *génie* (from Latin *genius* meaning 'a tutelary spirit'), used by the French translators of *The Arabian Nights* because it was similar in form and sense to the Arabic word.

2005 *Time* Nobody thinks the gambling genie can be put back in the bottle.

gentleman

a gentleman's agreement an arrangement or understanding which is based on the trust of both or all parties, rather than being legally binding.

1991 Charles Anderson *Grain: Entrepreneurs* There had been a 'gentleman's agreement' by the Grain Growers not to enter the markets of Saskatchewan Wheat Pool's predecessor.

the little gentleman in the velvet coat the mole. humorous

ℹ This expression was a toast used by the Jacobites, supporters of the deposed James II and his descendants in their claim to the British throne. It referred to the belief that the death of King William III resulted from complications following a fall from his horse when it stumbled over a molehill. The phrase is found in various other forms, including *the wee gentleman in black velvet*.

genuine

the genuine article a person or thing considered to be an authentic and excellent example of their kind.

George

let George do it let someone else do the work or take the responsibility. dated

get

(as) — as all get out to a great or extreme extent. North American informal

2013 *DVD Verdict* It's not a dark, dangerous performance, like Joe Spinell gave in *Maniac*, or an iconic one like Michael Rooker gave in *Henry: Portrait of a Serial Killer*, but it's entertaining as all get out.

be out to get someone be determined to punish or harm someone.

get in there take positive action to achieve your aim (often said as an exhortation). informal

get it on ❶ embark on an activity; get going. ❷ have sexual intercourse. informal, chiefly North American

❷ **2000** *Montreal Mirror* TechnicalVirgin.com has a similar message for horny teens who want to get it on without getting in the family way.

get it together get yourself or a situation organized or under control. informal

get it up (of a man) achieve an erection. vulgar slang

get off at — practise birth control by the withdrawal method. informal, euphemistic

ℹ The open slot in the phrase is filled by the name of any of a range of railway stations (e.g. Clapham Junction in London, Paisley in Glasgow) immediately preceding a terminus.

get out more used to suggest that someone is naive, or narrow-minded, or has too little experience of the world. informal

2001 *The Register* 'It's a war game. It's fun. It's better than sex.' No lads, it's not—and you really, really need to get out more.

get over yourself stop being conceited or pretentious. informal

get-up-and-go energy, enthusiasm, and initiative. informal

ℹ A mid-19th-century US colloquialism was 'get up and get'.

get you (him, her, etc.)! said as an invitation to notice or look at someone, especially in order to criticize or ridicule them. informal

get yours be killed. informal euphemistic

getting on for approaching (a specified time, age, or amount); almost. chiefly British

ℹ For other idioms containing *get*, see the entry for the main word in the idiom (for example, **get a life** at LIFE).

ghost

a ghost at the feast: *see* FEAST.

the ghost in the machine the mind viewed as distinct from the body.

ℹ This phrase was coined by the British philosopher Gilbert Ryle in *The Concept of Mind* (1949) for a viewpoint that he considered completely misleading.

the ghost walks money is available and salaries will be paid.

ℹ This expression has been explained in theatrical phrasebooks by the story that an actor playing the ghost of Hamlet's father refused to 'walk again' until the cast's overdue salaries had been paid.

give up the ghost ❶ (of a person) die. ❷ (of a machine) stop working; break down, especially permanently. ❸ stop making an effort; give up hope.

ℹ The Old English meaning of *ghost*, 'the soul or spirit as the source of life', survives only in this idiom.

❸ **2018 Brad Parks** *Closer Than You Know* Trying to go forward with some kind of murder-for-hire scenario would be both unjust and patently absurd, a terrible example of the government being unable to give up the ghost.

lay a (*or* the) ghost get rid of a distressing, frightening, or worrying memory or thought.

ℹ The image here is of exorcizing an unquiet or evil spirit.

look as if you have seen a ghost look very pale and shocked.

not have (*or* stand) the ghost of a chance have no chance at all.

giant

battle of the giants: *see* BATTLE.

giddy

my giddy aunt! used to express astonishment. dated

gift

beware the Greeks bearing gifts: *see* GREEK.

the gift of the gab the ability to speak with eloquence and fluency.

ℹ *Gab*, dating from the late 18th century, was an informal word for 'conversation or chatter'. In Scotland it was associated with *gab*, an early 18th-century dialect variant of *gob* meaning 'the mouth'.

the gift of tongues: *see* TONGUE.

God's (own) gift to —: *see* GOD.

in the gift of (of a church living or official appointment) in the power of someone to award.

look a gift horse in the mouth find fault with what has been given or be ungrateful for an opportunity.

ℹ The Latin version of the proverb *don't look a gift horse in the mouth* (*noli ... equi dentes inspicere donati*) was known to St Jerome in the early 5th century AD. The 16th-century English form was *do not look a given horse in the mouth*.

2013 *Daily Telegraph* The woman at the centre of a long-running divorce battle over a disputed fortune has been told by a judge she may have looked a gift horse in the mouth when turning down a £300 million settlement.

gild

gild the lily try to improve what is already beautiful or excellent.

ℹ This phrase adapts lines from Shakespeare's *King John*: 'To gild refined gold, to paint the lily ... Is wasteful and ridiculous excess'.

gill

green about the gills: *see* GREEN.

gilt

take the gilt off the gingerbread make something no longer appealing.

ℹ Gingerbread was traditionally made in decorative forms that were then ornamented with gold leaf.

g

ginger

ginger group a highly active faction within a party or movement that presses for stronger action on a particular issue. informal

ℹ An old horse dealer's trick (recorded from the late 18th century) to make a broken-down animal look lively was to insert ginger into its anus. From this developed the metaphorical phrase *ginger up*, meaning 'make someone or something more lively'; in the early 20th century the term *ginger group* arose, to refer to a highly active faction in a party or movement that presses for stronger action about something.

1970 *New Society* The appearance of ginger groups to fight specific proposals, is not necessarily a bad thing—particularly if the established bodies aren't prepared to fight.

gingerbread

take the gilt off the gingerbread: *see* GILT.

gird

gird (up) your loins prepare and strengthen yourself for what is to come.

ℹ This expression is of biblical origin, the idea being that the long, loose garments worn in the ancient Orient had to be hitched up to avoid impeding a person's movement. In 1 Kings 18:45–6, we find: 'And Ahab rode, and went to Jezreel. And . . . Elijah . . . girded up his loins, and ran before Ahab to the entrance of Jezreel'. The phrase was also used metaphorically in the New Testament: 'Wherefore gird up the loins of your mind, be sober, and hope to the end for the grace that is to be brought unto you . . .' (1 Peter 1:13).

girl

big girl's blouse: *see* BLOUSE.

the girl next door: *see* **the boy next door** *at* NEXT.

page three girl: *see* PAGE.

give

don't give me that! don't ask me to believe that! (used as an expression of annoyed incredulity). informal

2003 *The Times* 'You must be a millionaire,' he says. 'Pardon?' 'Don't give me that, you old rascal, you're made for life.'

give and take ❶ mutual concessions and compromises. ❷ exchange of words and views.

give as good as you get respond with equal force or vehemence when attacked.

give it to someone scold or punish someone. informal

give it up applaud enthusiastically. informal

2004 *New Zealand Listener* Ladiiieees and gentlemen, give it up for Joseph Lin and the Auckland Philharmonia conducted by Steven Smith, coming to you live from the Auckland Town Hall.

give me — I prefer or admire a specified thing.

2013 Eric S. Raymond *Armed & Dangerous* Awkward, poorly designed, unreliable, confusing, irritating, low productivity, hard on the wrists and arms. Give me Win7 any day. But if the comparison is with Linux/FLOSS desktops I regretfully agree—they all stink.

give someone one (of a man) have sexual intercourse with a woman. British vulgar slang

give or take — to within — (used to express the degree or accuracy of a figure). informal

2014 *New Zealand Herald* It used to think that was around 6 per cent; it now thinks 4.5 per cent, give or take half a percentage point.

what gives? what's the news?; what's happening? (often used as a friendly greeting). informal

ℹ For other idioms containing *give*, see the entry for the main word in the idiom (for example, **give the game away** at GAME).

gizzard

stick in your gizzard be a source of great and continuing annoyance. informal

glad

give someone the glad eye: *see* EYE.

give someone the glad hand offer someone a warm and hearty, but often insincere, greeting or welcome. informal

in your glad rags in your smartest clothes; in formal evening dress. informal

1922 H. B. Hermon-Hodge *Up Against It In Nigeria* We all turned out in our glad rags to join in the procession.

glass

the glass is half-full (*or* half-empty) used to refer to an optimistic (or pessimistic) outlook on life.

2013 *SeoBook* Yea, I do feel lucky. Maybe it's the old hippy in me. I always see the glass half full, and I'm always dreaming of a better tomorrow.

glassy

the (*or* just the) glassy the most excellent person or thing. Australian informal

ⓘ In mid-20th-century surfing slang, a *glassy* is an extremely smooth wave offering excellent surfing conditions.

gleam

a gleam (*or* twinkle) in someone's eye ❶ a barely formed idea. ❷ a child who has not yet been conceived. humorous

glitter

all that glitters is not gold the attractive external appearance of something is not a reliable indication of its true nature. proverb

gloom

doom and gloom: *see* DOOM.

glory

crowning glory: *see* CROWNING.

go to glory die or be destroyed.

in your glory in a state of extreme joy or exaltation. informal

glove

fit like a glove (of clothes) fit exactly.

1989 T. M. Albert *Tales of an Ulster Detective* McNinch invited him to try the shoe on his foot, which he did—and it fitted him like a glove.

the gloves are off (*or* with the gloves off *or* take the gloves off) used to express the notion that something will be done in an uncompromising or brutal way, without compunction or hesitation.

ⓘ The contrast implied in this phrase is with a gloved hand handling things gently or in a civilized way.

hand in glove: *see* HAND.

glutton

a glutton for punishment a person who is always eager to undertake hard or unpleasant tasks.

ⓘ *Glutton of*— was used figuratively from the early 18th century for someone inordinately fond of the thing specified, especially when translating the Latin phrase *helluo librorum* 'a glutton of books'. The possible origin of the present phrase is in early 19th-century sporting slang.

gnash

gnash your teeth feel or express anger or fury.

ⓘ The gnashing of teeth, along with weeping or wailing, is used throughout the Bible to express a mixture of remorse and rage (for example, in Matthew 8:12: 'But the children of the kingdom shall be cast out into outer darkness: there shall be weeping and gnashing of teeth').

1998 *Times* Prepare yourself for the usual wailing and gnashing of teeth after tomorrow's retail price index figures.

2013 Bryan Caplan, Arnold Kling & David Henderson *Library of Economics & Liberty—Econlog* How would you react if the world's laws barred you from every non-Haitian labor market on earth? With weeping and gnashing of teeth.

gnat

strain at a gnat: *see* STRAIN.

gnome

gnomes of Zurich Swiss financiers or bankers, regarded as having sinister influence. derogatory

ⓘ This phrase stems from a remark made by the British politician Harold Wilson in a speech in the House of Commons in 1956: 'all the little gnomes in Zurich . . . about whom we keep on hearing'.

go

be all go be very busy or active. informal

go-as-you-please untrammelled or free.

2005 *Article Alley: Travel & Leisure* So you're off on holiday, an adventure of a lifetime, you love to drive and explore. You're an independent go as you please type. So what's there to worry about?

go for it strive to the utmost to gain or achieve something (often said as an exhortation). informal

2005 *Dance Magazine* Remember: ultimate success depends on being able to identify what is—and isn't—working in your life. Then go for it!

go (to) it act in a vigorous, energetic, or dissipated way. British informal

2013 Derek Lowe *Corante—In the Pipeline* The purpose of this sort of paper matches a drug discovery person's worldview exactly: here's a reasonable way into a large number of good-looking compounds that no one's ever screened, so go to it.

go off on one become very angry or excited. British informal

2018 *Observer Magazine* The lightly spiced pumpkin purée and the thyme dressing feel like the gorgeous velvet box in which a diamond ring is presented. And now I've gone off on one, which is what happens when the food is this good.

g

go there refer to that particular (potentially embarrassing) subject. Usually used in the negative.

2004 Adam Roberts *The Amateur Gourmet* I, too, had a bad experience at Agnes and Muriel's (food poisoning from the pot roast, but let's not go there).

go well used to express good wishes to someone leaving. South African

have a go ❶ make an attempt; act resourcefully. ❷ take independent or single-handed action against a criminal or criminals.

have a go at attack or criticize someone. chiefly British

make a go of be successful in something. informal

ℹ An Australian and New Zealand variant of this expression is *make a do of it*, which dates from the early 20th century.

1987 Evelyn E. Smith *Miss Melville Returns* He'd been unable to make a go of life in the city, and so he'd returned to the small New England village he came from.

no go not possible or practicable. informal

on the go very active or busy. informal

to go (of food or drink from a restaurant or cafe) to be eaten or drunk off the premises. North American

ℹ For other idioms containing *go*, see the entry for the main word in the idiom (for example, **go commando** at COMMANDO).

goal

(score) an own goal ❶ (in football) (score) a goal by mistake against your own side. ❷ (do) something that has the unintended effect of harming your own interests. informal

❷ **2001** *Farmers Guardian* For a Government minister ... and a key adviser ... to state publicly their low estimation of farmers and farming is yet another spectacular own goal.

goalpost

move (*or* shift) the goalposts unfairly alter the conditions or rules of a procedure during its course.

2005 *Herald Express* (Torquay) Our schools have an excellent historical track record for teaching and learning. So why are measures being considered to move the goalposts on the pretext of religion and culture?

goat

get someone's goat irritate someone. informal

2003 S. Pax *Baghdad Blog* What really got my goat this time was finding out that the Human Shields get food coupons.

play (*or* act) the (giddy) goat fool around; act irresponsibly. informal

separate the sheep from the goats: *see* SHEEP.

god

act of God: *see* ACT.

by guess and by God: *see* GUESS.

find God: *see* FIND.

fit for the gods excellent; extremely pleasing.

God forbid: *see* FORBID.

God's acre a churchyard. archaic

ℹ This phrase comes from the German word *Gottesacker* meaning 'God's seed field' in which the bodies of the dead are 'sown'.

God's (own) gift (to —) the ideal or best possible person or thing for someone or something (used chiefly ironically or in negative statements).

2007 Paddy Crerand *Never Turn the Other Cheek* She thought she was God's gift, because she was the best-looking girl in the Gorbals.

God willing used to express the wish that you will be able to do as you intend or that something will happen as planned.

ℹ This is an expression found in many cultures: compare with Latin *deo volente* or Arabic *inshallah*.

in the lap of the gods: *see* LAP.

little tin god a self-important person.

ℹ *Tin* is implicitly contrasted here with precious metals. The phrase seems to have originated in Rudyard Kipling's *Plain Tales from the Hills*, where he described idols that he thought were given undeserved veneration: 'Pleasant it is for the Little Tin Gods When great Jove nods; But Little Tin Gods make their little mistakes In missing the hour when great Jove wakes'.

1987 Fannie Flagg *Fried Green Tomatoes at the Whistle Stop Cafe* This little tin God in the polyester suit and the three-pound shoes. So smug, so self-important, with the nurses fluttering around him like geisha girls.

man of God: *see* MAN.

play God behave as if all-powerful or supremely important.

put the fear of God in someone: *see* FEAR.

there but for the grace of God: *see* GRACE.

goes

anything goes there are no rules about acceptable behaviour or dress.

🛈 This phrase appeared earlier, in the late 19th century, as *everything goes*.

as (*or* so) far as it goes bearing in mind its limitations (said when qualifying praise of something).

what goes around comes around the consequences of your actions will have to be dealt with eventually. proverb

who goes there? said by a sentry as a challenge.

going

get someone going make someone angry or sexually aroused. British informal

going, going, gone! an auctioneer's traditional announcement that bidding is closing or closed, and that this is the last chance to have something. informal

— going on — used to suggest that someone's behaviour or attitudes are those of someone older or younger than their actual age. humorous

1994 Janice Galloway *Foreign Parts* Cassie, carrying this bloody windsurfing board through customs. Thirty-one going on fifteen.

have — going for you have a specified factor or factors in your favour. informal

1997 Marian Keyes *Rachel's Holiday* All we really had going for us was our hair; mine was long and dark and hers was long and blonde.

heavy going: *see* HEAVY.

not know if you are coming or going: *see* COMING.

while the going is good while conditions are favourable.

gold

all that glitters is not gold: *see* GLITTER.

fool's gold: *see* FOOL.

go gold (of a recording) achieve sales meriting a gold disc.

heart of gold: *see* HEART.

pot (*or* crock) of gold a large but distant or illusory reward.

🛈 This expression alludes to the traditional story that a pot of gold is to be found by anyone who succeeds in reaching the end of a rainbow.

worth your weight in gold: *see* WEIGHT.

gold dust

like gold dust very valuable and rare.

golden

a golden age a period in the past when things were at their best, happiest, or most successful.

🛈 According to Greek and Roman mythology, the Golden Age was the earliest and best age of the world, when human beings lived in a state of perfect happiness. The Ages of Silver, Brass, and Iron represented successive stages of a descent into barbarism and misery.

golden boy a very popular or successful man. informal

2005 Norman Lebrecht *La Scena Musicale* From the day he raised a baton as principal conductor in Birmingham in 1980, Rattle has been the golden boy of classical music.

a golden calf something, especially wealth, as an object of excessive or unworthy worship.

🛈 In the Bible, the golden calf was a statue of gold in the shape of a calf, made by Aaron in response to the Israelites' plea for a god while they awaited Moses' return from Mount Sinai, where he was receiving the Ten Commandments (Exodus, chapter 32).

a golden handshake a sum of money paid by an employer to a retiring or redundant employee.

🛈 On the same principle, the phrase *a golden hello* was coined in the late 20th century. It is explained in an Appointments section of the *New Scientist* in 1998: 'Employers . . . especially in the financial sector, are offering "golden hellos". These are advances of up to £2000, sometimes given on acceptance of a job offer or with the first month's salary.'

the golden mean the avoidance of extremes.

ⓘ This phrase translates the Latin phrase *aurea mediocritas*, which comes from the Roman poet Horace's *Odes*.

golden oldie ❶ an old song or film that is still well known and popular. ❷ someone who is no longer young but is still successful in their field. informal

the golden section the division of a line so that the whole is to the greater part as that part is to the smaller part.

ⓘ This is a mathematical term for a proportion known since the 4th century and mentioned in the works of the Greek mathematician Euclid. It has been called by several names, but the mid-19th-century German one *goldene Schnitt*, translating Latin *sectio aurea*, has given rise to the current English term.

kill the goose that lays the golden eggs: *see* GOOSE.

silence is golden: *see* SILENCE.

goldfish

goldfish bowl a place or situation lacking privacy.

gone

far gone: *see* FAR.

a gone coon: *see* COON.

gone a million: *see* MILLION.

gone with the wind: *see* WIND.

here today, gone tomorrow: *see* HERE.

gong

kick the gong around: *see* KICK.

good

all to the good to be welcomed without qualification.

as good as — very nearly —.

2003 *Washington Post* A situation in which so much of a population is immune to a disease that the few scattered 'susceptibles' are as good as immune to it.

as good as gold extremely well-behaved.

as good as new in a very good condition or state, especially close to the original state after damage, injury, or illness.

be as good as your word do what you have promised to do.

be good news: *see* NEWS.

be in good company: *see* COMPANY.

be on to a good thing: *see* THING.

be — to the good have a specified amount of profit or advantage.

2012 Eric S. Raymond *Armed & Dangerous* It looks like T-mobile would have been around 400 to the good at the end of two years if I had gone with the contract.

come up with (*or* deliver *or* produce) the goods do what is expected or required of you. informal

damaged goods: *see* DAMAGE.

do someone or something a power of good: *see* POWER.

fight the good fight: *see* FIGHT.

for good measure: *see* MEASURE.

get (*or* have) the goods on someone obtain (*or* possess) information about a person which may be used to their detriment. informal

give a good account of yourself: *see* ACCOUNT.

give as good as you get: *see* GIVE.

good and — used as an intensifier before an adjective or adverb. informal

1998 Barbara Kingsolver *The Poisonwood Bible* As soon as I had her good and terrified I'd slip away.

good call: *see* CALL.

good cop, bad cop: *see* COP.

good for a laugh: *see* LAUGH.

a good job: *see* JOB.

good offices: *see* OFFICE.

good oil reliable information. Australian informal

ⓘ This expression has behind it the image of oil that is used to lubricate a machine and so ensure that it runs well.

good on you! used as an exclamation of approval towards someone, especially for something that they have achieved. chiefly Australian

good riddance: *see* RIDDANCE.

good Samaritan: *see* SAMARITAN.

good show: *see* SHOW.

good to go in a fit state to proceed.

> **2013** *Mac Observer* After you've entered the original password, you'll type in the new one you want to change it to twice, and you're good to go!

the great and the good: *see* GREAT.

have a (good) mind to do something: *see* MIND.

have something on good authority: *see* AUTHORITY.

in good time ❶ with no risk of being late. ❷ in due course but without haste.

in someone's good books: *see* **in someone's bad books** *at* BOOK.

make good be successful.

make something good ❶ compensate for loss, damage, or expense. ❷ repair or restore after damage. ❸ fulfil a promise or claim.

never had it so good have never before enjoyed such prosperity.

> ℹ The expression was probably coined by George Meany, a 20th-century American trade-union leader, but it was popularized in Britain by the Conservative prime minister Harold Macmillan, who used it in a speech in 1957.

no good to gundy no good at all. Australian informal

> ℹ The origin of *gundy* remains obscure.

> **1955 Nina Pulliam** *I Traveled a Lonely Land* Just cards and races and booze—and fightin'. No good to Gundy!

of good cheer: *see* CHEER.

one good turn deserves another if someone does you a favour, you should take the chance to repay it. proverb

put in a good word for recommend or defend (someone)

so far, so good: *see* FAR.

take something in good part not be offended by something.

talk a good game: *see* TALK.

up to no good doing or intending to do something wrong. informal

> **2006 Ford Kiernan & Greg Hemphill** *Still Game: Scripts* I caught Tam and Eric up to no good in the foyer.

while the going is good: *see* GOING.

goodbye

kiss something goodbye: *see* KISS.

goog

full as a goog very drunk. Australian informal

> ℹ *Goog* is slang for 'egg', but its origins are uncertain.

goose

all someone's geese are swans someone habitually exaggerates the merits of undistinguished people or things.

> ℹ The goose is proverbially contrasted with the swan as being the clumsier, less elegant, and less distinguished bird; compare with **turn geese into swans** below.

cook someone's goose: *see* COOK.

kill the goose that lays the golden egg(s) destroy a reliable and valuable source of income.

> ℹ One of Aesop's fables tells the tale of a man who owned a miraculous goose that laid eggs of gold. However, he grew dissatisfied with its production of just one egg a day and killed it in the deluded expectation of finding a large quantity of gold inside it. For brevity's sake, the expression is often shortened (presumably by those unaware of its origin) to *kill the golden goose*.

> **2012** *The Age* (Melbourne) Fortescue chief executive Neville Power said Australia was at risk of 'killing the goose that lays the golden egg' from Labor's focus on the redistribution of wealth.

turn geese into swans exaggerate the merits of people.

what's sauce for the goose is sauce for the gander: *see* SAUCE.

a wild goose chase: *see* WILD.

wouldn't say boo to a goose: *see* BOO.

gooseberry

play gooseberry be a third person who stays in the company of two people, especially lovers, who would prefer to be on their own.

> ℹ *Gooseberry* is short for the earlier *gooseberry-picker*, referring to an activity as a pretext for lovers to be together.

Gordian knot

cut the Gordian knot solve or remove a problem in a direct or forceful way, rejecting gentler or more indirect methods.

> ℹ The knot referred to is that with which Gordius, king of ancient Phrygia (in Asia Minor), fastened the yoke of his wagon to the pole. Its complexity was such that it gave rise to the legend that whoever could undo it would

become the ruler of Asia. When Alexander the Great passed that way en route to conquer the East, he is said simply to have severed the knot with his sword.

gorge

your gorge rises you are sickened or disgusted.

ℹ *Gorge* is an obsolete term from falconry, meaning 'a meal for a hawk'; from this derives the more general sense of 'the contents of the stomach'.

g

gory

the gory details the explicit details of something.

2005 *Trav. Africa* There's a car-crash compulsiveness about this autobiographical account—we know that everything's going to get extremely messy, but can't help wanting all the gory details.

gospel

gospel truth the absolute truth. informal

1998 *Mirror* Any research that puts down men is accepted as gospel truth these days.

Gotham

a wise man of Gotham: *see* WISE.

gourd

out of your gourd ❶ out of your mind; crazy. ❷ under the influence of alcohol or drugs. North American informal

❶ **1988 Jay McInerney** *The Story of My Life* After ten minutes I'm bored out of my gourd.

❷ **1993 Stephen King** *Gerald's Game* I was 'on medication' (this is the technical hospital term for 'stoned out of one's gourd').

gown

town and gown: *see* TOWN.

grab

grab something (*or* someone) by the throat: *see* THROAT.

up for grabs available; obtainable. informal

ℹ This phrase was originally mid 20th-century US slang, relating especially to a woman who is open to sexual advances.

2018 Mel Sherratt *Hush Hush* There was so much up for grabs, and he wanted it. He'd earned it. And it was time he got what he was owed.

grace

airs and graces: *see* AIR.

be in someone's good (*or* bad) graces be regarded by someone with favour (*or* disfavour).

fall from grace ❶ fall into a state of sin. ❷ fall from favour. ❸ an instance of either of these.

❷ **2012** *New Yorker* George Valentin, a star with Fairbanksian dash, struggles to hold back the onset of sound, and, in so doing, falls from grace.

❸ **2004** *Times Literary Supplement* Celebrities ... seek publicity one day and then complain when their fall from grace becomes a tabloid scoop.

state of grace: *see* STATE.

there but for the grace of God (go I) used to acknowledge your good fortune in avoiding another's mistake or misfortune.

with good (*or* bad) grace in a willing and happy (*or* resentful and reluctant) manner.

grade

make the grade succeed; reach the desired standard. informal

grail

holy grail: *see* HOLY.

grain

against the grain contrary to the natural inclination or feeling of someone or something.

ℹ This phrase alludes to the fact that wood is easier to cut along the line of the grain than across or against it.

a grain of mustard seed a small thing capable of vast development.

ℹ Black mustard seed grows to a great height. In Matthew 13:31–2 it is stated that 'mustard seed... indeed is the least of all seeds: but when it is grown, it is the greatest among herbs'.

take something with a grain of salt: *see* **take something with a pinch of salt** *at* SALT.

grand

a (*or* the) grand old man of a man long and highly respected in a particular field.

ℹ Recorded from 1882, and popularly abbreviated as *GOM, Grand Old Man* was the nickname of the British statesman William Ewart Gladstone (1809–98), who went on to win his last election in 1892 at the age of eighty-three.

grandeur

delusions of grandeur: *see* DELUSION.

grandmother

teach your grandmother to suck eggs presume to advise a more experienced person.

ℹ The proverb *you can't teach your grandmother to suck eggs* has been used since the early 18th century as a caution against any attempt by the ignorant or inexperienced to instruct someone wiser or more knowledgeable.

granted

take for granted ❶ fail to properly appreciate (someone or something), especially as a result of overfamiliarity. ❷ assume that (something) is true without questioning it.

grape

sour grapes: *see* SOUR.

grapevine

hear something on the grapevine acquire information by rumour or by unofficial communication.

ℹ This phrase comes originally from an American Civil War expression, when news was said to be passed 'by grapevine telegraph'. Compare with **bush telegraph** (*at* TELEGRAPH).

grasp

grasp at straws: *see* **clutch at straws** *at* STRAW.

grasp the nettle tackle a difficulty boldly. British

ℹ This expression refers to a belief (recorded from the late 16th century onwards) enshrined in a rhyme quoted in Sean O'Casey's *Juno and the Paycock* (1925): 'If you gently touch a nettle it'll sting you for your pains; grasp it like a lad of mettle, an' as soft as silk remains'.

2012 *Independent* (Ireland) Labour Senator James Heffernan said it was time for the Government to 'grasp the nettle' by bringing in new abortion legislation.

grass

at the grass roots at the level of the ordinary voter; among the rank and file of a political party.

the grass is always greener other people's lives or situations always seem better than your own.

ℹ This is a shortened form of the proverb 'the grass is always greener on the other side of the fence', usually used as a caution against dissatisfaction with your own lot in life. There are a number of sayings about the attractions of something distant or inaccessible, for example *blue are the faraway hills*.

not let the grass grow under your feet not delay in acting or taking an opportunity.

put someone or something out to grass ❶ put an animal out to graze. ❷ force someone to retire; make someone redundant. informal

a snake in the grass: *see* SNAKE.

grasshopper

knee-high to a grasshopper: *see* KNEE-HIGH.

grave

dig your own grave: *see* DIG.

from the cradle to the grave: *see* CRADLE.

have one foot in the grave: *see* FOOT.

(on) this side of the grave in life.

silent (*or* quiet) as the grave very quiet.

take the (*or* your etc.) secret to the grave die without revealing a secret.

turn (*or* turn over) in their grave used to express the opinion that something would have caused anger or distress in someone who is now dead.

2010 *New Zealand Herald* On Monday, Samuel Parnell, the father of the eight-hour day, would have turned in his grave at the way the day set aside in his memory was desecrated.

graven

a graven image a carved representation of a god used as an object of worship.

ℹ This expression is from the second of the Ten Commandments: 'Thou shalt not make unto thee any graven image' (Exodus 20:4).

gravy

board (*or* climb on) the gravy train obtain access to an easy source of financial gain. informal

ⓘ *Gravy* is an informal term for 'money easily acquired'.

grease

grease (*or* oil) someone's palm bribe someone. informal

ⓘ This phrase comes from the practice of applying grease to a machine to make it run smoothly. The same expression exists in French as *graisser la patte*. The form with *palm* is now predominant but *hand* appears in the earliest recorded versions of the idiom, dating from the 16th century.

2005 *ArtThrob* If you were fortunate enough to encounter Canevari on opening night, he probably would have greased your palm with an artefact and gift from the exhibition—a very oily dollar bill peeled from a considerable wad.

grease (*or* oil) the wheels make things go smoothly, especially by paying the expenses.

greased

like greased lightning: *see* **like lightning** *at* LIGHTNING.

greasy

the greasy pole used to refer to the difficult route to the top of someone's profession.

ⓘ The original literal greasy pole was a pole covered with an oily substance to make it more difficult to climb or walk along, used especially as a form of entertainment.

greasy spoon a cheap, run-down restaurant or cafe serving fried foods.

1968 Len Deighton *Only When I Larf* Bob said he was hungry and wanted to pull up at every greasy spoon we passed.

great

the great and the good distinguished and worthy people collectively. often ironic

1998 *New Scientist* But last year, an ad hoc committee of the Internet's great and good unveiled its own plan.

the great outdoors: *see* OUTDOORS.

great and small of all sizes, classes, or types.

2013 *Washington Post* For hundreds of cartoonists great and small, some from Argentina and England and New Zealand, this is a must stop on any East Coast tour swing.

the Great Game: *see* GAME.

great minds think alike: *see* MIND.

a great one for a habitual doer of; an enthusiast for.

2011 Janet Dailey *Bannon Brothers* My dad was a great one for documenting everything.

Great Scott! expressing surprise or amazement. dated

ⓘ The phrase is an arbitrary euphemism for *Great God!* (it predates the Antarctic exploits of Captain R. F. Scott, with whom it sometimes associated).

no great shakes: *see* SHAKE.

the great unwashed: *see* UNWASHED.

Greek

it's all Greek to me I can't understand it at all. informal

ⓘ *Greek* meaning 'unintelligible language or gibberish' is recorded from the 16th century. In Shakespeare's *Julius Caesar*, Casca, having noted that Cicero speaks Greek, adds 'for mine own part, it was Greek to me'.

beware (*or* fear) the Greeks bearing gifts if rivals or enemies show apparent generosity or kindness, you should be suspicious of their motives. proverb

ⓘ This proverb refers to the Trojan priest Laocoon's warning in Virgil's *Aeneid*: '*timeo Danaos et dona ferentes*', in which he warns his countrymen against taking into their city the gigantic wooden horse that the Greeks have left behind on their apparent departure. The fall of Troy results from their failure to heed this warning.

green

green about (*or* around *or* at) the gills looking or feeling ill or nauseous. informal

ⓘ A person's *gills* are the fleshy parts between the jaw and the ears: this sense of the word dates from the early 17th century. Other colours are occasionally used to indicate a sickly appearance; much less common is *rosy about the gills* indicating good health.

green light permission to go ahead with a project.

ⓘ The green light referred to is the traffic signal indicating that traffic is free to move forward. Red and green lights were in use from the late 19th century in railway signals, but this figurative use of green light appears to date from the mid 20th century.

2005 *Independent* The report, which opponents see as giving the green light to designer babies . . . .

green with envy very envious or jealous.

the green-eyed monster jealousy. literary

ⓘ Green is traditionally the colour of jealousy, as shown in the previous idiom *green with envy* and in this one, where the green-eyed monster is jealousy personified. This expression is a quotation from Shakespeare's *Othello*, where Iago warns: 'O! beware my lord of jealousy; It is the green-eyed monster which doth mock The meat it feeds on'.

green shoots signs of reviving activity.

ⓘ The metaphor was popularized in Britain by its (over-optimistic) use in 1991 by the chancellor of the exchequer, Norman Lamont, to characterize signs of economic recovery.

have green fingers have a natural ability to grow plants successfully. British informal

ⓘ The equivalent North American expression is *have a green thumb*.

rub of the green: *see* RUB.

wear the green willow: *see* WILLOW.

wigs on the green: *see* WIG.

greener

the grass is always greener: *see* GRASS.

grey

a grey area an ill-defined situation or field not readily conforming to a category or to an existing set of rules.

ⓘ In the 1960s, *grey areas* in British planning vocabulary referred to places that were not in as desperate a state as slums but which were in decline and in need of rebuilding.

2001 *Rough Guide to Travel Health* In theory, it should be a cinch to diagnose appendicitis, but in practice it's much more of a grey area.

little grey cells brain cells (as symbolic of high intelligence or mental acuity).

ⓘ The phrase is particularly associated with the cerebral Belgian detective Hercule Poirot, invented by Agatha Christie.

2013 *New Statesman* Computers sometimes help, but the crucial work is done by those 'little grey cells', as Hercule Poirot would say.

grief

come to grief have an accident; meet with disaster.

2000 R. W. Holden *Taunton Cider & Langdons* The historian . . . will *see* no trace of the battlefield where Charles's grandson, the Duke of Monmouth, came to grief.

give someone grief be a nuisance to someone, especially by being argumentative or hostilely critical. informal

2013 *CNN Transcripts* Of course not every Red Sox player is fuzzy. Koji Uehara wore a beard for years and then shaved it before the season started. No one gives him grief because his relief pitching has been such a huge relief.

grig

merry (*or* lively) as a grig full of fun; extravagantly lively.

ⓘ The meaning and origin of the word *grig* are unknown. Samuel Johnson conjectured in his *Dictionary* that it referred to 'anything below the natural size'. A sense that fits in with the *lively* version of this idiom is 'a young or small eel in fresh water'. The phrases *merry grig* and *merry Greek*, meaning 'a lively, playful person', were both in use in the mid 16th century, but it is impossible to establish the precise relationship between them or to be certain which may be an alteration of the other.

grim

like (*or* for) grim death with intense determination.

ⓘ The variant *for grim death,* which makes no literal sense, probably arose by contamination with *for dear life* (*see* LIFE).

2014 *Daily Telegraph* With Ségolène spitting nails, and Valérie clinging on to her man for grim death, Hollande finally landed the top job in May 2012.

the Grim Reaper a personification of death in the form of a cloaked skeleton wielding a large scythe.

grin

grin and bear it suffer pain or misfortune in a stoical manner.

ⓘ The usual modern sense of *grin* is less sinister than its earliest senses: when it entered the language it primarily meant 'an act of showing the teeth' or 'a snarl'. From the mid 17th century to the mid 18th century, a *grin* was generally used in a derogatory way or in unfavourable contrast to a cheerful *smile*. The sense of *grin* in *grin and bear it* retains the earlier associations with showing your teeth in a grimace of pain or anger. *Grin and abide* is recorded as a proverb in the late 18th century; the modern version dates from the late 19th century.

grin like a Cheshire cat: *see* CHESHIRE.

grind

grind to a halt (*or* **come to a grinding halt**) move more and more slowly and then stop.

2013 **Joel Spolsky** *Joel on Software* If each of those companies had three or four engineers dedicating a few hours every day to picking off their competitors' applications, the number of granted patents to those companies would grind to a halt. Wouldn't that be something!

have an axe to grind: *see* AXE.

grindstone

keep your nose to the grindstone work hard and continuously.

ⓘ A *grindstone* was a thick revolving disc of stone on which knives and tools were sharpened. Appearing in various forms since the mid 16th century, this idiom originally referred to getting mastery over someone else by forcing them to work without a break.

grip

come (*or* **get**) **to grips with** ❶ engage in physical combat with. ❷ begin to deal with or understand.

get a grip keep or recover your self-control.

2000 Jo-Ann Goodwin *Danny Boy* I took a deep breath, trying desperately to get a grip, to hold myself together.

grist

grist to the mill experience, material, or knowledge which can be turned to good use.

ⓘ *Grist* in the sense of 'corn that is to be ground' is now used only in this phrase and in the proverb *all is grist that comes to the mill*. The word is related to Old Saxon *gristgrimmo* meaning 'gnashing of teeth'.

grit

grit your teeth make a great effort to keep your resolve when faced with an unpleasant or painful duty.

2012 *Daily Telegraph* The former French minister of finance lives her life according to the advice of her former synchronised swimming coach: 'When it's tough, grit your teeth and smile.'

true grit strength of character; stamina. informal

ⓘ *Grit* in this colloquial sense originated in early 19th-century US English. *True Grit* was the title of a 1969 Western starring John Wayne.

grody

grody to the max unspeakably awful. US informal

ⓘ *Grody* is probably an alteration of *grotesque* and *to the max* of *to the maximum point*.

groove

in (*or* **into**) **the groove** ❶ performing well or confidently, especially in an established pattern. ❷ indulging in relaxed and spontaneous enjoyment, especially dancing. informal

ⓘ A *groove* is the spiral track cut in a gramophone record that forms the path for the needle. *In the groove* is first found in the mid 20th century, in the context of jazz, and it gave rise to the adjective *groovy*, which initially meant 'playing or able to play jazz or similar music well'.

gross

by the gross in large numbers or amounts.

ⓘ A *gross* was formerly widely used as a unit of quantity equal to twelve dozen; the word comes from the French *grosse douzaine*, which literally means 'large dozen'.

ground

be on firm ground: *see* FIRM.

break new (*or* **fresh**) **ground** do something innovative which is considered an advance or positive benefit.

ⓘ Literally, to break new ground is to do preparatory digging or other work prior to building or planting something. In North America the idiom is *break ground*.

cut the ground from under someone's feet do something which leaves someone without a reason or justification for their actions or opinions. informal

from the ground up completely or complete. informal

2013 *Bit-Tech Hardware* Following on from the similar Euler we looked at recently, the Galileo is a slightly longer, more expensive case, which is designed from the ground up to be as skinny as possible.

get in on the ground floor become part of an enterprise in its early stages. informal

get off the ground (*or* get something off the ground) start (*or* cause to start) happening or functioning successfully.

go to ground ❶ (of a fox or other animal) enter its earth or burrow to hide, especially when being hunted. ❷ (of a person) hide or become inaccessible, usually for a prolonged period.

have an ear to the ground: *see* EAR.

have your feet on the ground: *see* FOOT.

hit the ground running start something and proceed at a fast pace with enthusiasm. informal

> **2000 Catherine Hanger** *World Food: Morocco* Don't plan on hitting the ground running, especially if you're on a long trip. It's worth allowing yourself time to adjust physically and mentally to your new environment and lifestyle.

kiss the ground: *see* KISS.

on the ground in a place where real, practical work is done.

on your own ground on your own territory or concerning your own range of knowledge or experience.

prepare the ground make it easier for something to occur or be developed.

run someone or something to ground: *see* **run someone or something to earth** *at* EARTH.

suit someone or something down to the ground: *see* SUIT.

thick (*or* thin) on the ground existing (*or* not existing) in large numbers or amounts.

Tom Tiddler's ground: *see* TOM.

work (*or* run) yourself into the ground exhaust yourself by working or running very hard. informal

grove

groves of Academe the academic community. literary

> ℹ This phrase alludes to the Roman poet Horace's *Epistles*, in which he says: *Atque inter silvas Academi quaerere verum* 'and seek for truth in the groves of Academe'. The Academia was a grove near ancient Athens where a number of philosophers, Plato among them, taught their pupils.

grow

grow on trees be plentiful or easily obtained.

> **2013** *Daily Telegraph* The atmosphere is great; that's what I enjoy. This baby will be a royal baby. And royal babies don't grow on trees.

not let the grass grow under your feet: *see* GRASS.

guard

lower (*or* drop *or* let down) your guard ❶ relax your defensive posture, leaving yourself vulnerable to attack. ❷ reduce your level of vigilance or caution.

> ℹ This is an expression connected in its literal sense with boxing, as is its opposite *raise your guard* meaning 'adopt a defensive posture'.

guernsey

get a guernsey ❶ be selected for a football team. ❷ gain recognition or approbation. Australian informal

> ℹ A *guernsey* is a type of knitted shirt or sweater; in Australia the word is specifically applied to a football shirt.

guess

anyone's (*or* anybody's) guess something very difficult or impossible to determine. informal

> **2002 Jeffrey Eugenides** *Middlesex* Where Lefty obtained the hash is anybody's guess.

by guess and by God without specific guidance or direction.

> ℹ This expression was originally used in a nautical context, where it meant to steer blind, without the guidance of landmarks. The euphemistic alternative *by guess and by Godfrey* is also sometimes found.

keep someone guessing leave someone uncertain or in doubt as to your intentions or plans. informal

there are no prizes for guessing: *see* PRIZE.

your guess is as good as mine I know as little about the matter as you (used in answer to a question).

guest

be my guest please do. informal

> **1988 Jay McInerney** *The Story of My Life* I'll hurt myself, Mannie screams. Be my guest, says Rebecca.

guid

the unco guid: *see* UNCO.

gullet

stick in your gullet: *see* **stick in your throat** *at* THROAT.

gum tree

up a gum tree in or into a predicament. informal

ⓘ This phrase is now found mainly in British English, but the phrase is recorded in the early 19th century in the USA, where *possum up a gum tree* was the title of a song or dance.

2012 *Independent* It was ... a complete cock-up, absolute folly, and I knew I was up a gum tree.

g

gun

a big gun: *see* **a big cheese** *at* BIG.

blow great guns be very windy. informal

give it the gun accelerate powerfully in a car. informal

go down with (all) guns firing (*or* blazing) fail or be beaten, but continue to offer resistance until the end.

go great guns perform forcefully, vigorously, or successfully. informal

1913 *Field* A moment later Louvois shot out, passed Sanquhar and Fairy King, and going great guns ... beat the favourite by a head.

hold (*or* put) a gun (*or* a pistol) to someone's head force someone to do something by using threats.

jump the gun: *see* JUMP.

smoking gun: *see* SMOKING.

son of a gun: *see* SON.

spike someone's guns: *see* SPIKE.

stick to your guns refuse to compromise or change, despite criticism. informal

ⓘ The image here is of a soldier maintaining his position under enemy fire.

2011 *Alf Grumble* Turns out if you're in the minority, you have less of an incentive to compromise than the majority does. Because if you stick to your guns, and reach that crucial 10%, your ideas eventually win out.

top gun a (or the) most important person.

under the gun under great pressure. North American informal

with (all) guns blazing with great determination and energy, often without thought for the consequences. informal

gundy

no good to gundy: *see* GOOD.

gurgler

go down the gurgler be wasted or lost. Australian & New Zealand informal

ⓘ A 'gurgler' is a drain.

gut

— your guts out perform a specified action as hard or as fully as possible. informal

2000 Anthony Bourdain *Kitchen Confidential* He'll take them out, get them liquored up so they blab their guts out, and I'll have a full report by noon next.

blood and guts: *see* BLOOD.

bust a gut: *see* BUST.

hate someone's guts feel a strong hatred for someone. informal

have someone's guts for garters punish or rebuke someone severely. informal

spill your guts: *see* SPILL.

gutser

come a gutser suffer a failure or defeat. informal

ⓘ *Gutser* (also spelled *gutzer*) is explained in Fraser and Gibbons' *Soldier and Sailor Words* (1925) as 'pre-war slang, and an old term among Scottish boys for falling flat on the water in diving, instead of making a clean header'. In air-force slang *come* (or *fetch) a gutser* meant 'crash'.

gyp

give someone gyp cause pain or severe discomfort to someone. British informal

ⓘ *Gyp* may be a dialect contraction of *gee-up*, a word of command used to urge a horse to move faster, the connection being that, in this phrase, whatever is giving someone *gyp* is preventing them from resting or taking things easy.

habit

creature of habit: *see* CREATURE.

kick the habit: *see* KICK.

hack

hack it manage; cope (usually used in the negative). informal

2011 Justin Cartwright *Other People's Money* Does she really want to be responsible for humiliating a family like the Tubals just for a story, for the sake of the *Globe and Mail* . . . ? Or is it for the editor, who couldn't hack it in London?

hackles

make someone's hackles rise make someone angry or indignant.

ⓘ *Hackles* are the long feathers on the neck of a fighting cock or the hairs on the top of a dog's neck, which are raised when the animal is angry or excited.

had

have had it: *see* HAVE.

never had it so good: *see* GOOD

hail

hail-fellow-well-met showing excessive familiarity.

1979 Steven Levenkron *The Best Little Girl in the World* Harold was accustomed to hail-fellow-well-met salesmen and deferential secretaries and even irate accountants.

hair

bad hair day: *see* BAD.

hair of the dog a small quantity of alcohol taken as a remedy for a hangover. informal

ⓘ The full form of this phrase is *hair of the dog that bit you*. Hair from a rabid dog was at one time thought to be a remedy against the effects of its bite; in this expression, the recommended cure for a hangover is a small amount of the cause of the problem.

1987 Bruce Allen Powe *The Ice Eaters* Murray, still feeling the effects of the previous evening, had suggested they go into a bar because he needed a hair of the dog.

a hair's breadth a very small amount or margin.

get someone by the short hairs: *see* **get someone by the short and curlies** *at* SHORT.

in (*or* out of) someone's hair annoying (*or* ceasing to annoy) someone. informal

keep your hair on! used to urge someone not to panic or lose their temper. British informal

let your hair down behave wildly or uninhibitedly. informal

make someone's hair curl: *see* CURL.

make someone's hair stand on end alarm or horrify someone.

neither hide nor hair of: *see* HIDE.

not harm a hair of someone's head: *see* HARM.

not turn a hair remain apparently unmoved or unaffected.

put hair (*or* hairs) on your chest (of alcoholic drink) revive your strength. informal

split hairs make small and overfine distinctions.

ⓘ This expression was first recorded in the late 17th century. *Split straws*, dating from the 19th century, is a less common version.

tear your hair out: *see* TEAR.

hairy

give someone the hairy eyeball: *see* EYEBALL.

hale

hale and hearty (of an old person) healthy and in good spirits.

ⓘ *Hale*, a relative of *whole*, is now obsolete except in this phrase.

2011 *New York Times* At 70, I am hale and hearty, exercising regularly and eating well.

half

a — and a half a particular person or thing considered as an impressive example of the kind specified. informal

1998 Sarah Waters *Tipping the Velvet* The daughter must be a beauty and a half... if the mother is so eager to keep her safe and close, away from young men's eyes.

at half cock when only partly ready. informal

ⓘ *At half cock* is used of a firearm with the cock lifted but not moved to the position at which the trigger will act. It is usually found in *go off at half cock* or *go off half-cocked* meaning 'go ahead without making proper preparation and therefore fail'.

the glass is half-full (*or* **half-empty):** *see* GLASS.

go halves (*or* **shares)** share something equally.

half the battle: *see* BATTLE.

half a chance the slightest opportunity. informal

1970 Nina Bawden *The Birds on the Trees* Give her half a chance and she'll make you think black's white.

half an eye: *see* EYE.

half a loaf not as much as you want but better than nothing.

ⓘ This phrase alludes to the proverb *half a loaf is better than no bread*, which has been in use since the mid 16th century.

the half of it the most important part or aspect of something. informal

1987 George Turner *Sea & Summer* Mum... would ask, 'But is this true?' and Billy... would tell her that wasn't the half of it.

half seas over fairly drunk. British informal, dated

ⓘ The expression originally meant literally 'halfway across the sea', hence implying a condition halfway between sobriety and drunkenness.

have half a mind to do something: *see* MIND.

hell's half acre: *see* HELL.

how the other half lives: *see* OTHER.

listen with half an ear: *see* EAR.

not do things by halves do things thoroughly or extravagantly.

not half ❶ not nearly as. ❷ not at all. informal ❸ to an extreme degree; very much so. British informal

six of one and half a dozen of the other: *see* SIX.

too — by half used to emphasize something bad.

2013 *New York Times* The 1998 New York premiere of 'Inishmaan' was too precious by half, and it wasn't until I saw Garry Hynes's straightforward staging ... that I began to think more fondly of it.

your better half: *see* BETTER.

halfpence

more kicks than halfpence: *see* KICK.

halfway

a halfway house ❶ a compromise. ❷ the halfway point in a progression. ❸ a place where ex-prisoners, mental patients, etc. can stay while they become reaccustomed to normal life.

ⓘ In the late 18th century, *a halfway house* was an inn or other establishment halfway between two places or at the midpoint of a journey.

meet someone halfway: *see* MEET.

halt

grind to a halt: *see* GRIND.

hames

make a hames of do (something) very badly or ineptly; make a mess of. Irish informal

ⓘ Hames are reinforcing pieces round a horse's collar, but why the word—if indeed it is the same word—came to be used in this expression remains unclear.

Hamlet

Hamlet without the prince a performance or event taking place without the principal actor.

ⓘ The phrase comes from an account given in the *Morning Post* of September 1775. The member of a theatrical company who was to play Hamlet in a production of Shakespeare's play ran off with an innkeeper's daughter before the performance; when the play was announced to the audience, they were told 'the part of Hamlet [was] to be left out, for that night'.

hammer

come (*or* **go) under the hammer** be sold at an auction.

hammer something home: *see* **drive something home** *at* HOME.

hammer and tongs with great energy and noise.

ⓘ The image here is of a blacksmith striking the hot iron removed from the forge with a pair of tongs.

2009 *Time Magazine* Safire had a long interview with Lee, which was posted online. It's still worth reading as an example of two first-class minds going at it hammer and tongs.

hand

all hands the entire crew of a ship.

ⓘ A US variant of this phrase is *all hands and the cook*, meaning 'absolutely everyone available', since the cook would not normally be expected to do the work of other team members except in cases of dire emergency.

all hands to the pumps used to indicate that everyone is urgently needed to help out in an emergency.

ⓘ The expression originated in nautical parlance, and *hand* in that context means 'a member of the crew'.

2009 Loz Flowers *blah blah flowers* With just the three biggest libraries in the Borough open today we had an all hands to the pumps atmosphere.

at first hand: *see* FIRST.

at second hand: *see* SECOND.

be a dab hand at: *see* DAB.

bind (*or* tie) someone hand and foot severely restrict someone's freedom to act or make decisions.

a bird in hand: *see* BIRD.

bite the hand that feeds you: *see* BITE.

cap in hand: *see* CAP.

cash in hand: *see* CASH.

change hands: *see* CHANGE.

do something with one hand (tied) behind your back do something easily.

a firm hand: *see* FIRM.

force someone's hand: *see* FORCE.

a free hand: *see* FREE.

get (*or* keep) your hand in become (*or* remain) practiced in something.

get (*or* lay) your hands on find or get (something).

get your hands dirty: *see* DIRTY.

give (*or* lend) a hand assist in an action or enterprise.

give someone the glad hand: *see* GLAD.

go hand in hand be closely associated (with each other).

hand in your dinner pail: *see* DINNER.

hand in glove in close collusion or association.

ⓘ This phrase appeared earlier (in the late 17th century) as *hand and glove*; the current form gained ground from the late 18th century.

hand in hand ❶ (of two people) with hands joined, especially as a mark of affection. ❷ closely associated or connected.

❷ **2014** *Telegraph* Cure's staff also try educate young mothers to eat healthily and take folic acid to avoid spina bifida in their babies, which sometimes goes hand in hand with hydrocephalus.

hand on the torch: *see* TORCH.

a hand's turn a stroke of work. informal

1982 Rodney Hall *Just Relations* Rich was she? A wallowing pig in jewels and wicked money she never did a hand's turn to earn for herself?

hand to hand (of fighting) at close quarters.

(from) hand to mouth satisfying only your immediate needs because of lack of money for future plans and investments.

1960 Lynne Reid Banks *The L-Shaped Room* I'm twenty-eight years old and I'm still living from hand to mouth like a bloody tramp.

hands down (especially of winning) easily and decisively.

ⓘ Originally a horse-racing expression, *win hands down* meant that a jockey was so certain of victory in the closing stages of a race that he could lower his hands, thereby relaxing his hold on the reins and ceasing to urge on his horse.

hands off! used to warn someone against touching or interfering with something.

have blood on your hands: *see* BLOOD.

have clean hands: *see* CLEAN.

have to hand it to someone used to acknowledge the merit or achievement of someone.

2001 *DVD Verdict* You've got to hand it to the people at Universal; they took a very fair and decent approach to their upcoming Jurassic Park trilogy box set.

have the upper hand: *see* UPPER.

have your hands full have as much work needing to be done as you can do

have your hands tied be unable to act freely

have your hand in the till: *see* **have your fingers in the till** *at* TILL.

have someone in the palm of your hand: *see* PALM.

hold someone's hand give a person comfort, guidance, or moral support in a sad or difficult situation.

I have only got one pair of hands: *see* PAIR.

an iron hand in a velvet glove: *see* IRON.

make (*or* lose *or* spend) money hand over fist make (*or* lose *or* spend) money very rapidly or in very large quantities. informal

🛈 This phrase first appeared in the mid 18th century as *hand over hand*. Found in nautical contexts, it referred to the movement of a person's hands when rapidly climbing a rope or hauling it in. By the mid 19th century, *hand over hand* was being used to mean 'advancing continuously and rapidly', especially of one ship pursuing another. *Hand over fist* is first recorded in the early 19th century, also in a nautical context, but it was soon used more generally to indicate speed, especially in the handling of money.

2013 Eric S. Raymond *Armed & Dangerous* It doesn't matter that Android is now the #1-selling smartphone in the U.S. and worldwide, Apple is making money hand over fist.

on (*or* off) someone's hands having (*or* not having) to be dealt with or looked after by the person specified.

overplay your hand: *see* OVERPLAY.

pair of hands: *see* PAIR.

play into someone's hands act in such a way as unintentionally to give someone an advantage.

put your hand in your pocket: *see* POCKET.

put your hands together applaud.

put your hand(s) up raise your hand(s) in surrender, to signify assent or participation, or as an admission of culpability.

2012 *CNN transcripts* All the other riders that were doping in this era have put their hands up. They all want to fix the sport and move on. But I don't know if Lance Armstrong's ever going to put his hands up.

the right hand doesn't know what the left hand's doing there is a state of confusion or a failure of communication within a group or organization.

rub your hands: *see* RUB.

a safe pair of hands: *see* SAFE.

set (*or* put) your hand to start work on.

🛈 A fuller version of this phrase is *set your hand to the plough*, which alludes to Luke 9:62: 'No man, having put his hand to the plough, and looking back, is fit for the kingdom of God'.

show your hand: *see* SHOW.

sit on your hands: *see* SIT.

stay someone's hand: *see* STAY.

strengthen someone's hand: *see* STRENGTHEN.

take a hand in become influential in determining something; intervene.

1988 *Shetland Times* The amenity trust is also taking a hand in restoring two old gravestones in the Ollaberry kirkyard.

take someone or something in hand take someone or something under your control, especially in order to improve them.

take your courage in both hands: *see* COURAGE.

take your life in your hands: *see* LIFE.

talk (*or* tell it) to the hand used to express dismissive disregard of, or indifference to, what a person has said or is saying, or to implore a person to stop speaking. US

🛈 The idea is also more fully expressed as *talk* (or *tell it*) *to the hand because the face isn't listening* (or *doesn't understand*, etc.). It is typically uttered with a hand outstretched and the palm facing the person addressed.

throw your hand in give up; withdraw from a contest.

🛈 In card games, especially poker, if you *throw your hand in* you retire from the game.

tip your hand: *see* TIP.

try your hand: *see* TRY.

turn your hand to something undertake an activity different from your usual occupation.

2013 *New Zealand Herald* A former All White's skipper is finding success off the soccer pitch as he turns his hand to the world of business.

wait on someone hand and foot attend to all of someone's needs or requests, especially when this is regarded as unreasonable.

1955 L. P. Hartley *A Perfect Woman* He has everything he wants and servants who wait on him hand and foot.

wash your hands (of): *see* WASH.

the whip hand: *see* WHIP.

with one hand (tied) behind your back ❶ with serious limitations or restrictions. ❷ used to indicate that you could do something without any difficulty.

with your hand in the cookie jar: *see* COOKIE.

wring your hands: *see* WRING.

handbasket

go to hell in a handbasket: *see* HELL.

handle

fly off the handle: *see* FLY.

get a handle on find a means of understanding, controlling, or approaching a person or situation.

2006 Polly Williams *The Rise & Fall of a Yummy Mummy* The lie hurts. But I can't explain the truth, partly because I haven't got a handle on it myself.

handshake

golden handshake: *see* GOLDEN.

handsome

handsome is as handsome does character and behaviour are more important than good looks. proverb

ℹ In this particular form the proverb dates from the mid 17th century. When used of behaviour, *handsome* really means 'chivalrous' or 'genteel', though in this saying it is often taken to refer to good looks. The original sense is made clear in the earlier version: *goodly is he that goodly dooth.*

high, wide, and handsome: *see* HIGH.

hang

get the hang of something learn how to operate or do something. informal

1990 Roddy Doyle *The Snapper* He was pretending to time them . . . because he couldn't get the hang of the stop-watch Bertie'd got him.

hang by a thread: *see* THREAD.

hang fire delay or be delayed in taking action or progressing.

ℹ In the late 18th century, *hang fire* was used to refer to the action of a firearm that was slow in communicating the fire through the vent to the charge and so did not go off immediately.

hang on to your hat: *see* **hold on to your hat** *at* HAT.

hang your head: *see* HEAD.

hang in there remain persistent and determined in difficult circumstances. informal, especially North American

hang a left (*or* right) make a left (*or* right) turn. US informal

hang loose: *see* LOOSE.

hang of a — (*or* a hang of) to a very high degree; very great. South African informal

ℹ In this expression *hang* is probably being used as a euphemism for *hell.*

1945 Frank Sargeson *When the Wind Blows* All this was because Charlie was hang of a funny to be with.

hang on someone's lips: *see* LIP.

hang one on ❶ punch (someone) hard. ❷ get drunk. informal, especially North American

hang someone out to dry leave someone in a difficult or vulnerable situation. informal

ℹ The image here is of hanging wet washing on a clothes line to dry. The idea of 'flapping uselessly or ineffectually' like clothes drying in the wind is also behind the cricketing metaphor *hanging your bat out to dry*, which dates from the late 19th century and means 'holding your bat away from your body at an ineffectual angle'.

2011 *Economist* The price rises will swiftly be reversed and the bosses responsible . . . could find themselves hung out to dry.

hang out your shingle: *see* SHINGLE.

hang tough be or remain inflexible or firmly resolved. North American informal

1992 Randall Kenan *Let the Dead Bury their Dead* Obviously, he intended to hang tough at first, but apparently Miss Jesse's psychic bullwhip lashed out and snap-crackled his brain.

hang up your boots stop working; retire. informal

ℹ *Boots* are seen in this expression as part of a person's working clothes. A common Canadian variant is *hang up your skates.*

1997 *Farmers Weekly* The hard fact is that all farmers, whether the pension scheme is attractive or not, are, mostly, reluctant to hang their boots up.

hang up your fiddle (when you come home): *see* FIDDLE.

hang your hat be resident. North American informal

2001 Kevin Sampson *Outlaws* End of the day though it ain't the Royal and that is where I want to hang my hat.

How's it hanging? How are you?; How are things?; Hello. US slang

ℹ The expression was originally used, with humorous reference, of the male genitals, and remains predominantly a male usage.

2012 Sue Townsend *The Woman Who Went to Bed for a Year* Alex, my man! How's it hanging, bro?

let it all hang out be uninhibited or relaxed. informal

not care (*or* give) a hang not care at all. informal

ℹ *Hang* here is a late 19th-century euphemism for *damn*.

thereby hangs a tale: *see* THEREBY.

h

hanging

a hanging offence a fault or crime so serious that the perpetrator should be executed.

2009 *Guardian* The sensational revelation that Jacqui Smith's husband used taxpayers' cash to view a couple of soft porn videos is not, in itself, a hanging offence.

someone's tongue is hanging out: *see* TONGUE.

ha'p'orth

spoil the ship for a ha'p'orth of tar: *see* SPOIL.

happen

shit happens: *see* SHIT.

happy

happy as a sandboy extremely happy; perfectly contented with your situation.

ℹ An 1823 dictionary describes a *sandboy* as an urchin who sold sand in the streets, and according to the same source the expression *jolly as a sandboy* was already proverbial by that date for 'a merry fellow who has tasted a drop'. A common British version of the phrase is *happy as Larry*, *Larry* being a pet name for *Lawrence*. This saying is sometimes connected with the renowned boxer Larry Foley (1847–1917); on the other hand, it may owe something to *larry*, a dialect word used by Thomas Hardy, meaning 'a state of excitement'. The North American version is *happy as a clam*, which apparently originated in the early 19th century on the east coast, where clams are plentiful: the full version *happy as a clam at high water* explains the source of the clam's satisfaction.

happy event the birth of a child. humorous

happy hunting ground a place where success or enjoyment is obtained.

ℹ This phrase originally referred to the optimistic hope of Native Americans that the afterlife will be spent in a country where there are good hunting grounds.

2008 *Jamaica Observer* That may have been part of the reason [the Australian cricket team] were shocked by India earlier this year at Perth, which has long been a happy hunting ground for Australia.

not a happy bunny (*or* camper) used to suggest that someone is displeased. informal

ℹ The variant *happy camper* alludes to the inmates of holiday camps, who stereotypically are constantly exhorted by the management to be happy.

2004 *This Is Wiltshire* Then Alan answered the phone. The majority of the conversation was unprintable. Basically the smoking chips hadn't been delivered again and Alan wasn't a happy bunny.

2009 *Express* He wasn't a happy camper, but sometimes the manager knows best.

hard

be hard put (to it) to find it very difficult to.

2011 *Ballet.co Magazine* Without knowing Lewis Carroll's book(s), you'd be hard put to understand why his Alice has endured as a classic read—and a frustrating challenge for film and ballet makers.

between a rock and a hard place: *see* ROCK.

die hard: *see* DIE.

a hard act to follow: *see* ACT.

hard and fast (of a rule or a distinction made) fixed and definitive.

hard as nails ❶ very hard. ❷ (of people) insensitive or callous; without pity.

hard at it busily working. informal

2005 *Gay Times* Will's been hard at it lately—and not just at the gym.

a hard case ❶ a tough or intractable person. ❷ an amusing or eccentric person. Australian & New Zealand

hard cheese: *see* CHEESE.

hard done by harshly or unfairly treated. British

hard feelings feelings of resentment.

2002 *Classical Net* It was Sir John Barbirolli who premiered the symphony in 1956, and Barbirolli who made its first recording. Boult apparently had no hard feelings, as his performances and recording quickly followed.

hard lines! used to commiserate with someone on a misfortune.

a hard nut (to crack): *see* **a tough nut** *at* NUT.

hard of hearing not able to hear well.

a hard row to hoe: *see* ROW.

the hard stuff strong alcoholic drink. informal

the hard way through suffering or learning from the unpleasant consequences of mistakes.

> **2009 Ronald Garay** *The Manship School* Veteran newspapermen who had come up the hard way, learning their skills in the hard school of experience.

hard yards arduous preparatory work necessary for success in an undertaking.

> ❶ The phrase originally referred to strenuous preparatory training for a sporting event.

> **2013** *Daily Telegraph* You don't turn around years of decline and stagnation overnight. It's a long haul and these are the months and years where we need to put in the hard yards.

hold hard used to exhort someone to stop or wait. British, dated

> ❶ *Hold hard* was originally an exclamation warning riders in the hunting field to pull hard on the reins to make their horses stop, similar to **hold your horses** (*see* HORSE).

play hard to get deliberately adopt an aloof or uninterested attitude, typically in order to make yourself more attractive or interesting. informal

put the hard word on ask a favour of someone, especially a sexual or financial favour. Australian & New Zealand informal

> **1997 Derek Hansen** *Sole Survivor* But if he'd come to put the hard word on her, why hadn't he picked a more appropriate time? Midmorning had never struck her as particularly conducive to romance.

the school of hard knocks: *see* SCHOOL.

hardball

play hardball use uncompromising and ruthless methods. informal

> ❶ In North America, *hardball* is literally baseball, especially as contrasted with softball.

> **2012 Ben Goldacre** *Bad Pharma* The pharmaceutical industry plays hardball with developing countries over the price of medicines.

hare

mad as a March hare: *see* **mad as a hatter** *at* MAD.

run with the hare and hunt with the hounds try to remain on good terms with both sides in a conflict or dispute. British

> ❶ This expression has been in use since the mid 15th century.

start a hare raise a topic of conversation. British, dated

> ❶ The rapid twisting and running of a hunted hare is here used as a metaphor for the pursuit of a topic in an animated conversation, especially one in which the participants hold strong views.

hark

hark who's talking: *see* **look who's talking** *at* TALK.

harm

not harm a hair of someone's head not cause someone the slightest harm.

out of harm's way in a safe place.

> **1996 Frank McCourt** *Angela's Ashes* Take down the Pope and hide him in the coal hole . . . where he won't be seen and he'll be out of harm's way.

wouldn't harm a fly: *see* **wouldn't hurt a fly** *at* FLY.

there is no harm in — the course of action specified may not guarantee success but is at least unlikely to have unwelcome repercussions.

> **2013** *Washington Post* There is no harm in preferring one fellow over another, of course. But there is some harm in suggesting . . . that their rival visions define the arc of our national history.

harness

die in harness: *see* DIE.

in harness ❶ in the routine of daily work. ❷ working closely with someone to achieve something.

> ❶ The image is of a horse or other animal being used for driving or draught work.

harp

harp on the same string dwell tediously on one subject.

Harry

play Old Harry with: *see* **play the devil with** *at* DEVIL.

Tom, Dick, and Harry: *see* TOM.

hash

make a hash of make a mess of; bungle. informal

> ℹ *Hash* comes from the French verb *hacher* meaning 'chop up small'. A *hash* is a dish of cooked meat cut into small pieces and recooked with gravy; from this comes the derogatory sense of *hash* meaning 'a jumble of incongruous elements; a mess'.

settle someone's hash deal with and subdue a person very forcefully. informal

sling hash: *see* SLING.

haste

more haste, less speed you make better progress with a task if you don't try to do it too quickly. proverb

> ℹ The primary meaning of 'speed' in this proverbial saying was 'success in the performance of an activity', rather than 'rapidity of movement', though it is the latter that is now generally assumed to be meant.

hasty

beat a hasty retreat: *see* BEAT.

hat

at the drop of a hat: *see* DROP.

be all hat and no cattle tend to talk boastfully without acting on your words. US informal

black hat (*or* white hat) used in reference to the bad (*or* good) party in a situation.

> ℹ This idiom refers to the colour of the hats traditionally worn by the bad (or good) characters in cowboy films.

hang your hat: *see* HANG.

hats off to — used to express admiration for someone who has done something praiseworthy. British

hold (*or* hang) on to your hat! said as a humorous warning that conditions are about to become more difficult or hazardous.

> **2008** *Guardian* Hold on to your hats, Hearts fans, Bertie Vogts is keen to return to Scotland and is heading for the Tynecastle manager's office.

I'll eat my hat: *see* EAT.

keep something under your hat keep something a secret.

old hat: *see* OLD.

pass the hat round collect contributions of money from a number of people for a specific purpose.

pick something out of a hat select something, especially the winner of a contest, at random.

pull one out of the hat bring off an unexpected trick in an apparently desperate situation.

> ℹ The image here is of a rabbit pulled out of a magician's hat.

> **1971 James McClure** *The Steam Pig* I must say you've really pulled one out of the hat this time.

pull a rabbit out of the hat: *see* RABBIT.

take your hat off (*or* raise your hat) to state your admiration for someone who has achieved something. British

> ℹ The image here is of the gesture of briefly removing your hat as a mark of courtesy or respect to someone.

talk through your hat: *see* TALK.

throw (*or* toss) your hat in (*or* into) the ring indicate willingness to take up a challenge or enter a contest.

> **2007 K. D. Ackerman** *Young J. Edgar* He announced ... that he was tossing his hat in the ring as a candidate for president of the United States.

tip your hat: *see* TIP.

wearing your — hat (*or* with your — hat on) used to indicate that someone is speaking or acting in a particular, especially professional capacity.

> **2013 Bruce Bond** *Passing Professional Skills Tests for Trainee Teachers* You are there as a teacher, not a friend. Remain professional throughout and always have your teacher's hat on.

hatch

batten down the hatches: *see* BATTEN.

down the hatch used to express friendly feelings towards your companions before drinking. informal

hatches, matches, and despatches the births, marriages, and deaths columns in a newspaper. humorous, dated

under (the) hatches ❶ below deck in a ship. ❷ concealed from public knowledge.

hatchet

bury the hatchet: *see* BURY.

do a hatchet job on criticize savagely.

hate

hate someone's guts: *see* GUT.

hatter

mad as a hatter: *see* MAD.

haul

haul ass: *see* **drag ass** *at* ASS.

haul someone over the coals: *see* COAL.

over the long haul: *see* LONG.

have

have had it ❶ be in a very poor condition; be beyond repair or past its best. ❷ be extremely tired. ❸ have lost all chance of survival. ❹ be unable to tolerate someone or something any longer. informal

have it away (on your toes) leave quickly. British informal

have it away (*or* off) with have sexual intercourse with. British vulgar slang

> **1998** *Oldie* Today, young Billy would be having it off with all three young ladies on a rota basis.

have (got) it in for have a particular dislike of someone and behave in a hostile manner towards them. informal

have (got) it in you to do something have the capacity or potential to do something. informal

have it out with someone attempt to resolve a contentious matter by confronting someone and engaging in a frank discussion or argument. informal

let's be having you used to tell someone to be quick in responding to instructions or in presenting themselves to take action. informal

> ❶ For other idioms containing *have*, see the entry for the main word in the idiom (for example, **have had your chips** at CHIP).

havoc

play havoc with completely disrupt; cause serious damage to.

> **2013** *New Zealand Herald* Utilities will have to rely on coal to plug gaps, playing havoc with Germany's greenhouse gas targets.

hawk

have eyes like a hawk: *see* EYE.

watch someone like a hawk keep a vigilant eye on someone, especially to check that they do nothing wrong.

hay

hit the hay go to bed. informal

make hay make good use of an opportunity while it lasts.

> ❶ This is a shortened version of the proverb *make hay while the sun shines*, which dates from the mid 16th century.

> **2013** *New Statesman* The optimists can never be that most desirable of things, a meliorist, because every setback is necessarily a disaster. For the pessimist, it's simply a matter of shit happens, but until it does, make hay.

a roll in the hay: *see* ROLL.

haystack

a needle in a haystack: *see* NEEDLE.

head

above your head beyond your ability to understand.

bang (*or* knock) people's heads together reprimand people severely, especially in an attempt to stop them arguing.

> **2004 David Peck** *Careers Services* He gained an early reputation as a right-wing critic of the Service who intended to change attitudes and bang heads together where necessary.

bang (*or* knock) your head against a brick wall doggedly attempt the impossible and have your efforts repeatedly and painfully rebuffed.

> **1995 Jayne Miller** *Voxpop* You're banging your head against a brick wall for years and still getting nowhere. It's soul-destroying.

be hanging over your head (of something unpleasant) threaten to affect you at any moment.

be on someone's (own) head be someone's sole responsibility.

bite (*or* snap) someone's head off reply sharply and brusquely to someone.

bury your head in the sand: *see* BURY.

butt heads: *see* BUTT.

come (*or* bring) to a head reach (or cause to reach) a crisis.

do someone's head in cause someone to feel annoyed, confused, or frustrated. British informal

2018 Gillian McAllister *Anything You Do Say* He'd go to parties and stuff but come home and tell me everything that he'd said ... ask me for reassurance. All of that. Did my head in.

h

do something standing on your head do something very easily.

enter someone's head occur to someone (usually used in the negative).

from head to toe (*or* foot) all over your body.

ⓘ An alternative formulation with the same meaning is *from top to toe*.

get your head down ❶ sleep. ❷ concentrate on the task in hand. British informal

get your head round (*or* around) something understand or come to terms with something. informal

give (someone) head perform oral sex on someone. vulgar slang

give someone their head allow someone complete freedom of action.

ⓘ The image is of allowing a horse to go as fast as it wants rather than checking its pace with the bit and reins. Compare with **allow free rein to** (*at* REIN).

2012 *Church Times* Lindy had married Robert the man, not Robert the priest, and, while he gave her her head, he also relied on her absolute candour.

go to your head ❶ (of alcohol) make you dizzy or slightly drunk. ❷ (of success) make you conceited.

hang your head (in shame) be deeply ashamed.

have eyes in the back of your head: *see* EYE.

have your head screwed on: *see* SCREWED.

have a swollen head: *see* SWOLLEN.

head and shoulders above by far superior to. informal

2006 *Ireland's Own* The one player who stands head and shoulders above the rest is button-accordion virtuoso Joe Burke

head for the hills: *see* HILL.

head (*or* cut) someone or something off at the pass forestall someone or something, especially at a critical moment or at the last possible moment.

ⓘ *Pass* is used here in the sense of a narrow route through mountains.

head over heels upside down; turning over completely in a forward motion, as in a somersault.

ⓘ The earlier, more logical, version of this phrase was *heels over head*; the normal modern form dates from the late 18th century. It is often used figuratively of an extreme condition, as in *head over heels in love*, 'madly in love', or *head over heels in debt*, 'deeply in debt'.

head south: *see* SOUTH.

heads I win, tails you lose I win whatever happens.

heads will roll there will be some people dismissed or disgraced.

1975 Sam Selvon *Moses Ascending* It appears he went back for reinforcements, and is returning to make some drastic changes in the administration of the Establishment. Heads will roll, they say.

hold (*or* put) a gun (*or* a pistol) to someone's head: *see* GUN.

hold your head (up) high be confident or unashamed.

keep (*or* lose) your head remain (*or* fail to remain) calm.

2005 Barbara Keating & Stephanie Keating *Blood Sisters* I made a hash of it ... Lost my head like an idiot.

keep your head above water avoid succumbing to difficulties, especially falling into debt.

keep your head down remain inconspicuous in difficult or dangerous times. informal

1995 Edward Toman *Dancing in Limbo* All his instincts told him to keep his head down. He didn't need Lily's constant nagging to remind him he was in deep trouble.

King Charles's head: *see* KING.

knock someone or something on the head: *see* KNOCK.

make head or tail of understand at all.

1994 S. P. Somtow *Jasmine Nights* I'm . . . trying to puzzle out why he has turned his animosity on me instead of those who are clearly his enemies. I can't make head or tail of it.

need your head examined (*or* examining) be foolishly irresponsible.

ℹ The implication here is that the examination will reveal proof of insanity.

2005 *Mimi in New York* Anyone who suggests diet and exercise are wrong needs their head examining.

off (*or* out of) your head ❶ mad or crazy. ❷ extremely drunk or severely under the influence of illegal drugs. informal

off the top of your head without careful thought or investigation. informal

1988 Jamaica Kincaid *A Small Place* He apologises for the incredible mistake he has made in quoting you a price off the top of his head which is so vastly different (favouring him) from the one listed.

an old head on young shoulders: *see* OLD.

on your (own) head be it used to indicate that you think someone should take full responsibility for anything that goes wrong if they persist in an inadvisable course of action.

over your head ❶ beyond your ability to understand. ❷ without your knowledge or involvement, especially when you have a right to this. ❸ with disregard for your own (stronger) claim.

a price on someone's head: *see* PRICE.

pull your head in mind your own business. Australian & New Zealand informal

put (*or* raise *or* stick) your head above the parapet speak out about something in spite of the risks involved.

ℹ A parapet is a protective wall along the top of a trench or similar military emplacement. Anyone showing their head over the top of it would be liable to be shot.

2013 *Daily Telegraph* The irony is that there is latent talent in Whitehall, although it is very difficult for good civil servants to stick their head above the parapet.

put your head in a noose: *see* NOOSE.

put your head on the block: *see* BLOCK.

put your heads together consult and work together.

put something into someone's head suggest something to someone.

rear its head: *see* REAR.

a roof over your head: *see* ROOF.

scratch your head: *see* SCRATCH.

stand (*or* turn) something on its head completely reverse the principles or interpretation of an idea, argument, etc.

take it into your head to do something decide impetuously to do something.

2009 Diana Gabaldon *An Echo in the Bone* Someone from the *Teal* might take it into his head to liberate the sailors in the hold.

turn heads attract a great deal of attention or interest.

turn someone's head make someone conceited.

two heads are better than one it's helpful to have the advice or opinion of a second person. proverb

1994 James Kelman *How Late It Was, How Late* Cause it's hard to do it yerself Keith, two heads are better than one.

wet the baby's head: *see* WET.

with your head in the clouds: *see* CLOUD.

— your head off laugh, talk, shout, etc. with a complete lack of restraint or without stopping.

2010 Christopher Grant *Teenie* Those girls look like straight-up groupies, screaming their heads off and trying to touch Greg.

headless

running about like a headless chicken: *see* CHICKEN.

headlights

like a rabbit (*or* deer) in the headlights used to refer to a state of fear, panic, or confusion so extreme that it is impossible to act or think normally.

headline

hit the headlines be written about or given attention as news.

heal

physician, heal thyself: *see* PHYSICIAN.

heap

at the top (*or* bottom) of the heap (of a person) at the highest (*or* lowest) point of a society or organization.

be struck all of a heap be extremely disconcerted. informal

heap coals of fire on someone's head: *see* COAL.

hear

be unable to hear yourself think be unable to think clearly as a result of an excessive amount of noise. informal

hear things: *see* THING.

never hear the end of something: *see* END.

you could hear a pin drop: *see* PIN.

hearing

hard of hearing: *see* HARD.

heart

after your own heart of the type that you like or understand best; sharing your tastes.

> **1988 Sebastian Barry** *Boss Grady's Boys* He took away every year I had to give a man, and then took away himself for good measure. He was a man after my own heart so I will not blame him.

bleeding heart: *see* BLEEDING.

break someone's heart overwhelm someone with sadness.

by heart from memory.

a change of heart: *see* CHANGE.

cross my heart: *see* CROSS.

cry from the heart: *see* CRY.

eat your heart out: *see* EAT.

a faint heart: *see* FAINT.

find it in your heart to do something: *see* FIND.

from the bottom of your heart (*or* from the heart) with sincere feeling.

have a heart be merciful, show pity (usually imperative).

have the heart be insensitive or hard-hearted enough.

> **2007 Robert Leleux** *The Memoirs of a Beautiful Boy* He'd say some perfectly exasperating thing, like someday we'd adopt children, and did I really have the heart to deny them a grandfather?

have (*or* put) your heart in be (*or* become) keenly involved in or committed to an enterprise.

have your heart in your mouth be greatly alarmed or apprehensive.

have your heart in the right place be sincere or well intentioned.

heart and soul great energy and enthusiasm.

> **1977 Michael Frayn** *Alphabetical Order* She hasn't been here long, I know. But she's put her whole heart and soul into this place.

heart of gold a generous nature.

heart of oak a courageous nature.

> ⓘ Literally, the *heart* is the solid central part of the oak tree traditionally used for timber for ships. The phrase was popularized by the words of an 18th-century song: 'Heart of oak are our ships, Heart of oak are our men'.

heart of stone a stern or cruel nature.

heart to heart candidly or intimately.

hearts and flowers used in allusion to extreme sentimentality.

hearts and minds used in reference to emotional and intellectual support or commitment.

> **2009 Robert Bothwell & Jean Daudelin** *Canada among Nations 2008* It [i.e. the aid programme] was ... forced to act as ... a hearts and minds operation for Canada's changeable political and security agendas.

in your heart of hearts in your innermost feelings.

lose heart become discouraged.

my heart bleeds for you: *see* BLEEDS.

pour your heart out: *see* POUR.

set your heart on decide you very much want to have.

a song in your heart: *see* SONG.

steal someone's heart: *see* STEAL.

take heart be encouraged.

take something to heart take something seriously; be much affected or upset by something.

> **1992 Ian Rankin** *A Good Hanging* Suicidal, just as actors can be. He took criticism to heart. He was a perfectionist.

to your heart's content: *see* CONTENT.

warm the cockles of someone's heart: *see* COCKLE.

wear your heart on your sleeve make your feelings apparent.

> ⓘ In medieval times, it was the custom for a knight to wear the name of a lady on his sleeve during a tournament; the phrase was later popularized by Shakespeare in *Othello*:

'For I will wear my heart upon my sleeve, For daws to peck at'.

2005 *Elle Girl* Even if you do find a bloke who's happy to wear his heart on his sleeve and shower you with gifts and public displays of affection, is that really you?

your heart's desire someone or something that is greatly wished for.

your heart sinks into your boots: *see* BOOT.

you're breaking my heart used ironically to suggest that the person referred to does not deserve the sympathy they are seeking.

heartbeat

a heartbeat (away) from very close to; the verge of.

hearth

hearth and home home and its comforts.

hearty

hale and hearty: *see* HALE.

heat

if you can't stand the heat, get out of the kitchen if you can't deal with the pressures and difficulties of a situation or task, you should leave others to deal with it rather than complaining. proverb

in the heat of the moment while temporarily angry, excited, or engrossed, and without stopping for thought.

pack heat: *see* PACK.

turn the heat on someone or something concentrate pressure or criticism on someone or something. informal

turn up the heat intensify pressure or criticism. informal

heather

set the heather on fire be very exciting. Scottish

heave

heave in sight (*or* into view) come into view. informal

ℹ *Heave* meaning 'rise up, as on the swell of a wave' occurs in several nautical expressions; here the allusion is to the way that objects appear to rise up over the horizon at sea. The past form of *heave* in this sense is *hove*, but because most English-speakers are completely unfamiliar with the verb in its literal usage, *hove* is often used as a present form (and a new past form, *hoved*, is created from it).

heave-ho

give (*or* get) the heave-ho expel (or be expelled) from an institution, association, or contest. informal

heaven

in seventh heaven in a state of ecstasy.

ℹ In late Jewish and Muslim theology, there were considered to be seven heavens, and the seventh of these was the highest, where a state of eternal bliss was to be enjoyed.

move heaven and earth make extraordinary efforts.

2001 *Independent* In the old days if a line went well you moved heaven and earth with your suppliers to get more—you never, ever put the price up.

pennies from heaven: *see* PENNY.

stink (*or* smell) to high heaven have a very strong and unpleasant odour.

the heavens opened it started to rain suddenly and very heavily.

heavy

heavy going difficult or boring to deal with.

2012 *New Statesman* Non-academic readers may find Robert Holland's latest volume heavy going at times but it will remain the definitive account of Anglo-Mediterranean history for years to come.

heavy hitter: *see* **big hitter** *at* BIG.

heavy lifting hard work; great, especially non-physical effort. chiefly US

2019 *Observer* Du Sautoy is open about his doubts when evaluating the new A[rtificial] I[ntelligence] … As he sees it, the creative heavy lifting is often being done by the programmer or the audience, and not the program itself.

the heavy mob a group of strong or violent criminals or bodyguards. British informal

heavy on using a lot of.

1984 Studs Terkel *The Good War* We were heavy on the Italian feeling in America. We were more Italian than Italians.

make heavy weather: *see* WEATHER.

heck

a (*or* one) heck of a — used for emphasis in various statements or exclamations. informal

ⓘ Of dialect origin, *heck* is a late 19th-century euphemism for *hell*.

2013 Mark Heuring *Mr Dilettante* Meyer, while irritating, is a heck of a coach.

hedge

hedge your bets try to minimize the risk of being wrong or incurring loss by pursuing two courses of action at the same time.

ⓘ *Hedging* your financial liabilities, especially bets or speculative investments, meant limiting your potential losses by also putting money on another outcome, in such a way as to balance, more or less, any potential loss on the initial transaction. In betting terms, this specifically means putting money on more than one runner in a race.

2004 Suketu Mehta *Maximum City* To hedge their bets, the stars usually work on three or four films at the same time.

heel

Achilles heel: *see* ACHILLES.

at (*or* to) heel (of a dog) close to and slightly behind its owner.

ⓘ *Bring someone to heel*, meaning 'get someone under control and make them act subserviently', is taken from this expression.

cool your heels be kept waiting.

ⓘ A British variant of this is *kick your heels*.

dig in your heels: *see* DIG.

down at heel ❶ (of a shoe) with the heel worn down. ❷ (of a person, place, or thing) with a poor, shabby appearance.

drag your heels: *see* **drag your feet** *at* DRAG.

head over heels: *see* HEAD.

hot on the heels of: *see* HOT.

kick up your heels have a lively, enjoyable time. chiefly North American

set (*or* rock) someone back on their heels astonish or discomfit someone.

show someone or something a clean pair of heels ❶ run away from someone or something as fast as possible. ❷ demonstrate clear superiority to someone or something.

❷ **2002** *Tom's Hardware Guide* How fast does a PC fitted with the most powerful hardware have to be in order to show a clean pair of heels to the world's best PC systems?

take to your heels (*or* legs) run away.

turn on your heel turn sharply round.

under the heel of dominated or controlled by.

2013 *New Statesman* Many of these states were under the heel of tyrant-warlords who had little or no lawful claim to their positions and power.

hell

all hell broke (*or* was let) loose suddenly there was chaos or uproar. informal

be hell on be unpleasant or harmful to.

come hell or high water no matter what difficulties may occur.

1995 Ian Rankin *Let It Bleed* It was the one appointment he'd known all day he would keep, come hell or high water.

for the hell of it just for fun. informal

— from hell an extremely unpleasant or troublesome instance or example of something. informal

2001 *Independent* Council tenants who racially harass asylum-seekers will face fast-track eviction under government plans to combat so-called neighbours from hell.

get the hell out (of) escape from a place or situation very quickly. informal

give someone (*or* get) hell reprimand someone (*or* be reprimanded) severely. informal

go to (*or* through) hell and back endure an extremely unpleasant or difficult experience.

go to hell in a handbasket undergo a rapid process of deterioration. North American informal

ⓘ This expression has been recorded since the early 20th century; variants of it include *go to hell in a handcart* and *go to hell in a basket*.

2004 Geoffrey Nunberg *Going Nuclear* The language is going to hell in a handbasket.

hell for leather as fast as possible.

ⓘ This phrase dates from the late 19th century, and originally referred to riding a horse at reckless speed.

a (*or* one) hell of a — used to emphasize something very bad or great. informal

1990 Stephen King *The Stand* If someone on the committee has been leaking, we're in a hell of a jam.

— the hell out of used in verbal phrases to emphasize force, speed, etc. informal

2004 *PopCult Magazine* All you can think of is, 'Get the hell out of my way so I can gamble'.

hell's bells an exclamation of annoyance or anger. informal

hell's half acre a great distance. North American

hell hath no fury like a woman scorned a woman who has been rejected by a man can be ferociously angry and vindictive. proverb

like a bat out of hell: *see* BAT.

like hell ❶ very fast, much, hard, etc. (used for emphasis). ❷ used in ironic expressions of scorn or disagreement. informal

❶ **2013 Kevin Barbieux** *The Homeless Guy* Putting stress on a broken or bruised bone hurts like hell.

not a cat in hell's chance: *see* CAT

not a hope (*or* chance) in hell no hope (*or* chance) at all. informal

ⓘ An elaboration of this phrase is *not a snowball's chance in hell.*

play (merry) hell with throw into turmoil; disrupt. informal

raise hell ❶ make a noisy disturbance. ❷ complain vociferously. informal

there will be hell to pay serious trouble will occur as a result of a previous action. informal

to hell with expressing your scorn or lack of concern for (someone or something). informal

until (*or* till) hell freezes over for an extremely long time or forever. informal

what the hell it doesn't matter. informal

hello

a golden hello: *see* **a golden handshake** *at* HANDSHAKE.

help

help a lame dog over a stile: *see* DOG.

so help me (God) used to emphasize that you mean what you are saying.

ⓘ This phrase alludes to the oath taken by witnesses in court when they swear to tell 'the truth, the whole truth, and nothing but the truth, so help me God'.

hen

like a hen with one chick (*or* chicken) absurdly fussy and overanxious.

rare (*or* scarce) as hen's teeth extremely rare.

ⓘ As hens do not possess teeth, the implication is that something is rare to the point of non-existence. The phrase was originally a US colloquialism, dating from the mid 19th century.

her

her indoors a humorous reference to a man's wife. British informal

Hercules

a labour of Hercules: *see* LABOUR.

herd

like herding cats: *see* CAT.

ride herd on: *see* RIDE.

here

here's looking at you: *see* LOOK.

here today, gone tomorrow soon over or forgotten; short-lived or transient.

2012 *SeoBook* In addition to the fickle here today, gone tomorrow nature of social media, the results are typically quite unpredictable.

neither here nor there of no importance or relevance.

2013 *Daily Telegraph* It's neither here nor there who they are or who pays them—what is important is for me to send our story out to the international community.

be out of here: *see* OUT.

same here: *see* SAME.

up to here having as much as or more than you can cope with or tolerate. informal

2000 *The Register* It's not clear why Richardson is off—perhaps she's had it up to here with lawsuits.

Herod

out-Herod Herod behave with extreme cruelty or tyranny.

ⓘ Herod, the ruler of Judaea at the time of Jesus's birth and the man responsible for ordering the massacre of boy babies in his realm, was portrayed in medieval miracle plays as a blustering tyrant. The phrase is from Shakespeare's *Hamlet*: 'I would have such a fellow whipp'd for o'erdoing Termagant; it out-herods Herod'.

herring

a red herring: *see* RED.

hewer

hewers of wood and drawers of water menial drudges; labourers.

ⓘ This expression refers to Joshua 9:21, which tells the story of how the Israelites were tricked into sparing the lives of some of the indigenous inhabitants of the Promised Land: 'And the princes said unto them, Let them live; but let them be hewers of wood and drawers of water unto all the congregation'.

hidden

a hidden agenda a person's real but concealed aims and intentions.

2013 *Business Insider* Finding out the reasons behind someone's decisions, the motivations behind someone's actions, the inside scoop about someone's hidden agenda—that stuff is hard to resist.

hidden depths: *see* DEPTH.

hide

hide your light under a bushel keep quiet about your talents or accomplishments.

ⓘ A *bushel* is a unit of measurement equal to eight gallons: in former times the word also referred to a container able to hold this amount. The expression has its source in Matthew 5:15: 'neither do men light a candle, and put it under a bushel, but on a candlestick'.

2013 *Daily Telegraph* Never one to hide his light under a bushel, Mr Robertson afterwards declared, to loud guffaws from the press room: 'Who dares wins.'

neither hide nor hair of someone not the slightest trace of someone.

tan someone's hide: *see* TAN.

hiding

on a hiding to nothing unlikely to succeed, or in a position to gain no advantage if you do. British

2013 *Keeping Stock* The overwhelmingly negative reaction demonstrates that when you put those two head to head, emotion will always win. Gareth Morgan was always going to be on a hiding to nothing with this campaign.

high

be for the high jump be about to be severely punished. British informal

ⓘ This expression was first recorded in the early 20th century as a military term meaning 'be put on trial before your commanding officer'. The image behind it is that of an execution by hanging.

come hell or high water: *see* HELL.

fly high: *see* FLY.

friends in high places: *see* FRIEND.

from on high ❶ from a very high place. ❷ from remote high authority or heaven.

high and dry ❶ (especially of ships left stranded by the sea as the tide ebbs) out of the water. ❷ in a difficult position, especially without resources.

❷ **1996 Frank McCourt** *Angela's Ashes* I hear he left you high and dry, eh? I don't know how a man in his right mind can go off and leave a wife and family to starve and shiver in a Limerick winter.

high and low in many different places.

2010 Francisca Goldsmith *Readers' Advisory Guide to Graphic Novels* An elegant vampire who has just broken off with a young woman looks high and low for a satisfying replacement partner.

high and mighty ❶ important and influential. ❷ thinking or acting as though you are more important than others; arrogant. informal

high as a kite: *see* KITE.

high days and holidays special occasions. informal

ⓘ In the Church's calendar a *high day* was the day of an important festival. A *holiday* (originally *holy day*) was similar but less specific. *Holiday* now refers to any day off, without any sacred significance, and so *holy day* is used if a specifically religious occasion is intended.

2013 *Gloucestershire Echo* One of the tasks delegated to me was ... to purchase cakes on colleagues' birthdays and other high days and holidays.

high old (of a time or state) most enjoyable or remarkable. informal

1955 Jean Potts *Death of a Stray Cat* You probably had a high old time chasing blondes.

high on the hog: *see* HOG.

high, wide, and handsome expansive and impressive; stylish and carefree in manner. informal ℹ This phrase originated in the USA, and *Yankee Slang* (1932) identifies 'Ride him, Cowboy, high, wide and handsome' as a shout commonly heard at rodeos.

2012 *Scotsman* It must be chastening for Japanese industry. It rode high, wide and handsome until the country's property/stock market bubble burst in 1990.

high words angry words. archaic

hit the high spots visit places of entertainment. informal

in high dudgeon: *see* DUDGEON.

in high feather: *see* **in fine feather** *at* FEATHER.

it is high time that it is past the time when (something should have happened or been done).

on a high in a state of euphoria. informal

ℹ This expression was originally mid-20th-century US slang, referring specifically to the euphoria induced by drugs.

on your high horse used to refer to someone behaving in an arrogant or pompous manner. informal

ride high: *see* RIDE.

run high be strong or tumultuous.

ℹ The image here is of waves or tides rising above their normal height, especially in stormy conditions.

2008 Simon Armitage *Gig* Amongst the women ... feelings are running high, especially after supper when they are packed off to bed while the gentlemen kick back with brandy and cigars.

stink to high heaven: *see* HEAVEN.

highway

my way or the highway: *see* WAY.

hike

take a hike go away (used as an expression of irritation or annoyance). informal

2004 R. B. Parker *Double Play* I know who you are ... I know who your father is. Now take a hike.

hill

a hill of beans: *see* BEAN.

ancient (*or* old) as the hills of very long standing or very great age.

ℹ *Hills* are used in the Bible as a metaphor for permanence.

head for (*or* take to) the hills run away; decamp.

2003 *The Press* (York) Marisa fears Marshall will head for the hills as soon as he discovers this elegant young woman's true identity.

over the hill past your best; declining. informal

up hill and down dale all over the place.

2001 *Observer* Why get ourselves bogged down with trials which may last many months and *see* our staff cross-examined up hill and down dale as defence counsel play the game of hunt the informant?

hilt

(up) to the hilt completely.

ℹ The image is that of plunging the blade of a knife deeply into something, so that only the hilt is visible.

hind

on your hind legs standing up to make a speech. British informal

talk the hind leg off a donkey: *see* TALK.

hindrance

let or hindrance: *see* LET.

hint

drop a hint: *see* DROP.

hip

in someone's hip pocket completely under someone's control. North American

joined at the hip: *see* JOIN.

shoot from the hip: *see* SHOOT.

hire

hire and fire engage and dismiss, especially as indicating a position of established authority over other employees.

2013 digby *Hullabaloo* Conservatives normally insist that the private sector can do anything it chooses, even hiring and firing on the basis of an owner's throwback religious or racist beliefs.

history

be history ❶ be perceived as no longer relevant to the present. ❷ used to indicate elimination, departure, dismissal, or death. informal

❷ **2013** *Daily Telegraph* The union bosses, it seemed, had delivered just what they wanted: New Labour was history. But they were misinformed. Ed Miliband is, it turns out, more Catholic than the Pope.

make history do something that is remembered in or influences the course of history.

the rest is history used to indicate that the events succeeding those already related are so well known that they need not be recounted again.

rewrite history: *see* REWRITE.

hit

h

hit-and-run ❶ (of a person) causing accidental or wilful damage and escaping before being discovered or stopped. ❷ (of an incident or accident) in which damage is caused in this way.

hit it off with feel a liking for; be friendly with. informal

ⓘ For other idioms containing *hit*, see the entry for the main word in the idiom (for example, **hit the hay** at HAY).

hitch

hitch horses together get on well together; act in harmony. US

hitch your wagon to a star make use of powers higher than your own.

ⓘ This phrase was used by the American philosopher and poet Ralph Waldo Emerson in 1870 in the context of idealistic aspiration; modern usage generally has the more cynical implication of attaching yourself to someone successful or famous in order to profit from the association.

2003 *The Hindu* There always have been, and always will be students who dream big and then work hard to hitch their wagon to a star.

hitter

big (*or* heavy) hitter: *see* BIG.

hob

play (*or* raise) hob cause mischief; make a fuss. North American

ⓘ *Hob* is short for *hobgoblin* and is used in this mid-19th-century expression to mean *'the devil'*. Compare with **raise Cain** (*at* CAIN) and **raise the devil** (*at* DEVIL).

1993 *Canadian Living* When rain finally came, it wouldn't stop and played hob with the lentils that were growing there for the first time in a big way.

Hobson

Hobson's choice: *see* CHOICE.

hock

in hock ❶ having been pawned. ❷ constrained by an onerous obligation.

ⓘ *Hock* here comes from the Dutch word *hok* meaning 'hutch' or 'prison'. Originally mid-19th-century US slang, this sense of *hock* is now found only in this phrase or, occasionally, in *out of hock*.

❷ **2019 Will Hutton** *Observer* America First nationalism, indulgent free market economics, Republican libertarianism and a political system in hock to corporate lobbying has just contributed to killing 356 innocent people.

hog

go the whole hog do something completely or thoroughly. informal

ⓘ The origin of the phrase is uncertain. It is recorded as a political expression in the USA in the early 19th century; an 1835 source maintains that it originated in Virginia 'marking the democrat from a federalist'.

live high on (*or* off) the hog have a luxurious lifestyle. North American

1991 Norman Mailer *Harlot's Ghost* Even the Joint Chiefs' flunkies live high on the military hog.

hog on ice an insecure person. North American informal

hoist

hoist with your own petard: *see* PETARD.

hold

hold water (of a statement, theory, or line of reasoning) appear to be valid, sound, or reasonable.

no holds barred no rules or restrictions apply in a particular conflict or dispute.

ⓘ *No holds barred* was originally a phrase used in wrestling, where it indicated that there were no restrictions on the kinds of holds used.

put something on hold temporarily defer taking action on or pursuing something.

ⓘ Originally, to put someone on hold was literally to make them wait for a telephone connection.

ⓘ For other idioms containing *hold,* see the entry for the main word in the idiom (for example, **hold your horses** at HORSE).

holding

be left holding the baby be left with an unwelcome responsibility, often without warning.

ⓘ A US variant of this expression is *be left holding the bag.*

there is no holding someone someone is particularly determined or cannot be prevented from doing something.

hole

blow a hole in ruin the effectiveness of something.

dig yourself into a hole: *see* DIG.

hole in the wall ❶ a small dingy place, especially a business or, in the USA, a place where alcoholic drinks are sold illegally. ❷ an automatic cash dispenser installed in the outside wall of a bank.

hole something below the waterline damage something irreparably.

ⓘ The image is of a ship with a hole or holes in its hull below the surface of the water, which will inevitably lead to its sinking.

2010 *Guardian* The former managing director, who led the Emirates project and the associated property development that could yet hole the club below the waterline financially, also exited.

in a hole in an awkward situation from which it is difficult to escape. informal

ⓘ This figurative use of *hole* has been in use since the mid 18th century (compare with **dig yourself into a hole** *at* DIG). The British politician Denis Healey described the first law of politics as 'when you are in a hole, stop digging'.

in the hole in debt. North American

money burns a hole in your pocket: *see* MONEY.

need something like a hole in the head used to emphasize that someone has absolutely no need or desire for something. informal

ⓘ The expression is a translation of Yiddish *ich darf es vi a loch in kop* 'I need it like a hole in the head'.

pick holes criticize.

a square peg in a round hole: *see* PEG.

top hole: *see* TOP.

watering hole: *see* WATERING.

holiday

a busman's holiday: *see* BUSMAN.

high days and holidays: *see* HIGH.

a Roman holiday: *see* ROMAN.

holier

holier than thou characterized by an attitude of self-conscious virtue and piety.

ⓘ This phrase comes from Isaiah 65:5: 'Stand by thyself, come not near to me; for I am holier than thou'.

hollow

beat someone hollow defeat or surpass someone completely or thoroughly.

hollow legs a large capacity for drinking alcohol without getting drunk, or for eating without becoming sated. humorous

in the hollow of your hand entirely in your power.

holy

holy grail something eagerly pursued or sought after.

ⓘ The literal Holy Grail was the cup or platter said to have been used by Christ at the Last Supper, which became the subject of a quest in Arthurian legend.

2014 digby *Hullabaloo* Acquiring great wealth isn't the holy grail for most people—the vast majority just want to live a decent, fulfilling life and provide well for their children.

holy of holies a place or thing regarded as sacrosanct.

ⓘ The reference here is to the Hebrew phrase for the inner chamber of the sanctuary in the Jewish Temple at Jerusalem, separated by a veil from the outer chamber.

home

bring something home to someone make someone realize the full significance of something.

chickens come home to roost: *see* CHICKEN.

close (*or* near) to home (of a remark or topic of discussion) relevant or accurate to the point that you feel uncomfortable or embarrassed.

come home to someone (of the significance of something) become fully realized by someone.

1981 Fannie Flagg *Daisy Fay & the Miracle Man* It came home to me that night that Momma has certainly lost her sense of humour.

drive something home make something clearly and fully understood by the use of repeated or forcefully direct arguments.

ⓘ The verbs *hammer*, *press*, and *ram* are also used in place of *drive*.

an Englishman's home is his castle: *see* ENGLISHMAN.

hearth and home: *see* HEARTH.

hit (*or* strike) home ❶ (of a blow or a missile) reach an intended target. ❷ (of a person's words) have the intended, often unsettling or painful, effect on their audience. ❸ (of the significance or true nature of a situation) become fully realized by someone.

home and dry successful in achieving your objective. chiefly British

ⓘ A fuller version of this phrase, which dates from the mid 20th century, is *home and dry on the pig's back*.

home and hosed successful in achieving your objective. chiefly Australian & New Zealand

2019 *Sunday Times* It was one of those pinch-yourself 40 minutes ... Scotland were dead, England were home and hosed, and then suddenly they were not.

home free successful in achieving your objective. North American

a home from home a place where you are as happy, relaxed, or at ease as in your own home.

ⓘ The North American version of this expression is *a home away from home*.

home, James (and don't spare the horses)! used as a humorous way of exhorting the driver of a vehicle to drive home quickly. dated

ⓘ This was the title of a popular song (1934) by Fred Hillebrand; it represents a parody of the instruction given to a coachman in the days of the horse and carriage.

home sweet home used as an expression of pleasure or relief at being in or returning to your own home.

house and home: *see* HOUSE.

the lights are on but no one is at home: *see* LIGHT.

long home: *see* LONG.

nothing to write home about: *see* WRITE.

who's—when—'s at home a humorously emphatic way of asking about someone's identity. British

1991 Joseph O'Connor *Mothers Were All the Same* The old lady said to tell that to Yuri Gagarin, but the hostess just giggled and said, 'Who's he when he's at home?'

homework

do your homework examine thoroughly the details and background of a subject or topic, especially before giving your own views on it.

honest

earn (*or* turn) an honest penny earn money by fair means, especially by hard work.

an honest broker a disinterested intermediary or mediator.

ⓘ This expression is a translation of the German *ehrlicher Makler*. In a speech in 1878 the German statesman Bismarck (1815–98) recommended adopting this role in peace-making, and the phrase became one of his sobriquets.

honest Injun: *see* INJUN.

make an honest woman of marry a woman, especially to avoid scandal if she is pregnant. dated or humorous

ⓘ *Honest* here originally meant 'respectable', but was probably associated with the archaic sense 'chaste or virtuous'.

honey

milk and honey: *see* MILK.

honour

do the honours ❶ perform a social duty or small ceremony for others. ❷ perform a particular function that is central to the proceedings. informal humorous

❷ **2007 David Kynaston** *A World to Build* Two men were hanged at Pentonville, with the lugubrious Albert Pierrepoint doing the honours.

honours are even there is equality in the contest. British

(in) honour bound obliged by your sense of honour.

Scout's honour: *see* SCOUT.

hoof

a cloven hoof: *see* CLOVEN.

on the hoof ❶ (of livestock) not yet slaughtered. ❷ without great thought or preparation.

❷ **2009** *Freaky Trigger* Spitting Image didn't always hit their targets dead on, but as it became more news-driven and writers had to script on the hoof, it had a freshness of feel for a while at least.

hook

by hook or by crook by one means or another; by fair means or foul.

ⓘ The *hook* referred to here is probably a billhook or heavy curved pruning knife; the *crook* is a hooked staff. One of the earliest recorded instances of the phrase is in Gower's *Confessio Amantis* (1390), which uses the rare word *hepe* (meaning 'a pruning knife') in place of *hook*. In 1822 William Cobbett wrote of people who lived near woodland being allowed, under the ancient forest law of England, to gather dead branches for fuel, which they may have brought down from the trees literally *by hook* or *by crook*.

1998 Adèle Geras *Silent Snow, Secret Snow* Till then, she would hang on. By hook or by crook. Come what may.

get (*or* give someone) the hook be dismissed from a job (*or* dismiss someone from a job). North American informal

get your hooks into get hold of or gain control of. informal

2001 *Bright Lights Film Journal* Horton, meanwhile, is in his own tizzy, terrified that gold-digging dames will get their hooks into Fred.

hook it run away. British informal, dated

hook, line, and sinker used to emphasize that someone has been completely tricked or deceived. informal

ⓘ This phrase is a fishing metaphor: all three are items attached to a fishing rod and likely to be gulped down by a greedy fish. The phrase has been in use since the mid 19th century.

2013 *Better Farming—Ontario Community of Professional Farmers* The liberals bought hook line and sinker McFlinty's dream of being able to have a legacy to be remembered. Well the truth is he will be remembered for all the wrong reasons.

off the hook ❶ no longer in trouble or difficulty. informal ❷ (of a telephone receiver) not on its rest, and so not receiving incoming calls.

ⓘ *Hook* in sense 1 is a long-standing (mid 15th-century) figurative use of the word to mean 'something by which a person is caught and trapped', as a fish hook catches a fish. Sense 2 is a fossilized expression from the late 19th century, the early years of telephony, when the receiver literally hung on a hook.

on the hook for (in a financial context) responsible for. North American informal

2001 *High Country News* Taxpayers are currently on the hook for anywhere from $32 billion to $72 billion in abandoned mine cleanup costs.

off the hooks dead. British informal

sling your hook leave; go away. British informal

ⓘ *Sling your hook* appears in a slang dictionary of 1874, where it is defined as 'a polite invitation to move on'. The underlying allusion may be to the raising of a ship's anchor and stowing it in a sling before setting sail.

2012 *Scribblings Jottings* So it seems that when the city of Liverpool told Warren to sling his hook and not come back he mistook a city's jeers for cheers.

hookey

play hookey stay away from school without permission or explanation; play truant. North American informal

ⓘ The origin of the phrase is not known for certain; it may be an adaptation of Dutch *hoekje spelen* 'play hide-and-seek'.

hoop

jump through hoops: *see* JUMP.

put someone (*or* go) through the hoops make someone undergo (*or* be made to undergo) a difficult and gruelling test or series of tests.

1994 *Legion* The crew was as fast and efficient as any they had put through the hoops.

hoot

not care (*or* give) a hoot (*or* two hoots) not care at all. informal

1990 Karen Lawrence *Springs of Living Water* Never think about anybody but yourself, do you? Never give two hoots about your poor little sister following you around.

hop

hop it depart suddenly. British informal

hop the twig (*or* stick) ❶ depart suddenly. ❷ die. British informal

on the hop unprepared. British informal

1991 M. S. Power *Come the Executioner* He went down to the dining-room, catching the staff on the hop, but they greeted him cheerfully enough.

hope

a forlorn hope: *see* FORLORN.

hope chest a chest containing linen, clothes, and household items stored by a woman in preparation for her marriage. North American

ⓘ The British equivalent of this expression is **bottom drawer** (*see* DRAWER).

hope against hope cling to a mere possibility.

2014 *DVD Verdict* I've met my Hyde and I hate him; it's extremely easy to step into Jekyll's shoes and hope against hope he can battle and come out on top.

hope springs eternal it is human nature always to find fresh cause for optimism.

ⓘ This is a shortened version of Alexander Pope's line in *An Essay on Man* (1733): 'Hope springs eternal in the human breast'.

2013 *Age* (Melbourne) When we make up our mind to throw a government out, hope springs eternal that the new lot will be much better.

not a hope in hell: *see* HELL.

white hope: *see* WHITE.

horizon

on the horizon just imminent or becoming apparent.

Horlicks

make a Horlicks of make a mess of. British informal

ⓘ *Horlicks* is the proprietary name of a malted milk drink. In this expression it is a euphemistic substitute for *bollocks*.

1988 Joanna Trollope *The Choir* He thought privately that they would make a fearful horlicks of running the choir.

horn

blow (*or* toot) your own horn talk boastfully about yourself or your achievements. North American

draw (*or* pull) in your horns become less assertive or ambitious; draw back.

ⓘ The image here is of a snail drawing in its retractile tentacles when disturbed.

1991 Paul Grescoe *Flesh Wound* Hollywood's major studios were pulling in their horns in the wake of a disastrous Christmas season.

lock horns: *see* LOCK.

on the horn on the telephone. North American informal

on the horns of a dilemma faced with a decision involving equally unfavourable alternatives.

ⓘ A mid-16th-century source described a *dilemma* as 'a horned argument' (after Latin *argumentum cornutum*), the idea being that if you avoided one 'horn' of the argument you ended up impaled on the other.

hornet

a hornets' nest a situation fraught with trouble, opposition, or complications.

2012 Eric S. Raymond *Armed & Dangerous* What we're doing just makes it easier to recruit new people who might have been on the edge before. Stirring up the hornets nest is completely unproductive.

horror

shock horror: *see* SHOCK.

horse

back the wrong horse: *see* BACK.

could eat a horse be extremely hungry. informal

a dark horse: *see* DARK.

don't change horses in midstream choose a sensible moment to change your mind. proverb

ⓘ This expression is quoted by Abraham Lincoln in 1864 as the saying of 'an old Dutch farmer'. Early versions of it used *swap* instead of *change*.

drive a coach and horses through: *see* COACH.

eat like a horse eat heartily and greedily.

flog a dead horse: *see* FLOG.

frighten the horses cause consternation or dismay; shock.

ⓘ The expression has been attributed, not altogether reliably, to the English actress Mrs Patrick Campbell (1865–1940), who allegedly said, in reference to a male homosexual affair, something along the lines of 'My dear, I don't care what they do, as long as they don't do it in the street and frighten the horses.'

2011 *Guardian* Did any performance look less than 100% mainstream? I mean don't frighten the horses or say bloody, anybody, otherwise Lauren 'Culture Vulture' Laverne will be jolly cross and not plug your new album.

(straight) from the horse's mouth from the person directly concerned or another authoritative source.

ⓘ This expression refers to the presumed ideal source for a racing tip and hence of other useful information.

2010 *Parklife* Just the other day I heard—from the horses mouth—that FIFA was in no way an 'interim government' before and during the World Cup.

hitch horses together: *see* HITCH.

a horse of another (*or* different) colour a thing significantly different.

1975 Sam Selvon *Moses Ascending* Two or three is okay, but when you start bringing in a battalion, it is a horse of a different colour.

hold your horses wait a moment; restrain your enthusiasm. informal

1999 Colin Dexter *The Remorseful Day* Hold your horses! One or two things I'd like you to check first, just to make it one hundred per cent.

horses for courses different people are suited to different things or situations.

ⓘ The earliest recorded instance of this expression, in A. E. T. Watson's *Turf* (1891), suggests its origin: 'A familiar phrase on the turf is "horses for courses" . . . the Brighton Course is very like Epsom, and horses that win at one meeting often win at the other'.

2004 *Guardian Unlimited* It's all a matter of horses for courses. Doubtless in its original incarnations at the Jermyn Street Theatre and the Mill at Sonning, this tribute to Jessie Matthews had a fragrant charm. Plonked down in the West End for a couple of weeks, however, it looks like a piece of anorexic nostalgia.

look a gift horse in the mouth: *see* GIFT.

put the cart before the horse: *see* CART.

a Trojan horse: *see* TROJAN.

wild horses won't drag someone to something (*or* something from someone) nothing will make someone go to a particular place (*or* divulge particular information). informal

2012 *New Zealand Herald* I loved Parliament. I didn't want to get dumped. But wild horses now couldn't drag me back.

hosed

home and hosed: *see* HOME.

hostage

a hostage to fortune an act, commitment, or remark which is regarded as unwise because it invites trouble or could prove difficult to live up to.

ⓘ The original *hostages to fortune* were a man's family, the allusion being to Francis Bacon's essay on marriage (1625): 'He that hath wife and children hath given hostages to fortune'.

hot

blow hot and cold alternate inconsistently between two moods, attitudes, or courses of action; be sometimes enthusiastic, sometimes unenthusiastic about something.

ⓘ This phrase refers to a fable involving a traveller who was offered hospitality by a satyr and offended his host by blowing on his cold fingers to warm them and on his hot soup to cool it.

drop someone or something like a hot potato quickly abandon someone or something. informal

ⓘ *Drop* here is used literally, but also in the figurative sense of 'end a social acquaintance with someone'. *A hot potato* can be used independently as a metaphor for a controversial or awkward issue or problem that no one wants to deal with.

go hot and cold experience sudden feelings of fear, embarrassment, or shock.

1973 Anthony Price *October Men* His wife had said . . . that she had gone 'all hot and cold' after nearly being run over.

have the hots for be sexually attracted to. informal

1996 Janette Turner Hospital *Oyster* One summer night, there was a man with a knife, a man on my own surveying team, a man I fancied, a man I knew had the hots for me.

hot air empty talk that is intended to impress.

2002 Andrew Taylor *Death's Own Door* Lydmouth's such a small place tongues are bound to wag. Ten to one it's just hot air.

hot and bothered: *see* BOTHERED.

hot and heavy intense; with intensity. North American informal

hot off the press (of information) completely new and previously unknown.

2005 *Sugar* The news that these thoroughbred A-listers exist isn't exactly hot off the press.

hot on the heels of following closely.

hot to trot ready and eager to engage in an activity. informal

hot under the collar angry, resentful, or embarrassed.

2000 Laurence McTaggart *Being Catholic Today* Do you get hot under the collar about vacuous musical moanings in church, or fired up at the thought of young people living 'in sin'?

in hot water in a situation of difficulty, trouble, or disgrace.

1997 *TV Quick* Hunter finds himself in hot water when a local TV reporter accuses him of police brutality—and is later found dead.

like a cat on a hot tin roof (*or* on hot bricks): *see* CAT.

make it (*or* things) hot for someone make life difficult for someone.

more — than someone has had hot dinners: *see* DINNER.

piping hot: *see* PIPING.

sell like hot cakes: *see* CAKE.

strike while the iron is hot: *see* STRIKE.

too hot to hold you (of a place) not safe to remain in because of your past misconduct.

1984 Gwyn Jones *A History of the Vikings* Of Naddod we read that he was . . . a viking of note who seems to have made Norway and other Norse settlements too hot to hold him.

hour

at the eleventh hour: *see* ELEVENTH.

your finest hour: *see* FINEST.

keep late (*or* regular) hours do the same thing, typically getting up and going to bed, late (*or* at the same time) every day.

the small hours: *see* SMALL.

till (*or* to) all hours till very late. informal

the witching hour: *see* WITCHING.

house

the angel in the house: *see* ANGEL.

bow down in the house of Rimmon: *see* BOW.

bring the house down make an audience respond with great enthusiasm, especially as shown by their laughter or applause.

clean house: *see* CLEAN.

eat someone out of house and home: *see* EAT.

front of house: *see* FRONT.

get on (*or* along) like a house on fire have a very good and friendly relationship.

go round (*or* all round) the houses ❶ take a circuitous route to your destination. ❷ take an unnecessarily long time to get to the point.

a halfway house: *see* HALFWAY.

house and home a person's home (used for emphasis).

a house divided a group or organization weakened by internal dissensions.

ℹ This phrase alludes to Matthew 12:25: 'Every city or house divided against itself shall not stand', that is, will be unable to withstand external pressures.

a house of cards an insecure or over-ambitious scheme.

ℹ Literally, a *house of cards* is a structure of playing cards balanced together.

2013 *Mac Observer* Eventually, the market share of cheap Android devices collapses like a house of cards.

on the house (of drinks or a meal in a bar or restaurant) free.

a plague on both your houses: *see* PLAGUE.

put (*or* set *or* get) your house in order make necessary reforms.

2002 *New York Times* There will be no moral credibility for the bishops to speak about justice, truth, racial equality, war or immigration if they can't get their own house in order.

safe as houses thoroughly or completely safe. British

houseroom

not give something houseroom be unwilling to have or consider something. British

ℹ The word *houseroom*, dating from the late 16th century, literally means 'lodging or accommodation in a house'.

1986 Liz Lochhead *True Confessions* Course I do get the Woman and the Woman's Own plus I swap Options for the Cosmopolitan off our Joy. I wouldn't give Woman's Realm houseroom.

housetop

proclaim (*or* shout) something from the housetops announce something publicly.

how

and how! very much so (used to express strong agreement). informal

how's your father: *see* FATHER.

Hoyle

according to Hoyle according to plan or the rules.

ℹ Edmond Hoyle (1672–1769) wrote a number of authoritative books about whist and other card games; his name, at first synonymous with expert opinion on card games, became a metaphor for the highest authority in all fields.

1989 Tom Bodett *The End of the Road* His divinely inspired plan had gone exactly according to Hoyle. He'd fooled them.

huff

huff and puff ❶ breathe heavily with exhaustion. ❷ express your annoyance in an obvious or threatening way.

hum

hum and haw (*or* ha) hesitate; be indecisive. British

ℹ The word *hum* has been used as an inarticulate syllable in hesitant speech since Chaucer; *ha* appears in a similar role from the early 17th century.

human

the milk of human kindness: *see* MILK.

humble

eat humble pie make a humble apology and accept humiliation.

ℹ *Humble pie* is from a mid-19th-century pun based on *umbles*, meaning 'offal', which was considered to be an inferior food.

2013 *Daily Telegraph* He said all the pro-independence campaign has offered are complaints of scaremongering and Alex Salmond needs to swallow 'big pieces of humble pie' to resolve the current 'crisis'.

your humble abode used to refer to your home with an ironic or humorous show of modesty.

hump

get (*or* have *or* give someone) the hump become (or be or make someone) annoyed or moody. British informal

live on your hump be self-sufficient. informal

ℹ The image here is of the camel, which is famous for surviving on the fat in its hump without feeding or drinking.

over the hump over the worst.

hunch

play a (*or* your) hunch make an instinctive choice.

hunt

witch hunt: *see* WITCH.

hunting ground

happy hunting ground: *see* HAPPY.

hurdle

fall at the first hurdle meet with failure at a very early stage of an undertaking.

hurrah

last hurrah: *see* LAST.

hurt

wouldn't hurt a fly: *see* FLY.

hustle

hustle your butt move or act quickly. North American informal

ℹ Other variants of this phrase include *hustle your buns* and, in vulgar slang, *hustle your ass*.

hymn sheet

sing from the same hymn sheet: *see* SING.

I

I

dot the i's and cross the t's: *see* DOT.

I ask you!: *see* ASK.

I'm all right, Jack: *see* JACK.

I tell a lie: *see* LIE.

I should cocoa: *see* COCOA.

ice

break the ice do or say something to relieve tension or get conversation started at the start of a party or when people meet for the first time.

cut no ice have no influence or effect. informal

> **1973 Joyce Porter** *It's Murder with Dover* MacGregor remembered ... that logical argument didn't cut much ice with Dover and he abandoned it.

hog on ice: *see* HOG.

on ice ❶ (of an entertainment) performed by skaters. ❷ (of wine or food) kept chilled by being surrounded by ice. ❸ (especially of a plan or proposal) held in reserve for future consideration.

> ❸ **1995** *Times Education Supplement* In Kent plans for 10 more nursery classes next year are on ice.

(skate) on thin ice (be) in a precarious or risky situation.

iceberg

the tip of an (*or* the) iceberg the small perceptible part of a much larger situation or problem which remains hidden.

> ℹ This phrase refers to the fact that only about one fifth of the mass of an iceberg is visible above the surface of the sea.

> **2002** *Focus* Rumours of BSE equivalents in lamb and chicken are just the tip of the dodgy-eating iceberg.

icing

the icing on the cake an attractive but inessential addition or enhancement.

> ℹ A North American variant of this phrase is *the frosting on the cake*.

> **2003 Anita Notaro** *Back after the Break* They were invited for a drink with the crew after the show, which was the icing on the cake as far as they were concerned: a chance to really mingle with the rich and famous.

idea

buck your ideas up: *see* BUCK.

get (*or* give someone) ideas become (*or* make someone) ambitious, big-headed, or tempted to do something against someone else's will, especially make a sexual advance. informal

what's the big idea?: *see* BIG.

if

if anything used to suggest tentatively that something may be the case (often the opposite of something previously implied).

ill

it's an ill wind: *see* WIND.

illusion

be under the illusion that wrongly believe that.

> **2012** *Daily Telegraph* If Barack Obama was under the illusion he didn't have a fight on his hands to win the 2012 US election then he received a rude awakening last night.

be under no illusion (*or* illusions) be fully aware of the true state of affairs.

> **1992** *Christian Scientist Monitor* It is crucial to the nation's security... that we be under no illusions about reasons for this zero-loss rate.

image

a graven image: *see* GRAVEN.

the living image of: *see* LIVING.

imitation

imitation is the sincerest form of flattery copying someone or something is an implicit way of paying them a compliment. proverb

immemorial

time immemorial: *see* TIME.

improve

improve the shining hour make good use of time; make the most of your time. literary

❶ This expression comes from Isaac Watts's *Divine Songs for Children* (1715): 'How doth the little busy bee Improve each shining hour'.

in

be in at the death: *see* DEATH.

be in for have good reason to expect (typically something unpleasant).

1988 Hugh Scott *The Shaman's Stone* The weather will break soon, then we'll be in for a storm.

be in like Flynn: *see* FLYNN.

be in on be privy to (something secret).

have it in for someone have hostile feelings towards someone. informal

in for a penny, in for a pound: *see* PENNY.

in on the act: *see* ACT.

in with enjoying friendly relations with. informal

1990 Jeffrey Masson *Final Analysis* I was in demand everywhere . . . simply because I was in with the right people.

the ins and outs all the details of something.

inch

give someone an inch once concessions have been made to someone they will demand a great deal.

❶ The full form of the saying is the proverb *give someone an inch and he will take a mile*. In former times, *ell* (an obsolete measure of length equal to a little over a metre) was sometimes substitued for *mile*.

within an inch of your life almost to the point of death.

2013 *Keeping Stock* The Police are following positive lines of inquiry in the hunt for the cowardly thugs who knocked Ryder to the round, then kicked him to within an inch of his life, leaving him for dead.

incline

incline your ear listen favourably. literary

❶ *Incline thine ear* is an expression used throughout the Bible, for example in Psalms 17:6: 'I have called upon thee, for thou wilt hear me, O God: incline thine ear unto me, and hear my speech'.

Indian

Indian summer ❶ a period of dry, warm weather occurring in late autumn. ❷ a tranquil or productive period in someone's later years.

❶ The expression originated in the USA, where it seems to have alluded to the relatively warm autumns experienced in the parts of the country mainly inhabited by Native Americans, in contrast with the cooler weather of the east coast.

❷ **1930 Vita Sackville-West** *The Edwardians* Meanwhile she was quite content that Sebastian should become tanned in the rays of Sylvia's Indian summer.

too many chiefs and not enough Indians: *see* CHIEF.

indoors

her indoors: *see* HER.

influence

under the influence affected by alcoholic drink, especially beyond the legal limits for driving a vehicle; drunk. informal

Injun

honest Injun honestly; really. dated

❶ *Injun* is a respelling of *Indian*, in the now discredited sense 'Native American'.

injury

do yourself an injury suffer physical harm or damage as a result of your own actions. informal

innings

have had a good innings have had a long and fulfilling life or career. British informal

❶ In cricket, an *innings* is the period that a team or batsman spends batting, and a *good innings* is one during which a lot of runs are scored.

2002 *Oldie* He keeps dropping heavy hints when he visits: he . . . said the other evening I have had a good innings (I am 86).

innocence

in all innocence without knowledge of something's significance or possible consequences.

2005 James Clarke *The Star* (South Africa) It was ... singularly unfair of the regional committee to strike from the book Alfred Zwane's 100 metre record ... simply because he took a banned substance in all innocence thinking he was eating jelly beans.

inside

on the inside in a position affording private information. informal

1932 *Daily Express* I have chatted with men who are believed to be on the inside, and they have informed me that there will certainly be changes at forward and in the three-quarter line.

i

inside out

know someone or something inside out know someone or something very thoroughly.

turn something inside out ❶ turn the inner surface of something outwards. ❷ change something utterly.

❷ **2002** *New Republic* My every preconception about Renaissance tapestry had been turned inside out.

insignificance

pale into insignificance: *see* PALE.

insult

add insult to injury do or say something that makes a bad or displeasing situation even worse.

ⓘ This phrase comes from Edward Moore's play *The Foundling* (1748): 'This is adding insult to injuries'.

intent

to (*or* for) all intents and purposes in all important respects.

2014 *New Zealand Herald* Today, the Herald looks back at some of the most high-profile unsolved murder and missing person files—all of which are still under active investigation by police, but are for all intents and purposes 'cold cases'.

interest

declare an (*or* your) interest make known your financial interests in an undertaking before it is discussed.

interesting

in an interesting condition pregnant. dated euphemistic

interference

run interference intervene on someone's behalf, typically so as to protect them from distraction or annoyance. North American informal

ⓘ *Run interference* is a metaphor from American football, where it refers to the legal blocking of an opponent to clear a way for the ball carrier.

intestinal

intestinal fortitude courage.

ⓘ The expression was coined around 1915 by Dr John W. Wilce of Ohio State University, USA, as a deliberately euphemistic avoidance of the word *guts*.

Irish

the luck of the Irish: *see* LUCK.

iron

blood and iron: *see* BLOOD.

clap someone in irons: *see* **clap someone in jail** *at* CLAP.

have many (*or* other) irons in the fire have many (*or* a range of) options or courses of action available or be involved in many activities or commitments at the same time.

ⓘ Various tools and implements made (or formerly made) of iron are called *irons*, for example grappling irons or branding irons. The metaphor is of a blacksmith or other worker who heats iron objects in a fire until they reach the critical temperature at which they can be shaped or used.

an iron curtain an impenetrable barrier, especially *the Iron Curtain*, the physical and other barriers preventing the passage of people and information between the Soviet bloc and the West during the cold war.

ⓘ In the late 18th century, an *iron curtain* was literally a fire curtain in a theatre, but the figurative sense was in use from the early 19th century, well before Winston Churchill observed in a speech in March 1946 that 'an iron curtain has descended across the Continent [of Europe]'.

the iron entered into someone's soul someone became deeply and permanently affected by imprisonment or ill-treatment. literary

ⓘ This expression comes from a phrase in the Latin Vulgate version of the Bible, *ferrum pertransit animam ejus*, a mistranslation of the Hebrew which literally translates as 'his person entered into the iron', meaning 'he was placed in fetters'.

an iron hand (*or* fist) in a velvet glove firmness or ruthlessness masked by outward gentleness.

iron out the wrinkles resolve all minor difficulties and snags.

ⓘ *Iron out* has been in figurative use since the mid 19th century; it often occurs with other nouns, especially *differences*.

1984 *New Yorker* Willa had sold her story to Universal Pictures and was in California ironing out some wrinkles in the deal.

pump iron: *see* PUMP.

rule someone or something with a rod of iron: *see* ROD.

strike while the iron is hot: *see* STRIKE.

issue

make an issue of treat too seriously or as a problem.

take issue with disagree with; challenge.

itch

your fingers itch: *see* FINGER.

the seven-year itch: *see* SEVEN.

itching

an itching palm an avaricious or greedy nature.

1937 Wyndham Lewis *The Revenge for Love* Had Alvaro been bribed? Had such a man an itching palm like the rest of them?

itchy

get (*or* have) itchy feet be restless; have a strong urge to travel or move from place to place. informal

item

be an item (of a couple) be involved in an established romantic or sexual relationship. informal

1997 *Independent* 'It is fair to say they are an item but they are not engaged,' said one of Mr Brown's closest confidantes.

ivory

tickle (*or* tinkle) the ivories play the piano. informal

ⓘ The *ivories* are the white keys of the piano, traditionally made of ivory.

jack

ball the jack: *see* BALL.

before you can say Jack Robinson very quickly or suddenly. informal

ⓘ This expression was in use in the late 18th century, but neither an early 19th-century popular song about Jack Robinson nor some mid-19th-century attempts to identify the eponymous Jack Robinson shed any light on its origins.

every man Jack each and every person. informal

ⓘ Jack is a pet name form of the forename John. It was sometimes used in informal American speech as a form of address to a man whose name you did not know, and as a generic name for any ordinary or working- class man.

I'm all right, Jack used to express or comment upon selfish complacency. informal

ⓘ *I'm all right, Jack* was (together with its more scabrous fuller form *Fuck you, Jack, I'm all right)* an early 20th-century catchphrase which became the title of a 1959 British film.

jack of all trades (and master of none) a person who can do many different types of work (but has special skill in none).

ⓘ *Jack* is used here to mean a 'general labourer' or 'odd-job man', a sense dating from the mid 19th century.

Jack the Lad a brash, cocky young man. British informal

ⓘ This originated as the nickname of Jack Sheppard, an 18th-century thief.

2017 *Somerset County Gazette* I was a bit of a Jack the Lad in my younger days.

on your Jack on your own. British informal

ⓘ This is an abbreviation of the rhyming slang expression *on your Jack Jones*.

jackpot

hit the jackpot ❶ win a jackpot. ❷ have great or unexpected success, especially in making a lot of money quickly. informal

ⓘ Originally, in the late 19th century, *jackpot* was a term used in a form of poker, where the pot or pool accumulated until a player could open the betting with a pair of jacks or higher cards. It is now used of any large money prize that accumulates until it is won.

jail

clap someone in jail: *see* CLAP.

jam

have (*or* want) jam on it have (or want) some additional pleasure, ease, or advantage.

1974 Olivia Manning *Rain Forest* Hugh . . . was free to leave at six . . . Pedley . . . said: 'You've got jam on it: walking home in the sunset.'

jam tomorrow a pleasant thing which is often promised but rarely materializes. British

ⓘ This expression comes from Lewis Carroll's *Through the Looking-Glass* (1871): 'The rule is jam tomorrow and jam yesterday—but never jam today'.

money for jam: *see* MONEY.

James

home, James (and don't spare the horses)!: *see* HOME.

Jane

plain Jane an unattractive girl or woman.

2002 *Guardian* [The film] assembles its stereotypes (the sexy exchange student, the plain Jane who's really a fox, the jock who is only dating her for a bet) then proceeds to gunk them all with a ton of scatalogical prankery.

jaw

your jaw drops you feel or appear amazed or shocked.

jazz

and all that jazz and such similar things. informal

ⓘ Of unknown origin, *jazz* was used informally to mean 'meaningless talk' within a decade of the word's first appearance in its musical sense, in the early 20th century. This phrase was a mid-20th-century development.

1960 *Punch* Politics, world affairs, film stars' babies and all that jazz, the things that the adult world seems obsessed with, do not interest us at all.

jeans

cream your jeans: *see* CREAM.

Jekyll

Jekyll and Hyde a person alternately displaying opposing good and evil personalities.

🛈 *The Strange Case of Dr Jekyll and Mr Hyde* (1886) is a novel by Robert Louis Stevenson, in which the physician Jekyll, in order to indulge his evil instincts, uses a drug to create the persona of Hyde, which at first he can assume at will but which gradually gains control of him.

jerk

put a jerk in it act vigorously, smartly, or quickly. informal, dated

1939 C. Day Lewis *Child of Misfortune* Put a jerk in it. I'm meeting my boy at the second house at the Royal.

jetsam

flotsam and jetsam: *see* FLOTSAM.

jewel

the family jewels: *see* FAMILY.

the jewel in the (*or* **someone's) crown** the most attractive or successful part of something.

🛈 In the early 20th century, this was used as a term for the British imperial colonies as a whole. *The Jewel in the Crown* was subsequently used by Paul Scott as the title of the first novel (1966) of his Raj Quartet, which is set in the last days of British rule in India.

jib

the cut of someone's jib the appearance or look of a person.

🛈 This was originally a nautical expression suggested by the prominence and characteristic form of the jib (a triangular sail set forward of the foremast) as the identifying characteristic of a ship.

jig

in jig time extremely quickly; in a very short time. North American informal

the jig is up the scheme or deception is revealed or foiled. North American informal

🛈 The sense of *jig* here dates from the late 16th century and means 'jest' or 'trick'. *The jig is over* is recorded from the late 18th century in the USA and the usual modern version with *up* appeared only slightly later.

Job

a Job's comforter a person who aggravates distress under the guise of giving comfort.

🛈 In the Bible, Job was a prosperous man whose patience and piety was tested by a series of undeserved misfortunes. The attempts of his friends to comfort him only add to his sense of despair and he tells them: 'miserable comforters are ye all' (Job 16:2). Despite his ordeals, he remains confident of the goodness and justice of God and in the end he is restored to his former situation.

job

big jobs a euphemistic way of referring to faeces or defecation. British informal

do a job on someone do something which harms or defeats an opponent. informal

give something up as a bad job decide that it is futile to devote further time and energy to something. informal

2005 Theresa Green *A Quiet Crusade* Sixth was startled to such a degree that he actually got up out of his basket and followed Maddie around for almost ninety seconds before giving it up as a bad job and going back to bed.

a good job a fortunate fact or circumstance. informal, chiefly British

2009 *All About Me* There wasn't much elbow room so it is a good job I sat in between Helen and Tony who I knew well.

jobs for the boys used in reference to the practice of giving paid employment to your friends, supporters, or relations. British derogatory

2002 *Guardian* The James Report found the unit operated a 'jobs for the boys' recruitment policy favouring Reed's friends and political acquaintances.

just the job exactly what is needed. British informal

make the best of a bad job: *see* **make the best of it** *at* BEST.

more than your job's worth not worth risking your job for.

ⓘ This phrase has given rise to the term *Jobsworth*, which is applied to the kind of person, usually a minor official, who says 'it's more than my job's worth' as a way of justifying an insistence on petty rules, even at the expense of common sense.

on the job ❶ while working. ❷ engaged in sexual intercourse. British informal

a snow job: *see* SNOW.

jockey

jockey for position manoeuvre in order to gain advantage over rivals in a competitive situation.

jog

jog someone's memory cause someone to remember something suddenly.

j

join

if you can't beat them, join them: *see* BEAT.

join the club: *see* CLUB.

join up the dots add the missing links in a line of reasoning (and reach the inevitable conclusion).

ⓘ The expression is based on the idea of an outline drawing made by tracing a line through a series of dots.

2003 *Scotland on Sunday* The Mercury Music Prize . . . really helped us to be taken seriously. I think a lot of people knew the songs but didn't necessarily know they were by us so it also helped to join up the dots for them.

join the great majority die. euphemistic

ⓘ This expression was first used by the poet Edward Young (1683–1765): 'Death joins us to the great majority'. However, the idea of the dead being 'the majority' is a very old one; it is found, for example, in the writings of the Roman satirist Petronius as *abiit ad plures*: 'he's gone to join the majority'.

joined at the hip inseparable in opinions or outlook. informal

ⓘ The metaphor is based on the idea of literal conjoined twins.

2002 *Fast Company Magazine* You can't look at Wall Street without looking at Washington. They're joined at the hip.

joint

case the joint: *see* CASE.

out of joint ❶ (of a specified joint) out of position; dislocated. ❷ in a state of disorder or disorientation.

❷ **1601 William Shakespeare** *Hamlet* The time is out of joint.

put someone's nose out of joint: *see* NOSE.

joke

be no joke be a serious matter or difficult undertaking. informal

2014 *Telegraph* The police already have access to much more violent means of crowd control. If you look at a baton round, it's no joke if you get that in the eye.

get (*or* be) beyond a joke become (*or* be) something that is serious or worrying. informal

2002 *Guardian* The rogue animal is believed to have attacked at least six residents in the past week, and his antics are now described by residents as 'well beyond a joke'.

the joke is on someone someone looks foolish, especially after trying to make someone else look so. informal

2011 *New York Times* It's terrifying to realize that this kind of cynical careerism . . . has probably ensured that we won't do anything about climate change until catastrophe is already upon us. So on second thought, I was wrong when I said that the joke was on the G.O.P.; actually, the joke is on the human race.

joker

the joker in the pack a person or factor likely to have an unpredictable effect on events.

ⓘ In a pack of playing cards, a *joker* is an extra card which does not belong to one of the four suits (clubs, diamonds, hearts, and spades) and usually bears the figure of a jester. It is used in some card games as a trump and in poker as a wild card.

1973 George Sims *Hunters Point* Fred Wheeler may be the joker in the pack. He might have got Dave involved in something wild.

jollies

get your jollies have fun or find pleasure. informal

Joneses

keep up with the Joneses try to maintain the same social and material standards as your friends or neighbours.

ⓘ This phrase originated as a comic-strip title, 'Keeping up with the Joneses—by Pop' in the

New York *Globe* (1913). *Jones*, one of the most common family names among English-speakers, is used as a generic name for neighbours or presumed social equals.

journey

a sabbath day's journey: *see* SABBATH.

jowl

cheek by jowl: *see* CHEEK.

joy

bundle of joy: *see* BUNDLE.

full of the joys of spring lively and cheerful.

your pride and joy: *see* PRIDE.

wish someone joy used to congratulate someone on something. British, chiefly ironic

> **2001** *Daily Telegraph* I . . . wish Lord Hamlyn, Tony and Cherie every possible joy of sex, money, and all the rest of it.

jubbly

lovely jubbly: *see* LOVELY.

Judas

a Judas kiss an act of betrayal, especially one disguised as a gesture of friendship.

> ❶ Judas Iscariot was the disciple who betrayed Jesus to the authorities in return for thirty pieces of silver: 'And he that betrayed him gave them a sign, saying, Whomsoever I shall kiss, that same is he: hold him fast' (Matthew 26:48).

judge

salute the judge: *see* SALUTE.

sober as a judge: *see* SOBER.

judgement

against your better judgement contrary to what you feel to be wise or sensible.

jugular

go for the jugular be aggressive or unrestrained in making an attack.

> **1997** *Cosmopolitan* Once she decides she wants a man, she goes for the jugular and doesn't give a hoot about any other woman (such as his girlfriend).

juice

stew in your own juice: *see* STEW.

jump

be for the high jump: *see* HIGH.

get (*or* have) the jump on get (*or* have) an advantage over someone as a result of your prompt action. North American informal

> **1912** **George Ade** *Knocking the Neighbors* Rufus was sinfully Rich . . . his Family had drilled into him the low-down Habit of getting the Jump on the Other Fellow.

go (and) jump in the lake go away and stop being a nuisance. informal

> **2013** *CNN transcripts* So far, Majority Leader Harry Reid has essentially told House of Representatives and the American people to go jump in the lake.

jump someone's bones have sex with someone. North American vulgar slang

jump down someone's throat respond to what someone has said in a sudden and angrily critical way. informal

jump the gun act before the proper or appropriate time. informal

> ❶ In athletics, a competitor who *jumps the gun* sets off before the starting pistol has been fired. The expression appears in the early 20th century as *beat the gun*.

jump in at the deep end: *see* DEEP.

jump on the bandwagon: *see* BANDWAGON.

jump out of your skin be extremely startled. informal

jump the queue ❶ push into a queue of people in order to be served or dealt with before your turn. ❷ take unfair precedence over others.

> ❶ The US version of this expression is *jump in line*.

jump the rails (*or* track) (of a train) become dislodged from the track; be derailed.

jump the shark (of a television series or film) reach a point at which far-fetched events are included merely for the sake of novelty, indicative of a decline in quality. US informal

> ❶ This phrase is said to refer to an episode of the long-running US television series *Happy Days*, in which the central character (the Fonz) jumped over a shark while waterskiing.

jump ship ❶ (of a sailor) leave the ship on which you are serving without having obtained permission to do so. ❷ suddenly abandon an organization, enterprise, etc.

jump through hoops be obliged to go through an elaborate or complicated procedure in order to achieve an objective.

2002 *Guardian* For the Going Underground single in 1980, the producer made Weller jump through hoops to deliver a convincing vocal performance.

jump (*or* leap) to conclusions (*or* the conclusion that) form an opinion hastily, before you have learned or considered all the facts.

jump to it take prompt and energetic action.

1974 Marian Babson *The Stalking Lamb* When you hear my signal—jump to it!

on the jump ❶ moving quickly. ❷ abruptly; swiftly. informal

❷ **1972 Judson Philips** *The Vanishing Senator* Get over here on the jump . . . Step on it, will you?

one jump ahead one step or stage ahead of someone else and so having the advantage over them.

see which way the cat jumps: *see* CAT.

take a running jump: *see* RUNNING.

that cat won't jump: *see* CAT.

jumping

be jumping up and down be very angry, upset, or excited. informal

jungle

blackboard jungle: *see* BLACKBOARD.

the law of the jungle the principle that those who are strong and apply ruthless self-interest will be most successful.

1989 Bessie Head *Tales of Tenderness & Power* And at the beer tank the law of the jungle prevailed, the stronger shoving the weaker.

jury

the jury is out a decision has not yet been reached on a controversial subject.

2013 *New Statesman* Is this really the way we want to watch films? The jury is out and the precise direction of simultaneous distribution is unclear.

just

get your just deserts: *see* DESERTS.

just the job: *see* JOB.

justice

do someone or something justice (*or* do justice to someone or something) treat or represent someone or something with due fairness or appreciation.

do yourself justice perform as well as you are able to.

poetic justice: *see* POETIC.

rough justice: *see* ROUGH.

kangaroo

have kangaroos in the (*or* your) top paddock be mad or eccentric. Australian informal

ⓘ In Australian English *paddock* is an enclosed field or tract of land.

1985 Peter Carey *Illywhacker* 'And he was a big man too, and possibly slow-witted.' 'Leichhardt?' 'No, Bourke . . . He had kangaroos in his top paddock.'

keel

on an even keel: *see* EVEN.

keen

keen as mustard extremely eager or enthusiastic. British informal

ⓘ In the literal sense of the phrase, *keen* means 'operating on the senses like a sharp instrument'.

keep

for keeps permanently, indefinitely. informal

ⓘ 2005 *Taipei Times* When he quits for keeps, Sanders probably will be asked to return to the TV studio.

keep yourself to yourself avoid contact or communication with others; be retiring and solitary.

play for keeps engage in an activity with ruthless determination and single-mindedness.

2003 *Inc. Magazine* The infamously tough buyers at Wal-Mart, he says, play for keeps. If you're a small vendor, and you fail them once, they'll never forget. You're on their shitlist for life.

you can't keep a good man (*or* woman) down a competent person will always recover well from setbacks or problems. informal

ⓘ For other idioms containing *keep*, see the entry for the main word in the idiom (for example, **keep up with the Joneses** at JONESES).

keeper

be your brother's keeper: *see* BROTHER.

keeping

in (*or* out of) keeping with in (or out of) harmony or conformity with.

ken

beyond your ken outside your range of knowledge or understanding.

ⓘ The now obsolete *ken* 'knowledge' is descended ultimately from the Old English verb *cennan* 'make known'.

kettle

a different kettle of fish a completely different matter or type of person from the one previously mentioned. informal

1993 *Empire* Meryl is the finest actress of her generation but Arnold is, er, a different kettle of fish.

the pot calling the kettle black: *see* POT.

a pretty (*or* fine) kettle of fish an awkward state of affairs. informal

ⓘ In late 18th-century Scotland, *a kettle of fish* was a large saucepan of fish, typically freshly caught salmon, cooked at Scottish picnics, and the term was also applied to the picnic itself. By the mid 18th century, the novelist Henry Fielding was using the phrase to mean 'a muddle'.

key

in (*or* out of) key in (*or* out of) harmony.

throw away the key used to suggest that someone who has been put in prison should or will never be released.

under lock and key: *see* LOCK.

kibosh

put the kibosh on put an end to; thwart the plans of. informal

ⓘ The meaning and origin of *kibosh* is uncertain. 'Put the kye-bosk on her' is used by 'a pot-boy' in Charles Dickens's *Sketches by Boz* (1836).

kick

alive and kicking: *see* ALIVE.

kick against the pricks hurt yourself by persisting in useless resistance or protest.

> ❶ In the Bible, on the road to Damascus Saul heard the words: 'It is hard for thee to kick against the pricks' (Acts 9:5). The image is that of an ox or other beast of burden fruitlessly kicking out when it is pricked by a goad or spur.

kick someone's ass (*or* butt) dominate, beat, or defeat someone. North American vulgar slang

kick (some) ass (*or* butt) act in a forceful or aggressive manner. North American vulgar slang

> **1995 Martin Amis** *Information* You got to come on strong. Talk big and kick ass.

a kick at the can (*or* cat) an opportunity to achieve something. Canadian informal

kick the bucket die. informal

> ❶ The *bucket* in this phrase may be a pail on which a person committing suicide might stand, kicking it away before they hanged themselves. Another suggestion is that it refers to a beam on which something can be hung up; in Norfolk dialect the beam from which a slaughtered pig was suspended by its heels could be referred to as a *bucket*.

kick the can down the road postpone making a decision or taking action. chiefly US

> **2013 Mark Heuring** *Mr Dilettante* Obamacare is still fundamentally broken, Washington politicians are still kicking the can down the road on the budget and the weather still sucks.

kick someone down the ladder reject or disown the friends or associates who have helped you to rise in the world, especially with the idea of preventing them from attaining a similar position.

kick the gong around smoke opium. informal

> ❶ *Gong* is early 20th-century US slang for an opium pipe.

kick the habit stop engaging in a habitual practice. informal

> **2011** *Spiked Magazine* Seven years have passed since Massachusetts became the sixth US state to introduce a state-wide indoor smoking ban. But officials there still haven't kicked the habit of lifestyle engineering. Now they are going after electronic cigarettes.

a kick in the pants (*or* up the arse *or* backside) something that prompts or forces fresh effort. informal

> **2013** *CNN transcripts* I was not even tested or considered to be a donor because of my weight. That was the kick in the pants I need.

kicking and screaming protesting vociferously, especially against being forced to accept innovations. informal

> **2004** *Gramophone Magazine* Some say he [Pierre Boulez] dragged the Philharmonic's generally conservative audience kicking and screaming into the harsh light of modernism.

a kick in the teeth a grave setback or disappointment, especially one seen as a betrayal. informal

> **1994** *Daily Mirror* The rates rise was a kick in the teeth for the housing market, which had been showing signs of recovery.

kick the tin make a contribution of money for a particular purpose. Australian informal

> ❶ The 'tin' was originally literally a tin can into which money was thrown.

kick over the traces become insubordinate or reckless.

> ❶ *Traces* are the straps by which a draught horse is attached to the vehicle it is pulling. If the animal kicked out over these straps, the driver would no longer be able to control it.

kick someone upstairs remove someone from an influential position in a business by giving them an ostensible promotion. informal

kick someone when they are down cause further misfortune to someone who is already in a difficult situation.

kick (*or* boot) something into touch remove something from the centre of attention or activity. British informal

> ❶ In football and rugby, the touchlines mark the sides of the playing area, and if the ball is kicked beyond these (*into touch*) it is no longer in play.

> **2009** *Guardian* The government has kicked into touch a decision on the future of its largest state-owned digital information business.

> ❶ The same idea is expressed by *kick something into the long grass.*

> **2019** *Observer* I never saw the Cameron that was all 'steady as she goes'. He'd get frustrated with people who would kick things into the long grass.

kick up a dust: *see* DUST.

kick up a fuss (*or* a stink) register strong disapproval; object loudly to something. informal

kick up your heels: *see* HEEL.

kick your heels: *see* **cool your heels** *at* HEEL.

kick yourself be annoyed with yourself for doing something foolish or missing an opportunity.

more kicks than halfpence (*or* ha'pence) more harsh treatment than rewards. British informal, dated

ℹ The idiom is usually pronounced in accordance with the variant spelling *ha'pence*.

kid

handle (*or* treat) someone or something with kid gloves deal with someone or something very gently or tactfully.

ℹ *Kid gloves* are those made with fine soft leather from a young goat's skin.

kids' stuff something that is childishly simple or naive. informal

1982 Vivien Alcock *The Sylvia Game* He had grown out of the game; it was kid's stuff. Besides it always landed him in trouble.

a new kid on the block: *see* BLOCK.

our kid your younger brother or sister (often used as a form of address). British informal

kill

be in at the kill be present at or benefit from the successful conclusion of an enterprise.

curiosity killed the cat: *see* CURIOSITY.

dressed to kill: *see* DRESSED.

go (*or* move in *or* close in) for the kill take decisive action to turn a situation to your advantage.

if it kills you whatever the problems or difficulties involved. informal

2001 Nancy Hope Wilson *Mountain Pose* I'm cracking that code if it kills me.

kill the fatted calf: *see* FATTED.

kill the goose that lays the golden egg: *see* GOOSE.

kill or cure (of a remedy for a problem) likely to either work well or fail catastrophically, with no possibility of partial success. British

2010 *Guardian* Andrew Smith, chief economist at KPMG, described Osborne's tough measures as 'a kill or cure' budget, adding: 'The aim is to eliminate the structural deficit over this parliament, but it risks choking off the recovery.'

kill time do things to make time seem to pass more quickly and to avoid getting bored, especially while waiting for something.

kill two birds with one stone achieve two aims at once.

kill someone with (*or* by) kindness spoil someone by overindulging them.

ℹ This expression dates back to the mid 16th century; it famously appears in the title of Thomas Heywood's play *A Woman Killed with Kindness* (1607).

kill yourself laughing be overcome with laughter.

killing

make a killing have a great financial success, especially on a stock exchange.

kilter

out of kilter out of harmony or balance.

ℹ *Kilter*, dating from the early 17th century, was a dialect word meaning 'frame or order'. It is now used only in this phrase.

kin

kith and kin: *see* KITH.

kind

be cruel to be kind: *see* CRUEL.

kindness

the milk of human kindness: *see* MILK.

king

a cat may look at a king: *see* CAT.

King Charles's head an obsession.

ℹ This expression alludes to the character of 'Mr Dick', in Charles Dickens's novel *David Copperfield*, who could not write or speak on any matter without the subject of Charles I's head intruding.

king of beasts the lion.

king of birds the eagle.

king of kings ❶ a king who has lesser kings under him. ❷ God.

king of terrors death personified.

king of the castle someone holding a pre-eminent position, rank, or place; a dominant or successful person.

ℹ The allusion is to a children's game in which someone stands on top of a mound and dares the other children to pull him or her off. This is accompanied by the rhyme 'I'm the king of the castle. Get down, you dirty rascal!'

2015 *Guardian* Hollywood's king of the castle, Steven Spielberg, has been in subdued mood for some time.

a king's ransom a huge amount of money; a fortune.

ⓘ In feudal times prisoners of war were freed for sums in keeping with their rank, so a king, as the highest-ranking individual, commanded the greatest ransom.

the sport of kings: *see* SPORT.

take the King's shilling: *see* SHILLING.

kingdom

come into (*or* to) your kingdom achieve recognition or supremacy.

till (*or* until) kingdom come forever. informal

to kingdom come into the next world. informal

ⓘ *Kingdom come* is the next world or eternity; it comes from the clause in the Lord's Prayer *thy kingdom come*.

1996 *Total Sport* Graham Gooch may be fast approaching his mid-forties but the old boy still clatters most bowlers to Kingdom come.

kiss

have kissed the blarney stone: *see* BLARNEY.

a Judas kiss: *see* JUDAS.

kiss and make up become reconciled.

2011 *Daily Telegraph* Ravens often squabble with each other, but they usually kiss and make up afterwards, new research suggests.

kiss and tell recount your sexual exploits, especially to the media concerning a famous person. chiefly derogatory

kiss someone's arse (*or* ass) behave obsequiously towards someone. vulgar slang

kiss ass behave in an obsequious or sycophantic way. North American vulgar slang

kiss my arse go away!; go to hell! vulgar slang

kiss of death an action or event that causes certain failure for an enterprise.

ⓘ This expression may refer to the kiss of betrayal given by Judas Iscariot to Jesus in the Garden of Gethsemane (Matthew 26:48–9).

2013 *New Statesman* He ends with those words often regarded as the political kiss of death: 'Ed Balls has the full confidence of the shadow cabinet, I'm sure.'

kiss of life ❶ mouth-to-mouth resuscitation. ❷ an action or event that revives a failing enterprise.

❷ **1997 Anthony Barnett** *This Time* She gave a decrepit institution the kiss of life, when she became its adversary.

kiss the dust submit abjectly; be overthrown.

kiss the ground prostrate yourself as a token of respect.

ⓘ This phrase refers to the practice, found particularly in courts of the ancient Eastern world, of throwing yourself on the ground in front of a monarch.

kiss the rod accept punishment meekly or submissively.

ⓘ This idiom refers to a former practice of making a child kiss the rod with which it was beaten. It is used by Shakespeare in *Two Gentlemen of Verona*: 'How wayward is this foolish love That, like a testy babe, will scratch the nurse And presently all humbled kiss the rod'.

kiss something goodbye (*or* kiss goodbye to something) accept the certain loss of something. informal

kit

get your kit off take off all your clothes. British informal

the whole kit and caboodle: *see* **the whole caboodle** *at* CABOODLE.

kitchen

everything but the kitchen sink everything imaginable. informal, humorous

ⓘ This expression was identified by Eric Partridge in his *Dictionary of Forces' Slang* (1948) as being used in the context of an intense bombardment in which the enemy fired everything they had *except the kitchen sink* (or *including the kitchen sink*).

1965 Ed McBain *Doll* Brown began searching. 'Everything in here but the kitchen sink,' he said.

if you can't stand the heat, get out of the kitchen: *see* HEAT.

kite

fly a kite: *see* FLY.

high as a kite intoxicated with drugs or alcohol. informal

ⓘ This expression is a play on *high* meaning 'lofty' and its informal sense 'intoxicated'.

kith

kith and kin your relations.

ℹ *Kith*, from an Old English word meaning 'native land' or 'countrymen', is now only used in this phrase, which itself dates back to the late 14th century. The variant *kith or kin* is also sometimes found.

kitten

have kittens be extremely nervous or upset. British informal

kitty

scoop the kitty: *see* **scoop the pool** *at* SCOOP.

knee

at your mother's (*or* father's) knee at an early age.

the bee's knees: *see* BEE.

bow (*or* bend) the knee: *see* BOW.

bring someone or something to their knees reduce someone or something to a state of weakness or submission.

2013 *CNN transcripts* The fall of Lehman Brothers nearly brought several of the world's financial institutions to their knees.

on bended knee: *see* BENDED.

on your knees ❶ in a kneeling position. ❷ on the verge of collapse.

weak at the knees overcome by a strong emotion.

your knees are knocking you are feeling very frightened. informal

knee-high

knee-high to a grasshopper very small or very young. informal, humorous

ℹ In this form the phrase apparently dates from the mid 19th century, but early 19th-century US versions include *knee-high to a toad* and *knee-high to a mosquito*.

knell

ring the knell of announce or herald the end of.

ℹ The image here is of the tolling of a bell to announce a death or funeral.

knickers

be all fur coat and no knickers: *see* FUR.

get your knickers in a twist become upset or angry. British informal

ℹ This expression was originally used specifically of women, a humorous masculine equivalent being *get your Y-fronts in a twist*.

2012 *New Zealand Herald* Anti-trade deal campaigners are getting their knickers in a twist at the prospect of New Zealand being part of two significant trading blocs.

knife

an atmosphere that you could cut with a knife: *see* ATMOSPHERE.

before you can say knife very quickly; almost instantaneously. informal, dated

get (*or* stick) the knife into (*or* in) someone do something hostile or aggressive to someone. informal

go (*or* be) under the knife have surgery. informal

like a (hot) knife through butter very easily; without any resistance or difficulty.

night of the long knives: *see* NIGHT.

twist (*or* turn) the knife deliberately make someone's grief or problems worse.

1991 Mavis Nicholson *Martha Jane & Me* While she and I were playing the cat-and-mouse game of these stories, I would sometimes, just to twist the knife a little further, ask about the little girl's father.

the knives are out (for someone) there is open hostility (towards someone). informal

knife-edge

on a knife-edge (*or* razor's edge) in a tense situation, especially one finely balanced between success and failure.

2000 *South African Times UK* With the game poised on a knife-edge, the Wallabies won a ruck and George Gregan's pass was floated to the flyhalf, who picked his line perfectly.

knight

a knight in shining armour an idealized or heroic person, especially a man who comes to the rescue of a woman in distress or in a difficult situation.

ℹ This expression, a variant of which is *a knight on a white charger*, is often used ironically of someone who presents himself in this guise but is in fact inadequate to the role. Compare with **a white knight** (*at* WHITE).

knight of the road a man who frequents the roads, for example a travelling sales representative, lorry or taxi driver, or tramp.

ⓘ Originally, in the mid 17th century, this phrase was ironically applied to a highwayman.

knight of the shires a British Conservative member of parliament who has the title 'Sir' and sits for a rural constituency, typically one of long service and with a high place in the party hierarchy.

2011 *Daily Telegraph* During the negotiations for entry, a Tory knight of the shires, Sir Derek Walker-Smith, was one of the few to draw attention to the significance of Article 3, Paragraph H of the Treaty of Rome.

a white knight: *see* WHITE.

knob

with knobs (*or* brass knobs) on and something more. British informal

2008 *Guardian* Obama praised her [Sarah Palin] as a skilled politician but rolled out his camp's new weapon—to depict her as a sort of McCain-Bush with brass knobs on.

knock

knock someone's block off hit someone very hard in anger. informal

ⓘ *Block* is used here in its informal sense of 'head'.

knock someone dead greatly impress someone. informal

1991 Julia Philips *You'll Never Eat Lunch In This Town Again* I'm good at public speaking. I've been knocking them dead at seminars.

knock someone for six: *see* **hit someone for six** *at* SIX.

knock someone into the middle of next week hit someone very hard. informal

knock it off used to tell someone to stop doing something that you find annoying or foolish. informal

knock someone off their perch: *see* PERCH.

knock on (*or* at) the door seek to join a particular group or sphere of action.

knock someone or something on the head decisively prevent an idea, plan, or proposal from being held or developed. British informal

ⓘ The image in this phrase is of stunning or killing a person or an animal by a blow to their head.

knock on wood: *see* **touch wood** *at* WOOD.

knock someone sideways affect someone very severely; make someone severely depressed or unable to cope. informal

1998 Penelope Lively *Spiderweb* It's always knocked me sideways—the thought of what we carry around, stashed away.

knock someone's socks off: *see* SOCK.

knock something into a cocked hat: *see* COCKED HAT.

knock spots off easily outdo. informal

ⓘ This expression may refer to shooting out the pips (spots) on a playing card in a pistol-shooting competition. Although it is now found chiefly in British English, the phrase originated in America.

2012 *Daily Telegraph* Julian Temperley, traditionalist cider-maker, faces down the Eurocrats' regulations that pander to the French by making his own English cider brandy (knocks spots off Calvados).

knock the stuffing out of someone: *see* STUFFING.

knock them in the aisles amaze and impress people. informal

knock your head against a brick wall: *see* **bang your head against a brick wall** *at* HEAD.

knock someone or something into shape: *see* **lick someone or something into shape** *at* SHAPE.

opportunity knocks: *see* OPPORTUNITY.

the school of hard knocks: *see* SCHOOL.

take a knock suffer a material or emotional setback.

you could have knocked me (*or* her, him, etc.) down with a feather I (*or* she, he, etc.) was greatly surprised. informal

ⓘ A similar idiom is found in Samuel Richardson's novel *Pamela* (1741) ('you might have beat me down with a feather'); the modern form of the expression with *knock* dates from the mid 19th century.

your knees are knocking: *see* KNEE.

knocker

on the knocker ❶ going from door to door, usually canvassing, buying, or selling. ❷ (of payment) immediately; on demand. Australian & New Zealand informal

up to the knocker in good condition; to perfection. informal

knot

at a rate of knots very fast. British informal

ⓘ A *knot* here is a nautical unit of speed, equal to one nautical mile per hour.

cut the knot: *see* CUT.

tie the knot get married. informal

tie someone (up) in knots make someone completely confused. informal

1996 *Daily Star* It looks like an open and shut case until the brilliant QC starts getting the prosecution witnesses tied up in knots.

knotted

get knotted used to express contemptuous rejection of someone. British informal

know

— as we know it as is familiar or customary in the present.

2001 *DJ* It's the real deal with live musicians playing some wonderful jazz over the kick drum, which is the only element that has anything to do with house music as we know it.

be in the know be aware of something known only to a few people.

before you know where you are (*or* before you know it) with baffling speed. informal

for all someone knows used to express the limited scope or extent of someone's information.

know a thing or two be experienced or shrewd.

2013 *Scary Duck* Hackett—a war hero who rose to become Deputy Chief of General Staff—can be safely assumed to know a thing or two about military and political strategy.

know all the answers: *see* ANSWER.

know something backwards: *see* BACKWARDS.

know better than be wise, well-informed, or well-mannered enough to avoid doing something specified.

1989 Anne Fine *Goggle-Eyes* Inspector McGee knows better than to tangle with Beth's granny.

know (*or* not know) from nothing be totally ignorant, either generally or concerning something in particular. North American informal

know how many beans make five: *see* BEAN.

know little (*or* nothing) and care less be completely unconcerned about something; be studiously ignorant.

know no bounds: *see* BOUND.

know on which side your bread is buttered: *see* BREAD.

know someone in the biblical sense have sex with someone. informal, humorous

ⓘ *Know* in this sense is an old use which is particularly associated with language in the Bible, e.g. Genesis 4:1: And Adam knew Eve his wife; and she conceived, and bare Cain'.

know someone or something inside out: *see* INSIDE OUT.

know something like the back of your hand: *see* BACK.

know the ropes be thoroughly acquainted with the way in which something is done. informal

ⓘ In its literal sense, this expression goes back to the days of sailing ships, when skill in handling ropes was essential for any sailor. The idiom is found in various forms, from the mid 19th century onwards, e.g. *learn* or *understand the ropes* and *show* or *teach someone the ropes*

know the score be aware of what is going on; be aware of the essential facts about a situation. informal

2012 *Keeping Stock* Taylor wants to appear in calm control, in demeanour and words, as if he's been there, done that, knows the score.

know the time of day be well informed about something.

know too much be in possession of too much important information to be allowed to live or continue as normal.

know what's what have enough knowledge or experience. informal

1992 *More* I know what's what at work, so no-one's going to trip me up.

know what you are about: *see* ABOUT.

know what you like have fixed or definite tastes, without necessarily having the knowledge or informed opinion to support them.

2002 *Sunday Herald* We adjourn to Starbucks where . . . I know what I like (grand skinny latte, £2.15).

know where the bodies are buried: *see* BODY.

know where you are (*or* stand) with know how you are regarded by someone; know the opinions of someone on an issue.

> **1991 Julian Barnes** *Talking It Over* Good old Stuart, he's so reliable. You know where you are with Stuart.

know who's who be aware of the identity and status of each person.

know your onions: *see* ONION.

know your own mind be decisive and certain.

not know beans about: *see* BEAN.

not know you are born: *see* BORN

not know someone from Adam: *see* ADAM.

not know if you are coming or going: *see* COMING.

not know shit (from Shinola): *see* SHIT.

not know what hit you be hit, killed, or attacked by someone or something without warning.

not know what to do with yourself be at a loss as to what to do, typically through boredom, embarrassment, or anxiety.

not know where (*or* which way) to look feel great embarrassment and not know how to react.

not know your arse from your elbow: *see* ARSE.

not want to know refuse to react or take notice. informal

the right hand doesn't know what the left hand's doing: *see* HAND.

what do you know (about that)? used as an expression of surprise. informal, chiefly North American

you never know you can never be certain; it's impossible to predict. informal

knowing

there is no knowing no one can tell.

known

have known better days: *see* **have seen better days** *at* DAY.

knuckle

go the knuckle fight with the fists. Australian informal

near the knuckle verging on the indecent or offensive. British informal

> ⓘ In the late 19th century this expression was used more generally to mean 'close to the permitted limit of behaviour'.

rap someone on the knuckles: *see* RAP.

labour

a labour of Hercules a task requiring enormous strength or effort.

ⓘ In Greek mythology, Hercules was a man of superhuman strength and courage who performed twelve immense tasks or labours imposed on him as a penance for killing his children in a fit of madness. After his death he was ranked among the gods.

a labour of love a task done for the love of a person or for the work itself.

labour the point explain or discuss something at excessive or unnecessary length.

lad

Jack the Lad: *see* JACK.

likely lad: *see* LIKELY.

ladder

kick someone down the ladder: *see* KICK.

lady

it isn't over till the fat lady sings there is still time for a situation to change.

ⓘ This phrase comes from the saying *the opera isn't over till the fat lady sings*, which originated in the 1970s in the USA; it is doubtful whether any particular operatic production or prima donna was ever intended.

ladies who lunch women with the money and free time to meet for social lunches. informal

ⓘ This expression comes from the title of a 1970s song by Stephen Sondheim: 'A toast to that invincible bunch... Let's hear it for the ladies who lunch'. While it is often used of women who raise money for charity by organizing fashionable lunches, it is also often used in a derogatory way of women with the money and leisure to lunch at expensive restaurants.

Lady Bountiful a woman who engages in ostentatious acts of charity to impress others.

ⓘ Lady Bountiful is the name of a character in *The Beaux' Stratagem* (1707), a play by the Irish Restoration dramatist George Farquhar.

Lady Luck chance personified as a controlling power in human affairs.

Lady Muck a haughty or socially pretentious woman. British informal

lady of the night used euphemistically to refer to a prostitute.

laldy

give it laldy do something with vigour or enthusiasm. Scottish

ⓘ *Laldy* or *laldie*, as in *give someone laldy*, means 'a punishment or beating'.

1993 Irvine Welsh *Trainspotting* A chorus ... echoes throughout the pub. Auld, toothless Willie Shane is giein it laldy.

lam

on the lam in flight, especially from the police. North American informal

lamb

like a lamb to the slaughter as a helpless victim.

ⓘ This expression is found in the Bible in Isaiah 53:7: 'he is brought as a lamb to the slaughter', an image later applied to Jesus.

mutton dressed as lamb: *see* MUTTON.

lame

help a lame dog over a stile: *see* DOG.

lame duck: *see* DUCK.

lamp

an Aladdin's lamp: *see* ALADDIN.

smell of the lamp: *see* SMELL.

lance

lance the boil take decisive action to put an end to an undesirable situation.

ⓘ The underlying image is of a boil being cut open with a lancet or other sharp surgical instrument, to release its pus.

2003 *Yorkshire Post Today* Mr Conway ... said ... it was time for Mr Duncan Smith to 'lance the boil' in his leadership. 'There's a growing feeling of "it's got to end".'

land

land on your feet: *see* **fall on your feet** *at* FOOT.

how the land lies what the state of affairs is.

in the land of the living alive or awake. humorous

ℹ This is a biblical idiom: see, for example, Job 28:13: 'Man knoweth not the price thereof; neither is it found in the land of the living' or Psalms 52:5: 'God shall likewise destroy thee for ever, he shall take thee away, and pluck thee out of thy dwelling place, and root thee out of the land of the living'.

land of Nod a state of sleep.

ℹ In the Bible, the Land of Nod was the place to which Cain was exiled after the murder of his brother Abel (Genesis 4:16). It has been used punningly to refer to sleep since the 18th century, notably by Jonathan Swift in *Polite Conversation* (1731–8): 'I'm going to the Land of Nod'.

live off the land (*or* **the country**) live on whatever food you can obtain by hunting, gathering, or subsistence farming.

2012 *New Statesman* Even today in what were the most populous areas it is easy to live off the land. All along the coast and rivers there were extensive stone fish traps. They didn't store food because it was so abundant!

never-never land: *see* NEVER.

no man's land: *see* NO.

landscape

a blot on the landscape: *see* BLOT.

lane

in the fast lane: *see* FAST.

language

speak the same language understand one another as a result of shared opinions and values.

2013 *Daily Telegraph* 'We speak the same language, we don't put up with any garbage from anybody,' says Mr Christie in his unmistakable tough-guy New Jersey tones.

lap

fall (*or* **drop**) **into someone's lap** (of something pleasant or desirable) come someone's way without any effort having been made.

in the lap of luxury in conditions of great comfort and wealth.

in the lap of the gods (of the success of a plan or event) open to chance; depending on factors that you cannot control.

ℹ This expression comes from one used in several passages in the works of the Greek epic poet Homer. The original Greek refers to the 'knees' of the gods, possibly because suppliants laid gifts on the knees of those who were sitting in judgement upon them.

lares

lares and penates the home.

ℹ In ancient Rome, the *lares* and *penates* were the protective gods of a household, and they came to be used to signify the home itself. The phrase *lares and penates* is generally used to refer to those things that are considered to be the essential elements of someone's home; in 1775 Horace Walpole wrote in a letter 'I am returned to my own Lares and Penates—to my dogs and cats'.

large

by and large: *see* BY.

give (*or* **have**) **it large** ❶ go out and enjoy yourself, typically with drink or drugs. British informal ❷ behave boisterously, extravagantly, or boastfully. British informal

❶ **1999** *London Student* Clubbers had it large to Americans Josh Wink and long-time Detroit supremo Derrick May.

large as life: *see* LIFE.

large it give it large. British informal

2018 Peter James *Absolute Proof* One moment she was lecturing him on their need to conserve and save money .... Next she was flying to Los Angeles and larging it in one of the city's swankiest hotels.

writ large: *see* WRIT.

larger

larger than life: *see* LIFE.

lark

up with the lark up very early in the morning.

ℹ References to the early-morning singing of the lark date back to the 16th century: the first recorded instance is found in John Lyly's *Euphues*. Early risers are often referred to as *larks*, while their late-to-bed counterparts may be described as *owls*. The phrase also employs a play on the word *up*, since the lark sings on the wing while flying high above its nest.

Larry

happy as Larry: *see* **happy as a sandboy** *at* HAPPY.

lash

be (*or* go) on the lash be engaged in (or go on) a heavy drinking session. British informal

have a lash at make an attempt at; have a go at. Australian & New Zealand

last

be the last word be the most fashionable or up-to-date.

1989 *Life* Thanks to a built-in microchip, Teddy Ruxpin became the last word in talking dolls.

breathe your last: *see* BREATHE.

die in the last ditch: *see* DIE.

every last: *see* EVERY.

famous last words: *see* FAMOUS.

have the last laugh: *see* LAUGH.

have the last word ❶ make or have the right to make the final decision or pronouncement about something. ❷ carry out a final and conclusive action in a process or course of events.

(drinking) in the last chance saloon having been allowed one final opportunity to improve or get something right. informal

1998 *Times* Gascoigne has finally found himself in the Last Chance Saloon.

in the last resort: *see* RESORT.

last but not least last in order of mention or occurrence but not of importance.

last hurrah a final act, performance, or effort, especially in politics. chiefly US

ⓘ The expression comes from the title of a novel (1956) by Edwin O'Connor about a US city boss.

the last of the Mohicans the sole survivor(s) of a particular race or kind.

ⓘ *The Last of the Mohicans* is the title of an 1826 novel by James Fenimore Cooper (1789–1851). The Mohicans, also spelled *Mohegans*, were an Algonquian people who formerly inhabited the western parts of the US states of Connecticut and Massachusetts.

the last roundup: *see* ROUNDUP.

the last straw: *see* STRAW.

last thing late in the evening, especially as a final act before going to bed.

on your last legs near the end of life, usefulness, or strength.

1987 Eric Newby *Round Ireland in Low Gear* It is certainly difficult to imagine how anyone who is in any way infirm, and some of the pilgrims who make the climb are literally on their last legs, can reach the top.

pay your last respects: *see* PAY.

stick to your last confine your activities to the area you have personal knowledge of or skill in.

ⓘ The expression derives from the proverb 'The cobbler should stick to his last', a last being a shoemaker's model for shaping or repairing a shoe.

your last gasp: *see* GASP.

late

better late than never: *see* BETTER.

late in the day at a late stage in proceedings, especially too late to be useful.

ⓘ A North American variant of this expression is *late in the game*.

the late unpleasantness: *see* UNPLEASANTNESS.

laugh

a barrel of laughs: *see* BARREL.

a bundle of laughs: *see* **a bundle of fun** *at* BUNDLE.

be having a laugh be attempting to playfully deceive someone. informal, chiefly British

2012 *Daily Telegraph* I said to one of the firemen, 'Why don't you go in?' and he said they couldn't if the water was higher than ankle deep. I said, 'You're having a laugh.' He said, 'No, that's health and safety.'

don't make me laugh don't say such ridiculous things. informal

enough to make a cat laugh: *see* CAT.

good for a laugh guaranteed to amuse or entertain.

1998 *Spectator* I'm now ashamed to admit it, but the fact remains that in 1979 voting Tory did seem good for a laugh.

have the last laugh be finally vindicated, thereby confounding earlier scepticism.

ⓘ There are various proverbial sayings expressing this idea, such as *he laughs best who laughs last* and *he who laughs last, laughs longest*.

laugh (*or* cry) all the way to the bank relish (or deplore) the fact that you are making a great deal of money, especially undeservedly or at the expense of others. informal

The original form of the phrase is *cry all the way to the bank*, which started life as an ironic observation by the flamboyant US pianist Liberace (1919–87), weighing the size of his takings against the low opinion of the critics.

1956 *Daily Mirror* On the occasion in New York at a concert in Madison Square Garden when he had the greatest reception of his life and the critics slayed him mercilessly, Liberace said: 'The take was terrific but the critics killed me. My brother George cried all the way to the bank.'

2013 Idiot Savant *No Right Turn* We should be demanding not just stronger safety practices, but also upfront liability bonds and insurance: so these scum can't ruin our environment, then laugh all the way to the bank.

laugh in someone's face show open contempt for someone by laughing rudely at them in their presence.

the laugh is on me (*or* you *or* him, etc.) the situation is reversed and now the other person is the one who appears ridiculous.

laugh like a drain laugh raucously; guffaw. British informal

a laugh a minute very funny.

laugh yourself silly (*or* sick) laugh uncontrollably or for a long time.

laugh on the other side of your face be discomfited after feeling satisfaction or confidence about something.

A North American variant of this expression is *laugh out of the other side of your mouth*.

laugh someone or something out of court dismiss someone or something with contempt as being obviously ridiculous.

laugh someone or something to scorn ridicule someone or something.

This is a biblical idiom: see, for example, Job 12:4: 'I am as one mocked of his neighbour, who calleth upon God, and he answereth him: the just upright man is laughed to scorn' or Matthew 9:24: 'He said unto them, Give place: for the maid is not dead, but sleepeth. And they laughed him to scorn.'

laugh up your sleeve be secretly or inwardly amused.

The use of *up* in this expression is a relatively recent development; the phrase dates from the mid 16th century in the form *laugh in your sleeve*.

play something for laughs (of a performer) try to arouse laughter in an audience, especially in inappropriate circumstances.

laughing

be laughing be in a fortunate or comfortable situation. informal

2012 *Scary Duck* With a great sales team, they say, the sky's the limit. And get a sales team that can sell ice to the Eskimoes, then you're laughing.

laughing stock a person subjected to general mockery or ridicule.

no laughing matter something serious that should not be joked about.

laurels

look to your laurels be careful not to lose your superior position to a rival.

rest on your laurels be so satisfied with what you have already done or achieved that you make no further effort.

In ancient Greece, a wreath made of bay-tree (laurel) leaves was awarded as a mark of distinction and, in particular, to victors at the Pythian Games held at Delphi.

lavender

lay something up in lavender preserve something carefully for future use.

The flowers and stalks of lavender were traditionally used as a preservative for stored clothes.

law

be a law unto yourself behave in a manner that is not conventional or predictable.

the law of diminishing returns: *see* DIMINISHING.

the law of the jungle: *see* JUNGLE.

the law of the Medes and Persians: *see* MEDES.

lay down the law issue instructions to other people in an authoritative or dogmatic way.

the letter of the law: *see* LETTER.

take the law into your own hands punish someone for an offence according to your own ideas of justice, especially in an illegal or violent way.

take someone to law initiate legal proceedings against someone.

there's no law against it used in spoken English to assert that you are doing nothing wrong, especially in response to an actual or implied criticism. informal

someone's word is law: *see* WORD.

lay

ℹ For idioms containing *lay*, see the entry for the main word in the idiom (for example, **lay a finger on** at FINGER).

lead

the blind leading the blind: *see* BLIND.

get the lead out move or work more quickly; hurry up. North American informal

ℹ This expression originated as mid-20th-century jazz slang, meaning 'play at a brisk speed'. A fuller version is *get the lead out of your pants*. Renowned for its weight, the metal *lead* appears in a number of expressions as a metaphor for inertness or heaviness (see, for example, **go down like a lead balloon** below and **swing the lead** *at* SWING).

go down (*or* over) like a lead balloon (especially of a speech, proposal, or joke) fail; be a flop. informal

1996 *Prospect* Simon Jenkins's book, *Accountable to None*, has gone down like a lead balloon with most Conservative reviewers.

lead someone a dance: *see* DANCE.

lead someone by the nose control someone totally, especially by deceiving them. informal

ℹ The image here is of an animal being controlled by a restraint round or in the nose. Shakespeare used this expression in *Othello* (1604): 'The Moor . . . will as tenderly be led by th'nose As asses are'.

lead from the front take an active role in what you are urging and directing others to do.

lead in your pencil vigour or energy, especially sexual energy in a man. informal

1972 Dan Lees *Zodiac* The couscous is supposed to put lead in your pencil but with Daria I needed neither a talking point nor an aphrodisiac.

lead someone up the aisle: *see* AISLE.

lead someone up the garden path: *see* GARDEN.

lead with your chin behave or speak incautiously. informal

ℹ This expression originated as mid-20th-century boxing slang, referring to a boxer's stance that leaves his chin unprotected.

swing the lead: *see* SWING.

leaf

shake (*or* tremble) like a leaf tremble greatly, especially from fear.

take a leaf out of someone's book closely imitate or emulate someone in a particular way.

2007 *Daily Telegraph* Parents thought British hotels should take a leaf out of the American book and allow up to five in a family room.

turn over a new leaf improve your conduct or performance.

ℹ The *leaf* referred to here is a page of a book. The phrase has been used in this metaphorical sense since the 16th century, and while it now always means 'change for the better', it could previously also mean just 'change' or even 'change for the worse'.

leak

have (*or* take) a leak urinate. informal

spring a leak (of a boat or container) develop a leak.

ℹ The expression was originally a nautical one, referring to the timbers of a wooden ship springing out of position and so letting in water.

lean

lean over backwards: *see* **bend over backwards** *at* BACKWARDS.

leap

a leap in the dark a daring step or enterprise whose consequences are unpredictable.

by leaps and bounds with startlingly rapid progress.

leap to the eye be immediately apparent.

look before you leap: *see* LOOK.

learn

live and learn: *see* LIVE.

lease

a new lease of (*or* on) life a substantially improved prospect of life or use after rejuvenation or repair.

2013 *Guardian* Alex Wares explains how the clever use of online channels and platforms is granting a new lease of life for TV sports online.

leash

strain at the leash: *see* STRAIN.

least

last but not least: *see* LAST.

least said, soonest mended a difficult situation will be resolved more quickly if there is no more discussion of it.

the line of least resistance: *see* RESISTANCE.

not least notably; in particular.

to say the least (*or* **the least of it**) used as an understatement or euphemism to imply that the reality is more extreme, usually worse.

2014 *Real Clear Markets* The tax bill and Obamacare double-play, coming with a midterm election fast approaching and the economy continuing to limp along ... are ill-timed to say the least.

l

leather

hell for leather: *see* HELL.

shoe leather: *see* SHOE.

leave

leave it out stop it. British informal

ℹ For other idioms containing *leave*, see the entry for the main word in the idiom (for example, **leave someone in the lurch** at LURCH).

leech

like a leech persistently or clingingly present.

ℹ This idiom refers to the way in which a leech attaches itself by suction to the person or animal from which it is drawing blood: the parasites are very difficult to remove once they are attached to the skin and feeding.

leeway

make up (the) leeway struggle out of a bad position, especially by recovering lost time. British

ℹ *Leeway*, which dates from the mid 17th century, was the nautical term for the drift of a ship towards the side downwind of its course. The figurative use of this phrase dates from the early 19th century.

left

be left at the post fail to compete. informal

ℹ The image here is of a racehorse that fails to leave the starting post along with its rivals.

be left holding the baby: *see* HOLDING.

from (*or* **out of**) **left field** from a position or direction that is unexpected or unconventional. informal, chiefly North American

ℹ The expression originated in the language of baseball: left field is the part of the outfield to the left of a right-handed batter as he faces the pitcher, which does not often come into play.

2013 *Sculpture Magazine* I am the only one who is an artist in the traditional sense. Sometimes my comments come out of left field. They're quirky and not just about technical or architectural issues.

hang a left: *see* HANG.

have two left feet be clumsy or awkward, especially as a dancer.

left out in the cold: *see* COLD.

left, right, and centre (*also* **left and right** *or* **right and left**) on all sides.

2008 Julie Burchill & **Chas Newkey-Burden** *Not in my Name* I just wish they'd stop finger-wagging at others in public while shagging left, right and centre in private!

left-handed

left-handed compliment a remark that is superficially complimentary but contains a strong element of adverse criticism.

leg

get your leg over (of a man) have sexual intercourse. vulgar slang

have the legs of be able to go faster or further than a rival. British

not have a leg to stand on have no facts or sound reasons to support your argument or justify your actions.

ℹ For other idioms containing *leg*, see the entry for the main word in the idiom (for example, **show a leg** at SHOW).

legend

a legend in their own lifetime a very famous or notorious person.

ℹ The expression originated with the biographer Lytton Strachey, who in his *Eminent Victorians* (1918) applied it to Florence Nightingale.

legit

go legit begin to behave honestly after a period of illegal activity. informal

ⓘ *Legit* was originally a late 19th-century theatrical abbreviation meaning 'a legitimate actor', that is, one who acts in 'legitimate theatre' (conventional or serious drama).

leisure

lady (*or* man *or* gentleman) of leisure a person who does not need to earn a living or whose time is free from obligations to others.

lemon

the answer's a lemon the response or outcome is unsatisfactory. informal

ⓘ A *lemon* here is used to represent a bad, unsatisfactory, or disappointing thing, possibly because the lemon is the least valuable symbol that can be achieved by playing a fruit machine.

hand someone a lemon pass off a substandard article as good; swindle someone.

lend

lend an ear (*or* your ears) listen to someone sympathetically or attentively.

lend colour to: *see* COLOUR.

lend your name to something allow yourself to be publicly associated with something.

length

the length and breadth of throughout the whole of (a place).

measure your length: *see* MEASURE.

Lenten

Lenten fare meagre rations that do not include meat.

ⓘ Lenten fare is literally food appropriate to *Lent*, the Christian season of fasting between Ash Wednesday and Easter Saturday in commemoration of Jesus's forty days of fasting in the wilderness.

leopard

a leopard can't change its spots people can't change their basic nature. proverb

less

in less than no time very quickly or soon. informal

less is more used to express the view that a minimalist approach to artistic or aesthetic matters is more effective.

no less used to suggest, often ironically, that something is surprising or impressive.

2014 Eric S. Raymond *Armed and Dangerous* I looked up his bio. Yeah, he's an idiot. Paid to teach philosophy, no less. I could do a better job.

lesser

the lesser evil (*or* the lesser of two evils) the less harmful or unpleasant of two bad choices or possibilities.

lesson

teach someone a lesson punish or hurt someone as a deterrent or warning.

let

let someone down gently seek to give someone bad news in a way that avoids causing them too much distress or humiliation.

let it go (*or* pass) choose not to react to an action or remark.

let yourself go ❶ act in an unrestrained or uninhibited way. ❷ neglect yourself or your appearance; become careless or untidy in your habits.

let or hindrance obstruction or impediment. formal

ⓘ *Let* in its Middle English sense of 'something that impedes' is now archaic and rarely occurs outside this phrase, in which it duplicates the sense of *hindrance*. It is, however, used in sports such as badminton and tennis.

1999 Marion Shoard *A Right to Roam* Citizens can claim routes as new public paths on the grounds that they have been used without let or hindrance for at least twenty years.

let someone have it attack someone physically or verbally. informal

ⓘ The interpretation of this idiom was crucial to the outcome of one of the most notorious English murder trials of the 20th century. In late 1952, Derek Bentley and Christopher Craig attempted to rob a warehouse in Croydon. They were trapped on the roof by the police, and Craig pulled out a gun. The police called on him to surrender the weapon. Bentley, who had already been apprehended, shouted out

'Let him have it, Chris!' Did he mean, literally, 'Give the gun to the policeman', or did he mean 'Shoot'? The jury evidently opted for the latter explanation, for Bentley was found guilty of murder and hanged. Craig, who actually fired the shot, was underage and so was only imprisoned.

❶ For other idioms containing *let*, see the entry for the main word in the idiom (for example, **let the cat out of the bag** at CAT).

letter

a bread-and-butter letter: *see* BREAD-AND-BUTTER.

a dead letter: *see* DEAD.

the letter of the law the precise literal interpretation of a rule or instruction (as opposed to its broad intention).

a man (*or* woman) of letters a scholar or writer.

a red letter day: *see* RED.

to the letter with adherence to every detail.

❶ The French equivalent of this phrase is *au pied de la lettre*, which has been used in English since the late 18th century.

level

do your level best do your utmost; make all possible efforts.

be level pegging be equal in score or achievement during a contest. British

a level playing field a situation in which everyone has a fair and equal chance of succeeding.

2013 digby *Hullabaloo* It's how we fight for people who have been hit with one economic blow or another and are out there trying to compete in the job market and just want a level playing field.

on the level honest and truthful. informal

liberty

take liberties ❶ behave in an unduly familiar manner towards a person. ❷ treat something freely, without strict faithfulness to the facts or to an original.

take the liberty venture to do something without first asking permission.

licence

licence to print money a very lucrative commercial activity, typically one perceived as requiring little effort.

lick

at a lick at a fast pace. informal

a lick and a promise a hasty performance of a task, especially of cleaning something. informal

2009 *Guardian* This will be the real test of each MP's sincerity: will they clean up politics, or just brush the surface mud off the present system with a lick and a promise?

lick someone's arse = lick someone's boots. vulgar slang

lick someone's boots be excessively obsequious towards someone, especially to gain favour.

lick someone or something into shape: *see* SHAPE.

lick (*or* smack) your lips (*or* chops) look forward to something with eager anticipation.

2012 Tim Harford *Dear Economist* Presumably the likes of Google and Facebook are licking their lips as they contemplate their role in creating digital identities where your punctuality on eBay, efficiency on TaskRabbit and cleanliness as an Airbnb guest can be stitched together in a seamless tapestry of reputational capital.

lick your wounds retire to recover your strength or confidence after a defeat or humiliating experience.

not be able to do something a lick be totally incompetent at the specified activity. US informal

2013 *DVD Verdict* The more the documentary reveals, the more impressed we become with this piano virtuoso who could not read a lick of sheet music.

lid

blow the lid off remove means of restraint and allow something to get out of control. informal

2013 *DVD Verdict* Anyone looking for a documentary that blows the lid off the business of beauty isn't going to find it here.

flip your lid: *see* FLIP.

keep a (*or* the) lid on ❶ keep an emotion or process from going out of control. ❷ keep something secret. informal

put the (*or* a) lid on put a stop to. informal

2013 *Motley Fool* The firm has huge resources and the know-how to recover market share in the UK, and its withdrawal from the US should finally put a lid on its failure there and help it to concentrate its efforts back home.

put the (tin) lid on be the culmination of a series of acts or events that makes things unbearable. British informal

2005 *The Press* (York) The Lancashire visitors made it 2–2 with seconds remaining. That put the tin lid on a frustrating afternoon for a much-changed York side who raced into an early lead through Fozzie Foster.

take (*or* lift) the lid off (*or* lift the lid on) reveal unwelcome secrets about. informal

lie

the big lie: *see* BIG.

give the lie to something serve to show that something previously stated or believed to be the case is not true.

I tell a lie (*or* that's a lie) an expression used to immediately correct yourself when you realize that you have made an incorrect remark. informal

let sleeping dogs lie: *see* SLEEPING.

let something lie take no action regarding a controversial or problematic matter.

lie back and think of England (of a woman) submit stoically to uncongenial but unavoidable sexual intercourse, especially with a husband. British

lie doggo: *see* DOGGO.

lie in state (of the corpse of a person of national importance) be laid in a public place of honour before burial.

lie like a trooper tell lies constantly and flagrantly. Compare with **swear like a trooper** (*at* SWEAR).

lie through your teeth (*or* in your throat) tell an outright lie without remorse. informal

lie low: *see* LOW.

live a lie lead a life that conceals your true nature or circumstances.

nail a lie: *see* NAIL.

lies

as far as in me lies to the best of my power.

how the land lies: *see* LAND.

life

the breath of life: *see* BREATH.

the change of life: *see* CHANGE.

do anything for a quiet life make any concession to avoid being disturbed.

a dog's life: *see* DOG.

a fact of life: *see* FACT.

the facts of life: *see* FACT.

for dear (*or* your) life as if or in order to escape death.

2006 *Vanity Fair* Bush is a 'dry drunk'—someone who quit one day and is just holding on for dear life.

for the life of me however hard I try; even if my life depended on it. informal

2013 Kevin Barbieux *The Homeless Guy* What I found was so simple and convenient, I can't for the life of me understand why the city's trip planner website didn't know.

frighten the life out of terrify.

get a life start living a fuller or more interesting existence. informal

1997 *J-17* All anybody seems to be talking about today is school. These people need to get a life.

it's the story of my life: *see* STORY.

kiss of life: *see* KISS.

large as life (of a person) conspicuously present. informal

ⓘ This expression was originally used literally, with reference to the size of a statue or portrait relative to the original: in the mid 18th century Horace Walpole described a painting as being 'as large as the life'. The humorous mid-19th-century elaboration of the expression, *large as life and twice as natural*, used by Lewis Carroll and others, is still sometimes found; it is attributed to the Canadian humorist T. C. Haliburton (1796–1865).

larger than life ❶ (of a person) attracting attention because their appearance or behaviour is more flamboyant than that of ordinary people. ❷ (of a thing) seeming disproportionately important.

❶ **2008** *Daily Telegraph* The characters are larger than life yet credible.

life and limb life and all bodily faculties.

2008 *Evening Standard* Any sudden surge of people, either in panic away from danger, or when attracted towards some 'happening', is a potential threat to life and limb.

the life of Riley: *see* RILEY.

the life and soul of the party a person whose vivacity and sociability makes a party enjoyable.

the light of your life: *see* LIGHT.

a matter of life and death a matter of vital importance.

a new lease of life: *see* LEASE.

not on your life said to emphasize your refusal to comply with some request. informal

see life gain a wide experience of the world, especially its more pleasurable aspects.

a slice of life: *see* SLICE.

the staff of life: *see* STAFF.

take your life in your hands risk being killed.

that's life an expression of your acceptance of a situation, however difficult.

there's life in the old dog yet despite appearances to the contrary, an old person is still full of vigour, enthusiasm, etc.

this is the life an expression of contentment with your present circumstances.

> **2001 Louise Rennison** *Knocked out by my Nunga-Nungas* Forced to go and sit in the pub with the elderly loons (and James) to 'celebrate'. Yippeee! This is the life ... (not).

to the life exactly like the original.

to save your life: *see* SAVE.

the time of your life: *see* TIME.

the university of life: *see* UNIVERSITY.

walk of life: *see* WALK.

within an inch of your life: *see* INCH.

lifeline

throw a lifeline to (*or* **throw someone a lifeline**) provide someone with a means of escaping from a difficult situation.

lifetime

a legend in their own lifetime: *see* LEGEND.

of a lifetime (of a chance or experience) such as does not occur more than once in a person's life; exceptional.

lift

heavy lifting: *see* HEAVY.

lift your elbow: *see* ELBOW.

lift (*or* **stir**) **a finger** (*or* **hand**) make the slightest effort to do something, especially to help someone.

> **2013** *Bookslut* No one, especially not her husband, so much as lifts a finger to help her with her heavy bags despite the added burden of a nursing infant.

light

according to your lights in accordance with your own personal standards of morality or propriety.

the bright lights: *see* BRIGHT.

be light on be rather short of.

be light on your feet be quick or nimble.

go out like a light fall asleep or lose consciousness suddenly. informal

green light: *see* GREEN.

have your name in lights: *see* NAME.

hide your light under a bushel: *see* HIDE.

in (the) light of drawing knowledge or information from; with regard to.

> **2013** *The Age* (Melbourne) In the light of the story about a petition circulating I asked Mr Rudd's office if his position had changed in relation to his planned China trip.

light at the end of the tunnel a long-awaited indication that a period of hardship or adversity is nearing an end.

light a fire under someone: *see* FIRE.

light the (*or* **a**) **fuse** (*or* **touchpaper**) do something that creates a tense or exciting situation.

> ❶ The image here is of lighting a fuse attached to gunpowder, fireworks, etc. in order to cause an explosion. A *touchpaper*, which is used in the same way as a fuse, is a twist of paper impregnated with saltpetre to make it burn slowly.

> **2012** *Real Clear Markets* As long as this mentality remains in Europe, yesterday's protests won't be the only source of instability in Europe's financial future: the [European Central Bank] itself could light the fuse.

the light of your life a much-loved person.

the lights are on but no one is at home used to refer sardonically to someone of limited mental capacity.

make light (*or* **little**) **of** treat as unimportant.

> **2014** *Washington Post* Davidson was named as an unindicted co-conspirator by a federal grand jury, which alleged that six peace activists ... had plotted to kidnap Kissinger .... Kissinger made light of the supposed scheme, joking that 'sex-starved nuns' must be after him, then apologized for his poor taste.

make light work of accomplish a task quickly and easily.

punch someone's lights out beat someone up.

see the light ❶ understand or realize something after prolonged thought or doubt. ❷ undergo religious conversion.

see the light of day ❶ be born. ❷ come into existence; be made public, visible, or available.

> ❷ **2003** *Screen Online* He soon finds himself caught between the moguls of the textile industry and the trade unions, all equally determined that his invention never sees the light of day.

strike a light: *see* STRIKE.

sweetness and light: *see* SWEETNESS.

throw (*or* cast *or* shed) light on help to explain (something) by providing further information about it.

trip the light fantastic: *see* TRIP.

lightbulb

lightbulb moment a moment of inspiration.

> ⓘ The allusion is to the turning on of a lightbulb, which provides instant illumination.
>
> **2012** *The Register* We've been beavering away on the Rocketry Experimental High Altitude Barosimulator (REHAB) element of our Low Orbit Helium Assisted Navigator (LOHAN) mission, and last week enjoyed a lightbulb moment as to how to create a decent seal between the metal hypobaric chamber and the glass lid.

lightning

lightning never strikes twice the same calamity never occurs twice.

> ⓘ This expression refers to the popular belief that lightning never strikes the same spot twice.
>
> **1983 Penelope Lively** *Perfect Happiness* It's nasty, isn't it?... Having to go to the same airport. Though in a way you can't help thinking well lightning never strikes twice.

like lightning (*or* like greased lightning) very quickly.

ride the lightning: *see* RIDE.

like

I like that! used as an exclamation expressing affront.

like it or not used to indicate that someone has no choice in a matter. informal

> **2012** *Time Out New York* Like it or not, you can't escape the guitar

like —, like — as — is, so is —.

> ⓘ Two familiar sayings which appear in this form are *like father, like son*, recorded in this form from the early 17th century onwards, and *like mother, like daughter*.
>
> **1982 Anita Desai** *A Village by the Sea* Did he teach you to tell me that—that rogue, your father? Like father, like daughter. A family full of liars, no-goods.

the likes of a similar type of person or thing. informal

> **2002 John McGahern** *That They May Face the Rising Sun* The decenter you treat the likes of him the more they'll walk all over you.

make like pretend to be; imitate. North American informal

> **1939 John Steinbeck** *The Grapes of Wrath* This rich fella ... makes like he's poor.

what are you (*or* is he *or* she, etc.) like? used as an expression of light-hearted incredulity at behaviour regarded as foolish or eccentric. British informal

what's not to like? used as a rhetorical expression of approval or satisfaction. informal

> ⓘ The expression originated in American English as a translation from Yiddish.

likely

likely lad ❶ a boy or young man viewed as capable or potentially successful; a promising youth. ❷ a working-class young man; a young man with characteristics stereotypically associated with the working class. British

> ⓘ The latter usage has been influenced by the title of *The Likely Lads*, a BBC television sitcom about two working-class young men from Newcastle-upon-Tyne, first broadcast in 1964.
>
> ❷ **2007 Steven Dunne** *The Reaper* A likely lad at the front of the queue bawled out 'Encore!' to gales of laughter and derisive hoots.

a likely story used to express disbelief of an account or excuse.

not likely! certainly not; I refuse. informal

lily

gild the lily: *see* GILD.

limb

life and limb: *see* LIFE.

out on a limb ❶ isolated or stranded. ❷ without support.

ⓘ A *limb* here is the projecting branch of a tree. A related expression is *go out on a limb*, meaning 'take a risk' or 'act boldly and uncompromisingly'.

2013 *PC World* I'm going out on a limb here and guessing that you don't have a tape backup drive. You may not even have an optical drive.

tear someone limb from limb violently dismember someone.

limit

be the limit be intolerably troublesome or irritating. informal

line

all (the way) along (*or* down) the line at every point or stage.

the bottom line the final reality; the important conclusion.

ⓘ Literally, *the bottom line* is the final total in an account or balance sheet.

1991 *Sun* The bottom line is that we would rather have Venables and Sugar than Gazza, Maxwell and Scholar.

come down to the line (of a race) be closely fought right until the end.

come (*or* bring someone or something) into line conform (*or* cause someone or something to conform).

cut in line jump the queue. US

do a line with someone have a regular romantic or sexual relationship with someone. Irish & New Zealand informal

draw the (*or* a) line at set a limit of what you are willing to do or accept, beyond which you will not go.

2013 *Daily Telegraph* The school, which had a Muslim headmistress ... had gone to great pains to devise a sensibly modest option for Muslim girls, but drew the line at the jilbab.

drop someone a line: *see* DROP.

the end of the line: *see* **the end of the road** *at* END.

fall in (*or* into) line conform with others or with accepted behaviour.

ⓘ This phrase originally referred to soldiers arranging themselves into military formation.

in the firing line: *see* FIRING.

get a line on learn something about. informal

1939 Raymond Chandler *The Big Sleep* I was trying to get a line on you, sure.

hard lines: *see* HARD.

hold the line ❶ not yield to the pressure of a difficult situation. ❷ maintain a telephone connection during a break in the conversation. dated

ⓘ Sense 1 is a military metaphor, from the idea of a line of soldiers withstanding an attack without moving from their positions.

❶ **1980 Shirley Hazzard** *The Transit of Venus* But if we made one exception we would naturally be in no position to hold the line on similar cases.

hook, line, and sinker: *see* HOOK.

in line for likely to receive.

lay (*or* put) it on the line speak frankly.

(draw) a line in the sand (state that you have reached) a point beyond which you will not go.

line of country: *see* COUNTRY.

the line of least resistance: *see* RESISTANCE.

line your pocket (*or* pockets) make money, usually by dishonest means.

out of line behaving in a way that breaks the rules or is considered disreputable or inappropriate.

read between the lines: *see* READ.

shoot a line: *see* SHOOT.

toe the line: *see* TOE.

linen

wash your dirty linen in public: *see* WASH.

lining

a silver lining: *see* SILVER.

link

the weak link: *see* WEAK.

lion

beard the lion in his den: *see* BEARD.

the lion's den a demanding, intimidating, or unpleasant place or situation.

the lion's mouth a place of great peril.

the lion's share the largest part of something.

2010 *Guardian* It's widely reported that Hungary is getting the lion's share of EU grants in the region.

throw someone to the lions cause someone to be in an extremely dangerous or unpleasant situation.

ℹ In ancient Rome, Christians and other religious or political dissidents were thrown to the lions in the arena to be killed.

twist the lion's tail: *see* TWIST.

lip

bite your lip repress an emotion; stifle laughter or a retort.

button your lip: *see* BUTTON.

curl your lip raise a corner of your upper lip to show contempt; sneer.

hang on someone's lips listen attentively to someone.

lick (*or* smack) your lips: *see* LICK.

pass someone's lips be eaten, drunk, or spoken by someone.

pay lip service to something express approval of or support for something without taking any significant action.

2005 *New York Times* The truth is that for all the lip service paid to supporting the troops, out of sight is often out of mind.

read my lips: *see* READ.

someone's lips are sealed a person is obliged to keep a secret.

a stiff upper lip: *see* STIFF.

liquid

liquid lunch a drinking session at lunchtime taking the place of a meal. informal humorous

lists

enter the lists issue or accept a challenge.

ℹ In medieval times, the *lists* were the enclosed area in which knights fought each other in tournaments.

little

have more something in your little finger than someone else has in their whole body: *see* FINGER.

a little bird told me: *see* BIRD.

little grey cells: *see* GREY.

little stranger a newly born baby. informal

2002 *Psychology Today* For anyone in the brand new role of caring for a little stranger so totally dependent on their ministrations, the early days of motherhood challenge anyone's sense of competence.

make little of: *see* **make light of** *at* LIGHT.

quite the little — used when ironically or condescendingly recognizing that someone has a particular quality or accomplishment.

2012 *New Zealand Herald* Mrs Tyrrell describes Katie as 'quite the little adventurer' and is worried the horses in paddocks near Long Bay Primary School will be too tempting for her daughter to resist.

twist someone around your little finger: *see* FINGER.

live

he who lives by the sword dies by the sword: *see* SWORD.

live and breathe something be extremely interested in or enthusiastic about a particular subject or activity; spend a great deal of your time pursuing a particular interest.

live and learn used, especially in spoken English, to acknowledge that a fact is new to you.

2006 Toni Schlesinger *Five Flights Up* I spent all my money on this lizard. I think you live and learn.

live and let live you should tolerate the opinions and behaviour of others so that they will similarly tolerate your own.

ℹ On its first appearance in English in 1622, this was referred to as a Dutch proverb (*Leuen ende laeten leuen*).

live by your wits: *see* WIT.

live in the past ❶ have old-fashioned or outdated ideas and attitudes. ❷ dwell on or reminisce at length about past events.

live in someone's pocket: *see* POCKET.

live in sin: *see* SIN.

live it up spend your time in an extremely enjoyable or extravagant way. informal

live a lie: *see* LIE.

live off the fat of the land: *see* FAT.

live off the land: *see* LAND.

live on your hump: *see* HUMP.

live on your nerves: *see* NERVE.

live out of a suitcase live or stay somewhere on a temporary basis and with only a limited selection of your belongings, typically because your occupation requires a great deal of travelling.

live over the shop live on the premises where you work.

live your own life follow your own plans and principles; be independent of others.

live rough live and sleep outdoors as a consequence of having no proper home.

live to fight another day survive a certain experience or ordeal.

ⓘ This idea, found in the works of the Greek comic playwright Menander, is expressed in the English proverbial rhyme *He who fights and runs away Lives to fight another day*.

live to tell the tale survive a dangerous experience and be able to tell others about it.

live wire an energetic and unpredictable person. informal

live with yourself be able to retain your self-respect as a consequence of your actions.

2012 *New Zealand Herald* It's been torment and torture and horrible and I don't know how some of your people who have done these things can live with yourselves.

man cannot live by bread alone: *see* BREAD.

where you live at, to, or in the right, vital, or most vulnerable spot. North American

2002 *New York Times* The movies hit [teenagers] where they live—in their own state of desperation and doubt.

lively

look lively: *see* LOOK.

lively as a grig: *see* **merry as a grig** *at* GRIG.

living

be (the) living proof that (*or* of) show by your or something's existence and qualities that something is the case.

beat the living daylights out of: *see* DAYLIGHT.

frighten the living daylights out of: *see* DAYLIGHT.

in the land of the living: *see* LAND.

in (*or* within) living memory within or during a time that is remembered by people still alive.

living on borrowed time: *see* BORROWED.

someone or something owes you a living: *see* OWE.

the living image of an exact copy or likeness of.

lo

lo and behold used to present a new scene, situation, or turn of events, often with the suggestion that, though surprising, it could in fact have been predicted.

load

get a load of used to draw attention to someone or something. informal

1994 Quentin Tarantino *Pulp Fiction* It's legal to carry it, but that doesn't matter, cause—get a load of this, alright—if the cops stop you, it's illegal for them to search you.

get (*or* have) a load on become drunk. US informal

load the dice against (*or* in favour of) someone put someone at a disadvantage (*or* advantage).

2012 *Daily Telegraph* I am no believer in the unfettered market, which loads the dice in favour of the haves rather than the have-nots.

take a (*or* the) load off your feet sit or lie down.

take a load off someone's mind bring someone relief from anxiety.

loaded

loaded for bear: *see* BEAR.

loaf

half a loaf: *see* HALF.

use your loaf use your common sense. British informal

ⓘ This expression probably comes from *loaf of bread*, rhyming slang for 'head'.

loath

nothing loath: *see* NOTHING.

lock

have a lock on have an unbreakable hold or total control over. North American informal

ⓘ *Lock* is here used in the sense of a hold in wrestling that prevents an opponent from moving a limb.

1974 Paul Erdman *Silver Bears* He would sooner *see* the whole bank go down the drain . . . than get beaten by us. Unless we develop an even better lock on him—and that won't be easy.

lock horns engage in conflict.

ⓘ The image here is of two bulls fighting head-to-head with their horns. Both the literal and figurative senses of the phrase originated in the USA, in the mid 19th century.

lock, stock, and barrel including everything; completely.

ⓘ *Lock, stock, and barrel* refers literally to the complete mechanism of a firearm.

under lock and key securely locked up.

locker

go to Davy Jones's locker: *see* DAVY JONES'S LOCKER.

a shot in the locker: *see* SHOT.

log

easy as falling off a log: *see* EASY.

sleep like a log: *see* SLEEP.

loggerheads

at loggerheads in violent dispute or disagreement.

ⓘ This expression is possibly a use of *loggerhead* in the late 17th-century sense of 'a long-handled iron instrument for heating liquids and tar'; the tool was perhaps also used as a weapon.

logic

chop logic: *see* CHOP.

loins

gird your loins: *see* GIRD.

loiter

loiter with intent stand or wait around with the intention of committing an offence. British

ⓘ This is a legal phrase which derives from an 1891 Act of Parliament; it is also used figuratively and humorously of anyone who is waiting around for some unspecified purpose.

Lombard

all Lombard Street to a China orange great wealth against one ordinary object; virtual certainty. dated

ⓘ *Lombard Street* in London was originally occupied by bankers from Lombardy, and it still contains a number of London's principal banks. This idiom dates from the early 19th century, but the use of a *China orange* to mean 'a worthless thing' is recorded earlier.

London

a London particular a dense fog formerly affecting London. dated

ⓘ This expression is first recorded in Charles Dickens's *Bleak House* (1853).

lone

lone wolf a person who prefers to act alone.

lonely

plough a lonely furrow: *see* PLOUGH.

lonesome

by (*or* on) your lonesome all alone. informal

long

the long arm of coincidence: *see* ARM.

the long arm of the law: *see* ARM.

as long as your arm: *see* ARM.

by a long chalk: *see* CHALK.

by a long shot: *see* SHOT.

how long is a piece of string?: *see* STRING.

in the long run (*or* term) over a long period of time; eventually.

1997 *New Scientist* But as the economist Maynard Keynes pointed out, in the long run we are all dead.

it's as broad as it's long: *see* BROAD.

the long and (the) short of it all that can or need be said.

2002 Jerzy Pilch *His Current Woman* The long and the short of it will be that for weeks on end everybody will be offended with everybody else to the point that no one will be speaking to anyone.

long home death. euphemistic, dated

ⓘ The expression is based on the idea of the soul's destination after death.

long in the tooth rather old.

ⓘ This phrase was originally used of horses, referring to the way their gums recede with age.

long time no see it's a long time since we last met (used as a greeting). informal ℹ This idiom developed as a humorous imitation of broken English spoken by a Native American.

night of the long knives: *see* NIGHT.

not be long for this world have only a short time to live.

2000 Patrick McGrath *Martha Peake* As he turned toward the door I saw at once that he could not be long for this world, so frail did he appear.

not by a long shot: *see* SHOT.

over (*or* for) the long haul over (or for) an extended period of time. chiefly North American

put something on the long finger: *see* FINGER.

so long ❶ goodbye till we meet again. informal ❷ in the meanwhile. South African

ℹ In its second sense, the expression is a translation of Afrikaans *solank*.

to cut a long story short: *see* SHORT.

longbow

draw the longbow make exaggerated claims or statements. dated

ℹ The longbow was the national weapon of England from the 14th century until the introduction of firearms, and prowess in its use was highly prized. The phrase has been used in this metaphorical sense since the mid 17th century.

look

a cat may look at a king: *see* CAT.

here's looking at you! used to express friendly feelings towards your companions before drinking. informal

look before you leap you shouldn't act without first considering the possible consequences or dangers. proverb

look daggers: *see* DAGGER.

look down your nose at despise. informal

look a gift horse in the mouth: *see* GIFT.

look lively used to tell someone to be quick in doing something. informal

ℹ A variant of this phrase is *look alive*, but this is now rather dated.

look on the bright side: *see* BRIGHT.

look over your shoulder: *see* SHOULDER.

look the part have an appearance or style of dress appropriate to a particular role or situation (even if not being actually very well suited to it).

2005 *Scotland on Sunday* Sharapova meanwhile was having problems of her own. Dressed to kill in a gold trimmed dress with gold trimmed and spangly shoes, she looked the part even if her game did not let her act it.

look someone in the eye (*or* face) look directly at someone without showing embarrassment, fear, or shame.

look someone up and down scrutinize someone carefully.

look the other way deliberately ignore wrongdoing by others.

2008 *New York Review of Books* In the buildup to today's mortgage market mess, numerous potentially helpful government agencies … either dropped the ball or looked the other way

look sharp: *see* SHARP.

look slippy: *see* SLIPPY.

look to your laurels: *see* LAURELS.

look who's talking: *see* TALK.

lookout

be on the lookout ❶ keep searching for someone or something that is wanted. ❷ be alert to danger or trouble.

ℹ The word *lookout*, which originated in naval and military contexts, was first applied, in the late 17th century, to sentries or other people employed to keep watch. The sense of 'the action of keeping watch', as used in this expression, dates from the mid 18th century.

loop

in (*or* out of) the loop aware (*or* unaware) of information known to only a limited number of people. informal

2012 *New Zealand Herald* He was concerned his group wasn't being kept in the loop and it was 'only by luck' he found out about today's hearing.

throw (*or* knock) someone for a loop surprise or astonish someone; catch someone off guard. North American

loose

cut loose ❶ distance yourself from a person, group, or system by which you are unduly influenced or on which you are over-dependent. ❷ begin to act without restraint. informal

❶ **1993 Isidore Okpewho** *Tides* When the time comes that I feel my friends are not sufficiently behind me in what I'm trying to do, I'm going to cut loose from them.

hang (*or* stay) loose be relaxed; refrain from taking anything too seriously. informal

have a screw loose: *see* SCREW.

a loose cannon a unpredictable person or thing likely to cause unintentional damage.

ⓘ A *loose cannon* was originally a cannon that had broken loose from its fastening or mounting, an accident especially dangerous on wooden ships of war.

loose end

at a loose end having nothing to do; not knowing what to do.

ⓘ A North American variant of this expression is *at loose ends*.

loosen

loosen someone's tongue make someone talk freely.

lord

drunk as a lord: *see* DRUNK.

Lord of the Flies the Devil.

ⓘ This expression (which is a translation of Hebrew *ba'al zebūb*, the source of English *Beelzebub*) is often used with allusive reference to the title of the 1954 novel by William Golding (1911–93), in which a group of schoolboys marooned on an uninhabited tropical island revert to savagery and primitive ritualistic behaviour.

lorry

fall off (the back of) a lorry (of goods) be acquired in illegal or unspecified circumstances.

ⓘ The traditional bogus excuse given to the police by someone caught in possession of stolen goods was that the items in question had 'fallen off the back of a lorry'.

1991 *Time Out* People buy so much stolen stuff that ... you can ... buy a video in Dixons and take it round the corner to a pub, say it fell off the back of a lorry and get 50 quid more than it cost you.

lose

lose it lose control of your temper or emotions. informal

2004 *Independent* I talk calmly, and then I lose it and start ranting angrily.

ⓘ For other idioms containing *lose*, see the entry for the main word in the idiom (for example, **lose the plot** at PLOT).

loser

be on (*or* on to) a loser be involved in a course of action that is bound to fail.

losing

a losing battle a struggle that is bound to end in failure.

losses

cut your losses abandon an enterprise or course of action that is clearly going to be unprofitable or unsuccessful before you suffer too much loss or harm.

ⓘ The sense of *cut* here is probably 'sever yourself from' rather than 'reduce in size'.

2012 *New York Times* Private, for-profit medicine has failed. When will we cut our losses and admit that the socialized or nationalized delivery systems that the rest of the modern world uses work far better by just about any measure?

lost

all is not lost used to suggest that there is still some chance of success or recovery.

be lost (*or* at a loss) for words be so surprised, confused, or upset that you cannot think what to say.

be lost in the shuffle: *see* SHUFFLE.

be lost on someone fail to influence or be noticed or appreciated by someone.

1990 Katherine Frank *Emily Brontë* Charlotte's lovely surroundings and the steady unfurling of one glorious summer day after the next were lost on her.

get lost go away (used, often in the imperative, as an expression of anger or impatience). informal

give someone up for lost stop expecting that a missing person will be found alive.

a lost soul ❶ a soul that is damned. ❷ a person who seems unable to cope with everyday life.

make up for lost time do something faster or more often in order to compensate for not having done it quickly or often enough before.

lot

all over the lot in a state of confusion or disorganization. US informal

a bad lot a dishonest person. British informal

fall to someone's lot become someone's task or responsibility.

have a lot on the ball: *see* BALL.

throw in your lot with decide to ally yourself closely with and share the fate of a person or group.

> ❶ Both this and the previous idiom come from the process of deciding something by drawing or casting lots.
>
> **2013** *Daily Telegraph* Theresa May lost for a second time today after failing to deport an Ethiopian who had 'thrown in his lot' with Islamist extremists 'committed to terrorism'.

loud

for crying out loud: *see* CRYING.

love

for the love of Mike used to accompany an exasperated request or to express dismay. British informal

> ❶ *Mike* is perhaps used here as a generic name for an Irishman; compare with *mickey* in **take the mickey out of** (*at* MICKEY).

a labour of love: *see* LABOUR.

love me, love my dog if you love someone, you must accept everything about them, even their faults. proverb

love rat a man who is sexually unfaithful or promiscuous. slang, chiefly British

> **2003 Cathy Hopkins** *Starstruck* 'Love rat.' 'That's a joke,' I said. 'I've only ever snogged three girls.'

love's young dream ❶ the relationship of young lovers. ❷ the object of someone's love. ❸ a man regarded as a perfect lover.

not for love or money not in any circumstances. informal

> **2007** *Salmagundi* Since the Christmas long weekend had just begun, there wasn't a dentist to be had for love or money, and Auntie Janet was forced to spend the next four days wearing a yashmak.

there's no (*or* little *or* not much) love lost between there is mutual dislike between two or more people mentioned.

tug of love: *see* TUG.

lovely

everything in the garden is lovely: *see* GARDEN.

lovely jubbly used to express delight or approbation; excellent. British informal

> ❶ The expression comes from *lovely Jubbly*, a 1950s advertising slogan for *Jubbly*, an orange-flavoured soft drink. It was adopted by comedy writer John Sullivan in his BBC television sitcom *Only Fools and Horses* (1981–93).

low

at a low ebb: *see* EBB.

high and low: *see* HIGH.

keep a low profile: *see* PROFILE.

lay someone low ❶ (of an illness) reduce someone to inactivity. ❷ bring to an end the high position or good fortune formerly enjoyed by someone.

lie low (especially of a criminal) keep out of sight; avoid detection or attention.

low-hanging fruit something that can be dealt with or acquired with comparatively little effort.

> **2012** *Independent* Foreign expats have always been a high-yielding target for HMRC, and with the organisation trying to boost its revenue, it's not surprising that they're targeting low-hanging fruit.

lower

lower the boom on ❶ treat someone severely. ❷ put a stop to an activity. informal

> ❶ It has been suggested that this phrase originally meant 'knocking out an adversary with one punch' in a fight.

lower the tone diminish the spirit or moral character of a conversation, place, etc.

> ❶ *Tone* here is used to mean the general character or attitude of a conversation, place, piece of writing, etc.

lower your guard: *see* GUARD.

lower your sights: *see* **raise your sights** *at* SIGHT.

lowest

the lowest of the low those regarded as the most immoral or socially inferior of all.

> **1995 Nicholas Whittaker** *Platform Souls* And fare dodgers, well, they're the lowest of the low, and should be strung up.

luck

as luck would have it used to indicate the fortuitousness of a situation.

1994 Beryl Gilroy *Sunlight on Sweet Water* As luck would have it, one day they met in the door of the rum shop.

beginner's luck: *see* BEGINNER.

down on your luck: *see* DOWN.

Lady Luck: *see* LADY.

the luck of the devil (*or* the devil's own luck) (undeserved) good luck.

2004 *Electric Newspaper* (Singapore) They [Manchester United] take on Fulham who ... have been having the 'luck of the devil'. But while they have looked fluent at times, their good fortune should run out at Old Trafford tonight.

the luck of the draw the outcome of chance rather than something you can control.

the luck of the Irish very good luck.

make your own luck be successful through your own efforts and opportunism.

push your luck: *see* PUSH.

ride your luck let favourable events take their course without taking undue risks.

take pot luck: *see* POT.

try your luck (at something) do something that involves risk or luck, hoping to succeed.

1964 Mary Stewart *This Rough Magic* I finally decided, after three years of juvenile leads in provincial rep that it was time to try my luck in London.

your luck is in (*or* out) you are fortunate (*or* unfortunate) on a particular occasion.

lucky

thank your lucky stars: *see* THANK.

third time lucky: *see* THIRD.

you, he, etc. will be lucky (*or* should be so lucky) used to say that someone's wishes or expectations are unlikely to be fulfilled.

lull

the lull before the storm: *see* STORM.

lump

a lump in the throat a feeling of tightness or dryness in the throat caused by strong emotion, especially grief.

take (*or* get) your lumps suffer punishment; be attacked or defeated. informal, chiefly North American

1971 Bernard Malamud *The Tenants* Now I take my lumps, he thought. Maybe for not satisfying Mary.

lunch

do lunch meet for lunch. informal, chiefly North American

ladies who lunch: *see* LADY.

liquid lunch: *see* LIQUID.

lose your lunch vomit. informal, euphemistic

2005 *Sunday Times* In March, Insanity—the Ride opened at the Stratosphere Hotel, offering a memorable way to lose your lunch. At a height of 906 ft, the ride uses centrifugal force to fling passengers 64 ft out over Sin City.

out to lunch: *see* OUT.

there's no such thing as a free lunch you never get something for nothing; any benefit received has eventually to be paid for.

2013 digby *Hullabaloo* But think what we would gain as a society in ... getting the myth out of their head that there is such a thing as a free lunch.

lurch

leave someone in the lurch leave an associate or friend abruptly and without assistance or support when they are in a difficult situation.

ⓘ *Lurch* as a noun meaning 'a state of discomfiture' dates from the mid 16th century but it is now used only in this idiom.

1987 Eileen Dunlop *The House on the Hill* What have Gilmores ever done but leave her in the lurch? Poor Jane, she just can't run the risk of being hurt again.

luxury

in the lap of luxury: *see* LAP.

lying

take something lying down accept an insult or injury without attempting retaliation.

2014 *Daily Telegraph* The second caller, also a woman, asked Mr Clegg whether he thought women should learn to stand up for themselves. After all, she said, his wife Miriam would surely never have taken the behaviour of Lord Rennard lying down.

lyrical

wax lyrical about (*or* **over**) talk in an effusive or enthusiastic way about something.

🛈 *Wax* (from Old English *weaxan*) was used to mean 'increase in size' right through until early modern English, but since then it has been superseded in all general contexts by *grow*. It now survives only in certain expressions, especially with reference to the moon's monthly increase and decrease (*waxing and waning*).

2013 *The Register* Brian waxes lyrical about Amazon, prompting Greg to ask: why are CIOs everywhere falling in love with private clouds?

machine

a cog in the machine: *see* COG.

the ghost in the machine: *see* GHOST.

mackerel

a sprat to catch a mackerel: *see* SPRAT.

mad

don't get mad, get even used to advise in favour of revenge rather than fruitless rage. informal

ⓘ This expression was a saying popularized by the US president John F. Kennedy, who called it 'that wonderful law of the Boston Irish political jungle'.

1998 *New Scientist* The Wellcome Trust doesn't get mad, it gets even.

like mad with great intensity, energy, or enthusiasm. informal

2013 *Mac Observer* The bloggers at CNET were freaking out . . . , the audience was cheering like mad, and a Rush fan site has already picked up on it.

mad as a box of frogs wildly eccentric or crazy. informal

2018 Sarah Langford *In Your Defence* Look, you'll see in evidence, but my client is as mad as a box of frogs, and somehow he's slipped it past both doctors.

mad as a hatter (*or* a March hare) completely crazy. informal

ⓘ In this expression, a *hatter* refers to Lewis Carroll's character, the Mad Hatter, in *Alice's Adventures in Wonderland* (1865). It is thought that hatters suffered from the effects of mercury poisoning because of the fumes arising from the use of mercurous nitrate in the manufacture of felt hats. The *March hare* version refers to the way hares leap about during the breeding season.

mad as a (cut) snake crazy or eccentric. Australian informal

madding

far from the madding crowd secluded or removed from public notice.

ⓘ The phrase was originally used in Thomas Gray's 'Elegy Written in a Country Churchyard' (1751). It is now better known as the title of one of Thomas Hardy's novels.

made

be made of money: *see* MONEY.

be made up ❶ be delighted. Northern English & Irish informal ❷ be assured of success; be lucky. Irish

have (got) it made be in a position where success or prosperity is certain. informal

2003 Clint McInnes *Gone Wylde: A Journey of Discovery* The secret to success in life is honesty and fair dealing. If you can fake that, you've got it made.

what you are made of your true abilities or qualities.

madness

that way madness lies it is ill-advised to pursue a particular course of action as it will cause distress or anxiety.

ⓘ This phrase is a quotation from *King Lear*, taken from the speech in which Lear shies away from contemplating the ingratitude of his daughters Regan and Goneril.

there is method in someone's madness: *see* METHOD.

maggot

act the maggot behave in a foolishly playful way. Irish informal

magic

a magic carpet: *see* CARPET.

wave a (*or* your) magic wand exercise an arbitrary (quasi-supernatural) power in order to make something happen.

2004 *Trinidad Guardian* It is not realistic to believe or to say that a UNC government would wave a magic wand and crime would dissipate.

magnitude

of the first magnitude: *see* **of the first order** *at* FIRST.

mailed

the mailed fist the use of physical force to maintain control.

ℹ *Mailed* in this context means 'wearing a glove of chain mail or plate armour'.

main

by main force through sheer strength.

ℹ *Main* derives from the Old English word *mægen* meaning 'physical force'. As an adjective meaning '(of strength or force) exerted to the full', it is a very ancient usage: *mægenstrengo* occurs in the Anglo-Saxon epic *Beowulf*.

with might and main: *see* MIGHT.

main brace

splice the main brace: *see* SPLICE.

majority

join the great majority: *see* JOIN.

the silent majority: *see* SILENT.

make

make do manage with the limited or inadequate means available.

ℹ This phrase can be used alone or in *make do and mend*, a UK slogan from the 1940s encouraging people to be frugal in wartime by mending and reusing worn-out clothes, sheets, etc. rather than throwing them away.

make or break be the factor which decides whether something will succeed or fail.

ℹ A variant of this phrase, found chiefly in British English, is *make or mar*. The use of *make* together with *mar* is recorded from the early 15th century, but since the mid 19th century *break* has become more common.

2014 *CNN transcripts* You know, big storms can test mayors, can make or break them. Imagine having to deal with it on your third day.

on the make ❶ intent on gain, typically in a rather unscrupulous way. ❷ looking for a sexual partner. informal

put the make on make sexual advances to. North American informal

1993 Anne River Siddons *Hill Towns* Put the make on you, did she, Joe? I should have warned you. Past a certain blood alcohol level Yolie gets snuggly.

ℹ For other idioms containing *make*, see the entry for the main word in the idiom (for example, **make hay** at HAY).

maker

meet your maker die. humorous or euphemistic

ℹ This expression alludes to the Christian belief that, after death, the soul goes to be judged by God, its creator.

making

be the making of someone ensure someone's success or favourable development.

malice

malice aforethought the intention to kill or harm which is held to distinguish unlawful killing from murder.

man

as — as the next man as — as the average person.

2011 *DVD Verdict* I appreciate a good dollop of gore as much as the next man (as long as he likes gore by the barrel full [sic]).

be your own man (*or* woman): *see* OWN.

every man for himself: *see* EVERY.

every man has his price: *see* PRICE.

man about town a fashionable male socialite.

man and boy throughout life from youth.

ℹ The Scottish poet William Dunbar used the phrase *baith man and lad* in the early 16th century, but the modern usage follows Shakespeare's *Hamlet*: 'I have been sexton here, man and boy, thirty years'.

man cannot live by bread alone: *see* BREAD.

a man for all seasons a man who is ready to cope with any contingency and whose behaviour is always appropriate to every occasion.

ℹ Robert Whittington applied this description to the English statesman and scholar Sir Thomas More (1478–1535), and it was used by Robert Bolt as the title of his 1960 play about More.

the man in black: *see* BLACK.

the man in the moon ❶ the imagined likeness of a face seen on the surface of a full moon. ❷ used, especially in comparisons, to refer to someone regarded as out of touch with real life.

❷ **1991** *Sight & Sound* You thought... you could mention even the most famous classic films as reference points in script meetings and not be looked at like the man in the moon.

the man in (*or* on) the street an ordinary person, usually with regard to their opinions, or as distinct from an expert.

ⓘ A specifically British variation of this expression is **the man on the Clapham omnibus** (*see* below).

man mountain a very large man; a giant.

ⓘ The expression was originally used as a name for Gulliver by the Lilliputians in Jonathan Swift's *Gulliver's Travels* (1726).

man of action: *see* ACTION.

man of the cloth a clergyman.

ⓘ Jonathan Swift used *cloth* as an informal term for the clerical profession in the early 18th century, but it was earlier applied to several other occupations for which distinctive clothing was worn, e.g. the legal or military professions.

man of God ❶ a clergyman. ❷ a holy man or saint.

a man of letters: *see* LETTER.

man of the moment a man of importance at a particular time.

man of straw (*or* straw man) ❶ a person compared to an effigy stuffed with straw; a sham. ❷ a sham argument set up to be defeated, usually as a means of avoiding having to tackle an opponent's real arguments.

❷ **2013 Bryan Caplan, Arnold Kling & David Henderson** *Library of Economics & Liberty* It sets up as a straw man a perfect, frictionless market and then concludes that because in reality there are no such things, the case for free markets is thereby undermined.

a man of the world: *see* WORLD.

the man on the Clapham omnibus the average man, especially with regard to his opinions. British

ⓘ This expression is attributed to the English judge Lord Bowen (1835–94), who used it as a metaphor for any ordinary reasonable person—such as a juror is expected to be. Clapham is a district in south London.

man's best friend an affectionate or humorous way of referring to a dog.

a man's man a man whose personality is such that he is more popular and at ease with other men than with women.

ⓘ This expression was apparently first used in George Du Maurier's story *The Martian* (1897), where the *man's man* is defined as 'a good comrade par excellence, a frolicsome chum, a rollicking boon-companion, a jolly pal'. A *man's woman*, which dates from the early 20th century, is a woman who is more at ease with men than with other women.

1991 *Men's Health* Masculinity used to be simple to define. If you had hair on your chest and a deep voice, and belonged to a club that excluded women, you were masculine, or, as was the phrase of the time, 'a man's man'.

man the barricades: *see* BARRICADE.

man to man in a direct and frank way between two men; openly and honestly.

the Man Upstairs God. informal humorous

men in black: *see* BLACK.

men in (grey) suits powerful men within an organization who exercise their influence or authority anonymously.

men in white coats psychiatrists or psychiatric workers (used to imply that someone is mad or mentally unbalanced). humorous

2009 *The Book Show* (ABC Radio) Most British prime ministers go mad at the end ... After year nine you can see the moonbeams start dancing around their heads and the men in white coats have to come and drag them out of 10 Downing St.

see a man about a dog: *see* DOG.

separate (*or* sort out) the men from the boys show or prove which people in a group are truly competent, brave, or mature.

1968 *House & Garden* The Dry Martini ... is a drink that will quickly separate the men from the boys and the girls from their principles.

to a man without exception.

twelve good men and true: *see* TWELVE.

yesterday's man: *see* YESTERDAY.

you are (*or* he is) the man used as a commendation of someone's sterling qualities. US slang

2010 *SeoBook* Can I just say, you are the man! You are 100% correct in your standpoint of both SEO outing practices, and also in your view of the media as a whole.

manger

dog in the manger: *see* DOG.

mangle

put someone through the mangle: *see* **put someone through the wringer** *at* WRINGER.

manner

bedside manner: *see* BEDSIDE.

in a manner of speaking in some sense; so to speak.

ⓘ *Manner of speaking* is recorded from the mid 16th century; compare with French *façon de parler*, which has been in use in English since the early 19th century.

to the manner born naturally at ease in a specified way of life, job, or situation.

ⓘ This comes from Shakespeare's *Hamlet*: 'though I am native here And to the manner born'. Punning on this expression, *to the manor born* is used to refer to someone who has aristocratic origins.

manse

son (*or* daughter) of the manse the child of a minister of religion, especially a Presbyterian.

ⓘ *Manse* is a Scottish English term for the house of a Presbyterian minister.

manure

rocking-horse manure: *see* ROCKING HORSE.

m

many

be too (*or* one too) many for outwit or baffle.

have one too many become slightly drunk.

many happy returns: *see* RETURN.

many's the — used to indicate that something happens often.

2000 *Taxi News* Many's the happy hour I've spent listening to cabbies thrash that one out.

there's many a slip ('twixt cup and lip): *see* SLIP.

map

all over the map *see* **all over the place** *at* ALL.

off the map (of a place) very distant or remote. Compare with **off the beaten track** (*at* BEATEN).

put something on the map make something prominent or important.

wipe something off the map obliterate something totally.

marble

lose your marbles go insane; become irrational or senile. informal

ⓘ *Marbles* as a term for 'a person's mental faculties' probably originated as early 20th-century American slang. The underlying reference is apparently to the children's game played with multicoloured glass balls.

2009 *Guardian* The uninhibited heroine loses her marbles and ends up doing herself unspeakable harm before being put out of her misery by her sensitive writer boyfriend.

marble orchard a cemetery. informal humorous

pick up your marbles and go home withdraw petulantly from an activity after having suffered a setback. informal, chiefly US

ⓘ The image here is of a child who refuses sulkily to continue playing the game of marbles.

March

mad as a March hare: *see* **mad as a hatter** *at* MAD.

march

an army marches on its stomach: *see* STOMACH.

march to (the beat of) a different tune (*or* drum *or* drummer) consciously adopt a different approach or attitude to the majority of people; be unconventional. informal

ⓘ The version with *drummer* comes ultimately from Henry David Thoreau's *Walden* (1854): 'If a man does not keep pace with his companions, perhaps it is because he hears a different drummer'.

2008 Uroskin *Put em all on an island* 'Islands are places apart, islanders are people apart,' he says. 'They march to the beat of very different drums.'

marching orders a dismissal or sending off.

ⓘ In military terminology, *marching orders* are literally instructions from a superior officer for troops to depart. The North American version of the idiom is *marching papers*.

steal a march on: *see* STEAL.

mare

a mare's nest a wonderful discovery which proves or will prove to be illusory.

ⓘ A *mare's nest* is here being used to symbolize something that does not exist, as horses do not make nests. The phrase is first recorded in the late 16th century, as is the variant *a horse's nest*, although the latter is now no longer in use.

marines

tell that to the marines (*or* the horse marines) a scornful expression of incredulity.

> ❶ This saying may have originated in a remark made by Charles II, recommending that unlikely tales should be referred to sailors who, from their knowledge of distant places, might be the people best qualified to judge their truthfulness. *Horse marines*, dating from the early 19th century, were an imaginary cavalry corps, soldiers mounted on horseback on board ship being a humorous image of ineptitude or of people out of their natural element. In 1823 Byron noted that *That will do for the marines, but the sailors won't believe it* was an 'old saying', and the following year Walter Scott used *Tell that to the marines—the sailors won't believe it!* in his novel *Redgauntlet*.
>
> **2003 Peter Lovesey** *House Sitter* So the official line was that the murders of Emma Tysoe and Axel Summers were unrelated. Tell that to the marines, he thought.

mark

be quick (*or* slow) off the mark be fast (*or* slow) in responding to a situation or understanding something.

> ❶ The *mark* here is the line or marker from which a competitor starts a race, as is also the case in **get off the mark** and **on your marks**.

a black mark: *see* BLACK.

full marks used to indicate that you think someone is worthy of much praise.

get off the mark get started.

hit the mark be successful in an attempt or accurate in a guess.

> ❶ The *mark* referred to here is a target in shooting.

leave (*or* make) its (*or* your *or* a) mark have a lasting or significant effect.

make your mark become famous and successful.

mark someone's card give someone information. informal

> ❶ This idiom, which dates from the mid 20th century, derives from the world of horse racing. The *card* is a *race card*, the list of runners at a race meeting, so to *mark someone's card* is to give them tips for possible winners.

the mark of Cain the stigma of a murderer; a sign of infamy.

> ❶ According to the book of Genesis, God placed a mark on Cain after the murder of his brother Abel, originally as a sign that he should not be killed or harmed; this was later taken to identify him as a murderer (Genesis 4:15).

mark time ❶ (of troops) march on the spot without moving forward. ❷ pass your time in routine activities until a more interesting opportunity presents itself.

near (*or* close to) the mark almost correct or accurate.

> ❶ The *mark* in this and the two following idioms is a target or goal.

off (*or* wide of) the mark ❶ a long way away from an intended target. ❷ incorrect or inaccurate.

on the mark correct or accurate.

on your marks used to instruct competitors in a race to prepare themselves in the correct starting position.

overshoot the mark: *see* OVERSHOOT.

up to the mark ❶ of the required standard. ❷ (of a person) as healthy or cheerful as usual.

market

be in the market for wish to buy.

a drug on the market: *see* DRUG.

play the market speculate in stocks.

marriage

marriage of convenience a marriage concluded to achieve a practical purpose.

> ❶ This expression was used by Joseph Addison in the early 18th century, translating the French *mariage de convenance*, which has itself been current in English since the mid 19th century.
>
> **1949 George Bernard Shaw** *Buoyant Billions* The proportion of happy love marriages to happy marriages of convenience has never been counted.

marrow

to the marrow to your innermost being.

> ❶ *Marrow* is the soft, fatty substance found in the cavities of bones.
>
> **2012** *Daily Telegraph* People may think of you as an outsider ('Phil the Greek', born in Corfu), but your mother, Princess Alice, was born in Windsor Castle, the daughter of Princess Victoria, one of Queen Victoria's favourite granddaughters.... You are royal to the marrow—related to kings, queens, emperors, kaisers, tsars.

marry

marry money marry a rich person. informal

m

mast

nail your colours to the mast: *see* COLOUR.

mat

go to the mat vigorously engage in an argument or dispute, typically on behalf of a particular person or cause.

ℹ The *mat* referred to is the thick mat in a gym on which wrestling is practised.

1924 P. G. Wodehouse *Leave it to Psmith* I... heard... you and Aunt Constance going to the mat about poor old Phyllis.

on the mat being reprimanded by someone in authority. informal

ℹ This idiom is a military reference: the orderly room mat was where a soldier accused of some misdemeanour would stand before the commanding officer.

match

game, set, and match: *see* GAME.

meet your match encounter your equal in strength or ability.

mix and match: *see* MIX.

put a match to set fire to.

the whole shooting match: *see* SHOOTING.

mate

mates' rates payment at less than the standard or usual rate, as charged to a friend or associate. British informal

2018 Peter James *Absolute Proof* 'How much are you charging?' ... 'Mates' rates? Two thousand for the searches. One thousand for each hit I get.'

math

do the math! work it out for yourself (used to suggest that the conclusion to be drawn about something is obvious). North American informal

ℹ *Math* is the American abbreviation of *mathematics*. When the phrase is used in British English, it is usually as *do the maths*.

2004 *BBC News: Business* I was faced with the choice of either topping up by using paid holiday or a vast reduction in earnings and a financial struggle when I least need it. You do the maths!

Matilda

waltz (*or* walk) Matilda carry a bundle of your personal possessions as you travel the roads. Australian

ℹ The name *Matilda* was one of a number of names given to the swag or pack carried by bushmen in Australia. The expression was famously used by A. B. ('Banjo') Paterson (1864–1941) in his 1903 song 'Waltzing Matilda'.

matter

a matter of course the usual or expected thing.

a matter of form a point of correct procedure.

a matter of life and death: *see* LIFE.

it is only a matter of time there will not be long to wait.

mind over matter: *see* MIND.

max

grody to the max: *see* GRODY.

to the max to the highest degree possible. informal

McCoy

the real McCoy the real thing; the genuine article. informal

ℹ The origin of this phrase is unknown, but it appears in the form 'the real Mackay' in a letter by Robert Louis Stevenson in 1883. *McCoy* is glossed as 'genuine liquor' in a 1930 edition of the *American Mercury*.

2010 Steven Kotler *A Small Furry Prayer* This is an air raid, take cover, this is the real McCoy.

meal

make a meal of treat a task or occurrence with more attention or care than necessary, especially for effect. British informal

1961 Colin Willock *Death in Covert* Dyson... was making a meal of everything. He had carefully paced the distance... He had stuck sticks in the ground.

mean

the golden mean: *see* GOLDEN.

mean business be in earnest.

2004 Harold Strachan *Make a Skyf, Man!* Industrial sabotage to show the big industrialists of the régime that we mean business.

mean to say really admit or intend to say.

1977 Jennifer Johnston *Shadows on our Skin* I mean to say, Joe Logan, where are you if you can't resist putting a small white tube of poison into your mouth every half an hour?

a means to an end a thing that is not valued or important in itself but is useful in achieving an aim.

ⓘ *End* and *means* are compared or contrasted in several proverbial sayings, for example **the end justifies the means** (*see* END) and *he who wills the end wills the means.*

no mean — a very good —.

ⓘ This expression was famously used by St Paul: 'I am . . . a Jew of Tarsus . . . a citizen of no mean city' (Acts 21:39).

2013 *The Stage* Getting any afternoon showcase audience to clap along with any real enthusiasm is no mean feat.

ways and means the methods and resources at someone's disposal for achieving something.

ⓘ In the British parliamentary system this phrase is used specifically of the various methods of raising government revenue.

1982 Frank McGuinness *The Factory Girls* He said too he couldn't afford opposition and there were ways and means of getting rid of it. Everybody thinks there's definitely going to be redundancies and pay-offs.

meaning

not know the meaning of the word behave as if unaware of the concept referred to or implied. informal

measure

for good measure in addition to what has already been done, said, or given.

get (*or* take *or* have) the measure of assess or have assessed the character, nature, or abilities of someone or something.

measure your length (of a person) fall flat on the ground. dated

meat

be meat and drink to be a source of great pleasure or encouragement to.

2009 *Guardian* The movement for universal suffrage and the abolition of slavery were meat and drink to a church that was built on democracy and the concept of all men and women being equal before God.

beat your meat: *see* BEAT.

dead meat: *see* DEAD.

easy meat: *see* EASY.

meat and potatoes ordinary but fundamental things; basic ingredients.

2012 *Pop Matters* I'm from Buffalo. I'm more of a meat and potatoes kind of person, never really thought of myself as a poet. Songwriter, yeah.

the meat in the sandwich: *see* SANDWICH.

strong meat: *see* STRONG.

medal

the reverse of the medal the opposite view of a matter.

Medes

the law of the Medes and Persians something which cannot be altered.

ⓘ This expression refers to Daniel 6:12: 'The thing is true, according to the law of the Medes and Persians, which altereth not.' The Medes were the inhabitants of Media, an ancient region of Asia to the southwest of the Caspian Sea.

medicine

a dose (*or* taste) of your own medicine the same bad treatment that you have given to others.

ⓘ The idea of taking or receiving *your own medicine* has been in metaphorical use since the mid 19th century.

2012 *Daily Telegraph* Paxman was given a taste of his own medicine in an amusingly bad-tempered exchange with John Humphrys on the *Today* programme on Friday.

meet

make ends meet: *see* END.

meet the case be adequate.

meet your eye (*or* ear) be visible (*or* audible).

meet someone's eye (*or* eyes *or* gaze) look directly at someone.

meet someone halfway make a compromise with someone.

meet your maker: *see* MAKER.

meet your match: *see* MATCH.

meet your Waterloo: *see* WATERLOO.

never the twain shall meet: *see* TWAIN.

there's more to someone or something than meets the eye a person or situation is more complex or interesting than they appear.

meeting

a meeting of minds an understanding or agreement between people.

megillah

the whole megillah something in its entirety, especially a complicated set of arrangements or a long-winded story. North American informal

ⓘ *Megillah* is the Hebrew word for a 'scroll' and refers particularly to each of five books of the Jewish Scriptures (the Song of Solomon, Ruth, Lamentations, Ecclesiastes, and Esther) appointed to be read in the synagogue on certain important days.

Melba

do a Melba ❶ return from retirement. ❷ make several farewell appearances. Australian & New Zealand informal

ⓘ The Australian operatic soprano Nellie Melba (the stage name of Helen Mitchell, 1861–1931) made repeated 'farewell' appearances.

melt

look as if butter wouldn't melt in your mouth: *see* BUTTER.

melt in the mouth (of food) be deliciously light or tender and need little or no chewing.

melting pot

in the melting pot in a process of change and with an uncertain outcome. British

memory

in living memory: *see* LIVING.

jog someone's memory: *see* JOG.

take a trip (*or* walk) down memory lane deliberately recall pleasant or sentimental memories.

mend

least said, soonest mended: *see* LEAST.

mend (your) fences make peace with a person.

ⓘ This expression originated in the late 19th century in the USA, with reference to a member of Congress returning to his home town to keep in touch with the voters and to look after his interests there. Similar notions are conjured up by the saying *good fences make good neighbours.*

1994 Louis de Bernières *Captain Corelli's Mandolin* He knew assuredly he should go and mend his fences with the priest.

mend your pace go faster; alter your pace to match another's.

mend your ways improve your habits or behaviour.

on the mend improving in health or condition; recovering.

mentioned

be mentioned in dispatches be commended for your actions. British

ⓘ In official military reports from the front line any soldiers who have been responsible for particular acts of bravery are commended by name.

mercy

tender mercies: *see* TENDER.

be thankful (*or* grateful) for small mercies be relieved that an unpleasant situation is alleviated by minor advantages.

merry

lead someone a merry dance: *see* DANCE.

merry as a grig: *see* GRIG.

play merry hell with: *see* HELL.

the more the merrier the more people or things there are the better a situation will be.

mess

mess with someone's head cause someone to feel frustrated, anxious, or upset. US informal

sell something for a mess of pottage: *see* POTTAGE.

message

get the message infer an implication from a remark or action. informal

2013 *Alf Grumble* The cops will be under fire for chasing a law-breaker ... who didn't get the message about being unfit to drive earlier that night when they took her car keys from her.

send the right (*or* wrong) message make a significant statement, either implicitly or by your actions.

messenger

shoot (*or* kill) the messenger treat the bearer of bad news as if they were to blame for it.

> ℹ Being the bearer of bad tidings has been a traditionally thankless task, as indicated in Sophocles' *Antigone*, 'No man loves the messenger of ill' and Shakespeare's *Antony and Cleopatra*, 'The nature of bad news infects the teller'.

method

there is method in someone's madness there is a sensible foundation for what appears to be foolish or strange behaviour.

> ℹ This expression comes from the scene in *Hamlet* in which Hamlet feigns madness, causing Polonius to remark: 'Though this be madness, yet there is method in't'.

mettle

be on your mettle be ready or forced to prove your ability to cope well with a demanding situation.

put someone on their mettle (of a demanding situation) test someone's ability to face difficulties in a spirited and resilient way.

> ℹ Originally the same word as *metal*, *mettle* was no more than a variant spelling that gradually became particularly associated with figurative uses of the word, meaning 'quality of temperament', and from that 'natural spirit' or 'courage'. These senses eventually developed so far from the literal senses that it was no longer apparent that they were originally the same word. The distinctive spellings *metal* and *mettle* to distinguish the two were in use by the early 18th century, though not necessarily universally applied until the following century.

Mexican

Mexican overdrive the neutral gear position used when coasting downhill. US informal

> ℹ This expression originated in the mid 20th century, especially in language used by long-distance truck drivers. Nowadays it is liable to be condemned for its xenophobic implications (alluding to the alleged laziness of Mexicans).

mice

when the cat's away, the mice will play: *see* CAT.

mickey

take the mickey tease or ridicule someone, especially in an unkind or persistent way. informal, chiefly British

> ℹ The origin of the phrase is not known for certain (a not entirely implausible explanation is that *Mickey* is short for *Mickey Bliss*, rhyming slang for *piss*—see **take the piss** at PISS); *take* (or *extract*) *the Michael* is a humorously formal variant.

Mickey Finn

slip someone a Mickey Finn give someone a drugged or otherwise adulterated drink.

> ℹ Recorded from the 1920s, this expression is of unknown origin, but it is sometimes said to be the name of a notorious Chicago barkeeper (*c.*1896–1906).

microscope

under the microscope under critical examination.

Midas

the Midas touch the ability to make money out of anything that you undertake.

> ℹ In classical legend, *Midas* was a king of Phrygia (in Asia Minor) who had the power to turn everything he touched into gold.

middle

knock someone into the middle of next week: *see* KNOCK.

the middle of nowhere somewhere very remote and isolated. informal

> ℹ This is one example of several derogatory expressions concerning rural life as viewed from an urban perspective: compare with **the back of beyond** (*at* BACK) and **in the sticks** (*at* STICK).

pig in the middle: *see* PIG.

play both ends against the middle: *see* PLAY.

steer (*or* take) a middle course adopt a policy which avoids extremes.

midnight

burn the midnight oil: *see* BURN.

midstream

in midstream ❶ in the middle of a stream or river. ❷ (of an activity or process, especially one that is interrupted) part-way through its course; unfinished.

might

might is right those who are powerful can do what they wish unchallenged, even if their action is in fact unjustified.

ℹ This was an observation made by both Greek and Latin writers and it was known in this form in English as far back as the early 14th century.

with might and main with all your force.

ℹ *Main* derives from the Old English word *mægen* meaning 'physical strength' (*see also* **by main force** *at* MAIN). The use of the two nouns *might* and *main* together dates from the mid 15th century; *main* in this sense is no longer used in modern English except in this phrase.

mightier

the pen is mightier than the sword: *see* PEN.

mighty

high and mighty: *see* HIGH.

m

Mike

for the love of Mike: *see* LOVE.

mile

be miles away be lost in thought and so unaware of what is happening around you. informal

a country mile: *see* COUNTRY.

go the extra mile be especially assiduous in your attempt to achieve something.

ℹ This origins of this expression can be traced back to the New Testament injunction 'And whosoever shall compel thee to go a mile, go with him twain' (Matthew 5:41). The revue song of 1957 by Joyce Grenfell, 'Ready . . . To go the extra mile', may have popularized its use.

a mile a minute very quickly. informal

ℹ As a noun, *mile a minute* is a popular nickname for the quick-growing climbing plant Russian Vine.

the mile-high club used in reference to having sex on an aircraft. humorous

2009 *The Book Show* (ABC Radio) If the stewardess spilled some wine on your partner's lap, would you assume it was a signal that she wanted to drag him into the cramped bathroom for an initiation into the mile high club?

run a mile used to show that someone is frightened by or very unwilling to do something. informal

2012 *National Business Review* (New Zealand) Both times I was advised he was returning over 25% for his investors. Immediately, instinct told me to run a mile.

see (*or* tell *or* spot) something a mile off recognize something very easily. informal

stand (*or* stick) out a mile be very obvious or incongruous. informal

milk

cry over spilt (*or* spilled) milk lament or make a fuss about a misfortune that has happened and that cannot be changed or reversed.

milk and honey prosperity and abundance.

ℹ This expression alludes to the prosperity of the Promised Land of Israel in the Bible (Exodus 3:8).

milk and water feeble, insipid, or mawkish.

milk the bull (*or* ram) engage in an enterprise doomed to failure.

the milk of human kindness care and compassion for others.

ℹ This phrase comes from *Macbeth*. In Lady Macbeth's soliloquy on the subject of her husband's character, she remarks: 'Yet I do fear thy nature; It is too full o' the milk of human kindness To catch the nearest way'.

mill

go (*or* put someone) through the mill undergo (*or* cause someone to undergo) an unpleasant experience.

grist to the mill: *see* GRIST.

run of the mill the ordinary or undistinguished type.

ℹ In this expression, the *run* is literally the material produced from a mill before it has been sorted or inspected for quality.

million

gone a million (of a person) completely defeated or finished. Australian informal

1976 *Australian (Sydney)* Gough's gone. Gone a million. He's had it.

a — in a million one of the very best of their kind.

2013 *Daily Telegraph* Most poignant of all was a Peppa Pig soft toy, wearing a T-shirt saying 'Daddy's Little Buddy', left by Drummer

Rigby's widow on behalf of their two-year-old son Jack, to whom the soldier had been 'a dad in a million'.

look (*or* feel) (like) a million dollars (of a person) look (*or* feel) extremely good. informal

millstone

a millstone round your neck a very severe impediment or disadvantage.

ⓘ A *millstone* was a large circular stone used to grind corn. The phrase alludes to a method of executing people by throwing them into deep water with a heavy stone attached to them, a fate believed to have been suffered by several early Christian martyrs.

mince

not mince words (*or* matters) speak candidly and directly, especially when criticizing someone or something.

mincemeat

make mincemeat of defeat decisively or easily in a fight, contest, or argument. informal

mind

at the back of your mind: *see* BACK.

be in (*or* of) two minds be unable to decide between alternatives.

be a weight off your mind: *see* WEIGHT.

bear in mind remember and take into account.

blow someone's mind affect someone very strongly. informal

ⓘ *Blow someone's mind* was originally a mid-20th-century expression for the effect of hallucinatory drugs such as LSD.

cast your mind back think back; recall an earlier time.

close (*or* shut) your mind to (*or* against) refuse to consider or acknowledge.

come (*or* spring) to mind (of a thought or idea) occur to someone; be thought of.

cross your mind (of a thought or idea) occur to you, especially transiently.

frame of mind: *see* FRAME.

give someone a piece of your mind: *see* PIECE.

great minds think alike used to flag up the coincidence when two people think of the same thing at the same time or have the same opinion.

have a mind of your own ❶ be capable of independent opinion or action. ❷ (of an inanimate object) seem capable of thought and desire, especially by behaving contrary to the will of the person using it.

have a (*or* a good *or* half a) mind to do something be very much inclined to do something.

have something on your mind be troubled by the thought of something.

hearts and minds: *see* HEART.

in your mind's eye in your imagination or mental view.

make up your mind make a decision; decide.

a meeting of minds: *see* MEETING.

mind over matter the power of the mind asserted over the physical universe; the use of willpower to overcome physical problems.

mind your Ps and Qs be careful to behave well and avoid giving offence.

ⓘ Various suggestions have been made concerning the significance of *P* and *Q*. One obvious one is that a child learning to read or write might have difficulty in distinguishing between the two tailed letters *p* and *q*. Another is that printers had to be very careful not to confuse the two letters when setting type.

mind the shop be temporarily in charge of affairs.

mind your back (*or* backs) used to warn inattentive bystanders that someone wants to get past. informal

never mind ❶ used to urge someone not to feel anxiety or distress. ❷ used to suggest that a problem or objection is not important. ❸ *also* **never you mind** used in refusing to answer a question. ❹ used to indicate that what has been said about one thing applies even more to another.

not pay someone any mind not pay someone any attention. North American

on someone's mind preoccupying someone, especially in a disquieting way.

open your mind to be prepared to consider or acknowledge; be receptive to.

out of your mind ❶ having lost control of your mental faculties; insane. ❷ used to express a belief in someone's foolishness or mental turmoil. ❸ suffering from the specified condition to a very high degree. informal

presence of mind: *see* PRESENCE.

put someone in mind of resemble and so cause someone to think of or remember.

2004 *MV Daily* Physically, he put me in mind of a cross between a young Michael Palin and the late, lamented David Munrow.

put your mind to something start to concentrate on something.

speak your mind: *see* SPEAK.

take a load off someone's mind: *see* LOAD.

minor

in a minor key in a lesser or understated way.

2007 David Poland *The Hot Blog—Movie City News* There are six categories with more than five nominees from the generously flexible group.... Surprises? Viggo Mortensen, Ryan Gosling, and (in a minor key) Amy Adams and Emile Hirsch.

minority

be (*or* find yourself) in a minority of one be the sole person to hold a particular view. often humorous

mint

in mint condition (of an object) new or as if new; in pristine condition.

ℹ The image behind this phrase is of a newly minted coin.

minute

a laugh a minute: *see* LAUGH.

one minute to midnight the last moment or opportunity. informal

2012 *CNN transcripts* I think the whole of this crisis is, you know, it's always one minute to midnight and the Germans come in and do something that buys a bit more time.

mirror

all done with mirrors achieved with an element of trickery.

ℹ This phrase alludes to the fact that conjuring tricks are often explained as being achieved through the skilful use of mirrors; compare with **smoke and mirrors** (*at* SMOKE).

smoke and mirrors: *see* SMOKE.

mischief

do someone (*or* yourself) a mischief injure someone or yourself. informal

make mischief create trouble or discord.

misery

put someone out of their misery release someone from suspense or anxiety, especially by telling them something they are anxious to know. informal

put something out of its misery end the suffering of a creature in pain by killing it.

miss

give something a miss decide not to do or have something. British informal

hit and miss done or occurring at random; succeeding by chance rather than through planning.

2013 *New Zealand Herald* As several reviewers have noted, Kinect's voice-recognition ability is hit and miss.

hit or miss as likely to be unsuccessful as successful.

miss the cut: *see* **make the cut** *at* CUT.

miss a beat hesitate or falter, especially in demanding circumstances or when making a transition from one activity to another.

miss the boat (*or* bus) be too slow to take advantage of an opportunity. informal

1987 Kathy Lette *Girls' Night Out* He'll never get divorced and marry her. She'll miss the boat.

1940 Neville Chamberlain *Speech at Central Hall, Westminster* Whatever may be the reason—whether it was that Hitler thought he might get away with what he had got without fighting for it, or whether it was that after all the preparations were not sufficiently complete—however, one thing is certain—he missed the bus.

not miss much be alert to or aware of everything that is happening around you. informal

not miss a trick never fail to take advantage of a situation. informal

1965 *Harper's Bazaar* Fenwicks... never misses a trick when it comes to picking up a new accessory idea.

mistake

and no mistake without any doubt. informal

2013 *Diamond Geezer* Whether soaring high above in your own exclusive pod, or pottering around the entertainment opportunities at ground level, you'll enjoy a memorable day out on the Dangleway and no mistake. Or so they say.

make no mistake (about it) do not be deceived into thinking otherwise. informal

1974 *Times* Make no mistake. We had a major work of television last night.

mistaking

there is no mistaking someone or something it is impossible not to recognize someone or something.

mite

a widow's mite: *see* WIDOW.

mitt

get your mitts on obtain possession of. informal

ⓘ *Mitt*, an abbreviation of *mitten*, is an informal term for a person's hand that dates back to the late 19th century.

mix

mix and match select and combine different but complementary items, such as clothing or pieces of equipment, to form a coordinated set.

mixed

a mixed bag a diverse assortment of things or people.

a mixed blessing something good which nevertheless has some disadvantages.

mixture

the mixture as before the same treatment repeated. British

ⓘ *The mixture as before* was an instruction which was formerly written on medicine bottles.

mo

curl the mo: *see* CURL.

mob

the heavy mob: *see* HEAVY.

mobile

downwardly (*or* upwardly) mobile moving to a lower (*or* higher) social position; losing (*or* gaining) wealth and status.

mockers

put the mockers on ❶ put an end to; thwart. ❷ bring bad luck to.

ⓘ This expression originated as early 20th-century British slang. An Australian variant is *put the mocks* on.

❶ **1966 Lionel Davidson** *A Long Way to Shiloh* Shimshon and the judo both seemed to have put the mockers on this particular idyll. We left soon after.

❷ **1970 Joyce Porter** *Dover Strikes Again* This investigation had got the mockers on it from the start.

mockery

make a mockery of something make something seem foolish or absurd.

2014 digby *Hullabaloo* A pressure cooker bomb is a 'weapon of mass destruction'? It's as if the Department of Justice is trying to make a mockery of the law.

Mohicans

the last of the Mohicans: *see* LAST.

molehill

make a mountain out of a molehill: *see* MOUNTAIN.

moment

at a moment's notice: *see* **at short notice** *at* NOTICE.

have your (*or* its) moments have short periods that are better or more impressive than others.

man of the moment: *see* MAN.

moment of truth a crisis; a turning point when a decision has to be made or a crisis faced.

ⓘ This expression is a translation of the Spanish *el momento de la verdad*, which refers to the final sword thrust in a bullfight.

never a dull moment: *see* DULL.

on the spur of the moment: *see* SPUR.

senior moment: *see* SENIOR.

Monday

Monday morning quarterback a person who is wise after the event. North American

ℹ In American football, a *quarterback* is the player stationed behind the centre who directs the team's attacking play. In North American English the word has also developed the sense of 'a person who directs or coordinates an operation or project'. A *Monday morning quarterback* is someone who passes judgement on something or criticizes it when it is too late for their comments to be of any use, since the particular game or project in question has finished or been completed.

money

be in the money have or win a lot of money. informal

be made of money be very rich. informal

a fool and his money are soon parted: *see* FOOL.

for my money ❶ in my opinion or judgement. ❷ for my preference or taste.

give someone or something a (good) run for their money: *see* RUN.

have money to burn have so much money that you can spend as lavishly as you want.

licence to print money: *see* LICENCE.

marry money: *see* MARRY.

money burns a hole in your pocket (*or* purse) you have an irresistible urge to spend money as soon as you have it.

money for jam (*or* old rope) ❶ money earned for little or no effort. ❷ an easy task. British informal

ℹ These expressions, which date back to the early 20th century, may have originated as military slang. In 1919, the *Athenaeum* stated that *money for jam* arose as the result of the 'great use of jam in the Army'.

money talks wealth gives power and influence to those who possess it. proverb

not for love or money: *see* LOVE.

on the money accurate; correct. chiefly North American

put money (*or* put your money) on ❶ place a bet on something. ❷ have confidence in the truth or success of something.

put your money where your mouth is take action to support your statements or opinions. informal

see the colour of someone's money: *see* COLOUR.

throw good money after bad incur further loss in a hopeless attempt to recoup a previous loss.

throw money at something try to solve a problem by recklessly spending more money on it, without due consideration of what is required.

time is money: *see* TIME.

you pays your money and you takes your choice: *see* PAY.

monkey

as artful (*or* clever) as a wagonload (*or* cartload) of monkeys extremely clever or mischievous. British informal

brass monkey: *see* BRASS.

have a monkey on your back ❶ have a burdensome problem. ❷ be dependent on drugs. informal

ℹ Sense 2 originated as mid-20th-century US slang; it can also mean 'experience withdrawal symptoms after ceasing to take a drug'.

have (*or* get) your monkey up be angry.

I'll be a monkey's uncle used to express great surprise. informal

like a monkey on a stick restless and agitated.

ℹ The image here is of a child's toy which consists of a figure of a monkey attached to a stick up and down which it can be moved.

make a monkey of (*or* out of) someone humiliate someone by making them appear ridiculous.

monkey see, monkey do used to suggest that someone has slavishly imitated another, especially in doing something foolish. informal, chiefly North American

2004 *Trinidad Guardian* Advanced technology has limited the independence of all nations and states. The world is now a global village, and monkey see monkey do as they all scramble for a dollar.

not give a monkey's be completely indifferent or unconcerned. informal

ℹ The expression is a euphemistic shortening of *not give a monkey's fuck* or *not give a monkey's toss*.

put (*or* get) a person's monkey up make someone angry. informal

monster

Frankenstein's monster: *see* FRANKENSTEIN.

the green-eyed monster: *see* GREEN-EYED.

month

flavour of the month: *see* FLAVOUR.

a month of Sundays a very long, seemingly endless period of time.

ⓘ This expression may be a reference to the traditionally slow passage of Sundays as a result of religious restrictions on activity or entertainment. In a letter written in 1849, G. E. Jewsbury talked of the absence of mail deliveries on Sundays, remarking: 'If I don't get a better letter from you . . . you may pass "a month of Sundays" at breakfast without any letter from me'.

2003 *American Photo* You'll experience more during this fun-filled photographic weekend than in a month of Sundays.

(that) time of the month: *see* TIME.

monty

the full monty the full amount expected, desired, or possible. informal

ⓘ The origin of this expression is unclear. Among various, though unsubstantiated theories, one cites as the source the phrase *the full Montague Burton*, apparently meaning 'a complete three-piece suit' (from the name of a tailor of made-to-measure clothing in the early 20th century). Another theory recounts the possibility of a military origin, with *the full monty* being 'the full cooked English breakfast' insisted upon by the British Second World War army commander Field Marshal Montgomery, whose nickname was 'Monty'.

moon

bay at the moon clamour or make an outcry to no effect.

ⓘ The barking of dogs at a full moon has been a metaphor for futile activity since the mid 17th century.

cry (*or* ask) for the moon ask for what is unattainable or impossible. British

ⓘ The *moon* in this expression, which dates from the mid 16th century, stands for something distant and unattainable, as it does in **promise someone the moon** below.

the man in the moon: *see* MAN.

many moons ago a long time ago. informal

ⓘ The reference here is to the phases of the moon marking out the months.

once in a blue moon: *see* BLUE.

over the moon extremely happy; delighted. informal

ⓘ This phrase comes from an old nursery rhyme which includes the lines *Heigh diddle diddle, the cat and the fiddle, the cow jumped over the moon*.

promise someone the moon (*or* earth) promise something that is unattainable. British

2009 *Gotta Get Drunk* They . . . filled their hearts with enthusiasm and instilled in their minds a new zest for life. They gave them hope! They promised them the moon, but alas, invariably they brought them to their doom.

moonlight

do a moonlight flit make a hurried, usually nocturnal, removal or change of abode, especially in order to avoid paying your rent. informal

ⓘ *Make a moonlight flitting* is recorded from the early 19th century and appears to have originated in northern England or Scotland. The expression is now often shortened to *do a moonlight*.

moonlight and roses used to characterize an atmosphere of romantic sentimentality.

ⓘ The expression comes from the title of a song (1925) by Neil Moret and Ben Black.

more

less is more: *see* LESS.

more — than someone has had hot dinners: *see* DINNER.

say no more: *see* SAY.

the more the merrier: *see* MERRY.

there's more to someone or something than meets the eye: *see* MEET.

morning

the morning after (the night before) the morning after an evening of drinking, when you have a hangover. humorous

morning, noon, and night all of the time; constantly.

2009 *Farmers Weekly Interactive* Plants are there but eaten to the ground. The first top dressings have sparked some life into them, only to be eaten off. Tiresome though it is, these fields must be patrolled morning, noon and night.

mortal

shuffle off this mortal coil: *see* COIL.

mortar

bricks and mortar: *see* BRICK.

clicks and mortar: *see* CLICK.

Morton

Morton's fork a situation in which there are two choices or alternatives whose consequences are equally unpleasant.

ⓘ John Morton (*c.*1420–1500) was Archbishop of Canterbury and chief minister of Henry VII. *Morton's fork* was the argument used by him to extract contributions to the royal treasury: the obviously rich must have money and the frugal must have savings, so neither could evade his demands.

mote

a mote in someone's eye a trivial fault in someone which is less serious than one in someone else who is being critical.

ⓘ A *mote* is a tiny speck of dust or a similar substance. The phrase comes from Matthew 7:3–5: 'Why beholdest thou the mote that is in thy brother's eye, but considerest not the beam that is in thine own eye?': the implication is that someone is ignoring a glaring fault of their own while criticizing a smaller one in someone else.

moth

like a moth to the flame irresistibly attracted to someone or something.

mothball

in mothballs unused but kept in good condition for future use.

mother

at your mother's knee: *see* KNEE.

the mother (*or* mother and father) of all — an extreme example or very large specimen of something. informal

2007 Michael Simkins *Fatty Batter* Our pet pug dog, little Oona, does the mother of all dumps on the flower bed.

motion

go through the motions ❶ do something perfunctorily, without any enthusiasm or commitment. ❷ simulate an action; act out something.

mould

be cast in a — mould be of the type specified.

1991 Jean Bow *Jane's Journey* He was certainly not cast in a common mould. She had never met anyone like him before.

break the mould put an end to a pattern of events or behaviour, especially one that has become rigid and restrictive, by doing things in a markedly different way.

ⓘ Originally this phrase referred to casting artefacts in moulds: destroying a mould ensured that no further identical examples could be produced. The expression became a catchphrase in Britain in the early 1980s with the foundation of the Social Democratic Party. Its founders promoted the party as breaking the 'out-of-date mould' of British politics, a phrase used by Roy Jenkins in a speech in 1980.

mountain

have a mountain to climb be facing a very difficult task.

if the mountain won't come to Muhammad, Muhammad must go to the mountain if one party will not compromise, the other party will have to make the extra effort.

ⓘ The story behind this expression is that Muhammad was once challenged to demonstrate his credentials as a prophet by summoning Mount Safa to come to him. When the mountain did not move in response to the summons, Muhammad observed that had the mountain moved it would undoubtedly have overwhelmed him and all his followers and that therefore he would go to the mountain to give thanks to God for his mercy in not allowing this disaster to happen.

make a mountain out of a molehill foolishly or pointlessly exaggerate the importance of something trivial.

ⓘ The contrast between the size of molehills and that of mountains has been made in this and related expressions since the late 16th century.

man mountain: *see* MAN.

move mountains ❶ achieve spectacular and apparently impossible results. ❷ make every possible effort.

ⓘ In sense 1, the phrase alludes to 1 Corinthians 13:2: 'And though I have the gift of prophecy, and understand all mysteries, and all knowledge; and though I have all faith, so that I could remove mountains, and have not charity, I am nothing'.

mourner

crowd the mourners: *see* CROWD.

mouse

play cat and mouse with: *see* CAT.

poor as a church mouse: *see* POOR.

quiet as a mouse: *see* QUIET.

mouth

be all mouth (and no trousers) tend to talk boastfully without any intention of acting on your words. informal

> **1998** *Oldie* What was the point of the Sitwells?... The image was the point, transcending mere achievement... The Sitwells were all mouth and no trousers.

down in the mouth: *see* DOWN.

(from) hand to mouth: *see* HAND.

froth at the mouth: *see* FROTH.

have your heart in your mouth: *see* HEART.

the lion's mouth: *see* LION.

make someone's mouth water ❶ cause someone to salivate at the prospect of appetizing food. ❷ cause someone to feel an intense desire to possess something.

melt in the mouth: *see* MELT.

put your money where your mouth is: *see* MONEY.

put the mouth on someone cause someone's performance to deteriorate by praising it. informal, chiefly Australian

put words in (*or* into) someone's mouth ❶ falsely report what someone has said. ❷ prompt or encourage someone to say something.

run off at the mouth talk excessively or indiscreetly. North American informal

shoot your mouth off: *see* SHOOT.

stop someone's mouth: *see* STOP.

(straight) from the horse's mouth: *see* HORSE.

take the words out of someone's mouth say what someone else was about to say.

watch your mouth be careful about what you say. informal

word of mouth: *see* WORD.

mouthful

give someone a mouthful talk to or shout at someone in an angry, abusive, or severely critical way; swear at someone. British informal

say a mouthful make a striking or important statement; say something noteworthy. North American informal

movable

a movable feast: *see* FEAST.

move

the earth moved: *see* EARTH.

move up a gear: *see* **change gear** *at* GEAR.

get a move on hurry up. informal

> **2012** *Guardian* When Sluizer finally flickered back into consciousness, he instructed the doctors to get a move on as he had to fly back to LA.

make a move ❶ take action. ❷ start on a journey; leave somewhere. British

make a move on (*or* put the moves on) make a proposition to someone, especially of a sexual nature. informal

move the goalposts: *see* GOALPOST.

move heaven and earth: *see* HEAVEN.

move mountains: *see* MOUNTAIN.

move with the times keep abreast of current thinking or developments.

not move a muscle: *see* MUSCLE.

the spirit moves someone: *see* SPIRIT.

mover

a mover and shaker someone at the centre of events who makes things happen; a powerful person.

> ❶ *Movers and shakers* is first recorded in Arthur O'Shaughnessy's 1874 poem 'Ode'.

> **2000** *Daily Telegraph* The Monte Carlo hotel restaurant [is] filled with actors and assorted movers and shakers attending the annual television festival.

mozz

put the mozz on exert a malign influence on (someone); jinx. Australian informal

> ❶ *Mozz* is short for Australian informal *mozzle* 'luck', which itself came from Hebrew *mazzāl* 'star, luck'.

Mr

Mr Clean: *see* CLEAN.

Mr Right: *see* RIGHT.

much

a bit much: *see* BIT.

not much in it little difference between things being compared.

so much the better (*or* worse) it is better (*or* worse) for that reason.

2013 *New Statesman* Never use a picture of a northerner in a suit unless it is . . . a celebrity footballer appearing at his drink-driving hearing. If you can get a mangy dog, a rat-faced kid in a cheap tracksuit or an old dear with a tartan shopping trolley, so much the better.

muchness

much of a muchness very similar; nearly the same. informal

ⓘ *Muchness*, used in Middle English in the sense 'large size, bigness', is now very seldom used outside this expression, which dates from the early 18th century.

muck

as common as muck of low social status. British informal

Lady Muck: *see* LADY.

make a muck of handle incompetently; bungle. British informal

where there's muck there's brass dirty or unpleasant activities are also lucrative. proverb

mucker

come a mucker fall heavily. British informal, dated

mud

clear as mud: *see* CLEAR.

drag someone through the mud: *see* **drag someone through the dirt** *at* DRAG.

fling (*or* sling *or* throw) mud make disparaging or scandalous remarks or accusations. informal

ⓘ The proverb *throw dirt* (or *mud) enough, and some will stick*, to which this phrase alludes, is attributed to the Florentine statesman Niccolò Machiavelli (1469–1527).

here's mud in your eye! used to express friendly feelings towards your companions before drinking. British informal

mud sticks disparaging or malicious allegations are difficult to disprove or shake off.

someone's name is mud someone is in disgrace or unpopular. informal

ⓘ *Mud* was a colloquial term for a fool from the early 18th century to the late 19th century.

2013 *Daily Telegraph* Although his name is mud amongst the Salmond Set, Jim Sillars . . . insists that the White Paper must include a 'Plan B' for the currency.

muddy

muddy the waters make an issue or a situation more confusing and harder to understand by introducing complications.

ⓘ The figurative use of *muddy* to mean 'make something hard to perceive or understand' occurs in Shakespeare; *muddy the waters* dates from the mid 19th century.

mug

a mug's game an activity which it is stupid to engage in because it is likely to be unsuccessful or dangerous. informal

ⓘ *Mug* was mid-19th-century slang for a fool, in particular someone who has been duped by a card sharper or criminal. *Mug's game* appeared in the early 20th century and has been applied to a wide variety of activities, especially horse racing and betting on horses.

2012 *National Business Review* (New Zealand) Borrowing $200 million a week for cheaper petrol is a mug's game.

Muhammad

if the mountain won't come to Muhammad, Muhammad must go to the mountain: *see* MOUNTAIN.

mule

stubborn as a mule: *see* STUBBORN.

mullock

poke mullock at ridicule someone. Australian & New Zealand informal

ⓘ In Middle English, *mullock* meant 'refuse or rubbish', a sense which only survives in dialect use. In Australian English it came to be used of rock that either did not contain gold or from which the gold had been extracted, and it then developed the extended sense of 'worthless information or nonsense'. This phrase dates from the early 20th century; compare with **poke borak at** (*at* BORAK).

multitude

cover a multitude of sins conceal or gloss over a lot of problems or defects.

ℹ This phrase refers to 1 Peter 4:8: 'For charity shall cover the multitude of sins'.

mum

keep mum remain silent about something; not reveal a secret. informal

mum's the word say nothing; don't reveal a secret. informal

ℹ In both of these idioms, *mum* stands for an inarticulate sound made with pursed lips indicating either unwillingness or inability to speak.

2009 Andrew *The 4th Avenue Blues* By the time an appointment rolls around, I feel better so mum's the word. I personally don't want to be put on any more medications.

murder

get away with murder succeed in doing whatever you choose without being punished or suffering any disadvantage. informal

murder will out murder cannot remain undetected.

ℹ This expression was used by Chaucer in *The Prioress's Tale*: 'Mordre wol out, certeyn, it wol nat faille'.

scream (*or* yell) blue murder make an extravagant and noisy protest. informal

ℹ A North American variant of this phrase is *scream bloody murder*.

1995 Iain Banks *Whit* I was now left with the ticklish problem of how to let my great-aunt know there was somebody there in the room with her without . . . causing her to scream blue murder.

Murphy

Murphy's law if anything can go wrong it will.

ℹ *Murphy's law* is said to have been the inspiration of a Californian project manager for the firm Northrop, referring to a remark made in 1949 by a colleague, Captain Edward Murphy of the Wright Field-Aircraft Laboratory. In 1955, *Aviation Mechanics Bulletin* explained Murphy's Law as 'If an aircraft part can be installed incorrectly, someone will install it that way'. A rather less polite British English equivalent is *sod's law* (*see* SOD).

muscle

flex your muscles: *see* FLEX.

not move a muscle not move at all.

mushroom

like mushrooms suddenly and in great numbers.

music

face the music: *see* FACE.

music to your ears something that is very pleasant or gratifying to hear or discover.

musketeers

three musketeers: *see* THREE.

mustard

cut the mustard come up to expectations; meet the required standard. informal

ℹ The origin of rhe phrase remains conjectural: in early 20th-century US slang, *(all) to the mustard* meant 'excellent', so perhaps there is some underlying idea of 'gathering excellence'.

2013 *DVD Verdict* Some of the kills are suitably icky and fun, even if the VFX [visual effects] are often sub par (a spear flying through the air on fishing wire just doesn't cut the mustard).

a grain of mustard seed: *see* GRAIN.

keen as mustard: *see* KEEN.

muster

pass muster be accepted as adequate or satisfactory.

ℹ This was originally a military expression, meaning 'come through a review or inspection without censure'. It is found earlier (late 16th century to late 17th century) in the now obsolete form *pass (the) musters* and has been in figurative use since the late 16th century.

mutton

dead as mutton: *see* **dead as a doornail** *at* DEAD.

mutton dressed as lamb a middle-aged or old woman dressed in a style suitable for a much younger woman. British informal

🛈 *Mutton* occurs in various derogatory contexts relating to women. It has been used as a slang term for prostitutes from the early 16th century, for example, while the phrase *hawk your mutton* means 'flaunt your sexual attractiveness' or (of a prostitute) 'solicit for clients'.

1988 Salman Rushdie *The Satanic Verses* Mutton dressed as lamb, fifty plus and batting her eyelashes like an eighteen-year-old.

nail

a bed of nails: *see* BED.

fight tooth and nail: *see* TOOTH.

hard as nails: *see* HARD.

hit the nail on the head state the truth exactly; find exactly the right answer.

> **2013 Ben** *Silent Words Speak Loudest* Bridget Christie hits the nail on the head with regard to Channel 4's extraordinary new show *Sex Box*. A concept apparently lifted straight out of Alan Partridge's notebook of programme ideas.

nail your colours to the mast: *see* COLOURS.

a nail in the coffin an action or event regarded as likely to have a detrimental or destructive effect on a situation, enterprise, or person.

> **1981 Roy Lancaster** *Plant Hunting in Nepal* A major nail in the coffin of the plant hunter, so some people believe, is the growing importance placed on plant conservation in the wild.

nail a lie expose something as a falsehood or deception.

> ❶ The reference here is to shopkeepers nailing forged coins to their shop counter to expose them and put them out of circulation, or to farmers pinning dead vermin to a barn door as a deterrent to others.

on the nail (of payment) without delay.

> ❶ The origins of this expression are uncertain. It may be related to the obsolete phrase *to the nail*, meaning 'to perfection' or 'to the utmost', which derived from the habit of sculptors giving a finishing touch to their work with a fingernail, or to joiners testing the accuracy of a joint in the same way. A North American equivalent is *on the barrelhead*.

> **2011 Alex Harrowell** *Yorkshire Ranter* They would surely have been likely to insist on payment in cash on the nail, rather than promises of future side-deals that would likely never be fulfilled.

right on the nail with complete accuracy.

naked

the naked truth the plain truth, without concealment or embellishment.

> ❶ This phrase may originally have developed as a translation of the Latin phrase *nudaque veritas*, found in Horace's *Odes*, or to any of various fables that personify Truth as a naked woman in contrast to the elaborate dress and artifice of Falsehood.

name

call someone names insult someone verbally.

drop names refer frequently to well-known people in such a way as to imply that they are close acquaintances.

give a dog a bad name: *see* DOG.

give your name to invent, discover, or found something which then becomes known by your name.

have to your name have in your possession.

have your name in lights ❶ (of an actor or performer) have their name displayed in lights outside a theatre, concert hall, etc. ❷ be famous.

have your name on it be destined or particularly suited to you.

> **2006** *Sunday Times* One round went through my already shattered rear window; another whistled past my head. But ... neither bullet had my name on it and I managed to get away.

in all but name existing in a particular state but not formally recognized as such.

> **2014** *Daily Telegraph* A long-awaited report ... in November concluded that while the Church should not marry same-sex couples, it should offer special services likely to amount to weddings in all but name.

in name only by description but not in reality.

> **2014** *Washington Post* RINO (Republican in name only) watchers will say he hasn't rolled back gun-control laws, but New Jersey is so anti-gun that any such attempt would only destroy his political capital.

lend your name to something: *see* LEND.

make a name for yourself become famous.

name and shame identify wrongdoers by name with the intention of embarrassing them into improving their behaviour.

2004 Helena Kennedy *Just Law* The case ... raised fundamental questions not just about the stigmatisation of those named and shamed, but also about the purpose of the judicial process.

name names mention specific names, especially of people involved in something wrong or illegal.

2000 *Times* A telephone hotline will ... enable the public to name names in the fight against counterfeiters.

name no names refrain from mentioning the names of people involved in an incident.

the name of the game the main purpose or most important aspect of a situation. informal

a name to conjure with: *see* CONJURE.

no names, no pack drill punishment or blame cannot be meted out if names and details are not mentioned.

ℹ *Pack drill* is a form of military punishment in which an offender has to perform parade-ground exercises while carrying a heavy pack. This early 20th-century expression is often used as an aside to recommend reticence about a particular subject.

put a name to know or manage to remember what someone or something is called.

someone's name is mud: *see* MUD.

something has your name on it you are destined or particularly suited to receive or experience a specified thing.

take someone's name in vain: *see* VAIN.

to name (but) a few giving only these as examples, even though more could be cited.

1996 *Mail on Sunday* A choice of sundried tomato bread, honey and walnut knots, dill and sesame knots, peppercorn rolls and croissants to name but a few.

what's in a name? names are arbitrary labels.

ℹ This phrase comes from Shakespeare's *Romeo and Juliet*: 'What's in a name? that which we call a rose By any other name would smell as sweet'.

you name it whatever you can think of (used to express the extent or variety of something). informal

2013 *Mac Observer* It's a crowd sourced stuff discovery service where people point Uncrate to all manner of—well—stuff. Cars, food, clothes, toys, you name it.

nana

do (*or* lose) your nana lose your temper. Australian

off your nana mentally deranged. Australian

ℹ *Nana* in these idioms is probably short for *banana*; compare with **go bananas** *at* BANANA.

nap

go nap ❶ win all the matches or games in a series. ❷ risk everything in one attempt.

not go nap on not be too keen on; not care much for. Australian informal

ℹ *Nap* is the name of a card game resembling whist in which a player attempts to take all five tricks. Its original name was *Napoleon*.

napping

catch someone napping (of an action or event) find someone off guard and unprepared to respond. informal

nappy

nappy brain a state of befuddlement supposedly suffered by parents of a new baby. informal

narrow

the straight and narrow: *see* STRAIGHT.

nasty

cheap and nasty: *see* CHEAP.

a nasty taste in the mouth: *see* **a bad taste in the mouth** *at* TASTE.

a nasty piece (*or* bit) of work an unpleasant or untrustworthy person. informal

something nasty in the woodshed: *see* WOODSHED.

nation

one nation a nation not divided by social inequality.

ℹ *One nation* was a political slogan of the 1990s, associated especially with the debate between the right and left wings of the British Conservative Party. It had its origins in the notion of the gulf between the 'Two Nations' of rich and poor, which Benjamin Disraeli referred to in his novel *Sybil* (1845) and which formed the basis of his vision of Tory democracy.

native

go native (of a person living away from their own country or region) abandon their own culture, customs, or way of life and adopt those of the country or region they are living in.

naturally

do what comes naturally engage in sexual intercourse. informal euphemistic

nature

call of nature used euphemistically to refer to a need to urinate or defecate.

get (*or* go) back to nature return to the type of life (regarded as being more in tune with nature) that existed before the development of complex industrial societies.

in the nature of things inevitable or inevitably.

> **2002** *Economist* The IMF sometimes makes mistakes. It is in the nature of things: the Fund practises battlefield medicine.

in a state of nature ❶ in an uncivilized or uncultivated state. ❷ totally naked. ❸ (in Christian theology) in a morally unregenerate condition, unredeemed by divine grace.

nature red in tooth and claw: *see* RED.

the nature of the beast the inherent or essential quality or character of something, which cannot be changed and must be accepted. informal

second nature: *see* SECOND.

your better nature the good side of your character; your capacity for tolerance, generosity, or sympathy.

> **2013 Eric S. Raymond** *Armed & Dangerous* Never appeal to a man's 'better nature'. He may not have one. Invoking his self-interest gives you more leverage.

naughty

naughty bits the parts of a person's body connected with sexual activity or attraction, especially their genitalia. informal humorous

naughty but nice reprehensible but irresistible. informal

> ℹ The expression, which often carries a sexual innuendo, was popularized in Britain especially as an advertising slogan for cream cakes in the 1970s.

navel

contemplate your navel spend time complacently considering yourself or your own interests; concentrate on one issue at the expense of a wider view.

near

as near as dammit: *see* DAMMIT.

near the knuckle: *see* KNUCKLE.

near the mark: *see* MARK.

a near thing: *see* **a close thing** *at* THING.

so near and yet so far a rueful comment on a situation in which you have narrowly failed to achieve an aim.

nearest

your nearest and dearest your close friends and relatives.

neat

neat as a new pin: *see* PIN.

necessary

a necessary evil something that is undesirable but must be accepted.

> **1997** *Internet World* Advertising may be a necessary evil. After all, someone has to support Internet ventures.

necessity

make a virtue of necessity: *see* VIRTUE.

neck

albatross round someone's neck: *see* ALBATROSS.

break your neck to do something exert yourself to the utmost to achieve something. informal

breathe down someone's neck: *see* BREATHE.

dead from the neck up: *see* DEAD.

get (*or* catch) it in the neck be severely criticized or punished. informal

have the (brass) neck to do something have the impudence or nerve to do something. informal

a millstone round your neck: *see* MILLSTONE.

neck and crop ❶ totally; altogether. ❷ (in cricket, with reference to a batsman being bowled out) comprehensively, emphatically.

ⓘ A 'crop' in this context is part of a bird's gullet.

❶ **1981 Ruth Rendell** *Best Man to Die* I knew a family—six children in that case there were—they got evicted neck and crop just because they cracked a drainpipe.

❷ **2005** *Guardian* Absolutely magnificent stuff from Stephen Harmison—a wonderful slower ball that bowled Michael Clarke neck and crop.

neck and neck level in a race, competition, or comparison.

ⓘ This phrase, together with **win by a neck** below, originally developed with reference to horse racing. A *neck* is the length of the head and neck of a horse as a measure of its lead in a race.

2014 *Daily Telegraph* Labour now has its smallest lead since December 2011, when the two parties were neck and neck on 38 per cent, according to ComRes.

neck or nothing risking everything on success.

1934 Leslie Charteris *The Saint Intervenes* In broad daylight, there was no chance of further concealment; and it was neck or nothing at that point.

neck of the woods a particular small geographical area or community.

ⓘ *Neck* in the sense of 'narrow strip of woodland' is recorded from the late 18th century.

2013 *New Statesman* In this (rural Scottish) neck of the woods, that season has less to do with shopping malls lit up like the QE2 from mid-October than with fetching in wood for the stove.

a pain in the neck: *see* PAIN.

put your neck on the block: *see* **put your head on the block** *at* BLOCK.

risk your neck: *see* RISK.

save someone's neck: *see* **save someone's skin** *at* SAVE.

stick your neck out risk incurring criticism, anger, or danger by acting or speaking boldly. informal

1969 Bessie Head *When Rain Clouds Gather* Things are so bad that if anyone sticks his neck out for a refugee, he's not likely to get promoted for five years.

up to your neck in ❶ heavily involved in something onerous or unpleasant. ❷ very busy with. informal

win by a neck succeed by a small margin.

wind your neck in: *see* WIND.

Ned Kelly

game as Ned Kelly: *see* GAME.

need

need something like a hole in the head: *see* HOLE.

needle

the eye of a needle: *see* EYE.

get the (dead) needle become very annoyed. British informal

a needle in a haystack something that is almost impossible to find because it is concealed by so many other similar things.

2002 *New York Times Magazine* Terrorists don't fit a consistent profile: you're looking for a needle in a haystack, but the color and shape of the needle keep changing.

sharp as a needle: *see* SHARP.

needs

must needs do something ❶ cannot avoid or help doing something. ❷ foolishly insist on doing something.

needs must sometimes you are forced to take a course of action that you would have preferred to avoid.

ⓘ This is a shortened form of the proverb *needs must when the Devil drives*, which is first found in a work by the medieval author John Lydgate.

neither

neither fish nor fowl (nor good red herring): *see* FISH.

Nellie

sit next to Nellie: *see* SIT.

nelly

not on your nelly certainly not.

ℹ This expression, modelled on the phrase *not on your life*, originated as *not on your Nelly Duff*, which is British rhyming slang for 'puff', meaning 'breath of life'.

nerve

a bag of nerves: *see* BAG.

get on someone's nerves irritate or annoy someone. informal

have nerves of steel not be easily upset or frightened.

live on your nerves (*or* your nerve ends) be extremely anxious or tense.

strain every nerve make every possible effort.

ℹ *Nerve* is used here in an earlier sense of 'tendon or sinew'.

touch (*or* hit) a (raw) nerve provoke a reaction by referring to a sensitive topic.

a war of nerves: *see* WAR.

Nessus

the shirt of Nessus used to refer to a destructive force or influence. literary

ℹ In Greek mythology, Nessus was a centaur killed by Hercules. While dying, Nessus told Deianira, Hercules' wife, that if she ever had cause to doubt her husband's love, she should wrap him in a shirt soaked in Nessus' blood as this would ensure his constancy. Deianira followed these instructions, but the centaur's blood was in fact a powerful poison that corroded Hercules' body and as he tried to remove the shirt chunks of his flesh were ripped away.

1922 Edith Wharton *The Glimpses of the Moon* It was as if a sickness long smouldering in him had broken out and become acute, enveloping him in the Nessus shirt of his memories.

nest

a cuckoo in the nest: *see* CUCKOO.

feather your (own) nest: *see* FEATHER.

fly the nest: *see* FLY.

foul your own nest: *see* FOUL.

a mare's nest: *see* MARE.

nester

empty nester: *see* EMPTY.

net

back of the net used in triumphant acclamation of success. informal

ℹ The underlying scenario is of a footballer scoring an emphatic goal.

2013 *New Musical Express* The footie fans' favourites return for another shot at musical greatness. Back of the net? Not quite.

cast the (*or* your) net search for suitable options or candidates in a specified way.

slip (*or* fall) through the net escape from or be missed by something organized to catch or deal with you.

1977 Margaret Drabble *The Ice Age* Britain is, after all, a welfare state, and not many slip through its net.

surf the net: *see* SURF.

nettle

grasp the nettle: *see* GRASP.

network

the old boy network: *see* OLD.

never

never a dull moment: *see* DULL.

never had it so good: *see* GOOD.

never in your wildest dreams: *see* DREAM.

never mind: *see* MIND.

never-never land an imaginary utopian place or situation.

ℹ This expression is often used with allusion to the imaginary country in J. M. Barrie's *Peter Pan* (1904). The term was used earlier to denote the remote and unpopulated northern part of the Northern Territory and Queensland in Australia (from which, it is implied, a person might never return).

never say die: *see* DIE.

never the twain shall meet: *see* TWAIN.

well I never! (*or* well I never did!) expressing surprise or indignation. informal

you never know: *see* KNOW.

new

a new one on (me, him, etc.) an account, idea, or joke not previously encountered by me, him, etc. informal

what's new? ❶ (used on greeting someone) what's going on? how are you? ❷ used to express the fact that a situation is entirely predictable.

❷ **2002** *The Mad Bull's Blog* Jamaica is 'Prison Break Paradise'! Prisoners escape from jail so often that we have come to expect it as an at least once-a-week occurrence.... Yesterday it was all over the radio that a warder had been beaten, and that a prisoner had escaped! What's new?

ℹ For other idioms containing *new*, see the entry for the main word in the idiom (for example, **the new rock and roll** at ROCK).

Newcastle

coals to Newcastle: *see* COAL.

news

be bad news be a problem or handicap. informal

2003 Gareth Joseph *Big Smoke* He wondered what was in store for him now. Those Biggs brothers were real bad news.

be good news be an asset; be commendable or admirable. informal

be news to be information not previously known to (someone), and perhaps regarded as implausible. informal

2004 *NZine—New Zealand Ezine* This was the first we had heard about it, and indeed it was news to the local community and the Hurunui District Council.

no news is good news without information to the contrary you can assume that all is well. proverb

yesterday's news: *see* YESTERDAY.

newt

pissed as a newt: *see* PISSED.

New York

a New York minute a very short time; a moment. US informal

next

the boy (*or* girl) next door a person or the type of a person perceived as familiar, approachable, and dependable, typically in the context of a romantic partnership.

next in line immediately below the present holder of a position in order of succession.

the next world (according to some religious beliefs) the place where you go after death.

nibs

his nibs a mock title used to refer to a self-important man, especially one who is in authority. informal

1989 Guy Vanderhaege *Homesick* Whatever his nibs prefers. I see that hasn't changed either. He still expects things to be organized to suit him and only him.

nice

make nice (*or* nice-nice) be pleasant or polite to someone, typically in a hypocritical way. informal, chiefly North American

2019 Polly Toynbee *Guardian* Theresa May and Jeremy Corbyn will go on making nice in an agreed charade to persuade the EU that delay could bring a cross-party pact.

naughty but nice: *see* NAUGHTY.

nice as pie: *see* PIE.

a nice little earner: *see* EARNER.

nice one used to express approval. informal

ℹ The expression was propelled into public consciousness by the phrase 'Nice one, Cyril', originally used in a 1972 television advert for Wonderloaf bread and subsequently taken up by Tottenham Hotspur supporters as a chant celebrating the footballer Cyril Knowles. It is often used ironically.

2013 *New Zealand Herald* The other downside is if the phone gets stolen or broken, you're stuck in the overpriced contract for two years with no phone. Nice one.

nice work if you can get it used to express envy of what is perceived to be another person's more favourable situation, especially if they seem to have reached it with little effort. informal

ℹ *Nice work if you can get it* was the title of an Ira Gershwin song from 1937.

no more Mr Nice Guy used to suggest that you will stop being lenient and begin to adopt more severe measures.

nicety

to a nicety precisely.

nick

in — nick in a specified condition. British informal

2010 Jason Fischer *JasoniJournal* The top result is in perfect condition, with a signed letter from the author—asking price about $400.

Mine isn't in perfect nick but it's still got the dust-jacket and everything.

in the nick of time only just in time; just at the critical moment.

ⓘ *Nick* is used here in the sense of 'the precise moment of an occurrence or an event'. This form of the phrase dates from the mid 17th century, but *in the* (*very*) *nick* is recorded from the late 16th century.

1985 Nini Herman *My Kleinian Home* Time and again, when all seemed lost, I somehow won through in the nick of time.

nickel

accept a wooden nickel be fooled or swindled. US

ⓘ A *wooden nickel* is a worthless or counterfeit coin.

not worth a plugged nickel of no value. US

ⓘ A *plugged* coin has had a part removed and the space filled with base material.

1991 R. Hawkey & R. Bingham *Wild Card* If as much as a whisper gets out . . . none of our lives are going to be worth a plugged nickel.

night

the dead of night: *see* DEAD.

lady of the night: *see* LADY.

make a night of it: *see* **make a day of it** *at* DAY.

morning, noon, and night: *see* MORNING.

night and day all the time; constantly.

night of the long knives a treacherous betrayal or ruthless action.

ⓘ *Night of the long knives* is especially associated with the massacre of the Brownshirts on Hitler's orders in 1934. Traditionally, the phrase referred to the legendary massacre of the Britons by Hengist in 472, described by Geoffrey of Monmouth in his *Historia Regum Britanniae*. In Britain it has been particularly used of the occasion in 1962 on which prime minister Harold Macmillan dismissed a third of his cabinet at the same time, of which the Liberal politician Jeremy Thorpe remarked 'Greater love hath no man than this, that he lay down his friends for his life'.

the watches of the night: *see* WATCH

nine

dressed (up) to the nines dressed very smartly or elaborately.

ⓘ This expression may come from the 99th Wiltshire Regiment, a military unit who were noted for their smart appearance.

a nine days' wonder: *see* WONDER.

nine to five typical office hours.

nine times out of ten on nearly every occasion.

on cloud nine: *see* CLOUD.

the whole nine yards everything possible or available. North American informal

ⓘ Numerous attempts have been made to elucidate the origins of the phrase, many outlandish, none successful.

1999 Salman Rushdie *The Ground Beneath Her Feet* Then the lovers throw a party, and what a party! Dancing, wine, the whole nine yards.

ninepence

— as ninepence used in similes expressing high satisfaction. informal

1968 Catherine Aird *Henrietta Who?* A rare old state it was in . . . but your mother . . . had it right as ninepence in next to no time.

2012 *The Register* Top archaeologists are chuffed as ninepence this week to announce that they have unearthed a massive statue . . . which was probably an 'idol' tumbled down by a terrible race of warriors referred to in the Bible.

no more than ninepence in the shilling of low intelligence. dated

ⓘ Since the decimalization of the British coinage, this phrase has gradually fallen out of use, but there are numerous other humorous variations on the theme of someone not possessing their proper share of brains or intelligence, for example **a sandwich short of a picnic** (*see* SANDWICH).

ninepin

go down (*or* drop *or* fall) like ninepins topple or succumb in large numbers.

2000 *Dunoon Observer & Argyllshire Standard* Post Offices and sub-offices have been going down like ninepins for years.

nineteen

talk nineteen to the dozen: *see* TALK.

nineteenth

nineteenth hole the bar in a golf clubhouse, as reached after a standard round of 18 holes. informal humorous

nip

in the nip naked. Irish informal

nip something in the bud suppress or destroy something at an early stage.

❶ This phrase refers to the horticultural practice of pinching out plant buds to prevent the development of shoots or flowers. *Nip* in this sense was used figuratively in the late 16th century, and *nip in the bud* in the early 17th century.

nip and tuck very closely contested; neck and neck.

❶ The phrase, which emerged in the US in the 19th century, probably came from the field of sewing or tailoring.

2002 *Journal of the Illinois State Historical Society* The rough and tumble Senate race is generally regarded as nip and tuck, likely to be decided by a close margin

put in the nips cadge, borrow, or extort money. Australian & New Zealand informal

nit

keep nit keep watch or act as a guard. Australian

❶ *Nit* here is possibly an alteration of *nix*, a warning signal by schoolchildren that a teacher is approaching.

pick nits look for and criticize small or insignificant faults or errors.

❶ The image here is of the painstaking removal of tiny parasitic *nits* (lice or lice eggs) from someone's hair. The phrase originated in the mid 20th century, chiefly in North American usage.

n

no

no can do I am unable to do it (used especially in refusing to comply with a request). informal

no man's land an intermediate or ambiguous area of thought or activity.

❶ This phrase was used literally in the late 16th century for a piece of land without an owner, but it is particularly associated with the terrain between the German trenches and those of the Allied forces in World War I. The figurative use of the phrase dates from the late 19th century.

the noes have it the negative votes are in the majority. Compare with **the ayes have it** (*at* AYE).

no two ways about it: *see* TWO.

not (*or* never) take no for an answer persist in spite of refusals.

no way under no circumstances; not at all. informal

no worries all right; fine. informal

— or no — regardless of the person, thing, or quality specified.

1995 Kazuo Ishiguro *The Unconsoled* I was thinking there's no reason we can't start doing all sorts of things together now, house or no house.

yes and no: *see* YES.

noble

the noble art boxing. chiefly archaic

❶ A fuller version of this phrase is *the noble art* (or *science*) *of self-defence*.

noblesse

noblesse oblige privilege entails responsibility.

❶ The phrase is a direct adoption from French, where it means literally 'noble rank entails responsibility'. It is first recorded in English in 1837. Nancy Mitford's *Noblesse Oblige* (1956) is subtitled 'An enquiry into the identifiable characteristics of the English aristocracy'.

nobody

be nobody's fool: *see* FOOL.

like nobody's business: *see* BUSINESS.

nod

get (*or* give someone or something) the nod ❶ be selected or approved (*or* select or approve someone or something). ❷ get (*or* give someone) a signal or information.

land of Nod: *see* LAND.

a nod's as good as a wink there's no need for further elaboration or explanation.

❶ This is a shortened form of the proverb, dating from the late 18th century, *a nod is as good as a wink to a blind horse*, used to convey that a mere hint or suggestion can be or has been understood. *A nod and a wink* is also used to mean 'a hint or innuendo'.

nod the nut plead guilty to a charge in court. Australian informal

❶ In colloquial terms, *nut* is the head, which is nodded to acknowledge guilt.

on the nod by general agreement and without discussion. British informal

nodding

be on nodding terms know someone slightly.

have a nodding acquaintance with someone or something know someone slightly; know a little about something.

1989 Donnie Radcliffe *Simply Barbara Bush* Their families had lived less than ten miles apart as they were growing up, and their fathers almost certainly had a nodding acquaintance on the golf course.

no-go

a no-go area an area which is dangerous or impossible to enter or to which entry is restricted or forbidden.

ℹ As a noun, *no-go* was first used in the late 19th century in the sense of 'an impracticable situation'. Its use in this phrase, with the sense of 'no entry', is particularly associated with Northern Ireland in the 1970s.

1971 *Guardian* For journalists and others, the Bogside and Creggan estates are 'no-go areas', with the IRA in total effective control.

noise

a big noise: *see* **a big cheese** *at* BIG.

make a noise speak or act in a way designed to attract a lot of attention or publicity.

nonce

for the nonce for the present; temporarily. dated

ℹ *Nonce* came from the Middle English phrase *then anes*, meaning 'the one (purpose)'; the first word came to be misinterpreted as *the*, and the *n* migrated to the second word.

none

be none the wiser: *see* WISER.

none the worse: *see* WORSE.

second to none: *see* SECOND.

will have (*or* want) none of something refuse to accept something (especially with reference to behaviour).

2000 Joe Pemberton *Forever & Ever Amen* It wasn't James's idea to board the *Christina*. He'd told Aunty Mary that it had sunk on the telly but she would have none of it.

non-linear

go non-linear become very excited or angry, especially about a particular obsession. informal

ℹ This expression may have originated as a humorous play on the phrase **go off the rails** (*see* RAIL).

nonsense

make nonsense (*or* a nonsense) of reduce the value of something to a ridiculous degree.

nook

every nook and cranny every part or aspect of something.

noon

morning, noon, and night: *see* MORNING.

noose

put your head in a noose bring about your own downfall.

north

up north to or in the north of a country. informal

nose

by a nose (of a victory) by a very narrow margin.

ℹ In horse racing, *by a nose* is the narrowest margin by which a horse can win.

cannot see further than (the end of) your nose be unwilling or fail to consider different possibilities or to foresee the consequences of your actions.

count noses count people, typically in order to determine the numbers in a vote.

cut off your nose to spite your face disadvantage yourself in the course of trying to disadvantage another.

ℹ This idea was proverbial for self-defeating malice in both medieval Latin and medieval French, and has been found in English since the mid 16th century.

follow your nose: *see* FOLLOW.

get your nose in front manage to achieve a winning or leading position.

get up someone's nose irritate or annoy someone. informal

give someone a bloody nose inflict a resounding defeat on someone.

have a nose for have an instinctive talent for detecting (something).

it's no skin off my nose: *see* SKIN.

keep your nose clean stay out of trouble. informal

keep your nose out of refrain from interfering in someone else's affairs.

keep your nose to the grindstone: *see* GRINDSTONE.

lead someone by the nose: *see* LEAD.

look down your nose at: *see* LOOK.

nose to tail (of vehicles) moving or standing close behind each other, especially in heavy traffic. British

on the nose ❶ to a person's sense of smell. ❷ precisely. informal, chiefly North American ❸ distasteful; offensive. Australian informal

pay through the nose: *see* PAY.

plain as the nose on your face: *see* **plain as day** *at* PLAIN.

poke your nose into: *see* POKE.

powder your nose: *see* POWDER.

put someone's nose out of joint upset or annoy someone. informal

rub someone's nose in something: *see* RUB.

thumb your nose at: *see* THUMB.

turn up your nose at show distaste or contempt for something. informal

under someone's nose (of an action) committed openly and boldly, but without someone noticing or noticing in time to prevent it. informal

with your nose in the air haughtily.

> **2012** *Pop Matters* When landing a well-placed barb, she stands tall, regal, and ramrod straight with her nose in the air.

not

not cricket: *see* CRICKET.

not half: *see* HALF.

not in my back yard expressing an objection to the siting of something regarded as undesirable in your own neighbourhood, with the implication that it would be acceptable elsewhere.

> ⓘ This expression originated in the USA in derogatory references to anti-nuclear campaigners. In Britain it is particularly associated with reports of the then Environment Secretary Nicholas Ridley's opposition in 1988 to housing developments near his own home. More recently, it has been used in association with the siting of housing for refugees and asylum seekers. The phrase has given rise to the acronym *nimby* as a term for someone with these attitudes.

not least: *see* LEAST.

not on your life: *see* LIFE.

note

compare notes: *see* COMPARE.

hit (*or* strike) the right (*or* wrong) note say or do something in exactly the right (*or* wrong) way.

strike (*or* sound) a — note express a feeling or view of a particular kind.

> **2000** *Times* John McCain . . . was expected to strike a hawkish note last night, calling for the upgrading of the Armed Forces.

nothing

be as nothing (compared) to be insignificant in comparison with.

> **2012** *Daily Telegraph* Had Arthur Scargill strolled into Christie's, I'd have seen him off with my gimlet eye. Had Michael Heseltine appeared, Tarzan would have been as nothing to my Jane.

double or nothing: *see* DOUBLE.

have nothing on someone or something ❶ have much less of a particular quality or ability than someone or something; be inferior to someone or something in a particular respect. ❷ (especially of the police) have no incriminating information about someone. informal

> ❶ **2013 Margaret Pomeranz** & **David Stratton** *At the Movies* The comparisons to *Little Miss Sunshine* are there in a way but this movie has nothing on that gem.

know from nothing: *see* KNOW.

like nothing on earth: *see* EARTH.

make nothing of (*or* not make anything of) not understand or decipher.

neck or nothing: *see* NECK.

nothing daunted without having been made fearful or apprehensive.

> ⓘ This use of *nothing* to mean 'not at all' is now archaic and is almost always found either in this phrase or in **nothing loath** below.

> **2012** *Music OMH—Classical & Opera* This production is also remarkable for the casting of the Bevan sisters, Sophie and Mary, as Elvira and Zerlina respectively. Follow that, as they say. Nothing daunted, Garsington embarks on Vivaldi's rarely seen L'Olimpiade on Sunday 3rd.

nothing doing ❶ there is no prospect of success or agreement. ❷ nothing is happening. informal

nothing less than used to express how extreme something is.

1990 Katherine Frank *Emily Brontë* Nothing less than the ultimate feminine destiny of marriage had been within her reach, and Charlotte had almost immediately spurned it.

nothing loath quite willing.

ℹ This expression was used by John Milton in *Paradise Lost*: 'Her hand he seis'd, and to a shadie bank... He led her nothing loath'.

nothing much in it: *see* MUCH.

nothing to it very simple to do. informal

nothing to write home about: *see* WRITE.

on a hiding to nothing: *see* HIDING.

something and nothing: *see* SOMETHING.

stop at nothing: *see* STOP.

sweet nothings words of affection exchanged by lovers.

thanks for nothing: *see* THANKS.

there's nothing (*or* nothing else) for it there's no alternative. British

2002 *Which?* If there's nothing for it other than to get a shiny new appliance, the next question to ask is: 'Where does the old one go?'

think nothing of (it): *see* THINK.

you ain't seen nothing yet there is something even more extreme or impressive in store. informal

ℹ This expression was popularized by Al Jolson's aside in the 1927 film *The Jazz Singer*, 'you ain't heard nuttin' yet' (alluding to the fact that it was the first movie to feature a recorded soundtrack, albeit a fairly limited one).

notice

at short (*or* a moment's) notice with little warning or time for preparation.

put someone on notice (*or* serve notice) warn someone of something about or likely to occur, often in a formal or threatening way.

sit up and take notice: *see* SIT.

now

now or never used to convey urgency and irrevocability.

2013 *Daily Telegraph* The 2017 Referendum will be a 'now or never' moment in our relationship with the European Union. The status quo for the EU is no longer an option.

now you're talking!: *see* TALK.

nowhere

in the middle of nowhere: *see* MIDDLE.

a road to nowhere: *see* ROAD.

nth

to the nth degree to any extent; to the utmost.

ℹ In mathematics, *nth* denotes an unspecified member of a series of numbers or enumerated items.

2000 *International Journal of Advertising* Benetton takes this principle of 'shock value' to its nth degree.

nudge

a nudge and a wink encouragement given secretly or implicitly; covert support.

ℹ Both a *nudge* and a *wink* are covert signs of complicity, with *wink* also having the implication of 'shutting your eyes' to something. The same idea is expressed by *a nod and a wink* (see **a nod's as good as a wink** at NOD).

2011 *CFO: Magazine for Senior Financial Executives* Give banks unlimited access to three-year funding from the European Central Bank and it wouldn't take much more than a nudge and a wink for them to buy the bonds of Europe's troubled peripheral countries instead of having the ECB do the job itself.

nudge nudge (wink wink) used to draw attention to an innuendo, especially a sexual one, in the previous statement. informal

ℹ This expression is a catchphrase from *Monty Python's Flying Circus*, a British television comedy programme.

nuff

nuff said there is no need to say any more.

ℹ *Nuff* is an informal or dialect shortening of *enough*.

nuisance

make a nuisance of yourself cause trouble and annoyance, usually deliberately or avoidably.

number

a back number: *see* BACK.

by numbers following simple instructions identified by numbers; mechanically.

ⓘ This phrase alludes to *painting by numbers*, a painting kit with a canvas on which numbers have been marked to indicate which colour of paint should be applied at which place. US English uses the variant *by the numbers*.

2013 *Daily Telegraph* Jonsson, 46, was also scathing about her former lover, saying he 'made love by numbers' and was devoid of passion.

do a number on treat someone badly, typically by deceiving, humiliating, or criticizing them in a calculated and thorough way. North American informal

have someone's number understand a person's real motives or character and thereby gain some advantage. informal

make your number report your arrival, pay a courtesy call, or report for duty.

ⓘ This expression has nautical origins: when ships *made their number*, they signalled to others the number by which they were registered. The literal sense was first recorded in the mid 19th century, with the figurative extension developing soon afterwards.

public enemy number one: *see* PUBLIC.

someone's or something's days are numbered: *see* DAY.

someone's number is up the time has come when someone is doomed to die or suffer some other disaster or setback. informal

ⓘ This phrase may allude to a lottery number or to the various biblical passages referring to the 'number of your days', i.e. the length of your life, for example in Job 38:21: 'Knowest thou it, because thou wast then born? or because the number of thy days is great?'

take care of (*or* look after) number one be selfishly absorbed in protecting your own person and interests. informal

there's safety in numbers: *see* SAFETY.

without number too many to count.

2013 *Bookforum* Times without number in this book we are treated to an evocation of beautiful houses, elegant clothing, glamorous gatherings.

nut

be nuts about (*or* on) be very enthusiastic about or fond of. informal

1934 Dashiell Hammett *The Thin Man* She told me she had this job with Wynant and he was nuts about her and she was sitting pretty.

do your nut be extremely angry or agitated. British informal

ⓘ In this phrase and in **off your nut** below, *nut* means 'head'.

for nuts even tolerably well. British informal

1934 Angela Thirkell *Wild Strawberries* That Miss Stevenson can't play for nuts.

from soup to nuts: *see* SOUP.

nod the nut: *see* NOD.

nuts and bolts the basic practical details of something. informal

off your nut out of your mind; crazy. informal

take (*or* use) a sledgehammer to crack a nut: *see* SLEDGEHAMMER.

a tough (*or* hard) nut (to crack) someone who is difficult to deal with or hard to beat; a formidable person. informal

nutmeg

a wooden nutmeg a false or fraudulent thing. US

ⓘ A *wooden nutmeg* was a piece of wood shaped to resemble a nutmeg and fraudulently sold as the real thing. This deception was particularly associated with the inhabitants of Connecticut, giving rise to the nickname 'the Nutmeg State'.

nutshell

in a nutshell in the fewest possible words.

ⓘ A *nutshell* is a traditional metaphor for a very small space. It is used by Shakespeare in *Hamlet*: 'I could be bounded in a nutshell, and count myself a king of infinite space, were it not that I have bad dreams'.

nutty

be nutty about like very much. informal

nutty as a fruitcake completely crazy. informal

ⓘ *Nutty* meaning 'mad or crazy' dates from the late 19th century, and this phrase, punning on the sense of 'full of nuts', from the 1930s. *Fruitcake* is also used on its own to mean 'a crazy or eccentric person'.

oak

heart of oak: *see* HEART.

oar

keep both oars in the water maintain a calm equilibrium in your life and affairs.

rest on your oars ❶ cease rowing by leaning on the handles of your oars, thereby lifting them horizontally out of the water. ❷ relax your efforts.

ℹ A US variant of this phrase is *lay on your oars*.

stick (*or* poke *or* put *or* shove) your oar in give an opinion or advice without being asked. informal

2013 Jayne *Our Great Southern Land* Public servants in the Federal Govt couldn't help but stick their oar in and have their tuppence ha'penny worth of drivel by interfering in discussions between the Tasmanian Aboriginal Centre and museums in England regarding the repatriation of Aboriginal remains.

oat

feel your oats feel lively and buoyant. US informal

ℹ Oats are used as feed for horses, making them friskier and more energetic.

get your oats have sexual intercourse. informal

1965 William Dick *A Bunch of Ratbags* I was kissing her excitedly and passionately... Cookie, you're gonna get your oats tonight for sure, I thought to myself.

off your oats lacking an appetite. informal

sow your wild oats go through a period of wild or promiscuous behaviour while young.

ℹ *Wild oats* are weeds found in cornfields which resemble cultivated oats: spending time sowing them would be a foolish or useless activity. The expression has been current since the late 16th century; from the mid 16th to the early 17th century, *wild oat* was also used as a term for a dissolute young man.

object

no object not influencing or restricting choices or decisions.

2013 *New Statesman* There has been ... a cross-party consensus in favour of the project. The result? Money is no object—so a scheme that was costed at £30 billion in 2010 is now estimated at £10 billion more.

the object of the exercise the main point or purpose of an activity.

Occam

Occam's razor the principle that in explaining something no more assumptions should be made than are necessary.

ℹ This principle takes its name from the English philosopher and Franciscan friar William of Occam (*c.*1285–1349): the image is that of the razor cutting away all extraneous assumptions.

occasion

rise to the occasion: *see* RISE.

ocean

a drop in the ocean: *see* DROP.

odd

odd one (*or* man) out ❶ someone or something that is different to the others. ❷ someone who is not able to fit easily or comfortably into a group or society.

odds

ask no odds ask no favours. US

at odds in conflict or at variance.

2014 *Alf Grumble* If 15 per cent of the population—the indigenous bit—are at odds over which Maori flag to fly, what are the chances of a consensus being reached on a national flag?

by all odds certainly. North American

it makes no odds it does not matter. informal, chiefly British

ℹ This phrase and **what's the odds** below come from an earlier use of *odds* to mean 'difference in advantage or effect'.

lay (*or* give) odds ❶ offer a bet with odds favourable to the other person betting. ❷ be very sure about something.

ⓘ The opposite of *lay odds* in sense 1 is *take odds* which means 'offer a bet with odds unfavourable to the other person betting'.

odds and ends miscellaneous articles and remnants.

ⓘ A racier alternative formulation is *odds and sods*.

over the odds above what is generally considered acceptable, especially for a price. British

shout the odds: *see* SHOUT.

what's the odds? what does it matter? informal

odour

be in good (*or* bad) odour with someone be in (*or* out of) favour with someone.

odour of sanctity ❶ a state of holiness. ❷ sanctimoniousness. derogatory

ⓘ This expression is a translation of the French idiom *odeur de sainteté*. It refers to a sweet or balsamic odour which was reputedly emitted by the bodies of saints at or after death, and which was regarded as evidence of their sanctity.

off

off and on intermittently; now and then.

off and running making good progress.

offence

a hanging offence: *see* HANGING.

office

a bad day at the office: *see* BAD.

good offices help and support, often given by exercising your influence.

2012 *Apollo Magazine* After it had been confiscated by the Nazis as 'decadent' in 1937 . . . , it was returned to the collection through the good offices of Curt Valentin . . . in 1949.

just another day at the office boring routine.

2013 *New Zealand Herald* I enjoy having to roll up my sleeves and have a go at a multitude of tasks that you may or may not know much about—there is certainly none of that 'just another day at the office' tedium.

the usual offices a toilet. euphemistic

offing

in the offing nearby; likely to happen or appear soon.

ⓘ This expression originated as a nautical term for a distance offshore, beyond a harbour or anchoring ground. It has been used figuratively since the late 18th century.

oil

banana oil: *see* BANANA.

burn the midnight oil: *see* BURN.

good oil: *see* GOOD.

oil someone's palm: *see* **grease someone's palm** *at* GREASE.

no oil painting not very attractive. British informal

oil and water two elements, factors, or people that do not agree or blend together.

ⓘ Water and oil are two liquid substances that repel each other and cannot be mixed together.

oil the wheels: *see* **grease the wheels** *at* GREASE.

pour oil on troubled waters: *see* POUR.

strike oil: *see* STRIKE.

ointment

a fly in the ointment: *see* FLY.

old

any old how in no particular order.

come the old soldier: *see* SOLDIER.

for old times' sake: *see* SAKE.

make old bones live to an advanced age.

money for old rope: *see* MONEY.

of the old school traditional or old-fashioned.

2012 *Manchester Music* The lad has a presence about him, he's an entertainer of the old school despite being about 20.

the old Adam: *see* ADAM.

old as the hills: *see* **ancient as the hills** *at* HILL.

the old boy network mutual assistance, especially preferment in employment, shown among those with a shared social and educational background.

an old chestnut: *see* CHESTNUT.

Old Dart England. Australian & New Zealand

ⓘ *Dart* originated as a variant form of *dirt*, as in *pay dirt*.

the old days a period in the past, often seen as significantly different from the present, especially noticeably better or worse.

old enough to be someone's father (*or* mother) of a much greater age than someone. informal

> **2013** *DVD Verdict* Naturally, she's smitten with this guy who's dead broke, has no prospects, talks about nothing besides himself, and is old enough to be her father.

the Old Firm (in Scotland) a name for Celtic and Rangers Football Clubs, either singly or collectively.

an old flame: *see* FLAME.

old hat used to refer to something considered passé and therefore banal or uninteresting. informal

an old head on young shoulders a mature or responsible attitude in a younger person.

an old one a familiar joke.

the old pals act used humorously to imply that someone is using a position of influence to help their friends. British informal

the old school tie the attitudes of group loyalty and traditionalism associated with wearing the tie of a particular public school. British

old Spanish customs: *see* SPANISH.

old trout: *see* TROUT.

an old wives' tale a widely held traditional belief that is now thought to be unscientific or incorrect.

> ℹ The phrase (and its earlier variant *old wives' fable*) is recorded from the early 16th century, with the earliest example being from Tyndale's translation of the Bible.

play Old Harry with: *see* **play the devil with** *at* DEVIL.

same old, same old: *see* SAME.

there's no fool like an old fool: *see* FOOL.

you can't teach an old dog new tricks: *see* DOG.

oldest

the oldest profession: *see* PROFESSION.

oldie

golden oldie: *see* GOLDEN.

olive

hold out (*or* offer) an olive branch offer a token of peace or goodwill.

> ℹ A branch of an olive tree is an emblem of peace. In the Bible, it was the token brought by a dove to Noah to indicate that God's anger was assuaged and that the flood had abated (Genesis 8:11).

Oliver

a Roland for an Oliver: *see* ROLAND.

omega

alpha and omega: *see* ALPHA.

on

be on about talk about tediously and at length. British informal

be on at someone nag or grumble at someone. British informal

be on to someone be close to discovering the truth about an illegal or undesirable activity that someone is engaging in. informal

be on to something have an idea or information that is likely to lead to an important discovery. informal

it's not on it's impractical or unacceptable. informal

on and off intermittently; now and then.

on it drinking heavily. Australian informal

on side supporting or part of the same team as someone else.

> **2001** *Daily Telegraph* In Oman, the policy of getting the local population on side was taken further, with the rebels who fought for the communists progressively being turned to fight against them.

what are you on? said to express incredulity at someone's behaviour, with the implication that they must be under the influence of drugs. informal

you're on said by way of accepting a challenge or bet. informal

once

once a —, always a — a person cannot change their fundamental nature.

> **1993 Margaret Atwood** *The Robber Bride* She was once a Catholic . . . and once a Catholic, always a Catholic, according to her mother.

once and for all (*or* once for all) now and for the last time; finally.

once and future denoting someone or something that is eternal, enduring, or constant.

ℹ This expression comes from T. H. White's *The Once and Future King* (1958), a series of novels about the Arthurian legends.

once bitten, twice shy a bad experience makes you wary of the same thing happening again.

ℹ This expression dates from the late 19th century. A variant common in the USA is *once burned, twice shy*.

once in a blue moon: *see* BLUE.

once (*or* every once) in a while from time to time; occasionally.

1989 Annie Dillard *The Writing Life* Every once in a while Rahm saw a peephole in the clouds and buzzed over for a look.

once upon a time: *see* TIME.

one

be in a minority of one: *see* MINORITY.

from day one: *see* DAY.

get something in one understand or succeed in guessing something immediately. informal

have one too many: *see* MANY.

(just) one of those things: *see* THING.

an old one: *see* OLD.

someone's one and only someone's one true love. informal

one and the same: *see* SAME.

one fine day: *see* FINE.

one for the road: *see* ROAD.

one in the eye for: *see* EYE.

one nation: *see* NATION.

one on one (*or* one to one) denoting or referring to a situation in which two parties come into direct contact, opposition, or correspondence.

2014 *CNN transcripts* But when it was just one on one, me talking with one of my students with my undivided attention and theirs, those were the moments that meant the most to me as well as them.

the one that got away something desirable that has eluded capture.

ℹ This phrase comes from the angler's traditional way of relating the story of a large fish that has managed to escape after almost being caught: 'you should have seen the one that got away'.

public enemy number one: *see* PUBLIC.

a right one: *see* RIGHT.

rolled into one: *see* ROLLED.

take care of number one: *see* NUMBER.

there's one born every minute: *see* BORN.

tie one on: *see* TIE.

with one eye on: *see* EYE.

one-horse

one-horse race a contest in which one candidate or competitor is clearly superior to all the others and seems certain to win.

2001 *PC Gamer* It's been looking increasingly like a one-horse race in recent times: nVidia have gone steaming ahead.

one-horse town a small town with few and poor facilities. informal

one-trick

one-trick pony (*or* horse) someone or something specializing in only one area, having only one talent, or of limited ability. chiefly US

2005 *DVD Verdict* Joan Collins . . . may be a one-trick pony (she's been playing nothing but variations on her Alexis Carrington for the past twenty years), but what a trick it is.

onion

know your onions be fully knowledgeable about something. informal

ℹ *Onions* is perhaps short for rhyming slang *onion rings*, meaning 'things'. The phrase dates from the 1920s.

only

the only game in town: *see* GAME.

someone's one and only: *see* ONE.

open

be open with speak frankly to; conceal nothing from.

an open book: *see* **a closed book** *at* CLOSED.

the heavens opened: *see* HEAVEN.

in (*or* into) the open ❶ out of doors; not under cover. ❷ not subject to concealment or obfuscation; made public.

keep open house provide general hospitality.

1950 Elizabeth Goudge *Gentian Hill* All well-to-do Devon farmhouses keep open house on Christmas Eve.

open-and-shut (of a case or argument) admitting no doubt or dispute; straightforward and conclusive.

open the door to: *see* DOOR.

open someone's eyes: *see* EYE.

open sesame a marvellous or irresistible means of achieving access to what would normally be inaccessible.

ⓘ In the tale of Ali Baba and the Forty Thieves in the *Arabian Nights*, the door of the robbers' cave was made to open by uttering this magic formula.

open up a can of worms: *see* CAN.

open your shoulders (in sport) give free play to the muscles of the shoulders in making a vigorous stroke.

2008 *Times of India* Montanes held his opening serve in the fourth, but it was a lost cause as Federer opened his shoulders once again to grab the final break he needed two games later.

push at an open door: *see* PUSH.

with your eyes open (*or* with open eyes): *see* EYE.

with open arms: *see* ARM.

opener

for openers to start with; first of all. informal

opium

the opium of the people (*or* masses) something regarded as inducing a false and unrealistic sense of contentment among people.

ⓘ This idiom is a translation of the German phrase *Opium des Volks*, used by Karl Marx in 1844 in reference to religion.

opportunity

opportunity knocks a chance of success occurs.

ⓘ This expression comes from the proverb *opportunity never knocks twice at any man's door* or *opportunity knocks but once*. The form of the saying with *opportunity* dates from the late 19th century, but *fortune* was used in the early 19th century and a version of the saying is recorded in medieval French. It reached a wider audience as the title of an ITV talent show (1956–78) hosted by Hughie Green.

option

keep (*or* leave) your options open avoid committing yourself.

2013 *Business Insider* The committee made few changes to the statement and appears willing to keep its options open at upcoming meetings.

soft option: *see* SOFT.

orange

all Lombard Street to a China orange: *see* LOMBARD.

apples and oranges: *see* APPLE.

squeeze (*or* suck) an orange take all that is profitable out of something.

orbit

into orbit into a state of heightened activity, performance, anger, or excitement. informal

1988 Candia McWilliam *A Case of Knives* I am a greedy girl, not merely swayed but waltzed into orbit by appearances.

orchard

marble orchard: *see* MARBLE.

order

be just what the doctor ordered: *see* DOCTOR.

in apple-pie order: *see* APPLE PIE.

in short order: *see* SHORT.

marching orders: *see* MARCH.

of the first order: *see* FIRST.

the order of the day ❶ the prevailing state of things. ❷ something that is required or recommended.

❷ **2014** *Daily Telegraph* The decree is meant to be a deterrent. In no way should there be the use of force, and utmost restraint will be the order of the day.

orders are orders commands must be obeyed, however much you may disagree with them.

out of order ❶ not in normal sequence. ❷ (of a machine) not working. ❸ (of behaviour) improper or unacceptable. informal

pecking order: *see* PECKING.

a tall order: *see* TALL.

other

have other fish to fry: *see* FISH.

how the other half lives used to express or allude to the way of life of a different group in society, especially a wealthier one. British informal

the other side of the coin: *see* COIN.

the other thing an unexpressed alternative. British dated, chiefly humorous

the other woman the lover of a married or similarly attached man.

pull the other one: *see* PULL.

significant other: *see* SIGNIFICANT.

out

at outs at variance or enmity.

ℹ A North American variant of this expression is *on the outs*.

1997 A. Sivanandran *When Memory Dies* Now the land had been taken from him . . . He was at outs with the world.

get out more: *see* GET.

go out like a light: *see* LIGHT.

out and about (of a person, especially after an illness) engaging in normal activity.

out and away by far.

out at elbows: *see* ELBOW.

out cold: *see* COLD.

O

out for having your interest or effort directed to; intent on.

out for the count: *see* COUNT.

out-Herod Herod: *see* HEROD.

out of the box: *see* BOX.

out of countenance: *see* COUNTENANCE.

be out of here be making a hasty departure. informal

2005 *Yorkshire Post Today* When the Customs officers saw this they approached him and identified themselves by shouting 'Customs and Excise' but as they did, the defendant was heard to say 'I'm out of here' and he ran off after locking both vehicles.

out of it ❶ not used or included in something. ❷ astray or distant from the centre or heart of anything. ❸ extremely drunk or under the influence of drugs. informal

out of order: *see* ORDER.

out of pocket: *see* POCKET.

out of sight, out of mind: *see* SIGHT.

out of your gourd: *see* GOURD.

out on your ear: *see* EAR.

out to lunch crazy; insane. informal

out there weird, offbeat, 'way out'; not mainstream. slang

1995 *Melody Maker* All the tracks on this record are very Derrick Carter and he has his own sound. It's really out there.

out with someone or something an exhortation to expel or dismiss someone or something unwanted.

out with it say what you are thinking.

1993 Margaret Atwood *The Robber Bride* She would be so squirrelly with desire—out with it, *lust*, capital L, the best of the Seven Deadlies—that she'd scarcely be able to sit still.

outdoors

the great outdoors the open air; outdoor life. informal

outside

get outside of eat or drink (something). informal

1981 Sam McAughtry *Belfast Stories* We'll get outside of a feed of bacon and egg and black pudding.

on the outside looking in (of a person) excluded from a group or activity.

oven

have a bun in the oven: *see* BUN.

over

all over bar the shouting: *see* SHOUTING.

over and done with completely finished.

over the counter: *see* COUNTER.

over the hill: *see* HILL.

overboard

go overboard ❶ be highly enthusiastic. ❷ behave immoderately; go too far.

ℹ The idea behind this idiom is that of recklessly jumping over the side of a ship into the water.

throw something overboard abandon or discard something.

ℹ The idea here is that something thrown over the side of a ship is lost forever.

overdrive

Mexican overdrive: *see* MEXICAN.

over-egg

over-egg the pudding (*or* cake) go too far in embellishing, exaggerating, or doing something.

ⓘ Excessive quantities of egg in a pudding could either make it too rich or cause it not to set or cook correctly.

2011 *Pop Matters* The combination of rich dialect and elaborate descriptions is to overegg the pudding, and . . . the unceasing pace of this formula page after page is akin to serving up bowl after bowl of it.

overplay

overplay your hand spoil your chance of success through excessive confidence in your position.

ⓘ In a card game, if you overplay your hand, you play a hand on the basis of an overestimate of your likelihood of winning.

overshoot

overshoot (*or* overstep) the mark go beyond what is intended or proper; go too far.

owe

owe someone one feel indebted to someone. informal

1990 Paul Auster *The Music of Chance* 'I guess I owe you one,' Floyd said, patting Nashe's back in an awkward show of gratitude.

someone or something owes you a living used to express disapproval of someone who expects to receive financial support or other benefits without doing any work.

own

as if you own the place in an overbearing or self-important manner. informal

be your own man (*or* woman *or* person) act independently and with confidence.

come into its (*or* your) own become fully effective, used, or recognized.

do your own thing: *see* THING.

get your own back take action in retaliation for a wrongdoing or insult. British informal

hold your own retain a position of strength in a challenging situation; not be defeated or weakened.

1953 Margaret Kennedy *Troy Chimneys* A young man so gifted may hold his own very well.

in your own sweet time (*or* way): *see* SWEET.

in your own time: *see* TIME.

on your own head be it: *see* HEAD.

score an own goal: *see* GOAL.

stand on your own (two) feet: *see* STAND.

oyster

the world is your oyster: *see* WORLD.

P

mind your Ps and Qs: *see* MIND.

pace

at a snail's pace: *see* SNAIL.

change of pace a change from what you are used to. chiefly North American

force the pace: *see* FORCE.

off the pace behind the leader or leading group in a race or contest.

put someone or something through their paces make someone or something demonstrate their qualities or abilities.

set the pace ❶ start a race as the fastest. ❷ lead the way in doing or achieving something.

stand (*or* stay) the pace be able to keep up with another or others.

pack

go to the pack deteriorate; go to pieces. Australian & New Zealand informal

> **1980 Frank Moorhouse** *Days of Wine and Rage* All the places overseas where the British have pulled out are going to the pack.

the joker in the pack: *see* JOKER.

pack your bag (*or* bags) put your belongings in a bag or suitcase in preparation for your imminent departure.

pack heat carry a gun. North American informal

pack it in stop what you are doing. informal

pack a punch ❶ be capable of hitting with skill or force. ❷ have a powerful effect.

pack drill

no names, no pack drill: *see* NAME.

packed

packed like sardines: *see* SARDINE.

packet

cop a packet: *see* COP.

packing

send someone packing make someone leave in an abrupt or peremptory way. informal

paddle

paddle your own canoe be independent and self-sufficient. informal

> ℹ This expression has been in figurative use from the early 19th century: it was the title of a popular song by Sarah T. Bolton in 1854.

page

on the same page (of two or more people) in agreement. US

page three girl a model whose nude or semi-nude photograph appears as part of a regular series in a tabloid newspaper.

> ℹ This sort of photograph featured on page three of the British tabloid newspaper *The Sun* until 2015.

paid

put paid to stop abruptly; destroy. informal

pain

feel no pain be insensible from drinking alcohol. informal

no pain, no gain suffering is necessary in order to achieve something.

> ℹ There has been a proverbial association between *pain* and *gain* since at least the late 16th century, and 'No Paines, no Gaines' was the title of a 1648 poem by Robert Herrick. The modern form, which dates from the 1980s, probably originated as a slogan used in fitness classes.
>
> **2009** *SeoBook* You could charge $1 each for votes, making them have a real economic cost. Such moves would clear out a big chunk of the current Sphinn audience, but no pain no gain.

a pain in the neck an annoying or tedious person or thing. informal

> ℹ There are a number of vulgar slang alternatives to *neck* in this idiom, such as *a pain in the arse* or, in the USA, *ass*.

paint

like watching paint dry (of an activity or experience) extremely boring.

not as black as you are painted: *see* BLACK.

paint the Forth Bridge used to indicate that a task can never be completed.

> ⓘ The steel structure of the Forth Railway Bridge in Scotland has required continuous repainting: it is so long that once the painters reach one end, they have to begin again at the other.

paint the town red go out and enjoy yourself flamboyantly. informal

paint yourself into a corner leave yourself no means of escape or room to manoeuvre.

painting

no oil painting: *see* OIL.

pair

another pair of shoes: *see* SHOE.

I have only got one pair of hands used to deflect further demands for you to do work when you are already extremely busy.

pair of hands a person seen in terms of their participation in a task.

pal

the old pals act: *see* OLD.

pale

beyond the pale outside the bounds of acceptable behaviour.

> ⓘ A *pale* (from Latin *palus* meaning 'a stake') is a pointed wooden post used with others to form a fence; from this it came to refer to any fenced enclosure. So, in literal use, *beyond the pale* meant the area beyond a fence. The term *Pale* was applied to various territories under English control and especially to the area of Ireland under English jurisdiction before the 16th century. The earliest reference (1547) to the *Pale* in Ireland as such draws the contrast between the English Pale and the 'wyld Irysh': the area *beyond the pale* would have been regarded as dangerous and uncivilized by the English.

pale into insignificance lose importance or value.

palm

cross someone's palm with silver: *see* CROSS.

grease someone's palm: *see* GREASE.

have (*or* hold) someone in the palm of your hand have someone under your control or influence.

an itching palm: *see* ITCHING.

pan

flash in the pan: *see* FLASH.

go down the pan reach a stage of abject failure or uselessness.

> **2011** *Spiked Magazine* As the conference kicked off, and as the world economy continued to shake and the Euro continued to go down the pan, the key issue was Tory leader David Cameron's use of sexist language.

pancake

flat as a pancake completely flat.

Pandora

a Pandora's box a process that once begun generates many complicated problems.

> ⓘ In Greek mythology, Pandora was the first mortal woman. One story recounts that she was created by Zeus and sent to earth with a box or jar of evils in revenge for the fact that Prometheus had disobediently given the gift of fire to the earth. She let all the evils out of the container to infect the earth; only hope remained to ease the lot of humankind. In another account, the box contained all the blessings of the gods which, with the exception of hope, escaped and were lost when the box was opened.

> **2003** *Times of Zambia* Though the case was withdrawn, the revelations that the butler had made in court have opened another pandoras box of marital scandals involving the prince and princess.

panic

panic stations a state of alarm or emergency. British informal

> ⓘ The usage is facetiously based on **action stations** (*at* ACTION) and **battle stations** (*at* BATTLE).

press (*or* push *or* hit) the panic button respond to a situation by panicking or taking emergency measures. informal

> ⓘ A *panic button* is a security device which can be used to raise the alarm in an emergency.

pants

beat the pants off: *see* BEAT.

by the seat of your pants by instinct rather than logic or knowledge. informal

ⓘ This expression was first used by pilots in the mid 20th century, in the form *fly by the seat of your pants*, meaning 'fly a plane by relying on human judgement rather than navigational instruments'.

1977 Martin Walker *National Front* Mussolini had governed by the seat of his pants, guided in part by his early Socialism, in part by his . . . bombastic nationalism.

catch someone with their pants (*or* trousers) down catch someone in an unprepared state or sexually compromising situation. informal

have ants in your pants: *see* ANT.

a kick in the pants: *see* KICK.

scare (*or* bore etc.) the pants off someone make someone extremely scared, bored, etc. informal

wearing (*or* in) short pants very young. informal

ⓘ A little boy was traditionally dressed in shorts before attaining a certain age, when he would be allowed to wear long trousers.

paper

make the papers be written about or given attention as news.

not worth the paper it is written on (of an agreement, promise, etc.) of no value or validity whatsoever.

on paper ❶ in writing. ❷ in theory rather than in reality.

paper over the cracks disguise problems or divisions rather than trying to solve them.

ⓘ The phrase is a translation of a German expression used by the statesman Otto von Bismarck in a letter of 1865, and early uses refer to this.

a paper tiger an apparently dangerous but actually ineffectual person or thing.

ⓘ This expression became well known in the West from its use by Mao Zedong, the Chinese Communist leader. In an interview in 1946, he expressed the view that 'all reactionaries are paper tigers'.

2013 *Business Insider* The problem that he finds himself in and has placed us in is that if he does not take action now after making these statements, then we become a paper tiger to the rest of the world.

send in your papers resign, especially (of an officer in the armed services) resign your commission. dated

paper bag

someone couldn't — their way out of a paper bag a person is completely unable to do something, either through ineptitude or weakness. informal

2003 *Atlanta Journal & Constitution* Last time I looked, the United Nations couldn't fight its way out of a paper bag.

par

above par ❶ at a premium. ❷ better than average.

ⓘ *Above par* is a stock exchange idiom. In this and the following idioms, *par* is the Latin for 'equal'.

at par at face value.

below (*or* under) par ❶ at a discount. ❷ worse than usual, often in relation to a person's health.

ⓘ As a golfing term, *under par* means 'better than the average score': *see* **par for the course** below.

on a par with equal in importance or quality to; on an equal level with.

2000 *Daily Telegraph* The listing puts cinemas on a par with cathedrals in the pantheon of English architecture

par for the course what is normal or expected in any given circumstances.

ⓘ In golf, *par* is the number of strokes that a first-class player would normally require to get round a particular course.

up to par at an expected or usual level or quality.

1989 Randall Kenan *A Visitation of Spirits* Why not him? Did he not look okay? Did he smell bad? Have bad breath? Were his clothes not up to par?

parade

rain on someone's parade: *see* RAIN.

parapet

put your head above the parapet: *see* HEAD.

parcel

pass the parcel a situation in which movement or exchange takes place, but no one gains any advantage.

ℹ *Pass the parcel* is the name of a children's game in which a parcel is passed round to the accompaniment of music. When the music stops, the child holding the parcel is allowed to open it.

2010 *Guardian* Cameron may talk of fixing broken politics, but Clegg has shown us how—stop Labour and the Tories playing pass the parcel with government, and allow a wider political spectrum to have their voices heard.

pardon

pardon my French: *see* **excuse my French** *at* FRENCH.

pare

pare something to the bone: *see* **cut something to the bone** *at* BONE.

parenthesis

in parenthesis as a digression or afterthought.

park

a walk in the park: *see* WALK.

parrot

sick as a parrot: *see* SICK.

part

be art and part of: *see* ART.

be part and parcel of be an essential feature or element of.

ℹ Both *part* and *parcel* ultimately come from Latin *pars* meaning 'part' and in this phrase they have virtually identical senses. The phrase is first recorded in mid-16th-century legal parlance; it is now used in general contexts to emphasize that the item mentioned is absolutely integral to the whole.

2002 *Sunday Mail* (Brisbane) Within a lifetime, man had landed on the moon and air travel became part and parcel of modern life.

look the part: *see* LOOK.

a man of (many) parts a man showing great ability in many different areas.

part brass rags with: *see* RAG.

part company ❶ (of two or more people) cease to be together; go in different directions. ❷ (of two or more parties) cease to associate with each other, usually as the result of a disagreement.

part of the furniture: *see* FURNITURE.

take something in good part: *see* GOOD.

particular

a London particular: *see* LONDON.

parting

a (*or* the) parting of the ways a point at which two people must separate or at which a decision must be taken.

ℹ This phrase has its origins in Ezekiel 21:21: 'the king of Babylon stood at the parting of the way, at the head of the two ways'.

party

bring something to the party: *see* **bring something to the table** *at* TABLE.

the life and soul of the party: *see* LIFE.

party animal a sociable person who enjoys parties. informal

the party's over a period of success, good fortune, or happiness has come to an end. informal

2011 *Motley Fool* This is going to be an enormous credit crunch. The party is over for the United States. We cannot continue borrowing to live beyond our means.

p

pass

come (*or* bring) to pass happen (or cause to happen). chiefly literary

make a pass at make an amorous or sexual advance to.

pass go successfully complete the first stage of an undertaking.

ℹ The phrase comes from the name of a manoeuvre in the board game Monopoly.

2007 *DVD Verdict* The worst thing (story-wise, anyway) is that because the film just wants to pass go and collect, its resolution is incredibly unsatisfying.

pass by on the other side avoid having anything to do with something that should demand your attention or concern.

ℹ This expression refers to the parable of the good Samaritan, recounted in Luke 10. A man travelling from Jerusalem to Jericho was attacked and robbed during the course of his journey. He was left lying by the road and the first two people who saw him 'passed by on the other side' of the road. It was the third traveller, the Samaritan (a man from Samaria) who helped him.

pass water urinate. dated, euphemistic

sell the pass betray a cause. British

ⓘ As in **head someone off at the pass** (*see* HEAD), *pass* is here used in the sense of a narrow route through mountains, viewed as a strategic point in time of war. *Selling the pass* was supplying information to the enemy that would enable them to circumvent or otherwise get through the obstacle (*turn the pass*). In the mid 19th century it was considered to be an Irish expression meaning 'betray your fellow countrymen by selling information to the authorities'.

2009 *Guardian My eye* was caught by an anguished attack by the Times religious affairs commentator Ruth Gledhill against Rowan Williams for ... selling the pass on gay rights and women in the Anglican church.

ⓘ For other idioms containing *pass*, see the entry for the main word in the idiom (for example, **pass the buck** at BUCK).

passage

a bird of passage: *see* BIRD.

passage of (*or* at) arms a fight or dispute.

rite of passage: *see* RITE.

a rough passage: *see* ROUGH.

work your passage work in return for a free place on a voyage.

past

a blast from the past: *see* BLAST.

not put it past someone believe someone to be psychologically capable of doing something, especially something you consider wrong or rash.

past it too old to be of any use or any good at anything. informal

past its sell-by date: *see* SELL-BY DATE.

run something past someone: *see* RUN.

pasture

(fresh fields and) pastures new a place or activity regarded as offering new opportunities.

ⓘ The expression is a slightly garbled version of a line from Milton's poem *Lycidas* (1637): 'Tomorrow to fresh woods and pastures new'.

put someone out to pasture force someone to retire.

pat

have something off (*or* down) pat have something memorized perfectly.

on your pat on your own. Australian informal

ⓘ This expression is from rhyming slang, *Pat Malone* meaning 'alone'.

pat someone on the back express approval of or admiration for someone.

stand pat stick stubbornly to your opinion or decision. chiefly North American

ⓘ In the card games poker and blackjack, *standing pat* involves retaining your hand as dealt, without drawing other cards.

patch

not a patch on greatly inferior to. British informal

1991 Mavis Nicholson *Martha Jane & Me* We thought the uniform of our soldiers was 'pathetic', not a patch on the American soldiers' uniform.

a purple patch: *see* PURPLE.

path

beat a path to someone's door: *see* BEAT.

lead someone up the garden path: *see* GARDEN.

the path of least resistance: *see* **the line of least resistance** *at* RESISTANCE.

the primrose path: *see* PRIMROSE.

patter

the patter of tiny feet used to refer to the expectation of the birth of a baby.

2003 *Belfast News Letter* Not quite the patter of tiny feet but the charge of a whole football team of little bairns.

Paul

rob Peter to pay Paul: *see* ROB.

pause

give pause to someone (*or* give someone pause (for thought)) cause someone to think carefully or hesitate before doing something.

pave

pave the way for create the circumstances to enable something to happen or be done.

pavement

pound the pavement: *see* POUND.

pay

above your pay grade ❶ above your level of professional responsibility. ❷ beyond your sphere of knowledge or influence.

> ❷ **2003** *Washington Times* Predicting the future of mankind is above my pay-grade.

the deuce to pay: *see* DEUCE.

the devil to pay: *see* DEVIL.

it (always) pays to — it produces good results to do a particular thing.

> **2014** *New Zealand Herald* Should Labour win this year's election, the package will be implemented progressively, the first stage not commencing until April 2016. It pays to read the fine print.

pay someone back in their own coin: *see* COIN.

pay a call go to the lavatory. dated, euphemistic

pay court to: *see* COURT.

pay its way (of an enterprise) earn enough to cover its costs.

pay lip service to something: *see* LIP.

pay the piper pay the cost of an enterprise. informal

> ⓘ This expression comes from the proverb *he who pays the piper calls the tune*, and is used with the implication that the person who has paid expects to be in control of whatever happens.

pay your respects make a polite visit to someone.

> ⓘ A similar expression is *pay your last respects*, meaning 'show respect towards a dead person by attending their funeral'.

pay through the nose pay much more than a fair price. informal

> **1998** *Country Life* We pay a lot of money for a fairly ordinary garment in order to advertise a name that is only well-known because we pay through the nose for the huge advertising budget.

pay your way meet all your expenses out of your own pocket.

rob Peter to pay Paul: *see* ROB.

there will be hell to pay: *see* HELL.

you pays your money and you takes your choice used to convey that there is little to choose between one alternative and another.

> ⓘ Both *pays* and *takes* are non-standard, colloquial forms, retained from the original version of the saying in a *Punch* joke of 1846.

pea

like peas (*or* like as two peas) in a pod so similar as to be indistinguishable or nearly so.

peace

hold your peace remain silent about something.

keep the peace refrain or prevent others from disturbing civil order.

no peace for the wicked: *see* WICKED.

peach

a peach of a — a particularly excellent or desirable thing of the kind specified. informal

> ⓘ *Peach* has been used since the mid 18th century as a colloquial term for an attractive young woman and more generally since the mid 19th century for anything of exceptional quality.

> **2012** *DVD Verdict* Survivors are scrambling down to the basement. There, they find Mickey, the building superintendent and a real peach of a guy, who has stocked the place with goods for just this very reason.

peaches and cream (of the complexion) of a cream colour with downy pink cheeks.

pearl

cast (*or* throw) pearls before swine give or offer valuable things to people who do not appreciate them.

> ⓘ This expression is a quotation from Matthew 7:6: 'Give not that which is holy unto the dogs, neither cast ye your pearls before swine, lest they trample them under their feet, and turn again and rend you'.

pearly

pearly whites a person's teeth. British informal

pear-shaped

go pear-shaped go wrong. informal

ℹ This phrase originated as RAF slang, as a humorously exaggerated allusion to the shape of an aircraft that has crashed nose first.

2013 *PC World* Even assuming you've hired a genuinely talented contractor to build your app, a lot can go pear-shaped on the road to project completion.

pebble

not the only pebble on the beach not the only person to be considered in a particular situation; (of a former lover) not unique or irreplaceable.

ℹ This expression is from an 1897 song title: *You're Not The Only Pebble On The Beach*. The original context was that of courtship: the way for a man to advance his suit was to make it plain to the woman that 'she's not the only pebble on the beach'. It is now often used more generally as a warning against selfish egocentricity.

pecker

keep your pecker up remain cheerful. British informal

ℹ *Pecker* is probably being used here in the sense of 'a bird's beak', and by extension 'a person's face or expression'. The phrase has been current in British English since the mid 19th century, but it has rather different connotations in the US, where *pecker* is an informal term for *penis*.

pecking

pecking order a hierarchy of status observed among a group of people or animals.

ℹ The expression originally referred literally to chickens and other birds, the more dominant of which in a group get to feed before the others.

pedal

with the pedal to the metal with the accelerator of a car pressed to the floor. North American informal

pedestal

put someone on a pedestal admire someone greatly but uncritically.

peg

off the peg (of clothes) ready-made as opposed to specially made for a particular person. chiefly British

ℹ A North American variant of this phrase is *off the rack*.

a peg to hang something on something used as a pretext or occasion for the discussion or treatment of a wider subject.

a square peg in a round hole a person in a situation unsuited to their abilities or character.

ℹ The variant *a round peg in a square hole* is also found, although it is less common.

take someone down a peg or two make someone realize that they are less talented or important than they think they are.

pegging

be level pegging: *see* LEVEL.

Pelion

pile (*or* heap) Pelion on Ossa add an extra difficulty or task to an already difficult situation or undertaking. literary

ℹ In Greek mythology, the mountain Pelion was held to be the home of the centaurs, and the giants were said to have piled Mounts Olympus and Ossa on its summit in their attempt to reach the heavens and destroy the gods.

pelt

at full pelt with great speed; as fast as possible.

in your pelt naked. Irish informal

pen

dip your pen in gall: *see* DIP.

the pen is mightier than the sword writing is more effective than military power or violence. proverb

penates

lares and penates: *see* LARES.

pencil

lead in your pencil: *see* LEAD.

penny

count the (*or* your) pennies be careful about how much you spend.

ℹ Variants of this expression are *watch the pennies* and, in the USA, *pinch the pennies*.

earn an honest penny: *see* HONEST.

in for a penny, in for a pound used to express someone's intention to see an undertaking through, however much time, effort, or money this entails.

not have a penny to bless yourself with be completely impoverished. dated

ⓘ This expression refers either to the cross on the silver pennies which circulated in England before the reign of Charles II or to the practice of crossing a person's palm with silver for luck.

the penny drops someone finally realizes or understands something. informal, chiefly British

ⓘ The image here is of the operation of a coin-operated slot machine.

not have two pennies to rub together lack money; be very poor.

a penny for your thoughts used to ask someone what they are thinking about. informal

pennies from heaven unexpected benefits, especially financial ones.

ⓘ *Pennies from Heaven* was the title of a 1936 song by the American songwriter Johnny Burke (1908–64). The expression is also well known as the title of a BBC drama series by Dennis Potter in the late 1970s.

penny wise and pound foolish careful and economical in small matters while being wasteful or extravagant in large ones.

a pound to a penny: *see* POUND.

a pretty penny: *see* PRETTY.

spend a penny urinate. British informal

ⓘ At one time coin-operated locks were commonly found on the doors of public lavatories. The phrase is now rather dated.

turn up like a bad penny (of someone or something unwelcome) inevitably reappear or return.

ⓘ A *bad penny* is a counterfeit coin which circulates rapidly as people try to pass it on to someone else.

two (*or* ten) a penny plentiful or easily obtained and consequently of little value. chiefly British

people

the opium of the people: *see* OPIUM.

Peoria

play in Peoria find favour with the average person, especially the average consumer. US informal

ⓘ Peoria is a town in the state of Illinois, and the expression originated in the world of touring theatre, denoting a play that would be commercially successful in an average middlebrow place.

percentage

play the percentages (*or* the percentage game) choose a safe and methodical course of action when calculating the odds in favour of success. informal

perch

knock someone off their perch cause someone to lose a position of superiority or pre-eminence. informal

perfect

practice makes perfect: *see* PRACTICE.

perish

perish the thought used, often ironically, to show that you find a suggestion or idea completely ridiculous or unwelcome. informal

2002 *Daily Telegraph* Perish the thought that sense of occasion is to die.

permitting

— permitting if the specified thing does not prevent you from doing something.

1997 *Classic Boat* Time and weather permitting rudderless sailing is also taught, along with spinnaker and trapezing.

person

be your own person: *see* **be your own man** *at* OWN.

perspective

in (*or* out of) perspective ❶ (of a work of art) showing the right (*or* wrong) relationship between visible objects. ❷ correctly (*or* incorrectly) regarded in terms of relative importance.

petard

hoist with (*or* by) your own petard have your plans to cause trouble for others backfire on you.

ⓘ The phrase is from Shakespeare's *Hamlet*: 'For 'tis the sport to have the enginer Hoist with his own petard'. In former times, a *petard* was a small bomb made of a metal or wooden box filled with explosive powder, while *hoist* here is the past participle of the dialect verb *hoise*, meaning 'lift or remove'.

Peter

rob Peter to pay Paul: *see* ROB.

Philip

appeal from Philip drunk to Philip sober: *see* APPEAL.

phoenix

(rise) like a phoenix from the ashes (emerge) renewed after apparent disaster or destruction.

ⓘ The phoenix was a mythical bird that lived for five or six centuries in the Arabian desert, after this time burning itself on a funeral pyre and rising from the ashes with renewed youth to live through another cycle.

phrase

to coin a phrase: *see* COIN.

turn of phrase a person's particular or characteristic manner of expression.

phut

go phut fail to work properly or at all. informal

ⓘ *Phut* is usually considered to be imitative of a dull, abrupt sound, like that made by a rifle or a machine breaking down. In fact, its earliest recorded use is by Rudyard Kipling in the late 19th century, and the context makes it likely that it was an Anglo-Indian word from Hindi and Urdu *phatnā* meaning 'to burst'.

physical

get physical ❶ become aggressive or violent. ❷ become sexually intimate with someone. ❸ take exercise. informal

physician

physician, heal thyself before attempting to correct others, make sure that you aren't guilty of the same faults yourself. proverb

ⓘ This expression alludes to Luke 4:23: 'And he said unto them, Ye will surely say unto me this proverb, Physician, heal thyself: whatsoever we have heard done in Capernaum, do also here in thy country'.

pick

have a bone to pick with someone: *see* BONE.

pick and choose select only the best or most desirable or appropriate from among a number of alternatives.

pick and mix denoting a method of assembling something by choosing items from among a large variety of different possibilities. British

pick someone's brains (*or* brain) question someone who is better informed about a subject than yourself in order to obtain information. informal

pick something clean completely remove the flesh from a bone or carcass.

pick a fight (*or* quarrel) talk or behave in such a way as to provoke a fight or argument.

pick something out of a hat: *see* HAT.

pick holes in: *see* HOLE.

pick nits: *see* NIT.

pick someone or something to pieces: *see* PIECE.

pick up the pieces restore your life or a situation to a more normal state, typically after a shock or disaster.

pick up the tab: *see* TAB.

pick up the threads resume something that has been interrupted.

pickle

a rod in pickle: *see* ROD.

picnic

be no picnic be difficult or unpleasant. informal

2001 *Rant* While Cheung looks elegant . . . in the 25 different versions of the *cheongsam* dress she wears in the film, moving in the garments was no picnic.

a sandwich (*or* two sandwiches) short of a picnic: *see* SANDWICH.

picture

be (*or* look) a picture (of a person or thing) be beautiful.

get the picture understand a situation. informal

in the picture fully informed about something.

out of the picture no longer involved; irrelevant.

a (*or* the) picture of — the embodiment of a specified state or emotion.

1989 *Woman's Realm* The... little girl looks a picture of health in her blue dungarees and red boots.

pretty as a picture: *see* PRETTY.

pie

easy as pie: *see* EASY.

eat humble pie: *see* HUMBLE.

have a finger in the (*or* in every) pie: *see* FINGER.

nice (*or* sweet) as pie extremely nice or agreeable.

a piece (*or* slice) of the pie a share in an amount of money or business regarded as something to be divided up.

pie in the sky something that is agreeable to contemplate but very unlikely to be realized. informal

ℹ This phrase comes from a 1911 song by the American labour leader Joe Hill (1879–1915), in which a preacher tells a slave: 'Work and pray, live on hay, You'll get pie in the sky when you die'.

piece

all of a piece with something entirely consistent with something.

2010 *Guardian* Who can forget the reaction of Bush to 9/11? Did he raise his head above the parapet and lead? He cowered in a bunker. That was all of a piece with his draft dodging.

bits and pieces: *see* BIT.

give someone a piece of your mind tell someone what you think, especially when you are angry about their behaviour.

go to pieces become so nervous or upset that you are unable to behave or perform normally.

in one piece unharmed or undamaged, especially after a dangerous journey or experience.

a nasty piece of work: *see* NASTY.

pick (*or* pull *or* tear) someone or something to pieces (*or* apart) criticize someone or something in a severe or detailed way.

a piece (*or* slice) of the action ❶ a share in the excitement of something. ❷ a share in the profits from something. informal

pick up the pieces: *see* PICK.

a piece of ass (*or* tail) a woman regarded in sexual terms. vulgar slang

a piece of cake: *see* CAKE.

a piece of piss: *see* PISS.

a piece of work an unpleasant person. informal

ℹ The phrase is a more concise version of a **nasty piece of work** (*see* NASTY).

2013 *Jon's Jail Journal* This man Sheriff Joe Arpaio is a real piece of work. The guards do everything they can to break a man's spirit and mind. There's no sunshine or fresh air.

say your piece give your opinion or a prepared statement.

the villain of the piece: *see* VILLAIN.

pierce

pierce someone's heart affect someone keenly or deeply.

pig

bleed like a (stuck) pig bleed copiously.

bring (*or* drive) your pigs to market succeed in realizing your potential.

in a pig's eye expressing scornful disbelief at a statement. informal, chiefly North American

1987 Evelyn E. Smith *Miss Melville Returns* Under other circumstances I think we could have been friends. 'In a pig's eye,' Susan thought.

make a pig of yourself overeat. informal

2004 *The Food Whore* They were so simple but so good. I couldn't help but make a pig of myself and eat them by the handful.

make a pig's ear of bungle; make a mess of. British informal

ℹ This probably developed with humorous reference to the phrase **make a silk purse out of a sow's ear** (*see* SILK).

on the pig's back living a life of ease and luxury; in a very fortunate situation. Irish informal

pig (*or* piggy) in the middle a person who is placed in an awkward situation between two others. chiefly British

ℹ This expression comes from the name of a game in which two people attempt to throw a ball to each other without a third person in the middle catching it.

a pig in a poke something that is bought or accepted without knowing its value or seeing it first.

ℹ In this expression, a *poke* is a small sack or bag, a sense which is now found chiefly in Scottish use.

2012 *The Age* (Melbourne) Is that what we will get with Abbott? No one knows; yet it seems Australians are preparing to buy a pig in a poke if and when they get offered the chance.

pigs might (*or* can) fly used ironically to express disbelief. chiefly British

ℹ *Pigs fly in the air with their tails forward* was a proverbial saying in the 17th century; the current version dates back to the late 19th century, and the first recorded use is by Lewis Carroll.

1973 Jack Higgins *A Prayer for the Dying* 'Something could come out of that line of enquiry.' 'I know... Pigs might also fly.'

squeal (*or* yell) like a stuck pig squeal or yell loudly and shrilly.

ℹ A *stuck pig* is one that is being butchered by having its throat cut; compare with **bleed like a stuck pig** above.

sweat like a pig sweat profusely. informal

pigeon

be someone's pigeon be someone's concern or affair.

ℹ In this phrase, the word *pigeon* derives from *pidgin*, as in *pidgin English*, the term for a grammatically simplified form of a language used for communication between people not sharing a common language. *Pidgin* itself represents a Chinese alteration of the English word 'business': it entered the English language with the meaning 'occupation' or 'affair(s)' in the early 19th century, emerging from the hybrid of English and other languages used at that time between Europeans and the Chinese for trading purposes.

put (*or* set) the cat among the pigeons: *see* CAT.

pike

come down the pike appear on the scene; come to notice. North American

ℹ In this expression, a *pike* is short for 'turnpike', the American term for a motorway on which a toll is charged.

1983 Ed McClanahan *The Natural Man* He was, in a word, the most *accomplished* personage who'd yet come down the pike in all the days of Harry's ladhood.

pikestaff

plain as a pikestaff: *see* PLAIN.

pile

at the top of the pile: *see* **at the top of the heap** *at* HEAP.

make a (*or* your) pile become rich. informal

ℹ *Pile* here means 'a pile of money'.

pile it on exaggerate for effect. informal

pile on the agony exaggerate or aggravate a bad situation. informal

pile Pelion on Ossa: *see* PELION.

pill

a bitter pill (to swallow) an unpleasant or painful necessity (to accept).

2013 *Daily Telegraph* The feeling of being victimised by one's own government is a bitter pill to swallow.

sugar (*or* sweeten) the pill make an unpleasant or painful necessity more acceptable.

ℹ The image here is of making bitter-tasting medicine more palatable by adding sugar.

pillar

from pillar to post from one place to another in an unceremonious or fruitless manner.

ℹ This expression may have developed with reference to the rebounding of a ball in a real-tennis court. It has been in use in this form since the mid 16th century, though its earlier form, *from post to pillar*, dates back to the early 15th century.

2011 *Financial Times* After almost a year of being bounced from pillar to post and asked to make changes to his product at his own expense, he was told that it failed to tick the right boxes.

a pillar of society a person regarded as a particularly responsible citizen.

ℹ The use of *pillar* to mean 'a person regarded as a mainstay or support for something' is recorded from medieval times; *Pillars of Society* was the English title of an 1888 play by the Norwegian dramatist Henrik Ibsen.

pilot

drop the pilot abandon a trustworthy adviser.

ℹ *Dropping the Pilot* was the caption of a famous cartoon by John Tenniel, published in *Punch* in 1890. It depicted Bismarck's dismissal as German Chancellor by the young Kaiser Wilhelm II. The pilot in this context is someone who directs the course of a ship; the phrase has nothing to do with flying aeroplanes.

pin

clean (*or* neat) as a new pin extremely clean or neat.

for two pins I'd, she'd, etc. — used to indicate that you are very tempted to do something, especially out of annoyance.

2005 *The Press* (York) I even wrote a *Street* script, aged nine, and sent it in. It included a line for Betty Turpin, talking about Annie Walker: 'For two pins I'd knock her block off.'

pin your colours to the mast: *see* COLOURS.

on pins and needles in an agitated state of suspense.

ⓘ *Pins and needles* is the pricking or tingling sensation in a limb recovering from numbness.

you could hear a pin drop there was absolute silence or stillness.

pin your ears back listen carefully.

pinch

at a pinch if necessary; in an emergency.

ⓘ A North American variant of this expression is *in a pinch*.

feel the pinch experience hardship, especially financial.

have to pinch yourself used to convey that a good situation is so surprising that the person involved has to make sure they are not imagining it.

take something with a pinch of salt: *see* SALT.

where the shoe pinches: *see* SHOE.

pineapple

the rough end of the pineapple bad treatment. Australian & New Zealand informal

1981 Peter Barton *Bastards I Have Known* There was no way that I was going to get 'the rough end of the pineapple' from Wally, so I kept out of his way.

pink

be tickled pink: *see* TICKLED.

in the pink in extremely good health and spirits. informal

ⓘ Literally, a *pink* is a plant with sweet-smelling pink or white flowers and slender leaves. In figurative use, *the pink* came to mean 'a supreme example of something', as in Shakespeare's *Romeo and Juliet*: 'I am the very pink of courtesy'. This led to the development of the phrase *in the pink of condition*, of which *in the pink* is a shortened version.

pint

get a quart into a pint pot: *see* QUART.

pip

give someone the pip make someone irritated or depressed. informal, dated

ⓘ *Pip* is a disease of poultry or other birds. In the late 15th century the word came to be used, often humorously, of various ill-defined or minor ailments suffered by people and so the informal sense of 'ill humour' developed.

1976 *Scotsman* I feel it's my duty but I'm not keen. My grandchildren give me the pip.

pip someone at (*or* to) the post defeat someone at the last moment.

ⓘ *Pip* was an informal late 19th-century term for 'defeat', but it is uncertain from which sense of the noun *pip* it derives. *Post* here is the winning post in a race.

squeeze someone until the pips squeak extract the maximum amount of money from someone. British

ⓘ This expression alludes to a speech made in 1918 by the British politician Sir Eric Geddes on the subject of Germany's payment of indemnities after World War I: 'The Germans . . . are going to pay every penny; they are going to be squeezed as a lemon is squeezed—until the pips squeak'. More recently, in the 1970s, the Labour Chancellor Denis Healey declared his intention to squeeze the rich until the pips squeaked.

pipe

pipe your eye weep. dated

put that in your pipe and smoke it used to indicate that someone should accept what has been said, even if it is unwelcome. informal

1947 W. Somerset Maugham *Creatures of Circumstance* I'm engaged to her, so put that in your pipe and smoke it.

pipeline

in the pipeline being planned or developed; about to happen.

1992 *Sunday Times of India* In effect, this means that two bio-pics on Buddha are in the pipeline for release in 1993.

piper

pay the piper: *see* PAY.

piping

piping hot very hot.

ℹ *Piping* describes the hissing or sizzling noise made by food taken very hot from the oven. The phrase was earliest used by Chaucer in *The Miller's Tale*: 'And wafres, pipyng hoot out of the gleede' (*gleede* is an obsolete word for a fire).

2013 Andrew *The 4th Avenue Blues* Dad brought me a chicken pot pie from KFC tonight and I can't wait to dig in. It was piping hot and needed to cool down some.

piss

vulgar slang

be (*or* go) on the piss be engaged in (or go on) a heavy drinking session. British

2000 Alexei Sayle *Barcelona Plates* They'd been on the piss the night before ... so there are thumping hangovers to contend with.

not have a pot to piss in be very poor. North American

a piece of piss a very easy thing to do. British

2018 Mark Billingham *The Killing Habit* 'Tom's got something he needs some help with.' 'It's a piece of piss,' Thorne said, turning to her. 'I swear.'

piss and vinegar aggressive energy.

piss and wind empty talk, bombast.

piss in someone's pocket try to ingratiate yourself with someone.

piss in the wind do something that is ineffective or a waste of time.

take the piss (out of) mock someone or something. British

2004 *Jockey Slut* It's quite anti-establishment from an Irish point of view, the way it takes the piss out of the church.

pissed

vulgar slang

pissed as a newt (*or* fart) very drunk.

pissed off annoyed; irritated.

pisser

pull someone's pisser: *see* PULL.

piste

go off piste depart from a planned or expected course of action.

ℹ A literal 'piste' is a prepared ski run: inexperienced skiers are advised to keep to it.

2013 *Scary Duck* Then you go live and there follows two minutes of terror hoping the presenter (who you cannot see) doesn't go too far off piste with the questions.

pistol

hold a pistol to someone's head: *see* **hold a gun to someone's head** *at* GUN.

pit

be the pits be extremely bad or the worst of its kind. informal

ℹ *Pits* is a mid-20th-century informal term for 'armpits' and has connotations of body odour; from this it came to refer generally to something regarded as bad or unpleasant.

dig a pit for: *see* DIG.

the pit of your (*or* the) stomach an ill-defined region of the lower abdomen seen as the seat of strong feelings, especially anxiety.

pit your wits against: *see* WIT.

pitch

make a pitch make a bid to obtain a contract or other benefit.

ℹ *Pitch* is used here in the late 19th-century colloquial sense of a sales pitch.

queer someone's pitch: *see* QUEER.

pitched

a pitched battle a fierce fight.

ℹ Literally, *a pitched battle* is one fought on a predetermined ground (the *pitch*), as opposed to either a casual skirmish or **a running battle** (*see* RUNNING).

pitchfork

rain pitchforks: *see* **rain cats and dogs** *at* RAIN.

pity

more's the pity used to express regret about a fact that has just been stated. informal

2004 *Noizyblog* The big bottles (no jugs, more's the pity) were coming out thick and fast, as a couple of the boys had had good wins on the fillies.

place

all over the place: *see* ALL.

fall into place (of a series of events or one event in a series) begin to make sense or cohere.

go places ❶ travel. ❷ be increasingly successful. informal

❷ **2010 Bola Agbaje** *Off the Endz* You are a grown man ... who I thought was looking to go places ... and you hang around lowlifes like that.

place in the sun a position of favour or advantage.

ⓘ In 1897 the German Chancellor, Prince Bernhard Von Bülow, made a speech in the Reichstag in which he declared: 'we desire to throw no one into the shade [in East Asia], but we also demand our place in the sun'. As a result, the expression has become associated with German nationalism; it is in fact recorded much earlier and is traceable to the writings of the French mathematician and philosopher Blaise Pascal (1623–62).

2002 *India Weekly* I think it is a great feeling, to know that after years of derision from the world, the Hindi film industry is achieving its place in the sun.

plague

a plague on both your (*or* their) houses used to suggest that each of two opposing sides is equally deserving of censure.

ⓘ The allusion here is to Shakespeare's *Romeo and Juliet*, in which Mercutio, mortally wounded in a brawl between the Montagues and the Capulets, says 'A plague o' both your houses!'

plain

plain as day (*or* the nose on your face) very obvious. informal

plain as a pikestaff ❶ very obvious. ❷ ordinary or unattractive in appearance.

ⓘ This phrase is an alteration of *plain as a packstaff*, which dates from the mid 16th century, the staff being that of a pedlar, on which he rested his pack of goods for sale. The version with *pikestaff* had developed by the end of the 16th century

plain Jane: *see* JANE.

plain sailing used to characterize a process or activity that goes well and is easy and uncomplicated.

plan

plan B: *see* B.

planet

what planet are you on? used to indicate that someone is out of touch with reality. British informal

plank

thick as two planks: *see* THICK.

walk the plank lose your job or position.

ⓘ The image here is of the traditional fate of the victims of pirates: being forced to walk blindfold along a plank over the side of a ship to your death in the sea.

plant

plant dragon's teeth: *see* **sow dragon's teeth** *at* DRAGON.

plate

on a plate with little or no effort from the person concerned. informal

1986 Max Egremont *Dear Shadows* They were handed an asset on a plate and treated it in a totally uncreative way.

on your plate occupying your time or energy. chiefly British

2013 *austie86* According to Austin I'm excited about some of the upcoming work I have on my plate, and it has continued to be a great learning experience.

step up to the plate: *see* STEP.

platinum

go platinum (of a recording) achieve sales meriting a platinum disc.

play

bring something into play cause something to begin to have an effect.

make a play for attempt to attract or attain. informal

2012 *The Register* Now Dell's making a play for the demographic that was lured by Apple, but it's not pushing Windows 8 or even Windows 7 on its hardware.

make (great) play of (*or* with) draw attention to in an ostentatious manner, typically to gain prestige or advantage.

2003 *Herald* (Glasgow) The embarrassing episodes, of which the Australian media made great play.

play with yourself masturbate. euphemistic

play yourself in become accustomed to the circumstances and conditions of a game or activity; get into a rhythm or pattern of working or performing. British

ℹ For other idioms containing *play*, see the entry for the main word in the idiom (for example, **play in Peoria** at PEORIA).

playing

a level playing field: *see* LEVEL.

not playing with a full deck: *see* DECK.

plea

cop a plea: *see* COP.

please

as — as you please used to emphasize the degree to which someone or something possesses the specified quality, especially when this is seen as surprising. informal

1989 Marilynne Robinson *Mother Country* Hearing themselves expound as slick as you please on every great question of the age . . . they must feel that their gift to the world of enlightenment exculpates the racism.

go-as-you-please: *see* GO.

please yourself used to express indifference, especially when someone does not cooperate or behave as expected.

2010 *Irish Times* The songs are all Elton John classics. What more could you want? I bet it's a little bit funny. Get it? Oh, please yourselves. Just go with it.

pretty please: *see* PRETTY.

pleased

pleased as Punch: *see* PUNCH.

pleasure

at Her (*or* His) Majesty's pleasure detained in a British prison.

pledge

sign (*or* take) the pledge make a solemn undertaking to abstain from alcohol.

plenty

there are plenty more fish in the sea: *see* FISH.

plight

plight your troth pledge your word in marriage or betrothal.

ℹ The verb *plight* is now virtually obsolete except in this particular phrase, as is the noun *troth*.

plot

lose the plot ❶ lose your ability to understand what is happening; lose touch with reality. ❷ become uncontrollably angry; lose it. informal

❶ **2013** *Daily Telegraph* As voters switch off from the David v Goliath contests favoured by the leader, both foes and friends are starting to ask whether Mr Miliband has lost the plot.

❷ **2002** *Glamour* On holiday in Spain I lost the plot because I thought my boyfriend was looking at a girl in the distance. I pushed him into a swimming pool.

the plot thickens the situation becomes more difficult and complex.

ℹ This expression comes from *The Rehearsal* (1671), a burlesque drama by George Villiers, 2nd Duke of Buckingham: 'now the plot thickens very much upon us'.

plough

plough a lonely (*or* your own) furrow follow a course of action in which you are isolated or in which you can act independently.

put (*or* set) your hand to the plough embark on a task.

ℹ This phrase alludes to Luke 9:62: 'And Jesus said unto him, No man, having put his hand to the plough, and looking back, is fit for the kingdom of God'.

pluck

pluck a rose (especially of a woman) urinate. dated euphemistic

plug

pull the plug prevent something from happening or continuing; put a stop to something. informal

ℹ This phrase alludes to an older type of lavatory flush which operated by the pulling out of a plug to empty the contents of the pan into the soil pipe.

2013 *Alf Grumble* Pulling the plug on funding for the Healthy Eating Healthy Action programmes and allowing the junk food industry free rein over our young kiwis is . . . creating a sad legacy of increasing diabetes and chronic diseases.

plugged

not worth a plugged nickel: *see* NICKEL.

plughole

go down the plughole be unsuccessful, lost, or wasted. informal

plum

have a plum in your mouth have a rich-sounding voice or affected accent. British

like a ripe plum (*or* ripe plums) used to convey that something can be obtained with little or no effort.

plumb

out of plumb not exactly vertical.

1984 T. Coraghessan Boyle *Budding Prospects* His bad eye, I noticed, had gone crazy. Normally it was just slightly out of plumb.

plumb the depths ❶ reach the extremes of evil or unhappiness. ❷ inquire into the most obscure or secret aspects of something.

plume

borrowed plumes: *see* BORROWED.

plunge

take the plunge commit yourself to a course of action about which you are nervous. informal

plus

plus-minus more or less; roughly. South African

1992 *Weekend Post* He expected 'plus-minus' 1000 files would eventually be forwarded for 'possible prosecution'.

poach

poach on someone's territory encroach on someone else's rights.

poacher

poacher turned gamekeeper someone who now protects the interests which they previously attacked.

pocket

have deep pockets have large financial resources. informal

2014 *New Zealand Herald* Going into a highly competitive market and competing with the big boys with deep pockets is a challenge.

in pocket ❶ having enough money or money to spare; having gained in a transaction. ❷ (of money) gained by someone from a transaction.

in someone's pocket dependent on someone financially and therefore under their influence.

line your pocket: *see* LINE.

live in someone's pocket live very close to someone and be closely involved with them.

out of pocket having lost money in a transaction.

pay out of pocket pay for something with your own money. US

piss in someone's pocket: *see* PISS.

put your hand in your pocket spend or provide your own money.

pod

in pod pregnant. informal, dated

like peas in a pod: *see* PEA.

poetic

poetic justice the fact of experiencing a fitting or deserved retribution for your actions.

ℹ This phrase is from Alexander Pope's satire *The Dunciad*: 'Poetic Justice, with her lifted scale'.

point

armed at all points: *see* ARMED.

brownie point: *see* BROWNIE.

case in point: *see* CASE.

the finer points of: *see* FINER.

not to put too fine a point on it: *see* FINE.

point the bone at: *see* BONE.

point the finger: *see* FINGER.

point of no return the point in a journey or enterprise at which it becomes essential or more practical to continue to the end.

score points (off) deliberately make yourself appear superior to someone else by making clever remarks.

1986 Jack Batten *Judges* There's nothing condescending or cruel about his wit. He doesn't score points off the people in the prisoners' box. He doesn't take advantage.

stretch a point: *see* STRETCH.

take someone's point accept the validity of someone's idea or argument. chiefly British

win on points win by accumulating a series of minor gains rather than by a single dramatic feat.

ⓘ In boxing, a fighter wins *on points* by having the referee and judges award him more points than his opponent, rather than by a knockout.

point-blank

ask (*or* tell, etc.) someone point-blank ask (*or* tell, etc.) someone something very directly, abruptly, or rudely.

ⓘ In its literal sense *point-blank* describes a shot or bullet fired from very close to its target. One of the earliest senses of the noun *blank* was 'the white spot in the centre of a target'.

poison

what's your poison? used to ask someone what they would like to drink. informal

poisoned

a poisoned chalice something that is apparently desirable but likely to be damaging to the person to whom it is given.

2000 *Observer* The growing feeling [is] that pole position has become something of a poisoned chalice, the winner during the past 12 races having come from elsewhere on the starting grid.

poke

be better than a poke in the eye with a sharp stick be welcome or pleasing. humorous

ⓘ Australian English substitutes *a burnt stick* for *a sharp stick*.

a pig in a poke: *see* PIG.

poke borak at: *see* BORAK.

poke fun at tease or make fun of.

1989 Basile Kerblay *Gorbachev's Russia* They used to poke fun at his boorish ways.

poke mullock at: *see* MULLOCK.

poke your bib in: *see* **stick your bib in** *at* BIB.

poke your nose into take an intrusive interest in; pry into. informal

poke your oar in: *see* **stick your oar in** *at* OAR.

take a poke at someone ❶ hit or punch someone. ❷ criticize someone.

pole

the greasy pole: *see* GREASY.

in pole position in an advantageous position.

ⓘ In motor racing, *pole position* is the position on the front row of the starting grid which will allow the driver to take the first bend on the inside. The phrase originated in the 19th century as a horse-racing term, referring to the starting position nearest the inside boundary rails.

poles apart greatly different in nature or opinion.

up the pole ❶ mad. British ❷ in difficulties. British ❸ wildly divergent from the facts or from reasonable behaviour. British ❹ pregnant. chiefly Irish

polish

spit and polish: *see* SPIT.

politics

play politics act for political or personal gain rather than from principle. derogatory

pomp

in your pomp in your period of greatest effectiveness; in your prime.

pomp and circumstance the ceremonial formality surrounding a public event.

ⓘ The expression originates in Shakespeare's *Othello*: 'Farewell . . . the royal banner, and all quality, pride, pomp, and circumstance of glorious war'; but its modern currency owes much to its use as the title of a set of orchestral marches (1901) by Sir Edward Elgar.

pony

dog-and-pony show: *see* DOG.

on Shanks's pony: *see* SHANKS'S PONY.

one-trick pony: *see* ONE-TRICK.

pool

scoop the pool: *see* SCOOP.

poor

poor as a church mouse (*or* as church mice) extremely poor.

ⓘ *Church mice* may be considered to be particularly poor or deprived in that they do not have the opportunity to find pickings from a kitchen or larder.

poor little rich girl (*or* boy) a wealthy young person whose money brings them no contentment (often used as an expression of mock sympathy).

ⓘ 'Poor Little Rich Girl' was the title of a 1925 song by Noel Coward.

the poor man's — an inferior or cheaper substitute for the thing specified.

2009 *One Summer Three Continents* Tomorrow we'll hopefully go on a boat tour of the Ballestas Islands (nicknamed the poor man's Galapagos).

poor relation a person or thing that is considered inferior or subordinate to others of the same type or group.

2003 *Ireland on Sunday* It has always been the poor relation of hurling and football but camogie has now unleashed a new weapon to attract a mass following—old-fashioned sex appeal.

take a poor view of: *see* **take a dim view of** *at* VIEW.

pop

— a pop costing a specified amount per item. informal

2014 *Diamond Geezer* At £12 a pop the exhibition's not cheap, but it is comprehensive and I didn't walk out feeling diddled.

have (*or* take) a pop at ❶ physically attack. ❷ criticize. informal

❷ **2012** *Spiked Magazine* It seems ... that there is no shortage of either the pathetic or the desperate, if the number of those queuing up to have a pop at Cameron et al for being born with mouths that doubled up as silver-cutlery storage units is any indication.

in pop in pawn. British informal

pop someone's cherry: *see* CHERRY.

pop the question propose marriage. British informal

pop your clogs die. British informal

ⓘ The expression, which is first recorded in 1970, probably comes from the idea of 'popping' (i.e. pawning) a person's clogs after they have died (and therefore have no further use for them). It may well also have been influenced, though, by the colloquial *pop off* meaning 'die', which dates back to the mid 18th century.

1998 *Oldie* We cannot claim any credit for foreseeing that Enoch was about to pop his clogs.

pope

Is the Pope (a) Catholic? used to indicate that something is blatantly obvious. informal

poppy

a tall poppy: *see* TALL.

port

any port in a storm in adverse circumstances any source of relief or escape is welcome.

ⓘ Literally, this expression applies to a ship seeking shelter from rough weather; it has been in use as a proverb from at least the mid 18th century.

pose

strike a pose: *see* STRIKE.

posh

too posh to push (of a mother-to-be, especially a well-to-do one) unwilling to suffer the discomfort and indignity of conventional labour, and therefore opting for a caesarean section.

2013 *Daily Telegraph* By choosing a natural birth, showing she is not 'too posh to push', the Duchess of Cambridge has made the right decision.

position

jockey for position: *see* JOCKEY.

possessed

like someone possessed very violently or wildly, as if under the control of an evil spirit.

possum

play possum ❶ pretend to be asleep or unconscious when threatened. ❷ feign ignorance.

ⓘ This expression, recorded from the early 19th century in the USA, refers to the opossum's habit of feigning death when threatened or attacked (*possum* is an informal US term for an opossum).

stir the possum stir up controversy; liven things up. Australian informal

post

ⓘ For idioms containing *post*, see the entry for the main word in the idiom (for example, **from pillar to post** at PILLAR).

postal

go postal go (violently) mad, especially from stress. US informal

ⓘ This expression arose as a result of several recorded cases in the USA in which postal-service employees ran amok and shot colleagues.

2001 *Brill's Content* Those adjustments [i.e. lay-offs] ... were ... accomplished in some instances by having guards escort employees immediately out of the building because ... Johnson ... feared they might 'go postal'.

postcard

answers on a postcard: *see* ANSWER.

posted

keep someone posted keep someone informed of the latest developments.

ⓘ *Posted-up* was a mid-19th-century Americanism meaning 'well informed'.

pot

for the pot for food or cooking.

1992 Doris Lessing *African Laughter* That was when we shot for the pot, just shooting what we needed.

go to pot deteriorate through neglect. informal

ⓘ The idea here is of chopping ingredients up into small pieces before putting them in the pot for cooking, and from this comes the sense 'be ruined or destroyed'.

keep the pot boiling: *see* BOILING.

not have a pot to piss in: *see* PISS.

the pot calling the kettle black someone making criticisms about someone else which could equally well apply to themselves.

2009 *Guardian* In what can only be described as a case of the pot calling the kettle black, HBOS chairman Lord Stevenson described its record in June last year as 'exceptionally bad'.

pot of gold: *see* GOLD.

put someone's pot on inform on a person. Australian & New Zealand informal

shit (*or* piss) or get off the pot used to convey that someone should stop wasting time and get on with something. vulgar slang

2018 Linwood Barclay *A Noise Downstairs* Look, maybe he'll actually do it ... But at some point, we have to—what did my father always like to say?—shit or get off the pot.

take pot luck take a chance that whatever is available will prove to be good or acceptable.

ⓘ The original idea behind the expression is of someone invited to an ordinary everyday family meal which will consist of whatever happens to be in the cooking pot that day.

potato

couch potato: *see* COUCH.

drop someone or something like a hot potato: *see* HOT.

meat and potatoes: *see* MEAT.

small potatoes: *see* SMALL.

Potemkin

a Potemkin village a sham or unreal thing.

ⓘ Count Potemkin (1739–91), a favourite of Empress Catherine II of Russia, reputedly ordered a number of fake villages to be built for the empress's tour of the Crimea in 1787.

pottage

sell something for a mess of pottage sell something valuable and irreplaceable for a ridiculously small amount.

ⓘ This expression comes from the biblical story of Esau, who sold his birthright to his brother Jacob in return for a dish of lentil broth (Genesis 25:29–34). *Mess* is a term for a serving of semi-liquid food and *pottage* is an archaic word for soup or stew. Although the phrase is recorded from 1526 it does not occur in the Authorized Version of the Bible (1611); it does, however, appear in chapter headings in the Bibles of 1537 and 1539 and in the Geneva Bible of 1560.

p

potty

potty mouth a tendency to use foul or obscene language. euphemistic

2005 *West Australian* The problem with a national TV show ... is that the big audience of all ages suppresses a comedian's natural potty mouth.

pound

in for a penny, in for a pound: *see* PENNY.

penny wise and pound foolish: *see* PENNY.

your pound of flesh an amount you are legally entitled to, but which it is morally offensive to demand.

ⓘ The allusion here is to Shylock's bond with the merchant Antonio in Shakespeare's *The Merchant of Venice* and to the former's insistence that he should receive it, even at the cost of Antonio's life.

pound the pavement move about on foot at a steady, regular pace in a town or city.

2013 *Daily Telegraph* Even as Tory activists pounded pavements and knocked on doors across the land, David Cameron and George Osborne were calculating the impossibility of the task.

a pound to a penny it is extremely likely. informal

pour

it never rains but it pours: *see* RAIN.

pour cold water on: *see* COLD.

pour your heart out express your deepest feelings or thoughts in a full and unrestrained way.

2004 Sean Taylor *Within the Legend of a Hero* She wished above all else to pour her heart out to him, to tell her sins without hesitation, to release that which she feared with all her soul.

pour it on progress or work quickly or with all your energy. North American informal

pour oil on troubled waters try to settle a disagreement or dispute with words intended to placate or pacify those involved.

pour on coal increase speed. US informal

ⓘ The metaphor is based on the shovelling of more coal into a locomotive's furnace.

powder

keep your powder dry be ready for action; remain alert for a possible emergency.

ⓘ When his troops were about to cross a river, the English statesman and general Oliver Cromwell (1599–1658) is said to have exhorted them: 'Put your trust in God; but mind to keep your powder dry'. The *powder* referred to is gunpowder.

2005 *Daily Telegraph* The suicide bombers seem to be less active than usual—but that may just be because they are keeping their powder dry for a post-constitution blitz.

powder your nose (of a woman) go to the lavatory.

ⓘ This is an early 20th-century euphemism, which is now rather dated. The term *powder room* has been used since the 1940s to refer to a ladies' toilet in a hotel, restaurant, or similar public building.

1972 L. P. Davies *What Did I Do Tomorrow?* I'll use your bathroom. To powder my nose, as nice girls say.

take a powder depart quickly, especially in order to avoid a difficult situation. North American informal

ⓘ The phrase is a shortening of an earlier *take a run-out powder,* but what the metaphorical underpinnings of that were remains obscure.

2002 *New York Times* Why don't you take a powder, jerk, or how'd you like a knuckle sandwich?

power

the corridors of power: *see* CORRIDOR.

do someone or something a power of good be very beneficial to someone or something. informal

more power to your elbow! said to encourage someone or express approval of their actions. British

power behind the throne a person who exerts authority or influence without having formal status.

the powers that be the authorities.

ⓘ This phrase comes from Romans 13:1: 'the powers that be are ordained of God'.

practice

old Spanish practices: *see* **old Spanish customs** *at* SPANISH.

practice makes perfect regular exercise of an activity or skill is the way to become proficient in it.

practise

practise what you preach do what you advise others to do.

praise

damn someone or something with faint praise: *see* DAMN.

sing the praises of: *see* SING.

pram

throw your toys out of the pram: *see* TOY.

prawn

come the raw prawn: *see* RAW.

prayer

not have a prayer have no chance at all of succeeding at something. informal

2012 *Guardian* His 'hell-raising' lasted about, what, in Hollywood terms, a month? He's a phony and wouldn't have a prayer in the company of Robert Shaw, Peter O'Toole, Oliver Reed, et al.

on a wing and a prayer: *see* WING.

preach

preach to the converted advocate something to people who already share your convictions about its merits or importance.

precautions

take precautions used euphemistically to refer to the use of contraceptives.

1969 Graham Greene *Travels with my Aunt* If we didn't have a child together, it was purely owing to the fact that it was a late love. I took no precautions, none at all.

precious

precious little (*or* few) extremely little (*or* few).

preen

preen yourself on something congratulate or pride yourself on something.

ℹ The implication of the phrase is generally that the self-congratulation is misplaced or unwarranted.

2005 *National Review* The multiculturalism upon which the liberal elite so preens itself would not appear to the extremist to be an expression of generosity and broadmindedness.

pregnant

a pregnant pause (*or* silence) a pause or silence that is laden with meaning or significance.

prejudice

terminate with extreme prejudice: *see* TERMINATE.

premium

at a premium ❶ scarce and in demand. ❷ above the usual or nominal price.

put (*or* place) a premium on regard as or make particularly valuable or important.

2001 Christopher Coker *Humane Warfare* Clearly, a society which puts a premium on individualism is likely to individualise every death—that of its own soldiers as well as the enemy's.

prepare

prepare the ground: *see* GROUND.

presence

make your presence felt have a strong and obvious effect on others or on a situation.

2004 *Casino City Times* Women are really now making their presence felt on the Internet.

presence of mind the ability to remain calm and take quick, sensible action when faced with difficulty or danger.

present

all present and correct used to indicate that not a single thing or person is missing.

1982 Bernard MacLaverty *A Time to Dance* She began to check it, scraping the coins towards her quickly and building them into piles. 'All present and correct,' she said.

(there is) no time like the present used to suggest that something should be done now rather than later.

present company excepted excluding those who are here now.

press

hot off the press: *see* HOT.

press the button: *see* BUTTON.

press something home: *see* **drive something home** *at* HOME.

press (the) flesh (of a celebrity or politician) greet people by shaking hands. informal, chiefly North American

2002 *New Republic* In 1972 he ... barnstormed across the state. 'He loved to get out and press the flesh.'

pretty

come to a pretty pass reach a bad or regrettable state of affairs.

not just a pretty face intelligent as well as attractive.

not a pretty sight not a pleasant spectacle or situation. informal

a pretty kettle of fish: *see* KETTLE.

a pretty penny a large sum of money. informal

1989 Russell Banks *Affliction* You can probably get a pretty penny for that place in a year or two.

pretty as a picture very pretty.

pretty please used as a wheedling form of request. informal

sitting pretty in an advantageous position or situation. informal

prey

fall prey to ❶ be hunted and killed by. ❷ be vulnerable to or overcome by.

price

cheap at the price: *see* CHEAP.

everyone has their price everyone can be won over by money.

a price on someone's head a reward offered for someone's capture or death.

price yourself out of the market be unable to compete commercially.

what price —? ❶ used to ask what has become of something or to suggest that something has or would become worthless. ❷ used to state that something seems unlikely.

❶ **1991** *New Scientist* What price modern medicine with its reliance on the prescription pad, and the slavish devotion to pills?

prick

kick against the pricks: *see* KICK.

prick up your ears ❶ (especially of a horse or dog) make the ears stand erect when on the alert. ❷ (of a person) become suddenly attentive.

a spare prick at a wedding a person who is out of place or has no role in a particular situation. British vulgar slang

pricking

a pricking in your thumbs a premonition or foreboding.

ℹ This expression comes from a speech by the Second Witch in Shakespeare's *Macbeth*: 'By the pricking of my thumbs, Something wicked this way comes'.

pride

pride goes (*or* comes) before a fall if you're too conceited or self-important, something will happen to make you look foolish.

ℹ This phrase is adapted from Proverbs 16:18: 'Pride goeth before destruction, and an haughty spirit before a fall'. *Goes before* here means 'precedes'.

pride of place the most prominent or important position amongst a group of things.

2004 *Gleaner* (Kingston, Jamaica) We are going to put agriculture first ... we are going to give agriculture its pride of place in terms of priority on the economic models.

your pride and joy someone or something of which you are very proud and which is a source of great pleasure.

prime

cut someone off (*or* down) in their prime bring someone's life or career to an abrupt end while they are at the peak of their abilities.

prime the pump stimulate or support the growth or success of something, especially by supplying it with money.

ℹ This phrase is used literally of a mechanical pump into which a small quantity of water needs to be poured before it can begin to function.

1977 Tom Sharpe *The Great Pursuit* Significance is all ... Prime the pump with meaningful hogwash.

primrose

the primrose path the pursuit of pleasure, especially when it is seen to bring disastrous consequences.

ℹ The allusion here is to 'the primrose path of dalliance' to which Ophelia refers in *Hamlet*.

prince

prince (*or* princess) of the blood a man (*or* woman) who is a prince (*or* princess) by right of their royal descent.

print

licence to print money: *see* LICENCE.

small print: *see* SMALL.

prisoner

prisoner of conscience a person detained or imprisoned because of their religious or political beliefs.

ⓘ This phrase is particularly associated with the campaigns of Amnesty International, a human-rights organization.

take no prisoners be ruthlessly aggressive or uncompromising in the pursuit of your objectives.

2012 *New York Times* Beyond nudity and yelling, 'common ingredients in performance art', the reputation of Ann Liv Young is that she is ruthless, shameless and takes no prisoners.

prize

(there are) no prizes for guessing used to convey that something is obvious.

pro

the pros and cons the arguments for and against something; the advantages and disadvantages of something.

ⓘ *Pro* is Latin for 'for'; *con* is an abbreviation of Latin *contra*, meaning 'against'.

problem

no problem used to express agreement or acquiescence.

Procrustean

a Procrustean bed something designed to produce conformity by unnatural or violent means.

ⓘ In Greek mythology, Procrustes was a robber who tied his victims to a bed, either stretching or cutting off their legs in order to to make them fit it.

2013 *Daily Telegraph* Can Europe do anything to help the Spanish, as a generation is maimed on the Procrustean bed of the euro?

prod

on the prod looking for trouble. North American informal

prodigal

prodigal son a person who leaves home to lead a spendthrift and extravagant way of life but later makes a repentant return.

ⓘ The biblical parable of the prodigal son in Luke 15: 11–32 tells the story of the spendthrift younger son of a wealthy man who leaves home and wastes all his money. When he repents of his extravagant ways and returns home, he is joyfully welcomed back by his father. *See also* **kill the fatted calf** *at* FATTED.

production

make a production of do something in an unnecessarily elaborate or complicated way.

profession

the oldest profession the practice of working as a prostitute. humorous

ⓘ Politics or the law is sometimes humorously awarded the status of 'second oldest profession', with the sarcastic implication that their practitioners are as immoral and mercenary as society traditionally considered prostitutes to be.

profile

keep (*or* maintain) a low profile avoid attracting public notice or comment.

program

get with the program do what is expected of you; adopt the prevailing viewpoint. North American informal

ⓘ Often used in the imperative.

prolong

prolong the agony cause a difficult or unpleasant situation to last longer than necessary.

promise

a lick and a promise: *see* LICK.

on a promise (of a person) confidently assured of something, especially of having sexual intercourse with someone. informal

promise someone the moon: *see* MOON.

promises, promises used to indicate that the speaker is sceptical about someone's stated intention to do something. informal

proof

be (the) living proof that: *see* LIVING.

the proof of the pudding is in the eating the real value of something can be judged only from practical experience or results and not from appearance or theory.

ⓘ *Proof* here means 'test', rather than 'verification'. A garbled version of the expression, *the proof is in the pudding*, is often heard, no doubt abbreviated for the sake of convenience.

2011 *Daily Telegraph* Much of what Mr Cameron said is music to my ears. But the proof of the pudding is in the eating. Many obstacles will confront him if he tries to give effect in legislation to things he has said in his speech.

prop

prop up the bar spend a considerable time drinking in a pub. informal

protest

under protest after expressing your objection or reluctance; unwillingly.

2013 *Farmers Weekly Interactive* They . . . said that they would seize the tractor unless a payment of £250 was made. The driver paid under protest.

proud

do someone proud ❶ act in a way that gives someone cause to feel pleased or satisfied. ❷ treat someone with lavish generosity or honour. informal

providence

tempt providence: *see* **tempt fate** *at* TEMPT.

prune

prunes and prisms used to denote a prim and affected speech, look, or manner.

ⓘ In Charles Dickens's *Little Dorrit* (1857), Mrs General advocates speaking this phrase aloud in order to give 'a pretty form to the lips'.

public

go public ❶ become a public company. ❷ reveal details about a previously private concern.

in the public eye the state of being known or of interest to people in general, especially through the media.

public enemy number one ❶ a notorious wanted criminal. ❷ a person or thing regarded as the greatest threat to a group or community.

❷ **2013** CNN transcripts Once upon a time, certain Americans probably considered you [Gloria Steinem] public enemy number one. I mean . . . some perceived you as this threat to societal order.

publish

publish or perish used to refer to an attitude or practice existing within academic institutions, whereby researchers are under pressure to publish material in order to retain their positions or to be deemed successful.

pudding

in the pudding club: *see* **in the club** *at* CLUB.

over-egg the pudding: *see* OVER-EGG.

the proof of the pudding is in the eating: *see* PROOF.

puff

huff and puff: *see* HUFF.

in all your puff in your whole life. informal, chiefly British

pull

on the pull in search of sexual conquests. informal

pull someone's leg deceive someone playfully; tease someone.

pull the other one used to express a suspicion that you are being deceived or teased. British informal

ⓘ A fuller form of this expression is *pull the other one, it's got bells on*. It extends the idea of *pulling someone's leg* (see above).

2004 Andrea Levy *Small Island* 'The Japs have surrendered,' Maxi informed me. 'Pull the other one,' I told him. 'Everyone knows Japs don't surrender.'

pull someone's pisser = pull someone's leg. vulgar slang

pull together cooperate in a task or undertaking.

pull yourself together recover control of your emotions.

ℹ For other idioms containing *pull*, see the entry for the main word in the idiom (for example, **pull your socks up** at SOCK).

pulp

beat (*or* smash) someone to a pulp beat someone severely.

pulse

feel (*or* take) the pulse of ascertain the general mood or opinion of.

ℹ The image here is of literally determining someone's heart rate by feeling and timing the pulsation of an artery.

2009 *Business Week Magazine* This is a stunning indictment of the financial establishment. Business leaders need only take the pulse of their employees, customers, suppliers, and shareholders to reach a similar conclusion.

have your finger on the pulse: *see* FINGER.

pump

all hands to the pumps: *see* HAND.

prime the pump: *see* PRIME.

pump iron exercise with weights. informal

pump ship urinate. euphemistic

ℹ The expression originated in nautical terminology, denoting the pumping of water from a ship's bilges.

punch

beat someone to the punch anticipate or forestall someone's actions.

pack a punch: *see* PACK.

pleased (*or* proud) as Punch feeling great delight or pride.

ℹ This expression alludes to the self-congratulatory glee displayed by the grotesque, hook-nosed Punch, anti-hero of the Punch and Judy puppet show.

pull your punches be less forceful, severe, or violent than you could be.

punch above your weight engage in an activity or contest perceived as being beyond your capacity or abilities.

ℹ This is a metaphor from boxing, in which contests are arranged between opponents of nearly equal weight.

2013 *Keeping Stock* We reckon that it is an excellent aspiration for New Zealand to be seeking a seat on the Security Council. We may be a small country, but on the world stage we punch above our weight.

punch the (time) clock ❶ (of an employee) clock in or out. ❷ be employed in a conventional job with regular hours. North American

punch someone's lights out: *see* LIGHT.

punch your ticket: *see* TICKET.

roll with the punches: *see* ROLL.

punishment

a glutton for punishment: *see* GLUTTON.

punt

take (*or* have) a punt at have a go at; attempt. Australian & New Zealand informal

2001 Louise Voss *To Be Someone* I'm willing to take a chance with you and put out your first record ... Like I said, I'm willing to take a punt on you guys and see how it goes.

pup

sell someone a pup swindle someone, especially by selling them something that is worthless. British informal

ℹ This phrase originated in the early 20th century; the idea behind it is presumably that of dishonestly selling someone a young and inexperienced dog when an older, trained animal had been expected.

1930 W. Somerset Maugham *Cakes and Ale* The public has been sold a pup too often to take unnecessary chances.

purdah

in purdah in seclusion.

ℹ *Purdah* comes from the curtain (*parda*) used in traditional Hindu and Muslim households, especially in the Indian subcontinent, to conceal women from the eyes of strangers. The transferred use of this expression to refer to seclusion generally dates from the 1920s.

1998 *Times* Treasury ministers are, of course, in purdah.

pure

pure and simple and nothing else.

1991 *Alabama Game & Fish* They are bred for waterfowling, pure and simple.

pure as the driven snow completely pure.

ⓘ When used of snow, *driven* means that it has been piled into drifts or made smooth by the wind. The phrase was famously parodied by the actress Tallulah Bankhead in 1947: 'I'm as pure as the driven slush'.

the real Simon Pure: *see* SIMON PURE.

purler

come (*or* go) a purler fall heavily, especially head first.

ⓘ The verb *purl* was in dialect or colloquial use in the mid 19th century in the senses 'turn upside down', 'capsize', or 'go head over heels'.

purple

born in (*or* to) the purple born into a reigning family or privileged class.

ⓘ In ancient times, purple garments were worn only by royal and imperial families because of the rarity and costliness of the dye. *Born in the purple* (rather than *to*) may have specific reference to the fact that Byzantine empresses gave birth in a room in the palace at Constantinople whose walls were lined with the purple stone porphyry. The title 'the Porphyrogenitos' or 'Porphyrogenita' was used for a prince or princess born in this room.

a purple patch an ornate or elaborate passage in a literary composition.

ⓘ This term is a translation of Latin *purpureus pannus*, and comes from the Roman poet Horace's *Ars Poetica*: 'Works of serious purpose and grand promises often have a purple patch or two stitched on, to shine far and wide'.

purpose

accidentally on purpose apparently by accident but in fact intentionally. humorous

at cross purposes: *see* CROSS.

to all intents and purposes: *see* INTENT.

purse

hold the purse strings have control of expenditure.

make a silk purse out of a sow's ear: *see* SILK.

tighten (*or* loosen) the purse strings restrict (or increase) the amount of money available to be spent.

push

at a push if necessary; in an emergency. British

2011 *Hair Today* No more than two of us can comfortably fit in there at a time—three at a push if you don't mind being intimately subjected to the specific perfume he/she may be wearing.

give someone (*or* get) the push (*or* shove) dismiss someone (*or* be dismissed) from a job; reject someone (*or* be rejected) in a relationship. British informal

push at (*or* against) an open door have no difficulty in accomplishing a task; fail to realize how easy something is.

push the boat out: *see* BOAT.

push someone's buttons: *see* BUTTON.

push the envelope: *see* ENVELOPE.

push your luck act rashly or presumptuously on the assumption that you will continue to be successful or in favour. informal

too posh to push: *see* POSH.

when (*or* if) push comes to shove when action must be taken; if the worst comes to the worst. informal

2001 *Financial Director* When push comes to shove, investors are not always impressed with promises of jam tomorrow.

pushing

pushing up the daisies: *see* DAISY.

put

not know where to put yourself feel deeply embarrassed. informal

1986 Robert Sproat *Stunning the Punters* He was begging and pleading with me . . . with tears rolling down his cheeks so I didn't know where to put myself.

put it (*or* yourself) about be sexually promiscuous. British informal

put it there used in the imperative to indicate that the speaker wishes to shake hands with someone in agreement or congratulation. informal

put it to someone make a statement or allegation to someone and challenge them to deny it.

put one over on deceive someone into accepting something false. informal

put something behind you get over a bad experience by distancing yourself from it.

put up or shut up defend or justify yourself or remain silent. informal

2014 *New Zealand Herald* Very soon, Cunliffe is going to have to put up or shut up about the alternative economy he has in mind.

ⓘ For other idioms containing *put*, see the entry for the main word in the idiom (for example, **put paid to** at PAID).

putty

be like putty (*or* wax) in someone's hands be easily manipulated or dominated by someone.

1975 Sam Selvon *Moses Ascending* Bob was there, and I gave him a little bit of crumpet, and afterwards he was like putty in my hands.

up to putty below the required standard; useless. Australian informal

Pyrrhic

Pyrrhic victory a victory gained at too great a cost.

ⓘ Pyrrhus was a king of Epirus, who defeated the Romans at Asculum in 279 BC, but in doing so sustained heavy losses and lost his finest troops.

Pythias

Damon and Pythias: *see* DAMON.

p

q.t.

on the q.t. secretly or secret; without anyone noticing. informal

ⓘ *q.t.* is a humorous abbreviation of *quiet*.

quake

quake in your shoes: *see* **shake in your shoes** *at* SHAKE.

quantity

unknown quantity: *see* UNKNOWN.

quantum

quantum leap a sudden large increase or advance.

ⓘ A literal quantum leap is the abrupt transition of an electron, atom, or molecule from one quantum state to another.

quart

get (*or* fit) a quart into a pint pot attempt to do the impossible, especially when this takes the form of trying to fit something into a space that is too small. British

quarter

a bad quarter of an hour: *see* BAD.

queen

Queen Anne's dead used humorously or ironically to suggest that a piece of supposed 'news' is in fact stale, or more broadly that a person who says something is simply stating the obvious or restating a well-worn or accepted truth. informal

ⓘ The expression is first recorded in 1798, by which time Queen Anne had indeed been dead for 84 years; but there is evidence of an earlier version, 'Queen Elizabeth is dead', from the 1730s.

2005 *Liverpool Daily Echo* 'McFadden's gone past the three French players there', said Lawrenson, who can also tell us that Queen Anne is dead, night follows day and bears defecate in the woods.

take the Queen's shilling: *see* **take the King's shilling** *at* SHILLING.

Queensberry

the Queensberry Rules standard rules of polite or acceptable behaviour.

ⓘ The *Queensberry Rules* are the code of rules which were drawn up in 1867 under the supervision of John Sholto Douglas (1844–1900), ninth Marquis of Queensberry (and persecutor of Oscar Wilde), to govern the sport of boxing in Great Britain.

queer

in Queer Street in difficulty, especially by being in debt. British informal, dated.

ⓘ *Queer Street* was an imaginary street where people in difficulties were supposed to live. The phrase has been used since the early 19th century to indicate various kinds of misfortune, but its predominant use has been to refer to financial difficulty.

1952 Angus Wilson *Hemlock and After* He enjoys a little flutter . . . and if he finds himself in Queer Street now and again, I'm sure no one would grudge him his bit of fun.

a queer fish a person whose behaviour seems strange or unusual. British informal, dated

queer someone's pitch spoil someone's chances of doing something, especially secretly or maliciously. British

ⓘ This phrase originated as 19th-century slang; early examples of its use suggest that the *pitch* referred to is the spot where a street performer stationed themselves or the site of a market trader's stall.

1973 Elizabeth Lemarchand *Let or Hindrance* He's a decent lad . . . he would never have risked queering Wendy's pitch with Eddy.

question

be a question of time be certain to happen sooner or later.

beg the question: *see* BEG.

no questions asked without any enquiries being made, especially ones thought likely to produce incriminating or embarrassing results. informal

pop the question: *see* POP.

the sixty-four thousand dollar question: *see* SIXTY-FOUR.

out of the question too impracticable or unlikely to merit discussion.

queue

jump the queue: *see* JUMP.

quick

be quick off the mark: *see* MARK.

be quick on the uptake: *see* UPTAKE.

cut someone to the quick cause someone deep distress by a hurtful remark or action.

ⓘ *Quick* means an area of flesh that is well supplied with nerves and therefore very sensitive to touch or injury.

quick and dirty makeshift; done or produced hastily. informal, chiefly US

quick as a flash: *see* FLASH.

quick on the draw very fast in acting or reacting.

ⓘ *The draw* is the action of taking a pistol or other weapon from its holster.

a quick one a rapidly consumed alcoholic drink. informal

quid

be quids in be in a position where you have profited or are likely to profit from something. British informal

ⓘ *Quids* 'pounds' is found only in this phrase, the normal plural being *quid*.

not the full quid not very intelligent. Australian & New Zealand informal

ⓘ As an informal term for a pound sterling (or, in former times, a sovereign or guinea) *quid* dates from the late 17th century: its origins are unknown. Compare with **not the full shilling** (*at* SHILLING).

quiet

anything for a quiet life: *see* LIFE.

quiet as a mouse (*or* lamb) (of a person or animal) extremely quiet or docile.

1982 Robertson Davies *The Rebel Angels* I shall be as quiet as a mouse. I'll just tuck my box . . . in this corner, right out of your way.

quiet as the grave: *see* **silent as the grave** *at* GRAVE.

quince

get on someone's quince irritate or exasperate someone. Australian informal

quite

quite the little —: *see* LITTLE

quits

call it quits ❶ agree or acknowledge that terms are now equal, especially on the settlement of a debt. ❷ decide to abandon an activity or venture, especially so as to cut your losses.

ⓘ The origin of the *-s* in *quits* is uncertain: the word may be an abbreviation of the medieval Latin *quittus*, meaning 'discharged', which was used on receipts to indicate that something had been paid for. The phrase is recorded from the late 19th century, but an earlier form, *cry quits*, dates back to the mid 17th century.

double or quits: *see* **double or nothing** *at* DOUBLE.

qui vive

on the qui vive on the alert or lookout.

ⓘ The French expression *qui vive?* (used in English since the late 16th century) means literally '(long) live who?' In former times a sentry would issue this challenge to someone approaching his post so as to ascertain where their allegiance lay.

1976 J. E. Weems *Death Song* They came in groups of four, five, or six—'all on the *qui vive*, apprehensive of treachery, and ready to meet it'.

quote

quote — unquote used parenthetically when speaking to indicate the beginning and end (or just the beginning) of a statement or passage that you are repeating, especially to emphasize the speaker's detachment from or disagreement with the original. informal

Rr

R

the three Rs reading, (w)riting, and (a)rithmetic, regarded as the fundamentals of elementary education.

rabbit

breed like rabbits reproduce prolifically. informal

let the dog see the rabbit: *see* DOG.

like a rabbit in the headlights: *see* HEADLIGHTS.

pull (*or* bring) a rabbit out of the (*or* a) hat used to describe an action that is fortuitous, and may involve sleight of hand or deception.

ℹ The image is of a conjuror producing a live rabbit from a hat as if by magic.

work the rabbit's foot on cheat or trick. US

ℹ A *rabbit's foot* is traditionally carried as a good-luck charm.

race

at the races in a position to compete successfully; in contention. informal

2011 *Daily Telegraph* If you don't have a credible economic policy, you are simply not at the races.

be in the race have a chance of success. Australian & New Zealand informal

1953 T. A. G. Hungerford *Riverslake* 'See that bloke?' He pointed down the road after the vanished car. 'A few years ago he wouldn't have been in the race to own a car like that.'

one-horse race: *see* ONE-HORSE.

a race against time a situation in which someone attempts to do or complete something before a particular time or before something else happens.

rack

go to rack and ruin gradually deteriorate in condition because of neglect; fall into disrepair.

ℹ *Rack* is a variant spelling of the word *wrack*, meaning 'destruction', but it is the standard one in this expression, which has been in use since the late 16th century.

2010 *Guardian* Now that the serfs have been emancipated, the estates are going to rack and ruin. Apparently they want something called 'wages'.

off the rack: *see* **off the peg** *at* PEG.

on the rack suffering intense distress or strain.

rack your brains (*or* brain) make a great effort to think of or remember something.

ℹ A *rack* was a medieval instrument of torture consisting of a frame on which a victim was stretched by turning rollers to which their wrists and ankles were tied. To *rack* someone was to torture them on this device and the image in this idiom is of subjecting one's brains to a similar ordeal in the effort to remember something.

2011 *Guardian* So come on, rack your brains, delve into your record collections (or your iTunes libraries: yes, I've heard how you people operate) and tell us the best songs about gossip.

radar

under (*or* off) the radar avoiding attention or detection.

2018 Isabelle Grey *Wrong Way Home* I need to stay under the radar. I don't want anyone remembering me later and giving the police a description.

raft

a (whole) raft of — a large collection of something.

ℹ *Raft* here is an alteration of a dialect word *raff*, meaning 'a great quantity'.

2004 *Times Literary Supplement* A prolific writer with a raft of books and pamphlets to his credit.

rag

be on the rag be menstruating. informal, chiefly North American

ℹ The expression is based on *rag* in the sense 'sanitary towel'.

chew the rag: *see* **chew the fat** *at* FAT.

(from) rags to riches used to describe a person's rise from a state of extreme poverty to one of great wealth.

2000 Imogen Edwards-Jones *My Canapé Hell* Much was made of his East End roots, his chance discovery on Oxford Street. He was truly a modern day tale of rags to riches.

in your glad rags: *see* GLAD.

lose your rag lose your temper. informal

2004 Sarah Hall *The Electric Michelangelo* Occasionally Cy lost his rag, and yelled at her to shut up.

part brass rags with quarrel and break off a friendship with.

ⓘ This expression is explained in W. P. Drury's short story *The Tadpole of an Archangel* (1898): 'When [sailors] desire to prove the brotherly love . . . with which each inspires the other, it is their . . . custom to keep their brasswork cleaning rags in a joint ragbag. But should relations . . . become strained between them, the bag owner casts forth upon the deck . . . his sometime brother's rags; and with the parting of the brassrags hostilities begin'. The phrase originated as late 19th-century nautical slang.

rag, tag, and bobtail a group of people perceived as disreputable or undesirable.

ⓘ A *bobtail* is a horse or dog with a docked tail, while *rag* and *tag* both express the idea of 'tattered clothes': the phrase literally means 'people in ragged clothes together with their dogs and horses'. The forms *tag, rag, and bobtail*, *ragtag and bobtail*, and *tagrag and bobtail* are also found.

a red rag to a bull: *see* RED.

take the rag off the bush (*or* hedge) surpass everything or everyone. chiefly US

rage

all the rage very popular or fashionable.

ⓘ *Rage* is used here in the sense of a widespread (and often temporary) enthusiasm or fashion.

2014 *New Statesman* After all, weren't valances—or something very like them—all the rage in 18th-century Bavaria?

ragged

run someone ragged exhaust someone by making them undertake a lot of physical activity.

rail

go off the rails begin behaving in a strange, abnormal, or wildly uncontrolled way. informal

2013 *New Zealand Herald* Out of the ring, she's a different person from the troubled teen who was going off the rails in Rotorua.

jump the rails: *see* JUMP.

on the rails ❶ behaving or functioning in a normal or regulated way. informal ❷ (of a racehorse or jockey) in a position on the racetrack nearest the inside fence.

ride the rails: *see* RIDE.

rain

it never rains but it pours misfortunes or difficult situations tend to follow each other in rapid succession or to arrive all at the same time.

rain cats and dogs rain very hard.

ⓘ Despite much speculation, there is no consensus as to the origin of *rain cats and dogs*. Suggestions range from the supernatural (cats being associated with witches who were credited with raising storms, dogs being attendants upon Odin, the Scandinavian storm god) to the down-to-earth (animals in medieval times drowning in flooded streets in times of heavy rain and their bodies being assumed by the credulous to have fallen from the skies). Other versions of the saying are *rain pitchforks* and, in Britain, *rain stair rods*, which date from the early 19th century and mid 20th century respectively, and reflect the shaft-like appearance of heavy rain. *Rain cats and dogs* is first recorded in Jonathan Swift's *Polite Conversation* (1738).

rain on somone's parade prevent someone from enjoying an occasion or event; spoil someone's plans. informal, chiefly North American

(come) rain or shine whether it rains or not; whatever the circumstances.

1994 *BBC Top Gear Magazine* But come rain or shine, there is a torrent of new convertibles about to reach the UK.

right as rain (of a person) perfectly fit and well, especially after a minor illness or accident. informal

2009 Thomas Emson *Skarlet* You'd only suffer tachycardia. Rapid heartbeat. Your blood pressure'd be normal, and you'd be right as rain in a couple of days.

take a rain check said when politely refusing an offer, with the implication that you may take it up at a later date. North American

ⓘ A *rain check* is a ticket given to spectators at US sporting events enabling them to claim a refund of their entrance money or gain admission on another occasion if the event is cancelled because of rain. The rain-check system is mentioned as operating in US sports grounds in the late 19th century; the figurative use of the word dates from the early 20th century.

rainbow

at the end of the rainbow used to refer to something much sought after but impossible to attain.

ⓘ This phrase refers to the story of a crock of gold supposedly to be found by anyone who succeeds in reaching the end of a rainbow.

chase rainbows (*or* a rainbow) pursue an illusory goal.

rainy

a rainy day a possible time of need, usually financial need, in the future.

ⓘ The expression may originate from the days when casual farm labourers needed to save a proportion of their wages 'for a rainy day', i.e. for occasions when bad weather might prevent them from working and earning money.

2002 *New York Times Book Review* The Russian walked out of K.G.B. headquarters with 'insurance against a rainy day'—the K.G.B.'s file on its secret mole inside the F.B.I.

raise

ⓘ For idioms containing *raise,* see the entry for the main word in the idiom (for example, **raise Cain** at CAIN).

rake

rake and scrape be extremely thrifty; scrimp and save. black English

rake over (old) coals (*or* rake over the ashes) revive the memory of a past event which is best forgotten. chiefly British

a rake's progress a progressive deterioration, especially through self-indulgence.

ⓘ A *rake* is a fashionable or wealthy man with dissolute or promiscuous habits. *A Rake's Progress* was the title of a series of engravings by William Hogarth (1697–1764). They depicted the rake's life progressing from wealthy and privileged origins to debt, despair, and death on the gallows.

thin as a rake (of a person or animal) very thin.

ram

ram something home: *see* **drive something home** *at* HOME.

rank

break rank (*or* ranks) ❶ (of soldiers or police officers) fail to remain in line. ❷ fail to maintain solidarity.

close ranks ❶ (of soldiers or police officers) come closer together in a line. ❷ unite in order to defend common interests.

❷ **2014** *Daily Telegraph* The media handling of the affair echoes the attitude of politicians, who, on both left and right, have largely closed ranks and professed outrage at the invasion of the president's privacy.

pull rank take unfair advantage of your seniority or privileged position.

rank and file the ordinary members of an organization as opposed to its leaders.

ⓘ The notion behind the expression is of the 'ranks' and 'files' into which privates and non-commissioned officers form on parade.

rise through (*or* from) the ranks ❶ (of a private or a non-commissioned officer) receive a commission. ❷ advance from a lowly position in an organization by your own efforts.

ransom

hold someone or something to ransom ❶ hold someone prisoner and demand payment for their release. ❷ demand concessions from a person or organization by threatening damaging action.

a king's ransom: *see* KING.

rap

beat the rap escape punishment for or be acquitted of a crime. North American informal

rap someone on (*or* over) the knuckles rebuke or criticize someone.

take the rap be punished or blamed, especially for something that is not your fault or for which others are equally responsible.

ⓘ The late 18th-century use of *rap* to mean 'criticism' or 'rebuke' was extended in early 20th-century American English to include 'a criminal charge' and 'a prison sentence'. Compare with **take the fall** (*at* FALL)

rare

rare as hen's teeth: *see* HEN.

rare bird an exceptional person or thing; a rarity.

ℹ The English expression is a literal translation of the Latin *rara avis*.

2005 *Apollo Magazine* Joseph Southall is that rare bird, an Arts and Crafts painter.

raring

raring to go very keen and eager to make a start. informal

ℹ Historically, *raring* is the present participle of *rare*, an obsolete dialectal variant of the verb *rear*.

raspberry

blow a raspberry make a derisive or contemptuous sound with your lips.

ℹ This expression is from rhyming slang, where *raspberry tart* means a fart.

2010 *Guardian* It would be easier to blow a raspberry at the malign forces of financial markets and the capricious judgments of rating agencies. But rational policymaking must be based in the world as it is, not how we would like it to be.

rat

like a drowned rat: *see* DROWNED.

like a rat up a drainpipe with great and opportunistic speed and vigour. informal

2005 *Scotland on Sunday* Give Bazalgette an opening, and he's in there, like a rat up a drainpipe.

love rat: *see* LOVE.

not give a rat's ass: *see* ASS.

rats deserting a sinking ship people hurrying to get away from an enterprise or organization that is failing. informal

smell a rat: *see* SMELL.

rate

at a rate of knots: *see* KNOT.

ration

come up (*or* be given) with the rations (of a medal) be awarded automatically and without regard to merit. military slang

rattle

rattle someone's cage make someone feel angry or annoyed, usually deliberately. informal

ℹ A humorous comparison is implied between the person annoyed in this way and a dangerous animal taunted by spectators outside its cage.

rattle sabres threaten to take aggressive action.

rattle your dags: *see* DAG.

raw

come the raw prawn attempt to deceive someone. Australian informal

ℹ In Australian English, a stupid person can be referred to as a *prawn*.

1959 Eric Lambert *Glory Thrown In* Don't ever come the raw prawn with Doc, mate. He knows all the lurks.

in the raw ❶ in its true state; not made to seem better or more palatable than it actually is. ❷ (of a person) naked. informal

a raw deal: *see* DEAL.

touch someone on the raw upset someone by referring to a subject about which they are extremely sensitive.

touch a (raw) nerve: *see* NERVE.

ray

ray of sunshine someone or something that brings happiness into the lives of others.

2012 *New Zealand Herald* There was spare money. Sometimes I saved it, sometimes I splurged on a treat. The point is that it was a little ray of sunshine. We all need those.

razor

Occam's razor: *see* OCCAM.

on a razor's edge: *see* **on a knife-edge** *at* KNIFE-EDGE.

razzle

on the razzle out celebrating or enjoying yourself. British informal

reach

reach for the stars: *see* STAR.

read

read between the lines look for or discover a meaning that is hidden or implied rather than explicitly stated.

> **2014** *Daily Telegraph* 'Reading between the lines, I think the Chinese are preparing for the loss of their rover,' said Lutz Richter, a planetary rover specialist with Kayser-Threde, a German aerospace company.

read someone like a book be able to understand someone's thoughts and motives clearly or easily.

read my lips listen carefully (used to emphasize the importance of the speaker's words or the earnestness of their intent). North American informal

> ℹ This expression was most famously used by the US Republican president George Bush in an election campaign pledge in 1988: 'Read my lips: no new taxes'.

read the riot act give someone a strong warning that they must improve their behaviour.

> ℹ The Riot Act was passed by the British government in 1715 in the wake of the Jacobite rebellion of that year and was designed to prevent civil disorder. The Act made it a felony for a group of twelve or more people to refuse to disperse after being ordered to do so and having being read a certain part of the Act by a person in authority. It was not repealed until 1967.

take something as read assume something without the need for further discussion. British

you wouldn't read about it used to express incredulity, disgust, or ruefulness. Australian & New Zealand informal

ready

ready for the off (of a person or vehicle) fully prepared to leave. informal

ready to roll (of a person or machine) fully prepared to start functioning or moving. informal

rough and ready: *see* ROUGH.

real

for real used to assert that something is genuine or is actually the case. North American informal

> **1992 Michael Bishop** *Count Geiger's Blues* The man . . . radiated only bluster and uncertainty. If challenged, he'd run. The other man facing Xavier was for real. He'd fight.

get real! used to convey that an idea or statement is foolish or overly idealistic. informal, chiefly North American

> **1995 Jayne Miller** *Voxpop* You might think living in a garret and starving for your art is wonderful, but get real!

the real deal a thing that is absolutely genuine or authentic; the real thing. informal

the real McCoy: *see* MCCOY.

the real Simon Pure: *see* SIMON PURE.

the real thing a thing that is absolutely genuine or authentic. informal

will the real — please stand up used rhetorically to indicate that the specified person should clarify their position or reveal their true character. informal

> **2012** *Daily Telegraph* From the people who brought you Will the Real Mitt Romney Please Stand Up? comes this riff on Obama's infamous 'you didn't build that' comment.

ream

ream someone's ass (*or* butt) criticize or rebuke someone. North American vulgar slang

reap

reap the harvest (*or* fruits) of suffer the results or consequences of.

reap the whirlwind: *see* WHIRLWIND.

you reap what you sow you eventually have to face up to the consequences of your actions.

> ℹ This proverbial saying exists in various forms. Its biblical source is Galatians 6:7: 'Be not deceived; God is not mocked: for whatsoever a man soweth, that shall he also reap'.

reaper

the Grim Reaper: *see* GRIM.

rear

bring up the rear ❶ be at the very end of a line of people or things. ❷ come last in a race or other contest.

rear its (ugly) head (of an unpleasant matter) emerge; present itself.

rearrange

rearrange someone's face injure or mutilate someone's face by hitting it. informal

reason

a feast of reason: *see* FEAST.

for reasons best known to himself (*or* herself, etc.) used when recounting someone's behaviour to suggest that it is puzzling or perverse. chiefly humorous

rhyme or reason: *see* RHYME.

see reason (*or* sense) realize that you have been wrong and adopt a sensible attitude.

(it) stands to reason it is obvious or logical.

theirs (*or* ours) not to reason why it is not someone's place to question a situation, order, or system.

> ℹ This phrase comes from Tennyson's poem 'The Charge of the Light Brigade' (1854), which describes how, in a notorious incident in the Crimean War, the British cavalry unquestioningly obeyed a suicidal order to ride straight at the Russian guns.

rebel

a rebel without a cause a person who is deeply dissatisfied with society in general but does not have a specific aim to fight for.

> ℹ *Rebel Without A Cause* was the title of a US film starring James Dean, released in 1955.

rebound

on the rebound while still affected by the emotional distress caused by the ending of a romantic or sexual relationship.

receiving

be at (*or* on) the receiving end be subjected to something unpleasant. informal

recharge

recharge your batteries regain your strength and energy by resting and relaxing for a time.

recipe

a recipe for disaster something that is very likely to lead to a bad outcome.

reckoned

a — to be reckoned with (*or* to reckon with) a thing or person of considerable importance or ability that is not to be ignored or underestimated.

> **2014** *DVD Verdict* As a seventh-grader, working on my first creative writing assignment of junior high, I was determined to show my new teacher that I was a force to be reckoned with.

reckoning

day of reckoning: *see* DAY.

record

for the record so that the true facts are recorded or known.

> **1992** *Sun* There was no need to ask if I had gone to the flat. For the record I have never been to the flat. The questions were calculated to make me look bad.

a matter of record something that is established as a fact through being officially recorded.

off the record not made as an official or attributable statement.

> **1990 Charles Allen** *The Savage Wars of Peace* I went to see him very much as somebody going in just to have a chat with him off the record after the interrogation.

on (the) record ❶ used in reference to the making of an official or public statement. ❷ officially measured and noted.

put (*or* set) the record straight give the true version of events that have been reported incorrectly; correct a misapprehension.

rewrite the record books: *see* REWRITE.

red

better dead than red the prospect of nuclear war is preferable to that of a Communist society.

> ℹ This expression was a cold-war slogan; it was reversed by the nuclear disarmament campaigners of the late 1950s as *better red than dead.*

in the red in debt, overdrawn, or losing money.

> ℹ *Red* ink was traditionally used to indicate debit items and balances in accounts. Compare with **in the black** (*at* BLACK).

paint the town red: *see* PAINT.

red as a beetroot (of a person) red-faced, typically through embarrassment.

the red carpet used in reference to privileged treatment of a distinguished visitor.

a red herring something, especially a clue, which is or is intended to be misleading or distracting.

ⓘ This expression derives from the former practice of using the pungent scent of a dried smoked herring to teach hounds to follow a trail (smoked herrings were red in colour as a result of the curing process).

red in tooth and claw involving savage or merciless conflict or competition.

ⓘ This phrase originated as a quotation from Tennyson's 'In Memoriam' (1850): 'Nature, red in tooth and claw'.

2001 *Observer* While there is a 'red in tooth and claw' aspect to this financial sharp end, there is a still larger element in the overclass who do not get their hands quite so dirty.

a red letter day a pleasantly memorable, fortunate, or happy day.

ⓘ In Church calendars, a saint's day or church festival was traditionally distinguished by being written in red letters.

(like) a red rag to a bull an object, utterance, or act which is certain to provoke or anger someone.

ⓘ The colour red was traditionally supposed to provoke a bull, and is the colour of the cape used by matadors in bullfighting.

2013 *New Statesman* There's no doubt that while the phrase 'tuition fees' is like a red rag to a student bull, a capped graduate tax is not.

reds under the bed used during the Cold War with reference to the feared presence and influence of Communist sympathizers in a society.

see red become very angry suddenly. informal

red-light

red-light district an area of a city or town containing many brothels, strip clubs, and other sex businesses.

redress

redress the balance take action to restore equality in a situation.

reduced

in reduced circumstances used euphemistically to refer to the state of being poor after being relatively wealthy.

reed

a broken reed a weak or ineffectual person, especially one on whose support it is foolish to rely.

ⓘ This expression refers to Isaiah 36:6, in which the Assyrian general taunts King Hezekiah of Jerusalem about the latter's supposed ally, the Egyptian pharaoh: 'Lo, thou trusteth in the staff of this broken reed, on Egypt'.

reel

off the reel ❶ without stopping, in an uninterrupted course or succession. ❷ immediately, quickly.

❶ **1946** *Sunday Dispatch* Won six races off the reel for Wembley Cubs.

rein

(a) free rein complete freedom of action or expression.

ⓘ The image here is of loosening grip on the reins of a horse, allowing it to choose its own course and pace, in contrast to the greater control implied by the next idiom.

keep a tight rein on exercise strict control over; allow little freedom to.

reinvent

reinvent the wheel waste a great deal of time or effort in creating something that already exists or doing something that has already been done.

relation

poor relation: *see* POOR.

relieve

relieve your feelings use strong language or vigorous behaviour when annoyed.

religion

get religion be converted to religious belief and practices. informal

remain

it remains to be seen something is not yet known or certain.

2001 *New York Times* It remains to be seen how long the downturn in the economy will last.

republic

banana republic: *see* BANANA.

residence

— in residence a person with a specified occupation (especially an artist or writer) paid to work for a time in a college or other institution.

2002 *Ashmolean Annual Report* Artist in Residence, Sarah Mulhall, demonstrates print-making techniques.

resistance

the line (*or* path) of least resistance an option which avoids difficulty or unpleasantness; the easiest course of action.

resort

in the last resort whatever else happens or is the case; ultimately.

2013 *Independent* 'Every private soldier,' writes Manning, was 'a man in arms fighting desperately for himself, and conscious that, in the last resort, he stood alone.'

respect

pay your respects: *see* PAY.

respecter

be no respecter of persons treat everyone the same, without being influenced by their status or wealth.

ⓘ This expression refers to Acts 10:34: 'God is no respecter of persons'.

rest

and the rest used to assert that something is an understatement. informal, chiefly British

2019 Daisy Coulam *Grantchester* 'How much did you put away?' 'A few whiskies.' 'And the rest!'

give it a rest used to ask someone to stop doing or talking about something that the speaker finds irritating or tedious. informal

lay something to rest soothe and dispel fear, anxiety, grief, and similar unpleasant emotions.

let it rest: *see* **let it drop** *at* DROP.

no rest for the wicked: *see* **no peace for the wicked** *at* WICKED.

rest your case ❶ conclude your presentation of evidence and arguments in a lawsuit. ❷ used humorously to show that you believe you have presented sufficient evidence for your views.

the rest is history: *see* HISTORY.

rest on your laurels: *see* LAURELS.

rest on your oars: *see* OAR.

rest (*or* God rest) his (*or* her) soul used to express a wish that God should grant someone's soul peace.

retreat

beat a hasty retreat: *see* BEAT.

return

many happy returns (of the day) used as a greeting to someone on their birthday

point of no return: *see* POINT.

return the compliment: *see* COMPLIMENT.

return to the charge: *see* CHARGE.

return to the fold: *see* FOLD.

revenge

revenge is a dish best served (*or* eaten) cold vengeance is often more satisfying if it is not exacted immediately. proverb

reverse

the reverse of the medal: *see* MEDAL.

reward

go to your reward die.

ⓘ This euphemistic expression is based on the idea that people receive their just deserts after death.

rewrite

rewrite history select or interpret events from the past in a way that suits your own particular purposes.

rewrite the record books (of a sports player) break a record or several records.

rhyme

rhyme or reason logical explanation or reason.

ribbon

cut a (*or* the) ribbon perform an opening ceremony, usually by formally cutting a ribbon strung across the entrance to a building, road, etc.

cut (*or* tear) something to ribbons ❶ cut (*or* tear) something so badly that only ragged strips remain. ❷ damage something severely.

ribs

stick to your ribs (of food) be very filling.

rich

a bit rich used to refer to something that causes ironic amusement or indignation.

> **2013** *Daily Telegraph* Lord Carey said it was a 'bit rich' to hear Mr Cameron tell religious leaders to face down aggressive secularisation when the Coalition seem to be 'aiding and abetting' such a practice.

crumbs from a rich man's table: *see* CRUMB.

(from) rags to riches: *see* RAG.

poor little rich girl: *see* POOR.

Richard

have had the Richard be irreparably damaged. Australian

> ❶ This expression comes from rhyming slang *Richard the Third*, meaning 'bird'. In the theatre, *get the bird* means 'be booed and hissed at'.

rid

be well rid of be in a better state for having removed or disposed of a troublesome or unwanted person or thing.

riddance

good riddance said to express relief at having got free of a troublesome or unwanted person or thing.

> ❶ Sometimes a fuller form is used: *good riddance to bad rubbish!*

riddle

talk (*or* speak) in riddles express yourself in an ambiguous or puzzling manner.

ride

for the ride for pleasure or interest, rather than any serious purpose.

> **2013** *Daily Telegraph* My mother Elizabeth, an anthropologist, went along for the ride but became absorbed by Tonga's intricate feudal system.

a free ride: *see* FREE.

let something ride take no immediate action over something.

— rides again used to indicate that someone or something has reappeared, especially unexpectedly and with new vigour.

> ❶ The expression arose from a title formula used in Westerns, most notably the 1939 US film *Destry Rides Again*.

> **1941** *Pleasures of Publishing* Our good friend Helen Bower of the Detroit *Free Press* sends us a circular which . . . is headed, 'Blackstone Rides Again', and is an announcement for a new edition of Blackstone's Commentaries.

ride for a fall act in a reckless or arrogant way that invites defeat or failure. informal

> ❶ This phrase originated as a late 19th-century horse-riding expression, meaning to ride a horse, especially in the hunting field, in such a way as to make an accident likely.

ride herd on keep watch over.

> ❶ Literally, this North American expression means 'guard or control a herd of cattle by riding round its edge'.

> **1999** *Coloradoan (Fort Collins)* That, in turn, would detract from his ability to ride herd on Washington special interests, allowing deficits to grow like mushrooms under a rotten log.

ride high be successful.

ride the lightning be executed in the electric chair. US informal

ride your luck: *see* LUCK.

ride off into the sunset achieve a happy conclusion to something.

> ❶ In the closing scenes of westerns, the characters are often seen riding off into the sunset after everything has been resolved satisfactorily.

ride on someone's coat-tails: *see* COAT-TAIL.

ride the pine (*or* bench) (of an athlete) not participate in a game or event, typically because of poor form. North American informal

ride the rails travel by rail, especially without a ticket. North American

ride roughshod over: *see* ROUGHSHOD.

ride shotgun ❶ travel as a guard in the seat next to the driver of a vehicle. ❷ ride in the passenger seat of a vehicle. ❸ act as a protector. chiefly North American

ride a tiger: *see* TIGER.

roller-coaster ride: *see* ROLLER-COASTER.

a rough (*or* easy) ride a difficult (*or* easy) time doing something.

take someone for a ride deceive or cheat someone. informal

rig

(in) full rig (wearing) smart or ceremonial clothes. informal

right

bang to rights (of a criminal) with positive proof of guilt. informal

> ❶ A North American variant of this expression is *dead to rights*.
>
> **1993 G. F. Newman** *Law & Order* He hadn't got the most vital piece of information he needed in order to capture the blaggers bang to rights.

a bit of all right: *see* BIT.

do the right thing marry a woman you have made pregnant in order to avoid a scandal. informal euphemistic

have your heart in the right place: *see* HEART.

in your own right as a result of your own claims, qualifications, or efforts, rather than an association with someone else.

left, right, and centre: *see* LEFT.

might is right: *see* MIGHT.

Mr Right the ideal future husband. informal

put (*or* set) someone right ❶ restore someone to health. ❷ make someone understand the true facts of a situation.

right as rain: *see* RAIN.

right as a trivet: *see* TRIVET.

right enough certainly; undeniably. informal

the right hand doesn't know what the left hand's doing: *see* HAND.

right on used as an expression of strong support, approval, or encouragement. informal

a right one a silly or foolish person. British informal

> **2008** *Guardian* Even expressions of irritation are likely to be abstracted, quasi-philosophical: 'He's a right one, he is.'

the right stuff character traits considered to be prerequisites of manliness, notably courage and resolution.

> ❶ The phrase was popularized as the title of a book (1979) by Tom Wolfe, in which the qualities were attributed to US test pilots, but it existed before then.

right you are used to acknowledge and assent to an instruction or suggestion. informal

see someone right make sure that a person is appropriately rewarded or looked after. British informal

serve someone right: *see* SERVE.

she's (*or* she'll be) right that will be all right; don't worry. Australian informal

somewhere to the right of Genghis Khan holding right-wing views of the most extreme kind.

> ❶ Genghis Khan (1162–1227), the founder of the Mongol empire, is used here as a supreme example of a repressive and tyrannical ruler. The name of the early 5th-century warlord Attila the Hun is sometimes substituted for that of Ghengis Khan in this expression.

too right used to express enthusiastic agreement with a statement. informal

Riley

the life of Riley (*or* Reilly) a luxurious or carefree existence. informal

> ❶ *Reilly* or *Riley* is a common Irish surname. A popular song of the early 20th century entitled 'My Name is Kelly' included the lines 'Faith and my name is Kelly Michael Kelly, But I'm living the life of Reilly just the same'. This may be the source of the expression but it is possible that the songwriter, H. Pease, was drawing on an already existing catchphrase.
>
> **1978** *Daily Telegraph* It is simply not true that we don't pay tax and are living the life of Riley.

Rimmon

bow down in the house of Rimmon: *see* BOW.

rinderpest

before (*or* since) the rinderpest a long time ago (*or* for a very long time). South African

> ❶ *Rinderpest* is a contagious viral disease of cattle that periodically caused heavy losses in much of Africa. The 1896 epidemic was so devastating that it was treated as a historical landmark, so giving rise to this expression.

ring

the brass ring: *see* BRASS.

hold the ring monitor a dispute or conflict without becoming involved in it.

> **2011** *CNN transcripts* He's looking to the military to restore order and essentially to hold the ring so that a democratic process can unfold.

make the welkin ring: *see* WELKIN.

ring a bell: *see* BELL.

ring the changes: *see* CHANGE.

ring down (*or* up) the curtain mark the end (*or* the beginning) of an enterprise or event.

> ❶ The reference here is to the ringing of a bell in a theatre as the signal to raise or lower the stage curtain at the beginning or end of a performance. Compare with **bring down the curtain on** (*at* CURTAIN).

ring in your ears (*or* head) linger in the memory.

ring the knell of: *see* KNELL.

ring of steel an encircling armed barrier preventing escape or restricting access.

ring off the hook (of a landline telephone) be constantly ringing due to a large number of incoming calls. North American

run (*or* make) rings round someone outclass or outwit someone very easily. informal

throw your hat in the ring: *see* HAT.

riot

read the riot act: *see* READ.

run riot ❶ behave in a violent and unrestrained way. ❷ (of a mental faculty or emotion) function or be expressed without restraint. ❸ proliferate or spread uncontrollably.

rip

let rip ❶ do something or proceed vigorously or without restraint. ❷ express yourself vehemently or angrily. informal

let something rip ❶ allow something, especially a vehicle, to go at full speed. ❷ allow something to happen forcefully or without interference. ❸ express something forcefully and noisily. informal

ripe

like a ripe plum: *see* PLUM.

rise

get (*or* take) a rise out of provoke an angry or irritated response from someone, especially by teasing them. informal

give rise to be the cause of.

rise and shine get out of bed smartly; wake up. informal

rise from the ashes be renewed after destruction.

> ❶ In classical mythology, the phoenix was a unique bird resembling an eagle that lived for five or six centuries in the Arabian desert. After this time it burned itself on a funeral pyre ignited by the sun and fanned by its own wings and was then born again from the ashes with renewed youth to live through another cycle of life. The simile *like a phoenix from the ashes* is used of someone or something that has made a fresh start after apparently experiencing total destruction.

rise like a rocket: *see* ROCKET.

rise to the bait react to a provocation or temptation exactly as intended.

> ❶ The image here is of a fish coming to the surface to take a bait or fly.
>
> **1966** *Listener* I should perhaps apologise for having risen to the bait of Mr Wilkinson's provocative letter.

rise to the occasion perform better than usual in response to a special situation or event.

rise with the sun (*or* lark) get up early in the morning.

your gorge rises: *see* GORGE.

rising

someone's star is rising: *see* STAR.

risk

risk your neck put your life in danger.

rite

rite of passage a ceremony or event marking an important stage in someone's life, especially birth, initiation, marriage, and death.

Ritz

put on the Ritz make a show of luxury or extravagance.

> ❶ The hotels in Paris, London, and New York founded by the Swiss-born hotelier César Ritz

(1850–1918) became synonymous with great luxury. This expression dates from the heyday of these grand hotels in the early 20th century.

river

sell someone down the river betray someone, especially so as to benefit yourself. informal

ℹ This expression originated in the USA, with reference to the practice in the slave-owning states of selling troublesome slaves to owners of sugar-cane plantations on the lower Mississippi, where conditions were harsher than those in the more northerly states.

2004 *On Earth* There is no one over here saying that the son of a gun sold us down the river.

up the river to or in prison. informal, chiefly North American

ℹ This phrase originated with reference to Sing Sing prison, which is situated up the Hudson River from the city of New York.

road

all roads lead to Rome: *see* ROME.

a bump in the road: *see* BUMP.

down the road: *see* DOWN.

the end of the road: *see* END.

get the show on the road: *see* SHOW.

hit the road set out on a journey; depart. informal

ℹ A US variant of this expression is *hit the trail.*

in (*or* out of) the (*or* your) road in (*or* out of) someone's way. informal

knight of the road: *see* KNIGHT.

one for the road a final drink, especially an alcoholic one, before leaving for home. informal

2018 Mel Sherratt *Hush Hush* He had planned on only having one more for the road, but that was two hours ago, and now he was struggling to stand up.

a road to nowhere a situation or course of action offering no prospects of progress or advancement.

the rocky road to —: *see* ROCKY.

royal road to: *see* ROYAL.

run out of road (of a motor vehicle) leave the road and crash, especially when going round a bend.

take to the road (*or* take the road) set out on a journey or series of journeys.

roaring

do a roaring trade (*or* business) sell large amounts of something; do very good business. informal

rob

rob Peter to pay Paul take something away from one person to pay another, leaving the former at a disadvantage; discharge one debt only to incur another.

ℹ This expression probably arose in reference to the saints and apostles Peter and Paul, who are often shown together as equals in Christian art and who therefore may be presumed to be equally deserving of honour and devotion. It is uncertain whether a specific allusion is intended; variants of the phrase include *unclothe Peter and clothe Paul* and *borrow from Peter to pay Paul.*

2009 *Daily Telegraph* Mr Levene was also running a 'rob Peter to pay Paul' scam in which the so-called profits were provided by using money from fresh investors.

rob someone blind get a lot of money from someone by deception or extortion. informal

robbery

daylight robbery: *see* DAYLIGHT.

rock

between a rock and a hard place in a situation where you are faced with two equally difficult or unpleasant alternatives. informal

2003 *Yours* You are between a rock and a hard place. Of course you want to see your sister and spend time with her but ... the time you have with her is really quite exhausting for you.

get your rocks off ❶ have an orgasm. ❷ obtain pleasure or satisfaction. vulgar slang

ℹ *Rocks* is a euphemism for *testicles.*

like a shag on a rock: *see* SHAG.

the new rock and roll something that is (temporarily) highly fashionable. informal

1998 Jeremy Paxman *The English* London, it was being confidently asserted, is the gastronomic capital of the world, food the new rock-'n'-roll.

on the rocks ❶ (of a relationship or enterprise) experiencing difficulties and likely to fail. ❷ (of a drink) served undiluted and with ice cubes. informal

rock bottom the lowest possible level.

2004 *Art Business News* By 1992, the Nunez family had hit rock bottom, in debt and living off their credit cards.

rock the boat: *see* BOAT.

rocker

off your rocker crazy. informal

🛈 A *rocker* in this expression is a concave piece of wood or metal placed under a chair or cradle enabling it to rock back and forth.

1932 Evelyn Waugh *Black Mischief* It's going to be awkward for us if the Emperor goes off his rocker.

rocket

not rocket science used to indicate that something is not very difficult to understand. humorous

rise like a rocket (and fall like a stick) rise suddenly and dramatically (and subsequently fall in a similar manner).

🛈 The origin of this phrase is a jibe made by Thomas Paine about Edmund Burke's oratory in a 1792 House of Commons debate on the subject of the French Revolution. Paine remarked: 'As he rose like a rocket, he fell like the stick'.

rocking horse

rocking-horse manure something extremely rare. Australian informal

rocky

the rocky road to — a difficult progression to something.

2001 *Star* So far A1 haven't put a foot wrong on the rocky road to superstardom.

rod

kiss the rod: *see* KISS.

make a rod for your own back do something likely to cause difficulties for yourself later.

a rod in pickle a punishment in store.

🛈 *In pickle* means 'preserved ready for future use'. This form, which dates from the mid 17th century, has superseded an earlier mid-16th-century variant *a rod in piss*.

rule someone or something with a rod of iron control or govern someone or something very strictly or harshly.

🛈 This expression comes from Psalm 2:9: 'Thou shalt break them with a rod of iron; thou shalt dash them in pieces like a potter's vessel'.

spare the rod and spoil the child if children are not physically punished when they do wrong their personal development will suffer. proverb

Roland

a Roland for an Oliver an effective or appropriate retort or response; tit for tat. archaic

🛈 The phrase alludes to the evenly matched single combat between Roland, the legendary nephew of Charlemagne, and Oliver, another of Charlemagne's knights (paladins). Neither man was victorious and a strong friendship subsequently developed between them. According to the French medieval epic the *Chanson de Roland*, Roland was in command of the rearguard of Charlemagne's army when it was ambushed at Roncesvalles (now Roncevaux) in the Pyrenees in 778; despite the urging of Oliver that he should blow his horn to summon aid, Roland refused to do so until too late, and they were slain along with the rest of the rearguard.

roll

heads will roll: *see* HEAD.

on a roll experiencing a prolonged spell of success or good luck. informal

2004 Brian Greene *The Fabric of the Cosmos* With general relativity, it's fair to say Einstein was on a roll.

ready to roll: *see* READY.

roll the dice take a chance.

🛈 The phrase is also used as a noun, *a roll of the dice*, meaning 'an instance of taking a chance'.

a roll in the hay (*or* the sack) an act of sexual intercourse. informal

2013 *The Age* (Melbourne) Someone turns up moidered. Turns out [it] was the butler's illegitimate son from a pre-war roll in the hay with Noni's half-sister.

a roll Jack Rice couldn't jump over a large quantity of money. Australian informal

roll of honour ❶ a list of those who have died in battle. ❷ a list of people whose deeds or achievements, typically in sport, are honoured.

roll up your sleeves prepare to fight or work.

roll with the punches ❶ (of a boxer) move their body away from an opponent's blows so as to lessen the impact. ❷ adapt yourself to difficult or adverse circumstances.

roll your own make your own cigarettes from loose tobacco.

strike someone off the rolls (*or* roll) debar a solicitor from practising after dishonesty or other misconduct.

ℹ The *rolls* here are the official lists or records, so called from the time when such records were kept on parchment or paper scrolls.

rolled

(all) rolled into one (of characteristics drawn from different people or things) combined in one person or thing.

1907 George Bernard Shaw *Major Barbara* My methods ... would be no use if I were Voltaire, Rousseau, Bentham, Mill, Dickens, Carlyle, Ruskin, George, Butler, and Morris all rolled into one.

roller-coaster

a roller-coaster ride an experience in which circumstances change rapidly and in a volatile manner from one extreme to another.

2004 *BBC News: Business* Shares have been on a rollercoaster ride, with US shares plunging and then recovering twice over.

rolling

be rolling in it (*or* in money) be very rich. informal

ℹ *Rolling in* (i.e. 'turning over and over in') here has the sense of 'luxuriating in'. The idea of wallowing in riches has been current since the late 16th century.

have people rolling in the aisles: *see* AISLE.

keep (*or* start) the ball rolling: *see* BALL.

a rolling stone a person who does not settle in one place for long.

ℹ This expression comes from the proverb *a rolling stone gathers no moss*, meaning that a person who is always moving on will not accumulate wealth or status, or responsibilities or commitments.

rolling drunk so drunk as to be swaying or staggering.

Roman

a Roman holiday an occasion on which enjoyment or profit is derived from the suffering or discomfort of others.

ℹ This expression comes from the poet Byron's description of the dying gladiator in *Childe Harold's Pilgrimage* as having been 'butchered to make a Roman holiday'.

Rome

all roads lead to Rome there are many different ways of reaching the same goal or conclusion.

ℹ This is an ancient saying which was based on the fact that Rome was the point of convergence of all the main roads of the Roman empire, and after that of the medieval pilgrimage routes through Europe. It can be compared with the medieval Latin phrase *mille vie ducunt hominem per secula Romam*, meaning 'a thousand roads lead a man forever towards Rome'.

fiddle while Rome burns: *see* FIDDLE.

Rome was not built in a day a complex or ambitious task is bound to take a long time and should not be rushed.

ℹ This warning against rashness and impatience has been current in English since the mid 16th century.

when in Rome (do as the Romans do) when abroad or in an unfamiliar environment you should adopt the customs or behaviour of those around you.

ℹ This proverbial expression may ultimately derive from St Ambrose of Milan (397), who is quoted in one of St Augustine's letters as saying that when he was in Rome he fasted as they did there, on a Saturday, although when he was in Milan he did not do this. A medieval Latin saying expresses the idea as *si fueris Romae, Romano vivito more; si fueris alibi, vivito sicut ibi*, 'if you are at Rome, live in the Roman manner; if elsewhere, live as they do there'.

1998 Pat Chapman *1999 Good Curry Guide* Cutlery is still for wimps (though you no longer have to ask for it). But when in Rome, eat the correct way, please, using a piece of Roti to scoop up your curry, in your right hand only.

roof

fall off the roof begin a menstrual period. US informal

go through (*or* hit) the roof ❶ (of prices or figures) reach extreme or unexpected heights; become exorbitant. ❷ suddenly become very angry. informal

raise the roof make or cause someone to make a lot of noise inside a building, for example through cheering.

2009 *CLUAS* [Irish music magazine] The reaction of the crowd (and look on the Quartet's faces) was classic as the anthemic choruses raised the roof!

the roof falls in a disaster occurs; everything goes wrong.

a roof over your head a place in which you can stay and find shelter.

rooftop

shout something from the rooftops talk about something openly and jubilantly, especially something previously kept secret.

🛈 This phrase is adapted from Luke 12:3: 'that which ye have spoken in the ear in closets shall be proclaimed upon the housetops'.

room

in a smoke-filled room (of political bargaining or decision-making) conducted privately by a small group of influential people rather than more openly or democratically.

🛈 This expression comes from a 1920 news report about the selection of the Republican presidential candidate: '[Warren] Harding of Ohio was chosen by a group of men in a smoke-filled room'.

no (*or* not) room to swing a cat used in reference to a very confined space. humorous

🛈 The *cat* in this expression is probably a 'cat-o'-nine-tails', a form of whip with nine knotted cords. In former times these whips were used to flog wrongdoers, especially at sea.

room at the top opportunity to join an elite or the top ranks of a profession.

🛈 The expression is attributed to the American politician Daniel Webster (1782–1852), who was cautioned against attempting to enter the overcrowded legal profession and is said to have replied: 'There is always room at the top'.

roost

chickens come home to roost: *see* CHICKEN.

rule the roost: *see* RULE.

root

at the grass roots: *see* GRASS.

put down roots begin to lead a settled life in a particular place.

root and branch used to express the thorough or radical nature of a process or operation.

2005 Lucy Kellaway *Who Moved My Blackberry?* Suggest you do not attempt to come home unless you are prepared to undergo a root and branch personal rebranding.

strike at the root (*or* roots) of have a potentially destructive effect on.

take root become fixed or established.

rope

give someone enough rope (*or* plenty of rope) give a person enough freedom of action to bring about their own downfall.

🛈 The fuller form of this expression is the proverb *give a man enough rope and he will hang himself*, which has been in use in various forms since the mid 17th century.

know the ropes: *see* KNOW.

money for old rope: *see* **money for jam** *at* MONEY.

on the ropes in a desperate position; in a state of near collapse or defeat.

🛈 This is an idiom from boxing, alluding to the situation of a losing boxer who is forced back by his opponent against the ropes that mark the sides of the boxing ring. First recorded, in its literal sense, in the early 19th century, the phrase has been in figurative use since at least the 1920s.

a rope of sand used in allusion to something that provides only illusory security or coherence. literary

rose

bed of roses: *see* BED.

the bloom is off the rose: *see* BLOOM.

come up roses (of a situation) develop in a very favourable way. informal

come up smelling of roses: *see* SMELLING.

everything's (*or* it's all) roses everything is going well. informal

(there is) no rose without a thorn every apparently desirable situation has its share of trouble or difficulty.

🛈 This expression has been proverbial since the mid 15th century. The earliest recorded instance is in a work by John Lydgate (1430–40): 'There is no rose . . . in garden, but there be sum thorne'.

moonlight and roses: *see* MOONLIGHT.

not all roses not entirely perfect or agreeable. informal

1938 Graham Greene *Brighton Rock* Sometimes he's bad to me . . . it's not all roses.

pluck a rose: *see* PLUCK.

roses, roses, all the way very successful or pleasant.

ℹ This expression is taken from the first line of Robert Browning's poem 'The Patriot' (1855), where it describes the throwing of roses at a popular hero as he passed through the streets.

1977 *World of Cricket Monthly* Although Australia lost the Ashes, it was roses, roses, all the way for him.

smell the roses: *see* SMELL.

under the rose in confidence; under pledge of secrecy. archaic

ℹ The origin of the rose as an emblem of secrecy is uncertain; the concept may have originated in Germany and there was a similar expression in early modern Dutch. *Under the rosse* appears in a 1546 State Paper of Henry VIII, with a gloss that suggests that it was then a new or unfamiliar expression. The Latin equivalent *sub rosa* has also been very commonly used in English since the mid 17th century in this metaphorical sense.

rot

the rot sets in a rapid succession of (usually unaccountable) failures begins.

rotten

a rotten apple: *see* APPLE.

rough

bit of rough a (usually male) sexual partner whose toughness or lack of sophistication is a source of attraction. informal

2006 *Movie City* Recall . . . his smart-dumb performance as Francis Bacon's bit of rough in *Love is the Devil*.

cut up rough behave in an aggressive, quarrelsome, or awkward way. British informal

ℹ *Cut up* is here being used in the sense of 'behave'. The phrase *cut up rough* is used by Dickens and the variant *cut up savage* (now no longer in use) by Thackeray.

2007 *Telegraph* Mr Miliband wants to prove a point to Mr Brown—who cut up rough with him over details of the Climate Change Bill, blocking his idea for personal carbon budgets.

live rough: *see* LIVE.

rough and ready ❶ rough or crude but effective. ❷ (of a person or place) unsophisticated or unrefined.

rough and tumble a situation without rules or organization; a free-for-all.

ℹ The expression originated in 19th-century boxing slang.

rough around the edges having a few imperfections.

rough as bags lacking refinement; coarse. Australian & New Zealand informal

a rough diamond a person who has genuinely fine qualities but uncouth manners. informal

ℹ Literally, *a rough diamond* is a diamond before it has been cut and polished. A North American variant of this expression is *a diamond in the rough*.

the rough edge (*or* side) of your tongue a scolding.

rough edges slight imperfections in someone or something that is basically satisfactory.

the rough end of the pineapple: *see* PINEAPPLE.

rough justice ❶ treatment, especially punishment, that is approximately fair. ❷ treatment that is not at all fair or not in accordance with the law.

a rough passage a difficult time or experience.

a rough ride: *see* RIDE.

sleep rough sleep in uncomfortable conditions, usually out of doors. British

take the rough with the smooth accept the difficult or unpleasant aspects of life as well as the good.

roughshod

ride roughshod over carry out your own plans or wishes with arrogant disregard for others.

1977 *Times Literary Supplement* Sociologists are notorious for their use of generalizing terms that ride roughshod over the particularities of history.

round

go the round (*or* rounds) (of a story or joke) be passed on from person to person.

in the round ❶ (of sculpture) standing free with all sides shown, rather than carved in relief against a ground. ❷ treated fully and thoroughly; with all aspects shown or considered. ❸ (of a theatrical performance) with the audience placed on at least three sides of the stage.

round the bend: *see* BEND.

round the clock: *see* CLOCK.

a square peg in a round hole: *see* PEG.

roundabout

swings and roundabouts: *see* SWING.

roundup

the last roundup death. informal euphemistic

ⓘ The metaphor was based on the idea of a final rounding-up of cattle in the American Wild West. The phrase itself seems to have originated as the title of a 1932 song by G. Brown.

roving

a roving eye a tendency to flirt or be constantly looking to start a new sexual relationship. informal

row

get your ducks in a row: *see* DUCK.

a hard (*or* tough) row to hoe a difficult task.

ⓘ *Hoeing a row* of plants is used here as a metaphor for very arduous work.

royal

battle royal: *see* BATTLE.

royal road to a way of attaining or reaching something without trouble.

ⓘ This expression alludes to a remark attributed to the Greek mathematician Euclid (*c.*300 BC). When the Egyptian ruler Ptolemy I asked whether geometry could not be made easier, Euclid is said to have replied: 'There is no royal road to geometry'.

rub

not have two — to rub together have none or hardly any of the specified items, especially coins. informal

2011 *TechDirt* I could go on but if you've got two brain cells to rub together you've got the point by now.

rub of the green the influence of luck, seen as being advantageous or more usually disadvantageous.

ⓘ The expression originated in the language of golf, where it denotes an accidental interference with the course or position of a ball on the green.

1962 *Guardian* If applications . . . reached fantastic proportions, the Government would have to consider the matter. 'At present we treat it as a rub of the green.'

rub your hands show keen satisfaction or expectation.

rub someone's nose in something (*or* rub it in) emphatically or repeatedly draw someone's attention to an embarrassing or painful fact. informal

ⓘ This expression comes from the mistaken belief that the way to house-train a puppy or kitten is to rub their noses in their faeces or urine if they have made a mess indoors.

1963 P. M. Hubbard *Flush as May* I'm sorry. I've said I'm sorry . . . Don't rub my nose in it.

rub salt into the wound: *see* SALT.

rub shoulders associate or come into contact with another person.

ⓘ A US variant of this expression is *rub elbows*.

1943 Graham Greene *The Ministry of Fear* It wasn't exactly a criminal world, though eddying along its dim and muted corridors you might possibly rub shoulders with genteel forgers.

rub someone (up) the wrong way irritate or repel someone.

ⓘ The image here is of stroking an animal against the lie of its fur.

there's (*or* here's) the rub that is the crucial difficulty or problem. literary

ⓘ This expression comes from Shakespeare's *Hamlet*: 'To sleep: perchance to dream: ay, there's the rub; For in that sleep of death what dreams may come When we have shuffled off this mortal coil, Must give us pause'. In the game of bowls, a *rub* is an impediment that prevents a bowl from running smoothly.

2004 Cheryl Holt *More than Seduction* But there's the rub, you see. I can't be linked to a scandal.

rubber

burn rubber drive very quickly. informal

2001 Marc Blake *24 Karat Schmooze* Two Squad cars burnt rubber and screamed to a halt by the gates.

rubber cheque a cheque that is returned unpaid. informal humorous

ⓘ The expression plays on the idea of a cheque that 'bounces', or is unpaid because there are insufficient funds in the drawer's account to cover it.

Rubicon

cross the Rubicon take an irrevocable step.

ⓘ The Rubicon was a small river in north-east Italy which in the first century BC marked the boundary of Italy proper with the province of Cisalpine Gaul. By taking his army across the Rubicon into Italy in 49 BC, Julius Caesar broke the law forbidding a general to lead an army out of his own province, and so committed himself to war against the Senate and Pompey. *See also* **the die is cast** *at* DIE.

rude

a rude awakening a sudden realization of the true (bad) state of affairs, having previously been under the illusion that everything was satisfactory.

2012 Mark Heuring *Mr Dilettante* New Yorkers of all income levels got a rude awakening yesterday when they saw in *The Post* how much more they will pay in taxes next year.

ruffle

ruffle someone's feathers cause someone to become annoyed or upset.

ruffled

smooth someone's ruffled feathers make someone less angry or irritated by using soothing words.

r

rug

cut a (*or* the) rug dance, typically in an energetic or accomplished way. North American informal

ⓘ The underlying idea is probably of dancing so vigorous that the floor covering is damaged.

1966 *Sky Magazine* The wide-open spaces around the bar ... mean, as it fills up, the place soon resembles a club and the punters are itching to cut a rug.

pull the rug (from under someone) abruptly withdraw support from someone.

ruin

go to rack and ruin: *see* RACK.

rule

as a rule usually, but not always.

divide and rule: *see* DIVIDE.

play by the rules follow what is generally held to be the correct line of behaviour.

rule of thumb a broadly accurate guide or principle, based on experience or practice rather than theory.

2014 Robert Cringely *I Cringely* Moore's Law doubles the performance of computers every couple of years and my old rule of thumb was that most people who make their living with computers are unwilling to be more than two generations behind.

— rule(s), OK? used to express your enthusiasm for a particular person or thing. informal, humorous

2000 *Elle* Here at ELLE we've always been big fans of Kerrigan's urban babewear, and this season ... she really rocked. Daryl K rules, OK?

rule the roost be in complete control.

ⓘ The original expression was *rule the roast*, which was common from the mid 16th century onwards. Although none of the early examples of its use shed any light on its source, we can surmise that it originally referred to someone being the most important person at a banquet or feast. *Rule the roost*, found from the mid 18th century, has now replaced the earlier version.

rule someone or something with a rod of iron: *see* ROD.

run the rule over examine cursorily for correctness or adequacy. British

2013 *Motley Fool* Our analysts at Motley Fool Share Advisor run the rule over such businesses daily. I want to invest in them. And so do you. But we both want to know that they won't be a one-generation wonder.

work to rule (especially as a form of industrial action) follow official working regulations exactly in order to reduce output and efficiency. chiefly British

rumour

rumour has it it is rumoured.

1993 Margaret Atwood *The Robber Bride* It's a good thing Roz didn't invest in that one, rumour has it that the backers are losing a shirt or two.

run

on the run ❶ trying to avoid being captured. ❷ continuously active and busy.

give someone or something a (good) run for their money provide someone or something with challenging competition or opposition.

2013 *The Stage* The slapstick fun of Dromgoole's production gives *Noises Off* a run for its money in terms of comic inventiveness.

have a (good) run for your money derive reward or enjoyment in return for your outlay or efforts.

(try to) run before you can walk attempt something difficult before you have grasped the basic skills required.

(make a) run for it attempt to escape someone or something by running away.

run something past someone mention something to someone as a suggestion, to elicit their views on it. informal

2003 Robert X. Cringely *I, Cringely* The business I am about to describe has not been legally tested. I have run it past a few lawyer friends of mine, but a true legal test can only be done in the courts.

ⓘ For other idioms containing *run*, see the entry for the main word in the idiom (for example, **run riot** at RIOT).

runaround

give someone the runaround deceive and confuse someone; avoid answering someone's questions directly. informal

rune

read the runes try to forecast the outcome of a situation by analysing all the significant factors involved. British

ⓘ The *runes* were an ancient Germanic alphabet once used in northern Europe, each character of which was supposed to have a secret magical significance. Small stones and pieces of bone engraved with these characters were used to try to foretell the future.

runner

do a runner leave hastily, especially to avoid paying for something or to escape from somewhere. informal, chiefly British

2010 *Cairns Post* (Queensland) The system ... prevents tenants from doing a runner without paying the power bill.

running

be running on empty: *see* EMPTY.

hit the ground running: *see* HIT.

in (*or* out of) the running in (*or* no longer in) contention for an award, victory, or a place in a team.

make the running set the pace in a race or activity.

off and running: *see* OFF.

a running battle a confrontation that has gone on for a long time.

ⓘ Literally, a *running battle* is one that is constantly changing its location, the opposite of **a pitched battle** (*see* PITCHED). The expression *running fight* was used in the late 17th century to describe a naval engagement in which the fight was continued as one party retreated or fled. *Running battle* appears to have originated in the mid 20th century.

the sands (of time) are running out: *see* SAND.

take a running jump used when angrily rejecting or disagreeing with someone.

1998 *Oldie* Get back to the studio and tell the focus groups to take a running jump!

take up the running take over as pacemaker in a race.

up and running taking place; active.

1998 *New Scientist* The arms race may be up and running again.

rush

be rushed off your feet: *see* FOOT.

fools rush in where angels fear to tread: *see* FOOL.

give someone the bum's rush: *see* BUM.

rush your fences act with undue haste. British

ⓘ This is a metaphor from horse riding: in the hunting field if you *rush your fences*, rather than tackling the obstacles steadily, you risk a fall.

a rush of blood (to the head) a sudden attack of wild irrationality in your thinking or actions.

rut

in a rut following a fixed (especially tedious or dreary) pattern of behaviour that is difficult to change.

ⓘ The *rut* in this expression is the deep groove worn by a wheel travelling many times along the same track.

2013 *CNN transcipts* In the 1960s and '70s, India was infamously stuck in a rut of slow growth with a mediocre two percent a year often.

sabbath

a sabbath day's journey a short and easy journey.

> ❶ Rabbinical law allowed a Jew to travel a certain distance on the Sabbath (about a kilometre); in the Bible, Mount Olivet is described as being 'from Jerusalem a sabbath day's journey' (Acts 1:12).

sabre

rattle sabres: *see* RATTLE.

sack

hit the sack go to bed. informal

hold the sack bear an unwelcome responsibility. North American

a roll in the sack: *see* **a roll in the hay** *at* ROLL.

sad sack: *see* SAD.

sackcloth

in sackcloth and ashes manifesting grief or repentance.

> ❶ In the Bible, the wearing of sackcloth and the sprinkling ashes on your head were signs of penitence or mourning.
>
> **2010** *Keeping Stock* Goff has demanded ... that he prostrate himself in sackcloth and ashes before a hostile media pack as a condition of returning to parliament.

sacred

a sacred cow: *see* COW.

sacrifice

sacrifice someone or something on the altar of: *see* ALTAR.

sad

sad sack an inept blundering person. informal, chiefly US

saddle

a burr under your saddle: *see* BURR.

in the saddle ❶ on horseback. ❷ in a position of control or responsibility.

safe

better safe than sorry: *see* BETTER.

play (*or* play it) safe (*or* for safety) take precautions; avoid risks.

safe as houses: *see* HOUSE.

a safe bet: *see* BET.

a safe pair of hands ❶ (in a sporting context) used to refer to someone who is reliable when catching a ball. ❷ used to denote someone who is capable, reliable, or trustworthy in the management of a situation.

to be on the safe side in order to have a margin of security against risks.

> **2000 Tom Clancy** *The Bear and the Dragon* To be on the safe side, the messages were super-encrypted with a 256-bit system specially made at the National Security Agency.

safety

there's safety in numbers being in a group of people makes you feel more confident or secure about taking action. proverb

said

enough said: *see* ENOUGH.

he said, she said used to characterize different and inconsistent versions of the same event, especially as offered by respectively a man and a woman, with no conclusive evidence as to which is correct.

> **2011** *TechDirt* All the complaints someone could possibly want to file can be filed, but that's not going to say that anything is going to be done about it. It's 'he said she said' and government will respond with it's national security, you don't like it don't fly.

least said, soonest mended: *see* LEAST.

nuff said: *see* NUFF.

when (*or* after) all is said and done when everything is taken into account (used to indicate that you are making a generalized judgment about a situation).

sail

sail close to (*or* near) the wind: *see* WIND.

sail under false colours: *see* COLOUR.

take the wind out of someone's sails: *see* WIND.

that ship has sailed: *see* SHIP.

trim your sails: *see* TRIM.

sailing

plain sailing: *see* PLAIN.

sake

for old times' sake in memory of former times; in acknowledgement of a shared past.

salad

your salad days ❶ the period when you are young and inexperienced. ❷ the peak or heyday of something.

ℹ This is a quotation from Shakespeare's *Antony and Cleopatra*. Cleopatra is commenting on her previous relationship with Julius Caesar: 'My salad days, When I was green in judgement, cold in blood To say as I said then!'

saloon

in the last chance saloon: *see* LAST.

salt

eat salt with be a guest of. British dated

like a dose of salts: *see* DOSE.

put salt on the tail of capture.

ℹ This phrase alludes to the humorous advice traditionally given to young children about the best way to catch a bird.

rub salt into the (*or* someone's) wound make a painful experience even more painful for someone.

salt the books fraudulently increase the apparent value of an invoice or account. informal

salt a mine fraudulently make a mine appear to be a paying one by placing rich ore into it. informal

the salt of the earth a person or group of people of great kindness, reliability, or honesty.

ℹ This phrase comes from Matthew 5:13: 'Ye are the salt of the earth: but if the salt have lost his savour, wherewith shall it be salted?'

sit below the salt be of lower social standing or worth.

ℹ This expression derives from the former custom of placing a large salt cellar midway down a long dining table at which people were seated in order of rank.

take something with a pinch (*or* grain) of salt regard something as exaggerated; believe only part of something.

ℹ The addition of a small amount of salt may make food more palatable. The sentiment is expressed in Latin by *cum grano salis*.

2013 *New Statesman* Perhaps his invectives against men who 'get down in the gutter and frankly worship dollars' can be taken with a pinch of salt, given Twain's obsession with profit and addiction to calamitous investments.

worth your salt good or competent at the job or profession specified.

ℹ Roman soldiers were paid a *salarium* (source of English *salary*), which was literally 'money to buy salt'.

2000 *Saga Magazine* Every place setting is measured with a ruler because no butler worth his salt wants to get to the end of a table with say, four settings left, and nowhere to put them.

salute

salute the judge (of a horse) win a race. Australian informal

Samaritan

good Samaritan a charitable or helpful person.

ℹ In the Bible, Jesus tells the parable of a man who 'went down from Jerusalem to Jericho and fell among thieves' (Luke 10). The first two people who came across him lying stripped and wounded by the side of the road 'passed by on the other side'. It was the third man, a Samaritan (i.e. a man from Samaria), who took pity on him and helped him.

same

be in the same boat: *see* BOAT.

by the same token: *see* TOKEN.

one and the same the same person or thing (used for emphasis).

2014 *The Retail Bulletin* Unlike in other companies, employees and shareholders are ultimately one and the same in the Partnership.

same difference used to express the speaker's belief that two or more things are essentially the same, in spite of apparent differences. informal

same here the same applies to me. informal

2012 *Daily Telegraph* It would be interesting to know what they were whispering to each other. ('How's your diary looking these days?' 'Pretty empty. Yours?' 'Same here.')

same old, same old used to convey that something is drearily predictable or familiar. informal

sing from the same hymn sheet: *see* SING.

sand

built on sand: *see* BUILT.

bury your head in the sand: *see* BURY.

(draw) a line in the sand: *see* LINE.

rope of sand: *see* ROPE.

run into the sand come to nothing.

2006 *New York Review of Books* What struck Jane Addams in retrospect ... was that immediately after this lecture, everything ran into the sand.

the sands (of time) are running out the allotted time is nearly at an end.

ⓘ The image here is of the sand in an hourglass moving from the upper chamber to the lower.

shifting sands: *see* SHIFTING.

sandboy

happy as a sandboy: *see* HAPPY.

S

sandwich

the meat (*or* filling) in the sandwich a person who is awkwardly caught between two opposing factions.

a sandwich (*or* two sandwiches) short of a picnic (of a person) stupid or crazy. informal

sardine

packed like sardines crowded very close together.

ⓘ The reference is to the close proximity of sardines in tins.

sauce

what's sauce for the goose is sauce for the gander what is appropriate in one case is also appropriate in the other case in question. proverb

ⓘ This expression is often used as a statement that what is right or wrong for one sex is right or wrong for the other as well. John Ray, who was the first to record this saying (in his *English Proverbs* of 1670), remarked 'This is a woman's Proverb'.

2010 *Guardian* Universities ... should not ... be 'rites of passage' for dullards who go there based on some liberal principle that what is sauce for the goose is sauce for the gander. Universities should be about academic achievement. The day some lefty decided that everyone should be going there is the day university education died.

saucer

have eyes like saucers have your eyes opened wide in amazement.

sausage

not a sausage nothing at all. British informal

save

save your breath: *see* BREATH.

save the day (*or* situation) find or provide a solution to a difficulty or disaster.

1990 Richard Critchfield *Among the British* When the postwar social fabric started to tear, amid a stagnant economy and global decline ... Edward Heath ... was supposed to save the day. He failed to deliver.

save (someone's) face: *see* FACE.

save someone's skin (*or* neck *or* bacon) rescue someone from danger or difficulty.

to save your life used in various expressions, especially *can't* (or *couldn't*) *do something to save your life*, to indicate that the person in question is very incompetent at doing something.

ⓘ The first recorded use of this expression is by Anthony Trollope in *The Kellys and O'Kellys* (1848): 'If it was to save my life and theirs, I can't get up small talk for the rector and his curate'.

saved

saved by the bell preserved from danger narrowly or by an unexpected intervention.

ℹ In boxing matches a contestant who has been knocked to the floor can be saved from being counted out by the ringing of the bell to mark the end of a round.

sawdust

spit and sawdust: *see* SPIT.

say

have something (*or* **nothing**) **to say for yourself** contribute (*or* fail to contribute) to a conversation or discussion.

say no more used to indicate that you understand what someone is trying to imply. informal

says you! used in spoken English to express disagreement or disbelief. informal, dated

say when said when helping someone to food or drink to instruct them to indicate when they have had enough. informal

you can say that again! used to express emphatic agreement. informal

you don't say (so)! used to express amazement or disbelief. informal

ℹ Also used ironically to suggest that the obvious has been stated.

ℹ For other idioms containing *say*, see the entry for the main word in the idiom (for example, **wouldn't say boo to a goose** at BOO).

saying

as the saying goes (*or* **is**) used to introduce or follow an expression, drawing attention to its status as a saying rather than part of your normal language.

go without saying be too well known or obvious to need to be mentioned.

there is no saying it is impossible to know.

scalded

like a scalded cat at a very fast speed.

2011 *Daily Telegraph* Research published this month revealed that deskbound workers have got bigger bottoms as the pressure of the weight causes fat cells to cluster. Yes, I too leapt up like a scalded cat when I first read that.

scale

the scales fall from someone's eyes someone is no longer deceived.

ℹ In the Bible, this expression described how St Paul, blinded by his vision on the road to Damascus, received his sight back at the hand of God (Acts 9:18).

throw something on (*or* **into**) **the scale** emphasize the relevance of something to one side of an argument or debate.

tip (*or* **turn**) **the scales** (*or* **balance**)**:** *see* TIP.

tip (*or* **turn**) **the scales at** have a weight of a specified amount.

scarce

make yourself scarce surreptitiously disappear; keep out of the way. informal

scare

scare the bejesus out of someone: *see* BEJESUS.

scare the daylights out of: *see* **frighten the daylights out of** *at* DAYLIGHT.

scarlet

scarlet woman a notoriously promiscuous or immoral woman.

ℹ The term was originally applied as a derogatory reference to the Roman Catholic Church, regarded as being devoted to showy ritual. It comes from Revelation 17.

scene

behind the scenes in private; secretly.

ℹ This expression alludes to the area out of sight of the public at the back of a theatre stage.

change of scene (*or* **scenery**) a move to different surroundings.

not your scene not something you are interested in. informal

set the scene ❶ describe a place or situation in which something is about to happen. ❷ create the conditions for a future event.

scenery

chew the scenery (of an actor) overact. informal

scent

on the scent ❶ (of an animal) following the scent of its quarry. ❷ in possession of a useful clue in a search or investigation.

put (*or* throw) someone off the scent mislead someone in the course of a search or investigation.

settle (*or* pay) a (*or* the) score take revenge on someone for something damaging that they have done in the past.

scheme

the scheme of things the organization of things in general; the way the world is.

schmear

the whole schmear everything possible or available; every aspect of something. North American informal

ℹ *Schmear* (also spelled *schmeer*, *shmear*, or *shmeer*) means 'bribery' or 'flattery', and comes from the Yiddish verb *schmirn* meaning 'grease' or 'flatter'.

1970 Lawrence Sanders *The Anderson Tapes* I want a complete list . . . Any thing and everything . . . The whole shmear.

school

of the old school: *see* OLD.

the old school tie: *see* OLD.

the school of hard knocks painful or difficult experiences that are seen to be useful in teaching someone about life.

school of thought a particular way of thinking, especially one not followed by the speaker.

too cool for school: *see* COOL.

science

blind someone with science: *see* BLIND.

the dismal science: *see* DISMAL.

S

scoop

scoop the pool (*or* the kitty) be completely successful; gain everything.

ℹ In gambling games, the *pool* or *kitty* is the total amount of money that is staked.

score

a cricket score: *see* CRICKET.

know the score: *see* KNOW.

on that (*or* this) score so far as that (*or* this) is concerned.

score an own goal: *see* GOAL.

score points: *see* POINT.

scorn

laugh someone or something to scorn: *see* LAUGH.

Scott

Great Scott!: *see* GREAT.

Scout

Scout's honour used to indicate that you have the honourable standards associated with Scouts, and so will stand by a promise or tell the truth. informal

ℹ A Scout is a member of the Scout Association, an organization originally for boys founded in 1908 by Lord Baden-Powell with the aim of developing their character by training them in self-sufficiency and survival techniques in the outdoors.

scrape

bow and scrape: *see* BOW.

rake and scrape: *see* RAKE.

scrape acquaintance with contrive to get to know. dated

1992 *Atlantic* I thought how lucky the Crimms were to have scraped acquaintance with me, for I seldom reveal my identity to ordinary people on my jaunts around the world.

scrape the barrel (*or* the bottom of the barrel) be reduced to using things or people of the poorest quality because there is nothing else available. informal

scratch

from scratch from the very beginning, especially without utilizing or relying on any previous work for assistance.

ℹ In certain sports, the *scratch* was originally the line or mark drawn to indicate the point from which competitors had to start a race unless they had been awarded an advantage and were able to start ahead of this line. So, a competitor starting *from scratch* would start from a position without any advantage. The expression **up to scratch** (see below) also comes from this sense of the noun *scratch*: a competitor who was up to scratch was of a good enough standard to start a race.

scratch a — and find a — an investigation of someone or something will soon reveal their true nature.

ℹ The first version of this expression used in English, in the early 19th century, was a translation of a remark attributed to Napoleon: *grattez le Russe et vous trouverez le Tartare*, 'scratch the Russian and you will find the Tartar'.

1924 George Bernard Shaw *St Joan* Scratch an Englishman and find a Protestant.

scratch your head ❶ think hard in order to find a solution to something. ❷ feel or express bewilderment. informal

scratch the surface ❶ deal with a matter only in the most superficial way. ❷ initiate the briefest investigation to discover something concealed.

up to scratch up to the required standard; satisfactory.

you scratch my back and I'll scratch yours if you do me a favour, I will return it. proverb

screaming

give someone the screaming abdabs: *see* ABDABS.

kicking and screaming: *see* KICK.

screen

the silver screen: *see* SILVER.

the small screen: *see* SMALL.

screw

have a screw loose be slightly eccentric or mentally disturbed. informal

put the screws on exert strong psychological pressure on someone so as to intimidate them into doing something. informal

screw up your courage summon up all your courage; force yourself to be brave.

tighten (*or* **turn**) **the screw** (*or* **screws**) exert strong pressure on someone. informal

a (final *or* **last) turn of the screw** an additional amount of pressure or hardship applied to a situation that is already extremely difficult to bear. informal

screwed

have your head screwed on (the right way) have common sense. informal

scrub

scrub up well have a smart and well-groomed appearance after making a deliberate effort. British informal

Scylla

Scylla and Charybdis used to refer to a situation involving two dangers in which an attempt to avoid one increases the risk from the other. literary

ℹ In classical mythology, *Scylla* was a female sea monster who devoured sailors when they tried to navigate the narrow channel between her and the whirlpool *Charybdis*. In later legends, *Scylla* was a dangerous rock, located on the Italian side of the Strait of Messina, a channel which separates the island of Sicily from the 'toe' of Italy.

sea

(all) at sea confused or unable to decide what to do.

2012 *The Age* (Melbourne) Ali never pretended to be perfect. In matters marital and fiscal, he was frequently all at sea. His humour was often scripted.

half seas over: *see* HALF.

there are plenty more fish in the sea: *see* FISH.

seal

put (*or* **set**) **the seal on** put the finishing touch to.

seal of approval: *see* APPROVAL.

seal someone's fate: *see* FATE.

set (*or* **put**) **your seal to** (*or* **on**) mark with your own distinctive character.

ℹ The reference in both of these idioms is to the former practice of stamping your personal seal on a completed letter or other document.

signed, sealed, and delivered: *see* SIGN.

someone's lips are sealed: *see* LIP.

seam

bursting (*or* **bulging**) **at the seams** (of a place or building) full to overflowing. informal

come (*or* **fall**) **apart at the seams** ❶ (of a thing) fall to pieces. ❷ (of a person); have an emotional breakdown; collapse. informal

ℹ *Seams* are the lines along which pieces of fabric or the planks of a boat are joined, perceived as the points most likely to be damaged or weakened.

search

search me! I do not know (used for emphasis). informal

season

a man for all seasons: *see* MAN.

the silly season: *see* SILLY.

seat

ℹ For idioms containing seat, see the entry for the main word in the idiom (for example, **by the seat of your pants** at PANTS).

second

at second hand by hearsay rather than direct observation or experience.

get your second wind: gain a new strength or energy to continue something that is an effort.

have a second string to your bow: *see* STRING.

on second thoughts having reconsidered a matter (and arrived at a different opinion or decision).

ℹ US English also uses *on second thought*.

play second fiddle to: *see* FIDDLE.

second banana: *see* BANANA.

second childhood a state of childishness that sometimes occurs in old age.

second nature a characteristic or habit in someone that appears to be instinctive because that person has behaved in a particular way so often.

a second thought a moment's further consideration; any worry or concern.

second to none surpassed by no other.

1961 Joseph Heller *Catch-22* He would stand second to none in his devotion to country.

S

secret

take the secret to the grave: *see* GRAVE.

section

the golden section: *see* GOLDEN.

see

see someone coming recognize a person who can be fooled or deceived. informal

see something coming foresee or be prepared for an event, typically an unpleasant one.

ℹ For other idioms containing *see*, see the entry for the main word in the idiom (for example, **see eye to eye** at EYE).

seed

go (*or* run) to seed ❶ (of a plant) cease flowering as the seeds develop. ❷ deteriorate in condition, strength, or efficiency.

sow the seed (*or* seeds) of do something which will eventually bring about a particular result.

1991 Philip Slater *A Dream Deferred* Each authoritarian government, groping toward modernization, would thereby sow the seeds of its own destruction.

seeing

be seeing things be hallucinating.

1987 Rohinton Mistry *Tales from Firozsha Baag* How much fun they made of me. Calling me crazy, saying it is time for old ayah to go back to Goa . . . she is seeing things.

seeing is believing you need to see something before you can accept that it really exists or occurs. proverb

seen

have seen better days: *see* DAY.

look as if you have seen a ghost: *see* GHOST.

seize

seize the day make the most of the present moment.

ℹ This expression is a translation of Latin *carpe diem*, originally a quotation from the Roman poet Horace.

sell

sell your soul (to the devil) do or be willing to do anything, no matter how wrong, in order to achieve your objective.

ℹ The reference here is to a contract supposedly made with the devil by certain people: in return for granting them all their desires in this life, the devil would receive their souls for all eternity. The most famous person reputed to have entered into such a contract was the 16th-century German astronomer and necromancer Faust, who became the subject of plays by Goethe and Marlowe and a novel by Thomas Mann.

ⓘ For other idioms containing *sell*, see the entry for the main word in the idiom (for example, **sell someone a pup** at PUP).

sell-by date

pass your sell-by date reach a point where you are useless or worn out. informal

ⓘ A sell-by date is that stamped on perishable goods indicating the latest date on which they may be sold.

2013 *Daily Telegraph* The Douglases, once considered to exemplify that most doomed category of 'most stable marriage in Hollywood,' illustrated still more sharply what happens when a sex god passes his sell-by date.

send

send in your papers: *see* PAPER.

send someone flying cause someone to be violently flung to the ground.

send someone packing: *see* PACKING.

send someone to Coventry: *see* COVENTRY.

senior

senior moment an untoward incident, especially one exhibiting forgetfulness, that is attributed to old age. informal humorous

sense

bring someone to their senses cause someone to think and behave reasonably after a period of folly or irrationality.

come to your senses become reasonable after acting foolishly.

see sense: *see* **see reason** *at* REASON.

take leave of your senses go mad.

separate

go your separate ways ❶ leave in a different direction from someone with whom you have just travelled or spent time. ❷ end a romantic, professional, or other relationship.

separate the men from the boys: *see* MAN.

separate the sheep from the goats: *see* SHEEP.

separate the wheat from the chaff: *see* WHEAT.

sepulcre

a whited sepulcre: *see* WHITED.

serve

first come, first served: *see* FIRST.

serve someone right be someone's deserved punishment or misfortune.

serve your time ❶ hold office for the normal period. ❷ spend time in office, an apprenticeship, or prison.

serve your (*or* its) turn be useful or helpful.

serve two masters take orders from two superiors or follow two conflicting or opposing principles or policies at the same time.

ⓘ This phrase alludes to the warning given in the Bible against trying to serve both God and Mammon (Matthew 6:24).

sesame

open sesame: *see* OPEN.

set

ⓘ For idioms containing *set*, see the entry for the main word in the idiom (for example, **set the scene** at SCENE).

settle

the dust settles: *see* DUST.

settle accounts with someone: *see* ACCOUNT.

settle someone's hash: *see* HASH.

settle a score: *see* SCORE.

seven

at sixes and sevens: *see* SIX.

seven-league boots: *see* BOOT.

the seven-year itch a supposed tendency to infidelity after seven years of marriage. informal

seventh

in seventh heaven: *see* HEAVEN.

sex

sex on legs an extremely sexually attractive person. informal

S

2004 *Northern Rivers Echo News* Yep, forget that sissy Richard Gere playing Lancelot, give me *Hornblower's* Ioan Gruffudd any day. The guy is sex on legs.

shade

in (*or* into) the shade in (*or* into) a position of relative inferiority or obscurity.

a shade — a little —. informal

2013 *New Statesman* I was a shade too young to be in on the Smiths from the start.

shades of — used to suggest reminiscence of or comparison with someone or something specified.

ⓘ The sense of *shade* alluded to here is 'shadow' or 'ghost'.

2013 *New York Times* She banishes her husband. Then, with shades of 'Eat, Pray, Love,' she spends many pages traveling the world trying to fathom her loss and recover from it.

shadow

afraid of (*or* frightened of) your own shadow unreasonably timid or nervous.

wear yourself to a shadow completely exhaust yourself through overwork.

shag

like a shag on a rock in an isolated or exposed position. Australian informal

ⓘ The *shag* in question is the cormorant-like seabird (the term is used in the Antipodes for any cormorant).

shaggy

a shaggy-dog story a long, rambling story or joke, especially one that is amusing only because it is absurdly inconsequential or pointless.

ⓘ The expression, dating back to the 1940s, comes from the subject of one such anecdote, a dog with shaggy hair.

1993 *New York Times Book Review* The book has the unhurried pace of the best of the shaggy dog stories; the pleasure is all in the journey rather than the destination.

shake

get (*or* give someone) a fair shake get (*or* give someone) just treatment or a fair chance. informal

in two shakes (of a lamb's tail) very quickly.

more — than you can shake a stick at used to emphasize the largeness of an amount. informal

1996 *Hong Kong & Macau: Rough Guide* There are more organised tours of Hong Kong than you can shake a stick at and . . . some are worth considering.

no great shakes not very good or significant. informal

1989 Guy Vanderhaeghe *Homesick* I got specs now. Catch better with them than before, but still am no great shakes at ball.

shake the dust off your feet leave a place indignantly or disdainfully.

ⓘ This expression comes from Jesus's instructions to his disciples: 'And whosoever shall not receive you . . . when ye depart out of that house or city, shake off the dust of your feet' (Matthew 10:14).

shake (*or* quake) in your shoes (*or* boots) tremble with apprehension.

shake a leg ❶ make a start; rouse yourself; make haste. informal ❷ dance. informal

❶ **2001** *Air Classics* We would have to 'shake a leg' to make it by sunset, so I advanced the throttles to high-speed cruise.

shake your booty: *see* BOOTY.

shaker

a mover and shaker: *see* MOVER.

shame

name and shame: *see* NAME.

shamrock

drown the shamrock drink, or go drinking on St Patrick's day.

ⓘ The *shamrock* with its three-lobed leaves was said to have been used by St Patrick, the patron saint of Ireland, to illustrate the doctrine of the Trinity. It is now used as the national emblem of Ireland.

Shanks's pony

on Shanks's pony using your own legs as a means of transport.

ⓘ *Shanks* (from the Old English word *sceanca*, 'leg bone') is now used as an informal term for 'legs'. The original form of the expression was *on Shanks's mare*.

shape

bent out of shape: *see* BENT.

get into shape (*or* get someone into shape) become (*or* make someone) physically fitter by exercise.

lick (*or* knock *or* whip) someone or something into shape act forcefully to bring someone or something into a fitter, more efficient, or better-organized state.

ℹ This expression originally referred to the belief, expressed in some early bestiaries, that bear cubs were born as formless lumps and were literally licked into shape by their mother. A bestiary was a treatise about different types of animal, popular especially in medieval times.

the shape of things to come the way the future is likely to develop.

shape up or ship out used as an ultimatum to someone to improve their performance or behaviour or face being made to leave. informal, chiefly North American

share

the lion's share: *see* LION.

share and share alike have or receive an equal share; share things equally.

shark

jump the shark: *see* JUMP.

sharp

look sharp be quick.

1953 Margaret Kennedy *Troy Chimneys* I had ... begun an idle flirtation with Maria, ... then, perceiving that I should be caught if I did not look sharp, I kept out of her way.

sharp as a needle extremely quick-witted.

ℹ A variant is *sharp as a tack*.

the sharp end ❶ the most important or influential part of an activity or process. ❷ the side of a system or activity which is the most unpleasant or suffers the chief impact. ❸ the bow of a ship. British humorous

shave

close shave (*or* call) a narrow escape from danger or disaster. informal

she

who's she—the cat's mother? ❶ used as a mild reproof, especially to a child, for impolite use of the pronoun *she* when a person's name would have been more well mannered. ❷ expressing the speaker's belief that a woman or girl has a high opinion of herself or is putting on airs. British informal

shed

shed light on: *see* **throw light on** *at* LIGHT.

sheep

the black sheep: *see* BLACK.

count sheep count imaginary sheep jumping over a fence one by one in an attempt to send yourself to sleep.

1977 Harvey Pitcher *When Miss Emmie was in Russia* Did you know that if you count sheep, it is watching the sheep jump that sends you off?

make sheep's eyes at someone look at someone in a foolishly amorous way.

separate the sheep from the goats divide people or things into superior and inferior groups.

ℹ This expression alludes to the parable of the Last Judgement in Matthew 25:32–3: 'And before him shall be gathered all nations: and he shall separate them one from another, as a shepherd divideth his sheep from the goats: and he shall set the sheep on his right hand, but the goats on the left'.

a wolf in sheep's clothing: *see* WOLF.

sheet

(as) white as a sheet: *see* WHITE.

between the sheets of, at, or related to sexual intercourse. informal, euphemistic

2005 *Montreal Mirror* Terror and oppression in managed circumstances are sexy for some folks, and let's face it, we need all the help we can get keeping things lively between the sheets.

a clean sheet: *see* CLEAN.

two (*or* three) sheets to (*or* in) the wind drunk. informal

ℹ The origins of this expression are nautical. *Sheets* here are the ropes attached to the corners of a ship's sail, used for controlling the extent and direction of the sail; if they are hanging loose in the wind, the vessel is likely to be out of control or taking an erratic course.

shelf

off the shelf not designed or made to order but taken from existing stock or supplies.

on the shelf ❶ (of people or things) no longer useful or desirable. ❷ (of a woman) past an age when she might expect to have the opportunity to marry. ❸ (of a music recording or a film) awaiting release on the market after being recorded.

shell

come out of (*or* retreat into) your shell become less (*or* more) shy and retiring.

shift

get a shift on hurry up. British informal

make shift do what you want to do in spite of not having ideal conditions; get along somehow.

shift for yourself manage as best you can without help.

shift the goalposts: *see* **move the goalposts** *at* GOALPOST.

shift your ground say or write something that contradicts something you have previously written or said.

shifting

shifting sands something that is constantly changing, especially unpredictably.

> **2012** *Guardian* The idea of a place's original inhabitants is a powerful one in uncertain times when countries and cultures look to fix a sense of their own identity, and the shifting sands of globalisation are driving the current round of indigenous cinema.

shilling

not the full shilling not mentally alert or quick-thinking.

take the King's (*or* Queen's) shilling enlist as a soldier. British

> ℹ It was once the practice to pay a shilling to a man who enlisted as a soldier.

shine

rain or shine: *see* RAIN.

rise and shine: *see* RISE.

take the shine off spoil the brilliance or excitement of; overshadow.

take a shine to take a fancy to; develop a liking for. informal

shingle

hang out your shingle begin to practise a profession. North American

> ℹ The main and oldest sense of *shingle* is 'a wooden roofing tile', but in the early 19th century the word developed the more general sense of 'a piece of board', while in the USA it also acquired the particular meaning 'a small signboard'. Literally, *hanging out your shingle* refers to hanging up a sign that advertises your profession.

shining

improve the shining hour: *see* IMPROVE.

a knight in shining armour: *see* KNIGHT.

ship

break ship fail to rejoin your ship after absence on leave.

jump ship: *see* JUMP.

pump ship: *see* PUMP.

rats deserting a sinking ship: *see* RAT.

run a tight ship: *see* TIGHT.

shape up or ship out: *see* SHAPE.

ships that pass in the night transitory acquaintances.

> ℹ This expression comes from Henry Wadsworth Longfellow's poem *Tales of a Wayside Inn* (1874).

spoil the ship for a ha'p'orth of tar: *see* SPOIL.

that ship has sailed that opportunity has passed.

> **2008 digby** *Hullabaloo* The hubris of these people, thinking they can throw around a bunch of shady facts and figures and bamboozle the public into loving George Bush again. That ship has sailed.

when someone's ship comes in (*or* home) when someone's fortune is made.

> ℹ This expression dates back to the period of Britain's maritime empire, when the safe arrival of a valuable cargo meant an instant fortune for the owner and those who had shares in the enterprise.

shipshape

shipshape and Bristol fashion with everything in good order.

> ℹ Recorded from the mid 19th century, this term originally referred to the commercial prosperity of the port of Bristol and the good condition of its shipping.

shires

knight of the shires: *see* KNIGHT.

shirt

keep your shirt on don't lose your temper; stay calm. informal

lose your shirt lose all your possessions, especially as the result of unwise financial transactions. informal

put your shirt on bet all you have on; be sure of. British informal

the shirt of Nessus: *see* NESSUS.

the shirt off your back your last remaining possessions as offered to another person.

shit

vulgar slang

be shitting bricks be extremely nervous or frightened.

a crock of shit: *see* CROCK.

Do bears shit in the woods?: *see* BEAR.

get your shit together organize yourself so as to be able to deal with or achieve something.

> **2003** *SEE Magazine* (Canada) Take Katie herself, doing just a really piss-poor job of getting her shit together to create a turkey dinner for her family.

give someone the shits make someone annoyed or angry. Australian & New Zealand

in the shit in trouble.

no shit used as a way of confirming or seeking confirmation of the truth of a statement.

> ❶ An ironic extension of the phrase, used to imply that something is a statement of the obvious, is *no shit, Sherlock,* invoking the name of the master detective Sherlock Holmes.

> **2018** *Observer* He told a tech industry conference that he had only recently grasped how much of Britain's commerce is dependent on free flows across the Channel between Dover and Calais. Britain is an island? No shit, Sherlock.

not give a shit not care at all.

not know shit not know anything.

not know shit from Shinola be very ignorant or innocent. US

> ❶ *Shinola* is the proprietary name of a US brand of boot polish.

shit for brains a stupid person. chiefly North American

shit happens used to express fatalism in the face of an unwelcome occurrence.

> ❶ A euphemistic alternative formulation is *stuff happens.*

shit or get off the pot: *see* POT.

tough shit: *see* TOUGH.

up shit creek in an awkward predicament.

when the shit hits the fan when a situation becomes critical; when the disastrous consequences of something become public.

shithouse

vulgar slang

be built like a brick shithouse (of a person) have a very solid physique.

shitless

vulgar slang

be scared (*or* **bored**) **shitless** be extremely frightened (*or* bored).

shock

future shock: *see* FUTURE.

shock and awe a name given to a US military strategy, developed in the 1990s, that relies on rapidly deployed overwhelming force to cow an enemy.

shock horror used as an ironically exaggerated reaction to something shocking.

> ❶ The expression encapsulates the hyperbole of newspaper headlines, especially those in tabloid papers.

> **2003** *Film Inside Out* She encourages one of the girls to consider a career in law—shock horror!—rather than deny her intellect and settle for homemaking.

short, sharp shock ❶ a brief but harsh custodial sentence imposed on offenders in an attempt to discourage them from committing further offences. ❷ a severe measure taken in order to effect quick results.

> ❶ The Home Secretary William Whitelaw advocated the *short sharp shock* as a form of corrective treatment for young offenders at the 1979 Conservative Party Conference; the deterrent value of such a regime was to be its severity rather than the length of time served.

shoe

another pair of shoes quite a different matter or state of things.

be in another person's shoes be in another person's situation or predicament.

dead men's shoes property or a position coveted by a prospective successor but available only on a person's death.

fill someone's shoes: *see* FILL.

if the shoe fits, wear it: *see* **if the cap fits, wear it** *at* CAP.

shake in your shoes: *see* SHAKE.

shoe leather used in reference to the wear on shoes through (much) walking. informal

> **2010** *Boston Globe* Calling himself humbled and honoured by the nomination, Shumlin vowed to use shoe leather and enthusiasm to run a positive but aggressive campaign.

wait for the other shoe to drop wait for the next or final thing to happen. North American

> ℹ The underlying scenario is the feeling of tense expectation experienced after hearing one shoe dropped on the floor, especially in the context of an unseen person undressing prior to sexual intercourse.

where the shoe pinches where your difficulty or trouble is.

shoestring

on a shoestring on a small or inadequate budget.

> ℹ *Shoestring* is a North American term for a shoelace, and the expression suggests metaphorically the 'thinness' of financial resources.

shoot

green shoots: *see* GREEN.

shoot the breeze (*or* the bull) have a casual conversation. North American informal

shoot your cuffs pull your shirt cuffs out to project beyond the cuffs of your jacket or coat.

shoot someone or something down in flames forcefully destroy an argument or proposal.

> **2013** *The Age* (Melbourne) I'm a reasonable guy. I'll have a chat. If there's an argument I'll either shoot it down in flames or say let's have a think about it.

shoot someone's fox thwart someone's plans or ambitions by pre-empting them.

> ℹ The expression comes from the world of fox-hunting, where shooting a fox, which robs the hunters of their sport, is viewed with great displeasure.

> **2004** *Scotland on Sunday* The Democrats had planned to make unemployment a key issue in their campaign: Dubya, with his tax cuts, has shot their fox.

shoot from the hip react suddenly or without careful consideration of your words or actions. informal

shoot it out engage in a decisive confrontation, typically a gun battle. informal

shoot a line describe something in an exaggerated, untruthful, or boastful way. British informal

shoot your mouth off talk boastfully or indiscreetly. informal

shoot yourself in the foot inadvertently make a situation worse for yourself; demonstrate gross incompetence. informal

> **2001** *AXM* I did gain a few Brownie points when I told her I'm a journalist ... But I proceeded to shoot myself in the foot by informing her that it doesn't pay anything more than chump change.

shooting

like shooting fish in a barrel: *see* FISH.

the whole shooting match everything. informal

> **1989 Patrick O'Brian** *The Thirteen Gun Salute* I have seen all the great houses brought down, Coutts, Drummonds, Hoares, the whole shooting match.

shop

all over the shop (*or* show) ❶ everywhere; in all directions. ❷ in a state of disorder or confusion. ❸ wildly or erratically. informal

> ℹ *All over the shop* was first recorded as British 'pugilistic slang' in Hotten's *Slang Dictionary* of 1874: to inflict severe punishment on an opponent was 'to knock him all over the shop'.

live over the shop: *see* LIVE.

mind the shop: *see* MIND.

shop till you drop go on an unrestrained shopping spree. informal

shut up shop ❶ cease trading, either temporarily or permanently. ❷ stop some activity. informal

talk shop discuss matters concerning your work, especially in circumstances where this is inappropriate.

> **1990 G. Gordon Liddy** *The Monkey Handlers* Lawyers talk shop, bounce ideas off one another all the time.

short

at short notice: *see* NOTICE.

be caught (*or* taken) short ❶ be put at a disadvantage. ❷ urgently need to urinate or defecate. British informal

a brick short of a load: *see* BRICK.

bring (*or* pull) someone up short make someone check or pause abruptly.

draw the short straw: *see* STRAW.

fall short (of) ❶ (of a missile) fail to reach its target. ❷ be deficient or inadequate; fail to reach a required goal.

get (*or* have) someone by the short and curlies (*or* short hairs) have complete control of a person. informal

have a short fuse: *see* FUSE.

in short order immediately; rapidly. chiefly North American

in the short run (*or* term) over a brief period of time.

the long and the short of it: *see* LONG.

make short work of accomplish, consume, or destroy quickly.

a sandwich short of a picnic: *see* SANDWICH.

sell someone or something short fail to recognize or state the true value of someone or something.

> **2005** *Tom Peters blog* He's right that Apple is an example of great brand harmony. But ... I think he's selling them short when he focuses on 'consistency.' What makes the Apple brand powerful is not how consistent the different touchpoints are, but how well they complement each other.

short and sweet brief and pleasant.

the short end of the stick the disadvantage in a situation; a bad deal.

> ⓘ A less polite alternative formulation is *the shitty end of the stick*.
>
> **2014** *DVD Verdict* Uchidas really cares about these characters too—they sometimes get the short end of the stick but, like a lot of classic comedies, you just know things will work out for everyone.

short, sharp shock: *see* SHOCK.

short shrift: *see* SHRIFT.

wearing short pants: *see* PANTS.

shot

a big shot: *see* **a big cheese** *at* BIG.

by a long shot by far; outstandingly. informal

> **2014** *Mac Observer* Many of the bloggers in question may actually be too young to realize just how revolutionary the iPhone was.... It beats the first Mac I bought years ago too, by a long shot.

call the shots (*or* tune) take the initiative in deciding how something should be done; be in control. informal

> ⓘ *Call the shots* was originally an American phrase, first recorded in the 1960s in the context of dice gambling. *Call the tune* comes from the saying *he who pays the piper calls the tune*, which dates from the late 19th century.
>
> **2014** *New Statesman* In the event of a future financial crisis, the UK chancellor calls the shots and can direct the Bank of England's governor to take specific action to restore financial stability.

get (*or* be) shot of get (*or* be) rid of. British informal

give it your best shot try as hard as you can to do something. informal

have shot your bolt: *see* BOLT.

like a shot without hesitation; willingly. informal

not a shot in your locker no money or chances left. British

> ⓘ The *locker* referred to in this expression is a compartment in which ammunition is kept.

not by a long shot by no means.

a shot in the arm stimulus or encouragement. informal

a shot in the dark: *see* DARK.

shot to pieces (*or* to hell) ruined. informal

a warning shot across the bows: *see* BOW.

shotgun

ride shotgun: *see* RIDE.

S

shoulder

be on someone's shoulder keep a close check on someone. informal

2010 *CNN transcripts* They make no mistake, they don't try to blend in, they're not trying to hide. They're trying to show you that they are there and they're on your shoulder. If you then go in a vehicle, then they're following you in pick-up trucks.

a chip on your shoulder: *see* CHIP.

the cold shoulder: *see* COLD.

head and shoulders above: *see* HEAD.

look over your shoulder be anxious or insecure about a possible danger.

1990 *Daily Star* The chief executive . . . toasted the lifting of the takeover threat. 'Now they can get on with running the business while not looking over their shoulders,' says one city analyst.

open your shoulders: *see* OPEN.

put your shoulder to the wheel set to work vigorously.

ⓘ The image here is of pushing with your shoulder against the wheel of a cart or other vehicle that has become stuck.

rub shoulders with: *see* RUB.

a shoulder to cry on someone who listens sympathetically to another person's problems.

shoulder to shoulder ❶ side by side. ❷ acting together towards a common aim.

ⓘ Sense 2 developed from the idea of soldiers standing side by side in unbroken ranks.

stand on someone's shoulders benefit from the previous experience of (a predecessor in your field).

straight from the shoulder: *see* STRAIGHT.

S

shout

give someone a shout call on or get in touch with someone. informal

in with a shout having a good chance. informal

shout something from the rooftops: *see* ROOFTOP.

shout the odds talk loudly and in an opinionated way.

shouting

all over bar the shouting (of a contest) almost finished and therefore virtually decided. informal

shove

when (*or* **if**) **push comes to shove:** *see* PUSH.

show

all over the show: *see* **all over the shop** *at* SHOP.

get (*or* **keep**) **the show on the road** start (*or* keep going) an enterprise or organization. informal

2000 Helen Simpson *Hey Yeah Right* It took an incredible amount to keep the show on the road, what with the mortgage and childcare.

give the (whole) show away demonstrate the inadequacies or reveal the truth of something.

good (*or* **bad** *or* **poor**) **show** used to express approval (*or* disapproval or dissatisfaction). British informal, dated

the only show in town: *see* **the only game in town** *at* GAME.

show someone a clean pair of heels: *see* HEEL.

show your colours: *see* COLOURS.

show your face appear or be seen in a particular place.

show the flag: *see* FLAG.

show your hand (*or* **cards**) disclose your plans.

ⓘ The image here is of players revealing their cards in a card game.

show a leg get out of bed; get up. British informal, dated

show of hands the raising of hands among a group of people to indicate a vote for or against something, with numbers typically being estimated rather than counted.

show your teeth reveal your strength; be aggressive. British

show someone the door dismiss or eject someone unceremoniously from a place or from your presence.

1991 Michael Curtin *The Plastic Tomato Cutter*Mr Yendall, would you credit I had applicants who scorned the wages? I showed them the door.

show someone who's boss: *see* BOSS.

steal the show: *see* STEAL.

stop the show: *see* STOP.

shower

send someone to the showers withdraw someone early on in a race or contest because of poor performance. North American informal

shred

tear someone or something to shreds: *see* TEAR.

a thing of shreds and patches something made up of scraps of fabric patched together. literary

ℹ In the third act of *Hamlet*, the prince describes his uncle Claudius, who has usurped the throne, as 'a king of shreds and patches'; this description was parodied by W. S. Gilbert in *The Mikado* as 'a thing of shreds and patches'.

shrift

short shrift rapid and unsympathetic dismissal; curt treatment.

ℹ *Shrift* literally denotes penance imposed after confession to a priest, and historically *short shrift* referred to a very brief allowance of time between condemnation and execution or other punishment.

2002 *Art in America* Edward Strickland's *Minimalism: Origins*, published in 1993, gives surprisingly short shrift to the Minimalists of the 1960s.

shrinking

shrinking violet an exaggeratedly shy person. informal

2004 *Sunday Times* Clough was no shrinking violet. He had absolute belief in himself and his methods, and wasn't afraid to say so to anybody.

shuffle

be (*or* get) lost in the shuffle be overlooked or missed in a confused or crowded situation. North American informal

shuffle the cards change policy or direction.

shuffle off this mortal coil: *see* COIL.

shut

be (*or* get) shut of be (*or* get) rid of. informal

ℹ For other idioms containing *shut*, see the entry for the main word in the idiom (for example, **shut up shop** at SHOP).

shutter

put up the shutters (of a business) cease trading either for the day or permanently.

shy

fight shy of: *see* FIGHT.

have a shy at try to hit something, especially with a ball or stone.

sick

on the sick receiving sickness benefit. British informal

sick and tired annoyed about or bored with something and unwilling to put up with it any longer. informal

sick as a dog extremely ill. informal

sick as a parrot extremely disappointed. British humorous

ℹ This expression established itself in the late 20th century as a catchphrase associated particularly with disappointed footballers or football managers. But in Aphra Behn's comedy *The False Count* (1682), we find Jacinta saying to her mistress 'Lord, Madam, you are as melancholy as a sick Parrot.'

2013 *Daily Telegraph* It's wonderful. I'm delighted, thrilled, over the moon. It is the Labour Party who should be sick as a parrot.

the sick man of — a country that is politically or economically unsound, especially in comparison with its neighbours in the region specified.

ℹ In the late 19th century, following a reported comment by Tsar Nicholas I of Russia about the moribund state of the Turkish empire, the Sultan of Turkey was described as *the Sick Man of Europe*. The term was later extended to Turkey itself and subsequently applied to other countries.

2013 *New Statesman* Japan is growing at roughly 4 per cent—making it, improbably, the fastest-growing Group of Seven economy. Business confidence is at a six-year high. The sick man of Asia has ... turned fleet of foot.

sick to death very annoyed by something and unwilling to put up with it any longer. informal

sick to your stomach ❶ feeling nauseous. ❷ disgusted.

worried sick so anxious as to make yourself ill.

side

let the side down fail to meet the expectations of your colleagues or friends, especially by mismanaging something. British

on the — side rather —.

> **2004** *Essentials* To find out if the meat is cooked, insert a skewer—if the juices are red or pink it is on the rare side.

on the side ❶ in addition to your regular job or as a subsidiary source of income. ❷ secretly, especially with regard to a sexual relationship in addition to your legal or regular partner. ❸ served separately from the main dish.

> ⓘ For other idioms containing *side*, see the entry for the main word in the idiom (for example, **a thorn in someone's side** at THORN).

sidelines

on (*or* from) the sidelines in (*or* from) a position where you are observing a situation but are unable or unwilling to be directly involved in it.

> ⓘ In sports such as football and basketball, the *sidelines* mark the long edges of a playing area, behind which spectators, coaches, and other non-players must remain.

sideways

knock someone sideways: *see* KNOCK.

sight

heave in sight: *see* HEAVE.

in (*or* within) your sights within the scope of your ambitions or expectations.

> ⓘ The image in this phrase and in **raise your sights** and **set your sights on** below is of a target visible through the sights of a gun.

S

not a pretty sight: *see* PRETTY.

out of sight extremely good; excellent (often used as an exclamation). informal dated

> ⓘ The expression originated in US slang in the 1890s, and is often spelled *outasight* to suggest its casual pronunciation.
>
> **2002 Randy Shandis** *The Filthy Archives* Meg Ryan is out of sight. This is her finest performance.

out of sight, out of mind you soon forget people or things that are no longer visible or present. proverb

raise (*or* lower) your sights become more (*or* less) ambitious; increase (*or* lower) your expectations.

set your sights on have as an ambition; hope strongly to achieve or reach.

> **2014 Esther** *A Catholic Mom in Hawaii* Then, should they succeed in Nigeria, they would set their sights on the South. If they should overrun Nigeria, it will be a steppingstone to conquering smaller countries.

a sight for sore eyes a person or thing that is very attractive or that you are extremely pleased or relieved to see. informal

a sight more — (*or* a sight — than *or* a sight too —) someone or something has a great deal or too much of a particular specified quality. informal

> **2012** *New Statesman* As a Labour supporter, I have to say Michael Dixon's comments (as a Conservative) seem a sight more informed than Tim Montgomerie's.

sign

sign of the times something typical of the nature or quality of a particular period, typically something undesirable.

sign on the dotted line agree formally.

> **1921 P. G. Wodehouse** *Indiscretions of Archie* I spoke to him as one old friend to another . . . and he sang a few bars from 'Rigoletto', and signed on the dotted line.

sign your own death warrant do something that ensures your own demise or downfall.

sign the pledge: *see* PLEDGE.

signed, sealed, and delivered (*or* signed and sealed) formally and officially agreed and in effect.

significant

significant other a person with whom someone has an established romantic or sexual relationship.

> **2001** *Journal of Sex Research* We asked: 'Are you currently in a relationship? (Do you have a significant other, boyfriend, girlfriend, sexual partner, spouse, etc.?)' and 'If you answered "YES", how long have you been in your current relationship?'

silence

a conspiracy of silence: *see* CONSPIRACY.

silence is golden it's often wise to say nothing. proverb

> ⓘ The fuller form of the saying is *speech is silver, but silence is golden*.

silent

silent as the grave: *see* GRAVE.

the silent majority the majority of people, regarded as holding moderate opinions but rarely expressing them.

> ℹ This phrase was first particularly associated with the US President Richard Nixon, who claimed in his 1968 presidential election campaign to speak for this segment of society.

> **2012** *New York Times* We've heard from people in the street. We've heard from those who have been hitting away at pots and pans. Now is the time for the silent majority.

the silent treatment a stubborn refusal to talk to someone, especially after a recent argument or disagreement.

> **2004 Julie Burchill** *Sugar Rush* If I hadn't been giving her the silent treatment because of my hurt pride, she'd never have even gone off with this psycho.

silk

make a silk purse out of a sow's ear turn something inferior into something of top quality.

> ℹ The observation that *you can't make a silk purse out of a sow's ear* has been proverbial since the late 16th century; there was an earlier version which featured *a goat's fleece* instead of *a sow's ear*.

silly

play silly buggers: *see* BUGGER.

— yourself silly be unable to act rationally because of doing something to excess.

> **2012** *National Business Review* One of the few times in life you are not free to check your newsfeed or Twitter yourself silly is when you're driving.

the silly season the months of August and September regarded as the time when newspapers often publish trivia because of a lack of important news. chiefly British

> ℹ This concept and phrase date back to the mid 19th century. In high summer Victorian London was deserted by the wealthy and important during the period in which Parliament and the law courts were in recess.

silver

be born with a silver spoon in your mouth be born into a wealthy family of high social standing.

cross someone's palm with silver: *see* CROSS.

have a silver tongue be eloquent or persuasive.

on a silver platter (*or* salver) without having been asked or sought for; without requiring any effort or return from the recipient.

> ℹ The image here is of a butler or waiter presenting something on a silver tray.

sell the family silver: *see* FAMILY.

a silver lining a positive or more hopeful aspect to a bad situation, even though this may not be immediately apparent.

> ℹ The full form of the phrase is the proverb *every cloud has a silver lining*.

the silver screen the cinema industry; cinema films collectively.

> ℹ In the early days of cinematography, a projection screen was covered with metallic paint to give a highly reflective, silver-coloured surface.

Simon Pure

the real Simon Pure the real or genuine person or thing.

> ℹ Simon Pure is a character in Susannah Centlivre's *A Bold Stroke for a Wife* (1717), who for part of the play is impersonated by another character.

simple

pure and simple: *see* PURE.

sin

— as sin having a particular undesirable quality to a high degree. informal

> **2013** *Bookslut* When Delia finally gives birth, she delegates all maternal responsibilities to her maid and calls her baby ugly as sin.

besetting sin: *see* BESETTING.

cover a multitude of sins: *see* MULTITUDE.

for your sins used to suggest that a task or duty is so onerous or unpleasant that it must be a punishment. chiefly British

> **2010** *Financial Times* I ran e-commerce back in 2000, I then ran the international business. I even, for my sins, was temporary finance director for a while.

like sin vehemently or forcefully. informal

live in sin live together as though married; cohabit. informal, dated

sing

sing a different tune (*or* song) change your opinion about or attitude towards someone or something.

sing for your supper: *see* SUPPER.

sing from the same hymn (*or* song) sheet present a united front in public by not disagreeing with one another. British informal

> **2000** *South China Morning Post* We're all singing from the same hymn sheet and there is a real will to clean up the game, though it may take a life ban to restore cricket's credibility.

sing the praises of express enthusiastic approval or admiration of.

singe

singe your wings suffer harm, especially in a risky attempt.

singing

all-singing, all-dancing: *see* ALL.

sink

everything but the kitchen sink: *see* KITCHEN.

sink or swim fail or succeed entirely by your own efforts.

sink without trace ❶ disappear and not be seen or heard of again. ❷ fail abjectly.

> ❷ **2003** *Down Democrat* Recently Paul Linehan's team sank without trace in the NCU Senior Cup, crushed by Division Two visitors Carrickfergus.

sink your teeth into: *see* **get your teeth into** *at* TEETH.

your heart sinks into your boots: *see* BOOT.

sinker

hook, line, and sinker: *see* HOOK.

sinking

a (*or* that) sinking feeling an unpleasant feeling caused by the realization that something unpleasant or undesirable has happened or is about to happen.

siren

siren song (*or* call) the appeal of something that is also considered to be harmful or dangerous.

> ℹ In classical mythology, the Sirens were sea nymphs whose beautiful singing lured sailors to their doom on submerged rocks.

sister

weak sister: *see* WEAK.

sit

sit at someone's feet be someone's pupil or follower.

sit next to Nellie learn how to do a job or task by watching and copying someone experienced in it. informal

sit on the fence: *see* FENCE.

sit on your hands take no action.

> **2013** *Daily Telegraph* It is ... only the latest in a long line of child abuse and neglect cases, from Baby P to Daniel Pelka, in which the authorities have sat on their hands until a child died.

sit (heavy) on the stomach (of food) take a long time to be digested.

sit on someone's tail drive extremely close behind another vehicle, typically while waiting for a chance to overtake.

sit tight ❶ remain firmly in your place. ❷ refrain from taking action or changing your mind. informal

> ❶ **1984 Studs Terkel** *The Good War* Our colonel told everyone to sit tight, don't leave the camp.

sit up (and take notice) suddenly start paying attention or have your interest aroused. informal

sitting

sitting duck a person or thing with no protection against an attack or other source of danger.

sitting pretty: *see* PRETTY.

six

at sixes and sevens in a state of total confusion or disarray.

> ℹ This phrase originated as gambling slang and may be an alteration or corruption of Old French *cinque* (five) and *sice* (six), these being the highest numbers on dice. The idea of risking all your goods on the two highest numbers led to the idea of carelessness and neglect of your possessions and eventually to the development of the phrase's current meaning.

2008 *Guardian* The countries of the European Union have been at sixes and sevens in their relations with Moscow.

hit (*or* knock) someone for six affect someone very severely; utterly overwhelm someone. British informal

🛈 In this expression, *six* stands for six runs, referring to a hit in cricket which sends the ball clear over the boundary of the playing area for a score of six runs.

six feet under dead and buried. informal

🛈 Six feet is the traditional depth of a grave.

six of the best: *see* BEST.

six of one and half a dozen of the other used to convey that there is no real difference between two alternatives.

sixpence

on a sixpence (of a stop or turn) within a small area or short distance. British informal

🛈 The old sixpenny coin was one of the smallest in circulation in Britain prior to decimalization in 1971.

sixteen

sweet sixteen: *see* SWEET.

sixty-four

the sixty-four thousand dollar question something that is not known and on which a great deal depends.

🛈 This expression dates from the 1940s and was originally *the sixty-four dollar question*, from a question posed for the top prize in a broadcast US quiz show. It has been hit by inflation, and much larger hypothetical prizes are now common, such as *the million dollar question* and even *the trillion dollar question*.

2010 *TechDirt* When you think about it, why would God want people not to work on Sunday? Now that is the 64-thousand dollar question.

size

cut someone down to size deflate someone's exaggerated sense of self-worth. informal

that's about the size of it said to confirm a person's assessment of a situation, especially one regarded as bad. informal

try something for size: *see* TRY.

skate

get your skates on make haste; hurry up. British informal

(skate) on thin ice: *see* ICE.

skeef

check someone or something skeef: *see* CHECK.

skeleton

a skeleton at the feast: *see* **a ghost at the feast** *at* FEAST.

a skeleton in the cupboard a discreditable or embarrassing fact that someone wishes to keep secret.

🛈 A US variant of this expression is *a skeleton in the closet*.

skid

hit the skids begin a rapid decline or deterioration. informal

🛈 The origin of *skid* is uncertain, but it may be connected with the Old Norse word from which English *ski* is derived. It is used here and in the next two entries in the sense of a plank or roller on which a heavy object may be placed in order to move it easily.

on the skids (of a person or their career) in a bad state; failing. informal

1989 Thomas Berger *The Changing Past* Jackie arrived at middle age with a career on the skids.

put the skids under hasten the decline or failure of. informal

skidoo

twenty-three skidoo: *see* TWENTY-THREE.

skin

be skin and bone be very thin.

by the skin of your teeth by a very narrow margin; only just.

get under someone's skin ❶ annoy or irritate someone intensely. ❷ fill someone's mind in a compelling and continual way. ❸ reach a deep understanding of someone. informal

❶ **2000 Joanne Harris** *Blackberry Wine* He argued constantly with his mother—*everything* got under his skin that year.

give someone (some) skin shake or slap hands together as a gesture of friendship or solidarity. African American slang

S

have skin in the game have a personal investment in an organization or undertaking, and therefore a vested interest in its success. informal

ℹ The idiom may be based either on the idea of the skin as representing the whole person (as in expressions such as *save someone's skin*), or on the US slang use of *skin* to mean 'dollar'.

1996 *Observer* We want to make a step change in our clients' business—and we're willing to risk our own capital to do it .... We're transforming the business by having skin in the game.

have a thick (*or* thin) skin be insensitive (*or* oversensitive) to criticism or insults.

it's no skin off my nose it's a matter of indifference to me; I am unaffected by it. informal

jump out of your skin: *see* JUMP.

make your skin crawl: *see* CRAWL.

save someone's skin: *see* SAVE.

skin (your) teeth laugh or smile. West Indian

there's more than one way to skin a cat there's more than one way of achieving your aim.

ℹ There are several traditional proverbs along these lines, for example *there are more ways of killing a cat than choking it with cream*.

under the skin in reality, as opposed to superficial appearances.

skirt

a bit of skirt: *see* **a bit of fluff** *at* BIT.

skittles

beer and skittles: *see* BEER.

S

skull

out of your skull ❶ out of your mind; crazy. ❷ very drunk. informal

skunk

drunk as a skunk: *see* **drunk as a lord** *at* DRUNK.

sky

blow something sky-high destroy something completely in an explosion. informal

gone to the big (*or* great) — in the sky having died. informal euphemistic

ℹ The open slot is filled by the name of a place or milieu typically occupied by the deceased in life.

2004 *DVD Verdict* Harold's pet goldfish has gone to the great fish bowl in the sky, but our favorite toddler doesn't grasp the meaning of death.

out of a clear (blue) sky: *see* CLEAR.

pie in the sky: *see* PIE.

the sky is the limit there is practically no limit.

2014 *Daily Telegraph* On Wednesday, at a school in Soweto, she focused on her other policy plank, telling 400 children: 'The sky is the limit if you work hard.'

to the skies very highly; enthusiastically.

1989 Gay Daly *Pre-Raphaelites in Love* Gabriel wrote to his little sister praising Lizzie to the skies.

slack

cut someone some slack allow someone some leeway; make allowances for someone's behaviour. North American informal

2013 Ben *Silent Words Speak Loudest* Perhaps ... we should cut Nash ... some slack. After all, to the 11-year-old Nash ... the Spice Girls' superficial sloganeering may have genuinely seemed like feminism.

take (*or* pick) up the slack ❶ pull on the loose end or part of a rope in order to make it taut. ❷ use up a surplus or improve the use of resources to avoid an undesirable lull in business.

slap

a face like a slapped arse: *see* ARSE.

slap and tickle physical amorous play. British informal

a slap in the face (*or* eye) an unexpected rejection or affront.

2013 *New Zealand Herald* One Maori media outlet snubbed last week's competition, saying the lack of full access was a slap in the face.

slap on the wrist a mild reprimand or punishment.

2013 *CNN transcripts* To think that he caused all of these deaths through, you know, essentially he deliberately drank all of this alcohol, a huge amount, and caused this accident. And to get a slap on the wrist I think is just stunning and shocking to the public.

slap someone on the back congratulate someone heartily.

slate

a clean slate: *see* **a clean sheet** *at* CLEAN.

on the (*or* **your**) **slate** to be paid for later; on credit. British

ℹ Shops and bars formerly kept a record of what a customer owed by chalking it on a tablet made of slate.

wipe the slate clean: *see* WIPE.

slaughter

like a lamb to the slaughter: *see* LAMB.

slave

slave over a hot stove: *see* STOVE.

sledgehammer

take (*or* **use**) **a sledgehammer to crack a nut** use disproportionately forceful means to achieve a simple objective.

ℹ A *sledgehammer* is a large, heavy hammer used for such jobs as breaking up rocks and driving in fence posts.

2013 *Daily Telegraph* What will it look like if we go at him all guns blazing? It'll be using a sledgehammer to crack a nut.

sleep

lose sleep: *see* LOSE.

not sleep a wink: *see* WINK.

put something to sleep ❶ kill (an animal, especially an old, sick, or badly injured one) painlessly. euphemistic ❷ put (a computer) on standby while it is not being used.

sleep easy: *see* EASY.

sleep like a log (*or* **top**) sleep very soundly.

the sleep of the just a deep, untroubled sleep.

ℹ The idea here is that only those with clear consciences can expect to have a peaceful night's sleep.

sleep rough: *see* ROUGH.

sleep with one eye open sleep very lightly so as to be aware of what is happening around you.

someone could do something in their sleep someone could do or accomplish something with no effort or conscious thought. informal

sleeping

let sleeping dogs lie avoid interfering in a situation that is currently causing no problems, but may well do so as a consequence of such interference. proverb

ℹ In the early 14th century the French phrase *n'esveillez pas lou chien qui dort* advised 'do not wake the sleeping dog', while Chaucer remarks in *Troilus and Criseyde* 'it is nought good a slepyng hound to wake'. The present form of the proverb seems to be traceable to Walter Scott's novel *Redgauntlet* (1824).

sleeve

have an ace up your sleeve: *see* ACE.

have a card up your sleeve: *see* CARD.

laugh up your sleeve: *see* LAUGH.

roll up your sleeves: *see* ROLL.

up your sleeve (of a strategy, idea, or resource) kept secret and in reserve for use when needed.

wear your heart on your sleeve: *see* HEART.

sleigh ride

take someone for a sleigh ride mislead someone.

ℹ A *sleigh ride* here is an implausible or false story or a hoax: if you *take someone for a sleigh ride* you mislead or cheat them. *Sleigh ride* can also mean 'a drug-induced high', so *take a sleigh ride* means 'take drugs, especially cocaine'.

sleight

sleight of hand the display of skilful, especially deceptive, dexterity or cunning.

ℹ Literally, the expression means 'manual dexterity in performing a conjuring trick'.

slice

slice and dice divide a quantity of information up into smaller parts, especially in order to analyse it more closely or in different ways.

a slice of the action: *see* **a piece of the action** *at* PIECE.

a slice of the cake a share of the benefits or profits. informal

1991 Robert Reiner *Chief Constables* Perhaps it's because they're such good spenders that our slice of the cake is sufficient for all we want.

a slice of life a realistic representation of everyday experience in a film, play, or book.

sliced

the best thing since sliced bread: *see* BREAD.

slide

let something slide negligently allow something to deteriorate.

sling

put someone's (*or* have your) ass in a sling land someone (*or* be) in trouble. North American vulgar slang

sling beer work as a bartender. North American informal

sling hash (*or* plates) serve food in a cafe or diner. North American informal

sling your hook: *see* HOOK.

sling mud: *see* **fling mud** *at* MUD.

slings and arrows adverse factors or circumstances.

ⓘ This expression is taken from the 'to be or not to be' speech in *Hamlet*: 'Whether tis nobler in the mind to suffer the slings and arrows of outrageous fortune, Or to take arms against a sea of troubles, And by opposing end them'.

2001 Ian J. Deary *Intelligence* The genetic lottery and the environmental slings and arrows influence the level of some of our mental capabilities.

slip

give someone the slip evade or escape from someone. informal

let something slip ❶ reveal something inadvertently in the course of a conversation. ❷ fail to take advantage of an opportunity.

let something slip through your fingers (*or* grasp) ❶ lose hold or possession of something. ❷ miss the opportunity of gaining something.

❷ **1925 W. Somerset Maugham** *Of Human Bondage* He was mad to have let such an adventure slip through his fingers.

a slip of a — a young, small, and slim person.

1980 Philip Larkin *Letter* After all you are a very young 51! Hardly 51 at all! A slip of a thing!

slip of the pen (*or* the tongue) a minor mistake in writing (*or* speech).

ⓘ The equivalent Latin phrases, *lapsus calami* and *lapsus linguae*, are also sometimes used in formal English.

slip on a banana skin make a silly and embarrassing mistake.

slip through the net: *see* NET.

there's many a slip ('twixt cup and lip) many things can go wrong between the start of something and its completion; nothing is certain until it has happened. proverb

slippery

slippery slope an idea or course of action which will lead inevitably to something unacceptable, wrong, or disastrous.

2013 *Rural Canadian* It bothers me greatly... when it appears that the local ... Green EDA (Electoral District Association) has once again got one foot on the slippery slope to de-registration due to lack of support.

slippy

look slippy be quick; make haste. British, dated

slow

be slow off the mark: *see* **be quick off the mark** *at* MARK.

be slow on the uptake: *see* **be quick on the uptake** *at* UPTAKE.

slow burn: *see* BURN.

slow but (*or* and) sure not quick but achieving the required result eventually. proverb

smack

a face like a smacked arse: *see* ARSE.

have a smack at make an attempt at or attack on. informal

a smack in the face (*or* eye) a strong rebuff. informal

smack your lips (*or* chops): *see* **lick your lips** *at* LICK.

small

great and small: *see* GREAT.

in small doses: *see* DOSE.

the (wee) small hours the early hours of the morning immediately after midnight.

small is beautiful the belief that something small-scale is better than a large-scale equivalent.

ℹ *Small is Beautiful* is the title of a book by E. F. Schumacher, published in 1973. The phrase is best known through its adoption as a slogan by environmentalists.

small beer something trivial or insignificant. chiefly British

ℹ Originally, *small beer* meant literally 'weak beer'.

2005 *Observer Music Monthly* Getting called a 'Paki' by ill-informed racists was very small beer compared to being shot at by Sinhalese government forces chasing her father.

a small fortune: *see* FORTUNE.

small potatoes something insignificant or unimportant.

ℹ This phrase originated in mid-19th-century American use, especially in the form *small potatoes and few in the hill*.

2012 *Guardian* Isn't a budget of $100m small potatoes by the standard of today's blockbuster movie?

small print inconspicuous details or conditions printed in an agreement or contract, especially ones that may prove unfavourable.

ℹ Such details are typically printed in small type.

the small screen television as a medium (as opposed to cinema).

it's (*or* what) a small world used to express surprise at meeting an acquaintance or discovering a personal connection in a distant place or an unexpected context.

with a small — used of the first letter of a word that has both a general and a specific use to show that in this case the general use is intended.

2012 *CNN transcripts* I am a Democrat, but I'm a democrat with a small d. I care about our democracy.

smart

look smart be quick. chiefly British

smart alec (*or* aleck) a person considered irritating because they know a great deal or always have a clever answer to a question.

ℹ From the male personal name *Alec*, a short form of *Alexander*.

smell

bells and smells: *see* BELL.

live (*or* survive) on the smell of an oil rag live in conditions of extreme want. Australian

smell blood discern weakness or vulnerability in an opponent.

smell of the lamp show signs of laborious study and effort.

ℹ The *lamp* here is an oil lamp, formerly used for night-time work or study.

smell a rat begin to suspect trickery or deception. informal

smell the roses enjoy or appreciate what is often ignored. North American informal

wake up and smell the coffee: *see* WAKE.

smelling

come up (*or* out) smelling of roses (*or* violets) make a lucky escape from a difficult situation with your reputation intact. informal

ℹ The fuller form of this expression, *fall in the shit and come up smelling of roses*, explains the idea behind it.

smile

come up smiling recover from adversity and cheerfully face the future. informal

1989 *Woman's Realm* But despite her ordeal courageous Kelly has come up smiling and is now looking forward to a bright future.

wipe the smile off someone's face: *see* WIPE.

smoke

the big smoke: *see* BIG.

go up in smoke ❶ be destroyed by fire. ❷ (of a plan) come to nothing. informal

in a smoke-filled room: *see* ROOM.

no smoke without fire (*or* where there's smoke there's fire) there's always some reason for a rumour. proverb

2012 *New York Times* Because many people believe there is 'no smoke without fire' he expected some of the stigma arising from the episode to remain with him for the rest of his life.

put that in your pipe and smoke it: *see* PIPE.

smoke and mirrors the obscuring or embellishing of the truth of a situation with misleading or irrelevant information. chiefly North American

2003 *Village Voice* (New York) In retrospect, the Bush administration's most publicized war stories have all been the products of smoke and mirrors.

smoke like a chimney smoke tobacco incessantly.

watch someone's smoke observe another person's activity.

ⓘ The implication of this phrase is that the activity in question will be so fast and furious that smoke will be generated.

1947 P. G. Wodehouse *Full Moon* Look at Henry the Eighth... And Solomon. Once they started marrying, there was no holding them—you just sat back and watched their smoke.

smoking

a smoking gun (*or* pistol) a piece of incontrovertible evidence.

ⓘ This phrase draws on the assumption, a staple of detective fiction, that the person found with a recently fired gun must be the guilty party. The use of the phrase in the late 20th century was particularly associated with the Watergate scandal in the early 1970s involving the US President Richard Nixon. When one of the Watergate tapes revealed Nixon's wish to limit the FBI's role in the investigation, Barber B. Conable famously commented: 'I guess we have found the smoking pistol, haven't we?'

2012 *New York Times* Incoming transactions in the chief justice's accounts, including deposits and bank transfers, totaled $28,740,497.93, the documents showed. This was when Mr Corona was earning less than $935 per month as a Supreme Court justice. 'It is the smoking gun,' Ramon C. Casiple, executive director of the Institute for Political and Electoral Reform in Manila, said of the disclosure.

S

smooth

in smooth water in quiet and serene circumstances, especially after difficulties.

smooth someone's ruffled feathers: *see* RUFFLED.

take the rough with the smooth: *see* ROUGH.

snail

at a snail's pace extremely slowly.

snake

a snake in the grass a treacherous or deceitful person.

ⓘ Since the late 17th century this expression has entirely superseded the earlier idiom *a pad in the straw. Pad* is an old dialect term for a toad, an animal that was formerly thought to be poisonous.

mad as a (cut) snake: *see* MAD.

snaky

go (*or* drive someone) snaky lose (*or* cause someone to lose) their self-control. Canadian

snap

in a snap in a moment; almost immediately. informal, chiefly North American

snap someone's head off: *see* **bite someone's head off** *at* HEAD.

snap out of it get out of a bad or unhappy mood. informal

snap your fingers at: *see* FINGER.

snappy

make it snappy be quick about it.

1994 Pete Hamill *A Drinking Life* Into bed! he said. Make it snappy! I retreated into the darkness of the second floor from the kitchen.

sneezed

not to be sneezed at not to be rejected without careful consideration; worth having or taking into account. informal

ⓘ The same sentiment is expressed by *not to be sniffed at*.

snook

cock a snook openly show contempt or a lack of respect for someone or something. informal, chiefly British

ⓘ Literally, if you cock a snook, you place your hand so that your thumb touches your nose and your fingers are spread out, in order to express contempt. Recorded from the late 18th century, the expression's origins are uncertain—as are those of the gesture itself, which occurs under a variety of names and in many countries, the earliest definite mention of it being by Rabelais in 1532.

snow

pure as the driven snow: *see* PURE.

a snow job a deception or concealment of your real motive in an effort to flatter or persuade. North American informal

snowball

not a snowball's chance in hell: *see* **not a hope in hell** *at* HELL.

snuff

up to snuff ❶ up to the required standard. ❷ in good health. informal

snug

snug as a bug (in a rug) extremely comfortable. humorous

so

so long: *see* LONG.

soap

no soap no chance of something happening or occurring. North American informal

> ℹ The origin of this expression, used to refuse a request, may lie in the mid-19th- century US informal use of *soap* to mean 'money'.

> **1929 Edmund Wilson** *I Thought of Daisy* If he tries to cut in on you, don't letum—I'll just tellum, no soap.

soft soap: *see* SOFT.

soapbox

on your soapbox energetically stating your opinions, especially ones which are already well known on a subject that you often revert to.

> ℹ Soapboxes (originally boxes in which soap was packed and transported) were in the past often used as makeshift platforms by public speakers.

sober

sober as a judge completely sober.

sock

bless your (*or* his/her/their) little cotton socks used as an expression of endearment. informal, chiefly British

knock (*or* blow) someone's socks off amaze or impress someone. informal

> **1991 Barbara Anderson** *Girls High* Years ago she saw a Hockney... the few lines which sketched the owlish face knocked her socks off.

> **1996** *Premiere* Ray Liotta strikes perfect notes as Hill while Joe Pesci blows your socks off as sociopathic side-kick Tommy.

knock the socks off someone beat or surpass someone. informal

pull your socks up make an effort to improve your work, performance, or behaviour. informal

put a sock in it stop talking. British informal

sock it to someone attack someone vigorously or make a forceful impression on them in some other way. informal

> **1991** *Baseball Today* Chicago socked it to the other teams in the American league.

— your socks off do something with great energy and enthusiasm. informal

> **2013** *Telegraph* It's arguable that he was not there enough throughout their childhood—ironically, because he was working his socks off to give other people's children a helping hand.

sod

chiefly British

sod all nothing. vulgar slang

> **2005 Hilary Mantel** *Beyond Black* That eventless realm ... where the dead ... pass the ages with sod all going on.

sod's law if anything can go wrong it will. informal *See also* **Murphy's law** *at* MURPHY.

soft

have a soft spot for be fond of or affectionate towards.

soft option an easier alternative.

soft soap persuasive flattery.

> ℹ The underlying idea is of soft soap (literally a type of semi-fluid soap) being lubricative and unctuous.

a soft touch: *see* TOUCH.

soften

soften (*or* cushion) the blow make it easier to cope with a difficult change or upsetting news.

S

soldier

come (*or* **play) the old soldier** use your greater age or experience of life to deceive someone or to shirk a duty. informal

ℹ In US nautical slang a *soldier* or an *old soldier* was an incompetent seaman.

soldier of fortune an adventurous person ready to take service under any person or state in return for money; a mercenary.

some

and then some and plenty more than that. informal, chiefly US

2014 *Daily Telegraph* Feltz, however, took the view that women can match men brain cell for brain cell—and then some.

something

something and nothing a trivial matter.

2018 Mel Sherratt *Hush Hush* We had a few words the week before last, that's all.... He said I was above myself just because I was the manager. It was something and nothing. He apologised when I next saw him.

something else an exceptional person or thing. informal

something for the weekend: *see* WEEKEND.

thirty-something (*or* **forty-something**, etc.) an unspecified age between thirty and forty (forty and fifty, etc.). informal

son

favourite son: *see* FAVOURITE.

son of a gun a humorous or affectionate way of addressing or referring to someone. informal

ℹ The term arose with reference to the guns carried on board ships: it is said to have been originally applied to babies born at sea by women accompanying their husbands.

S

song

for a song very cheaply. informal

ℹ The ultimate origin of this phrase is probably the practice, in former times, of selling written copies of ballads very cheaply at fairs. The expression was in common use by the mid 17th century.

1985 Nini Herman *My Kleinian Home* The place was going for a song, since anyone in his right mind would have steered well clear of it.

on song performing well; in good form. British informal

1996 *Times* The horse is in pretty good shape. I rode him out at Haydock and he felt on song.

song and dance ❶ a fuss or commotion. informal ❷ a long explanation that is pointless or deliberately evasive. North American informal

a song in your heart a feeling of great or euphoric happiness.

ℹ The expression originated in the title of a song, 'With a song in my heart' (1929), by Lorenz Hart.

wine, women, and song: *see* WINE.

sop

a sop to Cerberus something offered to appease someone.

ℹ In Greek mythology, Cerberus was the three-headed watchdog which guarded the entrance of Hades. In the *Aeneid* Virgil describes how the Sibyl guiding Aeneas to the underworld threw a drugged cake to Cerberus, thus enabling the hero to pass the monster in safety.

sorcerer

sorcerer's apprentice a person who having instigated a process is unable to control it.

ℹ This is a translation of the French *L'Apprenti sorcier*, the title of an 1897 symphonic poem by Paul Dukas based on *Der Zauberlehrling*, a 1797 ballad by Goethe. In this ballad the apprentice's use of magic spells sets in motion a series of events which he cannot control. The part of the apprentice was notably played by Mickey Mouse in the 1940 Walt Disney film *Fantasia*.

sorcery

sword and sorcery: *see* SWORD.

sore

like a bear with a sore head: *see* BEAR.

a sight for sore eyes: *see* SIGHT.

a sore point an issue about which someone feels distressed or annoyed and which it is therefore advisable to avoid raising with them.

stand (*or* **stick) out like a sore thumb** be very obviously and often embarrassingly different from the surrounding people or things.

sorrow

drown your sorrows: *see* DROWN.

more in sorrow than in anger with regret or sadness rather than with anger.

ℹ This is taken from *Hamlet*. When Hamlet asks Horatio to describe the expression on the face of his father's ghost, Horatio replies 'a countenance more in sorrow than in anger'.

sort

it takes all sorts people vary greatly in character, tastes, and abilities. proverb

ℹ The complete form of this expression is *it takes all sorts to make a world*, often used as a comment on what the speaker feels to be unconventional behaviour.

2013 *New Statesman* It is obviously Gilmour's prerogative, as a middle-aged writer, to be interested exclusively in other middle-aged writers. It may make him sound staggeringly narrow-minded and parochial, but so what: it takes all sorts.

out of sorts ❶ slightly unwell. ❷ in low spirits; irritable.

sort out the men from the boys: *see* **separate the men from the boys** *at* MAN.

soul

ℹ For idioms containing *soul*, see the entry for the main word in the idiom (for example, **sell your soul (to the devil)** at SELL).

sound

as sound as a bell: *see* **as clear as a bell** *at* BELL.

soup

alphabet soup: *see* ALPHABET.

duck soup: *see* DUCK.

from soup to nuts from beginning to end; completely. North American informal

ℹ Soup is likely to feature as the first course of a formal meal, while a selection of nuts may be offered as the final one.

in the soup in trouble. informal

soup and fish men's formal evening dress. British informal, dated

ℹ The allusion is to the traditional first two courses of a formal meal.

sour

sour grapes an attitude in which someone disparages or pretends to despise something because they cannot have it themselves.

ℹ In Aesop's fable *The Fox and the Grapes*, the fox, unable to reach the tempting bunch of grapes, comforts himself with the thought that they were probably sour anyway.

2012 *Washington Post* His comment, made on a conference call with donors, that President Obama won by offering 'gifts' to various constituencies reeked of sour grapes and a poor post-game analysis.

south

head (*or* go) south deteriorate.

2008 *Newsweek* Many months ago, McCain remarked, honestly, that he didn't know much about economics. As the economy heads south, he is routinely reminded of his candor.

sow

ℹ For idioms containing *sow*, see the entry for the main word in the idiom (for example, **make a silk purse out of a sow's ear** at SILK).

space

waste of space: *see* WASTE.

watch this space used to indicate that further developments are expected and more information will be given later. informal

ℹ The *space* referred to here is a section of a newspaper available for a specific purpose, especially for advertising.

1979 Julian Rathbone *The Euro-Killers* Where is he? Watch this space for exciting revelations in the next few days.

spade

call a spade a spade speak plainly or bluntly, without avoiding issues which are unpleasant or embarrassing.

ℹ A variation on this phrase, dating from the early 20th century and used for humorous emphasis, is *call a spade a shovel*.

2012 *New Zealand Herald* Mr Cunliffe today acknowledged that he created some strong feelings amongst his colleagues. 'I'm a reasonably strong personality, and I call a spade a spade, and I can be upfront,' Mr Cunliffe said.

in spades to a very high degree; as much as or more than could be desired. informal

ℹ This expression derives from the fact that spades are the highest-ranking suit in the card game bridge.

2014 *Washington Post* He repeatedly demonstrates that what really separates good people from bad people is the ability to empathize—an ability Dow possesses in spades.

Spain

build castles in Spain: *see* **build castles in the air** *at* CASTLE.

span

spick and span: *see* SPICK.

Spanish

old Spanish customs (*or* Spanish practices) long-standing though unauthorized or irregular work practices.

ⓘ This expression has been in use in printing circles since the 1960s; it is often used humorously to refer to practices in the British newspaper printing houses in Fleet Street, London, formerly notorious for their inefficiency. The reason for describing such practices as 'Spanish' is not known.

2009 *Guardian* With a postal strike ballot underway I see Royal Mail management again accusing the workforce of protecting 'old Spanish customs'.

spanner

a bag of spanners: *see* BAG.

a spanner in the works an event, person, or thing that prevents the smooth or successful implementation of a plan; a drawback or impediment.

ⓘ A variant, found chiefly in North American English, is *a monkey wrench in the works*, a *monkey wrench* being a spanner or wrench with adjustable jaws: to *throw a spanner* (or *a monkey wrench*) *into the works* is to deliberately wreck someone's plans or activities. In his 1974 novel *The Monkey Wrench Gang*, Edward Abbey used this as a metaphor for systematic industrial sabotage, and *monkey-wrenching* is now a colloquial term for such activity.

2011 Mark Heuring *Mr Dilettante* On balance, however, he's been much more of a hindrance than a help to his successors. It's time he stopped throwing spanners in the works.

spare

go spare become extremely angry or distraught. British informal

1991 Roddy Doyle *The Van* Remind me to replace this one . . . Veronica'll go spare if she goes to get it on Sunday and it's not there.

spare someone's blushes: *see* BLUSH.

a spare prick at a wedding: *see* PRICK.

spare the rod and spoil the child: *see* ROD.

to spare left over.

spark

bright spark: *see* BRIGHT.

sparks fly a discussion becomes heated or lively.

spark out completely unconscious. British informal

2005 *Mike da Hut* A good friend of mine who was playing away from home, got really pissed and before he passed out started a text to his amour. His wife found him on the settee spark out with his phone still in his hand.

strike sparks off each other (*or* one another) (of two or more people) creatively inspire each other while working on something.

speak

it speaks well for something places someone or something in a favourable light.

so to speak used to highlight the fact that you are describing something in an unusual or metaphorical way.

speak for yourself give your own opinions.

ⓘ The exclamation *speak for yourself!* indicates to someone that an opinion they have expressed is not shared by yourself and is resented.

speak in tongues speak in an unknown language during religious worship.

ⓘ Speaking in (*or* with) tongues is a phenomenon known more formally as *glossolalia*, which is regarded by some as a gift of the Holy Spirit. The Bible records that the apostles demonstrated this ability (e.g. Acts 10:46, 19:6), and it is a component of present-day charismatic Christian worship.

speak your mind express your feelings or opinions frankly.

1982 Marion Z. Bradley *The Mists of Avalon* Someday she would be too weary or too unguarded to care, and she would speak her mind to the priest.

speak of the devil: *see* DEVIL.

speak (*or* talk) out of turn speak in a tactless or foolish way.

speak volumes ❶ (of a gesture, circumstance, or object) convey a great deal. ❷ be good evidence.

❷ **2013** *Keeping Stock* It speaks volumes for Aaron Gilmore's inflated sense of self-importance that he may even entertain thoughts of a return to Parliament, let alone seeking a National electorate nomination.

speak as you find base your opinion of someone or something purely on personal experience; voice your frank opinion, even if it is interpreted as rude.

1988 Hilary Mantel *Eight Months on Ghazzah Street* Look, I don't have any theories. I just go issue by issue. I just speak as I find.

spec

on spec in the hope of success but without any specific plan or instructions. informal

ℹ The informal abbreviation of *speculation* to *spec* was originally American, but it has been used in British English since the early 19th century, and the phrase *on spec* itself dates from the mid 19th century.

2000 *Times* As large sculpture is commissioned before being produced, Barbara's routine became the opposite of Ben's, whose work was produced on spec.

spectre

a spectre at the feast: *see* **a ghost at the feast** *at* FEAST.

speed

full speed ahead: *see* **full steam ahead** *at* STEAM.

up to speed ❶ operating at full speed. ❷ (of a person or company) performing at an anticipated rate or level. ❸ (of a person) fully informed or up to date. informal

❷ **2013** *Daily Telegraph* Whatever option was chosen would be a 'technically complex and expensive' exercise, the Home Office said, with a separate Scotland needing time to get up to speed and prove to allies it could be trusted to share intelligence.

❸ **2014 Derek Lowe** *Corante—In the Pipeline* For reference and getting up to speed on the details, the comments section here has had reader recommendations for the Drug Metabolism and Pharmacokinetics Quick Guide.

spell

under someone's spell so devoted to someone that they seem to have magic power over you.

spend

spend a penny: *see* PENNY.

spice

variety is the spice of life: *see* VARIETY.

spick

spick (*or* spic) and span neat, clean, and well looked after.

ℹ Originally, in the 16th century, the phrase meant 'brand new'. It was short for *spick and span new,* itself an emphatic extension of *span new,* from Old Norse *span nýr,* literally 'chip new'; *spick* was influenced by Dutch *spiksplinternieuw,* literally 'splinter new'.

spike

spike someone's guns take steps to thwart someone's intended course of action.

ℹ First recorded in English in the late 17th century, the expression referred literally to the practice of hammering a metal spike into a captured enemy cannon so that it could not be fired.

spill

spill the beans reveal secret information, especially unintentionally or indiscreetly. informal

spill your guts reveal copious information to someone in an uninhibited way. informal

thrills and spills: *see* THRILL.

spilt

cry over spilt milk: *see* MILK.

spin

in a flat spin: *see* FLAT.

spin your wheels: *see* WHEEL.

spin a yarn: *see* YARN.

spirit

enter into the spirit join wholeheartedly in an event.

1994 Jonathan Coe *What a Carve Up!* His sarcasm was mischievous rather than icy, so I tried to enter into the spirit.

the spirit is willing (but the flesh is weak) someone has good intentions (but yields to temptation and fails to live up to them).

ℹ This expression quotes Jesus's words in Matthew 26:41, on finding his disciples asleep in the Garden of Gethsemane despite his instructions that they should stay awake.

the spirit moves someone someone feels inclined to do something.

ℹ This was a phrase originally used by Quakers, with reference to the inspiration of the Holy Spirit.

spit

be the spit (*or* the dead spit) of look exactly like. informal

ℹ The full form of the phrase is *be the spit and image of*, perhaps coming from the idea of a person apparently being formed from the spit of another, so great is the similarity between them. This fuller form also lies behind the expression *spitting image*.

spit and polish extreme neatness or smartness.

spit and sawdust (of a pub) old-fashioned, run-down, or dirty. British informal

ℹ Until the mid 20th century, the general bar of a pub would often have sawdust sprinkled on the floor, on to which the customers could spit.

spit blood be very angry. informal

spit chips be very angry. Australian informal

spit (out) the dummy behave in a petulant way. Australian informal

spit feathers be very thirsty. informal

spit in the eye (*or* face) of show contempt or scorn for.

spit it out used to urge someone to say, confess, or divulge something quickly. informal

spite

cut off your nose to spite your face: *see* NOSE.

spitting

spitting in (*or* into) the wind engaging in a futile or pointless activity.

2012 *TechDirt* This is one blog among many. Spitting into the wind here does nothing to stop more and more people from realizing that current copyright, trademark, and patent laws in various countries are crazy.

within spitting distance: *see* DISTANCE.

splash

make a splash attract a great deal of attention.

2013 *Urban Cinefile—Film in Australia* As to be expected, the special effects make a splash with some exceptional visuals like the funeral scene when a flaming boat flies over a waterfall.

spleen

vent your spleen: *see* VENT.

splice

splice the main brace ❶ (in the Royal Navy) serve out an extra tot of rum. ❷ serve out or start to consume alcoholic drinks. British informal

ℹ A sailing ship's main brace is a rope attached to its main spar. Splicing it (making a connection in it by interweaving strands) would have been a particularly onerous task, and the phrase probably arose from the custom of awarding sailors who did it an extra ration of rum.

split

split the difference take the average of two proposed amounts.

split hairs: *see* HAIR.

split your sides be convulsed with laughter. informal

split the ticket (*or* your vote) vote for candidates of more than one party. US

split the vote (of a candidate or minority party) attract votes from another candidate or party with the result that both are defeated by a third. British

spoil

spoil the ship for a ha'p'orth of tar risk the failure of a large enterprise by trying to economize on trivial things.

ℹ The expression originally referred to the use of tar to keep flies off sores on sheep (*ship* represented a dialectal pronunciation of *sheep*). *Ha'p'orth* is a contraction of *halfpennyworth*.

too many cooks spoil the broth: *see* COOK.

spoilt

be spoilt for choice have so many attractive possibilities to choose from that it is difficult to make a selection. British

spoke

put a spoke in someone's wheel prevent someone from carrying out a plan. British

ℹ It is not clear why a *spoke*, a normal component of many wheels, should have such a negative effect. It has been suggested that *spoke* here is a mistranslation of the Dutch word *spaak*, meaning 'a bar' or 'a stave', which is found in the identical Dutch idiom.

sponge

throw in the sponge: *see* **throw in the towel** *at* TOWEL.

spoon

be born with a silver spoon in your mouth: *see* SILVER.

greasy spoon: *see* GREASY.

the wooden spoon a hypothetical prize awarded to the least successful contestant; the booby prize.

ℹ A wooden spoon was originally presented to the candidate coming last in the Cambridge University mathematical tripos (the final honours examination for a BA degree).

sport

the sport of kings horse racing.

sporting

a sporting chance some possibility of success.

spot

a black spot: *see* BLACK.

a blind spot: *see* BLIND.

hit the high spots: *see* HIGH.

hit the spot be exactly what is required. informal

knock spots off: *see* KNOCK.

put someone on the spot force someone into a situation in which they must make a difficult decision or answer a difficult question. informal

spot on completely accurate or accurately. British informal

2007 Clarissa Dickson Wright *Spilling the Beans* She advised her solicitors to give the money to my mother for me, as she believed my father would fail to pass it on to me. She was spot on.

spout

up the spout ❶ no longer working or likely to be useful or successful. ❷ (of a woman) pregnant. British informal

sprat

a sprat to catch a mackerel a small expenditure made, or a small risk taken, in the hope of a large or significant gain. British

ℹ A *sprat* is a small sea fish, while a *mackerel* is rather larger. The phrase has been in use since the mid 19th century and is also found with *whale* in the place of *mackerel*.

spread

spread like wildfire: *see* WILDFIRE.

spread yourself too thin be involved in so many different activities or projects that your time and energy are not used to good effect.

spread your wings: *see* WING.

spring

ℹ For idioms containing *spring*, see the entry for the main word in the idiom (for example, **full of the joys of spring** at JOY).

spur

on the spur of the moment on a momentary impulse; without premeditation.

1988 Rodney Hall *Kisses of the Enemy* Now that was a witticism, an inspiration on the spur of the moment.

win your spurs: *see* WIN.

squad

the awkward squad: *see* AWKWARD.

square

back to square one: *see* BACK.

fair and square: *see* FAIR.

get square with pay a creditor.

have square eyes show the effects of habitually watching television to excess.

S

on the square ❶ honest; straightforward. ❷ having membership of the Freemasons.

ⓘ A square, or more fully a *set square*, is an L-shaped tool for drawing angles, and together with a pair of compasses it forms one of the main symbols of Freemasonry.

❷ **1997** *Guardian* One non-Masonic officer… claims he was moved sideways… and subsequently he discovered that the corrupt officers and the commander were all 'on the square'.

square accounts with: *see* **settle accounts with** *at* ACCOUNT.

square the circle do something that is considered to be impossible.

ⓘ In its literal sense, *square the circle* means 'construct a square equal in area to a given circle'. Since this problem is incapable of a purely geometrical solution, the phrase has developed a more general application and is used to refer to an attempt to do something impossible.

a square deal: *see* DEAL.

a square peg in a round hole: *see* PEG.

squeaky

squeaky clean beyond reproach; without vice.

ⓘ The expression originally refers literally to a surface so clean that it squeaks when a finger is rubbed across it.

2001 Sonia El Kahal *Business in the Asia Pacific* The quality of government is corrupt in Indonesia, squeaky clean in Singapore, and in-between elsewhere.

squeeze

put the squeeze on someone coerce or pressurize someone. informal

2013 *New Zealand Herald* I was sceptical about the LVR [loan-to-value ratio] policy precisely because it does put the squeeze on first-home buyers and makes it harder for them to get into the property market.

squeeze an orange: *see* ORANGE.

squeeze someone until the pips squeak: *see* PIP.

squib

a damp squib: *see* DAMP.

stab

a stab in the dark: *see* **a shot in the dark** *at* DARK.

a stab in the back a treacherous act or statement; a betrayal.

stable

shut (*or* lock) the stable door after the horse has bolted try to avoid or prevent something bad or unwelcome when it is already too late to do so. proverb

ⓘ This saying dates back to medieval times. Until the late 19th century it was used in the form *shut the stable door after the steed is stolen*.

stack

blow your stack: *see* **blow your top** *at* BLOW.

staff

the staff of life a staple food, especially bread.

stage

hold the stage dominate a scene of action or forum of debate.

set the stage for prepare the conditions for the occurrence or beginning of something.

2014 *Washington Post* Ideally, the president and her economic team would use this status to take measures that could set the stage for a future recovery.

stair

below stairs: *see* BELOW.

rain stair rods: *see* **rain cats and dogs** *at* RAIN.

stake

go to the stake for do anything to defend a specified belief, opinion, or person.

ⓘ In the past, especially during times of religious persecution, heretics were liable to be tied to a wooden stake and burned alive if they refused to recant their beliefs.

pull up stakes (of a person) move or go to live elsewhere. North American

ⓘ The *stakes* are the pegs or posts which secure a tent or which are put up as a palisade around a temporary settlement.

2000 Anthony Bourdain *Kitchen Confidential* Steven… has chosen to leave New York for Florida with his girlfriend, pulling up stakes, giving up his apartment, even bringing along his goldfish.

S

stake a claim declare your right to something.

ⓘ This expression refers to the practice of putting stakes around the perimeter of a piece of land to which a claim is laid. It is American in origin, dating from the California gold rush of 1849, when the prospectors registered their claims to individual plots of land in this way.

stalks

eyes out on stalks: *see* EYE.

stall

set out your stall ❶ display or show off your abilities, attributes, or experience in order to convince someone of your suitability for something. ❷ make your position on an issue very clear. British

stamp

stamp of approval: *see* APPROVAL.

stand

stand on me rely on me; believe me. informal

ⓘ For other idioms containing *stand,* see the entry for the main word in the idiom (for example, **stand and deliver!** at DELIVER).

standing

do something standing on your head: *see* HEAD.

leave someone or something standing (of a person or thing) be much better or faster than someone or something else.

stands

it stands to reason: *see* REASON.

star

have stars in your eyes be idealistically hopeful or enthusiastic, especially about a possible future in entertainment or sport.

reach for the stars have high or ambitious aims.

see stars see flashes of light, especially as a result of being hit on the head.

someone's star is rising someone is becoming ever more successful or popular.

thank your lucky stars: *see* THANK.

starch

take the starch out of someone shake someone's confidence, especially by humiliating them. US

staring

be staring someone in the face (of a fact or object) be glaringly apparent or obvious.

be staring something in the face (of a person) be on the verge of defeat, death, or ruin.

start

ⓘ For idioms containing *start,* see the entry for the main word in the idiom (for example, **start the ball rolling** at BALL).

starter

under starter's orders (of horses, runners, or other competitors) ready to start a race on receiving the signal from the starter.

state

in a state of nature: *see* NATURE.

state of the art the most recent stage in the development of a product, incorporating the newest ideas and the most up-to-date features.

state of grace a condition of being free from sin.

state of play ❶ the score at a particular time in a sports match. ❷ the current situation in an ongoing process, especially one involving opposing or competing parties. British

stations

action stations: *see* ACTION.

battle stations: *see* BATTLE.

panic stations: *see* PANIC.

stay

stay loose: *see* **hang loose** *at* LOOSE.

stay the course (*or* distance) ❶ hold out to the end of a race or contest. ❷ pursue a difficult task or activity to the end.

stay someone's hand restrain someone from acting.

a stay of execution a delay in carrying out a court order.

stay put remain in position without moving or being moved.

2014 *New Zealand Herald* New Zealand rates are widely tipped to go higher while Australia's are expected to stay put.

stead

stand someone in good stead (of something learned or acquired) be advantageous or useful to someone over time or in the future.

steady

go steady have a regular romantic or sexual relationship with a particular person. informal

1905 Edith Wharton *The House of Mirth* I thought we were to be married: he'd gone steady with me six months and given me his mother's wedding ring.

steady as she goes keep on with the same careful progress. informal

ⓘ In nautical vocabulary, *steady* is the instruction given to the helmsman to keep the ship on the same course.

2011 *Motley Fool* Thursday will bring us third-quarter numbers from Unilever ..., and it's going to be yet another 'steady as she goes' update.

steady the Buffs! an encouragement to remain calm, unflustered, and resolute, not giving way to panic. dated British

ⓘ 'The Buffs' was a nickname (from the colour of part of their uniform) given to the old third regiment of the line in the British army, and latterly to the East Kent Regiment.

2017 Chris Brookmyre *Want You Gone* He knows that the facility must boast near-impermeable insulation, so it must be only his own anxiety that is causing a chill to run through him. Steady the buffs, he tells himself. He's almost there.

S

steal

steal someone's clothes appropriate someone's ideas or policies. British informal

steal someone's heart win someone's love. dated

steal a march on gain an advantage over someone, typically by acting before they do.

steal the show attract the most attention and praise.

steal someone's thunder win praise for yourself by pre-empting someone else's attempt to impress.

ⓘ The critic and playwright John Dennis (1657–1734) invented a new method of simulating the sound of thunder in the theatre, which he employed in his unsuccessful play *Appius and Virginia*. Shortly after his play had finished its brief run, Dennis attended a performance of *Macbeth* in which the improved thunder effect was used, and he is reported to have exclaimed in a fury: 'Damn them! They will not let my play run, but they steal my thunder.'

steam

full steam (*or* speed) ahead used to indicate that you should proceed with as much speed or energy as possible.

get up (*or* pick up) steam ❶ generate enough pressure to drive a steam engine. ❷ (of a project, plan, or process in its early stages) gradually gain more impetus and driving force.

have steam coming out of your ears be extremely angry or irritated. informal

let (*or* blow) off steam get rid of pent-up energy or emotion. informal

ⓘ The image here is of the release of excess steam from a steam engine through a valve.

run out of (*or* lose) steam lose impetus or enthusiasm. informal

1992 Jeff Torrington *Swing Hammer Swing!* Eventually I ran out of steam and came to a halt.

under your own steam without assistance from others.

1996 Colin Bateman *Of Wee Sweetie Mice & Men* She was starting to move under her own steam, hesitant Bambi steps which weren't helped by being hurried along, but a good sign nevertheless.

steel

cold steel: *see* COLD.

have nerves of steel: *see* NERVE.

ring of steel: *see* RING.

steer

bum steer: *see* BUM.

steer a middle course: *see* MIDDLE.

steer clear of take care to avoid or keep away from.

2002 *ChartAttack Live Reviews* If you're looking for Hollywood gloss and spectacle, steer clear of this film.

stem

from stem to stern from the front to the back, especially of a ship.

step

mind (*or* watch) your step be careful.

step into the breach: *see* BREACH.

step on the gas: *see* GAS.

step on it ❶ make a motor vehicle go faster by pressing down on the accelerator pedal with your foot. ❷ hurry up. informal

step out of line behave inappropriately or disobediently.

step on someone's toes: *see* **tread on someone's toes** *at* TREAD.

step up to the plate take action in response to an opportunity, crisis, or challenge; take responsibility for something. chiefly North American

> ⓘ The expression originated in the language of baseball, where 'the plate' (in full, the 'home plate') is a rubber slab at one corner of the diamond where the batter stands when batting (roughly equivalent to the crease in cricket).
>
> **2004** *Boston Globe* Directors . . . need to step up to the plate in order for investors to feel comfortable that they are properly represented as shareholders.

take steps adopt a particular course of action in order to bring about a particular result.

Stephens

even Stephens: *see* EVEN.

sterner

be made of sterner stuff (of a person) have a stronger character and be more able to overcome problems than others.

> ⓘ This expression comes from Shakespeare's *Julius Caesar*: 'When that the poor have cried, Caesar hath wept; Ambition should be made of sterner stuff: Yet Brutus says he was ambitious; And Brutus is an honourable man'.
>
> **2014** *Daily Telegraph* Many people would have given up and just claimed on their insurance but Mr Woodhouse is made of sterner stuff.

stew

in a stew in a state of great anxiety or agitation. informal

stew in your own juice suffer the unpleasant consequences of your own actions or temperament without the consoling intervention of others. informal

stick

between the sticks playing as a goalkeeper. British informal

in the sticks in a remote rural area. informal

stick at nothing allow nothing to deter you from achieving your aim, even if it means acting wrongly or dishonestly.

stick 'em up! hands up! (said typically by a person threatening someone else with a gun). informal

stick it on ❶ make high charges. ❷ tell an exaggerated story. informal

stick it to someone treat someone harshly or severely. informal, chiefly US

stick one (*or* it) on someone hit someone. informal

a stick to beat someone or something with a fact or argument held over someone or something as a threat or an advantage.

up sticks go to live elsewhere. British informal

up the stick pregnant. British informal

> ⓘ For other idioms containing *stick*, see the entry for the main word in the idiom (for example, **stick to your guns** at GUN).

sticky

come to (*or* meet) a sticky end be led by your own actions to ruin or an unpleasant death. British informal

sticky fingers a propensity to steal. informal

a sticky wicket: *see* WICKET.

stiff

stiff as a board (of a person or part of the body) extremely stiff. informal

a stiff upper lip a quality of uncomplaining stoicism.

> ⓘ This is a characteristic particularly associated with the British but the phrase is apparently North American in origin, dating back to the mid 19th century. It is used, for example, in Harriet Beecher Stowe's novel *Uncle Tom's Cabin*, published in 1852.
>
> **2014** *New York Times* The ballet is a salute to Britain, and Balanchine catches several layers of the British persona: reverence and irreverence, the stiff upper lip and the twinkling eye.

still

still small voice the voice of your conscience.

ℹ In 1 Kings 19:12, the voice of God is described as *a still small voice*.

still waters run deep a quiet or placid manner may conceal a passionate nature. proverb

sting

sting in the tail an unpleasant or problematic end to something.

1992 Ronald Wright *Stolen Continents* At last Hendrick came to the sting in the tail of his speech.

stink

like stink extremely hard or intensely. informal

2008 *Guardian* All of the browser makers—Microsoft, Mozilla, Opera, and Apple—have been working like stink to improve their Javascript performance in their latest versions.

stink to high heaven: *see* HEAVEN.

stinking

cry stinking fish: *see* CRY.

stir

stir the blood make someone excited or enthusiastic.

stir a finger: *see* **lift a finger** *at* LIFT.

stir the possum: *see* POSSUM.

stir your stumps (of a person) begin to move or act. British informal, dated

ℹ *Stump* has been used as an informal term for 'leg' since the 15th century; the expression itself dates from the mid 16th century.

S

stitch

a stitch in time if you sort out a problem immediately, it may save a lot of extra work later. proverb

ℹ The fuller form of the expression is *a stitch in time saves nine. Nine* here has no particular significance as a number but was chosen because of its similarity in sound with the word *time*.

in stitches laughing uncontrollably. informal

ℹ *Stitch*, in the sense of 'a sudden localized jabbing pain', such as might be caused by a needle, is recorded in Old English. It is now generally used of a muscle spasm in the side caused especially by exertion. Shakespeare seems to have been the first to describe *stitches* brought on by laughter; in *Twelfth Night* (1601) Maria invites her fellow conspirators to observe the lovelorn Malvolio with the words: 'If you . . . will laugh yourselves into stitches, follow me'.

1981 D. M. Thomas *The White Hotel* She had them in stitches with her absurd—but true—anecdotes.

stock

laughing stock: *see* LAUGHING.

lock, stock, and barrel: *see* LOCK.

on the stocks in construction or preparation.

ℹ During construction, a ship is supported on a frame or scaffolding known as the *stocks*.

put (*or* **take**) **stock in** believe or have faith in.

ℹ The earliest example so far recorded of this expression is by Mark Twain in *Galaxy* (1870): 'The "chance" theory . . . is . . . calculated to inflict . . . pecuniary loss upon any community that takes stock in it'.

take stock ❶ make an inventory of the merchandise in a shop. ❷ review or make an assessment of a particular situation, typically as a prelude to making a decision.

stomach

an army marches on its stomach soldiers or workers can only fight or function effectively if they have been well fed.

ℹ The saying has been attributed to both Frederick the Great and Napoleon I. It is a version of the French phrase *c'est la soupe qui fait le soldat*.

have butterflies in your stomach: *see* BUTTERFLY.

have eyes bigger than your stomach: *see* EYE.

on a full (*or* **an empty**) **stomach** having (*or* without having) eaten beforehand.

the pit of your stomach: *see* PIT.

sick to your stomach: *see* SICK.

a strong stomach an ability to see or do unpleasant things without feeling sick or squeamish.

turn someone's stomach nauseate someone.

stompie

pick up stompies break into a conversation of which you have heard only the end. South African

ℹ In Afrikaans, a *stompie* is a cigarette butt.

stone

be carved (*or* set *or* written) in stone be fixed and unchangeable.

> ℹ The reference here is to the biblical Ten Commandments, written on tablets of stone by God and handed down to Moses on Mount Sinai (Genesis 31:18).

cast (*or* throw) the first stone be the first to accuse or criticize.

> ℹ The phrase comes from an incident recorded in St John's Gospel. A group of men preparing to stone an adulterous woman to death were addressed by Jesus with the words: 'He that is without sin among you, let him first cast a stone at her' (John 8:7).

have kissed the blarney stone: *see* BLARNEY.

heart of stone: *see* HEART.

leave no stone unturned try every possible course of action in order to achieve something.

like getting blood out of (*or* from) a stone: *see* BLOOD.

a rolling stone: *see* ROLLING.

stone me! (*or* stone the crows!) an exclamation of surprise or shock. British informal

a stone's throw a short distance.

> **1989 Joanna Trollope** *Village Affairs* Can't tell you the difference it will make, having you a stone's throw away.

throw stones criticize someone or something.

> ℹ This expression is often used with reference to the proverbial saying *those who live in glass houses should not throw stones*, the earliest variant of which is recorded in the mid 17th century.

stony

fall on stony ground (of words or a suggestion) be ignored or badly received.

> ℹ The reference here is to the parable of the sower recounted in both St Mark's and St Matthew's Gospels, in which some of the seed scattered by the sower fell on stony places where it withered away.

stool

fall between two stools fail to be or to take one of two satisfactory alternatives. British

> ℹ This phrase comes from the proverb *between two stools one falls to the ground*, first referred to in English by the medieval writer John Gower in *Confessio Amantis* (*c.*1390).

stop

the buck stops here: *see* BUCK.

pull out all the stops make a very great effort; go to elaborate lengths.

> ℹ The stops referred to here are those of an organ. Although this is an early 20th-century expression, Matthew Arnold, in the Preface to *Essays in Criticism* (1865) refers to an attempt on his behalf 'to pull out a few more stops in that... somewhat narrow-toned organ, the modern Englishman'.

stop at nothing recognize no obstacles or reasons for not doing something; be utterly ruthless or determined.

> **1991** *Time* Seen simplistically and from afar, Saddam Hussein comes across as... the villain who will stop at nothing.

stop your ears ❶ put your fingers in your ears to avoid hearing. ❷ refuse to listen.

stop a gap serve to meet a temporary need.

stop someone's mouth bribe or otherwise induce a person to keep silent about something.

stop the show (of a performer) provoke prolonged applause or laughter, causing an interruption.

stopper

put a (*or* the) stopper on cause something to end or become quiet.

store

in store coming in the future; about to happen.

set (*or* lay *or* put) store by (*or* on) consider something to be of a particular degree of importance or value.

storm

any port in a storm: *see* PORT.

the eye of the storm: *see* EYE.

go down a storm be enthusiastically received by an audience.

the lull (*or* calm) before the storm a period of unusual tranquillity or stability that seems likely to presage difficult times.

S

a storm in a teacup great excitement or anger about a trivial matter.

ⓘ A North American variant of this expression is *a tempest in a teapot*.

2013 *Independent* (Ireland) In the High Court today, Mr Justice Kevin Feeney said the matter had many appearances of 'a storm in a teacup' and it was a case that should be heard in the District Court.

take something by storm ❶ capture a place by a sudden and violent attack. ❷ have great and rapid success in a particular place or with a particular group of people.

❷ **2014** *New Zealand Herald* Kiwi toddler Kahlei Stone-Kelly is taking the world by storm with his skateboarding skills.

— up a storm perform a particular action with great enthusiasm and energy. chiefly North American

2013 Andrew *The 4th Avenue Blues* She looks really frail these days—George's incarceration taking a toll on her. She is still cooking up a storm, though.

weather the storm: *see* WEATHER.

story

end of story: *see* END.

it's (*or* **that's**) **the story of my life** used to lament the fact that a particular misfortune has happened too often in your experience. informal

to cut (*or* **make**) **a long story short** used to end an account of events quickly.

a likely story: *see* LIKELY.

stout

a stout heart courage or determination. literary

stove

slave over a hot stove work very hard preparing a meal. informal

straight

go straight live an honest life after being a criminal.

keep a straight face manage to not show any facial expression, even though you are amused.

put the record straight: *see* RECORD.

the straight and narrow morally correct behaviour.

ⓘ The full form of the expression is *the straight and narrow path* or *way*. It developed from a misunderstanding of Matthew 7:14, 'strait is the gate, and narrow is the way, which leadeth unto life', where *strait* is in fact being used as another word for *narrow*.

a straight arrow: *see* ARROW.

straight as a die: *see* DIE.

a straight fight a contest between just two opponents, especially in an election. British

straight from the shoulder ❶ (of a blow) well delivered. ❷ (of a verbal attack) frank or direct.

straight off (*or* **out**) without hesitation or deliberation. informal

straight up truthfully; honestly. informal

strain

don't strain yourself used sarcastically to accuse a person of laziness or dilatoriness. informal

strain at a gnat make a difficulty about accepting something trivial. literary

ⓘ The phrase derives from Matthew 23:24, 'Ye blind guides, which strain at a gnat, and swallow a camel'. The word *strain* here appears to mean 'make a violent effort', but it may in fact refer to the straining of a liquid to remove unwanted particles: the image is of a person quietly accepting a difficulty or problem of significant proportions while baulking at something comparatively trivial.

strain at the leash be eager to begin or do something.

strain every nerve: *see* NERVE.

strange

make strange (of a baby or child) fuss or be shy in company. Canadian

1987 Alice Munro *The Progress of Love* Her timid-looking fat son . . . usually liked Violet, but today he made strange.

stranger

little stranger: *see* LITTLE.

straps

hit your straps begin to perform as well as you can; hit your stride.

ⓘ The expression, which is used mainly in sporting contexts, originated in Australian English. It may have originated in the idea of looking for the straps of one's swag pack, interpreted metaphorically as seeking a new job.

2005 *Cricinfo news* A few players have started to hit their straps before the Test series, which is a good sign.

straw

clutch (*or* grasp *or* catch) at straws do, say, or believe anything, however unlikely or inadequate, which seems to offer hope in a desperate situation.

ⓘ This expression comes from the proverb *a drowning man will clutch at a straw*, which is recorded in various forms since the mid 16th century.

draw the short straw be the unluckiest of a group of people, especially in being chosen to perform an unpleasant task.

ⓘ One method of drawing lots involves holding several straws of varying lengths with one end concealed in your hand and then inviting other members of the group to take one each.

2019 *Guardian* It had been left to David Lidington, minister for the Cabinet Office, to open the latest Brexit debate the government had been hoping to avoid. He looked like a man who knew he had drawn the short straw.

the last (*or* final) straw a further difficulty or annoyance, typically minor in itself but coming on top of a whole series of difficulties, that makes a situation unbearable.

ⓘ The full version of this is the proverb *the last straw breaks the camel's back*. The modern form is traceable to Charles Dickens in *Dombey and Son* (1848), but earlier versions are recorded, including a mid-17th-century reference to *the last feather breaking a horse's back*.

make bricks without straw: *see* BRICK.

man of straw: *see* MAN.

not care two straws: *see* CARE.

a straw in the wind a slight but significant hint of future developments.

straws in your hair a state of insanity.

ⓘ In former times, the floors of mental institutions were covered with straw, and so having straw in the hair came to be regarded as a characteristic of a deranged person.

streak

like a streak (of lightning) very fast. informal

talk a blue streak: *see* BLUE.

stream

against (*or* with) the stream against (*or* with) the prevailing view or tendency.

on stream in or into operation or existence; available.

street

easy street: *see* EASY.

the man in the street: *see* MAN.

not in the same street far inferior in terms of ability. British informal

streets ahead greatly superior. British informal

1991 Alistair Campbell *Sidewinder* He has his shortcomings, sure, but he's streets ahead of Dr Nada.

up (*or* right up) your street well suited to your tastes, interests, or abilities. informal

ⓘ A North American variant of this expression is *up your alley*.

the word on the street: *see* WORD.

strength

give me strength! used as an expression of exasperation or annoyance.

go from strength to strength develop or progress with increasing success.

on the strength of on the basis of or with the justification of.

a tower (*or* pillar) of strength a person who can be relied upon to be a source of strong support and comfort.

ⓘ This phrase may come from the Book of Common Prayer: 'O Lord . . . be unto them a tower of strength'.

strengthen

strengthen someone's hand (*or* hands) enable or encourage a person to act more vigorously or effectively.

stretch

at full stretch ❶ with a part of your body fully extended. ❷ using the maximum amount of your resources or energy.

at a stretch ❶ in one continuous period. ❷ with much effort or difficulty.

by no (*or* not by any) stretch of the imagination used to emphasize that something is definitely not the case.

ℹ The phrase is often shortened to simply *by any stretch*.

2014 *DVD Verdict* I was extremely happy to find that *Brutalization*, also and more appropriately known as *Because of the Cats*, while not a great movie by any stretch, is really just a perfectly average police procedural about disaffected teens.

stretch your legs go for a short walk, typically after sitting in one place for some time.

stretch a point allow or do something not usually acceptable, typically as a result of particular circumstances.

1998 Penelope Lively *Spiderweb* I seem to recall that you are agnostic, but I would suggest, with all respect, that you stretch a point and attend Sunday Matins, at least on occasion.

stretch your wings: *see* WING.

stricken

stricken in years used euphemistically to describe someone old and feeble.

strictly

strictly for the birds: *see* BIRD.

stride

take something in your stride deal with something difficult or unpleasant in a calm and competent way.

strike

lightning never strikes twice: *see* LIGHTNING.

— strikes again something or someone acts again or reappears in characteristic fashion and with noticeable effect.

ℹ The expression originated in science-fiction and fantasy fiction and films, typically as the title of a sequel.

2004 *New Zealand Parliamentary Debates* They believe there is no legitimate place for Maori, except as subservient workers for their colonial masters. The tea planter strikes again!

strike a blow for (*or* against) act in support of (or opposition to).

strike a (*or* the right) chord: *see* CHORD.

strike a light used as an expression of surprise, dismay, or alarm. British informal, dated

strike at the root of: *see* ROOT.

strike it rich find a source of abundance or success. informal

strike lucky (*or* strike it lucky) have a lucky success. British

strike someone off the rolls: *see* ROLL.

strike oil attain prosperity or success.

1994 *Nature* S. P. Goldman . . . seems to have struck oil in the search for better ways of computing electronic states.

strike while the iron is hot make use of an opportunity immediately.

ℹ Iron can only be hammered into shape at a blacksmith's forge while it is hot.

striking

within striking distance: *see* DISTANCE.

string

have a second string to your bow have an alternative resource that you can make use of if the first one fails. British

ℹ This is a metaphor from archery; related expressions include *have several strings to your bow* and *add another string to your bow*. *Second string* can also be used on its own to mean simply 'an alternative resource or course of action'.

hold the purse strings: *see* PURSE.

how long is a piece of string? used as a rejoinder to indicate that it is unreasonable for someone to expect the speaker to be more precise about something. informal

no strings attached no special conditions or restrictions apply to an opportunity or offer. informal

on a string under your control or influence.

ℹ The idea here is of a puppeteer manipulating a puppet by its strings.

pull strings make use of your influence and contacts to gain an advantage unofficially or unfairly.

ℹ An American variant of this expression is **pull wires**: the image here and in the next idiom is of a puppeteer manipulating a marionette by means of its strings.

2012 *DVD Verdict* By then, his new wife, Megan, has descended in his esteem from a confident and ambitious copy writer at SCDP to a tearful, insecure actress who needs Don to pull strings and get her a part in a hokey TV ad.

pull the strings be in control of events or of other people's actions.

tighten the purse strings: *see* PURSE.

strip

tear someone off a strip: *see* TEAR.

stroke

different strokes for different folks: *see* DIFFERENT.

not (*or* **never**) **do a stroke of work** do no work at all.

put someone off their stroke disconcert someone so that they do not work or perform as well as they might; break the pattern or rhythm of someone's work.

stroke of genius an outstandingly brilliant and original idea.

stroke of luck (*or* **good luck**) a fortunate occurrence that could not have been predicted or expected.

stroke someone (*or* **someone's hair**) **the wrong way** irritate a person.

strong

the strong arm of the law: *see* **the long arm of the law** *at* ARM.

come it strong indulge in exaggeration. British informal

come on strong ❶ behave aggressively or assertively. ❷ make great efforts or advances. informal

going strong continuing to be healthy, vigorous, or successful. informal

strong meat ideas or language likely to be found unacceptably forceful or extreme. British

strong on ❶ good at; expert in. ❷ possessing large quantities of; rich in.

struck

be struck all of a heap: *see* HEAP.

strut

strut your stuff dance or behave in a lively, confident way. informal

> **2018 Isabelle Grey** *Wrong Way Home* I've followed her home, my blonde-haired woman in her tight black jeans. She can strut her stuff as much as she likes, but she's not going to win.

stubborn

stubborn as a mule extremely stubborn. informal

stuck

get stuck in (*or* **into**) start doing something enthusiastically or with determination. British informal

study

in a brown study: *see* BROWN.

stuff

do your stuff perform a task at which you are particularly skilled or which is in your particular area of expertise.

> **2005** *The Star* (South Africa) By now, he recommended that our entire house needed total rewiring, which he might as well do, he explained. I nudged my husband when he began to object. 'Let the expert do his stuff,' I hissed.

not give a stuff not care at all. British informal

the hard stuff: *see* HARD.

the right stuff: *see* RIGHT.

stuff happens: *see* **shit happens** *at* SHIT.

that's the stuff (*or* **the stuff to give the troops**) said in approval of what has just been done or said. British informal

stuffed

get stuffed said in anger to tell someone to go away or as an expression of contempt. British informal

stuffing

knock (*or* **take**) **the stuffing out of someone** severely impair someone's confidence or strength. informal

stump

beyond the black stump beyond the limits of settled, and therefore civilized, life. Australian

> ❶ This phrase comes from the custom of using a fire-blackened stump of wood as a marker when giving directions to travellers.

draw stumps cease doing something.

> ❶ In the game of cricket, the stumps are taken out of the ground at the close of play.

S

on the stump going about the country making political speeches or canvassing. chiefly North American

ⓘ In rural America in the late 18th century, the *stump* of a felled tree was often used as an impromptu platform for someone making a speech.

stir your stumps: *see* STIR.

up a stump in a situation too difficult for you to manage. US

style

cramp someone's style: *see* CRAMP.

like it is going out of style: *see* **like it is going out of fashion** *at* FASHION.

succeed

nothing succeeds like success success leads to opportunities for further and greater successes. proverb

suck

go suck an egg: *see* EGG.

suck someone dry exhaust someone's physical, material, or emotional resources.

suck it and see the only way to know if something will work or be suitable is to try it. British informal

suck it up accept something unpleasant or difficult. US informal

suck an orange: *see* **squeeze an orange** *at* ORANGE.

sudden

S

(all) of a sudden suddenly.

ⓘ As a noun *sudden* is now found only in this phrase, but from the mid 16th century to the early 18th century it was in regular use in the sense 'an unexpected danger or emergency'.

suffer

not suffer fools gladly be impatient or intolerant towards people you regard as unwise or unintelligent.

ⓘ This expression refers to 2 Corinthians 11:19: 'For ye suffer fools gladly, seeing ye yourselves are wise'.

2001 *Daily Telegraph* Such was her expertise as a Victorianist that her advice was widely sought, though she did not suffer fools gladly.

sugar

sugar the pill: *see* PILL.

suit

follow suit: *see* FOLLOW.

in your birthday suit: *see* BIRTHDAY.

men in suits: *see* MAN.

suit the action to the word carry out your stated intentions at once.

ⓘ The expression comes from the scene in *Hamlet* in which a troupe of actors arrive to present a play to the king and queen. Hamlet instructs them to 'suit the action to the word, the word to the action'.

suit someone's book: *see* BOOK.

suit someone or something down to the ground be extremely convenient or appropriate for a particular person or thing. British informal

2013 Margaret Pomeranz & **David Stratton** *At the Movies* I have not seen Jeremy Irons on the screen for some years and I thought that this part suited him down to the ground.

suitcase

live out of a suitcase: *see* LIVE.

suited

suited and booted wearing smart formal clothes.

2010 Andy Tibbs *Advertising* Unless otherwise requested, you probably won't need to turn up suited and booted, but think smart-casual.

summer

Indian summer: *see* INDIAN.

sun

catch the sun ❶ be in a sunny position. ❷ become tanned or sunburnt. British

make hay while the sun shines: *see* HAY.

place in the sun: *see* PLACE.

someone's sun is set the time of someone's prosperity is over.

the sun is over the yardarm it is the time of day when it is permissible to drink alcohol. informal

ⓘ This was originally a nautical expression: a *yardarm* is the outer extremity of a *yard*, a cylindrical spar slung across a ship's mast for a sail to hang from. The time of day referred to is noon, rather than 6 o'clock in the evening, as is often supposed.

1992 Angela Lambert *A Rather English Marriage* Have a snifter? Sun's over the yardarm, as they say in the senior service.

under the sun on earth; in existence.

Sunday

a month of Sundays: *see* MONTH.

sundry

all and sundry: *see* ALL.

sunny side

sunny side up (of an egg) fried on one side only. North American

sunset

ride off into the sunset: *see* RIDE.

sunset years the last years of a person's life. euphemistic

sunshine

ray of sunshine: *see* RAY.

sup

sup with the devil: *see* DEVIL.

supper

sing for your supper earn a benefit or favour by providing a service in return.

ⓘ This phrase comes from the nursery rhyme *Little Tommy Tucker*.

sure

slow but sure: *see* SLOW.

sure as eggs is eggs (*also* sure as fate) without any doubt; absolutely certain.

sure thing ❶ a certainty. ❷ certainly; of course. informal

❶ **2001** *Business Week* Any potential legal challenge to Microsoft's bundling decisions in XP is no sure thing.

❷ **2000 John Ballem** *Manchineel* 'Hand me your gun.' 'Sure thing, boss.'

surf

surf the net move from site to site on the Internet.

ⓘ *Surf* here comes from *channel-surfing*, the practice of switching frequently between channels on a television set in an attempt to find an interesting programme.

surf and turf a dish containing both seafood and meat, typically shellfish and steak. chiefly North American

surface

scratch the surface: *see* SCRATCH.

survival

survival of the fittest the continued existence of organisms which are best adapted to their environment, with the extinction of others, as a concept in the Darwinian theory of evolution.

ⓘ The phrase was coined by the English philosopher and sociologist Herbert Spencer (1820–1903) in *Principles of Biology* (1865). Besides its formal scientific use, the phrase is often used loosely and humorously in contexts relating to physical fitness (or the lack of it).

suss

on suss on suspicion of having committed a crime. British informal

ⓘ *Suss* is an abbreviation of *suspicion*, earlier and more correctly spelled *sus*. Until its abolition in 1981, a law nicknamed the *sus law* allowed the police to arrest a person on the suspicion that they were likely to commit a crime.

swallow

have swallowed a dictionary: *see* DICTIONARY.

one swallow doesn't make a summer a single fortunate event does not mean that what follows will also be good. proverb

2008 *Daily Telegraph* Just as one swallow doesn't make a summer, so one month of falling audiences doesn't spell the decline of Facebook or social networking.

swan

all someone's geese are swans: *see* GOOSE.

turn geese into swans: *see* GOOSE.

swathe

cut a swathe through pass through something causing great damage, destruction, or change.

ℹ A *swathe* was the area cut by a single sweep of a mower's scythe, and so the width of a strip of grass or corn cut in this way.

sway

hold sway have great power or influence over a particular person, place, or domain.

swear

swear black is white vigorously maintain anything, however unlikely, in order to get what you want.

swear blind affirm something in an emphatic manner. British informal

ℹ A North American variant of this expression is *swear up and down*.

swear like a trooper swear a great deal.

ℹ A *trooper* was originally a private soldier in a cavalry unit. Troopers were proverbial for their coarse behaviour and bad language at least as early as the mid 18th century: in *Pamela* (1739–40), Samuel Richardson writes 'she curses and storms at me like a Trooper'. Compare with **lie like a trooper** (*at* LIE).

sweat

blood, sweat, and tears: *see* BLOOD.

break sweat exert yourself physically. informal

ℹ US English prefers *break a sweat*.

by the sweat of your brow by your own hard work, typically manual labour.

ℹ This idiom is often used with reference to God's sentence on Adam after the Fall, condemning him to work for his food: 'In the sweat of thy face shalt thou eat bread' (Genesis 3:19).

don't sweat it don't worry. US

in a cold sweat in a state of sweating induced by fear, nervousness, or illness.

no sweat without any difficulty or problem. informal

1998 *GQ* Give me a date and I'll take it, no sweat. No problem. If I'm available.

sweat blood ❶ make an extraordinarily strenuous effort to do something. ❷ be extremely anxious. informal

sweat buckets sweat profusely. informal

sweat bullets be extremely anxious or nervous. North American informal

sweat it out ❶ endure an unpleasant experience, typically one involving extreme physical exertion in great heat. ❷ wait in a state of extreme anxiety for something to happen or be resolved. informal

sweat the small stuff worry about trivial things. US

sweep

make a clean sweep: *see* CLEAN.

sweep the board win all the money in a gambling game; win all possible prizes or rewards.

sweep someone off their feet: *see* FOOT.

sweep something under the carpet: *see* CARPET.

sweet

home sweet home: *see* HOME.

in your own sweet time (*or* way) when (or how) you want to, regardless of the possible inconvenience caused to others.

keep someone sweet keep someone well disposed towards yourself, especially by favours or bribery. informal

she's sweet all's well. Australian informal

1964 Kylie Tennant *Summer's Tales* 'Everything O.K.?' 'Yep,' said the scrawny man beneath us. 'She's sweet.'

short and sweet: *see* SHORT.

sweet Fanny Adams absolutely nothing at all. informal

ℹ Fanny Adams was the youthful victim in a famous murder case in 1867, her body being mutilated and cut to pieces by the killer. With gruesome black humour, her name came to be used as a slang term for a type of tinned meat or stew recently introduced to the Royal Navy; the current meaning developed early in the 20th century. *Sweet Fanny Adams* is often abbreviated in speech to *sweet FA*, which is understood by many to be a euphemism for *sweet fuck all*.

sweet nothings: *see* NOTHING.

sweet sixteen sixteen regarded as the characteristic age of prettiness and innocence in a girl.

the sweet spot a particularly fortunate or beneficial circumstance or factor.

ℹ The *sweet spot* on a tennis racket is the point believed by players to deliver the maximum power to the ball. In 1997 a physicist in Australia claimed to have disproved its existence.

2014 *New Statesman* Privately, senior shadow cabinet ministers admit that the economy could hit a 'sweet spot' for Osborne in time for the general election.

sweeten

sweeten the pill: *see* **sugar the pill** *at* PILL.

sweetness

sweetness and light ❶ social or political harmony. ❷ a reasonable and peaceable person.

ⓘ This is a phrase used by Jonathan Swift in *The Battle of the Books* (1704) and taken up by Matthew Arnold in *Culture and Anarchy* (1869): 'The pursuit of perfection, then, is the pursuit of sweetness and light'.

swim

in the swim involved in or aware of current affairs or events.

sink or swim: *see* SINK.

swim with the tide: *see* **go with the tide** *at* TIDE.

swine

cast pearls before swine: *see* PEARL.

swing

get (back) into the swing of things get used to (*or* return to) being easy and relaxed about an activity or routine you are engaged in. informal

go with a swing (of a party or other event) be lively and enjoyable. informal

in full swing (of an activity) proceeding vigorously.

no room to swing a cat: *see* ROOM.

swing both ways be bisexual. informal

2001 *Film Inside Out* Florence has baggage. At one moment, there is a hint that she might swing both ways, or, maybe, only one since the guy thing is a fake.

swing the lead malinger; shirk your duty. British informal

ⓘ This phrase originated in the armed forces and the *lead* in question is probably a sounding lead, a lump of lead attached to a line and slowly lowered to determine the depth of a stretch of water. The connection between this process and shirking one's duty is not entirely clear.

swings and roundabouts a situation in which different actions or options result in no eventual gain or loss. British

ⓘ This expression comes from the proverbial saying *you lose on the swings what you gain on the roundabouts.*

1983 Penelope Lively *Perfect Happiness* I have always reckoned on a fair share of that—swings and roundabouts, rough with smooth.

swollen

have a swollen head be conceited.

swoop

in one fell swoop: *see* FELL.

sword

beat (*or* turn) swords into ploughshares devote resources to peaceful rather than aggressive or warlike ends.

ⓘ The reference here is to the biblical image of God's peaceful rule: 'they shall beat their swords into plowshares, and their spears into pruning hooks' (Isaiah 2:4).

cross swords: *see* CROSS.

a double-edged sword: *see* DOUBLE-EDGED.

fall on your sword assume responsibility or blame on behalf of other people, especially by resigning from a position.

ⓘ The allusion is to a method of suicide in ancient Rome.

2013 *New Statesman* The time has come for you to fall on your sword. After 20 unbroken years at the heart of politics, you need a rest.

he who lives by the sword dies by the sword those people who commit violent acts must expect to suffer violence themselves. proverb

ⓘ The phrase was originally used with allusion to an incident in the Garden of Gethsemane. When the men came to arrest Jesus, one of his disciples drew his sword and cut off the ear of 'the servant of the high priest', earning this rebuke from Jesus: 'all they that take the sword shall perish with the sword' (Matthew 26:52). In contemporary versions *sword* is sometimes replaced by *gun, bomb*, etc.

the pen is mightier than the sword: *see* PEN.

put someone to the sword kill someone, especially in war.

sword and sorcery a genre of fiction characterized by heroic adventures and elements of fantasy.

sword of Damocles an imminent danger.

ⓘ When the courtier Damocles described Dionysius I, ruler of Syracuse (405–367 BC), as the happiest of men, Dionysius gave him a graphic demonstration of the fragility of his happiness:

S

he invited Damocles to a banquet, in the middle of which he looked up to *see* a naked sword suspended over his head by a single hair.

Sydney

Sydney or the bush all or nothing. Australian

syllable

in words of one syllable using very simple language; expressed plainly.

2005 Phil Gardner *Mulled Whines* Okay, can someone please explain 'Ring 2' to me in words of one syllable? I didn't have time to be scared, I was too busy trying to work out what the heck was going on.

sympathy

tea and sympathy: *see* TEA.

sync

in (*or* out of) sync working well (*or* badly) together; in (*or* out of) agreement.

ℹ *Sync* (or *synch*) is an informal abbreviation of *synchronization*.

2002 *Tikkun Magazine* One place to start should be pressure for the resignation of Attorney General John Ashcroft. His views are out of synch with most Americans.

system

all systems go everything functioning properly, ready to proceed.

beat the system: *see* BEAT.

get something out of your system get rid of a preoccupation or anxiety. informal

1988 Erich Segal *Doctors* First she let her get the crying out of her system.

S

Tt

T

to a T (*or* tee) exactly; to perfection. informal

> ❶ This origin of this idiom, which dates back to the late 17th century, is uncertain. Attempts to link *T* with either a golfer's tee or a builder's T-square are unconvincing. It is possible that the underlying idea is that of completing the letter T by putting in the cross stroke, but the early 17th-century expression *to a tittle* was identical in meaning, and it is possible that *T* may be an abbreviation of *tittle*.

> **2000** *Post (Denver)* He's got Ralphie's same non-charismatic charisma down to a T.

tab

keep tabs (*or* a tab) on monitor the activities or development of; keep under close observation. informal

> **1978 Mario Puzo** *Fools Die* Jordan knew that Merlyn the Kid kept tabs on everything he did.

pick up the tab pay for something. informal, chiefly North American

table

bring something to the table (*or* the party) contribute something of value to a discussion, project, etc.

crumbs from someone's table: *see* CRUMB.

drink someone under the table: *see* DRINK.

get your feet under the table: *see* FOOT.

lay something on the table ❶ make something known so that it can be freely and sensibly discussed. ❷ postpone something indefinitely. chiefly US

put your cards on the table: *see* CARD.

turn the tables reverse your position relative to someone else, especially by turning a position of disadvantage into one of advantage.

> ❶ Until the mid 18th century, *tables* was the usual name for the board game backgammon. Early instances of the use of this phrase, dating from the mid 17th century, make it clear that it comes from the practice of turning the board so that a player had to play what had previously been their opponent's position.

under the table drunk to the point of unconsciousness. informal

> **1921 W. Somerset Maugham** *The Trembling of a Leaf* Walker had always been a heavy drinker, he was proud of his capacity to see men half his age under the table.

tack

get (*or* come) down to brass tacks: *see* BRASS.

flat as a tack: *see* FLAT.

tackie

South African informal

a piece of old tackie an easy task.

> **1979** *Cape Times* Getting the news of the Zimbabwe Rhodesian ceasefire to the... guerillas might well make Paul Revere's famous midnight ride look like a piece of old tackie.

tread tackie drive or accelerate.

> ❶ *Tackies* are rubber-soled sports shoes. The origin of the word is uncertain, though there may be a connection with the English adjective *tacky*, meaning 'slightly sticky', perhaps referring to the effect of extreme heat on the shoes' soles.

> **1989** *Daily Dispatch* By the time they finally trod tackie on the road out, a full week had gone by.

tackle

wedding tackle: *see* WEDDING.

tag

tag, rag, and bobtail: *see* **rag, tag, and bobtail** *at* RAG.

tail

the tail wags the dog the less important or subsidiary factor or thing dominates a situation; the usual roles are reversed.

> **2012** *Washington Post* He said that primary challenges from the ideological fringe allow a relatively small minority to exert undue influence on electoral outcomes.... 'We've set up a system that allows the tail to wag the dog,' Edwards said.

turn tail turn round and run away. informal

with your tail between your legs in a state of dejection or humiliation. informal

with your tail up in a confident or cheerful mood. informal

ⓘ For other idioms containing *tail*, see the entry for the main word in the idiom (for example, **make head or tail of** at HEAD).

take

on the take taking bribes. informal

1990 Morley Torgov *St. Farb's Day* I seen plenty of cops drive Mercedes. The ones that're on the take.

take someone or something apart ❶ dismantle something. ❷ defeat someone or something conclusively. ❸ criticize someone or something severely. informal

take it submit to, tolerate, or endure a bad experience or hardship.

take it from me I can assure you.

take it or leave it said to convey that the offer you have made is not negotiable and that you are indifferent to another's reaction to it.

ⓘ For other idioms containing *take*, see the entry for the main word in the idiom (for example, **take no prisoners** at PRISONER).

taking

for the taking (of a person or thing) ready or available for someone to take advantage of.

1994 Jane Hamilton *A Map of the World* I try to imagine the land for the taking, and what it must have meant to have space for as far as the eye can see.

tale

ⓘ For idioms containing *tale*, see the entry for the main word in the idiom (for example, **tell tales** at TELL).

talk

chalk and talk: *see* CHALK.

look (*or* hark) who's talking used to convey that a criticism made applies equally well to the person who has made it. informal

money talks: *see* MONEY.

now you're talking! used to express your enthusiastic agreement with or approval of a statement or suggestion.

talk big talk confidently or boastfully. informal

talk of the devil: *see* **speak of the devil** *at* DEVIL.

talk a blue streak: *see* BLUE.

talk dirty: *see* DIRTY.

talk a good game talk convincingly yet fail to act effectively. US informal

2000 *Sunday Times* There were two types of people in the industry: the consultants who talk a good game but deliver little, and the wide boys and girls who get bums on seats but sacrifice standards.

talk the hind leg off a donkey talk incessantly. British informal

ⓘ In 1808 *talking a horse's hind leg off* was described as an 'old vulgar hyperbole' in *Cobbett's Weekly Political Register*, but the version with *donkey* was current by the mid 19th century. In 1879 Anthony Trollope mentioned *talk the hind legs off a dog* as an Australian variant.

1970 Nina Bawden *The Birds on the Trees* Talk, talk—talk the hind leg off a donkey, that one.

talk nineteen to the dozen talk incessantly. British

ⓘ No convincing reason has been put forward as to why nineteen should have been preferred in this idiom rather than twenty or any other number larger than twelve.

1998 Pamela Jooste *Dance with a Poor Man's Daughter* He hasn't even got his foot in the door before she's talking nineteen to the dozen and hanging round his neck and asking if he's got sweets in his pocket.

talk out of turn: *see* **speak out of turn** *at* SPEAK.

talk shop: *see* SHOP.

talk the talk speak fluently or convincingly about something or in a way intended to please or impress others. informal

2000 *South African Times UK* I'm sick and tired of seeing yet another little media performance of ministers talking the talk.

talk through your hat talk foolishly, wildly, or ignorantly. informal

ⓘ Vulgar variants of this expression include talking through your *backside*, *arse*, and *ass*.

talk to the hand: *see* HAND.

talk turkey: *see* TURKEY.

walk the talk: *see* WALK.

tall

a tall order something that is difficult to accomplish.

2013 Mirko Humbert *Designer Daily* As you can see, understanding typography is a pretty tall order! Luckily, there are plenty of really informative tutorials to be found.

a tall poppy a privileged or distinguished person.

ℹ The Roman tyrant Tarquin was reputed to have struck off the heads of poppies as a gruesomely graphic demonstration of the way in which the important men of a captured city should be treated. In recent years, the term *tall poppy syndrome* has also developed, referring to a tendency to discredit or disparage people who have become rich, famous, or socially prominent.

1991 Lynn Barber *Mostly Men* Journalists on the whole tend to be egalitarian-minded and contemptous of tall poppies, but I prefer the prima donnas.

walk tall: *see* WALK.

tan

tan someone's hide ❶ beat or flog someone. ❷ punish someone severely.

tandem

in tandem ❶ one behind another. ❷ alongside each other; together.

ℹ The Latin word *tandem* means 'at length': it was originally used in English as a term for a carriage drawn by two horses harnessed one in front of the other. Sense 1 preserves this late 18th-century sense, but since the mid 20th century the phrase has been commonly used to mean simply 'functioning as a team'.

tangled

a tangled web a complex, difficult, and confusing situation or thing.

ℹ This phrase comes from Sir Walter Scott's epic poem *Marmion* (1808); 'O what a tangled web we weave, When first we practise to deceive!'

tango

it takes two to tango both parties involved in a situation or argument are equally responsible for it. informal

ℹ *Takes Two to Tango* was the title of a 1952 song by Al Hoffman and Dick Manning.

2012 *New York Times* Strikes are never popular and are not meant to be. Whether they are justified is difficult to judge from the outside, except to say that it takes two to tango.

tank

a tiger in your tank: *see* TIGER.

tap

on tap ❶ ready to be poured from a tap. ❷ freely available whenever needed. informal ❸ on schedule to happen or occur. North American informal

tap someone's claret: *see* CLARET.

taped

have (*or* get) someone or something taped understand someone or something fully. British informal

ℹ Early examples of the phrase, dating from the early 20th century, do not make its development clear: the sense could derive either from the action of measuring someone with a tape measure or from that of tying someone or something up with tape (and thereby getting them under control).

2001 John Diamond *C: Because Cowards Get Cancer Too* After a few false starts you've learned how to do sending the meal back, dropping the girlfriend, getting through the job interview, making the marriage proposal: you think you've got it taped.

tapis

on the tapis (of a subject) under consideration or discussion.

ℹ This expression is a partial translation of the French phrase *sur le tapis*, meaning literally 'on the carpet'. A carpet in this context is a covering for a table rather than a floor, as indeed it was originally in the English idiom **on the carpet**. It refers to the covering of the council table around which a matter would be debated.

tar

beat (*or* whale) the tar out of beat or thrash severely. North American informal

spoil the ship for a ha'p'orth of tar: *see* SPOIL.

tar and feather smear with tar and then cover with feathers as a punishment.

ℹ This practice was introduced in Britain in 1189, when Richard I decreed that it should be the punishment for members of the navy found guilty of theft. It seems to have been intermittently imposed on other wrongdoers in Britain and has sometimes been inflicted on an unpopular or scandalous individual by a mob.

1981 Anthony Price *Soldier No More* The Russians . . . wouldn't have cared less if we'd tarred and feathered Nasser and run him out of Suez on a rail.

tar baby a difficult problem which is only aggravated by attempts to solve it.

ⓘ The allusion is to a doll smeared with tar as a trap for Brer Rabbit in Joel Chandler Harris's *Uncle Remus* (1881).

tar people with the same brush consider specified people to have the same faults.

task

take someone to task reprimand or criticize someone severely for a fault or mistake.

taste

a bad (*or* bitter *or* nasty) taste in the (*or* someone's) mouth a strong feeling of distress or disgust following an experience. informal

an acquired taste: *see* ACQUIRED.

a taste of your own medicine: *see* **a dose of your own medicine** *at* MEDICINE.

taste blood: *see* BLOOD.

there's no accounting for taste: *see* ACCOUNT

tea

go for your tea be murdered. informal euphemistic

ⓘ The expression arose among members of the IRA in the latter part of the 20th century.

not for all the tea in China not at any price; certainly not! informal

not your cup of tea: *see* CUP.

tea and sympathy hospitality and consolation offered to a distressed person.

teach

teach your grandmother to suck eggs: *see* GRANDMOTHER.

teach someone a lesson: *see* LESSON.

you can't teach an old dog new tricks: *see* DOG.

teacup

a storm in a teacup: *see* STORM.

team

a whole team and the dog under the wagon a person of superior ability; an outstandingly gifted or able person. US

tear

blood, sweat, and tears: *see* BLOOD.

end in tears: *see* END.

shed crocodile tears: *see* CROCODILE.

tear your hair out act with or show extreme desperation. informal

1991 Jill Churchill *A Farewell to Yarns*
Someplace people were having nervous breakdowns and tearing their hair out in a desperate effort to please Phyllis.

tear someone limb from limb: *see* LIMB.

tear someone off a strip (*or* tear a strip off someone) rebuke someone angrily. informal

ⓘ This expression was originally RAF slang, first recorded in the 1940s.

tear someone or something to shreds (*or* pieces) criticize someone or something aggressively. informal

vale of tears: *see* VALE.

wear and tear: *see* WEAR.

without tears (of a subject) presented so as to be learnt or achieved easily.

ⓘ The expression was first used in the titles of books by F. L. Mortimer, such as *Reading without Tears* (1857) and *Latin without Tears* (1877).

1991 William Fox *Willoughby's Phoney War*
[They] are going to be given their first lesson this afternoon. Skiing without tears, I hardly think.

teeter

teeter on the brink (*or* edge) be very close to a difficult or dangerous situation.

1997 James Ryan *Dismantling Mr Doyle*
Letting her secret teeter on the brink of becoming public was a game Eve played more and more.

teeth

cut your teeth acquire initial practice or experience of a particular sphere of activity or with a particular organization.

ⓘ The form *cut your eye teeth* is also found. The image is that of the emergence of a baby's teeth from its gums.

get (*or* sink) your teeth into work energetically and productively on (a task).

in the teeth of ❶ directly against (the wind). ❷ in spite of or contrary to (opposition or difficulty).

❷ **2001** *Fast Company Magazine* All of these solid performances occurred in the teeth of a global economic slowdown.

like pulling teeth extremely difficult or laborious to do. informal

2002 *Independent* It was like pulling teeth in the first half. I thought we were never going to score.

set your teeth ❶ clench your teeth together. ❷ become resolute.

ℹ For other idioms containing *teeth,* see the entry for the main word in the idiom (for example, **set someone's teeth on edge** at EDGE).

teething

teething troubles short-term problems that occur in the early stages of a new project.

ℹ The expression originally denoted the discomfort felt by babies when their teeth are growing.

telegraph

bush telegraph a rapid informal spreading of information or rumour; the network through which this takes place.

ℹ This expression originated in the late 19th century, referring to the network of informers who kept bushrangers informed about the movements of the police in the Australian bush or outback. Compare with **hear something on the grapevine** (*at* GRAPEVINE).

tell

I tell a lie: *see* LIE.

kiss and tell: *see* KISS.

live to tell the tale: *see* LIVE.

tell it like it is describe the true facts of a situation no matter how unpleasant they may be. informal

tell me about it used as an ironic acknowledgement of your familiarity with a difficult or unpleasant situation or experience described by someone else. informal

2004 *Milk Plus* 'We fought all night to get back HERE?' 'Yeah, tell me about it. Coney freakin Island. Paradise it ain't.'

tell me another used as an expression of disbelief or incredulity. informal

tell something a mile off: *see* **see something a mile off** *at* MILE.

tell tales (out of school) gossip about or reveal another person's secrets, wrong-doings, or faults.

1991 Mark Tully *No Full Stops in India* Indira trusted me throughout her life, and just because she's dead it's not right that I should break that trust and tell tales about her.

tell that to the marines: *see* MARINES.

tell someone where to get off (*or* where they get off) angrily rebuke someone. informal

tell someone where to put (*or* what to do with) something angrily or emphatically reject something. informal

time will tell: *see* TIME.

telling

that would be telling that would be divulging confidential information. informal

2000 Imogen Edwards-Jones *My Canapé Hell* 'Are you propositioning me?' I say, attempting to look provocative in my Devonshire home-knit and Angora Dutch cap. 'Now that would be telling,' he smiles.

there's no telling it's impossible to know what has happened or will happen.

you're telling me! used to emphasize that you are already well aware of something or in complete agreement with a statement. informal

tempest

a tempest in a teapot: *see* **a storm in a teacup** *at* STORM.

tempt

tempt fate (*or* providence) act rashly. informal

ten

count to ten: *see* COUNT.

ten a penny: *see* **two a penny** *at* PENNY.

ten out of ten full marks (used to congratulate someone for doing something perfectly).

tender

tender mercies used ironically to refer to attention or treatment not in the best interests of its recipient. chiefly British

2010 *Guardian* Bowie abandons his younger brother to the tender mercies of public school playground bullies and is consequently plagued with guilt.

tenterhooks

on tenterhooks in a state of suspense or agitation because of uncertainty about a future event.

ⓘ A *tenter* is a framework on which fabric can be held taut for drying or other treatment during the manufacturing process; in the past *tenterhooks* were hooks or bent nails fixed in the tenter to hold the fabric in position. The metaphorical use of the phrase for an agitated state of mind dates from the mid 18th century.

term

come to terms with come to accept a new and painful or difficult event or situation.

in no uncertain terms: *see* UNCERTAIN.

on terms ❶ in a state of friendship or equality. ❷ (in sport) level in score or on points.

terminate

terminate someone with extreme prejudice murder or assassinate someone. euphemistic, chiefly US

ⓘ The expression originated in the terminology of the Central Intelligence Agency in the 1970s.

terrible

terrible twos a period in a child's social development (typically around the age of two years) which is associated with very defiant or unruly behaviour. informal

territory

go (*or* come) with the territory be an unavoidable result of a particular situation.

ⓘ *Territory* is probably used here in its early 20th-century US sense of 'the area in which a sales representative or distributor has the right to operate'.

test

the acid test: *see* ACID.

stand the test of time last or remain popular for a long time.

test the water judge people's feelings or opinions before taking further action.

tether

at the end of your tether: *see* END.

Thames

set the Thames on fire: *see* **set the world alight** *at* WORLD.

thank

thank your lucky stars feel grateful for your good fortune.

2014 Kevin Barbieux *The Homeless Guy* Every day, as I watch the national weather reports, I thank my lucky stars that I relocated here when I did. I don't think I could have handled another Nashville winter.

thanks

no thanks to not because of; despite.

1993 Carl MacDougall. *The Lights Below* 'How's your mother?' 'Our mother's fine. No thanks to you. She was worried sick.'

thanks for the buggy ride used as a way of thanking someone for their help. North American dated

ⓘ A *buggy* was a light horse-drawn vehicle for one or two people.

thanks for nothing used ironically to indicate that what someone has done or said is extremely unwelcome to you.

that

and all that (*or* and that) and that sort of thing; and so on. informal

1982 Simon Brett *Murder Unprompted* I know he's the star and all that, but I'm damned if I'm going to be upstaged, even by him.

that's that there is nothing more to do or say about the matter.

that will be the day: *see* DAY.

them

them and us: *see* US.

there

been there, done that used to express past experience of or familiarity with something. informal

ⓘ This is often used as a flippant expression of boredom or world-weariness. A late 20th-century elaboration parodies the blasé tourist's attitude to experience: *been there, done that, got the T-shirt.*

2000 *New Yorker* He liked the idea of space-based interceptors but couldn't see the purpose of a new treaty that would once again give Russia a veto over our defenses. 'Been there, done that,' Cooper says.

be there for someone be available to provide support or comfort for someone, especially at a time of adversity.

2014 *Daily Telegraph* This has been such a difficult time and my head is all over the place. I just want to be there for my daughter but I am appreciative for all that has been done to help us.

get in there: *see* GET.

have been there (*or* here) before know all about a situation as a result of previous experience. informal

not all there: *see* ALL.

put it there: *see* PUT.

there you are (*or* go) ❶ this is what you wanted. ❷ expressing confirmation, triumph, or bemused resignation.

❷ **2005** *Film Inside Out* Whoever would have thought that Johnny Depp's appearance in the *Fast Show* would lead to Paul Whitehouse breaking into Hollywood, but there you go, anything can happen.

up there: *see* UP.

thereby

thereby hangs (*or* herein (*or* therein) lies) a tale used to indicate that there is more to be said about something.

2007 *DVD Verdict* How did they end up in the same car? Therein lies a tale, one that lone survivor Marian ... will tell reporter Mitch ... in flashbacks as she lies in a hospital bed.

1998 *Spectator* Now it has decided to fight back and clear its name. And herein lies a tale, however ludicrous.

thick

a bit thick more than you can tolerate; unfair or unreasonable. British informal

1991 Alistair Campbell *Sidewinder* I thought this was a bit thick, and to begin with I tried to defend myself.

give someone (*or* get) a thick ear punish someone (*or* be punished) with a blow, especially on the ear. British informal

have a thick skin: *see* SKIN.

lay something on thick (*or* with a trowel) grossly exaggerate or overemphasize something. informal

the thick of something the busiest or most crowded part of something.

1999 Christopher Brookmyre *One Fine Day in the Middle of the Night* They'd been in the thick of it, sharing God-knows-what experiences together, from foreplay to gunplay.

thick and fast rapidly and in great numbers.

thick as thieves (of two or more people) very close or friendly; sharing secrets. informal

thick as two (short) planks very stupid. informal

ⓘ Variants of this expression include *thick as a plank* and *thick as a brick*. There is a play on *thick* in its basic sense 'of relatively great depth from side to side' and its colloquial sense 'stupid'.

the thick end of something the greater part of something. informal

2014 *Keeping Stock* We haven't even got to the end of January and Labor and the Greens are already promising to spend the thick end of an extra three quarters of a million dollars a year.

thick on the ground: *see* GROUND.

through thick and thin under all circumstances, no matter how difficult.

thicken

the plot thickens: *see* PLOT.

thicker

blood is thicker than water: *see* BLOOD.

thin

have a thin skin: *see* **have a thick skin** *at* SKIN.

have a thin time have a wretched or uncomfortable time. British informal

into (*or* out of) thin air into (*or* out of) a state of being invisible or nonexistent.

on thin ice: *see* ICE.

spread yourself too thin: *see* SPREAD.

thin as a rake: *see* RAKE.

thin on the ground: *see* **thick on the ground** *at* GROUND.

the thin blue line used to refer to the police, typically in the context of maintaining order during unrest. informal

the thin end of the wedge an action or procedure of little importance in itself, but

t

which is likely to lead to more serious developments. informal

thin on top balding.

thing

be all things to all men (*or* people) ❶ please everyone, typically by regularly altering your behaviour or opinions in order to conform to those of others. ❷ be able to be interpreted or used differently by different people to their own satisfaction.

> ℹ This expression probably originated in reference to 1 Corinthians 9:22: 'I am made all things to all men'.

be on to a good thing have found a job or other situation that is pleasant, profitable, or easy. informal

a close (*or* near) thing a narrow avoidance of something unpleasant.

do the — thing engage in the particular form of behaviour typically associated with someone or something. informal, chiefly North American

> **1999 Tim Lott** *White City Blue* I was going to ask Tony there, oil us all with a few bevvies, and then do the best-man thing.

do your own thing follow your own interests or inclinations regardless of others. informal

first thing: *see* FIRST.

first things first: *see* FIRST.

have a thing about be obsessed with or prejudiced about. informal

hear (*or* see) things imagine that you can hear (*or* see) something that is not in fact there.

(just) one of those things used to indicate that you wish to pass over an unfortunate event or experience by regarding it as unavoidable or to be accepted.

know a thing or two: *see* KNOW.

last thing: *see* LAST.

make a thing of ❶ regard as essential. ❷ cause a fuss about. informal

the other thing: *see* OTHER.

sure thing: *see* SURE.

tell (*or* teach) someone a thing or two impart useful information or experience. informal

> **2013** *CNN transcripts* He's turning the tables on these teenagers and teaching them a thing or two about the power of social media.

a thing of shreds and patches: *see* SHRED.

things that go bump in the night ghosts; supernatural beings. informal

> ℹ This expression comes from *The Cornish or West Country Litany*: 'From ghoulies and ghosties and long-leggety beasties And things that go bump in the night, Good Lord deliver us!' The phrase is used as a humorous way of referring to nocturnal disturbances of all sorts.

think

come to think of it said when an idea or point occurs to you while you are speaking.

give someone furiously to think give a person cause to think hard.

> ℹ This is a literal translation of the French phrase *donner furieusement à penser*.

great minds think alike: *see* MIND.

have (got) another think coming used to express the speaker's disagreement with or unwillingness to do something suggested by someone else. informal

> **2000** *Sunday Herald (Glasgow)* The accelerating pretender has another think coming if it imagines that it has an easy shot at becoming world number one.

lie back and think of England: *see* LIE.

think better of: *see* BETTER.

think big: *see* BIG.

think nothing of consider (an activity others regard as odd, wrong, or difficult) as straightforward or normal.

> **2004** *Residential Architect* His foreign business partners think nothing of scheduling an hour-and-a-half meeting for 10:30 at night, then being back at work by 8 am.

think nothing of it do not apologize or feel bound to show gratitude (used as a polite response).

think on your feet react to events quickly and effectively.

think outside the box: *see* BOX.

think twice consider a course of action carefully before embarking on it.

think the world of: *see* WORLD.

thinking

not bear thinking about: *see* BEAR.

put on your thinking cap meditate on a problem. informal

third

third time lucky after twice failing to accomplish something, the third attempt may be successful.

ⓘ *Third time lucky* has been proverbial since the mid 19th century; a US variant is *third time is the charm*.

Thomas

a doubting Thomas: *see* DOUBTING.

thorn

no rose without a thorn: *see* ROSE.

a thorn in someone's side (*or* flesh) a source of continual annoyance or trouble.

ⓘ *A thorn in the side* comes from the biblical book of Numbers (33:55): 'those which ye let remain of them shall be pricks in your eyes, and thorns in your sides, and shall vex you in the land wherein ye dwell'. *A thorn in the flesh* quotes 2 Corinthians 12:7: 'And lest I should be exalted above measure through the abundance of the revelations, there was given to me a thorn in the flesh, the messenger of Satan to buffet me, lest I should be exalted above measure'.

those

those were the days: *see* DAY.

thought

ⓘ For idioms containing *thought*, see the entry for the main word in the idiom (for example, **perish the thought** at PERISH).

thousand

bat a thousand: *see* BAT.

thread

hang by a thread be in a highly precarious state.

lose the (*or* your) thread be unable to follow what someone is saying or remember what you are going to say next.

pick up the threads: *see* PICK.

three

page three girl: *see* PAGE.

three cheers for —: *see* CHEER.

three musketeers three close associates or inseparable friends.

ⓘ *The Three Musketeers* is a translation of *Les Trois Mousquetaires*, the title of a novel by the 19th-century French writer Alexandre Dumas père.

the three Rs: *see* R.

a three-ring circus: *see* CIRCUS.

three sheets to the wind: *see* **two sheets to the wind** *at* SHEET.

threescore

threescore and ten the age of seventy.

ⓘ In the Bible, threescore and ten amounts to the allotted span of a person's life: 'The days of our age are threescore years and ten' (Psalm 90:10).

thrill

thrills and spills the excitement of dangerous sports or entertainments, especially as experienced by spectators.

throat

be at each other's throats (of people or organizations) quarrel or fight persistently.

1990 Rian Malan *My Traitor's Heart* 'It's not only difficult for people outside to understand why blacks are at each others' throats,' he says. 'It's difficult for ourselves.'

cut your own throat bring about your own downfall by your actions.

force (*or* ram *or* shove) something down someone's throat force ideas or material on a person's attention by repeatedly putting them forward.

grab (*or* take) something or someone by the throat ❶ seize control of something. ❷ attract someone's undivided attention.

❶ **2008** *CNN transcripts* It would be great to see a candidate grab the mortgage issue by the throat and do something.

❷ **2012 Margaret Pomeranz and David Stratton** *At the Movies* Shot splendidly by Adam Arkepaw in an impressionistic style . . . , this film grabs you by the throat and refuses to let go.

have a frog in your throat: *see* FROG.

jump down someone's throat: *see* JUMP.

a lump in the throat: *see* LUMP.

stick in your throat (*or* gullet) be difficult or impossible to accept; be a source of continuing annoyance.

> ⓘ The literal sense refers to something lodged in your throat which you can neither swallow nor spit out. *See also* **stick in your craw** *at* CRAW and **stick in your gizzard** *at* GIZZARD.

throne

power behind the throne: *see* POWER.

throw

> ⓘ For idioms containing *throw,* see the entry for the main word in the idiom (for example, **throw your hat in the ring** at HAT).

thrown

be thrown in at the deep end: *see* **jump in at the deep end** *at* DEEP.

thrust

cut and thrust ❶ a spirited and rapid interchange of views. ❷ a situation or sphere of activity regarded as carried out under adversarial conditions.

> ⓘ In fencing, a *cut* is a slashing stroke and a *thrust* one given with the point of the weapon.

thumb

be all fingers and thumbs: *see* FINGER.

hold your thumbs fold your fingers over your thumbs to bring good luck; hope for luck or success. South African

> **1987** *Sunday Times* (South Africa) They say they are holding thumbs for her and praying that the pregnancy will be trouble-free.

a pricking in your thumbs: *see* PRICKING.

rule of thumb: *see* RULE.

stand out like a sore thumb: *see* SORE.

thumb your nose at show disdain or contempt for. Compare with **cock a snook** (*at* SNOOK).

thumbs up (*or* down) an indication of satisfaction or approval (*or* of rejection or failure). informal

> ⓘ The thumbs were used to signal approval or disapproval by spectators at a Roman amphitheatre, though they used 'thumbs down' to signify that a beaten gladiator had performed well and should be spared, and 'thumbs up' to call for his death.

twiddle your thumbs: *see* TWIDDLE.

under someone's thumb completely under someone's influence or control.

thunder

blood and thunder: *see* BLOOD.

steal someone's thunder: *see* STEAL.

tick

on tick on credit. informal

> ⓘ *Tick* is an abbreviation of *ticket*, a note recording money or goods received on credit.

tick all the (right) boxes fulfil all the necessary requirements. British informal

tight as a tick: *see* TIGHT.

what makes someone tick what motivates someone. informal

ticket

be tickets be the end. South African informal

have tickets on yourself be excessively vain or proud of yourself. Australian informal

punch your ticket deliberately undertake particular assignments that are likely to lead to promotion at work. US informal

split the ticket: *see* SPLIT.

work your ticket contrive to obtain your discharge from prison or the army.

write your (own) ticket dictate your own terms. North American informal

tickey

on a tickey in a very small area. South African

> ⓘ In the period before South African coinage was decimalized, a *tickey* was a very small silver coin worth three pennies.

tickle

be tickled pink (*or* to death) be extremely amused or pleased. informal

> **1992 Guy Vanderhaeghe** *Things As They Are* She made a big show of not being taken in by him, but I could see that all six feet . . . of her was tickled pink by his attentions.

slap and tickle: *see* SLAP.

tickle the ivories: *see* IVORY.

tide

go (*or* swim) with (*or* against) the tide act in accordance with (*or* against) the prevailing opinion or tendency.

time and tide wait for no man: *see* TIME.

tie

fit to be tied very angry. informal

1988 Joan Smith *A Masculine Ending* He was fit to be tied when I separated from Hugh, and he seems to blame me for the whole thing.

tie one on get drunk. North American informal

ℹ For other idioms containing *tie,* see the entry for the main word in the idiom (for example, **tie the knot** at KNOT).

tiger

have (*or* catch) a tiger by the tail = ride a tiger.

ℹ A similar difficulty confronts those who have a **wolf by the ears** (*see* WOLF).

1979 Peter Driscoll *Pangolin* You're taking on an organization with reserves you know nothing about. How do you know you won't be catching a tiger by the tail?

a paper tiger: *see* PAPER.

ride a tiger take on a responsibility or embark on a course of action which subsequently cannot safely be abandoned.

ℹ The expression comes from the Chinese proverb 'He who rides a tiger is afraid to dismount'.

1940 *Daily Progress* (USA) I believe that Hitler is riding a tiger in trying to keep all Europe under control by sheer force.

a tiger in your tank energy, spirit, or animation.

ℹ This expression originated as a 1960s advertising slogan for Esso petrol: 'Put a tiger in your tank'.

tight

keep a tight rein on: *see* REIN.

run a tight ship be very strict in managing an organization or operation.

sit tight: *see* SIT.

tight as a tick extremely drunk. informal

ℹ The simile *as full as a tick* occurs in a late 17th-century proverb collection, referring to the way in which the blood-sucking insects swell as they gorge themselves. In the modern expression, there is a play on *tight* as an informal synonym for 'drunk' and its literal meaning 'stretched taut', like a tick satiated with blood.

a tight corner (*or* spot *or* place) a difficult situation.

2013 *Daily Telegraph* A smile of immense satisfaction spread across Mr Cameron's face. 'Never underestimate the ability of Boris to get out of a tight spot,' he beamed.

tighten

tighten your belt: *see* BELT.

tighten the screw: *see* SCREW.

tile

on the tiles away from home having a wild or enjoyable time and not returning until late in the evening or early in the morning. informal, chiefly British

ℹ The image here is of a cat out on the rooftops at night. The expression has been in use since the late 19th century.

till

have (*or* with) your fingers (*or* hand) in the till stealing from your employer. Compare with **with your hand in the cookie jar** (*at* COOKIE).

tilt

(at) full tilt with maximum energy or force; at top speed.

1912 Edith Wharton *Letter* Just after we left Modena a crazy coachman drove full tilt out of a side road.

tilt at windmills attack imaginary enemies or evils.

ℹ In Cervantes' 17th-century mock-chivalric novel *Don Quixote*, the eponymous hero attacked windmills in the deluded belief that they were giants.

time

for the time being for the present; until some other arrangement is made.

give someone the time of day be pleasantly polite or friendly to someone.

2005 Barbara Keating & Stephanie Keating *Blood Sisters* The Britishers will never consider us as their own ... They won't give us the time of day when *Uhuru* comes.

have no time for dislike or disapprove of

2013 Jim Schrembi *The Age* A member of a socialist government like Carr would have no time for an anti-government free thinker like Julian Assange.

in your own time ❶ (*also* **in your own good time**) at a time and a rate decided by yourself (sometimes said sarcastically to a dilatory person). ❷ outside working hours; without being paid.

ⓘ In the second meaning, US English uses *on your own time*.

not before time used to convey that something now happening or about to happen should have happened earlier.

once upon a time ❶ at some time in the past (used as a conventional opening of a story). ❷ formerly.

pass the time of day exchange a greeting or casual remarks.

play for time use specious excuses or unnecessary manoeuvres to gain time.

take your time not hurry.

time and tide wait for no man if you don't make use of a favourable opportunity, you may never get the same chance again. proverb

ⓘ Although the *tide* in this phrase is now usually understood to mean 'the tide of the sea', it was originally just another way of saying 'time', used for alliterative effect.

time immemorial used to refer to a point of time so long ago that people have no knowledge or memory of it.

ⓘ In legal terms in Britain, *time immemorial* refers to the time up to the beginning of the reign of Richard I in 1189. A variant of the phrase is *time out of mind*.

the time of your life a period or occasion of exceptional enjoyment.

time is money time is a valuable resource, therefore it's better to do things as quickly as possible. proverb

ⓘ The present form of the expression seems to originate in a speech made by Benjamin Franklin in 1748, but the sentiment is much older. The saying 'the most costly outlay is time' is attributed to the 5th-century BC Athenian orator and politician Antiphon.

(that) time of the month used euphemistically to refer to a woman's menstrual period.

2002 Ricky Gervais & **Stephen Merchant** *Office: Scripts* Alright? What is it, time of the month?

time was there was a time.

2014 *Daily Telegraph* Time was when fireworks in this country were confined to Bonfire Night and great national occasions, such as a Royal wedding. Nowadays, they seem to accompany any event that is out of the ordinary.

(only) time will tell the truth or correctness of something will only be established at some time in the future.

ⓘ For other idioms containing *time*, see the entry for the main word in the idiom (for example, **in the nick of time** at NICK).

tin

do what it says on the tin function in precisely the way described, without any additional extraneous features.

ⓘ The expression derives from an advertising slogan (1994) for the wood preservative Ronseal: 'Does exactly what it says on the tin.'

2001 *Which?* A personal digital assistant … should do exactly what it says on the tin. It should help you out, make your life a bit easier.

have a tin ear be tone-deaf.

ⓘ For other idioms containing *tin*, see the entry for the main word in the idiom (for example, **kick the tin** at KICK).

tinker

not give (*or* care) a tinker's curse (*or* cuss *or* damn) not care at all. informal

ⓘ In former times, tinkers (itinerant menders of pots, pans, and other metal utensils) had a reputation for using bad language. The expression is often shortened to *not give a tinker's*.

1984 Patrick O'Brian *The Far Side of the World* When I was a squeaker nobody gave a tinker's curse whether my daily workings were right or wrong.

tinkle

tinkle the ivories: *see* **tickle the ivories** *at* IVORY.

tiny

the patter of tiny feet: *see* PATTER.

tip

on the tip of your tongue ❶ (of a particular word or name) almost but not quite able to be remembered. ❷ (of a comment or question) about to be uttered but then thought better of.

❷ **1977 Bernard MacLaverty** *Between Two Shores* It was on the tip of his tongue to ask her but he didn't have the courage.

tip your hand (*or* mitt) reveal your intentions inadvertently. US informal

ℹ This expression is the opposite of **keep your cards close to your chest** (see CARD).

1966 Martin Woodhouse *Tree Frog* We couldn't very well oppose it without tipping our hand.

tip your hat (*or* cap) raise or touch your hat or cap as a way of greeting or acknowledging someone.

the tip of an iceberg: *see* ICEBERG.

tip (*or* turn) the scales (*or* balance) (of a circumstance or event) be the deciding factor; make the critical difference.

tip (*or* turn) the scales at: *see* SCALE.

tip someone the wink give someone private information; secretly warn someone of something. British informal

tired

dog tired: *see* DOG.

sick and tired: *see* SICK.

tired and emotional drunk.

ℹ This is a humorous euphemism, used originally in newspapers in contexts where the word *drunk* would lay the publication open to a libel charge. It is particularly associated with the British satirical magazine *Private Eye*.

tit

arse over tit: *see* ARSE.

get on someone's tits irritate someone intensely. British vulgar slang

2002 *Sunday Herald* One thing that really gets on my tits is the no-can-do attitude.

go tits up collapse in failure. vulgar slang

ℹ The expression probably arose as a variant of **go belly up** (*see at* BELLY).

1983 Lynda La Plante *Widows* I don't want to see what's in those ledgers, cos if this is for real and it all goes tits up, I'm denying everything. The less I know, the better.

tit for tat a situation in which an injury or insult is given in return or retaliation.

tits and bums used in reference to the use of crudely sexual images of women. vulgar slang, chiefly British

ℹ The variant *tits and ass* is chiefly North American.

titty

tough titty: *see* **tough shit** *at* TOUGH.

toast

be toast be or be likely to become finished, defunct, or dead. informal

2011 *Business Insider* It's the sharp end of a simple belief of ours that if there is someone able and willing to do your job for less than you, you are toast.

have someone on toast be in a position to deal with someone as you wish. informal

2012 *The Age* (Melbourne) At the last election, Opposition Leader Tony Abbott reckoned he had her on toast but the electorate was in two minds and delivered a hung parliament.

warm as toast: *see* WARM.

tod

on your tod on your own; alone. British informal

ℹ In rhyming slang, *on your Tod Sloan* means 'on your own'. The Tod Sloan in question was a famous American jockey who made his name in horse racing in the 1890s.

toe

dig in your toes: *see* **dig in your heels** *at* DIG.

dip your toe into something: *see* DIP.

from head to toe: *see* HEAD.

from top to toe: *see* **from head to toe** *at* HEAD.

have it on your toes run away. British informal

make someone's toes curl bring about an extreme reaction in someone, either of pleasure or disgust. informal

1984 Paul Prudhomme *Louisiana Kitchen* This is so good it'll make your toes curl!

on your toes ready for any eventuality.

1921 John Dos Passos *Three Soldiers* If he just watched out and kept on his toes, he'd be sure to get it.

have (*or* get) a toe in the door: *see* **have a foot in the door** *at* FOOT.

toe the line accept the authority, principles, or policies of a particular group, especially under pressure.

ℹ Competitors in a race *toe the line* by placing their toes on the starting line.

2013 *Business Insider* Khodorkovsky has been in jail since he was arrested in 2003 in what supporters say was part of a Kremlin campaign to punish him for political challenges to Putin, gain control of his oil assets and warn other tycoons to toe the line.

tread on someone's toes: *see* TREAD.

turn up your toes die. informal

ⓘ This originated as a mid-19th-century expression, a more elaborate version being *turn your toes up to the daisies*.

toffee

not be able to do something for toffee be totally incompetent at doing something. British informal

2000 *Times* Wordsworth himself couldn't spell for toffee, and his punctuation was extraordinarily bad.

together

get it together: *see* GET.

get your shit together: *see* SHIT.

put your heads together: *see* HEAD.

toilet

go down the toilet be completely lost or wasted; fail utterly. informal

token

by the same token in the same way; for the same reason.

1975 Frederick Exley *Pages from a Cold Island* The student could ask anything he chose, and by the same token Wilson could if he elected choose not to answer.

toll

take its toll have an adverse effect.

ⓘ An alternative formulation with the same meaning is *take a heavy toll*.

Tom

Tom, Dick, and Harry used to refer to ordinary people in general.

ⓘ This expression is first recorded in an 18th-century song: 'Farewell, Tom, Dick, and Harry. Farewell, Moll, Nell, and Sue'. It is generally used in mildly derogatory contexts (*he didn't want every Tom, Dick, and Harry knowing his business*) to suggest a large number of ordinary or undistinguished people.

Tom Tiddler's ground a place where money or profit is readily made.

ⓘ *Tom Tiddler's ground* was the name of a children's game in which one of the players, named Tom Tiddler, marked out their territory by drawing a line on the ground. The other players ran over this line calling out 'We're on Tom Tiddler's ground, picking up gold and silver'. They were then chased by Tom Tiddler and the first (or, sometimes, the last) to be caught took his or her place.

Uncle Tom Cobley and all: *see* UNCLE.

tomorrow

as if there was (*or* as though there were) no tomorrow with no regard for the future consequences.

1980 *Guardian Weekly* Oil supplies that Americans at home continue to consume as though there were no tomorrow.

jam tomorrow: *see* JAM.

tomorrow is another day the future will bring fresh opportunities.

ⓘ This phrase was in use as long ago as the early 16th century, in the form *tomorrow is a new day*.

ton

come down like a ton of bricks: *see* BRICK.

tone

lower the tone: *see* LOWER.

tongs

hammer and tongs: *see* HAMMER.

tongue

be on the tip of your tongue: *see* TIP.

bite your tongue: *see* BITE.

the cat has got someone's tongue: *see* CAT.

the gift of tongues the power of speaking in unknown languages, regarded as one of the gifts of the Holy Spirit.

ⓘ When the disciples of Jesus were filled with the Holy Spirit after Pentecost (Acts 2:1–4), the *gift of tongues* was one of the ways in which this phenomenon manifested itself; compare with **speak in tongues** (*at* SPEAK).

have a silver tongue: *see* SILVER.

hold your tongue remain silent. informal

I could have bitten my tongue off: *see* BITTEN.

keep a civil tongue in your head: *see* CIVIL.

loosen someone's tongue: *see* LOOSEN.

the rough edge of your tongue: *see* ROUGH.

set tongues wagging be the cause of much gossip or rumour.

someone's tongue is hanging out someone is very eager for something, especially a drink.

speak in tongues: *see* SPEAK.

(with) tongue in cheek speaking or writing in an ironic or insincere way.

> ℹ This expression originated in the fuller form *put* or *thrust your tongue in your cheek*, meaning 'speak insincerely'. At one time, putting your tongue in your cheek could also be a gesture of contempt, but that shade of meaning has disappeared from the modern idiom.

with forked tongue: *see* FORKED.

tool

down tools: *see* DOWN.

tooth

fight tooth and nail fight very fiercely.

long in the tooth: *see* LONG.

red in tooth and claw: *see* RED.

top

blow your top lose your temper.

> ℹ Two chiefly North American variants are *blow your lid* and *blow your stack*.

from top to bottom completely; thoroughly.

from top to toe: *see* **from head to toe** *at* HEAD.

from the top from the beginning. informal

> **2005** *Bob's Yer Uncle* It was about putting yourself on the line, making new choices, trying new things, and feeling safe enough to fall flat on your face, say that didn't work, and then try it again from the top.

get on top of ❶ gain control of. ❷ be too much for (someone) to bear or cope with.

> ❶ **2013** *New Zealand Herald* My New Year's resolution was to really get on top of my financial affairs.

off the top of your head: *see* HEAD.

on top of the world happy and elated. informal

over the top to an excessive or exaggerated degree, in particular so as to go beyond reasonable or acceptable limits.

> ℹ The phrase *go over the top* originated in the First World War, when it referred to troops in the trenches charging over the parapets to attack the enemy. In modern use *over the top* is often abbreviated to *OTT*.

room at the top: *see* ROOM.

thin on top: *see* THIN.

top and tail ❶ remove the top and bottom of a fruit or vegetable while preparing it as food. ❷ wash the face and bottom of a baby or small child. British informal

top banana: *see* BANANA.

top the bill: *see* BILL.

top dollar a very high price. North American informal

> **2000** *Ralph* Klein has invested millions in building a non-conformist image . . . an image that has enabled the company to charge top dollar.

top drawer the highest level of society

> **1977 Colleen McCullough** *The Thorn Birds* Quite respectable, socially admissible, but not top drawer. Never top drawer.

top gun: *see* GUN.

top hole used, often as an exclamation, to indicate enthusiastic approbation or approval. British informal dated

the top of the tree the highest level of a profession or career.

top whack: *see* WHACK.

to top (*or* cap) it all as a culminating, typically unpleasant, event or action in a series.

up top in the brain (with reference to intelligence). British informal

torch

carry a torch for feel (especially unrequited) love for.

> **1996** *TV Times* A dentist carrying a torch for the local 'strawberry blonde' wonders if he married the right woman.

hand on (*or* pass) the torch pass on a tradition, especially one of learning or enlightenment.

> ℹ The image here is that of the runners in a relay passing on the torch to each other, as was the custom in the ancient Greek Olympic Games. The tradition of the torch relay is preserved as a prelude to the modern Olympics, with a team of runners carrying the Olympic torch vast distances across various countries until the site of the Games is reached.

put to the torch (*or* put a torch to) destroy by burning.

torn

that's torn it used to express dismay when something unfortunate has happened to disrupt your plans. British informal

toss

argue the toss: *see* ARGUE.

not give (*or* care) a toss not care at all. British informal

ℹ *Toss* probably originally denoted 'an act of tossing a coin', but in modern usage it is often interpreted as 'an act of masturbation'.

1998 *Country Life* I have swum in the Dart only a few yards from a mink, and the mink has not given a toss.

toss your cookies vomit. North American informal

t'other

tell t'other (*or* tother) from which tell one from the other. British humorous

ℹ *T'other* is a descendant of Middle English *the tother,* which arose from a misdivision of *thet other* 'the other'. The phrase is typically deployed as an example of 'humorous' northern dialect.

touch

the common touch: *see* COMMON.

kick something into touch: *see* KICK.

lose your touch not show your customary skill.

1991 *Times* The guv'nor is a former pork butcher who has clearly not lost his touch.

the Midas touch: *see* MIDAS.

a soft (*or* easy) touch someone who is easily manipulated; a person or task easily handled. informal

ℹ A *touch* was mid-19th-century criminal slang for the act of getting money from a person, either by pickpocketing or by persuasion. *Touch* was later extended to refer to the person targeted in this way, and a *soft touch* was specifically a person from whom money could easily be obtained.

2001 *Vanity Fair* He was also a soft touch for a sob story, possessed of nary a mean bone.

touch and go (of an outcome, especially one that is desired) possible but very uncertain.

touch base: *see* BASE.

touch bottom ❶ reach the bottom of water with your feet. ❷ be at the lowest or worst point. ❸ be in possession of the full facts. British

touch a (raw) nerve: *see* NERVE.

touch a (*or* the right) chord: *see* **strike a (*or* the right) chord** *at* CHORD.

a touch of the sun a slight attack of sunstroke.

touch wood: *see* WOOD.

touch your forelock: *see* FORELOCK.

would not touch someone or something with a bargepole: *see* BARGEPOLE.

touchpaper

light the touchpaper: *see* **light a fuse** *at* LIGHT.

tough

hang tough: *see* HANG.

a tough act to follow: *see* **a hard act to follow** *at* ACT

tough as old boots very sturdy or resilient.

ℹ Leather, of which boots are traditionally made, is notably strong and resistant to wear and tear. *As tough as leather* was in fact the earliest version of this phrase, although it has now been superseded by the current form.

1967 *Listener* This is no sweet old dolly . . . She is tough as old boots, working for a living.

tough it out endure a period of difficult conditions. informal

1998 *Cosmopolitan* Hang in there and tough it out. If you don't, you might be left with permanent fears about starting in new jobs, and that will stifle your career.

tough shit (*or* titty) used to express a lack of sympathy with someone or their problems. vulgar slang

towel

throw in the towel (*or* sponge) abandon a struggle; admit defeat.

ℹ Boxers or their trainers traditionally signal defeat by throwing the towel or sponge used to wipe a contestant's face into the middle of the ring.

tower

tower of strength: *see* STRENGTH.

town

go to town do something thoroughly or extravagantly, with a great deal of energy and enthusiasm. informal

1996 Dougie Brimson & Eddie Brimson *Everywhere We Go: Behind the Matchday Madness* When there is a major incident, the press still go to town and we are bombarded with graphic images of bloody faces.

man about town: *see* MAN.

on the town enjoying the entertainments, especially the nightlife, of a city or town. informal

one-horse town: *see* ONE-HORSE.

the only game in town: *see* GAME.

paint the town red: *see* PAINT.

run someone out of town force someone to leave a place. chiefly North American

town and gown non-members and members of a university in a particular place.

ⓘ The *gown* is the academic dress worn by university members, now required only on ceremonial or formal occasions. The distinction between *town and gown* was made in these specific terms in early 19th-century Oxford and Cambridge, but the traditional hostility between the native inhabitants of the two cities and the incoming students has been a long-standing phenomenon, as is evidenced by the St Scholastica's Day riot in Oxford in 1354.

toy

throw your toys out of the pram have a temper tantrum. British informal

2005 *Hecklerspray* Some might suggest that for Oprah to throw her toys out of the pram because a French woman told her she couldn't look at some clothes comes across as ... just a little arrogant.

trace

kick over the traces: *see* KICK.

sink without trace: *see* SINK.

track

cover your tracks: *see* COVER.

jump the track: *see* JUMP.

make tracks (for) leave (for a place). informal

1984 David Brin *Practice Effect* We have another big climb ahead of us and another pass to get through. Let's make tracks.

off the beaten track: *see* BEATEN.

the wrong side of the tracks a poor or less prestigious part of town. informal

ⓘ The expression, American in origin, comes from the idea of a town divided by a railroad track. In 1929, Thorne Smith wrote 'In most commuting towns ... there are always two sides of which the tracks serve as a line of demarcation. There is the right side and the wrong side. Translated into terms of modern American idealism, this means, the rich side and the side that hopes to be rich.'

1977 *Listener* Eva Duarte Peron ... came from the wrong side of the tracks.

trade

jack of all trades: *see* JACK.

traffic

as much as the traffic will bear as much as the trade or market will tolerate; as much as is economically viable.

trail

blaze a trail: *see* BLAZE.

trail (*or* drag) your coat deliberately provoke a quarrel or fight.

ⓘ If you trail your coat behind you someone is likely to step on it, either intentionally or unintentionally, so enabling you to pick a fight. This behaviour was traditionally associated with Irishmen at Donnybrook Fair, an annual fair once held in what is now a suburb of Dublin. Charlotte M. Yonge, in the novel *Womankind* (1877), alludes to this association: 'Party spirit is equally ready to give offence and to watch for it. It will trail its coat like the Irishman in the fair.'

1980 James Ditton *Copley's Hunch* I was trailing my coat ... Trying to get the Luftwaffe to come up and fight.

train

board (*or* climb on) the gravy train: *see* GRAVY.

in train (of arrangements) in progress; being proceeded with.

2005 *Architectural Review* 'China's New Dawn: an Architectural Transformation' is a mainly pictorial survey of some 50 projects, recently completed or in train.

transom

over the transom offered or sent without prior agreement; unsolicited. US informal

ⓘ A *transom* is a crossbar set above a door or window, and the word can also be used, especially in American English, as a term for a small window set above this crossbar. In former times, before the advent of air conditioning, many offices would leave these windows open for the purposes of ventilation, thereby allowing an aspiring author to take their manuscript to an editor's office and slip it through the open window to land on the floor inside. So, a manuscript that arrived *over the transom* was one that was unexpected. The phrase is still often used in publishing contexts, although it is no longer confined to them.

1976 Piers Anthony *But What of Earth?* Editors claim to be deluged with appallingly bad material 'over the transom' from unagented writers.

trap

shut your trap: *see* **shut your face** *at* FACE.

tread

tread the boards: *see* BOARD.

tread (*or* step) on someone's toes offend someone, especially by encroaching on their privileges.

tread tackie: *see* TACKIE.

tread water ❶ maintain an upright position in the water by moving the feet with a walking movement and the hands with a downward circular motion. ❷ fail to advance or make progress.

❷ **1996** *Financial Post* The NAPM index . . . has been treading water since the spring, and that is making a lot of people nervous.

tread on air: *see* **walk on air** *at* AIR.

treat

— a treat used to indicate that someone or something does something specified very well or satisfactorily. British informal

1988 Ray Pickernell *Yanto's Summer* A flared cream pleated skirt that complemented those long perfect brown legs, and a powder blue tee shirt that matched her eyes a treat.

treat someone like dirt: *see* DIRT.

tree

bark up the wrong tree: *see* BARK.

cannot see the wood for the trees: *see* WOOD.

grow on trees: *see* GROW.

out of your tree completely stupid; mad. informal

pull up trees perform remarkable exploits. informal

2019 *Sunday Times* While England went on their triumphal progress to World Cup glory, he was turning out for Nottinghamshire in the County Championship, where he hardly pulled up trees.

the top of the tree: *see* TOP.

up a tree in a difficult situation without escape; cornered. informal, chiefly North American

trend

buck the trend: *see* BUCK.

trial

trial and error the process of experimenting with various methods of doing something until you find the most successful.

trial by television (*or* the media) discussion of a case or controversy on television or in the media involving or implying accusations against a particular person.

triangle

eternal triangle: *see* ETERNAL.

trice

in a trice in a moment; very quickly.

ⓘ In late Middle English, *at a trice* meant 'at one pull or tug', and it soon developed the figurative meaning of 'in a moment, immediately'. By the late 17th century the original form of the expression had given way to the more familiar *in a trice*. *Trice* itself comes from a Middle Dutch verb meaning 'hoist'.

trick

a bag of tricks: *see* BAG.

a box of tricks: *see* BOX.

do the trick achieve the required result. informal

1990 Niki Hill *Death Grows On You* I figured a box of candy would do the trick, would bring some colour back.

every trick in the book every available method of achieving what you want. informal

how's tricks? used as a friendly greeting. informal

not miss a trick: *see* MISS.

the oldest trick in the book a ruse so hackneyed that it should no longer deceive anyone.

a trick worth two of that a much better plan or expedient. informal

ⓘ This phrase is from Shakespeare's *Henry the Fourth, Part 1*: 'I know a trick worth two of that i' faith'.

tricks of the trade special ingenious techniques used in a profession or craft especially those that are little known by outsiders.

turn a trick (of a prostitute) have a session with a client. informal

2018 Ruth Ware *The Death of Mrs Westaway* There's no way I'm turning tricks for some paedo pimp.

up to your (old) tricks misbehaving in a characteristic way. informal

tried

tried and true proved effective or reliable by experience.

ⓘ The same meaning is expressed by *tried and tested* and *tried and trusted*.

1967 *Listener* Miss Aukin had the good sense to use the tried and true concealment gambit by which eventually two young officers, bent on cuckolding a greengrocer, were compelled to hide in the same grandfather clock.

trim

in trim slim and healthy.

trim your sails make changes to suit your new circumstances.

ⓘ Literally, *trim a sail* means 'adjust the sail of a boat to take advantage of the wind'.

trip

get the trip (of a racehorse) be capable of competing successfully over a course of a particular length.

trip the light fantastic dance. humorous

ⓘ This expression comes from the invitation to dance in John Milton's poem 'L'Allegro' (1645): 'Come, and trip it as ye go On the light fantastic toe'.

trivet

right as a trivet perfectly all right; in good health. British informal

ⓘ A trivet is an iron tripod placed over a fire for a cooking pot or kettle to stand on. It is used in this expression to represent firmness and steadiness.

Trojan

work like a Trojan work extremely hard.

1974 Winifred Foley *A Child in the Forest* She put me to clean out all the fowls' cotes, and I worked at it like a Trojan.

a Trojan horse ❶ a person or device intended to undermine an enemy or bring about their downfall. ❷ a program designed to breach the security of a computer system, especially by ostensibly functioning as part of a legitimate program, in order to erase, corrupt, or remove data.

ⓘ In Greek mythology, the Trojan horse was a huge hollow wooden statue of a horse in which Greek soldiers concealed themselves in order secretly to enter and capture the city of Troy, an action which brought the ten-year siege of the city to an end.

trolley

off your trolley crazy. informal

ⓘ The *trolley* in this case is a pulley running on an overhead track that transmits power from the track to drive a tram; the idea is similar to that in **go off the rails** (*see* RAIL).

1983 Nathaniel Richard Nash *The Young and Fair* If you suspect Patty, you're off your trolley.

trolley dolly an air stewardess. British informal

trooper

lie like a trooper: *see* LIE.

swear like a trooper: *see* SWEAR.

troops

that's the stuff to give the troops: *see* **that's the stuff** *at* STUFF.

trot

hot to trot: *see* HOT.

on the trot ❶ in succession. ❷ continually busy. British informal

troth

plight your troth: *see* PLIGHT.

trouble

be asking for trouble: *see* ASKING.

borrow trouble: *see* BORROW.

get someone into trouble make (an unmarried woman) pregnant. dated euphemistic

meet trouble halfway distress yourself unnecessarily about what may happen.

teething troubles: *see* TEETHING.

troubled

fish in troubled waters: *see* FISH.

pour oil on troubled waters: *see* POUR.

trousers

ℹ For idioms containing *trousers,* see the entry for the main word in the idiom (for example, **wear the trousers** at WEAR).

trout

old trout an unattractive or bad-tempered old woman. informal

> **1972 Victor Canning**. *The Rainbird Pattern* She wasn't such a bad old trout. For all her money and position, life hadn't been all good to her.

trowel

lay something on with a trowel: *see* **lay something on thick** *at* THICK.

truck

have (*or* want) no truck with ❶ avoid dealing or being associated with. ❷ be unsympathetic or opposed to.

ℹ The earliest sense of *truck* was 'trading by the exchange of commodities' (from French *troquer*, meaning 'barter'), from which developed the sense 'communication or dealings'.

keep on trucking used as an encouragement to keep going, not to give up. informal

> **2004** *Something Awful* His most prized possession is a Denny's dinner plate which was signed by Gene Roddenberry reading, 'Dear Harlan, keep on trucking, some day you'll get the hang of this whole writing thing, sincerely Gene.'

truckload

by the truckload in large quantities or numbers. informal

true

out of true (*or* the true) not in the correct or exact shape.

> **1984 Jonathan Gash** *The Gondola Scam* They all look scarily out of true, and I do mean a terrible angle. Pisa's got one sloper.

tried and true: *see* TRIED.

true as Bob (*or* God) absolutely true. South African informal

true blue: *see* BLUE.

true grit: *see* GRIT.

true to form being or behaving as expected.

trump

come (*or* turn) up trumps ❶ (of a person or situation) have a better performance or outcome than expected. ❷ (of a person) be especially generous or helpful. informal, chiefly British

ℹ In bridge, whist, and similar card games, trumps are cards of the suit that has been chosen to rank above the other suits. The word *trump* is an alteration of *triumph*, which was once used in card games in the same sense.

trumpet

blow your own trumpet talk openly and boastfully about your achievements.

> **2012** *Daily Telegraph* I've just tried some of Heston's Coronation Chicken. Without wishing to blow my own trumpet, I made a better one last weekend.

trust

not trust someone as far as you can throw them not trust or hardly trust a particular person at all. informal

trust someone to — it is characteristic or predictable for someone to act in the specified way.

> **2003** *Blue Witch* 'Blimey, some of that furniture is a bit phallic, isn't it!' 'Trust you to notice that!'

truth

economical with the truth: *see* ECONOMICAL.

gospel truth: *see* GOSPEL.

moment of truth: *see* MOMENT.

naked truth: *see* NAKED.

the truth, the whole truth, and nothing but the truth the full and unvarnished truth.

ℹ These words are part of the statement sworn by witnesses giving evidence in court. They are often used informally to emphasize the absolute veracity of a statement.

try

try conclusions with: *see* CONCLUSION.

try a fall with contend with.

try it on ❶ attempt to deceive or seduce someone. ❷ deliberately test someone's patience to see how much you can get away with. British informal

❶ **2003** *This Is Essex* The watchdog Energywatch says that energy suppliers are too quick to assume that consumers who are genuinely disputing an inaccurate gas or electricity bill are 'trying it on'.

try something for size try out or test something for suitability.

try your hand see how skilful you are, especially at the first attempt.

1994 John Barth *Once Upon a Time* Since such dreaminess appeared to be my nature . . . why didn't I try my hand at writing fiction?

try your luck: *see* LUCK.

tube

down the tube (*or* tubes): *see* DOWN.

tuck

nip and tuck: *see* NIP.

tucker

your best bib and tucker: *see* BIB.

tug

tug of love a dispute over the custody of a child. British informal

tug your forelock: *see* **touch your forelock** *at* FORELOCK.

tumble

rough and tumble: *see* ROUGH.

tune

call the tune: *see* **call the shots** *at* SHOT.

change your tune: *see* CHANGE.

dance to someone's tune: *see* DANCE.

sing a different tune: *see* SING.

there's many a good tune played on an old fiddle someone's abilities do not depend on their age. proverb

2011 *Betty's Utility Room* On Friday night, U2's performance at Glastonbury was considered a triumph—proof indeed that many a good tune is played on an old fiddle.

to the tune of amounting to or involving the considerable sum of. informal

1996 *LSE Magazine* The average student also leaves in debt to the tune of several thousand pounds to the bank or the Student Loan Company.

tuned

tuned in aware of or able to understand something. informal

1994 *Today's Parent* It is more important to be tuned in to your child's needs than to be the boss.

tunnel

light at the end of the tunnel: *see* LIGHT.

turf

surf and turf: *see* SURF.

turkey

go cold turkey: *see* COLD.

like turkeys voting for Christmas used to suggest that a particular action or decision is hopelessly self-defeating. informal

talk turkey talk frankly and straightforwardly; get down to business. North American informal

ⓘ This phrase was first recorded in the mid 19th century, when it generally had the rather different sense of 'say pleasant things or talk politely'. Although several theories have been put forward, its origins are not clear.

turkey shoot something embarrassingly easily accomplished, especially the defeat of a hopelessly inferior opponent. informal, chiefly US

ⓘ The term originally denoted a shooting contest in which the target was a tethered turkey.

turn

to a turn to exactly the right degree (used especially in relation to cooking).

1931 *Good Housekeeping* The meal began with a magnificent bass, broiled to a turn over heart-wood coals.

turn and turn about one after another; in succession. chiefly British

turn it up stop doing or saying something annoying. informal

For other idioms containing *turn*, see the entry for the main word in the idiom (for example, **Buggins's turn** at BUGGINS).

turn-up

a turn-up for the book a completely unexpected event or occurrence; a surprise.

In this expression, *turn-up* refers to the turning up or over of a particular card in a game, while the *book* in question is one kept by a bookie to record bets made on a race.

turtle

turn turtle turn upside down.

If a turtle is flipped over on to its back, it becomes helpless and unable to move. The phrase has long been used figuratively of inanimate objects, especially boats, that have turned upside down or overturned.

1990 Stephen King *The Stand* His tractor turned turtle on him and killed him.

twain

never the twain shall meet two people or things are too different to exist alongside or understand each other.

This phrase comes from Rudyard Kipling's poem 'The Ballad of East and West' (1892): 'Oh, East is East and West is West, and never the twain shall meet'.

twelve

twelve good men and true a jury. dated

A jury in a court of law was traditionally composed of twelve men. Nowadays, of course, women also sit on juries, and so this phrase is falling out of use.

twenty-four

twenty-four seven all the time; twenty-four hours a day, seven days a week.

The phrase, which originated in the US, is often written *24/7*.

twenty-three

twenty-three skidoo a hasty departure. North American informal, dated

The expression is said to have been used originally in relation to male onlookers chased by police from the Flatiron Building, 23rd Street, New York City, where the skirts of female passers-by were raised by winds intensified by the building's design. The word *skidoo* itself, originally a verb meaning 'leave hastily', may be a variant of *skedaddle*.

twice

be twice the man or woman that someone is be much better or stronger than someone.

think twice: *see* THINK.

twiddle

twiddle your thumbs be bored or idle because you have nothing to do.

twig

hop the twig: *see* HOP.

twinkle

a twinkle in someone's eye something that is still in the pre-planning stage and on which no action has yet been taken, especially a child not as yet conceived. informal

twinkling

in a twinkling (*or* the twinkling of an eye) in an instant; very quickly.

A *twinkling* is the time taken to wink or blink an eye. The phrase can be traced back to 1 Corinthians 15:52: 'In a moment, in a twinkling of an eye, at the last trump: for the trumpet shall sound, and the dead shall be raised incorruptible, and we shall be changed', and it has been in figurative sense since medieval times.

twist

get your knickers in a twist: *see* KNICKERS.

round the twist: *see* **round the bend** *at* BEND.

twist someone's arm persuade someone to do something that they are or are thought to be reluctant to do. informal

twist in the wind be left in a state of suspense or uncertainty.

twist the knife: *see* KNIFE.

twist someone round your little finger: *see* FINGER.

twist the lion's tail provoke the resentment of the British. US

twitter

all of a twitter in a state of agitation or excitement. informal

two

no two ways about it used to convey that there can be no doubt about something.

put two and two together draw an obvious conclusion from what is known or evident.

ℹ An extension of this phrase is *put two and two together and make five*, meaning 'draw a plausible but incorrect conclusion from what is known or evident'.

that makes two of us you are in the same position or hold the same opinion as the previous speaker.

two can play at that game used to assert that one person's bad behaviour can be copied to that person's disadvantage.

ℹ For other idioms containing *two*, see the entry for the main word in the idiom (for example, **for two pins** at PIN).

two-edged

a two-edged sword: *see* **a double-edged sword** *at* DOUBLE-EDGED.

twopenn'orth

add (*or* put in) your twopenn'orth contribute your opinion. informal

ℹ The literal meaning of *twopenn'orth* is 'an amount of something that is worth or costs two pence'; by extension it can also be used to mean 'a small or insignificant amount of something'.

two-way

two-way street a situation or relationship between two people or groups in which action is required from both parties; something that works both ways.

ugly

an ugly duckling a young person who turns out to be beautiful or talented against all expectations.

ⓘ *The Ugly Duckling* is a fairy tale by Hans Christian Andersen in which the 'ugly duckling', mocked and jeered at by his peers, eventually develops into a beautiful swan.

win ugly: *see* WIN.

uncertain

in no uncertain terms clearly and forcefully.

1991 Kaye Gibbons *A Cure for Dreams* My mother got the doctor back out to our house and told him in no uncertain terms to do what he was paid to do.

uncertainty

the corridor of uncertainty: *see* CORRIDOR.

uncle

Bob's your uncle: *see* BOB.

cry (*or* say *or* yell) uncle surrender or admit defeat. North American informal

ⓘ *Uncle* in this context is probably a folk-etymological alteration of Irish Gaelic *anacol* 'mercy, quarter, safety'.

1989 Guy Vanderhaeghe *Homesick* Beat him six ways to Sunday and he still would never cry uncle or allow that there was an outside chance of his ever being wrong.

a Dutch uncle: *see* DUTCH.

I'll be a monkey's uncle: *see* MONKEY.

Uncle Tom Cobley (*or* Cobleigh) and all used to denote a long list of people. British informal

ⓘ *Uncle Tom Cobley* is the last of a long list of men enumerated in the ballad 'Widdicombe Fair', which dates from around 1800.

1966 *Guardian* It seems clear that a compromise, half-way solution had equally been ruled out by Government, Opposition, economists, press, TV, Uncle Tom Cobleigh and all.

unco

the unco guid strictly religious and moralistic people. Scottish, chiefly derogatory

ⓘ *Unco*, a Scottish alteration of *uncouth*, means 'remarkably or extremely', while *guid* is the Scottish form of *good*. The expression comes from Robert Burns's *Address to the Unco Guid, or the Rigidly Righteous* (1787), and it generally carries an implicit charge of hypocrisy.

under

ⓘ For idioms containing *under*, see the entry for the main word in the idiom (for example, **under age** at AGE).

university

the university of life the experience of life regarded as a means of instruction.

unknown

unknown country: *see* COUNTRY.

unknown quantity a person or thing whose nature, value, or significance cannot be determined or is not yet known.

unpleasantness

the late unpleasantness the war that took place recently.

ⓘ This phrase was originally used of the American Civil War (1861–5). It is now mainly used as a mock euphemism.

unstuck

come unstuck fail completely. informal

2001 *Irish Examiner* A Leinster victory would put the quarter-finals within touching distance, especially if French champions Toulouse come unstuck at Newcastle.

untracked

get untracked get into your stride or find your winning form, especially in sporting contexts. US

unwashed

the (great) unwashed the mass or multitude of ordinary people. derogatory

2013 Jayne *Our Great Southern Land* The North Melbourne to Coburg Railway Line was flung open, a whole 8.15 km of new track for the great unwashed to travel upon!

up

it is all up with it is the end or there is no hope for someone or something. informal

2002 *Guardian* The underlying problem is not the science itself, but the fact that the science is telling politicians something they are desperate not to hear: that it's all up with our current model of gung-ho globalisation.

be up on be well informed about a matter or subject.

on the up and up ❶ steadily improving. informal ❷ honest or sincere. informal, chiefly North American

❷ **2018 Brad Parks** *Closer than You Know* Once the judge sees that the confidential informant isn't on the up and up, he'll have no choice but to toss the warrant.

something is up something unusual or undesirable is afoot or happening. informal

1994 Marianne Williamson *Illuminata* It feels as though something is up, as though something significant and big is about to happen.

up against it facing some serious but unspecified difficulty. informal

up and about (*or* doing) having risen from bed; active.

up for it ready and willing to take part in a particular activity. informal

2003 *Observer* If the chance ever arose to do my singing and play football for Southampton, I'd be well up for it.

up there in the same high category.

2000 *Apollo Magazine* According to Charles Moffett, Co-director of Impressionist and Modern Art at Sotheby's, the painting is 'up there with Dr Gachet', Van Gogh's portrait of his doctor which was sold for $82.5 million in 1990.

up your game improve your performance.

2013 Idiot Savant *No Right Turn* If Labour wants to continue pretending to lead the opposition, they need to up their game significantly.

up yours! an exclamation expressing contemptuous defiance or rejection of someone. vulgar slang

ⓘ For other idioms containing *up,* see the entry for the main word in the idiom (for example, **up to scratch** at SCRATCH).

upgrade

on the upgrade improving or progressing.

upper

have (*or* gain) the upper hand have (*or* gain) advantage or control over someone or something.

on your uppers extremely short of money. informal

ⓘ In this expression, worn-out shoes are taken as an indication of someone's poverty; the *upper* is the part of a shoe above the sole, which is all that is left after the sole has been worn away.

a stiff upper lip: *see* STIFF.

the upper crust the aristocracy and upper classes. informal

ⓘ In Anne Elizabeth Baker's *Glossary of Northamptonshire Words and Phrases* (1854) 'Mrs Upper Crust' is explained as the nickname for 'any female who assumes unauthorized superiority'. The term was also current in informal American speech in the mid 19th century. The French word *gratin* has a similar pair of literal and metaphorical senses, being literally 'a crust of crumbs and cheese on top of a cooked dish' and metaphorically 'the highest class of society'.

upset

upset the apple cart: *see* APPLE CART.

upstairs

kick someone upstairs: *see* KICK.

the Man Upstairs: *see* MAN.

uptake

be quick (*or* slow) on the uptake be quick (*or* slow) to understand something. informal

upwardly

upwardly mobile: *see* **downwardly mobile** *at* MOBILE.

us

one of us a person recognized as an accepted member of a particular group, typically one that is exclusive in some way.

us and them expressing a sense of division within a group of people.

ⓘ The concept is also formulated as *them and us*. The underlying thought is generally that 'us' have a grievance against 'them'.

2019 *Guardian* Brexit plays out a conflict between Them and Us, but it is surely obvious after this week that the problem is not with Them on the continent. It's with the British Us.

use

use your loaf: *see* LOAF.

usual

the usual offices: *see* OFFICE.

Vv

vain

take someone's name in vain use someone's name in a way that shows a lack of respect.

ⓘ The third of the biblical Ten Commandments is: 'Thou shalt not take the name of the Lord thy God in vain' (Exodus 20:7).

vale

vale of tears the world regarded as a scene of trouble or sorrow. literary

ⓘ This phrase dates from the mid 16th century; earlier variants included *vale of trouble*, *vale of weeping*, and *vale of woe*.

1997 *Shetland Times* Then by God's grace we'll meet again, Beyond this vale of tears.

the vale of years the declining years of a person's life; old age.

ⓘ This expression comes from Shakespeare's *Othello*: 'for I am declin'd into the vale of yeares'.

valour

discretion is the better part of valour: *see* DISCRETION.

vanishing

do a vanishing act: *see* **do a disappearing act** *at* DISAPPEARING.

vantage

coign of vantage: *see* COIGN.

variety

variety is the spice of life new and exciting experiences make life more interesting.

ⓘ This proverbial expression comes from William Cowper's poem 'The Task' (1785): 'Variety's the very spice of life, That gives it all its flavour'.

veil

beyond the veil in a mysterious or hidden place or state, especially the unknown state of existence after death.

ⓘ The phrase was originally a figurative reference to the veil which concealed the innermost sanctuary of the Temple in Jerusalem; it was later taken as referring to the mysterious division between the next world and this.

draw a veil over avoid discussing or calling attention to something, especially because it is embarrassing or unpleasant.

take the veil become a nun.

velvet

an iron hand in a velvet glove: *see* IRON.

vengeance

with a vengeance in a higher degree than was expected or desired; in the fullest sense.

vent

give vent to express or release (a strong emotion, energy, etc.).

vent your spleen give free expression to your anger or displeasure.

2003 *Guardian* Woodgate's clumsy challenge on the striker was not contested, though the visitors wasted little time in venting spleen at both the culpable Danish midfielder and, erroneously, the young pretender.

verse

chapter and verse: *see* CHAPTER.

vest

keep your cards close to your vest: *see* **keep your cards close to your chest** *at* CARD.

victory

Pyrrhic victory: *see* PYRRHIC.

view

a bird's-eye view: *see* BIRD.

take a dim (*or* poor) view of regard someone or something with disapproval.

1996 C. J. Stone *Fierce Dancing* He says that . . . the Home Office . . . take a dim view of lifers talking to the press.

with a view to with the hope, aim, or intention of.

a worm's-eye view: *see* WORM.

village

a Potemkin village: *see* POTEMKIN.

villain

the villain of the piece the main culprit.

1928 P. G. Wodehouse *Money for Nothing* I'm sure you're on the right track. This bird Twist is the villain of the piece.

vine

die on the vine: *see* DIE.

wither on the vine: *see* WITHER.

vinegar

piss and vinegar: *see* PISS.

violet

shrinking violet: *see* SHRINKING.

viper

a viper in your bosom a person you have helped but who behaves treacherously towards you.

ⓘ The phrase comes from one of Aesop's fables, in which a viper reared in a person's bosom eventually bites its nurturer. The idea is also found in Latin (*in sinu viperam habere*) and the expression appears in various forms in English from the late 16th century.

Virginia

make a Virginia fence walk crookedly because you are drunk. US

ⓘ A *Virginia fence* is a fence made of split rails or poles joined in a zigzag pattern with their ends crossing.

virtue

make a virtue of (a) necessity derive some credit or benefit from an unwelcome obligation.

ⓘ This is a concept found in Latin in the writings of St Jerome: *facis de necessitate virtutem* 'you make a virtue of necessity'. It passed into Old French (*faire de necessité vertu*) and was apparently first used in English around 1374 by Chaucer in *Troilus and Criseyde*.

2002 *Australian Financial Review* Making in the best manner a virtue out of a necessity he went native with great success.

of easy virtue: *see* EASY.

visiting

visiting fireman a visitor to an organization given especially cordial treatment on account of their importance. US

voice

still small voice: *see* STILL.

a voice in the wilderness an unheeded advocate of reform.

ⓘ The phrase was originally used with reference to the words of John the Baptist, who proclaimed the coming of the Messiah: 'I am the voice of one crying in the wilderness' (John 1:23).

volumes

speak volumes: *see* SPEAK.

vote

like turkeys voting for Christmas: *see* TURKEY.

split the vote: *see* SPLIT.

vote with your feet indicate an opinion by being present or absent.

1982 *Christian Order* Uncounted thousands have 'voted with their feet', i.e., have left the Church.

vulture

culture vulture: *see* CULTURE.

wag

set tongues wagging: *see* TONGUE.

the tail wags the dog: *see* TAIL.

wagon

circle the wagons: *see* CIRCLE.

fix someone's wagon: *see* FIX.

hitch your wagon to a star: *see* HITCH.

on the wagon teetotal. informal

ⓘ This expression originated in early 20th-century American use in the form *on the water wagon*, the implication being that a person *on the water wagon* would eschew alcohol in favour of water.

1989 Michael Norman *These Good Men* I'll just have a club soda with a twist of lime... I'm on the wagon.

a whole team and the dog under the wagon: *see* TEAM.

wagonload

as artful as a wagonload of monkeys: *see* MONKEY.

wait

wait and see wait to find out what will happen before doing something.

ⓘ The expression became associated with the British prime minister Herbert Asquith, who said in speeches on numerous occasions in 1910, referring to the rumour that the House of Lords was to be flooded with new Liberal peers to ensure the passage of the Finance Bill, 'We had better wait and see.'

wait in the wings: *see* WING.

wait on someone hand and foot: *see* HAND.

waiting

play a waiting game employ the tactic of refraining from action for a time in order to act more effectively at a later date or stage.

2003 E. L. Skip Knox *The Punic Wars* If the Romans were to play a waiting game, refusing to meet him in open battle, then his plans would go awry.

wake

wake up and smell the coffee become aware of the realities of a situation, however unpleasant. informal, chiefly North American

wake-up

be a wake-up (*or* awake up) be fully alert or aware. Australian & New Zealand informal

a wake-up call something that alerts people to an unsatisfactory situation and prompts them to remedy it.

ⓘ A literal wake-up call is a phone call made at a prearranged time in order to wake someone up.

walk

cock of the walk: *see* COCK.

the ghost walks: *see* GHOST.

(try to) run before you can walk: *see* RUN.

walk all over ❶ defeat easily. ❷ take advantage of. informal

walk before you can run grasp the basic skills before attempting something more difficult.

walk the boards: *see* **tread the boards** *at* BOARD.

walk the chalk have your sobriety tested.

ⓘ A traditional method of ascertaining whether someone is sober or not is to see whether they can walk along a line chalked on the ground without wobbling.

walk free: *see* FREE.

a walk in the park something very easy or trouble-free. informal

2001 *Film Inside Out* She acts her socks off and yet the zany quality, that was a walk in the park for Hepburn, seems like a struggle for her.

walk it achieve a victory easily. informal

walk someone off their feet (*or* legs) exhaust a person with walking.

walk of life the position within society that a person holds or the part of society to which they belong as a result of their job or social status.

walk on air: *see* AIR.

walk on eggs (*or* eggshells) be extremely cautious about your words or actions.

walk the plank: *see* PLANK.

walk your (*or* the) talk suit your actions to your words. informal, chiefly North American

ⓘ This expression is also found as *walk the walk*, and elaborations are frequent, such as 'He can talk the talk, but can he walk the walk?'

walk tall feel justifiable pride. informal

2012 *Daily Telegraph* With such a major world player like this in Edinburgh, an independent Scotland really could walk tall.

walk Matilda: *see* **waltz Matilda** *at* MATILDA.

walkabout

go walkabout wander around from place to place in a protracted or leisurely way.

ⓘ In Australian English, a *walkabout* is a journey into the bush undertaken by an Aboriginal in order to live in a traditional manner and re-establish contact with spiritual sources.

walkies

go walkies go missing, especially as a result of theft. informal

walking

a walking — someone who notably embodies the characteristics of something. informal

1989 Charles Shaar Murray *Crosstown Traffic* He is . . . a dubious political philosopher and a walking disaster area as a businessman.

wall

between you and me and the wall: *see* **between you and me and the bedpost** *at* BEDPOST.

bounce off the walls: *see* BOUNCE.

climb the walls: *see* CLIMB.

come up against a brick wall: *see* BRICK.

drive someone up the wall make someone very irritated or angry. informal

a fly on the wall: *see* FLY.

the fourth wall: *see* FOURTH.

go over the wall escape from prison. informal

go to the wall ❶ (of a business) fail; go out of business. ❷ support someone or something, no matter what the cost to yourself. informal

hit the wall (of an athlete) experience a sudden loss of energy in a long race.

hole in the wall: *see* HOLE.

off the wall ❶ eccentric or unconventional. ❷ (of a person) crazy or angry. ❸ (of an accusation) without basis or foundation. North American informal

up against the wall in an inextricable situation; in great trouble or difficulty.

ⓘ The image here is of someone facing execution by a firing squad.

wall-to-wall ❶ (of a carpet or other floor covering) fitted to cover an entire floor. ❷ of great extent or number; allowing no unfilled space or interval. informal

❷ **1982 Sara Paretsky** *Indemnity Only* Why would he agree to see me? He'd never heard of me, he has wall-to-wall appointments.

walls have ears used to warn someone to be careful what they say as people may be eavesdropping. proverb

with your back to the wall: *see* BACK.

the writing is on the wall: *see* WRITING.

wallaby

on the wallaby (*or* wallaby track) (of a person) unemployed and having no fixed address. Australian informal

waltz

waltz Matilda: *see* MATILDA.

wand

wave a magic wand: *see* MAGIC.

wane

wax and wane: *see* WAX.

want

not want to know: *see* KNOW.

waste not, want not: *see* WASTE.

war

dogs of war: *see* DOG.

a war of nerves a struggle in which opponents try to wear each other down by psychological means.

a war of words a prolonged debate which is conducted by means of the spoken or printed word.

have been in the wars have been hurt or injured. informal

a war to end all wars a war, especially the First World War, regarded as making subsequent wars unnecessary.

warm

keep something warm for someone hold or occupy a place or post until another person is ready to do so.

like death warmed up: *see* DEATH.

make it (*or* things) warm for someone cause trouble or make things unpleasant for someone.

warm as toast pleasantly warm.

> **1991 W. P. Kinsella** *Box Socials* Scrunched down, warm as toast, between the cookstove and the woodbox, I couldn't see that getting something for nothing could be all that bad.

warm the cockles of someone's heart: *see* COCKLE.

warning

a warning shot across the bows: *see* BOW.

warpath

on the warpath ready and eager for confrontation.

> ⓘ The phrase originated with reference to Native Americans heading towards a battle with an enemy.

> **1999** *Cricketer* This summer, England are on the warpath against New Zealand in a four test series.

wart

warts and all including features or qualities that are not appealing or attractive. informal

> ⓘ This expression is said to stem from a request made by Oliver Cromwell to the portrait painter Peter Lely: 'Remark all these roughnesses, pimples, warts, and everything as you see me'.

> **2014** *Mac Observer* That was the beginning of my thirty-year love affair with Mac computing—warts and all.

wash

come out in the wash be resolved eventually with no lasting harm. informal

> **2013** *Daily Telegraph* By that stage in life, they are more relaxed, more philosophical, see more of the positive than the negative in the young and know that, in the end, most things will come out in the wash.

wash its face (of a business enterprise) earn enough income to cover its costs; break even. informal

> **2005** *Waterford News and Star* He said the Council's waste management collection was failing to make enough money to 'wash its face'.

wash your dirty linen in public discuss or argue about your personal affairs in public.

> ⓘ This expression dates from the early 19th century in English; a similar French expression about *linge sale* is attributed to Napoleon.

wash your hands go to the toilet. euphemistic

wash your hands of disclaim responsibility for.

> ⓘ This phrase originally alluded to the biblical description of Pontius Pilate, who, when he was forced to condemn Jesus to death, sent for a bowl of water and ritually washed his hands before the crowd as a sign that he was innocent of 'this just person' (Matthew 27:24).

won't wash will not be believed or accepted. informal

> **2011** *The Register* It's been very secretive about its protocols and security, refusing interoperability and asking users to just trust in Skype for their security. That won't wash in the real world.

waste

waste not, want not if you use a commodity or resource carefully and without extravagance you will never be in need. proverb

> ⓘ In this expression, *want* can be understood to mean either 'lack' or 'desire' according to the context.

waste of space a person perceived as useless or incompetent. informal

waste your breath: *see* BREATH.

watch

like watching paint dry: *see* PAINT.

set your watch by someone used to suggest that someone is reliably punctual, and by extension perhaps too predictable in their habits.

watch the clock: *see* CLOCK.

watch someone like a hawk: *see* HAWK.

watch the pennies: *see* **count the pennies** *at* PENNY.

watch someone's smoke: *see* SMOKE.

watch this space: *see* SPACE.

watch the time ensure that you are aware of the time, typically in order to avoid being late.

watch the world go by spend time observing other people going about their business.

1996 *Europe: Rough Guide* Outdoor seating allows you to watch the world go by or to play a game of chess with giant chess pieces under the trees.

watch your mouth: *see* MOUTH.

watch your step: *see* **mind your step** *at* STEP.

watch your (*or* someone's) back protect yourself (*or* someone else) against danger from an unexpected quarter.

the watches of the night the hours of night, especially viewed as a time when you cannot sleep. literary

ⓘ A *watch* was originally each of the three or four periods of time into which the night was divided, during which a guard would be stationed to keep a lookout for danger or trouble.

water

like water in great quantities.

2006 *Daily Telegraph* Twenty-something girls are ... spending money like water, reasoning that high house prices make the idea of saving for a home futile.

water under the bridge used to refer to events or situations in the past that are no longer to be regarded as important or a source of concern.

ⓘ The related expressions *there's been a lot of water under the bridge since* — or *a lot of water has flowed under the bridge since* — are used to indicate that a lot of time has passed and a great many events have occurred since a particular event. A North American variant is *water over the dam.*

ⓘ For other idioms containing *water,* see the entry for the main word in the idiom (for example, **tread water** at TREAD).

W

water cooler

water-cooler moment a moment, especially in a television programme, that provokes widespread and animated discussion.

ⓘ A water cooler is a dispenser of cooled drinking water, especially in an office or other place of work, and the image is of people gathering round it and talking about a particularly memorable passage in the previous evening's television broadcasts.

2009 Tim Footman *The Noughties* Multi-channel TV, coupled with online playback, meant that the televisual water cooler moment ('Did you see *Seinfeld/Miami Vice/Casualty* last night?') was increasingly restricted to live sports events.

waterfront

cover the waterfront: *see* COVER.

watering

watering hole a pub or bar. informal humorous euphemistic

ⓘ The expression developed from the original literal sense, 'a waterhole where animals regularly drink'.

waterline

hole something below the waterline: *see* HOLE.

Waterloo

meet your Waterloo experience a final and decisive defeat.

ⓘ The battle of Waterloo in 1815 marked the final defeat of Napoleon's army by the British and the Prussians.

wave

make waves ❶ create a significant impression. ❷ cause trouble. informal

❶ **2013** *Daily Telegraph* London-based singer FKA twigs and Adio Marchant (aka Bipolar Sunshine) are among the UK artists expected to make waves in 2014, according to Spotify.

on the crest of a wave: *see* CREST.

wave a magic wand: *see* MAGIC.

wavelength

on the same wavelength having the same ideas and way of thinking as another or each other, especially as affecting the ability to communicate.

wax

be wax in someone's hands: *see* **be putty in someone's hands** *at* PUTTY.

wax and wane undergo alternate increases and decreases.

> **2002** *New York Times* The level of security that people are psychologically able to accept changes as crisis situations wax and wane.

wax lyrical about: *see* LYRICAL.

the whole ball of wax: *see* BALL.

way

give way ❶ yield to someone or something. ❷ (of a support or structure) be unable to carry a load or withstand a force and so collapse or break. ❸ allow someone or something to go first.

give way to ❶ allow yourself to be overcome by or to succumb to (an emotion or impulse). ❷ be replaced or superseded by.

go all the way (*or* the whole way) ❶ continue a course of action to its conclusion. ❷ have full sexual intercourse with someone. euphemistic

go out of your way make a special effort to do something.

have it your (own) way used in the imperative to indicate angrily that although you disagree with something said or proposed, you are not going to argue further. informal

have your way with have sexual intercourse with (someone) (typically implying that it is against their better judgement). humorous

lose your (*or* the) way no longer have a clear idea of your purpose or motivation in an activity or business.

my way or the highway things must either be done in the way I wish or not done at all. informal

> **2018 Jeremy Clarkson** *Sunday Times* It won't make any difference in my house, where visitors face a simple choice: my way or the highway. I have my own very simple set of extra rules, which are: the word must be in common usage and you must be able to explain its meaning.

on the way out ❶ going down in status, estimation, or favour; going out of fashion. ❷ dying. informal

put someone in the way of give a person the opportunity of. dated

way to go used to express pleasure, approval, or excitement. North American informal

> ℹ The expression is apparently an abbreviation of 'That's the (right) way to go!'

> **1990 Robert Oliver** *Making Champions* You had Bechard shakin'. He wasn't gonna mess with you. Way to go!

> ℹ For other idioms containing *way,* see the entry for the main word in the idiom (for example, **in the family way** at FAMILY).

wayside

fall by the wayside ❶ fail to persist in an endeavour or undertaking. ❷ be left without attention or help.

> ℹ In sense 1 the phrase alludes to the biblical parable of the sower in Mark 4:3–20, and in particular to verse 4: 'And it came to pass, as he sowed, some fell by the way side, and the fowls of the air came and devoured it up'.

wazoo

up (*or* out) the wazoo in great quantities. informal

> ℹ *Wazoo* is an informal American term for the buttocks or anus. Its origins are unknown.

> **2018 Linwood Barclay** *A Noise Downstairs* He thinks he can get you off with a suspended sentence or something, that there are extenuating circumstances up the wazoo that the court will be sympathetic to.

weak

weak at the knees: *see* KNEE.

the weak (*or* weakest) link the point at which a system, sequence, or organization is most vulnerable; the least dependable element or member.

weak sister a weak, ineffectual, or unreliable member of a group. North American informal

wear

wear and tear damage or deterioration sustained from continuous use.

wear the trousers be the dominant partner in a marriage or the dominant person in a household. informal

wear (*or* wear your years) well remain young-looking.

> ❶ For other idioms containing *wear*, see the entry for the main word in the idiom (for example, **the worse for wear** at WORSE).

weasel

weasel words words or statements that are intentionally ambiguous or misleading.

weather

fine (*or* lovely) weather for ducks wet, rainy weather. humorous

keep a weather eye on observe a situation very carefully, especially for changes or developments.

make good (*or* bad) weather of it (of a ship) cope well (*or* badly) in a storm.

make heavy weather (*or* work) of have unnecessary difficulty in dealing with a task or problem. informal

> ❶ In a nautical context, *heavy weather* means 'violent wind accompanied by heavy rain or rough sea'.

under the weather ❶ slightly unwell. ❷ in low spirits. informal

weather the storm survive a period of difficulty.

weave

bob and weave: *see* BOB.

get weaving set briskly to work; begin action. British informal

> **1992 George MacDonald Fraser** *Quartered Safe Out Here* Come on, come on, come on! . . . Let's get weaving!

web

a tangled web: *see* TANGLED.

wedding

wedding tackle a man's genitalia. British vulgar slang

wedge

the thin end of the wedge: *see* THIN.

week

knock someone into the middle of next week: *see* KNOCK.

week in, week out every week without exception.

weekend

dirty weekend: *see* DIRTY.

something for the weekend a condom or packet of condoms. informal

> ❶ The expression originated as a euphemism used by barbers when asking their customers if they wished to buy some condoms.

weekend warrior a person who participates in an activity only in their spare time. North American informal

weigh

weigh something in the balance: *see* BALANCE.

weight

be a weight off your mind come as a great relief after you have been worried.

be worth your (*or* its) weight in gold be extremely useful or helpful.

carry weight: *see* CARRY.

pull your weight do your fair share of work.

take the weight off your feet sit or lie down and rest.

throw your weight about (*or* around) be unpleasantly self-assertive. informal

throw your weight behind someone use your influence to help support someone. informal

> **2000** *South African Times* Tony Blair and . . . Bill Clinton have thrown their weight behind a South African-engineered 'Marshall Plan' to rescue the developing world from deepening poverty.

welcome

welcome to the club: *see* **join the club** *at* CLUB.

outstay your welcome stay as a visitor longer than you are wanted.

welkin

make the welkin ring make a very loud sound.

ⓘ *Welkin* is a poetic term for 'the sky or heaven', which is now found only in literary contexts and in this expression.

well

alive and well: *see* ALIVE.

go well: *see* GO.

leave well alone refrain from interfering in or changing something, for fear of making it worse.

welly

give it some welly exert more effort or strength. informal

ⓘ *Welly* or *wellie*, an informal abbreviation of *Wellington boot*, acquired an informal sense of 'power or vigour' in the 1970s.

1997 *BBC Top Gear Magazine* Drop down a gear, give it some welly and that long bonnet rises towards the horizon in the best traditions of . . . a traditional British Sports Car.

wend

wend your way go in a specific direction, typically slowly or by an indirect route.

west

go west be killed or lost; meet with disaster. British informal

ⓘ The image here is of the sun setting in the west at the end of the day.

wet

all wet mistaken; completely wrong. North American

get your feet wet: *see* FOOT.

wet the baby's head celebrate a baby's birth with a drink, usually an alcoholic one. British informal

wet behind the ears lacking experience; immature. informal

ⓘ The image is of a baby or young animal which is still damp after it has been born.

a wet blanket someone who has a depressing or discouraging effect on others.

ⓘ A dampened blanket can be used to smother a fire; the image here is of a person extinguishing a lively or optimistic mood by their gloominess or negativity.

2012 *Guardian* How does an actor known for her versatility . . . embody the grown-up girlfriend who gets in between the boy and his bear without seeming like the wet blanket who's spoiling the party.

wet your whistle have a drink. informal

whack

out of whack out of order; not working. North American & Australian

2001 *Boat* Somewhere along the line the connection between big business and the consumer went out of whack.

top (*or* full) whack the maximum price or rate.

1989 *Holiday Which?* Tour prices vary; you pay top whack if you book in large hotels.

whale

a whale of a — an extremely good example of a particular thing. informal

2013 digby *Hullabaloo* This summer, House Republicans have promised, in Speaker John Boehner's words, 'a whale of a fight' before they raise the debt ceiling—if they even raise it at all.

wham-bam

wham-bam-thank-you-ma'am used in reference to sexual activity conducted roughly and quickly, without tenderness.

what

and (*or* or) what have you and (*or* or) anything else similar. informal

2013 Bob Jacobson & Paula Thornton *Corante—Total Experience* There aren't any basic amines on that list (or esters, or amides, or what have you), are there?

and what not and other similar things. informal

2013 *New Zealand Herald* We walked them through streets and shops and what not, getting people not to touch them and socialising them with other animals as well.

be just what the doctor ordered: *see* DOCTOR.

give someone what for punish or scold someone severely. British informal

have what it takes have the necessary qualities or attributes for success. informal

know what's what: *see* KNOW.

what gives?: *see* GIVE.

what with because of (used typically to introduce several causes of something).

> **2014** *Daily Telegraph* They were a strange-looking lot, I thought. What with those funny-looking mod suits and pudding-bowl haircuts, they could have been aliens from another planet.

wheat

separate (*or* sort) the wheat from the chaff distinguish valuable people or things from worthless ones.

> ⓘ Chaff is the husks of corn or other seed separated out when the grain is winnowed or threshed. The metaphorical contrast between wheat and chaff is drawn in several passages in the Bible, for example in Matthew 3:12: 'he will thoroughly purge his floor, and gather his wheat into the garner; but he will burn up the chaff with unquenchable fire'.

wheel

a big wheel: *see* **a big cheese** *at* BIG.

a cog in the wheel: *see* COG.

grease the wheels: *see* GREASE.

reinvent the wheel: *see* REINVENT.

put your shoulder to the wheel: *see* SHOULDER.

put a spoke in someone's wheel: *see* SPOKE.

set the wheels in motion do something to begin a process or put a plan into action.

silly as a wheel very silly. Australian

> **1985 John Clanchy** *The Lie of the Land* Father Tierney was mad. Cracked as an egg, some boys said, silly as a wheel.

spin your wheels waste your time or efforts. North American informal

> **2001** *Time* As long as our national energy policy is demand-driven . . . we will continue to spin our wheels.

the wheels come off things go disastrously wrong (causing an enterprise to fail).

> **2006** *Sunday Times* There is not much a captain can do when the wheels come off and batsmen and bowlers underperform.

wheel and deal engage in commercial or political scheming.

> ⓘ The verb *wheel* is here used to mean 'control events'. The sense is related to the noun *a big wheel*, meaning 'an important person who makes things happen'.

the wheel has turned full circle: *see* CIRCLE.

the wheel of Fortune the wheel which the goddess Fortune is said to turn as a symbol of random luck or change.

wheels within wheels used to indicate that a situation is complicated and affected by secret or indirect influences.

> ⓘ The image here is of the cogs found in pieces of intricate machinery.

when

say when: *see* SAY.

where

tell someone where to get off: *see* TELL.

where it's at: *see* AT.

where's the fire?: *see* FIRE.

where there's a will there's a way: *see* WILL.

whet

whet someone's appetite stimulate someone's interest by partial revelation.

while

once in a while: *see* ONCE.

whip

a fair crack of the whip: *see* CRACK.

whip the cat ❶ complain or moan. ❷ be sorry; show remorse. Australian & New Zealand informal

the whip hand a position of power or control over someone.

> **2012** *New York Times* Aung San Suu Kyi took the opportunity to strike a conciliatory tone toward the military rulers who kept her under house arrest for 15 years and still hold the whip hand in deciding the fate of Myanmar's fragile reforms.

whips of large quantities of. Australian & New Zealand

whirl

give it a whirl give it a try. informal

> **1979 Snoo Wilson** *A Greenish Man* You've nothing to lose. Give it a whirl, try it for a month.

W

whirlwind

reap the whirlwind suffer serious consequences as a result of your actions.

ⓘ This expression alludes to the proverb *they that sow the wind shall reap the whirlwind*, which is taken from Hosea 8:7. Probably the most celebrated (or some would say notorious) instance of its use was by Air Chief Marshal Arthur 'Bomber' Harris, head of RAF Bomber Command, in 1942, commenting on the aerial bombardment of German cities: 'The Nazis entered this war under the rather childish delusion that they were going to bomb everybody else and nobody was going to bomb them .... They sowed the wind, and now they are going to reap the whirlwind.'

2012 *The Age* (Melbourne) The ALP government created this disaster with cheap populist politics when it dismantled the Pacific Solution with much fanfare and cheering. Now they are reaping the whirlwind in lost lives and human misery.

whisker

have (*or* have grown) whiskers (especially of a story) be very old. informal

within a whisker of extremely close or near to doing, achieving, or suffering something. informal

whistle

bells and whistles: *see* BELL.

blow the whistle on bring an illicit or disreputable activity to an end by informing on the person responsible. informal

ⓘ This idiom comes from football, in which the referee blows a whistle to indicate that a player has broken the rules. Those who inform on others engaged in an illicit activity are now referred to as *whistle-blowers*.

clean as a whistle: *see* CLEAN.

wet your whistle: *see* WET.

whistle Dixie: *see* DIXIE.

whistle in the dark pretend to be confident or unafraid.

2012 *New York Times* Western talk of success in building up the Afghan state seems little more than whistling in the dark.

whistle in the wind try unsuccessfully to influence something that cannot be changed.

whistle something down the wind let something go; abandon something.

ⓘ This phrase comes from falconry. It originally referred to the action of letting a trained hawk loose by casting it off with the wind instead of against the wind in pursuit of prey.

white

(as) white as a sheet (of a person) very pale, especially from shock.

big white chief: *see* CHIEF.

bleed someone white: *see* **bleed someone dry** *at* BLEED.

in black and white: *see* BLACK.

men in white coats: *see* MAN.

show the white feather appear cowardly. British dated

ⓘ A white feather in a game bird's tail was considered to be an indication of bad breeding.

swear black is white: *see* SWEAR.

a white elephant a possession that is useless or troublesome, especially one that is expensive to maintain or difficult to dispose of.

ⓘ In former times, the rare albino elephant was regarded as holy. It was highly prized by the kings of Siam (now Thailand), and its upkeep was extremely expensive. It was apparently the practice for a king of Siam to give one of the elephants to a courtier they disliked: the unfortunate recipient would usually be financially ruined by the attempt to maintain the animal.

white hat: *see* **black hat** *at* HAT.

white hope a person expected to bring much success to a team or organization.

ⓘ The expression originated in the USA in the 1910s as an epithet applied to a white heavyweight boxer who it was hoped (by whites) might beat Jack Johnson, the first black boxer to hold the world heavyweight title (1908–15). Its racial connotations make it prudent nowadays to avoid it.

1941 Lord Berners *Far from the Madding War* He was a composer: the white hope (so a critic had described him) of English music.

a white knight a company that makes a welcome bid for a company facing an unwelcome takeover bid.

ⓘ The image here is of the traditional figure from chivalric romances, who rides to the rescue of someone in danger. *See also* **a knight in shining armour** *at* KNIGHT.

the white man's burden: *see* BURDEN.

whited

a whited sepulchre a hypocrite; someone who is ostensibly virtuous but inwardly corrupt. literary

ⓘ This expression comes from Matthew 23:27: 'Woe unto you . . . for ye are like unto whited sepulchres, which indeed appear beautiful outward, but are within full of dead men's bones, and of all uncleanness'. A *sepulchre* is a room or monument, cut in rock or built of stone, in which a dead body is laid or buried.

whiter

whiter than white ❶ extremely white. ❷ morally beyond reproach.

who

who goes there?: *see* GOES.

whoa

from go to whoa from start to finish. Australian & New Zealand

whole

on the whole taking everything into account; in general.

ⓘ For other idioms containing *whole*, see the entry for the main word in the idiom (for example, **the whole nine yards** at NINE).

whoop

whoop it up ❶ enjoy yourself or celebrate in a noisy way, usually in a group. ❷ create or show excitement or enthusiasm. US informal

whoopee

make whoopee ❶ celebrate wildly. ❷ make love. informal

why

the whys and wherefores the reasons for or details of something.

2014 *Big-Tech Hardware* With so much brain power and so many column inches used up deliberating the whys and wherefores of the latest big tech products . . . it's often easy to overlook the little things that can actually make even more difference day to day.

W

wick

dip your wick (of a man) have sexual intercourse. vulgar slang

get on someone's wick annoy someone. British informal

wicked

no peace (*or* rest) for the wicked someone's heavy workload or lack of tranquillity is punishment for a sinful life. humorous

ⓘ This expression comes from Isaiah 48:22: 'There is no peace, saith the Lord, unto the wicked'.

wicket

a sticky wicket ❶ a pitch that has been drying out after rain and is therefore difficult to bat on. Cricket ❷ a tricky or awkward situation. informal

wide

give someone or something a wide berth: *see* BERTH.

high, wide, and handsome: *see* HIGH.

the wide blue yonder: *see* BLUE.

wide of the mark: *see* **off the mark** *at* MARK.

widow

a widow's cruse an apparently small supply that proves inexhaustible.

ⓘ In the Bible, 1 Kings 17 tells the story of the widow to whom Elijah was sent for sustenance. When he asked her for bread, she replied that all she had for herself and her son was 'an handful of meal in a barrel and a little oil in a cruse' (a *cruse* was a small earthenware pot or jar). Elijah told her to make him a cake from these ingredients and then to make food for herself and her son as God had decreed that the containers should be continually replenished.

a widow's mite a small monetary contribution from someone who is poor.

ⓘ This phrase comes from a story recounted in Mark 12:41–4. A poor widow donated two mites (coins of very low value) to the treasury of the Temple in Jerusalem, a sum which constituted all the money she possessed. Witnessing this act, Jesus told his disciples that she had given more than the richest contributor because she had given all that she had.

wife

the world and his wife: *see* WORLD.

wig

flip your wig: *see* **flip your lid** *at* FLIP.

wigs on the green violent or unpleasant developments; ructions.

> The image here is of wigs becoming dislodged or being pulled off during a brawl.
>
> **1996 Frank McCourt** *Angela's Ashes* Mam threatens us from the bed that we're to help our small brother. She says, If ye don't fix yeer brother's shoes an' I have to get out of this bed there will be wigs on the green.

wiggle

get a wiggle on get moving; hurry. informal

wild

sow your wild oats: *see* OATS.

the wild blue yonder: *see* **the wide blue yonder** *at* BLUE.

wild horses won't drag someone to something: *see* HORSE.

wild and woolly uncouth in appearance or behaviour.

> This phrase was originally applied to the American West. The adjective *woolly* probably refers to sheepskin clothing worn with the wool still attached to it, seen as characteristic clothing of the pioneers and cowboys who opened up the western US.

wilderness

a voice in the wilderness: *see* VOICE.

wildest

beyond your wildest dreams: *see* DREAM.

never in your wildest dreams: *see* DREAM.

wildfire

spread like wildfire spread with great speed.

wild goose

a wild goose chase a foolish and hopeless search for or pursuit of something unattainable.

> This expression is first recorded in the late 16th century. It was then the term for a kind of equestrian sport in which all the competitors had to follow accurately the course of the leader at definite intervals, like a flight of wild geese. Later, the term was applied to an erratic course taken by one person or thing and followed by another.
>
> **2013** *New Statesman* Journals full of happy accidents send future researchers off on wild goose chases, or cost them money and time trying to replicate, which they can never quite do.

will

where there's a will there's a way determination will overcome any obstacle. proverb

> This form of the saying was quoted by William Hazlitt in 1822, but George Herbert recorded a variant as one of his *Outlandish Proverbs* in 1640: *To him that will, wais are not wanting.*

with the best will in the world however good your intentions (used to imply that success in a particular undertaking, although desired, is unlikely).

with a will energetically and resolutely.

> **1984 Bernard MacLaverty** *Cal* Dunlop told Cal to muck out the byre and because it was something he could do he went at it with a will.

willies

give someone the willies give someone a strong feeling of nervous discomfort. informal

willing

God willing: *see* GOD.

the spirit is willing (but the flesh is weak): *see* SPIRIT.

willow

wear the green willow 1 grieve for the loss of a loved one. 2 suffer unrequited love. literary

> A willow branch or leaves traditionally symbolized grief or unrequited love. In *Othello*, Desdemona sings the mournful 'willow song', about a maid forsaken by her lover, shortly before she is murdered.

W

win

win the day: *see* **carry the day** *at* DAY.

win by a neck: *see* NECK.

win (*or* earn) your spurs gain your first distinction or honours. informal

ⓘ In the Middle Ages a knight who had *won his spurs* had attained knighthood by performing an act of bravery: a pair of gilt spurs were the distinguishing mark of a knight.

win ugly gain victory through solid application and hard work rather than elegantly and with apparent effortlessness.

ⓘ The phrase gained popularity as the title of the book *Winning Ugly: Mental Warfare in Tennis* (1993) by the Australian tennis coach Brad Gilbert and Steve Jamison.

2005 *Croydon Guardian* Manager Bob Langford said he was happy to 'win ugly' to ensure Ryman Division One safety.

you can't win them all (*or* win some, lose some) said to express consolation or resignation after failure in a contest. informal

wind

between wind and water at a vulnerable point.

ⓘ This is a nautical metaphor referring to the part of a ship's side near the waterline that is sometimes above the water and sometimes submerged; damage to the ship at this level is particularly dangerous. The phrase is first recorded in its literal sense at the time of the Spanish Armada (1588): 'One of the shot was betweene the winde and the water, whereof they thought she would haue sonke'. By the mid 17th century, it was also being used of people.

1967 Michael Gilbert *The Dust and the Heat* Mallinson *must* have guessed what was coming. Nevertheless, it hit him between wind and water.

blow with the wind act according to prevailing circumstances rather than a consistent plan.

break wind release gas from the anus; fart.

get wind of begin to suspect that something is happening; hear a rumour of. informal

get your second wind: *see* SECOND.

gone with the wind gone completely; having disappeared without trace.

ⓘ This expression comes from Ernest Dowson's poem 'Cynara' (1896): 'I have forgot much, Cynara, gone with the wind', but it is best known as the title of Margaret Mitchell's 1936 novel about the American Civil War.

it's an ill wind few things are so bad that no one profits from them. proverb

ⓘ The full form of this nautical saying is *it's an ill wind that blows nobody any good* or *that profits nobody*. Recorded since the mid 16th century, it is used especially as a comment on a situation in which one person's bad luck is the cause of another's good fortune.

piss and wind: *see* PISS.

piss in the wind: *see* PISS.

put (*or* have) the wind up alarm or frighten (*or* be alarmed or frightened). British informal

ⓘ One of the earliest recorded uses of this expression was in a letter from the poet Wilfred Owen in 1918: 'Shells so close that they thoroughly put the wind up a Life Guardsman in the trench with me'.

raise the wind obtain money for a purpose. British

ⓘ When it first entered the language in medieval times, this phrase referred to the belief that spirits or witches were able to cause the winds to blow in order to help or hinder ships; the figurative use dates from the late 18th century.

sail close to (*or* near) the wind verge on indecency, dishonesty, or disaster. informal

ⓘ This originated as a nautical expression, meaning 'sail as nearly against the wind as is possible'. It has been in figurative use since the mid 19th century.

1996 Martin Dove *How To Win Any Consumer Competition* I like the extra thrill of writing to a tight deadline but sometimes I do sail a bit close to the wind with closing dates.

a straw in the wind: *see* STRAW.

take the wind out of someone's sails frustrate a person by unexpectedly anticipating an action or remark.

1977 Eva Figes *Nelly's Version* She could so easily have taken the wind out of my sails and put me in my place for good.

throw caution to the wind(s): *see* CAUTION.

to the wind(s) (*or* the four winds) ❶ in all directions. ❷ so as to be abandoned or neglected.

❶ **1995 Kate Atkinson** *Behind the Scenes at the Museum* My little flock scatters to the four winds and are hugged and congratulated by their respective parents for being so pretty, charming, cute, delightful, and so on.

twist in the wind: *see* TWIST.

two (*or* three) sheets to the wind: *see* SHEET.

which way the wind blows how a situation is likely to develop.

whistle something down the wind: *see* WHISTLE.

whistle in the wind: *see* WHISTLE.

wind down the windows (of a skier) make circular motions with the arms in an effort to maintain balance.

ⓘ The comparison is with someone turning a handle to lower a car window.

wind someone round your little finger: *see* **twist someone round your little finger** at FINGER.

wind your neck in stop behaving in an annoyingly conspicuous manner, especially talking too much. British informal

windmill

fling (*or* throw) your cap over the windmill(s) act recklessly or unconventionally. dated

1933 John Galsworthy *One More River* I suggest that both of you felt it would be mad to fling your caps over the windmill like that?

tilt at windmills: *see* TILT.

window

go out (of) the window (of a plan or pattern of behaviour) no longer exist; disappear. informal

2011 *Guardian* The result is that right and wrong go out of the window.

window of opportunity a favourable opportunity for doing something that must be seized immediately if it is not to be missed.

windward

to windward of in an advantageous position in relation to. dated

wine

new wine in old bottles something new or innovatory added to an existing or established system or organization.

ⓘ The proverb *you can't put new wine into old bottles* is a reference to Matthew 9:17: 'Neither do men put new wine into old bottles: else the bottles break, and the wine runneth out, and the bottles perish'.

wine and dine someone entertain someone by offering them drinks or a meal.

wine, women, and song the hedonistic life of drinking, sexual pleasure, and carefree entertainment proverbially required by men.

wing

clip someone's wings: *see* CLIP.

in the wings ready to do something or to be used at the appropriate time.

ⓘ This idiom comes from the theatre, in which the *wings* here are the areas screened from public view where actors wait for their cue to come on stage.

on a wing and a prayer with only the slightest chance of success.

ⓘ This expression comes from the title of a 1943 song by the American songwriter Harold Adamson, 'Comin' in on a Wing and a Prayer'. He himself took it from a contemporary comment made by a wartime pilot speaking to ground control before making an emergency landing.

spread (*or* stretch *or* try) your wings extend your activities and interests or start new ones.

under your wing in or into your protective care.

1991 Mickey Mantle *My Favorite Summer* He kind of took me under his wing and showed me the ropes in my first year.

wait in the wings stand ready to do something or to be used at the appropriate time.

winged

winged words highly significant or apposite words. literary

ⓘ The image, taken from Homer's *Iliad*, is of the words travelling as directly as arrows to their intended target.

wink

forty winks: *see* FORTY.

in the wink of an eye (*or* in a wink) very quickly.

a nod's as good as a wink: *see* NOD.

not sleep (*or* get) a wink (*or* not get a wink of sleep) not sleep at all.

a nudge and a wink: *see* NUDGE.

nudge nudge (wink wink): *see* NUDGE.

tip someone the wink: *see* TIP.

winking

as easy as winking very easy or easily. informal

winter

the dead of winter: *see* DEAD.

wipe

wipe someone's eye get the better of a person. British informal, dated

wipe the floor with inflict a humiliating defeat on. informal

wipe the slate clean forgive or forget past faults or offences; make a fresh start.

ℹ In former times, shopkeepers and pub landlords would keep a record of what was owing to them by writing the details on a tablet of slate; a *clean slate* was one on which no debts were recorded.

wipe the smile off someone's face cause someone to stop feeling so contented, complacent, or proud.

wire

down to the wire used to denote a situation whose outcome is not decided until the very last minute. informal

ℹ This expression comes from horse racing and originated in North America, where a *wire* is stretched across and above the finishing line on a racecourse.

get your wires crossed: *see* CROSSED.

live wire: *see* LIVE.

under the wire at the last possible opportunity, just before a time limit. North American informal

wisdom

in someone's wisdom used ironically to suggest that an action is not well judged.

1992 *Rugby World & Post* In their wisdom Ciaran Fitzgerald and his selectors decided to dispense with the incumbent, Rob Saunders, and bring Aherne back for his thirteenth Irish cap.

wise

be wise after the event understand and assess an event or situation only after its implications have become obvious.

ℹ The French version of this expression can be traced back to the late 15th century: the chronicler Philippe de Commynes used the phrase *saiges après le coup* in his *Mémoires*, remarking of it 'comme l'on dit des Bretons' (as the Bretons say).

crack wise: *see* CRACK.

put someone wise give someone important information. informal

1950 Graham Greene *The Third Man* He was a year older and knew the ropes. He put me wise to a lot of things.

a wise man of Gotham a foolish person. dated

ℹ *Gotham* is a village in Nottinghamshire which is associated with the folk story *The Wise Men of Gotham*, in which the inhabitants of the village demonstrate their cunning by feigning stupidity. *Gotham* is now a nickname for New York City, used originally by Washington Irvine but later linked particularly with the Batman stories.

a word to the wise: *see* WORD.

wiser

be none (*or* not any) the wiser know no more than before.

wish

if wishes were horses, beggars would ride if you could achieve your aims simply by wishing for them, life would be very easy. proverb

ℹ This expression was first recorded in the early 17th century as a Scottish proverb.

the wish is father to the thought we believe a thing because we wish it to be true.

ℹ This expression is used by Shakespeare in *2 Henry IV*: 'Thy wish was father, Harry, to that thought'. However, observations on this kind of self-delusion are found in much earlier writings, including those of Julius Caesar and Demosthenes.

1980 Alice Thomas Ellis *The Birds of the Air* Somewhere in that area of the human mind where the wish is father to the thought activity was taking place. Hunter, Barbara decided, had wangled this invitation in order to be with her.

wish someone joy: *see* JOY.

wit

be at your wits' end be overwhelmed with difficulties and at a loss as to what to do next.

be frightened (*or* scared) out of your wits be extremely frightened.

gather (*or* collect) your wits bring yourself back to a state of equanimity.

1984 Geraldine McCaughrean *The Canterbury Tales* Poor old man, he was too astonished to speak. And before he could collect his wits, he was sitting at table . . . with his lord on one side and his daughter on the other.

have (*or* keep) your wits about you be constantly alert and vigilant.

live by your wits earn money by clever and sometimes dishonest means, having no regular occupation.

pit your wits against compete with someone or something.

2013 *Daily Telegraph* Do you know your Elizabeth from your Anne? Pit your wits against our Royal baby quiz and collect your score at the end.

witch

witch hunt a campaign directed against a person or group holding unorthodox or unpopular views.

ⓘ The expression was inspired by the persecution in former times of people believed to be witches, often culminating in execution by burning.

witching

the witching hour midnight.

ⓘ In Shakespeare's *Hamlet*, Hamlet declares: 'Tis now the very witching time of night, When churchyards yawn and hell itself breathes out contagion to this world'. He is referring to the popular superstition that witches and other supernatural powers are active at midnight.

wither

wither on the vine fail to be implemented or dealt with because of neglect or inaction.

ⓘ The image of grapes failing to grow is probably a reference to various passages in the Bible in which a withered vine is used as a metaphor for a state of physical or spiritual impoverishment.

withers

wring someone's withers: *see* WRING.

wives

an old wives' tale: *see* OLD.

wobbly

throw a wobbly have a fit of temper or panic. British informal

2000 *Sunday Business Post* The scene in which Dustin Hoffman's autistic character throws a wobbly in the airport had never quite left me.

woe

woe betide used humorously to warn (someone) that they will be in trouble if they do a specified thing.

ⓘ The same warning can be expressed by *woe to*.

2012 *Daily Telegraph* This is an essential point to grasp about the Home Secretary. Woe betide the unwary colleague who trespasses on her territory.

wolf

cry wolf call for help when it is not needed; raise a false alarm.

ⓘ An old fable tells the tale of a shepherd boy who constantly raised false alarms with cries of 'Wolf!', until people no longer took any notice of him. When a wolf did actually appear and attack him, his genuine cries for help were ignored and no one came to his aid.

have (*or* hold) a wolf by the ears be in a precarious position.

ⓘ The saying became current in English in the mid 16th century, but the Roman comic dramatist Terence (195–159 BC) mentions its Latin equivalent, *lupum auribus tenere*, as already being an old saying in his time. Compare with **have a tiger by the tail** (*at* TIGER).

1990 George Will *Suddenly* A Communist Party administering an economy is holding a wolf by the ears.

lone wolf: *see* LONE.

keep the wolf from the door have enough money to avert hunger or starvation.

ⓘ The phrase has been used in this sense since the mid 16th century, but the image of the wolf as a symbol of a devouring and destructive force is found much earlier than this. In Matthew 10:16, for example, Jesus tells his disciples: 'Behold I send you forth as sheep in the midst of wolves: be ye therefore wise as serpents, and harmless as doves'.

throw someone to the wolves leave someone to be roughly treated or criticized without trying to help or defend them. informal

ⓘ This phrase probably arose in reference to tales about packs of wolves pursuing travellers in horse-drawn sleighs, in which one person was pushed off the sleigh to allow it to go faster, so enabling the others to make their escape.

1958 *Listener* This able and agreeable doctor was thrown to the wolves by a Prime Minister who had good reason to know that his own position was desperate.

a wolf in sheep's clothing a person or thing that appears friendly or harmless but is really hostile and dangerous.

ⓘ This expression comes from Jesus's words in Matthew 7:15: 'Beware of false prophets, which come to you in sheep's clothing, but inwardly they are ravening wolves'.

woman

ⓘ For idioms containing *woman,* see the entry for the main word in the idiom (for example, **the other woman** at OTHER).

wonder

a nine days' wonder something that attracts enthusiastic interest for a short while but is then ignored or forgotten.

wonders will never cease used, often ironically, as an exclamation of great surprise at something pleasing.

work (*or* do) wonders have a very beneficial effect on someone or something.

1997 Paul Wilson *Calm at Work* While it is true that holidays work wonders for the relief of stress, the relief is only temporary.

wood

babes in the wood: *see* BABE.

cannot see the wood for the trees fail to grasp the main issue because of over-attention to details.

ⓘ The North American version of this expression is *cannot see the forest for the trees.*

dead wood: *see* DEAD.

Do bears shit in the woods?: *see* BEAR.

have the wood on have the advantage over. Australian and New Zealand informal

neck of the woods: *see* NECK.

out of the wood (*or* woods) out of danger or difficulty.

ⓘ A proverbial warning against *hallooing before you are out of the wood* dates from the late 18th century.

touch wood said in order to prevent a confident statement from bringing bad luck.

ⓘ A North American variant is *knock on wood.* The phrase refers to the traditional custom of touching something wooden to avert possible bad luck.

1991 Rohinton Mistry *Such a Long Journey* Sohrab and Gustad did not shout or argue like they used to, touch wood.

wooden

accept a wooden nickel: *see* NICKEL.

win the wooden spoon: *see* SPOON.

wooden nutmeg: *see* NUTMEG.

woodshed

something nasty in the woodshed a shocking or distasteful thing kept secret. British informal

ⓘ This expression is taken from Stella Gibbons's comic novel *Cold Comfort Farm* (1933), in which Aunt Ada Doom's dominance over her family is maintained by constant references to her having seen *something nasty in the woodshed* in her youth. The details of the experience are never explained.

take someone to the woodshed reprove or punish someone, especially discreetly. US informal, dated

ⓘ This expression referred to the former practice of taking a naughty child to a woodshed to be punished, out of sight of other people.

woodwork

vanish into (*or* come *or* crawl out of) the woodwork (of an unpleasant person or thing) disappear into (*or* emerge from) obscurity. informal

ⓘ The implication here is that the people or things concerned are like cockroaches or other unpleasant creatures living in the crevices of skirting boards and cupboards.

wool

all wool and a yard wide of excellent quality; thoroughly sound.

ⓘ Literally, this expression refers to cloth of the finest quality.

1974 Anthony Gilbert *A Nice Little Killing* No one will ever catch her . . . with an alibi all wool and a yard wide.

dyed in the wool: *see* DYED.

pull the wool over someone's eyes deceive someone, especially by telling untruths.

2012 *New Statesman* The business about wealth taxes is another pack of lies from him to pull the wool over the eyes of the Lib Dem rank and file.

woolly

wild and woolly: *see* WILD.

word

eat your words: *see* EAT.

be as good as your word: *see* GOOD.

be the last word: *see* LAST.

be lost for words: *see* LOST.

from the word go from the very beginning. informal

2013 *Farmers Weekly Interactive* While the continental approach is to give potash-hungry oilseed rape crops the nutrients they require from the word go, growers in Britain often fail to feed the crop sufficiently for high yields.

get a word in edgeways: *see* EDGEWAYS.

have the last word: *see* LAST.

have a word in someone's ear speak to someone privately and discreetly, usually to give them a warning. informal

have words talk angrily; argue. euphemistic

2004 *Fast Company Magazine* They don't kick him out, lock horns, or have words—although Ron Harbour certainly gives them plenty of reasons.

high words: *see* HIGH.

in words of one syllable: *see* SYLLABLE.

a man (*or* woman) of few words a taciturn person.

a man (*or* woman) of his (*or* her) word a person who keeps the promises that they make.

not the word for it not an adequate or appropriate description.

1992 *European Travel & Life* The landscape of Alaska has the power to overwhelm. 'Beautiful' is not the word for it.

put in a good word for: *see* GOOD.

put the hard word on: *see* HARD.

put words into someone's mouth: *see* MOUTH.

say the word give permission or instructions to do something.

someone's word is law someone must be obeyed without question.

someone's word is their bond someone keeps their promises.

ℹ A variant of this expression, now rather dated, is *an Englishman's word is his bond*.

take someone at their word interpret a person's words literally or exactly, especially by believing them or doing as they suggest.

take someone's word (for it) believe what someone says or writes without checking for yourself.

take the words out of someone's mouth: *see* MOUTH.

too — for words extremely —. informal

1990 Rosamund Pilcher *September* I'm not saying 'Isn't it beautiful' all the time, because if I do, it'll just sound too banal for words.

a war of words: *see* WAR.

weasel words: *see* WEASEL.

winged words: *see* WINGED.

the – word ❶ used euphemistically to replace a taboo word beginning with the specified letter (e.g. *the f-word* for *fuck*). ❷ used ironically to replace a word, beginning with the stated letter, denoting something despised or deplored (e.g. *the l-word* for *liberal*).

❶ **2005 Nick Hornby** *A Long Way Down* If I'd known what Maureen was like, then I would have toned it down a bit, probably, but I didn't; I think I might even have used the c-word, for which I've apologized.

❷ **2005** *Courier-Mail* (Brisbane) The f-word—feminism—is tossed around like a worn old sock as the audience tried to fathom how the movement's desire for women to be sexually fulfilled has morphed into a push to simply be sexy.

word for word in exactly the same or, when translated, exactly equivalent words.

word of mouth spoken language; informal or unofficial discourse.

1987 Bruce Duffy *The World As I Found It* His ideas were repeated by word of mouth or passed around as transcripts of the shorthand notes that his students doggedly took down during his lectures.

the word on the street a rumour or piece of information currently being circulated. informal

2001 *Sci Fi* Word on the street is that the Hughes brothers are calling this an 'urban thriller'.

a word to the wise a hint or brief explanation given, that being all that is required.

ℹ The equivalent Latin phrase is *verbum sapienti sat est* (a word to the wise is enough); the abbreviation of this, *verb. sap.*, is sometimes used in English.

1983 Penelope Lively *Perfect Happiness* A word to the wise. If you don't know the place I'm told the thing to do is steer clear of the guided tours.

work

give someone the works ❶ give someone everything. ❷ treat someone harshly. informal

have your work cut out be faced with a hard task.

2013 Derek Lowe *Corante—In the Pipeline* The clinical trials for the biggest diseases in this area are well-known to be expensive and tricky to run. You've got your work cut out for you over there.

in the works being planned, worked on, or produced. chiefly North American

2003 *N. Y. Magazine* Movie-star-of-the-moment Jennifer Lopez... is in talks to star in *Monster in Law*, a new comedy in the works at New Line Cinema.

ⓘ For other idioms containing *work*, see the entry for the main word in the idiom (for example, **make short work of** at SHORT).

workman

a bad workman blames his tools someone who has done something badly will seek to lay the blame on the equipment rather than admit to their own lack of skill. proverb

ⓘ A similar 13th-century French proverb observed *mauveés ovriers ne trovera ja bon hostill*, 'bad workmen will never find a good tool', and variants of this early saying can be found in English until the mid 19th century until the emergence of the modern version.

world

the best of both (*or* all possible) worlds the benefits of widely differing situations, enjoyed at the same time.

ⓘ The variant *all possible worlds* alludes to the catchphrase of the eternally optimistic philosopher Dr Pangloss in Voltaire's *Candide* (1759): *Dans ce meilleur des mondes possibles... tout est au mieux*, usually quoted in English as 'Everything is for the best in the best of all possible worlds'.

brave new world: *see* BRAVE.

carry the world before you have rapid and complete success.

citizen of the world: *see* CITIZEN.

W

come (*or* go) up in the world rise in status, especially by becoming richer.

dead to the world: *see* DEAD.

the end of the world: *see* END.

for all the world exactly, in every respect.

2007 Charles Stross *Halting State* She pauses and looks straight at the phonecam, for all the world as if she's reading from a teleprompter.

go (*or* come) down in the world drop in status, especially by becoming poorer.

in a world of your own concerned with your own thoughts and not aware of what is happening around you.

a man (*or* woman) of the world a person who is experienced and practical in human affairs.

the next world: *see* NEXT.

not be long for this world: *see* LONG.

on top of the world: *see* TOP.

out of this world extremely enjoyable or impressive. informal

1995 *Daily Express* I thought the rest of the team, and especially the defence, were out of this world.

set the world alight (*or* on fire) achieve something sensational. informal

ⓘ A British variant of this expression is *set the Thames on fire*.

1976 Dick Francis *In the Frame* He was the same sort of man my father had been, middle-aged, middle-of-the-road, expert at his chosen job but unlikely to set the world on fire.

it's a small world: *see* SMALL.

think the world of have a very high regard for.

watch the world go by: *see* WATCH.

the way of the world the manner in which people typically behave or things typically happen (used to express your resignation to it).

with the best will in the world: *see* WILL.

the world and his wife everyone; a large number of people. British

ⓘ This expression is first recorded in Jonathan Swift's *Polite Conversation* (1738).

the world, the flesh, and the devil all forms of temptation to sin.

the world is your oyster you are in a position to take the opportunities that life has to offer.

ⓘ This expression may come from Shakespeare's *The Merry Wives of Windsor*: 'Why, then the world's mine oyster, Which I with sword will open'. The humorously malapropistic variant *the world is your lobster* was popularized by the Thames TV series *Minder* (1979–94).

2013 **Ben** *Silent Words Speak Loudest* When you finish your career as a professional footballer, the world is your oyster—there are so many options.

a (*or* the) world of a very great deal of.

worlds apart very different or distant.

worm

a worm's-eye view the view looking up at something from ground level.

ℹ This expression was formed on the pattern of **bird's-eye view** (*see* BIRD). It usually refers to the viewpoint of a humble or insignificant person who is witnessing important events or people.

(even) a worm will turn even a meek person will resist or retaliate if pushed too far. proverb

food for worms a dead person.

open up a can of worms: *see* CAN.

wormwood

wormwood and gall a source of bitter mortification and grief. literary

ℹ *Gall* is bile, a substance secreted by the liver and proverbial for its bitterness, while *wormwood* is an aromatic plant with a bitter taste. The expression originated in reference to various passages in the Bible, for example Lamentations 3:19: 'Remembering mine affliction and my misery, the wormwood and the gall'.

worry

not to worry used to reassure someone by telling them that a situation is not serious.

no worries: *see* NO.

worse

none the worse for ❶ not adversely affected by. ❷ not to be considered inferior on account of.

❶ **1991 Alistair Campbell** *Sidewinder* Two days have passed, and I am up and about, feeling none the worse for my attack of sunstroke.

so much the worse for used to suggest that a problem, failure, or other unfortunate event or situation is the fault of a person specified and that the speaker does not feel any great concern about it.

the worse for wear ❶ damaged by use or weather over time; battered and shabby. ❷ (of a person) feeling rather unwell, especially as a result of drinking too much alcohol. informal

worst

be your own worst enemy: *see* ENEMY.

do your worst do as much damage as you can (often used to express defiance in the face of threats).

get (*or* have) the worst of it be in the least advantageous or successful position; suffer the most.

if the worst comes to the worst if the most serious or difficult circumstances arise.

worth

for all someone is worth ❶ as energetically or enthusiastically as someone can. ❷ so as to obtain everything you can from someone. informal

❶ **1995 Kate Atkinson** *Behind the Scenes at the Museum* In the kitchen, Brian, Adrian's lover, is wearing Bunty's pink rubber gloves and washing up for all he's worth.

ℹ For other idioms containing *worth,* see the entry for the main word in the idiom (for example, **not worth the candle** at CANDLE).

wound

lick your wounds: *see* LICK.

rub salt into the wound: *see* SALT.

wrap

keep something under wraps conceal or be secretive about something. informal

2013 *New Zealand Herald* It's never simple, keeping a surprise present under wraps.

wrap someone in cotton wool: *see* COTTON WOOL.

wrap someone round your little finger: *see* **twist someone round your little finger** at FINGER.

wrap it up be quiet. British informal

wrap yourself in the flag: *see* FLAG.

wring

wring someone's withers stir someone's emotions or conscience.

ℹ This phrase is taken from *Hamlet*. In the play-within-the-play scene, Hamlet remarks ironically that there is no need for King

Claudius, his usurping uncle, to feel troubled by the plot, remarking: 'let the galled jade wince, our withers are unwrung'. The *withers* are the bony ridge between the shoulders of a horse which is liable to be chafed by an ill-fitting saddle.

wring your hands show great distress.

wringer

put someone through the wringer (*or* the mangle) subject someone to a very stressful experience, especially a severe interrogation. informal

1984 Louise Erdrich *Love Medicine* I saw that he had gone through the wringer. He was red-eyed, gaunt, and he was drunk.

wrinkle

iron out the wrinkles: *see* IRON.

wrist

slap on the wrist: *see* SLAP.

writ

writ large clear and obvious.

ⓘ The literal sense of *written in large characters* has long fallen out of use. As the past participle of *write*, *writ* has been superseded by *written* except in this phrase and analogous phrases such as *writ small*.

2012 *Daily Telegraph* He [Max Bygraves] was, as one critic said, 'The boy next door writ large'.

your writ runs you have authority of a specified extent or kind.

write

nothing to write home about of little interest or value. informal

1970 Nina Bawden *The Birds on the Trees* I daresay what I did was nothing to write home about, but it put food in her belly and shoes on her feet!

write your ticket: *see* TICKET.

writing

the writing is on the wall there are clear signs that something unpleasant or unwelcome is going to happen.

ⓘ This phrase comes from the biblical story of Belshazzar's feast, at which a disembodied hand appeared and wrote a message on the wall foretelling the fall of the Babylonian kingdom to the Medes and Persians (Daniel 5:5, 25–8). A North American variant is *the handwriting is on the wall*.

2014 *Daily Telegraph* Church leaders fear the writing is on the wall for traditional church magazines after one of the oldest in the country closes after more than 100 years.

written

be (*or* have something) written all over your face used to convey that the presence of a particular quality or feeling is clearly revealed by a person's expression. informal

wrong

get in wrong with (*or* on the wrong side of) someone incur the dislike or disapproval of someone. informal

get someone wrong misunderstand someone, especially by falsely imputing malice to them.

get (hold of) the wrong end of the stick misunderstand someone or something completely.

go down the wrong way (of food) enter the windpipe instead of the gullet.

ⓘ For other idioms containing *wrong*, see the entry for the main word in the idiom (for example, **put a foot wrong** at FOOT).

wrote

(and) that's all she wrote used to convey that there is or was nothing more to be said about a matter. North American informal

2001 *Chicago Tribune* The snap was a little high, and . . . I tilted up for a second and that's all she wrote . . . I took my eye off the ball.

wrote the book on know everything there is to know about; be the expert on. informal, chiefly North American

yank

yank someone's chain: *see* **pull someone's chain** *at* CHAIN.

yard

by the yard in large numbers or quantities.

> **2002** *Guardian* Culture became a commodity: painters sold landscapes cut up by the foot for home decoration; booksellers offered books by the yard; publishers traded copyrights.

hard yards: *see* HARD.

not in my back yard: *see* NOT.

the whole nine yards: *see* WHOLE.

yardarm

the sun is over the yardarm: *see* SUN.

yarn

spin a yarn tell a story, especially a long and complicated one.

> ℹ A *yarn* is one of the long fibres from which a rope is made. The expression is nautical in origin and has been used in this figurative sense since the early 19th century.

year

for donkey's years: *see* DONKEY.

full of years having lived to a considerable age. archaic

> ℹ *Full of years* is an expression originating in the Authorized Version of the Bible: 'an old man, and full of years' (Genesis 25:8).

put years on (*or* take years off) someone make someone feel or look older (*or* younger).

the vale of years: *see* VALE.

the year dot: *see* DOT.

year in, year out continuously or repeatedly over a period of years.

yes

yes and no partly and partly not.

> **1981 Brian Murphy** *The Enigma Variations* 'Do you believe that if you continue seeing me you'll be damned?' 'Yes and no.'

yesterday

I wasn't born yesterday: *see* BORN.

yesterday's man a man, especially a politician, whose career is finished or past its peak.

yesterday's news a person or thing that is no longer of interest.

yonder

the wide blue yonder: *see* BLUE.

you

you and yours you together with your family and close friends.

> **1937** *American Home* So it's natural . . . to take good care of the home that gives you and yours this steadfast protection.

young

angry young man: *see* ANGRY.

bright young thing: *see* BRIGHT.

young blood: *see* **new blood** *at* BLOOD.

yours

up yours!: *see* UP.

you and yours: *see* YOU.

Zz

zone

in the zone (especially in sport) in a state of such concentration that you are able to perform at the peak of your physical or mental capabilities.

Zs

catch (*or* bag) some Zs get some sleep. US

> ℹ The expression is based on the graphic use of a series of Zs to represent snoring.

Index

This section contains groups of idioms which are linked by a common theme or subject. The themes are listed in alphabetical order and the word in bold print indicates where individual idioms may be found in the dictionary itself. For example, the idiom 'take the **plunge**' is listed in the dictionary at the main entry **plunge**.

Action

start the **ball** rolling
get the **bit** between your teeth
at the **coalface**
get **cracking**
go for the **doctor**
get (*or* pull) your **finger** out
keep your nose to the **grindstone**
hammer and tongs
hard yards
heavy lifting
hit the ground running
hot to trot
have many **irons** in the fire
rest on your **laurels**
lead from the front
put your money where your **mouth** is
rest on your **oars**
put your hand to the **plough**
take the **plunge**
press the button
roll up your sleeves
set the wheels in motion
shake a leg
put your **shoulder** to the wheel
get the **show** on the road
watch someone's **smoke**
stir your stumps
strike while the iron is hot
get **weaving**
no peace for the **wicked**

Age

out of the **ark**
have seen **better** days
the **bloom** is off the rose
you can't teach an old **dog** new tricks
there's no **fool** like an old fool
have one **foot** in the grave
full of years
ancient (*or* old) as the **hills**
over the **hill**
have had a good **innings**
on your last **legs**
long in the tooth
an **old** head on young shoulders
pass your sell-by date
past it
second childhood
stricken in years
sweet sixteen
terrible twos
threescore years and ten
there's many a good **tune** played on an old fiddle
the **vale** of years
put **years** on someone

Ambition

think **big**
bite off more than you can chew
fire in the belly
fly high
holy grail
punch above your weight
room at the top
try to **run** before you can walk
set your heart on
raise your **sights**
set your **sights** on
reach for the **stars**
punch your **ticket**

Anger and annoyance

bent out of shape
get off your **bike**
make your **blood** boil
blow your top
have a **cob** on
count to ten
have a **cow**
go **crook**
get your **dander** up
give someone the hairy **eyeball**
breathe **fire**
fit to be tied
flip your lid
fly off the handle
froth (*or* foam) at the mouth
have a short **fuse**
blow a **gasket**
go off on one
make someone's **hackles** rise
hot under the collar
get the **hump**
have your **monkey** up
do your **nana**
go **non-linear**
put someone's **nose** out of joint
do your **nut**
get on someone's **quince**
give someone the **pip**
lose your **rag**
rattle someone's cage
a **red** rag to a bull

Anger and annoyance (*cont.*)

Anxiety and worry

Appearance

Argument and conflict

Beauty

Boastfulness and conceit

Bribery, corruption, and extortion

Caution

Certainty

Change

Chaos and disorder

Class

Danger

Death

Debt

Deception and lying

Departure

Doubt and uncertainty

Drinking

Drugs

Duty and responsibility

Embarrassment, shame, and humiliation

Equality

Excess and extravagance

Expense

Experience

Failure

Family

Fate and chance

Food

Fools and foolishness

Foresight and the future

Forgiveness and reconciliation

Friends and acquaintances

Futility

Gossip and rumour

Happiness, pleasure, and enjoyment

Haste and speed

Justice (*cont.*)

Language, speech, and conversation

Laziness

Love

Madness

Marriage

Misfortune and adversity

Mistakes

Money, wealth, and prosperity

Nakedness

Opportunity

Poverty

Power

Power (*cont.*)

Pregnancy

Preparation and readiness

Reputation and fame

Revenge and retribution

Secrecy

Self-Interest

Sex

Strength

Success

Surprise

Warfare

Weakness

Weather

Work and employment

Youth

Oxford Quick Reference

The Concise Oxford Dictionary of English Etymology
T. F. Hoad

A wealth of information about our language and its history, this reference source provides over 17,000 entries on word origins.

'A model of its kind'

Daily Telegraph

New Oxford Rhyming Dictionary

From writing poems to writing birthday cards, and from composing advertising slogans to music lyrics, this dictionary has what every writer (or budding writer) needs. It contains rhymes for over 45,000 words, including proper names, place names, and foreign terms used in English.

'All wordsmiths are bound to enjoy feeling indebted (fetid, minareted, rosetted ...)'

Julia Donaldson (author of *The Gruffalo*)

Oxford Dictionary of English Idioms
John Ayto

Containing over 6,000 idioms from all over the English-speaking world, this authoritative and entertaining dictionary is a breath of fresh air for anyone fascinated by the colourful nature of the English language.

'Anyone who is addicted to the richness of the English language or simply intrigued by the origin and meaning of an idiom like "teach your grandmother to suck eggs" will relish this work'

Library Journal

OXFORD

Oxford Quick Reference

The Concise Oxford Dictionary of Quotations
SIXTH EDITION
Edited by Susan Ratcliffe

Based on the highly acclaimed seventh edition of *The Oxford Dictionary of Quotations*, this dictionary provides extensive coverage of literary and historical quotations, and contains completely up-to-date material. A fascinating read and an essential reference tool.

Oxford Dictionary of Quotations by Subject
Edited by Susan Ratcliffe

The ideal place to discover what's been said about what, the dictionary presents quotations on nearly 600 areas of special interest and concern in today's world.

The Oxford Dictionary of Humorous Quotations
Edited by Gyles Brandreth

From the sharply witty to the downright hilarious, this sparkling collection will appeal to all senses of humour.

The Oxford Dictionary of Political Quotations
Edited by Antony Jay

This lively and illuminating dictionary from the writer of 'Yes Minister' presents a vintage crop of over 4,900 political quotations. Ranging from the pivotal and momentous to the rhetorical, the sincere, the bemused, the tongue-in-cheek, and the downright rude, examples include memorable words from the old hands as well as from contemporary politicians.

'funny, striking, thought-provoking and incisive ... will appeal to those browsing through it at least as much as to those who wish to use it as a work of reference'

Observer